Johannes Hein
Verb Doubling and Dummy Verb

Linguistische Arbeiten

Edited by
Klaus von Heusinger, Agnes Jäger,
Gereon Müller, Ingo Plag,
Elisabeth Stark and Richard Wiese

Volume 574

Johannes Hein

Verb Doubling and Dummy Verb

Gap Avoidance Strategies in Verbal Fronting

DE GRUYTER

Zugl.: Leipzig, Univ., Diss., 2018

ISBN 978-3-11-099188-8
e-ISBN (PDF) 978-3-11-063560-7
e-ISBN (EPUB) 978-3-11-063543-0
ISSN 0344-6727

Library of Congress Control Number: 2020939083

Bibliographic information published by the Deutsche Nationalbibliothek
The Deutsche Nationalbibliothek lists this publication in the Deutsche Nationalbibliografie;
detailed bibliographic data are available on the Internet at http://dnb.dnb.de.

© 2022 Walter de Gruyter GmbH, Berlin/Boston
This volume is text- and page-identical with the hardback published in 2020.
Printing and binding: CPI books GmbH, Leck

www.degruyter.com

Für Momo und Halbmondaugen
Danke für das perfekte Timing

Contents

List of Tables —— XI

Abbreviations —— XIII

Introduction and overview —— 1

Part I: Verbal fronting: Typology and theory

1 Properties of verbal fronting —— 13
1.1 Terminology —— 13
1.2 Fronting from below auxiliaries and verb-embedding verbs —— 16
1.3 Morphological form of the fronted verb —— 17
1.4 Verb copy and dummy verb as repairs —— 21
1.5 Category of the moved constituent —— 29
1.6 The role of information structure —— 31

2 Patterns in verbal fronting —— 33
2.1 Repair patterns in languages with both verb and verb phrase fronting —— 33
2.1.1 Symmetric verb doubling —— 34
2.1.2 Symmetric dummy verb insertion —— 36
2.1.3 A new, asymmetric pattern —— 37
2.1.4 Generalization I —— 71
2.2 Repair patterns in languages with either verb or verb phrase fronting —— 72
2.2.1 Verb fronting only —— 73
2.2.2 Verb phrase fronting only —— 75
2.2.3 Generalization II —— 77
2.3 Summary and overview of sample languages' properties —— 78

3 Previous approaches —— 83
3.1 Linearization conflict —— 85
3.2 P-recoverability and Economy of Pronunciation —— 91
3.3 Parallel Chains —— 97
3.4 An edge constraint on copy deletion —— 104
3.5 Non-syntactic head movement —— 111

4 An analysis in terms of order of operations — 116
4.1 The general idea and basic assumptions — 116
4.1.1 Ā-head movement in syntax — 120
4.1.2 Head movement as a post-syntactic operation — 134
4.1.3 Heads, copies and copy deletion — 145
4.1.4 Variable order of post-syntactic operations — 148
4.2 Deriving the typology — 154
4.2.1 Generalization I — 155
4.2.2 Generalization II — 181
4.2.3 Summary — 185

5 Predictions and further issues — 187
5.1 Emergent predictions — 187
5.1.1 Gratuitous verb doubling under Ā-head movement — 191
5.1.2 Optionality of repairs in verb fronting — 197
5.1.3 Summary — 202
5.2 Further issues — 203
5.2.1 Availability of Ā-head movement — 204
5.2.2 Nominalization of the fronted constituent — 206
5.2.3 Order as a consequence of haplology avoidance — 214

6 Conclusion — 218

Part II: Language data

7 Languages with only one kind of verbal fronting — 229
7.1 Languages with verb fronting only — 229
7.1.1 Basaa — 229
7.1.2 Berbice Dutch Creole — 235
7.1.3 Edo — 240
7.1.4 Ewe — 244
7.1.5 Fongbe — 245
7.1.6 Gungbe — 252
7.1.7 Haitian Creole — 255
7.1.8 Kisi — 264
7.1.9 Leteh (Larteh) — 265
7.1.10 Nupe — 267
7.1.11 Nweh — 273
7.1.12 Papiamentu — 275

7.1.13	Pichi —— **277**	
7.1.14	Saramaccan —— **279**	
7.1.15	Tuki —— **281**	
7.1.16	Turkish —— **286**	
7.1.17	Vata —— **287**	
7.2	Languages with verb phrase fronting only —— **293**	
7.2.1	Danish —— **293**	
7.2.2	Hausa —— **297**	
7.2.3	Japanese —— **305**	
7.2.4	Norwegian —— **309**	
7.2.5	Skou —— **316**	
7.2.6	Swedish —— **320**	
7.2.7	Welsh —— **326**	
7.2.8	Wolof —— **331**	
8	**Languages with both kinds of verbal fronting —— 337**	
8.1	Languages with symmetric dummy verb insertion —— **337**	
8.1.1	Basque —— **337**	
8.1.2	Breton —— **345**	
8.1.3	Dutch —— **354**	
8.1.4	German —— **357**	
8.2	Languages with symmetric verb doubling —— **374**	
8.2.1	Brazilian Portuguese —— **374**	
8.2.2	Buli —— **383**	
8.2.3	Dagaare —— **392**	
8.2.4	Hebrew —— **395**	
8.2.5	Hungarian —— **403**	
8.2.6	Korean —— **406**	
8.2.7	Krachi —— **416**	
8.2.8	Mandarin Chinese —— **420**	
8.2.9	Mani —— **430**	
8.2.10	Polish —— **432**	
8.2.11	Russian —— **444**	
8.2.12	Spanish —— **450**	
8.2.13	Tiv —— **460**	
8.2.14	Vietnamese —— **461**	
8.2.15	Yiddish —— **470**	
8.2.16	Yoruba —— **481**	

Bibliography —— 485

Index —— 507

Language Index —— 511

List of Tables

Tab. 2.1   Overview of properties of verbal fronting in languages of the sample —— 81

Tab. 7.1   Properties of verbal fronting in Basaa —— 235
Tab. 7.2   Properties of verbal fronting (type one) in Berbice Dutch Creole —— 240
Tab. 7.3   Properties of verbal fronting in Edo —— 243
Tab. 7.4   Properties of verbal fronting in Ewe —— 245
Tab. 7.5   Properties of verbal fronting in Fongbe —— 252
Tab. 7.6   Properties of verbal fronting in Gungbe —— 255
Tab. 7.7   Properties of verbal fronting in Haitian Creole —— 264
Tab. 7.8   Properties of verbal fronting in Kisi —— 265
Tab. 7.9   Properties of verbal fronting in Leteh (Larteh) —— 266
Tab. 7.10 Properties of verbal fronting in Nupe —— 273
Tab. 7.11 Properties of verbal fronting in Nweh —— 275
Tab. 7.12 Properties of verbal fronting in Papiamentu —— 277
Tab. 7.13 Properties of verbal fronting in Pichi —— 279
Tab. 7.14 Properties of verbal fronting in Saramaccan —— 281
Tab. 7.15 Properties of verbal fronting in Tuki —— 286
Tab. 7.16 Properties of verbal fronting in Turkish —— 287
Tab. 7.17 Properties of verbal fronting in Vata —— 293
Tab. 7.18 Properties of verbal fronting in Danish —— 296
Tab. 7.19 Properties of verbal fronting in Hausa —— 305
Tab. 7.20 Properties of verbal fronting in Japanese —— 309
Tab. 7.21 Properties of verbal fronting in Norwegian —— 316
Tab. 7.22 Properties of verbal fronting in Skou —— 320
Tab. 7.23 Properties of verbal fronting in Swedish —— 326
Tab. 7.24 Properties of verbal fronting in Welsh —— 330
Tab. 7.25 Properties of verbal fronting in Wolof —— 336

Tab. 8.1   Properties of verbal fronting in Basque —— 345
Tab. 8.2   Properties of verbal fronting in Breton —— 353
Tab. 8.3   Properties of verbal fronting in Dutch —— 357
Tab. 8.4   Properties of verbal fronting in German —— 374
Tab. 8.5   Properties of verbal fronting in Brazilian Portuguese —— 383
Tab. 8.6   Properties of verbal fronting in Buli —— 391
Tab. 8.7   Properties of verbal fronting in Dagaare —— 395
Tab. 8.8   Properties of verbal fronting in Hebrew —— 403
Tab. 8.9   Properties of verbal fronting in Hungarian —— 406
Tab. 8.10 Properties of verbal fronting in Korean —— 416
Tab. 8.11 Properties of verbal fronting in Krachi —— 420
Tab. 8.12 Properties of verbal fronting in Mandarin —— 430
Tab. 8.13 Properties of verbal fronting in Mani —— 432
Tab. 8.14 Properties of verbal fronting in Polish —— 444

Tab. 8.15	Properties of verbal fronting in Russian —— **450**
Tab. 8.16	Properties of verbal fronting in Spanish —— **459**
Tab. 8.17	Properties of verbal fronting in Tiv —— **461**
Tab. 8.18	Properties of verbal fronting in Vietnamese —— **470**
Tab. 8.19	Properties of verbal fronting in Yiddish —— **481**
Tab. 8.20	Properties of verbal fronting in Yoruba —— **484**

Abbreviations

AfA	Afro-Asiatic
AuA	Austro-Asiatic
CD	copy deletion
CR	chain reduction
CUC	Chain Uniformity Condition
DP_{ext} / DP_S	external argument
DP_{int} / DP_O	internal argument
ECCD	Edge Condition on Copy Deletion
FF-Elimination	Formal Feature Elimination
FOFC	Final-over-final Condition
HM	head movement
IE	Indo-European
LCA	Linear Correspondence Axiom
LD	Local Dislocation
LF	Logical Form (module of grammar)
MLC	Minimal Link Condition
NC	Niger-Congo
n.d.	no data
PF	Phonological Form (module of grammar)
SCC	Strict Cycle Condition
V2	verb-second

Glosses

ACC	accusative	NCM	nominal class marker
C/COMP	complementizer	NMLZ	nominalizer
CL	clitic	NOM	nominative
DEF	definite	PFV	perfective aspect
DEM	demonstrative	PROG	progressive aspect
DET	determiner	PROSP	prospective aspect
FOC	focus marker	PRS	present tense
FUT	future tense	PST	past tense
INF	infinitive	SM	subject marker
IPFV	imperfective aspect	TOP	topic marker

Introduction and overview

Displacement is a pervasive property of natural languages. Components of a sentence may appear in a position in the string which is not their usual or canonical position in the sense that it is not the position associated with the grammatical function of the component. Thus, in the English sentence in (1-a) the constituent *black olives* which has the grammatical function of a direct object appears in the usual direct object position immediately following the lexical verb. In sentence (1-b), in contrast, the phrase is displaced into the sentence-initial position. The canonical position of the displaced element is indicated by underlined empty space.

(1)   a.   Elizabeth likes *black olives* but she absolutely detests the green ones.
       b.   *Black olives*$_1$ Elizabeth likes ___$_1$ but she absolutely detests the green ones.

The sentence in (1-b) puts more of a contrast on black vs. green olives compared to sentence (1-a). Nonetheless, the phrase *black olives* clearly still functions and is interpreted as an object despite not occurring in the canonical object position.

In order to account for this, Chomsky (1965) has suggested that the grammar has two levels: deep structure (D-structure), where all elements occur in their canonical or base positions, and surface structure (S-structure), where elements may occur in positions different from their base positions. Displacement is then achieved by transformational rules that operate on deep structures and yield surface structures. Later, transformational rules developed into the concept of Move-α (Chomsky 1977, 1980, 1986), which could apply to any constituent α of D-structure and displace it into some other position in S-structure. Within recent minimalism, movement has been subsumed under the basic operation Merge as a case of Internal Merge where an element that has already been introduced into the structure at an earlier stage of the derivation is again merged with the current root node.

In general, movement may apply to any category subject to language specific restrictions. Thus, English allows displacement of DPs (2-a), PPs (2-b), CPs (2-c), adverbials (2-d), and VPs (2-e).

(2)   a.   [$_{DP}$ The first bus of the day] Peter didn't catch ___$_{DP}$ so he had to take the next one.
       b.   [$_{PP}$ In our house] we usually had enough room for unexpected guests ___$_{PP}$.

c. [_CP_ That getting drunk was a bad idea] Kate only realized ___CP the next morning.
d. [_Adv_ Certainly] he ___Adv didn't want to hurt anybody.
e. [_VP_ Sing the melody] she can ___VP but can she also play it on the piano?

In many Slavic languages it is additionally possible to displace an attributive adjective as the example (3) from Bosnian/Croatian/Serbian (BCS) demonstrates.

(3) [_A_ Lijepe] je vidio ___A kuće.
 beautiful is seen houses
 'Beautiful houses, he saw.' (*BCS*, Bošković 2004: 16)

Commonly, movement of a constituent results in a gap in its base position, as is the case with the examples above. However, displacement of verbal constituents into the left periphery behaves differently. When the main lexical verb or its verb phrase is fronted and there is no other verbal element, e.g. an auxiliary or modal, present in the clause, a copy of the lexical verb appears instead. In Hebrew, for instance, displacement of a verb (4-a) or a verb phrase (4-b) into sentence-initial position requires the presence of an inflected copy of the displaced verb in the usual verb position (4). The verb inside the fronted constituent takes the form of an infinitive.

(4) a. **Liknot** hi **kanta** et ha-praxim.
 to.buy she bought ACC the-flowers
 'As for buying, she bought the flowers.'
 b. [**Liknot** et ha-praxim], hi **kanta**.
 buy.INF ACC the-flowers she bought
 'As for buying the flowers, she bought (them).'
 (*Hebrew*, Landau 2006: 37)

Although this verb doubling is widely attested there are also languages in which a semantically largely vacuous dummy verb, usually meaning 'do' or 'make', occurs instead of a gap. For example, when a Dutch verb (5-a) or verb phrase (5-b) occurs in the left periphery of the clause and no modal or temporal auxiliary is present, a form of *doen* 'do' occupies the canonical position of the inflected verb (5). The fronted verb is an infinitive just like in Hebrew.

(5) a. **Verraden doet** hij haar niet.
 betray does he her not
 'He doesn't betray her.'

b. [Haar **verraden**] **doet** hij niet
   her betray does he not
   'He doesn't betray her.'
   (*Dutch*, Broekhuis & Corver 2015: 1045, 1043)

This peculiarity of verbal fronting to repair a gap with a verb copy or a dummy verb sets it apart from other displacement phenomena and has attracted the interest of many linguists over time who have investigated several distinct languages with the same pattern and tried to provide a theoretical account for it. One implicit assumption of all these accounts is that both dimensions of variation, (i) fronted verb vs. fronted verb phrase and (ii) verb copy vs. dummy verb, are independent of each other such that a language uniformly displays either verb doubling or dummy verb insertion with both types of fronting but not one repair strategy with one type of fronting and the other repair strategy with the other type of fronting.

In this monograph, I present novel data from Asante Twi (Kwa, Niger-Congo; Ghana) and Limbum (Grassfields, Niger-Congo; Cameroon) that show that this assumption cannot be upheld. Both languages allow a single verb or a full verb phrase to be fronted. While in the first scenario a copy of the verb appears in the base position, a dummy verb is inserted in the second case. This is shown for Asante Twi in (6) and for Limbum in (7).

(6) a. **Sí**(-é) na Kofí á-**sí**/*á-yɔ́ dán.
       build-NMLZ FOC Kofi PRF-build/PRF-do house
       'Kofi has BUILT a house. (not e.g. bought one)'
    b. [Dán **sí**](-é) na Kofí *á-sí/á-**yɔ́**
       house build-NMLZ FOC Kofi PRF-build/PRF-do
       'Kofi has BUILT A HOUSE. (not e.g. bought a boat)' (*Asante Twi*)

(7) a. Á r-**yū** (cí) njíŋwè fɔ́ bí **yū**/*gī̄ msāŋ
       FOC 5-buy (COMP) woman DET FUT1 buy/do rice
       'The woman will BUY rice.'
    b. Á r-[**yū** msāŋ] (cí) njíŋwè fɔ́ bí *yū/**gī̄**
       FOC 5-buy rice (COMP) woman DET FUT1 buy/do
       'The woman will BUY RICE.' (*Limbum*)

The repair strategy can, thus, apparently be variable within a language depending on the type of fronting. Free recombination of repair strategy and type of fronting yields the typology of four logically possible patterns in (8).

(8) *Typology of repair patterns in verbal fronting*

	Fronted element		Languages
	Verb	Verb phrase	
I	verb copy	verb copy	Hebrew, ...
II	dummy verb	dummy verb	Dutch, ...
III	verb copy	dummy verb	Asante Twi, Limbum
IV	dummy verb	verb copy	—

The typology shows a gap for the fourth pattern, dummy verb insertion with a fronted verb and verb doubling with a fronted verb phrase. An investigation of 45 languages that exhibit verbal fronting (see part II) supports the treatment of this gap as systematic since no language displays even rudimentary lexicalized traces of such a pattern. In the absence of evidence to the contrary, it is therefore plausible to formulate this observation as the generalization in (9).[1]

(9) *Generalization I*
If a language shows both verb and verb phrase fronting it either exhibits the same repair strategy in both frontings (verb doubling or dummy verb insertion), or verb doubling in verb fronting and dummy verb insertion in verb phrase fronting. The reverse pattern is inexistent.

In this book, I develop an account of verbal fronting within the copy theory of movement that captures the abovementioned generalization. It is able to derive the attested patterns including the asymmetric one found in Asante Twi and Limbum but fails to derive the unattested one thereby correctly predicting its absence from the data. The account relies on three main concepts: (i) regular head movement is a post-syntactic operation (see among others Chomsky 1995b, Boeckx & Stjepanović 2001, Schoorlemmer & Temmerman 2012) while a different type of head movement, namely $\bar{A}$-head movement, that is, movement of a head into a specifier, takes place in narrow syntax (see Koopman 1984, Landau 2006, Vicente 2007, 2009, Harizanov 2019, Arregi & Pietraszko 2020); (ii) the lowest copy of an $\bar{A}$-head movement chain cannot be affected by copy deletion because it is a head supporting a whole projection line; and (iii) there is a strict language-specific order of application (<) between the post-syntactic operations head movement (HM) and copy deletion

---

[1] Unfortunately, verbal fronting, although attested for many languages, has been documented and investigated to a sufficient level only in a couple of languages. Any claim about its typology or supposed universal patterns is therefore necessarily a bold one. My hope is that the purported generalization triggers more research on the issue be it only with the goal to disconfirm it in the end.

(CD) (see among others Müller 2009a, Arregi & Nevins 2012, Schoorlemmer 2012, for the ordering of syntactic and post-syntactic operations).

Within the copy theory of movement, verb doubling of the kind found in verbal fronting can be modelled as the result of multiple copy spell out (Abels 2001, Nunes 2004). In other words, it is the consequence of an exceptional failure of the system to delete low copies of a moved item. In case of verb phrase fronting, the moved item is a full verb phrase, i.e. a verb and its internal argument(s) (10). In case of verb fronting, however, there are two possible movement types that lead to it. One is movement of a remnant verb phrase, that is, a verb phrase that only consists of the verbal head because its internal argument(s) have moved out of it (11-b). The other is Ā-head movement of the verbal head directly into the left periphery (SpecCP or SpecFocP or SpecTopP) (11-a).

(10) *Syntactic structure of verb phrase fronting*
 [CP [VP V DP] [C' C [TP T ... [VP V DP]]]]

(11) *Syntactic structures of verb fronting*
 a. [CP V [C' C [TP T ... [VP V DP]]]]
 b. [CP [VP V DP] [C' C [TP T ... DP [VP V DP]]]]

In each of these cases, there is a copy of the main verb left in the base position that, if pronounced in addition to the highest copy in SpecCP, will surface as verb doubling.

With verb phrase fronting (10), the general intuition here (which can also be found in Houser et al. 2006) is that deletion of the low copy of the verb can be prevented when it previously head-moves out of the deletion site (12) (see also Goldberg 2005 for a similar approach to verb-stranding VP-ellipsis).

(12) *Verb doubling in verb phrase fronting: HM ≺ CD*
 a. HM: [CP [VP V DP] [C' C [TP T ... [VP V DP]]]]
 b. CD: [CP [VP V DP] [C' C [TP V+T ... [VP V DP]]]]

Conversely, when copy deletion applies first, the low copy is deleted before it can head-move to a higher position which is then filled with a dummy verb (13). Crucially in order for this to be possible, both operations have to apply in the post-syntactic component of grammar and have to apply in a given order.

(13) *Dummy verb insertion in verb phrase fronting: CD ≺ HM*
 a. CD: [CP [VP V DP] [C' C [TP T ... [VP V DP]]]]
 b. HM: [CP [VP V DP] [C' C [TP do+T ... [VP V DP]]]]

The effect of the order of operations can then be summarized as in table (14).

(14)   *Effect of order of operations in verbal fronting (incomplete)*

Moved item	Order of post-syntactic operations		Surface
	HM < CD	CD < HM	
full verb phrase	verb doubling	dummy verb insertion	verb phrase fronting

With verb fronting via remnant movement, the effect of the order of operations is the same as in verb phrase fronting because what is fronted syntactically is actually a complete verb phrase. Copy deletion just has to be able to delete the object copy inside the fronted verb phrase. Thus, if head movement applies first, the low verb copy inside the verb phrase copy can move to T prior to copy deletion (15).

(15)   *Verb doubling in verb fronting via remnant movement: HM < CD*
   a.   HM: [$_{CP}$ [$_{VP}$ V DP] [$_{C'}$ C [$_{TP}$ T ... DP [$_{VP}$ V DP]]]]
   b.   CD: [$_{CP}$ [$_{VP}$ V ~~DP~~] [$_{C'}$ C [$_{TP}$ V+T ... DP ~~[$_{VP}$ V DP]~~]]]

Again, if copy deletion applies first the low verb copy will be deleted before it can move to T and a dummy is inserted to support T's inflectional features (16).

(16)   *Dummy verb insertion in verb fronting via remnant movement: CD < HM*
   a.   CD: [$_{CP}$ [$_{VP}$ V ~~DP~~] [$_{C'}$ C [$_{TP}$ T ... DP ~~[$_{VP}$ V DP]~~]]]
   b.   HM: [$_{CP}$ [$_{VP}$ V ~~DP~~] [$_{C'}$ C [$_{TP}$ *do*+T ... DP ~~[$_{VP}$ V DP]~~]]]

Consequently, verb fronting that arises by remnant movement of a verb phrase is affected by the order of post-syntactic operations in the same fashion as verb phrase fronting (17).

(17)   *Effect of order of operations in verbal fronting (incomplete)*

Moved item	Order of post-syntactic operations		Surface
	HM < CD	CD < HM	
full verb phrase	verb doubling	dummy verb insertion	verb phrase fronting
remnant verb phrase	verb doubling	dummy verb insertion	verb fronting

Thus far, the account is able to derive the symmetric verb doubling pattern as found in Hebrew and the symmetric dummy verb insertion pattern as found in Dutch. The former arises if a language has the order HM < CD in the post-syntax and the movement underlying verb fronting is remnant verb phrase movement. The latter is a consequence of a language having the order CD < HM with verb fronting being the result of remnant verb phrase movement.

With verb fronting via Ā-head movement, the situation is different. As the low verb copy in an Ā-head movement chain is immune to copy deletion by virtue of being a projecting head the order of operations has no effect on its spell-out. Whether head movement applies before copy deletion or vice versa, the low verb copy can move to T (although it does not have to in order to be spelled out) and will be pronounced. Ā-head movement thus neutralizes the effect of the order of operations in favour of verb doubling (18).

(18) *Effect of order of operations in verbal fronting*

	Order of post-syntactic operations		
Moved item	**HM < CD**	**CD < HM**	**Surface**
full verb phrase	verb doubling	dummy verb insertion	verb phrase fronting
remnant verb phrase	verb doubling	dummy verb insertion	verb fronting
bare verb	verb doubling	**verb doubling**	verb fronting

The asymmetric pattern in Asante Twi and Limbum then arises as follows: These languages show the order CD < HM which in combination with full verb phrase movement leads to dummy verb insertion in verb phrase fronting. Verb fronting, however, is achieved by Ā-head moving the bare verb, which inevitably results in verb doubling. Exceptional non-deletion of a low verb copy in an Ā-head movement chain thus leads to exceptional verb doubling in a language that might otherwise (i.e. in verb phrase fronting) exhibit dummy verb insertion due to it having the order where copy deletion applies before head movement.

A language that employs Ā-head movement in verb fronting like Asante Twi and Limbum but has the order HM < CD will display a symmetric verb doubling pattern just like Hebrew because both Ā-head movement and full verb phrase movement result in verb doubling.

The patterns resulting from the interaction between type of movement and order of operations is summarized in table (19).

(19) *Repair patterns resulting from order of operations and type of movement*

	Ā-head movement	**Remnant movement**
CD < HM	asymmetric pattern	symmetric dummy verb insertion
HM < CD	symmetric verb doubling	symmetric verb doubling

It is evident from (19) that although there are four ways in which the two orders of operations can combine with the two types of movement used in verb fronting only three different repair patterns arise. The account is hence unable to generate the mirror image of the asymmetric pattern of Asante Twi and Limbum and therefore correctly derives the typological gap.

A second observation that can be made about the present sample of languages is that those which display verb fronting to the exclusion of verb phrase fronting never show dummy verb insertion. They exclusively exhibit verb doubling. In contrast, the languages that solely allow verb phrase fronting but not verb fronting never show verb doubling but only dummy verb insertion.

The first part of the observation follows directly from the fact that verb fronting in these languages must necessarily be brought about through $\bar{A}$-head movement rather than remnant movement of the verb phrase. This is because remnant verb phrase movement presupposes the possibility of verb phrase movement, which is obviously absent from languages which do not exhibit any kind of verb phrase fronting. $\bar{A}$-head movement always results in verb doubling and, therefore, these languages exclusively display verb doubling.

The second observation about languages that only show verb phrase fronting does not ensue and might actually be a consequence of the very small number of languages of this type in the sample. Only eight of the 47 languages solely exhibit verb phrase fronting three of which belong to the same sub-family of the Indo-European phylum, namely Germanic. In addition, I will argue that with this type of language dummy verb insertion is expected to be more frequent than verb doubling because the former requires fewer properties to come together in a single language than the latter.

Part I of this book is concerned with the typology and the theory of verbal fronting.

The first chapter presents some general properties of verbal fronting that show variability cross-linguistically. After first clarifying some terminological issues, it discusses the behaviour of verbal fronting from below a verb-embedding verb like an auxiliary or modal, the morphological form of the fronted verb, the verb copy's and the dummy verb's status as a repair element, the size and category of the fronted constituent, and the fact that the information structural interpretation of the fronted consituent does not have any effect on whether a verb copy or a dummy verb appears inside the clause.

In the subsequent chapter, the main typological one, I will present the relevant patterns of verbal fronting based on a selection of examples from the relevant languages and provide a more detailed description of verbal fronting in Asante Twi and Limbum. I will then argue that in the majority of languages, and in Asante Twi and Limbum in particular, there is evidence for movement as well as evidence that verb doubling and dummy verb insertion are not derived from some independently available verb doubling or dummy verb construction. It will also be shown that the repair strategies are not linked to the information-structural function associated with verbal fronting. The two generalizations briefly introduced above will be properly established from the data.

Chapter three is concerned with previous approaches to verbal fronting. As a lot of approaches have been proposed over the years I will concentrate on five fairly recent ones which try to account for the exceptional spell-out of a second verb copy within the minimalist framework. These pursue strategies as diverse as linearization conflicts (Nunes 2004), P-recoverability and economy of pronunciation (Landau 2006), parallel chains (Aboh 2006, Aboh & Dyakonova 2009, Kandybowicz 2008), an edge constraint on copy deletion (Trinh 2011), and non-syntactic head movement (LaCara 2016a). I will argue that none of these is able to derive the asymmetric repair pattern of Asante Twi and Limbum and the typological gap.

A new approach in terms of an order of application between post-syntactic operations is presented in the main theoretical chapter of the book, chapter four. After recapitulating the general idea of the proposal I will introduce and discuss its basic tenets, namely (i) $\bar{A}$-head movement in syntax, regular head movement in the post-syntax, (ii) copy deletion and its unapplicability to heads, (iii) cross-linguistically variable but language-specific strict orders of the post-syntactic operations. Arguments from the literature in favour of each of these will be reported if existent and where possible new arguments from Asante Twi and Limbum will be presented. I will then demonstrate how the proposal derives the attested patterns in detail based on example sentences from one representative language for each pattern. Those languages are Hebrew for the symmetric verb doubling pattern with $\bar{A}$-head movement, German for the symmetric dummy verb insertion pattern, Asante Twi for the asymmetric pattern, and Polish for the symmetric verb doubling pattern with remnant movement. Thereafter, the observations about languages with only one type of verbal fronting will be scrutinized.

In chapter five, I will deduce three predictions from the proposed analysis, one of which is a variation of Generalization IIa, while the other, more interesting two concern the presence of verb copies below auxiliaries and modals in $\bar{A}$-head movement dependencies (called gratuitous verb doubling) and optionality between verb doubling and dummy verb insertion in verb fronting. As I show, the first of the latter can be validated. The two candidate languages, Basque and Breton, that seem likely to provide evidence for the validity of the second one, however, turn out to not entirely exhibit the expected optionality. Thereafter, I will discuss three further issues. The first one concerns the question how a language can be said to lack a certain type of movement, the second one deals with nominalization of the fronted verbal constituent prevalent in African languages, and the third has to do with the idea that the order of operations may be a consequence of haplology avoidance.

Chapter six concludes part I of the monograph and summarizes its main points.

Part II provides descriptions of verbal fronting for each of the 45 languages including, if available, evidence for movement, evidence against verbal fronting being derived from an independent verb doubling or dummy verb construction, and other notable properties. It is meant to be both an encyclopedia that the reader can consult to obtain more details on the patterns and examples adduced throughout the book as well as a compendium of verbal fronting that brings together the knowledge and data currently scattered across the manifold works on this issue. As such it may also serve as a reference point for future research in verbal fronting.

Chapter seven comprises the languages that allow only one type of verbal fronting, that is, either verb fronting or verb phrase fronting.

Chapter eight contains languages that show both types of verbal fronting. First, languages with symmetric dummy verb insertion are discussed, then languages with symmetric verb doubling.

Part I: **Verbal fronting: Typology and theory**

1 Properties of verbal fronting

After clarifying the terminology and defining what falls under the term 'verbal fronting', this chapter presents and discusses some general properties of verbal fronting which exhibit various degrees of variation cross-linguistically. First, as pointed out in the introduction, fronting of a verbal category from under an auxiliary, modal, or another verb-embedding verb oftentimes results in a gap rather than verb doubling or dummy verb insertion and will therefore not be the focus of this book. Second, there is variation in the morphological form of the verb in the fronted constituent ranging from infinitives over nominalizations to fully inflected verbs. Third, the status of the verb copy or dummy verb as an actual repair is investigated, followed by a short discussion on the size/category of the the fronted constituent. The chapter closes by arguing that the information structural status of the fronted category does not have an effect on whether a verb copy or a dummy verb appears inside the clause.

1.1 Terminology

At the beginning, let me clarify a few issues that might otherwise cause confusion. First, verbal fronting has figured under various terms including VP-topicalization, verb focus, predicate fronting, or predicate cleft(ing), some of which are narrower than others while some presuppose a specific underlying structure. In this monograph, I understand verbal fronting to refer to a construction in which the main contentful lexical verb of a sentence is displaced (either with or without its internal argument(s)) from its canonical or base position into the left (or probably also the right) periphery compared to a corresponding simple declarative sentence. In addition, this displacement has to be associated with an information-structural interpretation of (a part of) the fronted constituent as focus, topic, or contrast.

Thus, taking German as an example, sentence (1-a) is an instance of verbal fronting, because the verb (together with its object) appears in sentence-initial position. This is not its canonical position in a main clause as we can see in the neutral declarative clause (1-b). The verb also appears sentence-initially in jokes like (2) where it does not receive a special interpretation as focus or topic. These examples therefore are not instances of verbal fronting as understood in this book.

(1) a. [Das Auto waschen] tut Hans jede Woche, aber den Rasen
the car wash.INF does Hans every week but the lawn
mäht er nur einmal im Monat.
mows he only once in.the month
'As for washing the car, Hans does it every weeky but he mows the lawn only once a month.'
  b. Hans wäscht das Auto jede Woche aber den Rasen mäht er
Hans washes the car every week but the lawn mows he
nur einmal im Monat.
only once in.the month
'Hans washes the car every week but he mows the lawn only once a month.' *(German)*

(2) Kommt ein Neutron in eine Bar. Sagt der Barkeeper: "Tut mir leid,
comes a neutron in a bar says the barkeeper does me pity
heute nur für geladene Gäste."
today only for invited/charged guests
'A neutron walks into a bar and the barkeeper says: "I'm sorry, today for charged guests only."' *(German)*

Within verbal fronting one can distinguish two kinds, verb fronting and verb phrase fronting. In the former, the verb strands its internal argument(s) inside the clause, whereas in the latter, at least one of them accompanies the verb into the left periphery. Thus, the Hebrew example (3-a) instantiates verb fronting while example (3-b) is a case of verb phrase fronting.

(3) a. **Liknot** hi **kanta** et ha-praxim.
to.buy she bought ACC the-flowers
'As for buying, she bought the flowers.'
  b. [**Liknot** et ha-praxim], hi **kanta**.
buy.INF ACC the-flowers she bought
'As for buying the flowers, she bought (them).'
(Hebrew, Landau 2006: 37)

Languages may vary with regard to whether they allow both kinds of fronting, like Hebrew above (see section 8.2.4), or only one kind, either verb fronting but not verb phrase fronting, like Nupe (4) (see section 7.1.10), or verb phrase fronting but not verb fronting, like Norwegian (5) (see section 7.2.4).

(4) a. Bi-**ba** Musa à **ba** nakàn o.
RED-cut Musa FUT cut meat cut/RED-cut FOC
'It is CUTTING that Musa will do to the meat (as opposed to say, *cooking*.)'

    b. *[Du-**du** cènkafa] Musa à **du** (cènkafa) o.
        RED-cook rice   Musa FUT cook rice   FOC
        'It is COOKING RICE that Musa will do.'
    c. *[Cènkafa du-**du**] Musa à **du** (cènkafa) o.
        rice   RED-cook Musa FUT cook rice   FOC
        'It is COOKING RICE that Musa will do.'

                                      (*Nupe*, Kandybowicz 2008: 79, 86)

(5) a. [(Å) **lese** bøk-er]   **gjør**/*leser han hele   dag-en.
        to read.INF book.PL-PL.INDEF does/reads he   whole day-DEF
        'Reading books he does all day.'
    b. *(Å) **lese**   **gjør/leser** han bøk-er   hele   dag-en.
        to read.INF does/reads he   book.PL-PL.INDEF whole day-DEF
        'Reading he does to books all day.'

                                      (*Norwegian*, Siri M. Gjersøe p.c.)

Importantly, the terms 'verb fronting' and 'verb phrase fronting' are used as purely descriptive terms for surface strings. This is particularly crucial for 'verb fronting' which does not imply that the fronted consituent is structurally a bare V head. It could equally well be a VP that has been bereft of its arguments. Consequently, verb fronting could be the result of either a bare V head in SpecCP (or whichever position it is that constitutes the clausal periphery) or a remnant VP in that position. It is particularly vital, in light of the analysis and discussion in the following chapters, to bear in mind that 'verb fronting' and 'verb phrase fronting' do not refer to actual syntactic movements. When talking about syntactic movement processes of a verbal head or a verb phrase, I will (try to) be consistent in calling those 'movement' or 'preposing' rather than 'fronting'.

    In order to correctly determine whether a language shows one or the other kind of fronting it is not sufficient to consider only examples of fronted intransitive verbs. Not selecting any interal arguments, a fronted intransitive *per se* can instantiate both verb or verb phrase fronting. Hence, a language that displays verb phrase fronting with transitive verbs, but where the only examples for purported verb fronting come from intransitive verbs will be treated as a lánguage that lacks verb fronting. Equally, in the absence of explicit evidence showing a fronted verb accompanied by its internal argument(s) it will be concluded that a language lacks verb phrase fronting.

1.2 Fronting from below auxiliaries and verb-embedding verbs

As mentioned in the introduction, verbal fronting is different from other displacement phenomena in that under certain circumstances there occurs a copy of the verb or a dummy verb instead of the usual gap. Compare, for instance, regular object focus (6-a) with verb focus (6-b) in Leteh (Kwa, Niger-Congo; Ghana). While (6-a) shows a gap in the base position of the object, the base position of the verb is occupied a copy of the fronted verb in (6-b).

(6) a. Sika₁ né Ananse bè-wúrì ___₁ a.
money FOC Ananse FUT-steal DEF
'Ananse will steal MONEY.'
b. **Fókyè** né Ama **fòkyè** daa a.
sweep.NMLZ FOC Ama PRS.sweep everyday DEF
'Ama SWEEPS everyday.' (*Leteh*, Ansah 2014: 167, 174)

However, this divergent behaviour of verbal fronting can usually only be observed if the verb's base position is not embedded under an auxiliary, a modal, or any other verb-embedding verb. This restriction holds independent of the type of repair that the language would display otherwise and independent of the kind of fronting. Consider the examples from German and Polish. While the former shows dummy verb insertion in the relevant auxiliary-less environment (7) the latter displays verb doubling (8).

(7) a. **Waschen tut** Hans das Auto jede Woche.
wash.INF does Hans the car every week
'As for washing, Hans washes the car every week.'
b. [Das Auto **waschen**] **tut** Hans jede Woche.
the car wash.INF does Hans every week
'As for washing the car, Hans does it every week.' (*German*)

(8) a. **Pić** (to) Marek **pije** herbatę, ale jej nie robił.
drink.INF TO Marek drinks tea but it not make.PST
'As for drinking, Marek drinks tea, but he did not make it.'
b. [**Pić** herbatę] (to) Marek **pije**, ale jej nie robił.
drink.INF tea TO Marek drinks but it not make.PST
'As for drinking tea, Marek drinks it, but he did not make it.'
(*Polish*, Joanna Zaleska p.c.)

However, if the clause contains an auxiliary, modal or verb-embedding verb, verbal fronting shows a gap in the base position of the verb in both languages, as shown in (9) for German and in (10) for Polish.

(9) a. **Waschen**₁ will Hans das Auto jede Woche ___₁.
 wash.INF wants Hans the car every week
 'As for washing, Hans wants to wash the car every week.'
 b. [Das Auto **waschen**]₁ will Hans jede Woche ___₁
 the car wash.INF wants Hans every week
 'As for washing the car, Hans wants to do it every week.' (*German*)

(10) a. **Wypić**₁ (to) Marek chce ___₁ herbatę, ale nie chce jej robić.
 drink.INF TO Marek wants tea but not wants it make
 'As for drinking, Marek wants to drink tea but he doesn't want to make it.'
 b. [**Wypić** herbatę]₁ (to) Marek chce ___₁, ale nie chce jej robić.
 drink tea TO Marek wants but not wants it make
 'As for drinking tea, Marek wants to drink it, but he doesn't want to make it.' (*Polish*, Joanna Zaleska p.c.)

Although examples like (9) and (10) clearly are cases of verbal fronting, I will ignore them for the most part in this monograph. As they do not display any repairs they are of no interest in establishing the possible patterns of repairs in verbal fronting constructions across languages. However, I will come back to verb doubling under auxiliaries, modals, or verb-embedding verbs briefly in section 5.1.1 because the analysis makes an interesting prediction about it.

1.3 Morphological form of the fronted verb

In general, fronted verbs appear as non-finite forms in both verb and verb phrase fronting. This form is either the infinitive, which is the predominant pattern for Indo-European languages but not restricted to them, or a nominalization of the verbal constituent, which is the preferred pattern in the African languages. To give a few examples, in the verbal fronting constructions from Dutch (11-a), Hebrew (11-b), and Tuki (11-c) the fronted verb is an infinitive whereas the examples from Kisi (12-a), Buli (12-b), and Hausa (12-c) show a nominalized form in the left periphery.

(11) a. **Verraden doet** hij haar niet.
 betray.INF does he her not
 'He doesn't betray her.'
 (*Dutch*, Broekhuis & Corver 2015: 1045)
 b. [**Liknot** et ha-praxim] hi **kanta**.
 buy.INF ACC the-flowers she bought
 'As for buying the flowers, she bought (them).'
 (*Hebrew*, Landau 2006: 37)

  c. O-**nyá** ówú vítsu tu-**nyám** cwí.
    INF-eat FOC we SM-eat fish
    'We ATE fish.'   (*Tuki*, Biloa 2013: 75)

(12) a. **Pùé**ŋ-ndáŋ yá **púé**ŋ ní.
    forget-NMLZ I forget FOC
    'It's forgetting that I did.'   (*Kisi*, Childs 1997: 50)
  b. (Ká) **dē**-kā àlī/àtì Àtìm **dè** mángò-kŭ dīēm.
    FOC eat-NMLZ C Àtìm ate mango-DEF yesterday
    'It is eating that Àtìm ate the mango yesterday. (not e.g. throwing it
    away)'   (*Buli*, Hiraiwa 2005a: 262)
  c. [**Araa** masa littaafii] na **yi**.[1]
    lend.VN to.him book 1s do
    'Lending him a book I did.'   (*Hausa*, Tuller 1986: 430)

For a few languages, in particular the Creoles, the Asian languages, and Wolof, the literature was not explicit with regard to whether the fronted verb is an infinitive, a nominalization, or something different altogether. In general, in those languages the fronted verb is simply glossed as an uninflected stem as in Saramaccan (13-a), Japanese (13-b), and Wolof (13-c).

(13) a. **Sùku** a **sùku** en.
    look.for he look.for him
    'He LOOKED FOR him.'   (*Saramaccan*, Byrne 1987: 97)
  b. [Sushi-o **tabe**-sae] John-ga **si**-ta.
    sushi-ACC eat-even John-NOM do-PST
    'Even eat sushi, John did.'
             (*Japanese*, Nishiyama & Cho 1998: 467)
  c. [**Suub** simis b-i]   l-a-a **def**.
    dye shirt CL-DEF.PROX *l*-C-1SG do
    'Dye the shirt is what I did.'   (*Wolof*, Torrence 2013a: 68)

In determining whether a non-finite fronted verb is an infinitive or a nominalization, I relied on the classification in the respective grammar or language description either mentioned in the text or manifested in the glossing. However, I would like to point out here that this distinction is not necessarily real but might be terminological in nature. A lot of African languages just do not show any dedicated infinitive forms. Rather, the functions of the infinitive are taken over by other constructions including deverbal nominalizations and serial verb constructions. Ultimately, when one compares the language-internal distribution of infinitives and deverbal

---

[1] The gloss VN here stands for 'verbal noun', a form of deverbal nominalization in Hausa.

nominalizations I expect there to be a considerable overlap to the effect that infinitives and (certain) nominalizations are identical or at least equivalent in their distribution and use.

Interestingly, the Scandinavian languages in the sample also allow for the fronted verb to have a finite form (14). In fact, this seems to be the preferred option in Swedish (Lødrup 1990, Teleman et al. 1999) if not the only grammatical one (Platzack 2012).

(14) a. ...og [køre/kørde   bilen] gjorde han.
         and drive.INF/drive.PST car.DEF did   he
         '...and drive the car, he did.'
                                            (*Danish*, Platzack 2008: 280)
     b. [Spille/spiller   golf] gjør jeg aldri.
        play.INF/play.PRS golf do.PRS I   never
        'Play golf, I never do.'
                                            (*Norwegian*, Lødrup 1990: 3)
     c. ...och [körde/*köra   bilen] gjorde han.
         and drive.PST/drive.INF car.DEF did   he
         '...and drive the car, he did.'
                                            (*Swedish*, Platzack 2008: 281)

Tense-marking is commonly assumed to be hosted in T which is not part of the fronted VP in (14) (see sections 7.2.1, 7.2.4 and 7.2.6 for arguments). With regard to the question of how tense-marking can appear on the fronted verb I follow LaCara (2016b) in assuming that T optionally agrees with the verb as soon as the former is merged and its tense features are copied onto V before the VP undergoes movement into the left periphery (arguably SpecCP). This operation must independently be available in Danish, Norwegian and Swedish because in embedded clauses, where in contrast to matrix V2-clauses there is no V-to-T movement, the embedded verb is nonetheless marked for tense (15) (Holmberg & Platzack 1991).

(15) a. Vi ved   [at Peter ofte drikke-r kaffe om morgenen].
        we know that Peter often drink-PRS coffee in morning
        'We know that Peter often drinks coffee in the morning.'
                                            (*Danish*, Vikner 1995: 47)
     b. Jeg tro-r   [at Hanne ikke like-r   kaffe].
        I   believe-PRS that Hanne not like-PRS coffee
        'I believe that Hanne doesn't like coffee.'
                                            (*Norwegian*, Siri M. Gjersøe p.c.)
     c. ...[att jag inte kyss-te henne].
             that I not kiss-PST her
        '...that I didn't kiss her.'   (*Swedish*, Holmberg 1999: 1)

There is another issue with the Scandinavian languages. Usually – that is, in sentences without an auxiliary – they do not display verb fronting (16).[2]

(16) a. ***Å lese** gjør han bøk-er hele dag-en.
 to read.INF does he book.PL-PL.INDEF whole day-DEF
 (*Norwegian*, Siri M. Gjersøe p.c.)
 b. ***Säljer gör** han den inte, men han kanske lånar ut den ibland.
 sell.PRS does he it no but he perhaps lend out it sometimes
 (*Swedish*, Holmberg 1999: 12)

However, as soon as the base position of the fronted verb is embedded under a form of the perfect auxiliary *ha* 'have', which selects the participle of the lexical verb, stranding of the object of a transitive verb becomes possible (17).

(17) a. **Lest** har han bok-en ikke ennå, bare sett den på sokkel-en.
 read.PTCP has he book-DEF not yet only put it on shelf-DEF
 'As for reading, he hasn't read the book yet, only put it on the shelf.'
 (*Norwegian*, Siri M. Gjersøe p.c.)
 b. **Kysst** har jag henne inte, bara hållit henne i handen.
 kiss.PTCP have I her not onyl held her in hand.DEF
 'As for kissing, I haven't kissed her, only held her by the hand.'
 (*Swedish*, Holmberg 1999: 7)

According to the definition given in section 1.1, the sentences in (17) are examples of verb fronting because the main contentful verb is displaced into the left periphery and associated with a topic interpretation. However, the bipartition of verbal fronting into verb and verb phrase fronting in this book is relevant only in conjunction with the repair strategy associated with one or the other. As no repair can be observed in (17), I will ignore these examples for the time being and treat the Scandinavian languages as only displaying verb phrase fronting.[3]

---

[2] For Danish, I could not find an example showing the ungrammaticality of verb fronting directly. However, the only examples where a single verb appears sentence-initially are of intransitive verbs or of transitive verbs without an overt object (see section 7.2.1). In the absence of any positive evidence for verb fronting with stranded internal arguments, I conclude that it is ungrammatical in the language.

[3] Ultimately, the surface terms 'verb fronting' and 'verb phrase fronting' are linked to underlying syntactic movements such that a verb fronting configuration is the consequence of either $\bar{\text{A}}$-head movement of the verbal head or remnant movement of the verb phrase. The absence of verb

1.4 Verb copy and dummy verb as repairs

Because it is different from regular displacement in not displaying a gap, it has been proposed that the fronted verbal constituent is either base generated in a separate clause (the biclausal analysis of verbal fronting, see Lumsden & Lefebvre 1990, Lumsden 1990, Larson & Lefebvre 1991, Dekydspotter 1992) or independently generated (e.g. as a cognate object or a low copy) and subsequently moved into the left periphery (see among others Bamgbose 1972, Nylander 1985, Stewart 1998, Cable 2004, Kandybowicz 2004, Harbour 2008). If one of these analyses were true, we would be mistaken in treating the verb copy or the dummy verb as a repair phenomenon. Rather, both would constitute inherent parts of an independent construction from which verbal fronting is derived either by adding another regularly generated clause like the first part of the proper biclausal cleft sentence '*It was*

---

fronting in auxiliary-less sentences even if Object Shift took place then indicates that remnant verb phrase movement is not available in these languages. Additionally, for Swedish Holmberg (1999: 7–9) argues that any derivation of (17-b) that involves remnant verb phrase movement violates Holmberg's Generalization stating that Object Shift cannot cross an unmoved verb. The examples in (17) can therefore not be generated by remnant verb phrase movement. Holmberg (1999: 9) suggests that they involve $\bar{\text{A}}$-head movement of the verb to SpecCP. However, if this were the case, we would expect verb fronting to be possible in (16-b) and in (i), where instead of an auxiliary there is a modal verb selecting the infinitive form of the main verb.

(i)   *?Träffa   ska   jag henne inte, men vi   ska   hålla kontakt per e-mail.
      meet.INF shall I   her   not but we shall keep contact by e-mail
                                                                                                                        (*Swedish*, Holmberg 1999: 12)

The fact that it is ungrammatical in these examples indicates that $\bar{\text{A}}$-head movement is not licit in Swedish. Consequently, (17-b) cannot involve either of the movements that are associated with regular verb fronting and hence, Swedish does not show the kind of general verb fronting intended by the definition in section 1.1.

Instead, I would suggest that the apparent verb fronting in (17) is due to the participial status of the main verb. Assuming that a head Part encoding the participial feature(s) is merged above VP the verb would move to this head thereby enabling Object Shift across it in accordance with Holmberg's Generalization (ii-a). The resultant remnant PartP could subsequently undergo movement to SpecCP (ii-b).

(ii)   a.   [$_{PartP}$ Part [$_{VP}$ V DP]]

       b.   [$_{CP}$ [$_{PartP}$ V+Part [$_{VP}$ ___V ___DP]] [$_{C'}$ ... DP ___$_{PartP}$]]

Since due to the absence of the Part head the crucial V-to-Part movement is unavailable in simple present tense sentences as well as in sentences containing a modal, Object Shift is precluded from creating a frontable remnant phrase that contains just the main verb.

eating that Peter did.' or by movement of, for instance, a cognate object like *dance* in '*Peter danced a dance.*'

The biclausal base generation analysis can be argued to be false if verbal fronting shows evidence for movement or monoclausality. This is indeed the case for most languages in the sample where data on the issue were available. Verbal fronting generally appears to behave like wh-movement in the language meaning that it is usually able to cross finite clause boundaries but not permitted from inside a syntactic island like a wh-constituent or a complex noun phrase. In addition, if verbal fronting cannot cooccur with wh-movement (or other types of Ā-movement) in the same sentence this is another indication that it involves movement, the most elegant explanation for the impossibility of coccurrence being that verbal fronting targets the same landing position as wh-movement and is therefore blocked if this position is occupied by some other movee. To give an example, consider the following data from Fongbe (Kwa, Niger-Congo; Benin). Verb fronting is allowed to take place across two finite clause boundaries in (18).

(18) **Xò** wɛ̀ Sìká lìn [$_{CP}$ ɖɔ̀ Kɔ̀fí ɖɔ̀ [$_{CP}$ ɖɔ̀ Àsíbá **xò** Kɔ̀kú]].
hit FOC Sika think   C Kofi say   C Asiba hit Koku
'It is hit that Sika thinks that Kofi said that Asiba did to Koku.'
(*Fongbe*, Law & Lefebvre 1995: 32)

In (19), the copy of the fronted verb is located inside an island, a wh-clause in (19-a) and a complex noun phrase in (19-b). Both sentences are ungrammatical although verb fronting with verb doubling is grammatical in a simple sentence (20).

(19) a. *****Bló** (wɛ̀) Bàyí kànbyɔ̀ [$_{CP}$ ɖɔ̀ étɛ̀$_1$ (wɛ̀) Kɔ̀kú **bló** ___$_1$].
do FOC Bayi ask   C what FOC Koku do
b. *****Gbà**   (wɛ̀) ùn tùn [$_{DP}$ súnû [$_{CP}$ ɖé-è **gbà**   xwé ɔ́]].
destroy FOC 1SG know man   OP-RES destroy house DEF
(*Fongbe*, Ndayiragije 1993: 107f.)

(20) **Xò** wɛ̀ Àsíbá **xò** Kɔ̀kú; e hù è ǎ.
hit FOC Asiba hit Koku he kill him NEG
'It's HIT that Asiba did to Koku; he did not kill him.'
(*Fongbe*, Law & Lefebvre 1995: 35)

Demonstrated in (21) is the ungrammaticality of verb fronting cooccurring with other types of Ā-movement in the same clause such as wh-extraction (21-a), regular noun phrase focus (21-b), and relativization (21-c).

1.4 Verb copy and dummy verb as repairs — 23

(21) a. *Été₁ wè, **dù** wè Kɔ̀kú **dù** ___₁.
what FOC eat FOC Koku eat
b. *[Àsɔ́n ɔ́]₁ wè, **dù** wè Kɔ̀kú **dù** ___₁.
crab DEF FOC eat FOC Koku eat
c. *[Àsɔ́n ɔ́]₁, **dù** wè, ɖé-è Kɔ̀kú **dù** ___₁ ɔ́.
crab DEF eat FOC OP-RES Koku eat DEF
(*Fongbe*, Law & Lefebvre 1995: 16)

The arguments and examples in favour of movement are similar in the majority of languages investigated in this book (see part II).

A further argument in favour of base generation has been made based on so-called genus-species effects. The term describes a situation where the denotation of the fronted verbal constituent deviates from that of the clause-internal subject to the restriction that one is taxonomically related to the other, that is, a subset or superset of it. Consider the Yiddish examples in (22).

(22) a. ?[Essen *fish*] est Maks *hekht*.
eat.INF eats Max pike
'As for eating fish, Max eats pike.'
b. ?[*Forn* keyn amerike] bin ikh *gefloygn* keyn amerike.
travel.INF to America am I flown to America
'As for travelling to America, I have flown to America.'
c. ?[*Forn* keyn amerike] bin ikh *gefloygn keyn nyu-york*.
travel.INF to America am I flown to New York
'As for travelling to America, I have flown to New York.'
(*Yiddish*, Cable 2004: 9)

Evidently, the clause-internal counterparts to the fronted verbal constituents, here further specify the denotation of the latter by denoting themselves a taxonomical subset of them. Thus, in (22-a) *hekht* 'pike' is a subclass of *fish* 'fish', in (22-b) *gefloygn* 'flown' is a more specific form of *forn* 'travel' and in (22-c) *gefloygn keyn nyu-york* 'flown to New York' is a specification of the more general *forn keyn amerike* 'travel to America'. According to Cable (2004), the difference in lexical material in these constructions is hard to explain if the fronted constituent is related to the clause-internal one by movement and therefore supports a base generation analysis. However, I would like to point out that this is not an inevitable conclusion. First, under the copy theory of movement there is, usually implicitly assumed, an operation that creates a copy of the moving item. This copy operation, if properly defined, could be able to alter the featural constitution of the copy such that it only copies a subset of the semantic features of the original element. Assuming that the copy stays behind while the attracted original moves this could give rise to the observed genus-species effect. Alternatively, under a late insertion approach to morphology (e.g. Distributed Morphology, Halle & Marantz 1993, 1994), post-syntactic operations like Impoverishment might change the features of a terminal such that only a more general Vocabulary Item can be inserted. These are just two rough suggestions meant to highlight the fact that genus-species effects do not immediately preclude a movement-based analysis. In light of the rarity of such effects in the languages of the sample, however, I will adopt the stance that the occurrence of genus-species effects provides a weak argument against movement for the time being.

The second explanation for the absence of a gap with verbal fronting is that it is derived from constructions that independently contain a verb copy or a dummy verb. These can, for instance, be cognate object constructions, low verb doubling constructions, or *do*-periphrases. The cognate object, low verb copy, or complement of the dummy verb is then moved from its base position into the left periphery stranding the finite lexical or dummy verb.

There are two main cross-linguistically applicable arguments against this analysis (besides possible language-specific arguments): (i) The purported independent base construction is not productive (enough) in a language meaning that there are grammatical instances of verbal fronting for which no corresponding base construction exists, and (ii) verbal fronting and the alleged base construction may cooccur. A case at hand for the first line of argumentation is provided by Nupe (see also section 7.1.10), which shows verb fronting as in (23-a) and also comprises of a class of verbs that take a cognate object as in (23-b).

(23)   a.   Bi-**ba**   Musa à   **ba** nakàn o.
           RED-cut Musa FUT cut meat   FOC
           'It is CUTTING that Musa will do to the meat.'
   b.   Musa à   nyà   enyà.
           Musa FUT dance dance(N)
           'Musa will dance.'   (*Nupe*, Kandybowicz 2008: 79, 99)

However, the purported base construction of (23-a), in which the fronted verb *biba* 'cut' appears as a cognate object of *ba* 'cut' is ungrammatical (24-a). This also holds if *ba* is nominalized by the prefix *è-* instead of reduplication (24-b).

(24)   a.   *Musa ba nakàn bi-ba.
           Musa cut meat   RED-cut
   b.   *Musa ba nakàn è-ba.
           Musa cut meat   NMLZ-cut   (*Nupe*, Kandybowicz 2008: 99)

Conversely, although it is possible to front the cognate object *enyà* 'dance(N)' as demonstrated in (25), the result does not have the same semantics as a regular verb fronting sentence would, namely that of contrastive verb focus. Rather, its interpretation is similar to that of topicalization (Kandybowicz 2008: 100).

(25) È-**nyà**   Musa à **nyà**   (*enyà)   o.
      NMLZ-dance Musa FUT dance   dance(N) FOC
      'It is a dance that Musa will do.'
      NOT: 'It is DANCING that Musa will do (as opposed to say, performing a ritual).' (*Nupe*, Kandybowicz 2008: 100)

Taken together, verb fronting therefore cannot be derived from the cognate object construction in Nupe.

The second type of counter-argument is the cooccurrence of verbal fronting with its alleged base construction in the same clause. If the former were indeed derived from the latter we would expect this cooccurrence to be impossible as the former necessarily presupposes the deconstruction of the latter. An example for this line of argumentation is provided by Buli, which like Nupe displays both cognate object constructions (26-a) and verb fronting (26-b) independently.

(26) a. Àtìm pù:sì   pū:s-ā.
          Atim greeted greeting-ID.PL
          'Atim greeted greetings.'
      b. (Ká) **pū:s**-ā   àlī/àtì Àtìm **pù:sì**.
          FOC greeting-ID.PL C   Atim greeted
          'It is greetings that Atim greeted.'   (*Buli*, Hiraiwa 2005a: 267)

However, (26-b) cannot be derived from (26-a) by movement of the cognate object *pū:s-ā* 'greeting-ID.PL' into the left periphery because it may appear in its base position in a sentence that also exhibits verb fronting (27).

(27) (Ká) **pū:sī**-kā   àlī/àtì Àtìm **pù:sì**   pū:s-ā.
      FOC greet-NMLZ.SG C   Atim greeted greeting-ID.PL
      'It is greeting that Atim greeted.'   (*Buli*, Hiraiwa 2005a: 267)

For many languages in the sample under consideration here (that are documented well enough) one of these two arguments can be made (see chapter II). Sometimes additional language-specific evidence can be brought up against deriving verbal fronting from independent constructions. However, there are also a few languages to which none of these arguments is applicable. One example is Edo (see section 7.1.3), which shows both verb fronting (28-a) and a cognate object construction (28-b).

(28) a. Ù-**khién**-mwèn ɔ́ré Òzó **khién** èbé.
    NMLZ-sell-NMLZ FOC Ozo sell book
    'It is selling that Ozo did to the book (not say give as a gift).'
  b. Òzó bgé èkhù ù-gbé-mwèn.
    Ozo hit door NMLZ-hit-NMLZ
    'Ozo hit the door a hitting.' (*Edo*, Stewart 2001: 92, 95)

The cognate object construction is available for a large range of verbs and cannot cooccur with verb fronting in the same clause (29). Thus, arguments (i) and (ii) do not pertain to Edo.

Other languages for which it is not immediately clear that verbal fronting cannot be derived from an independent construction include German and Welsh. In both of these there exists a *do*-periphrase that may optionally be used instead of a regular synthetically inflected verb without an associated change of meaning (although there may well be a change in register; see among others Abraham & Fischer 1998, Schwarz 2009, Weber 2017 for German, and Sproat 1985, Borsley et al. 2007 for Welsh). Examples of a regular synthetic form of German and Welsh are given in (29-a) and (30-a), while the corresponding *do*-periphrases are provided in (29-b) and (30-b).

(29) a. Er wäscht jede Woche das Auto.
    he washes the car every week
    'He washes the car every week.'
  b. Er tut jede Woche das Auto waschen.
    he does every week the car wash.INF
    'He washes the car every week.' (colloquial) (*German*)

(30) a. Gwelodd Siôn ddraig.
    see.3SG.PST John dragon
    'John saw a dragon.'
  b. Gwnaeth Siôn weld draig.
    do.3SG.PST John see dragon
    'John saw a dragon.' (*Welsh*, Sproat 1985: 176)

With verbal fronting the observed repair in both languages is the respective verb meaning 'do', i.e. *tun* in German (31-a) and *gwneud* in Welsh (31-b), the same verb that is used in the periphrases in (30) and (29).

(31) a. [Das Auto **waschen**] **tut** er jede Woche.
    the car wash.INF does he every week
    'As for washing the car, he does it every week.' (*German*)

b. [**Cau** y glwyd] y **gwnaeth** y ffermwr.
　　shut the gate　　c did　　　the farmer
　　'Shut the gate, the farmer did.'　　　　(*Welsh*, Rouveret 2012: 918)

It would therefore seem like an elegant solution to analyse (31) as the result of VP-movement applying to (29-b) and (30-b), respectively. The fact that a dummy verb meaning 'do' appears in verbal fronting would then simply be due to it being present in the basal *do*-periphrase.

At least for German, there is one issue with this approach. As Bayer (2008) notes, the *do*-periphrase is ungrammatical with individual-level predicates like *besitzen* 'to own' (32-a) and *ähneln* 'to resemble' (32-b) (see also Freitag 2019, Bayer & Freitag to appear).[4]

(32)　a.　*Der Klaus **tut**　einen guten Charakter **besitzen**.
　　　　　the Klaus does a　　good character　own
　　　　　'Klaus has good character.'
　　　b.　*Der Klaus **tut**　seinem Vater **ähneln**.
　　　　　the Klaus does his　　father resemble
　　　　　'Klaus resembles his father.'　　　(*German*, Bayer 2008: 4)

Nonetheless, the respective verb and verb fronting counterparts of (32) are fine.

(33)　a.　**Besitzen tut**　der Klaus einen guten Charakter nicht erst seit
　　　　　own.INF does the Klaus a　　good character not　　first since
　　　　　er im　Internat　　war, aber man bemerkt ihn seitdem
　　　　　he in.the boarding.school was but　one notices　him since
　　　　　sicherlich noch deutlicher.
　　　　　certainly　more obviously
　　　　　'As for having, Klaus does not only have good character since he went to a boarding school but one surely notices it more obviously since then.'
　　　b.　[Einen guten Charakter **besitzen**] **tut**　der Klaus nicht erst seit
　　　　　 a　　good character　own　　　does the Klaus not　first since
　　　　　er im　Internat　　war.
　　　　　he in.the boarding.school was
　　　　　'As for having good character, Klaus does not only have it since he went to bearding school.'　　　　　　　　　　　　　(*German*)

---

4 To me these examples are not necessarily ungrammatical. However, they are definitely degraded compared to those in (29).

(34) a. **Ähneln tut** der Klaus seinem Vater nur äußerlich.
resemble does the Klaus his father only outwardly
'As for resembling, Klaus only resembles his father concerning their looks.'
b. [Seinem Vater **ähneln**] **tut** der Klaus nur äußerlich.
his father resemble does the Klaus only outwardly
'As for resembling his father, Klaus only resembles him concerning their looks.' *(German)*

Also, if dummy verb insertion is supposed to be derived from an independent construction in German, Welsh, and similar languages, we would still have to account for its occurrence in languages like Danish, Norwegian, and Swedish, which do not comprise of a German-style *do*-periphrase (35).

(35) a. *Han gør ikke sulte og …
he does not starve and
Intended: 'He doesn't starve and …' *(Danish, Houser et al. 2006: 5)*
b. *Jeg **gjør** aldri **spille** golf
I do never play golf
Intended: 'I never play golf.' *(Norwegian, Lødrup 1990: 9)*
c. *Johan gjorde köra bilen.
Johan did drive car.DEF
Intended: 'Johan drove the car.' *(Swedish, Platzack 2008: 1)*

In this regard, note that even in languages with a *do*-periphrase, the analysis of dummy verb insertion as derived from this independent construction is not forced by the data. One could equally well analyse the dummy verb that occurs in verbal fronting as a verbal fronting-induced repair that has nothing to do with the dummy verb that appears in the *do*-periphrase.

Although the former explanation appears to be more elegant than the latter, it does not account for the fact that verbal fronting requires there to be a dummy verb at all. In other words, one would have to postulate an additional restriction on verbal fronting that confines it to only apply to sentences that independently contain a *do*-periphrase. The same holds, of course, for verb doubling languages, where verbal fronting would have to be restricted to cognate object or low verb doubling constructions. Thus, deriving verbal fronting from independently available verb doubling or dummy verb constructions by restricting its applicability is not more or less elegant than allowing that it applies across the board but triggers a repair in case the finiteness would otherwise remain unexpressed. Both solutions are, in a sense, two opposite sides of the same coin. Nonetheless, treating verb doubling and dummy verb insertion as a repair is able to account for both, languages that have an independent verb doubling or dummy verb construction and those that do not, whereas treating them as parts of independent constructions does not extend to languages where these constructions are not attested outside of verbal fronting. From the cross-linguistic perspective taken in this book an analysis of verb doubling and dummy verb insertion as repairs triggered by verbal fronting is to be preferred due to its wider empirical coverage. I will, therefore, also regard them as repairs in languages where they could plausibly be derived from independent constructions with the consequence that the proposed analysis in chapter 4 applies to those languages as well.

1.5 Category of the moved constituent

Languages with verbal fronting vary with regard to the (non-object) material that may accompany the fronted constituent. In languages like Swedish (36-a) and Yoruba (36-b), for example, the fronted verb may be marked with tense/aspect and agreement markers while this is not possible in, for instance, Krachi (37-a) and Papiamentu (37-b).

(36) a. [**Läse**-r boken] **gör** han nu.
          read-PRS book does he now
          'Reading the book he is now.'
                                              (*Swedish*, Källgren & Prince 1989: 47)
     b. Mí-[máa-**ra**   iwé] ni Ajé máa **ra** iwé.
          NMLZ-PROG-buy paper FOC Aje PROG buy paper
          'It is continuous book-buying that Aje does/did.'
                                                (*Yoruba*, Manfredi 1993: 20)

(37) a. *Kɛ-[ɛ/kɛ-**dıkɛ**   i-gyo] yı ɔkyı wʊ ɛ/kɛ-**dıkɛ**.
          NMLZ-PST/FUT-cook PL-yam FOC woman the PST/FUT-cook
                                      (*Krachi*, Kandybowicz & Torrence 2016: 233)
     b. *Ta a **traha** e a **traha**.
          FOC ASP work he ASP work   (*Papiamentu*, Muysken 1977: 93)

In other languages, we find that nominal modifiers like determiners or adjectives may accompany the verb in sentence-initial position. Examples thereof are Dagaare (38-a) and Fongbe (38-b).

(38) a. [À bóɔ́/bó-vèlàà ná **dááó**] lá ká ń (dà) **dà**.
          DEF goat/goat-good DEM buy.NMLZ FOC C 1SG PST buy
          'It is buying that (good) goat that I did.'
                                        (*Dagaare*, Hiraiwa & Bodomo 2008: 805)

b. **Yì** ɔ́ wɛ̀ Kɔ̀kú **yì**.
leave DEF FOC Koku leave
'It is leave (as expected) that Koku did.'

(*Fongbe*, Lefebvre & Brousseau 2002: 506)

Note that the presence of nominal modifiers and other nominal markers like number and case constitutes an argument against the analysis of verb phrase fronting as incorporation of the object into the verbal head (in the sense of Baker 1988) followed by verb fronting. As Baker (2009: 153) points out, the appearance of such additional material in the structure precludes an analysis in terms of genuine noun incorporation. However, it may well be possible that varying degrees of pseudo noun incorporation are at play regulating how much and what kind of material can be fronted alongside the object (see Massam 2001, Dayal 2011). While there are some approaches to pseudo noun incorporation where the object undergoes head movement into the verbal head (i.e. proper incorporation, see Chung & Ladusaw 2004, Baker 2014), in the most recent ones the object stays inside the VP (Kalin 2014, 2018, Tyler 2018, Levin 2019, Driemel 2020). Pseudo noun incorporation of the internal argument (to varying degrees) is therefore not an argument against treating a fronted string containing a verb and its object as constituting a proper verb phrase (rather than a complex verbal head).

While no examples of verbal fronting with high sentence adverbs appearing in the fronted constituent are attested in the languages of the sample, there are a number of languages which permit low adverbs in this position. Thus, for instance, Krachi (39-a) and Hausa (39-b) both allow a manner adverb to accompany the fronted verb (phrase).

(39) a. Kɛ-[**mɔ** bireŋ] yɪ Kofi ɛ-**mɔ** a-kyuŋ.
NMLZ-kill quickly FOC Kofi PST-kill PL-fowl
'It was SLAUGHTERING QUICKLY that Kofi did to fowls.'

(*Krachi*, Kandybowicz & Torrence 2016: 231)

b. [**Cin** abinci da saurii] suka **yi**.
eat.VN food with haste 3P.REL.PERF do
'Eating food in a hurry they did.' (*Hausa*, Tuller 1986: 430)

Adverbs in particular may be helpful in determining the category of the fronted constituent on a language-specific basis. Given that there is evidence that low adverbs attach to either VP or *v*P in a given language, then their presence or absence in the fronted constituent indicates what that constituent's category is. Thus, suppose that manner adverbs like *bireŋ* 'quickly' in Krachi could be shown to adjoin to *v*P. Their ability to appear in verbal fronting then strongly indicates that what is fronted in Krachi is a *v*P rather than a VP because if it were a VP we would expect the manner adverb to obligatorily be stranded. Of equal use are aspectual markers which, assuming that aspect is hosted either on its own Asp-head or on v, provide another cue to whether the fronted constituent is at least an AspP or a vP.

The presence of an adverb in verb fronting could also help to determine whether this fronting involves a bare head or a remnant phrase. In the former case, adverbs in general should be excluded from occuring with the fronted constituent because as adjuncts they necessarily require a phrasal category to adjoin to. In the latter case, depending on whether the constituent is a remnant VP or vP, VP-adverbs or vP-adverbs, respectively, should be able to accompany the fronted verb. As a consequence, the presence of any adverb in verb fronting indicates that the fronted constituent must be phrasal rather than a bare head and that verb fronting therefore cannot involve $\bar{A}$-head movement.

Unfortunately, information on the possibility of adverbs or TAM-markers inside the fronted constituent is only inconsistently, if at all, available for most languages in the sample. I included the data that could be found in the language descriptions in part II in the hope that a more systematic investigation of the matter may fill the gaps in the future.

1.6 The role of information structure

Since verbal fronting is associated with one of two different information structural interpretations, namely either focus or topic, one might suggest that each kind of repair, verb doubling and dummy verb insertion, may be uniquely linked to one of these interpretations. However, this is not the case. For each of the four combinations in the cross-classification of type of repair and information-structural function there are at least three languages that instantiate the relevant cross-classification as demonstrated in the table in (40).

(40) *Cross-classification of repair and information structural function*

	Focus	Topic
verb doubling	Nupe, Buli, Dagaare	Polish, Br. Portuguese, Vietnamese
dummy verb insertion	Hausa, Wolof, Welsh	Dutch, Swedish, Skou

Of course, the classification of verbal fronting in a particular language as focalization or topicalization here relies on the classification made in the respective literature which is often not extensively argued for or justified in detail. The terms 'topic' and 'focus' are therefore somewhat vague and imprecise also because different researchers in different times may have used and understood (and thus diagnosed) them quite differently from each other. Consequently, closer inspection of the interpretation of verbal fronting in some languages might find that what has been claimed to be a topic is actually a focus or vice versa. However, until further research proves the consulted literature wrong I will proceed on the assumption that the classifications therein are correct. In this light, the information-structural function of the fronted constituent has no determining effect on the kind of repair.

Interestingly, though, there is a clear trend in the data such that verbal fronting in African languages and African-influenced creoles receive a focus interpretation whereas it tends to have a topic reading in the non-African languages. I will not pursue this observation further here.

2 Patterns in verbal fronting

In this chapter, I will first present the familiar symmetric patterns of verbal fronting in languages that have both types in more detail arguing that in most of them there is evidence that verbal fronting involves movement but is not derived from independent constructions containing a verb copy or a dummy verb. I will then introduce the asymmetric pattern of Asante Twi and Limbum and argue that they too involve movement and a proper repair of the gap. Based on these three patterns a first generalization will be established that states the inexistence of the fourth logically possible pattern. Further, I will show that the type of repair cannot be linked to the information-structural role of the fronted constituent. In the last part of the chapter, I then take a look at languages that only have one of the two types of verbal fronting. These languages will give rise to a second generalization.

2.1 Repair patterns in languages with both verb and verb phrase fronting

Having discussed some general properties of verbal fronting in the previous sections we can now turn to the interaction of the kind of verbal fronting, i.e. verb or verb phrase, and the observed repair. First, we will take a look at languages which exhibit both verb and verb phrase fronting. These have implicitly been assumed to employ the same type of repair in both kinds of verbal fronting, an assumption that is refuted by the asymmetric pattern of Asante Twi and Limbum. In the second part of this section, we will then closer scrutinize languages that show only one kind of verbal fronting observing that a one-to-one correspondence holds between the type of repair and the kind of fronting. Languages which allow a fronted transitive verb to drag its objects along as well as strand them can *a priori* be expected to show four different patterns of repairs (assuming that optionality between two repairs is barred). These are given in table (1).

(1)   *Possible repair patterns in languages with both kinds of verbal fronting*

	Verb fronting	Verb phrase fronting
I	verb copy	verb copy
II	dummy verb	dummy verb
III	verb copy	dummy verb
IV	dummy verb	verb copy

Patterns I and II are symmetric patterns in the sense that the same repair strategy is used in both verb and verb phrase fronting. Patterns III and IV are asymmetric patterns because the repair strategy is different depending on the kind of verbal fronting. I will discuss each pattern in turn.

2.1.1 Symmetric verb doubling

In the present sample, the most frequent of the patterns in (1) is pattern I where verb doubling is the repair in both verb and verb phrase fronting. This pattern is attested in 16 of the 20 (22, counting Asante Twi and Limbum) languages that show both kinds of verbal fronting. Languages that instantiate it are in alphabetical order:

1. Brazilian Portuguese
   (Romance, Indo-European; Bastos-Gee 2009, see also section 8.2.1)
2. Buli
   (Gur, Niger-Congo; Hiraiwa 2005a,b, see also section 8.2.2)
3. Dagaare
   (Gur, Niger-Congo; Hiraiwa & Bodomo 2008, see also section 8.2.3)
4. Hebrew
   (Semitic, Afro-Asiatic; Landau 2006, 2007, see also section 8.2.4)
5. Hungarian
   (Uralic; Ürögdi 2006, Vicente 2007, Lipták & Vicente 2009, see also section 8.2.5)
6. Korean
   (Koreanic; Hagstrom 1995, Cho 1997, Nishiyama & Cho 1998, Choi 2000, 2003, Cho & Kim 2002, Jo 2000, 2013, see also section 8.2.6)
7. Krachi
   (Kwa, Niger-Congo; Kandybowicz & Torrence 2016, see also section 8.2.7)
8. Mandarin Chinese
   (Chinese, Sino-Tibetan; Cheng 2008, Cheng & Vicente 2013, see also section 8.2.8)
9. Mani
   (Mel, Niger-Congo; Childs 2011, see also section 8.2.9)
10. Polish
    (Slavic, Indo-European; Bondaruk 2009, 2012, see also section 8.2.10)
11. Russian
    (Slavic, Indo-European; Abels 2001, Verbuk 2006, Aboh & Dyakonova 2009, see also section 8.2.11)

2.1 Repair patterns in languages with both verb and verb phrase fronting — 35

12. Spanish
    (Romance, Indo-European; Vicente 2007, 2009, Lipták & Vicente 2009, see also section 8.2.12)
13. Tiv
    (Southern Bantoid, Niger-Congo; Angitso 2015, Táíwò & Angitso 2016, see also section 8.2.13)
14. Vietnamese
    (Viet-Muong, Austro-Asiatic; Tran 2011, Trinh 2011, see also section 8.2.14)
15. Yiddish
    (Germanic, Indo-European; Davis & Prince 1986, Källgren & Prince 1989, Cable 2004, see also section 8.2.15)
16. Yoruba
    (Defoid, Niger-Congo; Manfredi 1993, see also section 8.2.16)

A few examples of this very widespread pattern are given below from Brazilian Portuguese (2), Buli (3), Korean (4), and Vietnamese (5).

(2) a. **Temperar** o cozinheiro **temperou** o peixe (não a carne).
       season.INF the cook seasoned the fish not the meat
       'As for seasoning something, the cook seasoned the fish (not the meat).'
    b. [**Temperar** aquele peixe] o cozinheiro sempre **temperou** (mas...)
       season.INF that fish the cook always seasoned
       but
       'As for seasoning that fish, the cook always seasoned it (but...)'
       (*Br. Portuguese*, Bastos-Gee 2009: 162)

(3) a. (Ká) **dē**-kā àlī/àtì Àtìm *(dè) máŋgò-kú dīēm.
       FOC eat-NMLZ C Àtìm ate mango-DEF yesterday
       'It is eating that Àtìm ate the mango yesterday. (not e.g. throwing it away)'
    b. (Ká) [máŋgò-kú **dē**]-kā àlī/àtì Àtìm *(dè) dīēm.
       FOC mango-DEF eat-NMLZ C Àtìm ate yesterday
       'It is eating the mango that Àtìm ate yesterday. (not e.g. buying a banana)' (*Buli*, Hiraiwa 2005a: 262)

(4) a. **Masi**-ki-nun Chelsu-ka mayckwu-lul **masi**-ess-ta.
       drink-NMLZ-TOP Chelsu-NOM beer-ACC drink-PST-DECL
       'As for drinking, Chelswu drank beer.' (*Korean*, Jo 2000: 97, en. 4)
    b. [Sakwa-lul **mek**]-ki-nun John-i **mek**-ess-ta.
       apple-ACC eat-NMLZ-TOP John-NOM eat-PST-DECL
       'As for eating apples, John did.' (*Korean*, Cho & Kim 2002: 679)

(5) a. **Doc** thi toi co **doc** quyen sach nay, nhung khong hieu.
 read TOP I ASR read CL book this but not understand
 'As for reading this book, I read, but I don't understand.'
 b. [**Doc** quyen sach nay] thi toi co **doc**, nhung khong hieu.
 read CL book this TOP I ASR read but not understand
 'As for reading this book, I read, but I don't understand.'

(Vietnamese, Tran 2011: 60f.)

The fact that verb doubling occurs in both verb fronting and verb phrase fronting, if a language has both processes, seems hardly surprising, at least under the most intuitive and widespread explanation for verb doubling, namely that the verb has to fulfill two conflicting requirements: On the one hand it needs to move into a focus/topic position in the left periphery of the clause while on the other hand it has to express finiteness, e.g. host inflectional affixes TP-internally. This conflict is then resolved by doubling the verb such that one copy of it is moved to the designated focus/topic position while another copy of the same verb is placed within TP to encode finiteness (see e.g. Cho & Nishiyama 2000, Abels 2001, Travis 2003, Kobele 2006, Landau 2006, Bayer 2008, Fleischer 2008, Kandybowicz 2008, Aboh & Dyakonova 2009, Vicente 2009, Müller 2009b, Trinh 2011). As these conflicting requirements arise in verb fronting and verb phrase fronting alike, the most economical, and hence expected, strategy is for a language to employ the same repair in both configurations.

2.1.2 Symmetric dummy verb insertion

The abovementioned repair does not necessarily have to be verb doubling. It is also conceivable to insert a default, semantically largely vacuous verb that acts as a host for finiteness inflection, thus instantiating pattern II. Indeed, this pattern is attested in the clear minority of four of the 20 (22) languages with both kinds of fronting. These are in alphabetical order:

1. Basque
 (isolate; Haddican 2007, Elordieta & Haddican 2016, see also section 8.1.1)
2. Breton
 (Celtic, Indo-European; Anderson 1981, Borsley et al. 1996, Jouitteau 2011, see also section 8.1.2)
3. Dutch
 (Germanic, Indo-European; Broekhuis & Corver 2015, see also section 8.1.3)
4. German
 (Germanic, Indo-European; Diedrichsen 2008, see also section 8.1.4)

Examples for this pattern II are given below from Breton (6) and German (7).

(6) a. **Debriñ** a **raio** Yannig krampouezh e Kemper hiziv.
      eating PRT will.do Johnny crêpes   in Quimper today
      'Johnny will eat crêpes in Quimper today.'
   b. [**Debriñ** krampouezh] a **raio** Yannig e Kemper hiziv.
      eat   crêpes   PRT will.do Johnny in Quimper today
      'Johnny will eat crêpes in Quimper today.'

      (*Breton*, Anderson 1981: 34, 30)

(7) a. **Waschen tut** er das Auto nie.
      wash.INF does he the car never
      'He never washes the car.'
   b. [Das Auto **waschen**] **tut** er nie.
      the car wash.INF   does he never
      'Something that he never does is wash the car.'

      (*German*, Diedrichsen 2008: 221)

Hitherto, neither of the asymmetric patterns had been attested indicating that the choice of repair is completely independent of the kind of verbal fronting. The implicit generalization could be formulated as in (8).

(8) *Verbal fronting generalization (to be refuted)*
    If a language shows some repair mechanism in verb fronting it also shows that same repair mechanism in verb phrase fronting and vice verse (provided it displays both kinds of fronting).

This generalization seems very reasonable from an economical perspective. When there are two very similar constructions, verb and verb phrase fronting, that evidently cause the same problem of leaving the clause without a finite verb, then the most economical and straightforward way to resolve the issue is to use the same repair in both kinds of construction. However, in the following section, I will present evidence that (8) does not hold in the form of two languages manifesting the asymmetric pattern III.

2.1.3 A new, asymmetric pattern

In this section, verbal fronting in Asante Twi (Kwa, Niger-Congo; Ghana) and Limbum (Narrow Grassfields Bantu, Niger-Congo; Cameroon) will be examined. As can be observed in (9) and (10) the repair pattern in both languages is the asymmetric pattern III, where verb doubling occurs with verb fronting (9-a)/(10-a) but dummy verb insertion appears with verb phrase fronting (9-b)/(10-b).

(9) a. **Sí**(-é)   na Kofi **á-sí**/*á-yɔ́   dán.
         build-NMLZ FOC Kofi PRF-build/PRF-do house
         'Kofi has BUILT a house. (not e.g. bought one)'

     b. [Dán **sí**]-(é)   na Kofi *á-sí/**á-yɔ́**.
         house build-NMLZ FOC Kofi PRF-build/PRF-do
         'Kofi has BUILT A HOUSE. (not e.g. bought a boat)'   (*Asante Twi*)

(10) a. Á r-**yū** (cí)   njíŋwè fɔ́ bí **yū**/*gī msāŋ.
         FOC 5-buy (COMP) woman DET FUT1 buy/do rice
         'The woman will BUY rice.'

     b. Á r-[**yū** msāŋ] (cí) njíŋwè fɔ́ bí *yū/**gī**.
         FOC 5-buy rice (COMP) woman DET FUT1 buy/do
         'The woman will BUY RICE.'   (*Limbum*)

The examples in (9) and (10) are syntactic configurations where a (nominalised) verbal constituent – the verb alone in (9-a) and (10-a) and the verb with its internal argument in (9-b) and (10-b) – appears in the left periphery of the clause expressing focus of that constituent. As in many other West African languages, there are two copies of the main verb in (9-a) and (10-a), one of them fronted and nominalised/nonfinite, the other in its base position and finite. In (9-b) and (10-b), on the other hand, the finite copy of the main verb is replaced by a dummy verb *yɔ* and *gī*, respectively (both translatable as 'do'), while the only occurrence of the main verb is in the fronted nominalised object-verb complex. In (9) and (10), dummy verb insertion occurs in verb phrase fronting but verb doubling in verb fronting, thus proving (8) wrong.

In the following, I will present verbal fronting in both languages in detail showing that verb and verb phrase fronting behave alike within each language and like verbal fronting constructions in other languages. In particular, I will address various properties of verbal fronting some of which have been discussed in section 1 and provide evidence that verbal fronting involves movement as well as evidence that verb doubling and dummy verb insertion are indeed repairs.

2.1.3.1 Asante Twi

Asante Twi, a dialect of Akan, is a Kwa language of the Niger-Congo family spoken by about nine million people in Ghana, centered around the city of Kumasi. It has a two-way tone distinction with high tones marked with an acute and low tones left unmarked. Its basic word order is SVO (11).[1]

(11) Kofí á-si   dán.
      Kofi PRF-build house
      'Kofi has built a house.'

The language shows both verb and verb phrase fronting. Interestingly, however, it does not behave like most other languages that have both constructions in exhibiting the same repair, either verb doubling or dummy verb insertion, in both. Rather, verb fronting in Asante Twi leads to verb doubling (12-a) while verb phrase fronting results in dummy verb insertion (12-b). The respective alternative repair in each case renders the sentence ungrammatical.

(12) a. **Sí**-(é)   na Kofí **á-sí**/*á-yɔ́   dán.
          build-NMLZ FOC Kofi PRF-build/PRF-do house
          'Kofi has BUILT a house. (not e.g. bought one)'
      b. [Dán **sí**]-(é) na Kofí *á-sí/**á-yɔ́**.
          house build-NMLZ FOC Kofi PRF-build/PRF-do
          'Kofi has BUILT A HOUSE. (not e.g. bought a boat)'

The preposed constituent can optionally be marked with a nominalizing suffix -é. While this is generally true for both verb and verb phrase fronting, my informant stresses that there is a strong preference to omit the nominalizer, in verb fronting even more than in verb phrase fronting. The focus marker *na* is the same that appears in standard nominal focus constructions (13-a, b) (and *ex-situ* wh-questions (13-c, d)). Hence, as expected, verbal fronting, too, has a (contrastive) focus interpretation.[2]

(13) a. Kofí na ɔ-bóá-a   Afiá.
          Kofi FOC 3SG-help-PST Afia
          'It is Kofi who helped Afia.'   (Marfo 2005: 9)

---

1 Unless otherwise noted, all data in this section were elicited from my informant Sampson Korsah. Any occurring errors are mine.
2 While both verb and verb phrase fronting in (12) may be used to answer the questions in (i-a, b), and are therefore interpreted as contrastive focus, only verb phrase fronting (12-b) is felicitous as an answer to question (i-c), and may therefore serve to express new information focus.

(i)   a. Did Kofi buy a house?
      b. Did Kofi buy a car?
      c. What did Kofi do?

      b. Dán   na Kofí á-sí.
          house FOC Kofi PRF-build
          'It is a house that Kofi has built.'
      c. Hwán na Baá ré-séré   nó?
          who   FOC Baa PROG-laugh 3SG
          'Who is Baa laughing at?'   (Marfo 2005: 81)
      d. Déén na Ám!má pέ?
          what FOC Ama   like
          'What does Ama like?'   (Korsah & Murphy 2019: 5, ex. 8-b.)

This asymmetric pattern of gap avoidance in verbal fronting has hitherto remained unnoticed and has, to my best knowledge, not been described in the literature.

    In this section, I will investigate the syntactic properties of verb and verb phrase fronting. Besides having the same information structural interpretation, both constructions behave alike with respect to Ā-diagnostics, negation, and additional material in the fronted constituent. Further, there is evidence for Ā-head movement in verb fronting and for the fronted constituent being of category V rather than v. In addition, I present an argument against an approach that derives verb phrase fronting from cognate object constructions or an underlying yɔ-periphrase.

    Before we delve into this matter, however, let me take you on a short digression. In Asante Twi there is a default verbal element *yɛ* which is phonologically similar to the dummy verb *yɔ* and can also be translated as 'do' (and 'make' and 'be', among others). This element has a curious distribution, obligatorily occurring in simple past tense clauses with intransitive verbs (unergative and unaccusative) (14-a, b) and monotransitive simple past tense clauses where the object is moved (14-c).

(14)   a. Kofí sa-a   *(yɛ).
           Kofi dance-PST yɛ
           'Kofi danced.'
      b. Dua nó shi-i   *(yɛ).
           tree DEF burn-PST yɛ
           'The tree burned.'
      c. Déén na Ám!má di-i   *(yɛ)?
           what FOC Ama   eat-PST yɛ
           'What did Ama eat?'
      d. Kofí ré-sa   (*yɛ). / Kofí á-sa   (*yɛ).
           Kofi PROG-dance yɛ / Kofi PFV-dance yɛ
           'Kofi is dancing. / Kofi has danced.'
                                                    (Kandybowicz 2015: 244, 264; tones added)

Kandybowicz (2015) analyses the occurrence of *yɛ* in these cases as prosodically conditioned. Under the Match theory of syntactic-prosodic constituency correspondence (Selkirk 2011) *yɛ* is inserted late as a Last Resort to avoid a mapping of prosodically vacuous domains from empty syntactic Spell-Out domains which would violate his proposed constraint against prosodic vacuity. The relevant Spell-Out domain here is AspP, which is, as Kandybowicz (2015) argues, the sister of the phase head *v*. *Yɛ* is ungrammatical if the verb is marked for aspect (14-d) because in this case the verb has only moved to Asp and hence the AspP is not empty (15-a). However, if a verb shows an overt past tense affix it has moved out of AspP to T (see also Kobele & Torrence 2006: 163) and, in case it is intransitive, left behind a fully evacuated AspP (15-b) which triggers *yɛ*-insertion (14-a, b). In case the object of a transitive verb with an overt past tense affix has been moved away, too (16), *yɛ* also occurs, because both the verb and the object have left AspP (14-c).

(15) a.

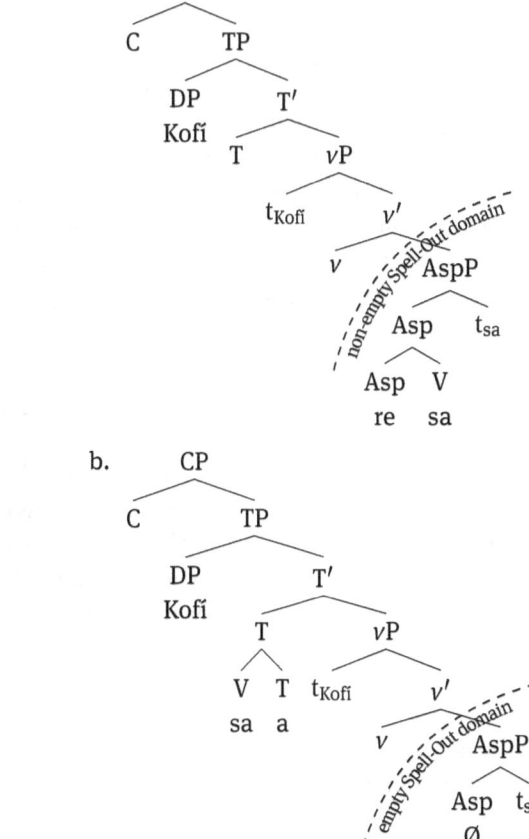

b.

(16)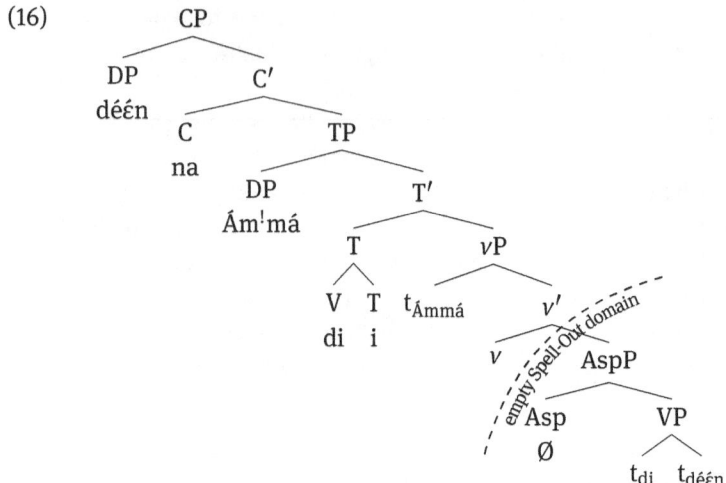

With this in mind let us consider verbal fronting. Since *yɔ* is phonologically and semantically similar to *yɛ* one might be tempted to treat them as variants of the same underlying element *yE*, whose insertion is conditioned by prosodic vacuity as proposed in Kandybowicz (2015). This is, however, not possible. As shown in (17), *yɔ* occurs in cases where the AspP is not empty but contains an overt aspectual affix. The constraint against prosodic vacuity not being violated here, insertion of *yE* is unexpected and unexplained under the approach sketched above.

(17) [Dán **sí**](-é)   na Kofi ré-**yɔ́**.
      house build-NMLZ FOC Kofi PROG-do
      'Kofi is BUILDING A HOUSE.'

One might argue that the aspect exponent in (17) is only inserted very late, as would be the case in Distributed Morphology (DM), and that prosodically conditioned *yE*-insertion happens earlier, at a point where the AspP is still devoid of any phonological material. *Yɔ* might then be regarded as the affix-bearing allomorph of *yE*. But this would suggest that prosodic domains are created (and prosodic vacuity is determined) before vocabulary insertion into f-morphemes[3] (roughly, functional heads) has taken place, i.e. before all the phonological material of a Spell-Out domain has been assembled (e.g. via Vocabulary Insertion). New phonological material, like the aspect affix, that becomes available only after construction of prosodic structure would have to be integrated into it, uneconomically requiring a second instance of prosodic structure creation.

---

3 In DM, the term 'morpheme' denotes a syntactic terminal node and its morphosyntactic feature bundle, not the phonological exponent of that node. Terminals for which there is no free choice

2.1 Repair patterns in languages with both verb and verb phrase fronting — 43

However, even if one adopts the Late Insertion account, this cannot be the whole story because there are instances of yɔ in Spell-Out domains that contain more than just affixal material. Consider the grammatical sentence in (18) which combines VP fronting with simple past tense, where Asp is empty and the verb moves to T (Kandybowicz 2015), and exhibits both yɛ and yɔ.

(18) [Dán sí](-é) na Kofí **yɔ́**-ɔ́ yɛ.
house build-NMLZ FOC Kofi do-PST yɛ
'Kofi BUILT A HOUSE.'

According to an analysis that conflates yɛ and yɔ, both instances of the default verbal element should be triggered by the need to avoid prosodically empty Spell-Out domains. Yɛ is inserted upon Spell-Out of the first phase domain that is sent to PF, which is the sister of v, i.e. the empty AspP. Under standard assumptions about phases, the next domain that is spelled out is the TP which is the domain of the next phase head C. This domain, however, is not empty in the above example as it contains the subject which, as an l-morpheme, crucially must have undergone Vocabulary Insertion before prosodic domain construction (otherwise every syntactic domain would map onto an empty prosodic domain reducing the whole approach to absurdity). Nevertheless, yɔ is inserted, although this, crucially, does not happen to avoid a prosodically empty domain but rather to provide a host for the past tense affix. I thereby conclude that Kandybowicz's (2015) conditions for yɛ-insertion are different from those of the phonologically and semantically similar element yɔ and that they therefore cannot be the same element.

That said, we can now turn towards examining the properties of verbal fronting. First, note that verb phrase fronting with definite objects (19-a) is considerably degraded compared to verb phrase fronting with indefinites (19-b).[4]

---

as to Vocabulary Insertion, i.e. whose phonological realisation is solely determined by their morphosyntactic content are f-morphemes. L-morphemes, on the other hand, allow for a choice, i.e. they may be filled by Vocabulary Items that denote language specific concepts. The distinction is roughly that between functional and lexical heads (cf. Halle 1992, Embick 1997, Marantz 1997, Harley & Noyer 1998, 1999).

4 At first glance, this might be taken as an indication that the object in verb phrase fronting constructions incorporates into the verb which is subsequently nominalized and displaced into the left periphery. However, the fronted object may be overtly marked for plural (i), which is untypical for incorporated nouns (Baker 1988, 2009).

(i) [A-dán **sí**](-é) na Kofí á-**yɔ́**.
PL-house build-NMLZ FOC Kofi PFV-do
'Kofi has BUILT HOUSES. (not e.g. bought cars)'

(19) a. ??[Dán nó **sí**](-é) na Kofí á-**yɔ́**.
    house DEF build-NMLZ FOC Kofi PRF-do
    'Kofi has BUILT THE HOUSE (not, say, bought the car).'
  b. [Dán **sí**](-é) na Kofí á-**yɔ́**.
    house build-NMLZ FOC Kofi PRF-do
    'Kofi has BUILT A HOUSE (not, say, bought a car).'

With regard to the question whether verbal fronting involves Ā-movement there are several arguments in favour of this. First, the dependency can cross finite clause boundaries (20) and is sensitive to islands such as Wh-Islands (21), Complex NP Islands (22), Subject Islands (23), Relative Clause Islands (24), Adjunct Islands (25), and the Coordinate Structure Constraint (26).[5]

(20) a. **Sí**(-é) na Ama ká-a [CP sɛ́ Kofí á-**si** dán].
    build-NMLZ FOC Ama say-PST COMP Kofi PRF-build house
    'Ama said that Kofi has BUILT a house.'
  b. [Dán **sí**](-é) na Ama ká-a [CP sɛ́ Kofí á-**yɔ́**].
    house build-NMLZ FOC Ama say.PST COMP Kofi PRF-do
    'Ama said that Kofi has BUILT A HOUSE.'

Furthermore, if the structure were indeed derived by noun incorporation, this would require massive look-ahead, because it would have to only be possible in case the incorporation structure is moved to the left periphery at a very late stage of the derivation. As (ii) attests, noun incorporation and the connected word order change is not possible if the object-verb complex stays *in-situ*.

(ii) *Kofí dán-si.
    Kofi house-build
    Intended: 'Kofi house-builds.'

I conclude that the impossibility of definite marking must be caused by something else. One possible explanations is that definites obligatorily have to leave their thematic (i.e. base-merged) position in order to be licensed (Diesing 1992). In that case, the definite objects have to move out of the VP and are thus exempt from being fronted in verb phrase fronting structures.

5 This contradicts Saah & Goodluck (1995), who show that Asante Twi does not exhibit island effects in question formation, relativization, and topicalization. However they only tested cases of Ā-movement from argument positions the island insensitivity of which is, as Korsah & Murphy (2019) argue, due to Asante Twi having obligatory resumption with DP-movement, where resumption can obviate island effects (Borer 1984). Under certain conditions, i.e. for inanimates, the resumptive pronoun can be deleted making it look like a gap. Consequently, verb doubling and *do*-support in Asante Twi cannot be treated on a par with resumption (i.e. as "verbal resumption") because one would expect them, as overt resumptive elements, to render the dependency insensitive to islands, contrary to fact.

(21) *Wh-Island*
   a. ***Sí**(-é)   na Ama bísá-a [_CP_ sɛ   dabɛ́n na Kofí **sí**-i
      build-NMLZ FOC Ama ask-PST   COMP when FOC Kofí build-PST
      dán   ].
      house
      'Ama asked when Kofí BUILT a house.'
   b. *?[Dán **sí**](-é)   na Ama bísá-a [_CP_ sɛ   dabɛ́n na Kofí
      house build-NMLZ FOC Ama ask-PST   COMP when FOC Kofí
      yɔ́-ɔɛ́].
      do-PST
      'Ama asked when Kofí BUILT A HOUSE.'

(22) *Complex NP Island*
   a. ***Sí**(-é)   na mé-ń-té-e   [_DP_ atétésɛ́m bíárá [_CP_ sɛ
      build-NMLZ FOC 1SG-NEG-hear-PST   rumour.PL any   COMP
      Kofí á-**si**   dán   ]].
      Kofí PRF-build house
      'I didn't hear any rumours that Kofí has BUILT a house.'
   b. *?[Dán **sí**](-é)   na mé-ń-té-e   [_DP_ atétésɛ́m bíárá [_CP_
      house build-NMLZ FOC 1SG-NEG-hear-PST   rumour.PL any
      sɛ́   Kofí á-**yɔ́**   ]].
      COMP Kofí PRF-do
      'I didn't hear any rumours that Kofí has BUILT A HOUSE.'

(23) *Subject Island*
   a. ***Sí**(-é)   na [_CP_ sɛ́   Kofí á-**si**   dán nó] má-a Ama
      build-NMLZ FOC   COMP Kofí PRF-build house CD give-PST Ama
      ání gyé-eɛ́.
      eye collect-PST
      'That Kofí has BUILT a house made Ama happy.'
   b. *[Dán **sí**](-é)   na [_CP_ sɛ́   Kofí á-**yɔ́**   nó] má-a Ama ání
      house build-NMLZ FOC   COMP Kofí PRF-do   CD give Ama eye
      gye-eɛ́.
      collect
      'That Kofí has BUILT A HOUSE made Ama happy.'

(24) *Relative Clause Island*
   a. ***Sí**(-é)   na Ama bísá-a ɛdá [_CP_ áa Kofí **sí**-i   dán]
      build-NMLZ FOC Ama ask-PST day   REL Kofí build-PST house.
      'Ama asked for the day that Kofí BUILT a house.'
   b. *?[Dán **sí**](-é)   na Ama bísá-a ɛdá [_CP_ áa Kofí **yɔ́**-ɔɛ́].
      house build-NMLZ FOC Ama ask-PST day   REL Kofí do-PST
      'Ama asked for the day that Kofí BUILT A HOUSE.'

(25) *Adjunct Island*
    a. ***Sí**(-é)   na Kofí nóm nsúó [cp ésánsé ɔ-a-**sí** dán].
         build-NMLZ FOC Kofi drink water   because 3.SG-PRF-build house
         'Kofi drinks water because he has BUILT a house.'
    b. *?[Dán **sí**](-é)   na Kofí nóm nsúó [cp ésánsé ɔ́-á-**yɔ́**].
         house build-NMLZ FOC Kofi drink water   because 3.SG-PRF-do
         'Kofi drinks water because he has BUILT A HOUSE.'

(26) *Coordinate Structure Constraint*
    a. ***Nóm** na Kofí [&P á-di   bayéré ne á-**nóm**   nsúó].
         drink FOC Kofi   PFV-eat yam   and PFV-drink water
         'Kofi has eaten a yam and DRUNK water.'
    b. *[Nsúó **nóm**](-é)   na Kofí [&P á-di   bayéré ne á-**yɔ́**].
         water drink-NMLZ FOC Kofi   PFV-eat yam   and PFV-do
         'Kofi has eaten yam and DRUNK WATER.'

Second, there are a number of TAM constructions and some morphosyntactic processes in Asante Twi that lead to tonal changes on the verb (Boadi 2008, Paster 2010). Among these changes is a process of low tone raising on verbs with underlying L tones. It is triggered in certain syntactic environments, all of which typically involve Ā-movement, like *ex situ* wh-questions (27-b) and nominal focus fronting (28-b). It raises all L tones on the verb and attached aspectual (but not tense) affixes. The following examples illustrate this for the *pɛ* 'like' (27-a) and *boá* 'help' (28-a) which contain at least one L tone (unmarked).

(27)   a.   Ám¡má **pɛ** bayéré.
             Ama   like yam
             'Ama likes yam.'
       b.   Déén na Ám¡má **pɛ**?
             what FOC Ama   like
             'What does Ama like?'   (Korsah & Murphy 2019: 5)

(28)   a.   Kofí **boá**-a   Afíá.
             Kofi help-PST Afia
             'Kofi helped Afia.'
       b.   Kofí na   ɔ-**bóá**-a   Afíá.
             Kofi FOC 3SG-help-PST Afia
             'It is Kofi who helped Afia.'   (Marfo 2005: 9)

Korsah & Murphy (2019) argue that L tone raising is not a specific property of the *na*-construction (pace Marfo 2005, Marfo & Bodomo 2005), as one might suspect from (28) and (27), because it is also attested in relative clauses (29-b) and affects every verb in a long-distance dependency, where only one instance of *na* is present (30-b) (with (30-a) as baseline).

(29) a. Kofí **waré**-e ɔbáá nó.
Kofi marry-PST woman DEF
'Kofi married the woman.'
b. [_DP_ ɔbáá_i_ [_CP_ áa ɔ_i_-**wáré**-e Kofí nó]] fi Aburí.
woman REL 3SG-marry-PST Kofi CD be.from Aburi
'The woman who married Kofi is from Aburi.' (Saah 2010: 92)

(30) a. Kofí **nim** [_CP_ sɛ́ Ésí á-**ka** [_CP_ sɛ́ Ám¡má **pɛ** bayéré]].
Kofi know COMP Esi PRF-say COMP Ama like yam
'Kofi knows that Esi has said that Ama likes yam.'
b. Déén na Kofí **ním** [_CP_ sɛ Esi á-**ká** [_CP_ sɛ Ám¡má **pɛ́**]]?
what FOC Kofi know COMP Esi PRF-say COMP Ama like
'What does Kofi know that Esi has said that Ama likes?'

(Korsah & Murphy 2019: 8)

Since tonal changes as reflexes of movement are well-attested cross-linguistically (Lahne 2008b, Georgi 2014) and they are associated with verbs (i.e. *v*) in Asante Twi thus corresponding to what is standardly assumed to be a phase head (Chomsky 2000, 2001), Korsah & Murphy (2019) analyse low tone raising on verbs in Asante Twi as a reflex of successive-cyclic Ā-movement through Spec*v*P. Crucially, this tonal change also occurs on the lower verb copy or *yɔ* in the predicate cleft constructions under discussion here (31).

(31) a. **Pɛ** na Ama **pɛ́** bayéré.
like FOC Ama like yam
'Ama LIKES yam.'
b. [Bayéré **pɛ**](-é) na Ama **yɔ́**.
yam like-NMLZ FOC Ama do
'It is liking yam that Ama does.'

If Korsah and Murphy's analysis is on the right track, this means that these constructions involve an Ā-dependency, too. In conclusion, this means that verb and verb phrase fronting in Asante Twi cannot be a case of base-generation.

Third, this is further corroborated by the absence of any genus-species effects. Those are found in Yiddish (32-a) and Brazilian Portuguese (32-b) and describe a phenomenon where the lexical material in the fronted constituent is different from that in the base position with a semantic entailment relation holding between the two.

(32) *Genus-species effects*
    a. ?*Forn*   *keyn amerike* bin   ikh *gefloygn keyn nyu-york*.
        travel.INF to   america be.1SG I   flown to   New York
        'As for travelling to America, I have flown to New York.'

                                                        (*Yiddish*, Cable 2004: 9)
    b. *Comer peixe*, eu normalmente *como   samão*.
        eat.INF fish   I usually   eat.1SG salmon
        'As for eating fish, I usually eat salmon.'

                                           (*Br. Portuguese*, Cable 2004: 11)

Cable (2004) argues that the fronted constituent in those languages be better analyzed as being base-generated rather than ($\bar{\text{A}}$-)moved because it is unclear how lexical material can change during movement.[6] As (33) attests, Asante Twi does not allow for any lexical mismatch between the fronted constituent and the copies left in base position except for inflectional affixes.

(33)   a. *[Tuna di](-e)   na Ama yɔ-ɔ/di-i   nam.
             tuna eat-NMLZ FOC Ama do-PST/eat-PST fish
             Intended: 'It was eating tuna that Ama did/ate fish.'
    b. *Tia(-e)   na Kofi *kasa*-a.
             shout-NMLZ FOC Kofi speak-PST
             Intended: 'It was shouting that Kofi spoke.'
    c. *[Nam di](-e)   na Ama yɔ-ɔ/di-i   tuna.
             fish eat-NMLZ FOC Ama do-PST/eat-PST tuna
             Intended: 'It was eating fish that Ama did/ate tuna.'
    d. *Kasa(-e)   na Kofi *tia*-a.
             speak-NMLZ FOC Kofi shout-PST
             Intended: 'It was speaking that Kofi shouted.'

Constructions like (33-a, c) are additionally ruled out by the impossibility to have a copy of the object appear alongside the verb in verb phrase fronting (34).

(34) *[Nam di](-e)   na Ama a-yɔ/a-di   nam.
       fish eat-NMLZ FOC Ama PFV-do/PFV-eat fish

---

[6] In a late-insertion approach to phonological realization of syntactic material including late insertion of roots (Haugen & Siddiqi 2013, Harley 2014) this argument might not be completely convincing. It is imaginable that certain post-syntactic processes analogous to Impoverishment (Bonet 1991, Harley 1994, Harris 1997) or Enrichment (Müller 2007) change the featural composition of terminal nodes such that a semantically related phonological form is inserted.

2.1 Repair patterns in languages with both verb and verb phrase fronting — 49

I take the absence of genus-species effects to indicate that base-generation does not play a role in verbal fronting constructions.

Fourth, verbal fronting shows reconstruction effects for Principle C (35), which are usually associated with Ā-dependencies.

(35) *[$_{VP}$ Kofí$_i$ ḿfóníŕí **hú**](-é)   na   ɔ$_i$-á-**yɔ́**   ___vp.
      Kofi picture see -NMLZ FOC 3SG-PRF-do
      'He$_i$ has SEEN A PICTURE OF KOFI$_i$.'

Reconstruction for Principle A could not be tested due to the ban on fronting of definite objects. As an anaphor is necessarily definite its fronting always leads to ungrammaticality independent of the coindexation pattern (36-a). Fronting the object anaphor on its own, however, shows reconstruction (36-b).

(36) a. ??[Ne-hó$_i$ **pírá**](-é) na ɔ$_i$-á-**yɔ́**.
        3SG-REFL hurt-NMLZ FOC 3SG-PRF-do
        'He$_i$ has HURT HIMSELF$_i$.'
   b. Ne-hó$_i$ na   ɔ$_i$-á-pírá   ___ne-hó.
        3SG-REFL FOC 3SG-PFV-hurt
        'Himself$_i$, Kofi$_i$ has hurt.'

Fifth, it is impossible to front both a wh-expression and a verbal constituent (37), which indicates that both elements occupy the same structural position and undergo the same kind of movement, namely Ā-movement.

(37) a. *[Déɛ́n] na [**ńóm**](-é)   na Esi **ńóm**?
       what FOC drink-NMLZ FOC Esi drink
       'What does Esi DRINK?'
   b. *[**Ńóm**](-é)   na [déɛ́n] na Esi **ńóm**?
       drink-NMLZ FOC what FOC Esi drink
       'What does Esi DRINK?'
   c. ??[Déɛ́n] [**ńóm**](-é)   na Esi **ńóm/yɔ́**?
       what drink-NMLZ FOC Esi drink/do
       'What does Esi DRINK?'

In conclusion, the five arguments presented above all corroborate treating verbal fronting in Asante Twi as an Ā-dependency rather than a base-generated structure.

Let us then turn to the size/category of the fronted constituent. The verb inside it can neither be marked with negation (38-a, c) nor with aspectual affixes (38-b, d).

(38) a. *N-**sí**(-é)   na Kofi á-(n-)**sí**   dán.
       NEG-build(-NMLZ) FOC Kofi PRF-NEG-build house
       'Kofi has NOT BUILT a house.'

b. *Á-**sí**(-é)   na Kofí á-**si**   dán.
   PRF-build-NMLZ FOC Kofi PRF-build house
   'Kofi has BUILT a house.'

c. *[Dán   n-**sí**](-é)   na Kofí á-(n-)**yɔ́**.
   house NEG-build-NMLZ FOC Kofi PRF-NEG-do
   'Kofi has NOT BUILT A HOUSE.'

d. *[Dán   á-**sí**](-é)   na Kofí á-(n-)**yɔ́**.
   house PFV-build-NMLZ FOC Kofi PRF-do
   'Kofi has NOT BUILT A HOUSE.'

Taking the phrase structure proposed by Kandybowicz (2015) as a basis, where aspect is located between *v* and V, this implies that the fronted constuent is a V(P) rather than a *v*(P).

Concerning the phrasal status of the sentence-initial constituent in verb fronting, there are two possibilities: (i) The verb is the head of a remnant verb phrase or (ii) it is a bare head. In order for the first option to hold, it is necessary to show that Asante Twi comprises of an independent VP-evacuating object movement. The simplest evidence for such a movement would be the possibility to have the object appear either pre-verbally (39-b) (or before the indirect object in ditransitive constructions (39-d)) or after low VP-adverbs like *ntɛm* 'quickly' (40-b) which linearize verb phrase finally. As is evident from the examples below, neither option is grammatical.

(39) a. Kofí á-si   dán.
         Kofi PRF-build house
         'Kofi has built a house.'
      b. *Kofí dán   á-si.
         Kofi house PRF-build
         'Kofi has built a house.'
      c. Kofí ma-a   mmɔfŕá nó kŕataá.
         Kofi give-PST children DET book
         'Kofi gave the children a book.'
      d. *Kofí ma-a   kŕataá mmɔfŕá nó.
         Kofi give-PST book   children DET
         'Kofi gave a book to the children.'

(40) a. Kofí á-si   dán   ntɛm.
         Kofi PFV-build house quickly
         'Kofi has quickly built a house.'
      b. *Kofí á-si   ntɛm   dán.
         Kofi PFV-build quickly house
         'Kofi has quickly built a house.'

2.1 Repair patterns in languages with both verb and verb phrase fronting — 51

Nonetheless, there is an environment in which the direct object appears before the verb, namely when the verb is embedded under a restructuring verb like *kyiri* 'hate', *gyae* 'stop', or *pɛ* 'like' (41-a). These verbs require their complements to exhibit OV order rather than the standard VO order which is ungrammatical in this context (41-b) (this has also been noted by Kobele & Torrence 2004).

(41) a. Ghánàní bíárá pè [ǹsúó nóḿ]
Ghanaian every like water drink
'Every Ghanaian likes to drink water.'
b. *Ghánàní bíárá pè [nóḿ ǹsúó]
Ghanaian every like drink water

Curiously, this 'object shift' looks very similar to the order reversal found in verb phrase fronting, where the fronted constituent also shows OV instead of VO order. This suggests that they are both plausibly derived by the same syntactic mechanism.

As I will suggest in section 5.2.2 (also see Hein & Murphy to appear), this mechanism could be a Last Resort flexible linearization to avoid a violation of the Final-over-Final Condition (FOFC, Biberauer et al. 2008) in nominalized verb phrases. Nominalization is achieved by late attachment of a dissociated nominalizing head *n* Embick & Noyer (2001). Since the verb phrase is head-initial but the nominalizer is a suffix the resulting structure [$_{nP}$ [$_{VP}$ V Obj] *n*] violates the FOFC. Thus, the word order of the verb phrase is reversed so as to avoid this violation. If both OV constructions indeed share a common analysis, (41) cannot be evidence for VP-evacuating movement of the object since the object clearly has not moved out of the VP in examples of verb phrase fronting.

Consequently, verb fronting in Asante Twi cannot be remnant verb phrase fronting but must in fact be a case of Ā-head movement (see section 4.1.1).

Concerning where and with what verbal fronting can appear, verb phrase fronting seems to be subject to more restrictions than verb fronting. Thus, verb fronting is possible with all kinds of verbs, including unergatives (42-a), unaccusatives (42-b), ditransitives (42-c), and individual-level predicates (42-d, e).

(42) a. **Sá** na Kofí á-**sá**/*á-yɔ́.
dance FOC Kofi PRF-dance
'Kofi has DANCED.'
b. **Da** na Kofí á-**dá**/*á-yɔ́ wɔ Accra.
fall.asleep FOC Kofi PRF-fall.asleep/PRF-do at Accra
'Kofi has FALLEN ASLEEP in Accra.'
c. **Má** na Kofí á-**má** mmofrá sika.
give FOC Kofi PRF-give children money
'Kofi has GIVEN money to children.'

d. **Dɔ́/Pɛ́** na Kofí **dɔ́/pɛ́** bayéré.
   love/like FOC Kofi loves/likes yam
   'Kofi LOVES/LIKES yam.'
e. **Sɛ́** na Kofí **sɛ́** kraman.
   resemble FOC Kofi resemble dog
   'Kofi RESEMBLES a dog.'

Verb phrase fronting, whether partial or full, however is not possible with ditransitives (43). Equally degraded is verb phrase fronting of individual-level predicates like *pɛ* 'like' and *sɛ* 'resemble' (44).

(43) a. *[Mmɔfŕá sika **má**](-é) na Kofí á-**má**/á-**yɔ́**.
       children money give-NMLZ FOC Kofi PRF-give/PRF-do
       'Kofi has GIVEN MONEY TO CHILDREN.'
   b. *[Mmɔfŕá **má**](-é) na Kofí á-**má**/á-**yɔ́** sika.
       children give-NMLZ FOC Kofi PRF-give/PRF-do money
       'Kofi has GIVEN CHILDREN money.'
   c. ??[Sika **má**](-é) na Kofí á-**má**/*á-**yɔ́** mmɔfŕá.
       money give-NMLZ FOC Kofi PRF-give/PRF-do children
       'Kofi has GIVEN MONEY to children.'

(44) a. *[Bayéré **dɔ́/pɛ́**](-é) na Kofí **yɔ́**.
       yam love/like-NMLZ FOC Kofi does
       'Kofi LOVES/LIKES YAM.'
   b. *[Kraman **sɛ́**](-é) na Kofí **yɔ́**.
       dog resemble-NMLZ Kofi does
       'Kofi RESEMBLES A DOG.'

Additionally, while verb fronting stranding a PP-adverb like *wɔ Accra* 'in Accra' is perfectly grammatical (45-b), verb phrase fronting stranding the PP is slightly degraded (45-c). Any attempts to front the PP-adverb together with either the verb (45-d) or the verb phrase (45-e) result in ungrammaticality.

(45) a. Kofí á-si dán wɔ Accra.
       Kofi PRF-build house at Accra
       'Kofi has built a house in Accra'
   b. **Sí** na Kofí á-**sí** dán wɔ Accra.
       build FOC Kofi PRF-build house at Accra
       'Kofi has BUILT a house in Accra.'
   c. ?[Dán **sí**](-é) na Kofí á-**yɔ́** wɔ Accra.
       house build-NMLZ FOC Kofi PRF-do at Accra
       'Kofi has BUILT A HOUSE in Accra.'

d. *[(Wɔ Accra) **sí**(-é)   (wɔ Accra)] na Kofí á-**sí**/á-**yɔ́**
   at Accra build-NMLZ in Accra FOC Kofi PRF-build/PRF-do
   dán.
   house
   'Kofi has BUILT a house IN ACCRA.'
e. *[(Wɔ Accra) dán   **sí**(-é)   (wɔ Accra)] na Kofí á-**yɔ́**.
   in Accra house build-NMLZ in Accra FOC Kofi PRF-do
   'Kofi has BUILT A HOUSE IN ACCRA.'

The ungrammaticality of fronted adverbs is part of a larger pattern. In general, Asante Twi does not seem to allow the fronted constituent to be accompanied by any type of adverb, neither in verb nor in verb phrase fronting. Thus, the examples of verb fronting with a low adverb *ntɛm* 'quickly' (46-a) and a high adverb *ampá* 'truly' (46-b) are equally ungrammatical as their verb phrase fronting counterparts (47-a, b).

(46) a. *[**Sí**   ntɛm](-e)   na Kofí á-**sí**   dán.
        build quickly(-NMLZ) FOC Kofi PRF-build house
        'Kofi has QUICKLY BUILT a house.' / 'It is quickly building that Kofi does to a house.'
     b. *[**Sí**   ampá](-e)   na Kofí á-**sí**   dán.
        build truly(-NMLZ) FOC Kofi PRF-build house
        'Kofi has TRULY BUILT a house.' / 'It is truly building that Kofi does to a house.'

(47) a. *[Dán **sí**   ntɛm](-e)   na Kofí á-**yɔ́**.
        house build quickly(-NMLZ) FOC Kofi PRF-do
        'Kofi has QUICKLY BUILT A HOUSE.' / 'It is building a house quickly that Kofi has done.'
     b. *[Dán **sí**   ampá](-e)   na Kofí á-**yɔ́**.
        house build truly(-NMLZ) FOC Kofi PRF-do
        'Kofi has TRULY BUILT A HOUSE.' / 'It is truly building a house that Kofi has done.'

Considering these differences between verb and verb phrase fronting, one might be tempted to conclude that they are two different constructions. Indeed, one of their main differences is syntactic, namely the kind of movement involved, $\bar{\text{A}}$-head movement in verb fronting and phrasal $\bar{\text{A}}$-movement in verb phrase movement. However, apart from the slight degradation of PP-stranding verb phrase fronting (45-c) and the curious unavailability of (partial) verb phrase fronting with ditransitives (43), both verb and verb phrase fronting show the same (morpho-)syntactic behaviour: They can span finite clause boundaries, are sensitive to islands, trigger tonal raising, do not show genus-species effects, optionally allow for nominalization, and disallow the presence of negation, inflectional affixes, and any type of adverb in the fronted constituent. I therefore suggest that they share a common derivational syntax with the main difference being that verb fronting involves Ā-head movement whereas verb phrase fronting is the result of phrasal Ā-movement.

Before we can accept the Asante Twi pattern as a real asymmteric repair pattern for verbal fronting, we need to test if the dummy verb *yɔ* and the verb copy are indeed repairs and not just elements that can be found independently in other constructions. Two structures come to mind that cross-linguistically show independent verb copies and dummy verbs, respectively and might therefore serve as the basis for verbal fronting: The first are cognate object constructions as in Edo (see section 7.1.3) and the second are so-called *do*-periphrases as in German (see section 8.1.4).

Cognate objects are rare in Asante Twi. In fact, my informant could only think of one example involving the verb *sa* 'dance' (48-a). A similar construction with a cognate object of the verb *si* 'build' and the actual direct object *dán* 'house' in the same clause is ungrammatical (48-b).

(48) a. Kofí sa   a-sa.
          Kofi dance NMLZ-dance
          'Kofi dances (a dance).'
      b. *Kofí si   a-si   dán.
          Kofi build NMLZ-building house

The cognate object construction is thus not productive enough to serve as the basis from which verb fronting could be derived by moving the cognate object into the left periphery (and slightly modifying its morphological form.) The verb copy that appears in the canonical verb position in verb fronting is therefore most probably the result of a genuine repair operation.

With regard to verb phrase fronting, the approach that suggests deriving it from a periphrase by moving a nominalized verb phrase complement of the dummy verb *yɔ* into the left periphery is doomed to fail. Example (49) attests to the fact that the putative base construction is ungrammatical.

(49) a. *Kofí á-yɔ   dán   sí(-é).
          Kofi PFV-do house build-NMLZ
      b. *Kofí dán   sí(-é)   á-yɔ.
          Kofi house build-NMLZ PFV-do

A related *do*-support-like construction can be observed with *in situ* wh-questions where the questioned element could be a verb phrase. The placeholder verb in this case is *yé* 'do' (50-a). Even if *yé* could somehow turn into *yɔ*, this construction may not serve as the independent basis for verb phrase fronting either due to it being ungrammatical with a full nominalized verb phrase in place of the wh-word *déɛ́n* 'what' (50-b).

(50) a. Kofi re-yé déɛ́n?
      Kofi PROG-do what
      'What is Kofi doing?'
  b. *Kofi re-yé dán sí(-é)
      Kofi PROG-do house build-NMLZ

We can therefore safely conclude that insertion of the dummy verb in verb phrase fronting constructions is a proper repair operation. Consequently, verbal fronting constructions in Asante Twi display a repair pattern that has hitherto been undescribed and has remained uninvestigated in the literature. It demonstrates that symmetric repair patterns, though very frequent, are not the only possible repair patterns in verbal fronting.

2.1.3.2 Limbum

Limbum, a Grassfields language of the Niger-Congo family, is spoken by an estimate of 73 000–90 000 (Fransen 1995: 21) (130 000 according to Ethnologue based on a census from 2005) predominantly in the Northwestern region of Cameroon. It is the native language of the Wimbum people and shows a three-way tone contrast between low (à), mid (ā), and high (á) tones. The basic word order is SVO, exemplified in (51).[7]

(51) Ŋwè fɔ̄ àm tí ŋgū
     man DET PST3 cut wood
     'The man cut the wood.'   (Becker & Nformi 2016: 58)

Like Asante Twi, Limbum shows both verb and verb phrase fronting but does not display the same repair in both of them. Rather, verb fronting triggers verb doubling (52-a) whereas verb phrase fronting leads to the insertion of a dummy verb *gī* meaning 'do' (52-b).

(52) a. Á **r-yū** (cí) njíŋwè fɔ̄ bí **yū**/*gī msāŋ.
     FOC 5-buy (COMP) woman DET FUT1 buy/do rice
     'The woman will BUY rice.'

---

[7] Unless otherwise noted, all data in this section were elicited from my informant Jude Nformi. Any occurring errors are mine.

b. Á r-[**yū** msāŋ] (cí) njíŋwè fɔ́ bí **gī**/*yū.
   FOC 5-buy rice (COMP) woman DET FUT1 do/buy
   'The woman will BUY RICE.' (Becker & Nformi 2016: 74f.)

In contrast to Asante Twi, the fronted constituent has to obligatorily be nominalized, seemingly exceptionlessly by being marked with the nominal class marker of noun class five. The focus marker *á* is the same that appears in regular nominal focus constructions, like subject (53-a) and object (53-b) focus, as well as *ex situ* wh-questions (53-c, d).

(53) a. Á Nfòr (cí) í bā zhē bāā.
        FOC Nfor COMP 3SG PST1 eat fufu
        'NFOR ate fufu.'
     b. Á Ngàlá (cí) mè bí kɔ̄nī.
        FOC Ngala COMP I FUT1 meet
        'I will meet NGALA.'
     c. Á ndá (cí) í bā zhē bāā?
        FOC who COMP 3SG PST1 eat fufu
        'Who is it that ate fufu?'
     d. Á kéɛ́ wè bā yɛ́?
        FOC what you.SG PST1 see
        'What is it that you saw?' (Becker & Nformi 2016: 60, 72)

The optional *cí* marker is glossed as COMP in this book reflecting the intuition that it is a realization of the C head whose specifier is occupied by the focussed phrase. This entails that the *á* marker is actually a focus particle (possibly heading its own focus phrase, see Becker et al. 2019, Cable 2010). The regular complementizer in embedded clauses is *nɛ* and shows agreement with the matrix subject in the form of a prefix (Nformi 2018).

Becker & Nformi (2016) argue that the *á*-focus construction encodes new information focus. There also is a second focus construction with a different focus marker *bá*, which they argue to convey contrastive (exhaustive) focus. Examples of regular nominal *bá*-focus as well as *bá*-wh-questions are given in (54).

(54) a. À bā zhē bá Nfòr bāā.
        EXPL PST1 eat FOC Nfor fufu
        'It is Nfor who has eaten fufu.'
     b. Mè bí kɔ̄nī bá Ngàlá.
        I FUT1 meet FOC Ngala
        'It is Ngala whom I will meet.'

c. À   bā zhē bá ndà bāā?
   EXPL PST1 eat FOC who fufu
   'Who (if not X / of them) ate fufu?'
d. Wè   bā yɛ́ bá kɛ́ɛ́?
   you.SG PST1 see FOC what
   'What (if not X) did you see?'   (Becker & Nformi 2016: 60, 72)

This latter focus with a contrastive interpretation is also available for verbs with the result of verb doubling (55). However, in contrast to regular nominal focus the marker *bá* is absent in these examples.

(55) Njíŋwè fɔ́ bí **yū** msāŋ **yú**.
      woman DET FUT1 buy rice buy
      'It is buying that the woman will do to the rice.'
                                              (Becker & Nformi 2016: 74)

Since it is the sentence-final verb copy that is prosodically more prominent, Becker & Nformi (2016) conclude that it must be this copy that occupies the low focus position, i.e. has moved into its surface position. Based on this, they show that low verb phrase focus, in contrast to high verb phrase focus with *á*, is ungrammatical with both verb doubling (56-a) and dummy verb insertion (56-b).

(56) a. *Njíŋwè fɔ́ bí yū (bá) yū msāŋ.
         woman DET FUT1 buy FOC buy rice
      b. *Njíŋwè fɔ́ bí gī (bá) yū msāŋ.
         woman DET FUT1 do FOC buy rice   (Becker & Nformi 2016: 75)

Therefore, contrastive *bá*-focus is of minor interest to us here, since this section is supposed to establish Limbum as providing a second instantiation of the asymmetric repair pattern in verbal fronting that we saw in Asante Twi. As only the high *á*-focus construction displays this pattern, I will leave aside verb focus with *bá* for the time being. In the following, I will investigate the syntactic properties of the *á*-focus construction in more detail, demonstrating that verb and verb phrase fronting behave in the same fashion with regard to Ā-diagnostics, negation, and possible additional material in the fronted constituent. Furthermore, it will be argued that verb fronting involves Ā-head movement rather than remnant movement and that the category of the fronted constituent is plausibly V rather than *v*. Finally, I provide evidence that a purported independent construction displaying dummy verb insertion cannot be the basis for deriving verb phrase fronting. Equally, verb doubling in verb fronting is shown not to be derivable from an independent cognate object construction or verb doubling construction.

First, note that, just like Asante Twi, Limbum does not tolerate verb phrase fronting with a definite object. Thus, example (57) is judged ungrammatical when *njíŋwè* 'woman' is followed by the definite determiner *fɔ́* (57-a) while it is fine when *fɔ́* is omitted.

(57) a. *Á r-[klɔnì njíŋwè fɔ́] (cí) mè bí **gī**.
FOC 5-meet woman DET COMP 1SG FUT1 do
'I will MEET THE WOMAN.'

b. Á r-[**klɔnì** njíŋwè] (cí) mè bí **gī**.
FOC 5-meet woman COMP 1SG FUT1 do
'I will MEET A WOMAN.'

This behaviour is expected given that definite DPs are usually discourse-old (or unique) and should therefore not occur in a position associated with new information.

Further, *á*-focus fronting is not a root phenomenon. Nominal elements (58-a) and wh-elements (58-b) as well as verbs (58-c) and verb phrases (58-d) may occur in the focus position in an embedded clause, in the latter two cases we find the regular repair of verb doubling and dummy verb insertion respectively.

(58) a. Mè kwàshī [$_{CP}$ mè-nɛ á **ndāp** (cí) Nfor bí bō].
1SG think 1SG-COMP FOC house COMP Nfor FUT1 build
'I think that Nfor will build A HOUSE.'

b. Shey à mū bípshī [$_{CP}$ í-nɛ á **kɛ́ɛ́** (cí) Nfor bí zhē lɛ̄].
Shey 3SG PST2 ask 3SG-COMP FOC what COMP Nfor FUT1 eat Q
'Shey asked WHAT Nfor will eat.'

c. Mè kwàshī [$_{CP}$ mè-nɛ á r-**bō** (cí) Nfor bí **bō** ndāp].
1SG think 1SG-COMP FOC 5-build COMP Nfor FUT1 build house
'I think that Nfor will BUILD a house.'

d. Mè kwàshī [$_{CP}$ mè-nɛ á r-[**bō** ndāp] (cí) Nfor bí **gī**].
1SG think 1SG-COMP FOC 5-build house COMP Nfor FUT1 do
'I think that Nfor will BUILD A HOUSE.'

Turning to the evidence in favour of verbal fronting involving $\bar{\text{A}}$-movement we first find that it may cross finite clause boundaries as shown in (59-b, c).

(59) a. Mè kwàshī mè-nɛ Nfor bí bō ndāp.
1SG think 1SG-COMP Nfor FUT1 build house
'I think that Nfor will build a house.'

2.1 Repair patterns in languages with both verb and verb phrase fronting — 59

    b. Á r-**bò** (cí) mè kwàshī [mè-nɛ Nfor bí **bō** ndāp].
       FOC 5-build COMP 1SG think 1SG-COMP Nfor FUT1 build house
       'I think that Nfor will BUILD a house.'

    c. Á r-[**bò** ndāp] (cí) mè kwàshī [mè-nɛ Nfor bí **gī**].
       FOC 5-build house COMP 1SG think 1SG-COMP Nfor FUT1 do
       'I think that Nfor will BUILD A HOUSE.'

Further, it is impossible to front a verb or verb phrase from inside a Complex NP Island (60-b, c), an Adjunct Island (61-b, c), or from a coordinate structure (62).

(60) *Complex NP Island*

    a. Mè mū yō? [_DP_ nsūŋ [_CP_ zɨ̄-nɛ Nfor bí bō ndāp]].
       1SG PST2 hear news 3SG-COMP Nfor FUT1 build house
       'I heard a rumour that Nfor will build a house.'

    b. *Á r-**bò** (cí) mè mū yō? [_DP_ nsūŋ [_CP_ zɨ̄-nɛ Nfor
       FOC 5-build COMP 1SG PST2 hear news 3SG-COMP Nfor
       bí **bō** ndāp]].
       FUT1 build house
       'I heard a rumour that Nfor will BUILD a house.'

    c. *Á r-[**bò** ndāp] (cí) mè mū yō? [_DP_ nsūŋ [_CP_ zɨ̄-nɛ
       FOC 5-build house COMP 1SG PST2 hear news 3SG-COMP
       Nfor bí **gī**]].
       Nfor FUT1 do
       'I heard a rumour that Nfor will BUILD A HOUSE.'

(61) *Adjunct Island*

    a. Nfor à mū vɨ̄ ŋkà? kà? [_CP_ àndzhɔ́? í mū sī bō
       Nfor 3SG PST2 come party not because he PST2 PROG build
       ndāp].
       house
       'Nfor didn't come to the party because he was building a house.'

    b. *Á r-**bò** (cí) Nfor à mū vɨ̄ ŋkà? kà? [_CP_ àndzhɔ́? í
       FOC 5-build COMP Nfor 3SG PST2 come party not because he
       mū sī **bō** ndāp].
       PST2 PROG build house
       'Nfor didn't come to the party because he was BUILDING a house.'

    c. *Á r-[**bò** ndāp] (cí) Nfor à mū vɨ̄ ŋkà? kà? [_CP_
       FOC 5-build house COMP Nfor 3SG PST2 come party not
       àndzhɔ́? í mū sī **gī**].
       because he PST2 PROG do
       'Nfor didn't come to the party because he was BUILDING A HOUSE.'

(62)   *Coordinate Structure Constraint*
  a. Nfor bí [&P bō   ndāp kìr yū ntùmntùm].
      Nfor FUT1   build house and buy motorbike
      'Nfor will build a house and buy a motorbike.'
  b. *Á r-**yù** (cí)   Nfor bí [&P bō   ndāp kìr **yū** ntùmntùm].
      FOC 5-buy COMP Nfor FUT1   build house and buy motorbike
      'Nfor will build a house and BUY a motorbike.'
  c. *Á r-[**yù** ntùmntùm] (cí)   Nfor bí [&P bō   ndāp kìr **gī**].
      FOC 5-buy motorbike COMP Nfor FUT1   build house and do
      'Nfor will build a house and BUY A MOTORBIKE.'

The situation with Wh-Islands, however, is different. In Limbum the wh-word in an embedded interrogative most naturally occurs *in situ* (63-a). Consequently, due to the absence of wh-movement, embedded interrogatives do not constitute proper islands for extraction of a nominal (63-b) or another wh-element (63-c) as expected.

(63) a. Shey à   mū bípshī [CP í-nɛ   Nfor bí zhē kɛ́ɛ́].
          Shey 3SG PST2 ask   3SG-COMP Nfor FUT1 eat what
          'Shey asked what Nfor will eat.'
      b. Á Nfor (cí)   Shey à   mū bípshī [CP í-nɛ   í   bí zhē
          FOC Nfor COMP Shey 3SG PST2 ask   3SG-COMP 3SG FUT1 eat
          kɛ́ɛ́].
          what
          'Shey asked what NFOR will eat.'
      c. Á kɛ́ɛ́ (cí)   Shey à   mū bípshī [CP í-nɛ   Nfor bí
          FOC what COMP Shey 3SG PST2 ask   3SG-COMP Nfor FUT1
          zhē àsí?kɛ̀]?
          eat when
          'What is it that Shey asked when Nfor will eat (it)?'

Even if the wh-element in the embedded interrogative has undergone movement, extraction of a nominal (64-a) or another wh-element, be that an argument (64-b) or an adjunct (64-c), does not incur a Wh-Island violation.[8]

---

8 When a wh-element is displaced from its base position there obligatorily appears a question particle in sentence-final position. This question particle is usually *lē* for argument wh-items and *à* for non-argument wh-items. Curiously, when both types of wh-item occur in the same clause and both undergo movement, we find that only *à* is present if the argument wh-item leaves the clause and the non-argument wh-item stays inside it (64-b), but that a combination of *lē* and *à* shows up in the reversed case (64-c). I currently have no suggestion as to why this happens.

2.1 Repair patterns in languages with both verb and verb phrase fronting — 61

(64) a. Á Nfor (cí)   Shey à   mū bípshī [$_{CP}$ í-nɛ   á   kɛ́ɛ́
       FOC Nfor COMP Shey 3SG PST2 ask   3SG-COMP FOC what
       (cí)   í   bí   zhē lɛ̄].
       COMP 3SG FUT1 eat Q
       'Shey asked WHAT NFOR will eat.'

   b. Á kɛ́ɛ́ (cí)   Shey à   mū bípshī [$_{CP}$ í-nɛ   á   àsí?kè
       FOC what COMP Shey 3SG PST2 ask   3SG-COMP FOC when
       (cí)   Nfor bí   zhē à].
       COMP Nfor FUT1 eat Q
       'Shey asked WHAT Nfor will eat WHEN.'

   c. Á àsí?kè (cí)   Shey à   mū bípshī [$_{CP}$ í-nɛ   á   kɛ́ɛ́
       FOC when COMP Shey 3SG PST2 ask   3SG-COMP FOC what
       (cí)   Nfor bí   zhē lɛ̄/à].
       COMP Nfor FUT1 eat Q
       'Shey asked WHEN Nfor will eat WHAT.'

Verb and verb phrase fronting are also possible from inside an embedded interrogative, independently of whether the wh-element has undergone movement (65) or not (66).

(65) a. Á r-bò   (cí)   Shey à   mū bípshī [$_{CP}$ í-nɛ   á   àsí?kè
       FOC 5-build COMP Shey 3SG PST2 ask   3SG-COMP FOC when
       (cí)   Nfor bí   bō   ndāp à].
       COMP Nfor FUT1 build house Q
       'Shey asked when Nfor will BUILD a house.'

   b. Á r-[bò   ndāp] (cí)   Shey à   mū bípshī [$_{CP}$ í-nɛ   á
       FOC 5-build house COMP Shey 3SG PST2 ask   3SG-COMP FOC
       àsí?kè (cí)   Nfor bí   gī   à].
       when COMP Nfor FUT1 do Q
       'Shey asked when Nfor will BUILD A HOUSE.'

(66) a. Á r-bò   (cí)   Shey à   mū bípshī [$_{CP}$ í-nɛ   Nfor bí
       FOC 5-build COMP Shey 3SG PST2 ask   3SG-COMP Nfor FUT1
       bō   ndāp àsí?kè].
       build house when
       'Shey asked when Nfor will BUILD a house.'

   b. Á r-[bò   ndāp] (cí)   Shey à   mū bípshī [$_{CP}$ í-nɛ   Nfor
       FOC 5-build house COMP Shey 3SG PST2 ask   3SG-COMP Nfor
       bí   gī   àsí?kè].
       FUT1 do when
       'Shey asked when Nfor will BUILD A HOUSE.'

With respect to extraction from embedded interrogative clauses, verbal fronting thus behaves parallel to wh-extraction and regular nominal focus which can be interpreted as evidence for it involving the same kind of movement, namely Ā-movement.

This view is supported by the fact that there is reconstruction for Principle A. When the fronted verb phrase contains the anaphor *zhɨ tu* '3SG.POSS head' as in (67-b) it is still coreferent with the subject of the clause *Nfor* like it is in the neutral declarative version in (67-a) despite being outside the latter's c-command domain on the surface.

(67) a. Nfor$_i$ à mū jàasi zhɨ$_i$ tu.
Nfor 3SG PST2 criticize 3SG.POSS head
'Nfor$_i$ criticized himself$_i$.'

b. Á r-[jàasi zhɨ$_i$ tu] (cí) Nfor$_i$ à mū gī.
FOC 5-criticize 3SG.POSS head COMP Nfor 3SG PST2 do
'Nfor$_i$ CRITICIZED HIMSELF$_i$.'

Let us now turn to the category of the fronted constituent. As demonstrated below, neither negation (68) nor any tense (69) or aspect markers (70) may cooccur with the fronted verb (phrase).

(68) a. *Á r-[bò kà?] (cí) Nfor bí bō ndāp (kà?).
FOC 5-build NEG COMP Nfor FUT1 build house NEG

b. *Á r-[bò ndāp kà?] (cí) Nfor bí gī (kà?).
FOC 5-build house NEG COMP Nfor FUT1 do NEG

(69) a. *Á r-[bí bò] (cí) Nfor (bí) bō ndāp.
FOC 5-FUT1 build COMP Nfor FUT1 build house

b. *Á r-[bí bò ndāp] (cí) Nfor (bí) gī.
FOC 5-FUT1 build house COMP Nfor FUT1 do

(70) a. *Á r-[ce bò] (cí) Nfor (ce) bō ndāp.
FOC 5-PROG build COMP Nfor PROG build house

b. *Á r-[ce bò ndāp] (cí) Nfor (ce) gī.
FOC 5-PROG build house COMP Nfor PROG do

Assuming that tense and aspectual markers are located in T and *v* respectively this means that the fronted constituent cannot be of these categories. Rather, it must belong to a category that is lower in the phrase structure than both T and *v*. The fronted constituent in verbal fronting in Limbum is hence of the category V.

Given this, it is clear that the fronted constituent in verb phrase fronting is a VP. However, for verb fronting there are two possible analyses of the fronted verb: (i) It may either be the head of a remnant VP or (ii) it is a bare V head.

2.1 Repair patterns in languages with both verb and verb phrase fronting — 63

Option (i) presupposes the availability of a productive VP-evacuating movement like scrambling or object shift. As evidenced by (71), however, it is not possible to scramble the direct object across the indirect object in a ditransitive constructions. The order where the direct object precedes the indirect object is, like in English, only licit when the indirect object is a PP (72-a). However, in this DP-PP-construction, changing the order of both objects results in ungrammaticality again (72-b).

(71) a. Nfor à mū fā Shey bzhɨ.
    Nfor 3SG PST2 give Shey food
    'Nfor gave Shey some food.'
  b. *Nfor à mū fā bzhɨ Shey.
    Nfor 3SG PST2 give food Shey
    'Nfor gave Shey some food.'

(72) a. Nfor à mū fā bzhɨ nì Shey.
    Nfor 3SG PST2 give food PREP Shey
    'Nfor gave some food to Shey.'
  b. *Nfor à mū fā nì Shey bzhɨ.
    Nfor 3SG PST2 give PREP Shey food
    'Nfor gave some food to Shey.'

A productive VP-evacuating movement is thus not available in Limbum. Therefore, verb fronting cannot be movement of a remnant VP. Rather, it must be the case that the fronted verb is a bare head with verb fronting being an instance of $\bar{\text{A}}$-head movement.

Concerning possible restrictions of verbal fronting to a subclass of verbs we find that there are none. In fact, both verb and verb phrase fronting are available for a variety of different verb classes. Besides the transitive verbs above unergatives like *fàʔ* 'work' (73-a) as well as unaccusatives like *gwè* 'fall' (73-b) may undergo fronting.

(73) a. Á r-**fàʔ** (cí) Nfor bí **fàʔ/gī**.
    FOC 5-work COMP Nfor FUT1 work/do
    'Nfor will WORK.'
  b. Á r-**gwè** (cí) ndāp fɔ̄ à Ø **gwè/*gī**.
    FOC 5-fall COMP house DET 3SG PFV fall/do
    'The house FELL.'   (Becker & Nformi 2016: 7)

Interestingly, unergatives optionally allow both kinds of repair, verb doubling or dummy verb insertion, which is expected since fronted constituent here is ambiguous between a bare verbal head and a verb phrase.

Verb and verb phrase fronting are also available for ditransitives like *fā* 'give'. A regular declarative sentence containing *fā* is given in (74-a). Example (74-b) shows verb fronting which, as expected, triggers verb doubling, while (74-c) is an instance of verb phrase fronting and results in insertion of the dummy *gī*.

(74) a. Nfor à mū fā Shey bzhī.
Nfor 3SG PST2 give Shey food
'Nfor gave Shey some food.'
b. Á r-**fá** (cí) Nfor à mū **fā** Shey bzhī.
FOC 5-give COMP Nfor 3SG PST2 give Shey food
'Nfor GAVE Shey some food.'
c. Á r-[**fá** Shey bzhī] (cí) Nfor à mū **gī**.
FOC 5-give Shey food COMP Nfor 3SG PST2 do
'Nfor GAVE SHEY SOME FOOD.'

Partial verb phrase fronting, that is, the fronting of the verb and only one of its two objects, however, is not licit in Limbum as shown in (75-a) for the direct object and in (75-b) for the indirect object.

(75) a. *Á r-[**fá** bzhī] (cí) Nfor à **fā/gī** Shey.
FOC 5-give food COMP Nfor PST2 give/do Shey
'Nfor GAVE SOME FOOD to Shey.'
b. *Á r-[**fá** Shey] (cí) Nfor à **fā/gī** bzhī.
FOC 5-give Shey COMP Nfor PST2 give/do food
'Nfor GAVE SHEY some food.'

This can be interpreted as another argument against VP-evacuating object movement and, by extension, against a remnant movement analysis of verb fronting. In order for a partial verb phrase to undergo fronting, one of its objects must have moved out of it. The fact that partial verb phrase fronting is ungrammatical indicates that no such movement is available.

In contrast to Asante Twi, which only allowed verb fronting, Limbum displays both kinds of verbal fronting with individual-level predicates like *yòb* 'resemble' (76) and *kɔ̀ŋ* 'love' (77) . The a. examples here provide a neutral sentence containing the respective predicate while the b. and c. examples respectively show verb fronting and verb phrase fronting.

(76) a. Nfor à yòb zhɨ̀ tāà.
Nfor 3SG resemble 3POSS father
'Nfor resembles his father.'
b. Á r-**yòb** (cí) Nfor à **yòb** zhɨ̀ tāà.
FOC 5-resemble COMP Nfor 3SG resemble 3POSS father
'Nfor RESEMBLES his father.'

2.1 Repair patterns in languages with both verb and verb phrase fronting — 65

  c. Á r-[yòb zhɨ̀ tāà] (cí) Nfor à **gī**.
   FOC 5-resemble 3POSS father COMP Nfor 3SG do
   'Nfor RESEMBLES his father.'

(77) a. Nfor à kɔŋ Shey.
   Nfor 3SG love Shey
   'Nfor loves Shey.'
  b. Á r-**kɔ̀ŋ** (cí) Nfor à **kɔ̀ŋ** Shey.
   FOC 5-love COMP Nfor 3SG love Shey
   'Nfor LOVES Shey.'
  c. Á r-[**kɔ̀ŋ** Shey] (cí) Nfor à **gī**.
   FOC 5-love Shey COMP Nfor 3SG do
   'Nfor LOVES SHEY.'

However, the behaviour of locative PP-adverbials like *ní Yaounde* 'in Yaounde' under verbal fronting is parallel to what we observed in Asante Twi. Adverbs in general have to always occur sentence-finally like in (78-a). While both verb fronting and verb phrase fronting is grammatical when stranding the PP (78-b, c) the PP incurs ungrammaticality when it is fronted alongside a verb or a verb phrase (78-d, e).

(78) a. Nfor bí bō ndāp ní Yaounde.
   Nfor FUT build house in Yaounde
   'Nfor will build a house in Yaounde.'
  b. Á r-**bō** (cí) Nfor bí **bō** ndāp ní Yaounde.
   FOC 5-build COMP Nfor FUT1 build house in Yaounde
   'Nfor will BUILD a house in Yaounde.'
  c. Á r-[**bō** ndāp] (cí) Nfor bí **gī** ní Yaounde.
   FOC 5-build house COMP Nfor FUT1 do in Yaounde
   'Nfor will BUILD A HOUSE in Yaounde.'
  d. *Á r-[**bō** ní Yaounde] (cí) Nfor bí **bō** ndāp.
   FOC 5-build in Yaounde COMP Nfor FUT1 build house
  e. *Á r-[**bō** ndāp ní Yaounde] (cí) Nfor bí **gī**.
   FOC 5-build house in Yaounde COMP Nfor FUT1 do

Just like in Asante Twi, the ungrammaticality extends to other fronted adverbs. Thus verb fronting as well as verb phrase fronting where the fronted constituent is accompanied by the adverb *chéchér* 'quickly' is ungrammatical (79).

(79) a. Nfor bí bō ndāp chéchér.
   Nfor FUT1 build house quickly
   'Nfor will quickly build a house.'

    b. *Á   r-**bō**   chéchér (cí)   Nfor bí **bō** ndāp (chéchér).
       FOC 5-build quickly   COMP Nfor FUT1 build house quickly
    c. *Á   r-[**bō** ndāp chéchér] (cí)   Nfor bí **gī** (chéchér).
       FOC 5-build house quickly   COMP Nfor FUT1 do quickly

As was the case for Asante Twi above, in order for Limbum to serve as a convincing instantiation of the asymmetric repair pattern it needs to be shown that verb doubling as well as dummy verb insertion are not derived from independent constructions like cognate object constructions or *do*-periphrases.

Starting with cognate object constructions we find that Limbum indeed exhibits a few verbs that can take cognate objects. One example is *bī* 'dance' (80).

(80)   Nfor bí   bī   bī.
       Nfor FUT1 dance(V) dance(N)
       'Nfor will dance (a dance).'

An argument against verb fronting being derived from constructions like (80) is that cognate objects are quite restricted in their distribution in the language. They can only occur with a handful of verbs and do not cooccur with the direct object of a transitive verb. It is, for instance, not possible for the transitive verb *bō* 'build' to take a cognate object in addition to its direct object *ndāp* 'house' in the following example.

(81)   *Nfor bí   bō   (r-)bō   ndāp.
       Nfor FUT1 build(V) 5-build(N) house

Thus, cognate object formation is not productive enough to provide the necessary base construction for all attested verb fronting examples. It is, therefore, clear that verb doubling in verb fronting cannot be reanalysed as fronting of a cognate object.

Concerning dummy verb insertion in verb phrase fronting, a purported base construction with a dummy verb embedding a verb phrase is ungrammatical (82).

(82)   a. *Njíŋwè fɔ̄   bí   gī (r-)yū msāŋ.
       woman DET FUT1 do 5-buy rice
       'The woman will buy rice.'
    b. *Nfor à   mū gī (r-)bò   ndāp.
       Nfor 3SG PST2 do 5-build house
       'Nfor built/did build a house.'

Consequently, dummy verb insertion as it occurs in verb phrase fronting cannot be traced back to an independent construction containing a dummy verb that selects a verb phrase.

In conclusion, both verb doubling and dummy verb insertion in Limbum verbal fronting must be considered proper repair strategies for an illicit gap. In turn, besides Asante Twi, Limbum then constitutes a second instance of the asymmetric repair pattern, whose status as a real pattern is thereby further strengthened.

2.1.3.3 Other languages showing the asymmetric pattern III

There are two additional languages that potentially exhibit the same pattern as Asante Twi and Limbum, namely Haitian Creole (see also section 7.1.7) and Afrikaans. As I do not dispose of enough data for both languages to convincingly argue the case, I will only briefly discuss them here. Further research is necessary to clarify whether they indeed instantiate pattern III or not. One verbal fronting construction in Mandarin might also instantiate this asymmetric pattern (see section 8.2.8).

Let us begin with Haitian Creole, a French-based creole spoken by approximately ten million people in Haiti. It clearly comprises of a verb fronting construction, associated with contrastive focus on the verb, in which the verb is doubled (83-a). At the same time, fronting of a verb phrase with concomitant doubling is ungrammatical (83-b) (see section 7.1.7 for more details).

(83)   a.   Se te **manje** li tre di Jan t' ap **manje** pen an.
             SE TNS eat   he TNS say John TNS ASP eat   bread DET
             'It was eating the bread he said that John did.'   (Lefebvre 1987: 169)
      b.   *Se [**manje** yon pòm] Jan   **manje** (yon pòm).
             SE eat   an apple John eat   an apple
             Intended: 'It is eating an apple that John did.'   (Harbour 2008: 856)

However, there is an additional verb fronting construction which warrants closer scrutiny because it exhibits the opposite repair operation, namely dummy verb insertion (84).

(84)   Se **vini** li a Jan te **fè**.
       SE coming his DET John PST do
       'It's his visit (that we knew would happen) that John did.'
                                        (Lumsden & Lefebvre 1990: 766)

This construction is less common than the verb focalization in (83) but still grammatical and, at first sight, presents a case of apparent verb fronting with dummy verb insertion. However, what is fronted in (84) might equally well be a full verb phrase (headed by an intransitive verb) rather than a verbal head on its own. Under this perspective, Haitian Creole actually disposes of both verb fronting and verb phrase fronting. Exhibiting verb doubling with the former but dummy verb insertion with the latter, it would pattern with Asante Twi and Limbum.

However, the situation is somewhat more intricate than that. First, note that the construction in (84) does not permit the fronting of the object together with the transitive verb. In this respect, it behaves like the doubling construction in (83).

(85)   *Se [achté flè   mwé an] m' ap fè flè.
         SE buying flower POSS DET I   ASP do flower
         'It is the buy of flowers (that I was supposed to do) that I am doing.'
                                                    (Lumsden & Lefebvre 1990: 774)

At first glance, this restriction speaks against an analysis of the dummy verb as a consequence of verb phrase fronting. As the internal argument is part of the verb phrase, we would expect it to front with the verb, contrary to fact. However, the construction's behaviour is not completely identical to that of verb fronting with verb doubling. Consider example (86) which is equally ungrammatical as (85).

(86)   *Se [achté mwé an] m' ap fè flè.
         SE buying POSS DET I   ASP do flower
         'It is the buy of flowers (that I was supposed to do) that I am doing.'
                                                    (Lumsden & Lefebvre 1990: 774)

This example shows that it is not possible to front a transitive verb while stranding its object. As we have seen in (83-a) above, this is perfectly grammatical with verb doubling. Thus, examples like (86) cannot involve the same kind of verb fronting used in the latter.

If fronting of a transitive verb with its object is impossible but stranding the object is also not allowed, the fronting construction is in effect restricted to intransitive verbs which do not have any internal arguments. As pointed out in section 1.1, there is an inherent ambiguity with intransitive verb fronting: It may either be understood to be verb fronting or verb phrase fronting where the phrase in this case only consists of the verb itself. As it stands, the dummy verb construction might therefore equally well be verb phrase fronting rather than verb fronting. This ambiguity is additionally supported by data like (87-b) where just like in Hebrew (see section 8.2.4) and Vietnamese (see section 8.2.14) fronting of an intransitive is optionally triggers either verb doubling or dummy verb insertion.

Note further that the fronted verb in the dummy verb construction has nominal characteristics. It can appear with determiners (86), possessive pronouns (87-a) and the question particle *ki* (87-b).

(87)   a.   Se [vini   m'nan] m' fè.
             SE coming POSS.DET I do
             'It is the visit (I was supposed to do) that I did.'

2.1 Repair patterns in languages with both verb and verb phrase fronting — 69

b. Se [ki **vini**] Jan ap **fè/vini**?
SE WH coming John AP do/come
'It is what visit that John is doing?' (= a visit to dine or to pay a debt...)
(Lumsden & Lefebvre 1990: 774)

As demonstrated by Filipovich (1987) and Brousseau et al. (1989), verb-to-noun conversion in Haitian Creole is restricted to verbs that do not assign case to their complements, i.e. to intransitive verbs. Considering the fact that nominalization (of any kind) does not appear with the verb doubling constructions in the language, we may assume that the nominalization is forced by verb phrase fronting and that verb phrase fronting, like in Asante Twi and Limbum, triggers dummy verb insertion. As nominalization is only available for intransitive verb phrases, only these can occur in fronted position with a dummy verb clause-internally. The lack of overt objects in the fronted verb phrase would then be due a conspiracy of two factors: (i) only verbs that do not assign case to their complement can be nominalized and (ii) the fronted verb phrase is obligatorily nominalized. If this is correct, Haitian Creole might serve as another manifestation of the asymmetric pattern III.

Turning to Afrikaans, a very cursory assessment of verbal fronting reveals that it shows verb doubling with verb fronting (88-a) while the opposite repair of dummy verb insertion is ungrammatical (88-b). Contrarily, verb phrase fronting entails the presence of a dummy verb (89-a) with verb doubling being ungrammatical (89-b).

(88) a. **Skryf skryf** hy die boek.
write write he the book
'Write the book he certainly does.' (Biberauer 2009: 12)
b. *__Skryf doen__ hy die boek, maar hy wil dit nie publiseer nie.[9]
write does he the book but he will it not publish not
Intended: 'He does write the book, but he will not publish it.'
(Erin Pretorius p.c.)

(89) a. [Die boek **skryf**] **doen** hy, maar hy wil dit nie publiseer nie.
the book write does he but he will it not publish not
'As for writing the book, he writes it, but he doesn't want to publish it.'
b. *[Die boek **skryf**] skryf hy, maar hy wil dit nie publiseer nie.
the book write writes he but he will it not publish not
(Erin Pretorius p.c.)

---

[9] This sentence's grammaticality status is based on its average rating of 1.14 on a 5-point Likert scale ranging from 1 (completely ungrammatical) to 5 (completely grammatical) in an online questionnaire with 205 native speaker participants carried out by Cora Pots.

Apparently, fronting of a ditransitive verb phrase is also possible. This holds for the double object construction (90-a) as well as for the prepositional object construction (90-b). The respective repair is dummy verb insertion in both.

(90) a. [Die kinders lekkergoed **gee**] **doen** hy, maar hy gee nie die
 the children sweets give does he but he gives not the
 volwassene sjokolade nie.
 adults chocolate not
 'As for giving the children sweets, he does that, but he doesn't give the adults chocolate.'
 b. [Lekkergoed aan die kinders **gee**] **doen** hy, maar hy gee nie
 sweets to the children give does he but he gives not
 sjokolade aan die volwassene nie.
 chocolate to the adults not
 'As for giving sweets to the children, he does that, but he doesn't give chocolate to the adults.' (Erin Pretorius p.c.)

There is also some evidence that the object in the fronted verb phrase may be modified, for instance by an adjective (91).

(91) [Die kort artikel **skryf**] **doen** hy vandag, maar die lang boekresensie
 the short article write does he today but the long book.review
 kan hy nie klaarmaak nie.
 can he not finish not
 'As for writing the short article, he does that today, but he won't be able to finish the long book-review.' (Erin Pretorius p.c.)

An indication that the dummy verb in verb phrase fronting is indeed a repair comes from the fact that a *doen*-periphrasis is not existent in the language (92).

(92) *Vandag doen hy die kort artikel skryf.
 today does he the short article write
 Intended: 'Today, he'll write the short article.' (Erin Pretorius p.c.)

Based on this limited set of data, Afrikaans also instantiates pattern III in addition to Asante Twi, Limbum, and possibly Haitian Creole, and in contrast to its sister language Dutch, which exhibits pattern II. In order to properly evaluate the status of Afrikaans, however, more data on verbal fronting need to be investigated, in particular concerning the $\bar{\text{A}}$-status of the dependency between the fronted constituent and its clause-internal counterpart (i.e. the verb copy or the dummy verb).

2.1.4 Generalization I

Having shown that verb and verb fronting have the same distribution and are subject to the same restrictions within Asante Twi and Limbum we are forced to accept their asymmetric pattern as a proper repair pattern in the realm of verbal fronting. Provided that pattern III in Haitian Creole and Afrikaans can be confirmed, these two would lend further weight on the reality of this pattern. This raises two questions, one typological and the other theoretical. First, if verb doubling and dummy verb insertion legitimately coexist as repair strategies in verbal fronting in one and the same language as evidenced by Asante Twi and Limbum, are there languages that instantiate the reverse asymmetric pattern IV, namely exhibiting dummy verb insertion with verb fronting and verb doubling with verb phrase fronting? This question may be answered negatively. At least in this sample (and to my knowledge), there are no languages that show verb doubling in verb phrase fronting contexts but dummy verb insertion with verb fronting. It therefore seems plausible that there is a systematic gap in the typology of repair patterns for verbal fronting. Second, how can the attested asymmetric and symmetric patterns be derived under Minimalist assumptions about syntax and PF to the exclusion of the unattested one? In chapter 4, I will present an account that derives patterns I–III but is unable to derive pattern IV. The attested patterns are shown with two example languages each in (93).

(93)   *Attested repair patterns in languages with both kinds of verbal fronting*

	Verb fronting	Verb phrase fronting	Languages
I	verb copy	verb copy	Hebrew, Dagaare, ...
II	dummy verb	dummy verb	Breton, German, ...
III	verb copy	dummy verb	Asante Twi, Limbum, ...

Given that pattern III has now been discovered in at least Asante Twi and Limbum while pattern IV remains unattested we can formulate the first generalization over the present sample of languages as in (94).

(94)   *Generalization I*
If a language shows both verb and verb phrase fronting it either exhibits the same repair strategy in both frontings (verb doubling or dummy verb insertion), or verb doubling in verb fronting and dummy verb insertion in verb phrase fronting. The reverse pattern is inexistent.

The theoretical part of this book in chapter 4 is devoted to account for this generalization within current Minimalism.

Concluding this part on repair patterns in languages that show both kinds of verbal fronting, a final note on their proportions in the sample seems in order. Pattern I is by far the most frequent with a total of 16 languages exhibiting it. Both, pattern II and pattern III are much rarer with four and two (four, counting Haitian Creole and Afrikaans) languages displaying them, respectively (95).

(95) Numbers and proportions of each attested pattern

	Pattern			
	I	II	III	Total
number of languages	16	4	2	22
proportion in languages with both frontings	73 %	18 %	9 %	100 %
proportion in complete sample	34 %	9 %	4 %	47 %

As is evident from (95), more than half of the languages in the sample allow only one kind of verbal fronting. We will turn to these languages in the following section.

2.2 Repair patterns in languages with either verb or verb phrase fronting

Not all languages allow both kinds of verbal fronting. There is a considerable number of predominantly African and creole languages in which a verb's object(s) may not accompany it into the left periphery. Other languages, in contrast, obligatorily require the object(s) to be fronted together with the verb. I will refer to the former as verb fronting only languages and to the latter as verb phrase fronting only languages. Similar to what was the case for languages with both types of fronting there are *a priori* four logically possible repair patterns, namely two for each language type (96).

(96) Possible repair patterns in languages with only one kind of verbal fronting

	Verb fronting	Verb phrase fronting
A	verb copy	—
B	dummy verb	—
C	—	verb copy
D	—	dummy verb

A language that only allows verb fronting would instantiate pattern A if it used verb doubling as a repair and pattern B if it used dummy verb insertion. Similarly, a language that only permits verb phrase fronting would be an example of pattern C if it used verb doubling as a repair, but of pattern D if it used dummy verb insertion instead. However, again not all four patterns are attested.

2.2.1 Verb fronting only

In the majority of languages that exhibit only one kind of verbal fronting this kind is verb fronting. Of 25 languages there are 17 that fall into this category. They are given in alphabetical order below:

1. Basaa
   (Southern Bantoid, Niger-Congo; Bassong 2014, see also section 7.1.1)
2. Berbice Dutch Creole
   (Dutch-lexicon creole; Kouwenberg 1994, see also section 7.1.2)
3. Edo
   (Gur, Niger-Congo; Stewart 1998, see also section 7.1.3)
4. Ewe
   (Kwa, Niger-Congo; Ameka 1991, 1992, 2010, see also section 7.1.4)
5. Fongbe
   (Kwa, Niger-Congo; Lefebvre 1992, Ndayiragije 1993, Law & Lefebvre 1995, Lefebvre & Brousseau 2002, see also section 7.1.5)
6. Gungbe
   (Kwa, Niger-Congo; Aboh 1998, Aboh & Dyakonova 2009, see also section 7.1.6)
7. Haitian Creole[10]
   (French-based creole; Piou 1982, Lefebvre 1987, Lumsden & Lefebvre 1990, Larson & Lefebvre 1991, Harbour 2008, see also section 7.1.7)
8. Kisi
   (Mel, Niger-Congo; Childs 1997, see also section 7.1.8)
9. Leteh/Larteh
   (Kwa, Niger-Congo; Ansah 2014, see also section 7.1.9)
10. Nupe
    (Nupoid, Niger-Congo; Kandybowicz 2008, see also section 7.1.10)
11. Nweh
    (Grassfields, Niger-Congo; Nkemnji 1995, Koopman 1997, see also section 7.1.11)

---

10 Haitian Creole might actually allow both verb and verb phrase fronting. There are three examples of fronting of an intransitive verb with dummy verb insertion in the clause that could be analysed as verb phrase fronting (see sections 2.1.3.3 and 7.1.7). In that case, Haitian Creole would actually also instantiate the asymmetric pattern III found in Asante Twi and Limbum.

12. Papiamentu
    (Portuguese-based creole; Muysken 1977, 1978, Kouwenberg & Murray 1994, see also section 7.1.12)
13. Pichi
    (English-lexicon creole; Yakpo 2009, see also section 7.1.13)
14. Saramaccan
    (English- and Portuguese-based creole; Byrne 1987, see also section 7.1.14)
15. Tuki
    (Southern Bantoid, Niger-Congo; Biloa 2013, see also section 7.1.15)
16. Turkish
    (Turkic; Lee 2002, Göksel & Kerslake 2005, see also section 7.1.16)
17. Vata
    (Kru, Niger-Congo; Koopman 1984, see also section 7.1.17)

Interestingly, all 17 languages use verb doubling as a repair, that is, they all display pattern A. There is no language in the sample (and to my knowledge) that exhibits pattern B, namely allowing verb fronting only but using dummy verb insertion as a repair. A few examples of pattern A are given below from Basaa (97), Haitian Creole (98), Saramaccan (99), and Tuki (100). Where available I include examples showing the ungrammaticality of verb phrase fronting. Otherwise the absence of any such examples is taken as an indication that verb phrase fronting is illicit.

(97) a. N-**nígl**-ak   wɔ́-n hí-bí-**nígíl**   mínsɔngí.
       3.NMLZ-learn-NMLZ 3-FOC 19.SM-PST2-learn 4.mathematics
       'The boy LEARNED MATHEMATICS (he did not teach it/play football).'
    b. *[N-**nígl**-ak   mínsɔngí]   wɔ́-n hí-bí-**nígíl**.
       3.NMLZ-learn-NMLZ 4.mathematics 3-FOC 19.SM-PST2-learn
       (*Basaa*, Bassong 2014: 146)

(98) a. Se **manje** Jan **manje** pen.
       SE eat   Jan eat   bread
       'It is eating bread that John did.' (he did not bake it)
                                              (Lefebvre 1987: 170)
    b. *Se [**manje** yon pòm] Jan **manje** (yon pòm).
       SE eat   an apple John eat   an apple
                                        (*Haitian Creole*, Harbour 2008: 856)

(99) a. **Sùku**   a **sùku**   en.
       look.for he look.for him
       'He LOOKED FOR him.'
    b. *[**Sùku** en] a **sùku**.
       look.for him he look.for   (*Saramaccan*, Byrne 1987: 97)

(100) a. O-**nyá** ówú nǔ ngu-nú-**nyám** cwí.
 INF-eat FOC I SM-F1-eat fish
 'I will EAT fish.'
 b. *[O-**nyá** cwí] ówú nǔ ngu-nú-**nyám** cwí.
 INF-eat fish FOC I SM-F1-eat fish (*Tuki*, Biloa 2013: 76)

Thus, the languages which solely allow verb fronting only ever exhibit verb doubling as a repair, never dummy verb insertion. Of the *a priori* expectable two patterns A and B, the latter turns out to be unattested. This immediately raises the question whether a similar observation, i.e. only one of two possible patterns being attested, holds for the languages in which only verb phrase fronting is possible. Indeed, this is the case.

2.2.2 Verb phrase fronting only

A considerably smaller number of eight languages in the sample are restricted in so far as they do not exhibit verb fronting but do display verb phrase fronting. These are in alphabetical order again:
1. Danish
 (Germanic, Indo-European; Platzack 2008, Houser et al. 2006, 2011, Ørsnes 2011, see also section 7.2.1)
2. Hausa
 (Chadic, Afro-Asiatic; Tuller 1986, Jaggar 2001, Hartmann 2006, see also section 7.2.2)
3. Japanese
 (Japonic; Nishiyama & Cho 1998, Aoyagi 2006, Ishihara 2010, see also section 7.2.3)
4. Norwegian
 (Germanic, Indo-European; Lødrup 1990, Siri M. Gjersøe p.c., see also section 7.2.4)
5. Skou
 (Western Skou; Donohue 2004, see also section 7.2.5)
6. Swedish
 (Germanic, Indo-European; Källgren & Prince 1989, Holmberg 1999, Platzack 2012, see also section 7.2.6)
7. Welsh
 (Celtic, Indo-European; Sproat 1985, Tallerman 1996, Borsley et al. 2007, Rouveret 2012, see also section 7.2.7)

8. Wolof
(Atlantic, Niger-Congo; Torrence 2013a,b, Martinović 2015, 2017, see also section 7.2.8)

In stark contrast to the languages in the previous section, these eight unanimously employ dummy verb insertion, that is, they instantiate pattern D. There are no deviations from this pattern that I know of. Pattern C, therefore, can be regarded as hitherto unattested. Examples of pattern D are given below from Norwegian (101), Skou (102), Welsh (103), and Wolof (104-a). Where available I include examples showing the ungrammaticality of object stranding. As usual, the absence of any such examples is interpreted as them being ungrammatical.

(101) a. [(Å) **lese** bøk-er] **gjør**/*leser han hele dag-en.
to read.INF book.PL-PL.INDEF does/reads he whole day-DEF
'Reading books he does all day.'
b. *(Å) lese gjør/leser han bøk-er hele dag-en.
to read.INF does/reads he book.PL-PL.INDEF whole day-DEF
(*Norwegian*, Siri M. Gjersøe p.c.)

(102) a. [Moerító ke=k-**ang**]=inga, bàng ke=**li**.
fish(sp.) 3SG.NF=3SG.NF-eat=the yesterday 3SG.NF=do
'Eating Yellowtail scad, he did (it) yesterday.'
b. *Ke=k-ang=inga, bàng ke=baléng moerító.
3SG.NF=3SG.NF-eat=the yesterday 3SG.NF=man fish(sp.)
(*Skou*, Donohue 2004: 126f.)

(103) [**Pori'r** comin a'r cloddiau] a **wnaeth** Ifas am y
browse.the common and.the hedges PRT did.3SG Ifas for the
lleill.
others
'Ifas BROWSED THE COMMON AND THE HEDGES for the others.'
(*Welsh*, Tallerman 1996: 100)

(104) a. [**Suub** simis b-i] l-a-a *(**def**).
dye shirt CL-DEF.PROX *l*-C-1SG do
'Dye the shirt is what I did.'
b. *Suub l-a-a suub simis b-i.
dye *l*-C-1SG dye shirt CL-DEF.PROX
Intended: 'I DYED the shirt.' (*Wolof*, Torrence 2013a: 68)

Languages that only allow verb phrase fronting thus seem to behave exactly opposite to those that permit only verb fronting as the former exclusively display dummy verb insertion while the latter show only verb doubling.

2.2.3 Generalization II

In contrast to the largely symmetric patterns in languages that show both kinds of verbal fronting, the repair in languages that allow only one kind is not independent of this kind. Verb fronting in the latter never gives rise to dummy verb insertion. A fact that is surprising given the observation that this repair is in principle able to occur in this kind of fronting as evidenced by languages like German or Dutch. On the other hand, verb phrase fronting never leads to verb doubling, which again runs counter to our expectations because verb doubling is a possible repair of verb phrase fronting in languages like Hebrew or Dagaare. Of the four expected repair patterns, thus, only two are attested given in (105) each with two of the languages in the sample that instantiate them.

(105) *Possible repair patterns in languages with only one kind of verbal fronting*

	Verb fronting	Verb phrase fronting	Languages
A	verb copy	—	Tuki, Saramaccan, …
D	—	dummy verb	Danish, Wolof, …

Given these observations one can formulate a second generalization about verbal fronting over the languages in the sample that display only one kind of fronting (106).

(106) *Generalization II*
    a. If a language allows only verb fronting it exclusively shows verb doubling as repair.
    b. If a language allows only verb phrase fronting it exclusively shows dummy verb insertion as repair.

The proposed analysis in chapter 4 will be able to account for (106-a). The second part (106-b), however, does not follow from it. In section 4.2.2.2, I will discuss (106-b) in more detail against the background of the presented analysis. I will conclude that the observation underlying it may be flawed due to the small number of languages instantiating pattern D and due to the fact that pattern D is expected to be more likely compared to pattern C because the latter presupposes a very specific combination of properties while the former emerges under various different combinations of properties.

Concerning the numbers we find that, within the languages that show only one kind of verbal fronting in the sample, pattern A is markedly more frequent than pattern D (107).

(107) *Numbers and proportions of each attested pattern*

	Pattern		
	A	D	Total
number of languages	17	8	25
proportion in languages with one fronting	68 %	32 %	100 %
proportion in complete sample	36 %	17 %	53 %

In total, more than half (25) of the languages in the sample (47) show only one kind of verbal fronting with pattern A being instantiated by the most languages in the sample.

2.3 Summary and overview of sample languages' properties

In this chapter, I have introduced the terms verb fronting and verb phrase fronting as referring to surface configurations in which the main verb of a clause appears not in its base position but in the left periphery either stranding its object(s), a case of verb fronting, or having them accompany it, a case of verb phrase fronting. Verbal fronting is used as the overarching term connecting the two. The fronted verb can take different morphological forms in different languages. Commonly, it is nominalized or an infinitive but there are rare cases where it may also appear in tensed form. Cross-linguistic variation is also observed in the kind of non-object material that may cooccur with a fronted verb. While some languages allow the verb to be marked with TAM-exponents or even nominal modifiers like adjectives, determiners, and demonstratives, other languages permit no such marking. These elements serve well as diagnostics for the underlying category of the fronted constituent as V(P), v(P), or Asp(P). A similar diagnostic is presented by adverbs. Knowing at which level certain adverbs usually adjoin their presence or absence in the fronted constituent reveals whether it is a VP or a vP.

A further issue concerning verbal fronting is the question whether it involves ($\bar{\text{A}}$-)movement or not. In the majority of languages, standard diagnostics for ($\bar{\text{A}}$-)movement, like unboundedness, island-tests, cooccurrence with other $\bar{\text{A}}$-movements, or reconstruction effects support the treatment of the fronted constituent as having been moved into the left periphery rather than being base-generated.

All abovementioned properties are of interest to research on verbal fronting and have therefore been included in the language descriptions in part II where relevant data were available. An overview of the behaviour of the 47 investigated languages with respect to them is provided in table 2.1 at the end of this chapter.

2.3 Summary and overview of sample languages' properties — 79

In the absence of any other inflectable material in the clause, verb and verb phrase fronting commonly trigger one of two repair strategies in order to avoid a gap. Either a copy of the displaced verb occurs in the base position or a dummy verb, usually equivalent to *do* in English, is inserted instead. In some languages there are independent verb doubling or dummy verb constructions such that verbal fronting could be claimed to be derived from these by moving the main verb while stranding the other verb copy or dummy verb. However, many languages do not have the necessary independent constructions or, if they have them, they are not productive enough. A conception of verb doubling and dummy verb insertion as repairs directly related to verbal fronting is therefore necessary for these latter languages. In trying to account for the observed typology and generalizations, which hold for all languages alike, it is therefore reasonable to treat all verb doubling and dummy verb insertion in verbal fronting as repairs.

The observed patterns fall into two categories: (i) Patterns in languages with both verb and verb phrase fronting and (ii) patterns in languages with only one kind of verbal fronting. Concerning (i), new data from Asante Twi and Limbum were presented that instantiate one of the two hitherto unattested asymmetric patterns. The absence of the second asymmetric pattern in the sample lead to the formulation of the generalization in (108).

(108)   *Generalization I*
If a language shows both verb and verb phrase fronting it either exhibits the same repair strategy in both frontings (verb doubling, i.e. pattern I, or dummy verb insertion, i.e. pattern II), or verb doubling in verb fronting and dummy verb insertion in verb phrase fronting, i.e. pattern III. The reverse pattern, i.e. pattern IV, is inexistent.

Concerning (ii), it was found that there is a one-to-one correspondence between the kind of verbal fronting and the observed repair, which is formulated as the generalization in (109).

(109)   *Generalization II*
   a. If a language allows only verb fronting it exclusively shows verb doubling as repair (pattern A).
   b. If a language allows only verb phrase fronting it exclusively shows dummy verb insertion as repair (pattern D).

The overall picture that emerges here is that five of eight logically possible repair patterns in verbal fronting are attested whereas three patterns remain unattested (110).

(110) *Attested and unattested repair patterns in the sample*

Pattern	Verb fronting	Verb phrase fronting	# of langs	% of langs
attested				
I	verb copy	verb copy	16	34
II	dummy verb	dummy verb	4	9
III	verb copy	dummy verb	2	4
A	verb copy	—	17	36
D	—	dummy verb	8	17
unattested				
IV	dummy verb	verb copy		
B	dummy verb	—		
C	—	verb copy		

The conclusion drawn from this observation is that these patterns constitute systematic typological gaps that any account of verbal fronting should ideally be able to derive. In the next chapter, I will discuss a few prominent approaches to verb doubling and dummy verb insertion in verbal fronting and show that none of them adequately accounts for all observed patterns. I will then proceed to develop a new analysis of verbal fronting and its repair mechanisms in chapter 4 that derives all attested patterns to the exclusion of the two unattested patterns IV and B. Pattern C will be argued to be absent from the data due to additional factors.

Tab. 2.1: Overview of properties of verbal fronting in languages of the sample

Language	Genealogy	V	VP	copy	dummy	unbd	Wh	CNP	Subj	Adj	Rel	Coord	Recon	Wh-Co	GS	TAM	L-Adv	H-Adv	Neg	Det	Nom	Inf	Dir	F/T-M	Foc	Top
Asante Twi	NC > Kwa	✓	✓	✓	✓	✓	✓	✓	✓	✓	–	✓	✓	–	–	–	–	–	–	–	S	–	L	✓	✓	–
Basaa	NC > S Bantoid	✓	–	✓	–	✓	✓	✓	✓	✓	–	✓	?	–	–	–	?	?	–	–	✓	(–)	L/R	–	✓	–
Basque	Isolate	✓	✓	S	–	✓	?	?	?	?	?	✓	?	?	?	?	?	?	?	–	–	✓	L	–	✓	–
B. Dutch Creole	Creole	✓	–	✓	–	✓	?	?	?	?	?	?	?	?	?	?	?	?	?	–	–	✓	L	✓	–	✓
Br. Portuguese	IE > Romance	S	✓	S	–	S	S	✓	✓	?	S	✓	?	–	–	S	?	?	?	?	–	✓	L	–	–	–
Breton	IE > Celtic	✓	✓	✓	–	✓	✓	?	?	?	S	?	?	?	?	?	?	?	?	?	–	✓	L	–	?	?
Buli	NC > Gur	✓	✓	✓	–	✓	✓	?	S	S	S	✓	?	?	?	?	?	?	?	?	–	✓	L	–	✓	–
Dagaare	NC > Gur	–	✓	–	–	✓	✓	?	?	S	✓	✓	?	?	?	?	?	?	?	S	S	✓	L	–	–	✓
Danish	IE > Germanic	✓	✓	✓	✓	✓	✓	?	✓	?	✓	✓	?	?	?	?	?	?	?	?	✓	✓	L	–	✓	✓
Dutch	IE > Germanic	✓	✓	✓	–	✓	✓	–	✓	?	✓	✓	?	?	?	✓	✓	?	?	✓	✓	✓	L	–	✓	✓
Edo	NC > Edoid	✓	S	✓	–	?	?	?	?	?	?	?	?	?	?	?	?	?	?	?	?	?	L	–	–	–
Ewe	NC > Kwa	✓	–	✓	–	?	?	?	?	?	?	✓	?	–	–	✓	?	?	?	?	?	?	L	–	–	–
Fongbe	NC > Kwa	✓	✓	✓	–	✓	–	✓	✓	✓	✓	✓	?	–	–	?	✓	?	?	✓	✓	✓	L	S	✓	✓
German	IE > Germanic	✓	✓	✓	✓	S	–	–	–	?	–	✓	?	–	–	–	?	?	?	?	?	–	L	–	–	✓
Gungbe	NC > Kwa	✓	✓	S	–	✓	✓	?	✓	?	?	✓	?	–	–	✓	✓	✓	?	✓	✓	✓	L	S	✓	–
Haitian Creole	Creole	✓	✓	✓	–	✓	✓	?	?	?	?	✓	?	?	?	?	?	?	?	?	?	✓	L	S	✓	–
Hausa	AfA > Chadic	–	✓	–	–	✓	✓	?	?	?	?	✓	?	–	–	–	✓	?	?	?	?	✓	L	–	✓	✓
Hebrew	AfA > Semitic	✓	✓	✓	–	✓	✓	?	?	?	?	✓	?	?	?	?	?	?	?	?	?	✓	L	–	✓	–
Hungarian	Uralic	✓	✓	S	–	✓	✓	?	?	?	?	✓	?	?	?	?	✓	?	?	?	?	?	L	–	✓	–
Japanese	Japonic	–	✓	–	–	✓	?	?	?	?	?	✓	?	–	–	–	?	?	?	?	?	✓	L	–	✓	✓
Kisi	NC > Mel	✓	✓	✓	–	✓	✓	?	?	?	?	✓	?	?	?	?	✓	?	?	?	?	?	L	–	✓	–
Korean	Koreanic	✓	✓	✓	–	✓	✓	?	?	?	?	✓	?	?	?	?	?	✓	?	?	?	?	L	–	✓	✓
Krachi	NC > Kwa	✓	✓	✓	–	✓	✓	?	?	?	?	✓	?	?	?	?	?	✓	?	?	?	?	L	–	✓	–
Leteh	NC > Kwa	✓	–	✓	–	✓	✓	?	?	?	?	✓	?	?	?	?	?	?	?	?	?	–	L	–	✓	–
Limbum	NC > Grassfields	✓	✓	✓	–	✓	✓	?	?	?	?	✓	?	–	–	✓	✓	?	?	?	?	✓	L	–	✓	✓
Mandarin	ST > Chinese	✓	✓	S	–	?	?	?	?	?	?	?	?	?	?	?	?	?	?	?	?	?	L	–	✓	✓
Mani	NC > Mel	✓	–	✓	–	✓	✓	?	?	?	?	✓	?	?	?	?	?	?	?	?	?	?	L	–	✓	–
Norwegian	IE > Germanic	✓	✓	✓	✓	✓	✓	?	?	?	?	✓	✓	?	?	✓	✓	?	?	?	?	✓	L	✓	✓	✓
Nupe	NC > Nupoid	✓	–	✓	–	?	?	?	?	?	?	?	?	?	?	?	?	?	?	?	?	?	L	–	✓	✓
Nweh	NC > Grassfields	✓	✓	✓	–	✓	–	?	?	?	?	✓	?	✓/–	–	–	✓	?	?	?	?	S	R	–	✓	✓
Papiamentu	Creole	✓	✓	✓	–	?	?	?	?	?	?	?	?	?	?	?	?	?	?	?	?	?	L	–	✓	–
Pichi	Creole	✓	–	✓	–	?	?	?	?	?	?	?	?	?	?	?	?	?	?	?	?	?	L	S	✓	✓
Polish	IE > Slavic	✓	✓	✓	–	S	✓	✓	✓	✓	?	✓	✓	✓	–	S	✓	–	–	–	–	✓	L	S	–	✓

Tab. 2.1: Continued

Language	Genealogy	V	VP	copy	dummy	unbd	Wh	CNP	Subj	Adj	Rel	Coord	Recon	Wh-Co	GS	TAM	L-Adv	H-Adv	Neg	Det	Nom	Inf	Dir	F/T-M	Foc	Top
Russian	IE > Slavic	✓	✓	–	–	–	?	?	?	?	?	?	?	?	?	✓	–	?	?	?	–	✓	L	(✓)	–	✓
Saramaccan	Creole	✓	–	✓	–	(✓)	?	?	?	?	?	?	?	?	(–)	?	?	?	?	?	?	?	L	–	–	–
Skou	Skou > W Skou	–	✓	–	✓	?	✓	?	?	?	?	?	?	?	?	✓	?	?	?	?	?	?	L	–	✓	✓
Spanish	IE > Romance	✓	✓	–	–	✓	–	?	?	?	?	?	–	?	–	?	?	?	?	?	?	?	L	–	–	✓
Swedish	IE > Germanic	–	✓	–	–	✓	?	?	?	?	?	?	?	?	?	(✓)	?	?	?	?	?	(✓)	L	?	?	✓
Tiv	NC > S Bantoid	✓	✓	✓	–	✓	?	✓	✓	✓	✓	✓	✓	?	?	✓	?	?	?	?	?	✓	L	✓	✓	–
Tuki	NC > S Bantoid	✓	✓	–	–	✓	?	?	?	?	?	?	?	?	?	✓	?	?	?	–	?	✓	L	✓	✓	✓
Turkish	Turkic	✓	?	✓	?	?	?	?	?	?	?	?	?	?	?	?	?	?	?	?	?	?	L	?	?	–
Vata	NC > Kru	✓	✓	–	–	✓	✓	?	✓	✓	?	?	–	?	?	✓	?	?	?	?	?	?	L	✓	✓	✓
Vietnamese	AuA > Viet-Muong	✓	✓	–	?	?	?	?	?	?	✓	?	?	?	?	?	?	?	?	–	?	?	L	?	✓	–
Welsh	IE > Celtic	–	✓	✓	–	✓	–	?	?	?	?	?	?	?	–	?	?	?	?	?	?	?	L	?	✓	✓
Wolof	NC > Atlantic	–	✓	–	–	✓	?	?	?	?	?	?	?	?	?	✓	?	?	?	?	?	?	L	✓	✓	–
Yiddish	IE > Germanic	–	✓	–	–	✓	?	?	?	?	?	?	?	?	?	(✓)	?	?	?	?	?	✓	L	✓	✓	–
Yoruba	NC > Defoid	✓	✓	✓	–	–	?	?	?	?	?	?	?	?	✓	?	?	?	?	✓	✓	?	L	?	✓	✓

Abbreviations: NC – Niger-Congo; IE – Indo-European; AfA – Afro-Asiatic; AuA – Austro-Asiatic; ST – Sino-Tibetan; V – verb fronting; VP – verb phrase fronting; unbd – unbounded; Wh – Wh-Island; CNP – Complex NP Island; Subj – Subject Island; Adj – Adjunct Island; Rel – Relative Clause Constraint; Coord – Coordinate Structure Constraint; Recon – Reconstruction; Wh-Co – Wh-cooccurrence; GS – Genus-species effects; TAM – tense-aspect-mood markers; L-Adv – low (VP) adverbs; H-Adv – high (TP) adverbs; Neg – Negation; Det – Determiners and other nominal modifiers; Nom – nominalized; Inf – infinitive; Dir – direction of fronting (left or right periphery); F/T-M – overt focus/topic marker; Foc – focus interpretation; Top – topic interpretation

3 Previous approaches

Of course, verbal fronting has not escaped the watchful eyes of linguists around the world. Particularly the predicate cleft constructions found in many West African languages and derived creoles have sparked interest among the early missionaries/hobby linguists due to their verb doubling features. The first generally received and highly influential work on verb doubling verbal fronting within the Chomskyan generative tradition is probably Koopman's (1984) work on Vata and Nweh. This was quickly followed more research leading to a by now vast body of theoretical work on the topic supplemented by an ever-growing base of empirical data from various languages. Formal approaches to verb doubling predicate clefts fall into one of four quite different categories (Kandybowicz 2008: 80f.). The first type of approach analyses verbal fronting as a bi-clausal structure that is base-generated (e.g. Lumsden & Lefebvre 1990, Lumsden 1990, Larson & Lefebvre 1991, Dekydspotter 1992). In the second type of analysis, the copy is independently generated (i.e. as a cognate object or low copy) and subsequently moved to the left periphery (e.g. Bamgbose 1972, Nylander 1985, Hutchinson 2000, Massam 1990, Manfredi 1993, Lefebvre 1994, Hoge 1998, Stewart 1998, Cable 2004, Kandybowicz 2004, Harbour 2008). The third and fourth type of approach are quite similar to each other: Both involve movement of the verbal category to the left periphery coupled with the exceptional spell-out of a trace or copy of it. They differ with regard to the kind of the relevant movement in verb fronting: It can either be head-movement (e.g. Piou 1982, Bernabé 1983, Koopman 1984, Ndayiragije 1992, 1993, Aboh 1998, 2006, Nunes 2004, Landau 2006, Vicente 2007, 2009, Harbour 2008, Kandybowicz 2008, Aboh & Dyakonova 2009, Bastos-Gee 2009, Trinh 2011, LaCara 2016a) or phrasal movement (e.g. Koopman 1997, Nishiyama & Cho 1998, Cho & Nishiyama 2000, Abels 2001, Nunes 2004, Hiraiwa 2005b).

It is worth mentioning that the majority of these publications are concerned with a single language or a comparison between two languages, none of which shows the asymmetric pattern of verb doubling and dummy verb insertion. Notable exceptions are Aboh & Dyakonova (2009) and Trinh (2011). The former devote half a page to English (Germanic) *do*-support where they speculate that their analysis may extend to these languages encoding the difference between symmetric dummy verb insertion and symmetric verb doubling insertion as the existence vs. non-existence of a dummy element in the language. The latter develops an analysis that supposedly accounts for the difference between the presence of verb doubling in Hebrew and Vietnamese on the one side its absence in German and Dutch (plus Swedish and Norwegian) on the other (although he does not consider the dummy verb strategies in those languages at all). Unfortunately, he does not explicitly discuss verb phrase fronting. In addition, LaCara (2016a) asserts that he aims at extending his account, that currently only accounts for symmetric verb doubling, to cases of symmetric dummy verb insertion. Apart from these two to three accounts, all the other approaches are concerned exclusively with verb doubling in languages that exhibit either verb and verb phrase fronting or verb fronting alone.

In this chapter I will present and discuss a selection of previous approaches in order to show that without considerable modification they are not able to account for the asymmetric repair pattern found in Asante Twi and Limbum (and potentially Haitian Creole and Afrikaans), let alone derive Generalization I. I chose to disregard approaches of type one and two, which involve some kind of base-generation of the two copies. While there are languages that show good evidence for low copying (Haitian Creole, Harbour 2008), cognate object fronting (Edo, Stewart 1998) or biclausality (a number of creoles with proper cleft structures) in most languages this evidence is absent. It is also clearly absent in Asante Twi and Limbum, which are the main focus of explanation here. Hence, unless there is evidence to the contrary, it seems plausible to assume that copies/dummy verbs are a repair triggered by the $\bar{\text{A}}$-movement of the original verb (on its own or as part of the verb phrase) into the left-periphery, which disqualifies approaches of type one and type two as explanations. Of the remaining two types of accounts, the one that makes use of head-movement is more prominent and relevant for our discussion. First, it features in the most recent publications on the topic indicating that there is some emergent consensus in the field that this type of analysis is on the right track. Second, the two publications that actually engage with verb doubling and dummy verb insertion as two sides of the same coin fall into this category. And third, the new approach presented in this book is of type three as well. Of the most recent type three analyses I chose to discuss Nunes (2004), Landau (2006), Aboh & Dyakonova (2009), Trinh (2011) and LaCara (2016a). These are, in my opinion, clear and explicit enough to be evaluated. Additionally, they sufficiently differ from each other and thus represent a wide range of possible explanations of verb doubling.[1] In what follows, I will briefly present each of these accounts and discuss how they fail to derive the asymmetric pattern.

---

[1] I do not discuss Vicente (2007, 2009) because he explicitly adopts Landau's (2006) account and hence does not add a new proposal as to why the lower copy is not deleted. Similarly, Bastos-Gee (2009) merely applies Nunes's (2004) approach to Brazilian Portuguese without further modifications. Both Vicente (2007, 2009) and Bastos-Gee (2009) can therefore be regarded as simple applications of Landau (2006) and Nunes (2004) to different data respectively.

3.1 Linearization conflict

In the Copy Theory of Movement (Chomsky 1995b), each movement step leaves behind a copy of the moved item rather than a trace, which used to be the case in Government and Binding approaches to movement. This conception of movement requires an explanation for the fact that, in most cases, these lower copies are not pronounced. Nunes (2004) is, to my knowledge, the first attempt at providing such an explanation without simply restating the facts. Revising and extending the ideas presented in his dissertation (Nunes 1995), Nunes (2004) proposes that the deletion of lower copies of a movement chain is the consequence of contradicting linearization statements. Consider his example of an English passive sentence in (1), where the element *John* has moved from the complement position of V to the specifier position of T leaving behind a copy of itself.

(1) [$_{TP}$ John^i was [$_{vP}$ kissed John^i]]   (Nunes 2004: 24)

As both instances of *John* in this movement chain bear the same selectional index[2] they are indistinguishable from each other. When this structure is linearized according to the Linear Correspondence Axiom (LCA, Kayne 1994) we obtain the following partial linearization statements:

– ⟨was, John^i ⟩, because *was* asymmetrically c-commands *John^i* and has to precede it according to the LCA.
– ⟨John^i, was ⟩, because *John^i* asymmetrically c-commands *was* and has to precede it according to the LCA.

These two statements are contradictory and, therefore, the structure in (1) needs to be repaired to be linearizable. Nunes proposes that this is done by an operation Chain Reduction (2), which applies post-syntactically.

(2) *Chain Reduction* (Nunes 2004: 27)
Delete the minimal number of constituents of a nontrivial chain CH that suffices for CH to be mapped into a linear order in accordance with the LCA.

---

[2] A selectional index is assigned to an item when it is selected from the lexicon into the numeration (Chomsky 1995b: 227). It is simply copied along when the whole item is copied in the syntax as a result of movement and thus serves as a means to determine the distinctiveness of two syntactic elements. If they share the same index, they are nondistinct.

Given this operation, the structure in (1) could be made fit for linearization in two ways: (i) by deleting the lower copy of *John^i* or (ii) by deleting the higher one. What we find, however, is that only deletion of the lower copy leads to a well-formed output sentence. In order to account for this, Nunes (2004), following Chomsky (1995b: 230–231), suggests another operation called Formal Feature Elimination (FF-Elimination) that is active at the PF branch of grammar and takes care that formal features, which are not legible in this component, are deleted (3).

(3) *Formal Feature Elimination (FF-Elimination)* (Nunes 2004: 31–32)
Given the sequence of pairs $\sigma = \langle (F, P)_1, (F, P)_2, \ldots, (F, P)_n \rangle$ such that σ is the output of Linearize, F is a set of formal features, and P is a set of phonological features, delete the minimal number of features of each set of formal features in order for σ to satisfy Full Interpretation at PF.

Since higher copies usually have fewer formal features, because these have been satisfied/deleted by movement/checking, fewer applications of FF-Elimination are required if Chain Reduction deletes the lower copy (and their formal features with them) rather than the higher one. Thus, simple economy considerations ensure that Chain Reduction, all else being equal, applies to the lower copy.

As elegant as this proposal may be, it is empirically inadequate for structures in which more than one copy in a movement chain is phonetically realized, as is the case in verb doubling verb fronting, for instance. Consider the Vata verb fronting examples in (4).

(4) a. **Lī** ɔ̄ dā sáká **lī**.
eat s/he PERF rice eat
'S/he has EATEN rice.'
b. **Lī** à lī-dā zué sáká.
eat we eat-PST yesterday rice
'We ATE rice yesterday.' (Koopman 1984: 38)

Nunes argues that in these cases, the higher copy of the verb is morphologically reanalysed as forming a single terminal together with the Focus head to which it has moved (5). Appealing to a proposal by Chomsky (1995b), Nunes assumes that the LCA does not apply word-internally and that the higher copy therefore becomes invisible for the LCA as soon as it is fused with the Foc^0 head (only the newly formed VFoc terminal node plays a role for linearization). Consequently, it will not trigger Chain Reduction because it no longer causes a linearization conflict.

(5)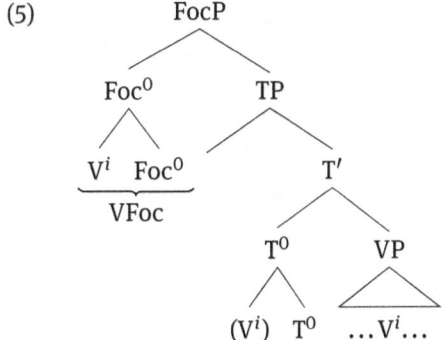

The lower copy of V will not be deleted in any case, whether it moves to T^0 or not.[3] If it does move to T^0 (as is presumably the case in (4-a)) there are two chain links visible to the LCA/Chain Reduction, one in the complex T^0 head and the other in the base position of V. Deleting the latter will suffice for the structure to be linearized according to the LCA. If an auxiliary occupies T^0 and the V head stays *in-situ* (as is presumably the case in (4-b)), there will only be one chain link of a trivial chain and no linearization conflict arises. Note that head movement of the verb to T^0, which is analogous to head movement of the verb to Foc^0, does not suffice to render it invisible to the LCA. This is achieved only by morphological reanalysis of the complex head as one single terminal.

Evidence for a morphological reanalysis for the higher V copy, according to Nunes (2004), comes from the fact that none of the material that usually accompanies the verb, like tense particles or negation, can occur with it (6).

(6) a. *Lī-dā à lī-dā zué saká.
 eat-PST we eat-PST yesterday rice
 b. (*Ná`-)lē wá ná`-lē-kā.
 NEG-eat they NEG-eat-FT
 'They will not EAT.' (Koopman 1984: 38, 156)

He argues that if the Foc^0 head did not obligatorily trigger morphological reanalysis, we would expect sentences like (6) to be grammatical as nothing would prevent copying the tense or negation particle along with the verb. However, if it does

---

[3] Here, it is not entirely clear to me whether Nunes assumes that head movement of V applies successive-cyclically via T^0 to Foc^0 or whether he envisages this more as counter-cyclic parallel movement of the verb into both positions at the same time (i.e. parallel chains, see Aboh 2006, Chomsky 2008, Aboh & Dyakonova 2009). For the ensuing discussion, I will take him to mean the former.

obligatorily trigger fusion, the presence of copied particles renders the verbal head too complex for reanalysis, correctly predicting the ungrammaticality of (6). A further argument that Nunes presents concerns verbs that cannot appear in the verb doubling verb fronting construction. These are auxiliaries, the defective verb *na/la/lɔ* 'to say' and the verbs *lɛ̀* 'to be' and *kà* 'to have', whose common property is that they cannot be affected by morphological processes that all other verbs can be subjected to (Koopman 1984: 158). Nunes argues, that it is plausible that they also cannot undergo the morphological process of obligatory fusion with the Foc^0 head in verb fronting constructions and are therefore precluded from fronting. Their inertness to fronting thus receives a simple explanation if morphological reanalysis is obligatorily triggered by Foc^0.

In summary, the pronunciation of two links of a verb movement chain is the result of one of these links being morphologically fused with another head thereby becoming invisible for the LCA and consequently for Chain Reduction.

There are a number of problems with Nunes' (2004) account of verb doubling when one tries to apply it to other languages beyond Vata. First, there are a lot of languages with verb doubling verb fronting, in which the Foc^0 head (or Top^0 head) is (at least optionally) overtly realized.[4] A few examples are given in (7).

(7) a. **Sí**(-é)   na Kofi á-**sí**   dán.
       build-NMLZ FOC Kofi PRF-build house
       'Kofi has BUILT a house. (not e.g. bought one)'   (*Asante Twi*)

   b. **Dááó**   lá ká ń   dà **dà**   bóɔ́.
       buy.NMLZ FOC C 1SG PST buy goat
       'It is buying that I did to a goat (as opposed to e.g. selling it).'
                                              (*Dagaare*, Hiraiwa & Bodomo 2008: 803)

   c. **dù** wè Kɔ̀kú **dù** àsòn ɔ́
       Eat FOC Koku eat crab DET
       'It is eat that Koku did to the crab (not e.g. throw it away).'
                                              (*Fongbe*, Lefebvre 1992: 58)

---

4 In my sample, these languages are: AsanteTwi (see section 2.1.3.1), Berbice Dutch Creole (see section 7.1.2), Buli (see section 8.2.2), Dagaare (see section 8.2.3), Ewe (see section 7.1.4), Fongbe (see section 7.1.5), Gungbe (see section 7.1.6), Haitian Creole (see section 7.1.7), Japanese (see section 7.2.3), Kisi (see section 7.1.8), Krachi (see section 8.2.7), Leteh (see section 7.1.9), Limbum (see section 2.1.3.2), Mandarin Chinese (see section 8.2.8), Mani (see section 8.2.9), Nupe (see section 7.1.10), Papiamentu (see section 7.1.12), Pichi (see section 7.1.13), Polish (see section 8.2.10), Russian (see section 8.2.11), Tiv (see section 8.2.13), Tuki (see section 7.1.15), Turkish (see section 7.1.16), Vietnamese (see section 8.2.14), and Yoruba (see section 8.2.16).

d. Ù-**bán**　　kɔ́　　ḿbòm wɔ̀ **bán** wɔ́m-yɛ̀.
　　NCM-build PRO.FOC Mbom 3SG build boat-STAT
　　'It is building a boat that Mbom did (built a boat).'
　　　　　　　　　　　　　　　　　　(*Mani*, Childs 2011: 219)

e. O-**nyá**　ówú nǔ ngu-nú-**nyám** cwí.
　　INF-eat FOC I　SM-F1-eat　fish
　　'I will EAT fish.'　　　　　　　　(*Tuki*, Biloa 2013: 76)

f. **Doc** thi toi co **doc** quyen sach nay, nhung khong hieu.
　　read TOP I ASR read CL　book this but　not　understand
　　'As for reading this book, I read, but I don't understand.'
　　　　　　　　　　　　　　　　　　(*Vietnamese*, Tran 2011: 60)

In these languages it seems implausible to assume that morphological reanalysis of V and Foc⁰ takes place because if it did, we would expect there to be a single terminal node in which only one phonological exponent can be inserted, i.e. either the fronted verb or the focus marker, not both. Further, an alternative approach where it is the copy in T⁰ that fuses with its sister and evades Chain Reduction is untenable for the same reasons. Among the languages in (7), many show tense or aspect markers which are usually assumed to be hosted in T⁰ or Asp⁰/*v*⁰. If these heads show overt expression and the V head that has moved to them also is overtly realized, then fusion into a single terminal cannot have taken place

A further issue concerns the availability of verb doubling with verb phrase fronting in some languages, where the verb and its object(s) are displaced into the left periphery and a copy of the verb appears in the canonical verb position (8).

(8) a. [Bɔ́ɔ́ **dááó**]　lá　ká ń　dà **dà** (*ò/*bɔ́ɔ́).
　　　goat buy.NMLZ FOC C 1SG PST buy　it/goat
　　　'It is buying a goat that I did (as opposed to e.g. selling a hen).'
　　　　　　　　　　　　　　　　　(*Dagaare*, Hiraiwa & Bodomo 2008: 805)

b. Ù-[**bán**　wɔ́m] kɔ́　　ḿbòm wɔ̀ **báŋ**-yɛ̀.
　　NCM-build boat PRO.FOC Mbom 3SG build-STAT
　　'It is building a boat Mbom built a boat.'　　(*Mani*, Childs 2011: 219)

c. [**Doc** quyen sach nay] thi toi co **doc**, nhung khong hieu.
　　read CL　book this TOP I ASR read but　not　understand
　　'As for reading this book, I read, but I don't understand.'
　　　　　　　　　　　　　　　　　(*Vietnamese*, Tran 2011: 60f.)

One can in principle conceive of two different structures for verb phrase fronting: In the first structure, the VP moves as a whole phrase into the specifier of FocP (or

CP) (9-a).[5] In the alternative structure, first the V head adjoins to Foc⁰, then the object DP moves into the specifier of FocP (or CP) (9-b).

(9)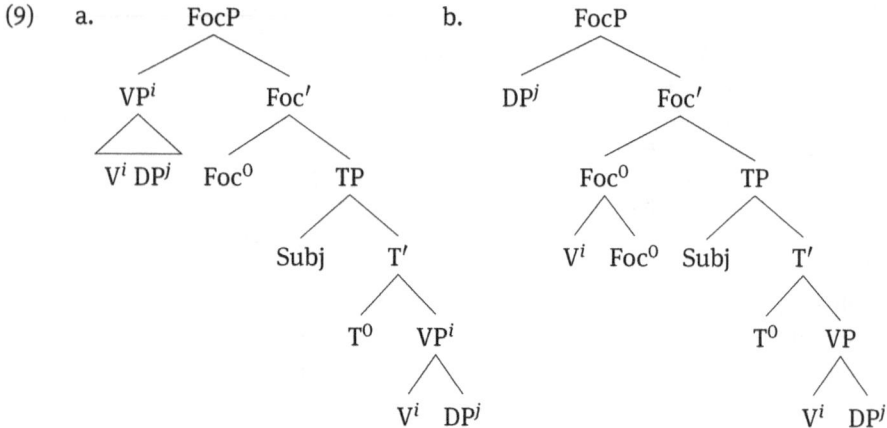

Both options pose problems for Nunes' approach to verb doubling. In (9-a), morphological reanalysis of the V head in the fronted VP with the Foc⁰ head is not possible. Hence, we would expect that Chain Reduction applies to the movement chain of VPs and deletes the lower VP copy. This would leave us with one token of V in the fronted VP and possibly a dummy verb that acts as a host for tense-markers in T. While this accounts for the Asante Twi and Limbum pattern of verb phrase fronting it leaves unexplained the vast number of languages in section 8.2 which show verb doubling rather than dummy verb insertion with verb phrase fronting. Note that head-movement of V to T⁰ does not remedy the situation. In such a case there would be two movement chains, one linking the two VP^{i}s, and the other linking the three V^{i}s. As it stands, Chain Reduction would apply to both chains and delete the copies with more formal features. For the V-chain, these would be the two copies dominated by VP. For the VP-chain, it would be the lower copy. We would thus wrongly expect the structure to surface as in (10), with the single V copy appearing in T⁰ and a headless VP occupying SpecFocP.

(10) [$_{FocP}$ [$_{VP}$ V̶ DP] [$_{Foc'}$ Foc⁰ [$_{TP}$ Subj [$_{T'}$ [$_{T⁰}$ V T⁰] [$_{VP}$ V̶ D̶P̶]]]]]

---

5 Concerning distinctiveness of phrasal objects, Nunes (2004: 23) assumes that "their labels encode the relevant piece of information regarding distinctiveness". I take this to mean that they either inherit the selectional index of their head (and are distinguished from their head by their phrase structure status) or that they get assigned a unique new index when they are moved and thus copied.

Turning to the second structural option in (9-b), Nunes' approach basically runs into the same problems mentioned for verb fronting above because it basically is the same structure as the one for verb fronting in (5). The only difference is that in (9-b), the specifier position of FocP is occupied by the object. Therefore, morphological reanalysis of V and Foc⁰ is necessary to prevent deletion of lower V copies and to ensure double pronunciation. However, as was already argued above, this reanalysis is not possible in all languages that show verb doubling and thus cannot be the correct way to resolve the issue of verb doubling. Note also that the verb and its object no longer form a constituent to the exclusion of other material in the structure in (9-b). In addition, this structure leads us to expect that the linear order in a fronted verb phrase should always be OV. This expectation is not borne out. While there are languages that exhibit a switch from VO to OV order (e.g. Asante Twi, Buli, Dagaare; see Hein & Murphy to appear for discussion), there are also many languages where the basic VO order is retained (e.g. Limbum, Vietnamese, Hebrew, Polish).

In summary, for Nunes (2004) verb doubling is the result of one of the verb copies to be invisible to Chain Reduction. This invisibility is achieved by morphological reanalysis of a V with the head that it is adjoined to. Crucially, though, many verb doubling languages show overt focus and/or tense markers in verb doubling constructions which makes it seem very implausible that a morphological reanalysis has taken place in these structures. Consequently, Nunes (2004) is unable to account for verb doubling in a number of languages, let alone derive the whole typology that we have seen in the previous chapter in a satisfactory manner.

3.2 P-recoverability and Economy of Pronunciation

Landau (2006) pursues a somewhat distinct approach to spell-out of multiple copies. The decision whether a copy is spelled-out or deleted is not made based on linearization conflicts and the most economic application of Chain Reduction and FF-Elimination. Rather, the phonological/prosodic properties of copies are taken to determine whether they surface or not. Working in the Copy Theory of Movement, Landau's explanation for the fact that not all copies of a movement chain are pronounced is the existence of the economy constraint in (11).

(11) *Economy of Pronunciation* (Landau 2006: 57)
 Delete all chain copies at PF up to P-recoverability.

Thus, similar to Chain Reduction, the deletion operation applies in the PF component of grammar but, in contrast to it, it does not need to be specifically triggered by a linearization conflict. Rather, it applies freely up to a certain boundary. This boundary is set by P-recoverability.

(12) *P(honological)-Recoverability* (Landau 2006: 56)
In a chain $\langle X_1 \ldots X_i \ldots X_n \rangle$, where some X_i is associated with phonetic content, X_i must be pronounced.

In the standard cases, (12) ensures that at least one copy in a chain of non-empty elements is pronounced simply because all copies in such a chain have phonetic content themselves that would be irrecoverably lost if they were all deleted.[6] Now the key to both spell-out of the highest copy and spell-out of multiple copies is what it means for a copy to be "associated with phonetic content". Landau (2006) proposes the following definition (13).

(13) X is associated with phonetic content iff:
    a.   X has phonetic content, or
    b.   X is in a position specified with some phonological requirement.

The crucial part of (13) is the second. According to Landau, certain syntactic positions can impose phonological requirements on the elements in these positions. One example is head movement of V to T, where V adjoins to T and has the phonological requirement to provide a lexical host for the affixes in T (14), an idea that, as Landau acknowledges, is not new (see Davis & Prince 1986, Dekydspotter 1992, Abels 2001).

(14)   [$_{TP}$ [$_T$ [$_V$ work] [$_T$ -ed]] [… [$_V$ work]]]

In this case, according to clause b. of (14), V is associated with phonetic content and therefore will be pronounced. The lower copy of the V-movement chain, which is associated with phonetic content as stated in clause a. of (13), however, will be deleted because its phonological features can be recovered from the higher copy and it does not fulfill a specific phonological requirement in its position that cannot be recovered from the higher copy. Another example of clause b. is the requirement of English interrogative C (in wh-questions), whose specifier must be spelled out. The reason for why it is usually the highest copy that will be spelled out is that it is the one that has moved and is therefore most likely to be imposed

---

6 Note that this requires syntactic terminals to either start out with phonological information specified or be equipped with it (e.g. via Vocabulary Insertion in Distributed Morphology) prior to the application of the deletion operation.

with some additional phonological requirement that lower copies do not have to fulfill.

The situation is different with multiple copy spell-out. Based on data from Hebrew V(P) fronting, Landau claims that in verb doubling structures, the two overtly realized copies both fulfill a distinct phonological requirement. Consider the Hebrew verb fronting examples in (15) and its simplified underlying structure in (16).

(15) **Lirkod,** hu **rakad.**
INF.dance he danced
'As for dancing, he danced.' (Landau 2006: 57)

(16)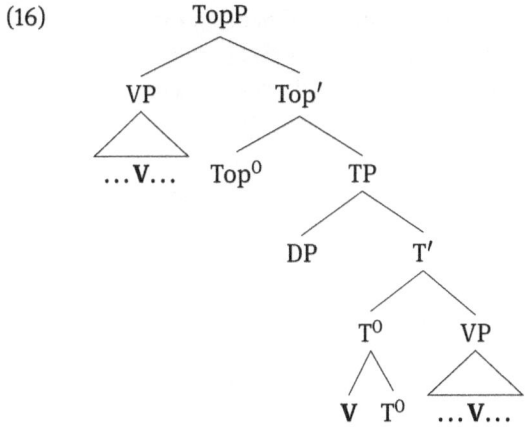

There are three copies of the verb in the structure. At first glance, only the position of the sister of T⁰ is associated with a phonological requirement, i.e. providing a lexical host for tense and agreement features as an active *do*-support strategy is absent from Hebrew (Landau 2006: 37). However, Landau claims that the position SpecTopP equally imposes a phonological requirement on V as the head of VP, namely, the specific intonational pattern of fronted VPs. This pattern consist of a high pitch accent on the stressed syllable of the fronted verb followed by a low tone plateau (Landau 2006: 39). Consequently, both the V copy in SpecTopP and the one in T fulfill some phonological requirement that is not recoverable from any of the other copies and, hence, they are both unaffected by deletion. The lowest copy of V, in contrast, only has phonetic content that can be recovered by the higher copies. It will therefore undergo deletion resulting in the presence of two pronounced verbs in the structure (16).

In summary, Landau (2006) attributes the pronunciation of two verb copies to each of them serving an additional phonological purpose in the positions that they have moved to. Therefore, one prerequisite of double pronunciation is that the verb moves at least twice in order for there to be two different target positions with different additional phonological demands because the verb's base position does not have any such requirements. Commonly, at least one of these movements is V-to-Asp/T/C movement.

Even though Landau's (2006) proposal is successful in deriving Hebrew verb doubling in V(P) fronting without making reference to any dependency of PF-deletion on LF-recoverability there are, in my opinion, several issues, both empirical and conceptual, that cast doubt on it.

First, let us have a look at the empirical side. As stated above, in order for the account to work, the verb has to move at least twice with one movement usually being head movement of V to some higher functional head in order to act as a host for the affixes in this head. While this movement is well motivated for Hebrew and a lot of the Indo-European languages in my sample, it is not clear that it is as prevalent in the verb doubling languages of other families. Consider, in particular, the examples in (17) of verb doubling in languages where tense/aspect or agreement is expressed by a free morpheme rather than by a bound one that requires a lexical host to attach to.

(17) a. [Bóɔ́ **dááó**] lá ká ń dà **dà**.
 goat buy.NMLZ FOC C 1SG PST buy
 'It is buying a goat that I did (as opposed to e.g. selling a hen).'
 (*Dagaare*, Hiraiwa & Bodomo 2008: 805)

 b. Bi-**ba** Musa à **ba** nakàn o.
 RED-cut Musa FUT cut meat FOC
 'It is CUTTING that Musa will do to the meat (as opposed to say, *cooking*.)'
 (*Nupe*, Kandybowicz 2008: 79)

 c. Á r-**yū** (cí) njíŋwè fɔ́ bí **yú** msaŋ.
 FOC 5-buy COMP woman DET FUT1 buy rice
 'The woman will BUY rice.' (*Limbum*)

 d. À kɛ̀ʔ n-**cù** ká **cǔ**.
 s/he PST N-boil crab boil
 'She BOILED the crab (as opposed to frying it).'
 (*Nweh*, Koopman 1997: 71)

 e. Ta **pòst** mi no a **pòst** e karta.
 FOC mail 1SG not ASP mail the letter
 'It's just that I hadn't mailed the letter.'
 (*Papiamentu*, Kouwenberg & Murray 1994: 36)

 f. Nà **go** à dè **go** ò.
 FOC go 1SG.SBJ IPFV go SP
 '[Mind you] I'm going.' (*Pichi*, Yakpo 2009: 297)

In these languages, in the absence of any supporting evidence, the null hypothesis is most plausibly that V does not move to any higher functional head at all. According to Landau's account, it should then be deleted, contrary to fact.

Another way in which the crucial head movement of V can be absent even in a language that usually shows it is when the higher functional head is realized by an overt auxiliary or modal. Whereas in many Indo-European languages, a copy of the lexical verb will be ungrammatical in such a case, it is by no means unattested cross-linguistically.[7] Particularly interesting in this regard is the Vata example (18) that we have already seen in the previous section.

(18) a. **Lī** à lī-dā zué sáká.
      eat we eat-PST yesterday rice
      'We ATE rice yesterday.'
   b. **Lī** ɔ̄ dā sáká **lī**.
      eat s/he PERF rice eat
      'S/he has EATEN rice.' (*Vata*, Koopman 1984: 38)

As (18-a) indicates, the verb may move to T in the past tense, where T is occupied by the marker *dā*. However, present perfect is expressed with the same marker in T and the lexical verb in its base position (18-b). Nonetheless, when the verb is fronted, the lower copy is expressed overtly and thus must have evaded deletion by Economy of Pronunciation even though it cannot be said to serve some additional phonological requirement. If it did, we would incorrectly expect it to also be pronounced in this position in (18-a). Two further examples of verb doubling in the presence of auxiliaries are given in (19).

(19) a. (Ká) **dē**-kā àlī/àtì Àtìm bòrò-à **dè** máŋgò, àtì ǹ jàm
      FOC eat-NMLZ C Àtìm PROG-PROG ate mango C 1SG came
      lǎ.
      DEM
      'When I came, it was eating that Àtìm was eating a mango.'
      (*Buli*, Hiraiwa 2005b: 556)
   b. **Doc** thi no nen **doc** sach.
      read TOP he should read book
      'As for reading, he should read books.' (*Vietnamese*, Trinh 2009: 191)

---

7 The distinction between auxiliaries and free tense/aspect morpheme is, of course, rather fuzzy. Here, I remain agnostic as to what exactly distinguishes them and rely on the status assigned to these elements by the authors of the language sources. What is relevant to the argument is that these elements, instead of the lexical verb, express tense/aspect and are thus most plausibly hosted by the T/Asp head which renders movement of V to T/Asp unlikely.

Asante Twi and Limbum's[8] asymmetric pattern – where only verb fronting leads to verb doubling while verb phrase fronting results in dummy verb insertion – presents a further problem. As Landau (2006: 58) himself insinuates, in Hebrew the phonological requirement of T to have a lexical host for its affixes is tied to the absence of any kind of *do*-support strategy in the language. Taking this idea and developing it, one could assume that in a language that has such a strategy at its disposal, a higher functional head would not impose a phonological requirement on an adjoined V head because a dummy verb could take its place. In effect, for verbal fronting this would predict that the V in this position should always be deleted due to Economy of Pronunciation because it does not fulfil a phonological requirement that could not be recovered from spell-out of the highest copy of V in the left periphery. In contrast, what happens is that the V copy in T is deleted only if the higher copy is part of a VP but evades deletion in case the higher copy is a bare head. One could, of course, assume that V only moves to T in verb fronting and stays *in situ* when a whole VP is preposed. However, this would be an *ad hoc* solution and seems dubious in light of the fact that run-of-the-mill phrasal movement in Asante Twi does not appear to block head movement of V to a higher functional head like Asp or T (20).

(20) a. Dán na Kofí á-si.
house FOC Kofi PFV-build
'It is a house that Kofi has built.'
b. Dán na Kofí si-i.
house FOC Kofi build-PST
'It was a house that Kofi built.' (*Asante Twi*)

Additionally, the trigger for insertion of a dummy verb in those cases where the lexical verb is not available is usually assumed to be the need to provide a host for any inflectional affixes in higher functional heads like Asp and T. If, indeed, the non-pronunciation of Asp/T-adjoined V heads in verbal fronting with dummy verb insertion were due to the absence of a lexical host requirement on Asp/T, the need to insert a dummy verb would disappear leaving us with no explanation as to why there actually has to be a dummy verb instead of a simple gap in this position.

Aside from these empirical arguments against Landau (2006), there are two conceptual difficulties that I want to point out here. The first one concerns the information flow between syntax and prosody when the system determines that

---

8 Note that Limbum does not seem to show any evidence for V-to-higher functional head movement and hence only indirectly bears on the issue here because it shows the asymmetric repair pattern.

the V copy in SpecTopP in Hebrew cannot be deleted because a particular prosodic pattern will be realized on it. In the standard theory of the syntax-prosody interface (*Match Theory*, Selkirk 2011), however, syntactic consituency only indirectly translates into prosodic structure governed by a set of mapping constraints. This means that information about the intonation, which is determined based on prosodic structure, cannot be tied to a particular syntactic position. The detailed syntactic information necessary for this has simply been lost in the mapping procedure. Hence, an intonational pattern cannot be said to be specified of a particular position like SpecTopP and therefore cannot determine that a copy in this position is to be pronounced. A second issue, although perhaps only terminological in nature, is that it seems odd to me to refer to a copy as having or being associated with phonetic content if what one is trying to account for is whether this copy actually gets to have phonetic content, i.e. is pronounced. Copies may have phonological content, e.g. bear phonological features, before they are deleted. Phonetic features, however, are, in my opinion, tied to actual articulation rather than abstract representation.

To conclude this section, double pronunciation of a verb in verb fronting in Landau (2006) is the result of two copies fulfilling two distinct phonological requirements in their respective positions. As, commonly, such a requirement is absent from the verb's base position, there have to be at least two movement steps into two distinct positions in order for verb doubling to occur. Crucially, one of these movement steps, i.e. head movement of V to a higher functional head, appears to be unattested in some of the verb doubling languages I have investigated. Equally, it is sometimes blocked by the presence of an auxiliary in the higher functional head with the lower verb copy still being overtly realized. Landau's (2006) account is therefore unsuitable as a general explanation for verb doubling, dummy verb insertion and the resulting typology developed in the previous chapters.

3.3 Parallel Chains

Similar to what was the case in Landau's (2006) and Nunes's (2004) approach, the verb in Aboh's (2006), Aboh & Dyakonova's (2009), and Kandybowicz's (2008) account of verb doubling undergoes two movement steps into distinct positions. In contrast to Nunes (2004), however, where the two copies in these positions were part of the same chain, they propose that the higher copies are each the highest copy of their respective separate movement chain sharing a common tail in the base position of the verb. The two chains are reduced in a regular manner, that is, the lower copy is deleted while the highest one of each chain is pronounced resulting in double spell-out of the verb. This is an instance of Chomsky's (2008) *parallel chains* where the lowest copy of a moved element is part of both an Ā-chain and an A-chain. For Chomsky (2008) parallel chains are created when a phase head H_1 that carries both a movement-triggering Edge-feature and some movement-triggering Agree-feature transmits the latter to another head H_2 c-commanded by H_1 and both features then probe for the same goal G. This goal, then, moves into the specifier position of each head separately creating two distinct chains CH_1 and CH_2 with different heads but a single common foot (21).

(21) $[_{\text{Spec}H_1P}$ G $[H_1^{[\text{EDGE}]} [_{\text{Spec}H_2P}$ G $[H_2^{[\text{AGREE}]} [\ldots G]]]]]$
              $\underbrace{}_{CH_1}$ $\underbrace{}_{CH_2}$

Originally, this approach was meant to eliminate chains that link A and Ā positions such as the one in English subject *wh*-questions. There, the *wh*-subject standardly has to undergo A-movement to SpecTP first before being Ā-moved to SpecCP in a second step thereby creating an Ā-A-chain. On a parallel chains account, both movements are independent of one another and each constitutes its own chain with one being and Ā-chain and the other being an A-chain (22).

(22) $[_{\text{SpecCP}}$ who $[C^{[\text{WH}]} [_{\text{SpecTP}}$ who $[T^{[\text{EPP}]} [_{\text{Spec}vP}$ who $[v$ see John $]]]]]]$
              $\underbrace{}_{\text{Ā-chain}}$ $\underbrace{}_{\text{A-chain}}$

Kandybowicz (2008: 114) notes that both movements do not necessarily have to take place at the same time. He argues that the longer chain is likely created first because inheritance of the Agree-feature by the lower head only takes place after the higher head is merged into the structure. However, he also mentions that feature inheritance is not a necessary requirement. Rather, the minimal condition for creating parallel chains is two separate Agree operations applying to the same goal.

The proposals by Aboh (2006), Aboh & Dyakonova (2009) and Kandybowicz (2008) differ from Chomsky's original one in that at least one of the two parallel movements is head movement. Investigating verb doubling in a verb fronting construction in Nupe, Kandybowicz (2008), referring to Vicente's (2007) arguments against the ban on Ā-head movement, argues that the verb root moves into Spec-FocP. Probing of Foc for the verb root is possible because under the revised Phase Impenetrability Condition (Chomsky 2001) transfer of the domain of the v phase head, which contains the verb root, is delayed until the next higher phase head is merged. Thus, Foc must not be merged higher than C, for which independent evidence exists in Nupe (Kandybowicz 2008: chap. 2). Independent of verb fronting, the verb root has to move to v in the language (Kandybowicz 2008: chap. 2). Since both Foc and v separately probe for the verb root, two parallel chains are created, one being a head movement chain and the other being an Ā-head movement chain (23).

(23)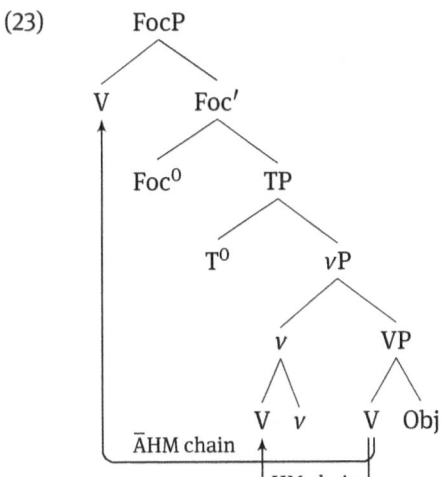

An ordinary mechanism of chain reduction then inspects each chain separately and deletes its lower copy.[9]

Aboh & Dyakonova (2009) investigate VP fronting in Russian and V fronting in Gungbe and assume a checking approach, where two elements both bear the relevant feature which is checked (and possibly deleted) under Agree. Working under the split-C hypothesis (Rizzi 1997), where C has a finer structure consisting of the heads Foc and Top projecting between the higher Force and the lower Fin heads, they propose that Agree-Tense-Aspect features on an Asp head, which are inherited from Fin, trigger the short V-to-Asp head movement. The Foc or Top head, on the other hand, bears a discourse-related feature probing for a focus feature on

---

9 Kandybowicz (2008) claims that a linearization conflict (which is the trigger for deletion of all but one copy in Nunes 2004) between the two non-distinct elements in the heads of the separate chains does not arise because the lower chain between V and v is entirely contained within the vP phase. In cyclic phase-based spell-out, this chain will pass the interfaces and thus undergo Chain Reduction and Linerization before the V-to-SpecFocP chain becomes available at PF. However, in standard conceptions of phase transfer, the phase head itself, v in this case, is not part of the domain that is sent off to PF. As v contains the higher chain link of the V-to-v chain, we would expect it to not be visible by Chain Reduction and therefore, the lower link of that chain should not be deleted. Instead, upon transfer of the domain of the CP phase, both the V copy in SpecFocP and the lower one in the complex v head become available at PF and should cause a linearization conflict that should result in the deletion of the V copy in v, contrary to fact.

V and triggering V-to-Foc head movement (24) (for details see Aboh & Dyakonova 2009: §4).[10]

(24)
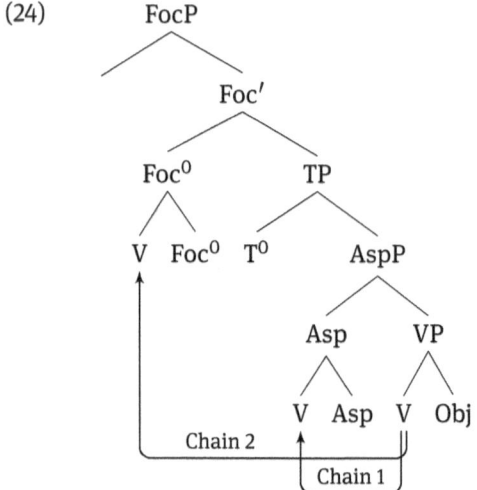

Probing of Foc/Top for V is possible because under the revised Phase Impenetrability Condition Chomsky (2001) transfer of the domain of the *v* phase head, which contains V, is delayed until the next higher phase head is merged. Thus, Foc/Top must not be merged higher than the next phase head and must not constitute a phase head itself.

Example (25) illustrates that V-to-Foc movement skips intermediate tense and aspect markers and cannot successively adjoin to these heads on its way to Foc. This violates the Head Movement Constraint (HMC Travis 1984) and thus belongs to a class of movement phenomena called long head movement (see Lema & Rivero 1990, 1991, Rivero 1991, 1993, Roberts 1994)

(25) a. **Xɔ̀** Sɛ́ná ná nɔ̀ **xɔ̀** wémà ná Kòfí.
buy Sena FUT HAB buy book PREP Kofi
'Sena will habitually BUY a book to Kofi.'
b. *Xɔ̀-nɔ̀-ná Sɛ́ná **xɔ̀** wémà ná Kòfí.
buy-HAB-FUT Sena buy book PREP Kofi
(*Gungbe*, Aboh & Dyakonova 2009: 1055)

---

10 VP/vP movement is supposed to be the result of Generalized Pied-piping (Chomsky 1995b: 262) where the whole VP/vP moves instead of the V head and lands in SpecFocP/SpecTopP instead of adjoining to Foc/Top.

Aboh & Dyakonova (2009) claim that this failure to obey the HMC is a result of the fact that both movements are due to distinct probes. As distinct features are activated in the two Agree-relations, intervention is not expected. Competition and hence intervention may only take place between features of the same kind, e.g. tense and aspect, but not across types of features, e.g. tense and focus. Consequently, an auxiliary, modal, or restructuring verb, which bears tense/aspect features and is merged above the lexical verb, intervenes for V-to-Asp movement thereby blocking it and eventually preventing double pronunciation of the verb (26). The lexical verb may still move to Foc/Top, as the auxiliary is not specified for a discourse-related feature.

(26) a. Kupat'sja(-to) my budem, ...
 swim.INF-PRT we.NOM AUX.FUT.1P
 'As for swimming, we will swim...'
 b. Pomoč'(-to) emu ja konečno smogu (*pomoč'), ...
 help.INF-PRT him.DAT I.NOM certainly can help
 'Speaking of helping him, I certainly can do it, ...'
 c. Gotovit'sja k ekzamenu(-to) my uže načali
 prepare.INF to exam.DAT-PRT we.NOM already start.PST.MASC.S
 (*gotovit'sja), ...
 prepare.INF
 'As for preparing for the exam, we have already started it indeed,...'
 (*Russian*, Aboh & Dyakonova 2009: 1056f.)

Concerning English VP topicalization as in (27) (or V(P) fronting in Germanic languages in general), where instead of a copy of the lexical verb there is a form of *do* inside the clause, Aboh & Dyakonova (2009) suggest that these obligatorily involve intervention of *do* between the inflectional head (Fin, T, or Asp) and the lexical verb.

(27) I asked John to repair the car and [repair the car] he did.

The difference between languages that show verb doubling and those that exhibit dummy verb insertion is then attributed to the fact that the latter dispose of a dummy element that always agrees with the inflectional head and, thus, always adjoins to it blocking the creation of two parallel V chains whereas the former do not comprise of such an element.

In summary, pronunciation of two verb copies in verbal fronting structures is due to the fact that there are two distinct chains of verb (head-)movement, one to SpecFocP (Kandybowicz 2008) or to Foc/Top (Aboh & Dyakonova 2009) and the other to v/Asp, which are both rooted in the same position, namely the verb's base position. Whatever the mechanism is that ensures that in the common cases only the highest copy of a chain is pronounced, it also applies to these verb chains and deletes the lower copies while retaining the highest one in a regular fashion. Consequently, two copies of the verb are phonetically realized. Therefore, like in Landau (2006), verb doubling is contingent on the verb moving to *v* or Asp (or T) in addition to its displacement into the left periphery. The consistent occurrence of a dummy instead of a verb copy in some languages is a consequence of it blocking the crucial V-to-Asp/T movement like any other auxiliary, modal, or restructuring verb.

Having presented the general functioning of a parallel chains approach as presented in Aboh (2006), Aboh & Dyakonova (2009) and Kandybowicz (2008) for single languages let me now turn to its evaluation with regard to the typological variation shown in the previous chapters. The first thing to note is that because of the dependency of doubling on V-to-higher inflectional head movement, the account suffers from the same empirical flaw as Landau (2006). It is unable to explain why some languages which seem to show no evidence for movement of V to *v*/Asp or T still pronounce two copies of the verb in verbal fronting constructions. Even in Gungbe itself the aspect and tense markers are free morphemes that do not require a lexical verb to lean on to (28) and hence do note require the verb to move to Asp.[11]

(28)   Xɔ́ Séná ná nɔ̀ xɔ́ wémà ná Kòfí.
        buy Sena FUT HAB buy book PREP Kofi
        'Sena will habitually BUY a book to Kofi.'

(*Gungbe*, Aboh & Dyakonova 2009: 1055)

In conjunction with the language data raised against Landau (2006) in (17) this challenges the present approach.

---

[11] Based on evidence from the closely related language Gengbe Aboh & Dyakonova (2009) argue that all Gbe languages have V-to-Asp movement. If I understood their argumentation correctly, in Gungbe, this movement is blocked if the aspect head is realized by a free morpheme, just like V-to-T(-to-C) movement is blocked in Germanic languages when T is realized by an auxiliary. Crucially, Gungbe allows aspect stacking (of, at least, habitual over progressive) which Aboh and Dyakonova take to imply that both Asp heads are present in the structure. Thus, if both are overtly expressed, V has to stay *in situ*. When the progressive Asp is empty, V raises to it. When both of them are empty, V raises all the way to the habitual Asp. If this analysis of Gungbe is correct, all verb doubling examples found in the paper are unproblematic for their account. However, if both aspect heads are overtly realized, V-to-Asp movement should be blocked. Therefore, in verb fronting constructions with two overt aspect markers, the verb copy in the base position should be deleted as the foot of the V-to-Foc chain and, consequently, verb doubling should not occur. Unfortunately, an example with this configuration has not been provided in the literature.

Equally problematic for Aboh & Dyakonova (2009) and Kandybowicz (2008) are languages like Buli, Vata, and Vietnamese, where the lower copy is pronounced even when an auxiliary or modal blocks the V-to-*v*/Asp/T movement as in (18-b) and (19) in the previous section. In these cases, Aboh & Dyakonova as well as Kandybowicz counterfactually predict that the lower copy of the single V-to-Foc/Top chain should undergo deletion.

The asymmetric repair pattern of verbal fronting constitutes another problem. Both Limbum and Asante Twi show verb doubling in verb fronting. Disregarding the fact that Limbum does not seem to have V-to-*v*/Asp/T movement, this means that according to a parallel chains account, the verb moves to at least Asp. In verb phrase fronting, however, instead of a copy of the verb there is a dummy verb inside the clause. Head movement of V to Asp thus must have been blocked by the intervening dummy. There are two questions that this pattern raises: (i) Although a dummy element occurs in verb phrase fronting in Asante Twi and Limbum this element does not seem to be independently available in a position between the verb and the higher Asp or T head (29), at least not in the way it is in English (30).

(29) a. *Kofí á-yɔ sí dán.
  Kofi PFV-do build house
 b. *Kofí á-yɔ dán sí(-é).
  Kofi PFV-do house build-NMLZ (*Asante Twi*)
 c. *Njíŋwè fɔ́ bí gī r-yū msāŋ.
  woman DET FUT1 do 5-buy rice
  Intended: 'The woman will buy rice' (*Limbum*)

(30) John did (indeed) build a house.

How, then, could we make sure – without encountering a look-ahead problem – that it is selected and merged in the structure in exactly those cases where at a later step in the derivation the verb phrase moves to Foc? (ii) Given that verb phrase fronting is triggered by the same mechanism as verb fronting (i.e. a probe on Foc probing for V plus optional Generalized Pied-piping of VP) why is an intervening dummy element obligatorily merged in the former but is obligatorily absent in the latter? As far as I can see, there is no straightforward way to capture the asymmetric pattern in a parallel chains account.

A last point of criticism is of conceptual nature. In order for parallel chains to be created two distinct heads have to probe for the same goal. The subsequent movements of the goal to the two heads necessarily violate the Strict Cycle Condition (Chomsky 1973: 243). Although this generally holds for syntactic head movement (see Heck 2016 for a discussion of this problem and possible solutions) the point here is that the violation would be incurred even if the movements were phrasal movements into specifier positions.

In conclusion, Kandybowicz (2008) and Aboh & Dyakonova (2009) analyse double pronunciation of the verb in verbal fronting as the spell-out of the heads of two different chains that have been created by parallel (head-)movement of the verb into a higher information structural head like Foc or Top and into a higher inflectional head like *v*/Asp or T. Just as in Landau's (2006) approach, verb doubling thus requires the verb to undergo at least two distinct movements. Consequently, verb doubling languages that do not show any evidence for movement of V to *v*/Asp/T or where this movement is blocked by an auxiliary occupying *v*/Asp/T are incorrectly precluded by this account. Further, it is unclear how the asymmetric pattern instantiated by Asante Twi and Limbum could be derived. On the one hand, in verb phrase fronting only, the dummy verb has to enter the structure early enough to block V-to-Asp movement, on the other hand, it must not be contained in the structure at all in verb fronting. This problem is aggravated by the fact that both verb and verb phrase fronting are supposed to be triggered by the same mechanism, a head probing for V, with the difference being that in the latter, the verb phrase is pied-piped along with the verb. In light of these empirical challenges, I believe that an analysis in terms of parallel chains is not the right approach to derive the three attested patterns and the gap in the typology of verbal fronting.

3.4 An edge constraint on copy deletion

The proposal by Trinh (2009, 2011) is similar to Nunes (2004) and Landau (2006) in the sense that within the Copy Theory of Movement, it tries to account for multiple copy spell-out in verbal fronting by constraining the application of a PF operation Copy Deletion in a certain way. In contrast to all the previous proposals, Trinh (2011) explicitly tries to account for those languages, where doubling occurs despite the two verb copies not being morphologically distinct (as in Nunes 2004) or the verb not moving to *v*/Asp/T (as in Landau 2006, Aboh 2006, Aboh & Dyakonova 2009, Kandybowicz 2008). Starting from an observation by Vicente (2007) that morphological distinctness (and V-to-*v*/Asp/T movement) is likely not the sole factor conditioning multiple copy spell-out, he postulates the Edge Condition on Copy Deletion (ECCD) (31).

(31)   *Edge Condition on Copy Deletion* (Trinh 2011: 31)
       For any chain (α, β) where α is the higher and β the lower copy of the moved constituent, deletion of β requires that β ends an XP.

3.4 An edge constraint on copy deletion — 105

In this formulation, β ends an XP if and only if the last morpheme of β coincides with the last morpheme of the XP. Against the background assumption of Pronunciation Economy, that states that Copy Deletion must apply when it can, this condition is claimed to account for the distribution and (un)availability of verb doubling in various languages, including Hebrew, Vietnamese, Dutch, German, Swedish and Norwegian. The underlying observation leading to (31) is that a majority of verb doubling languages are VO languages while multiple verb spell-out is absent from OV languages despite them exhibiting verbal fronting. Accepting the possibility that verb fronting in addition to being remnant VP movement, can also be derived by Ā-head movement of the verb into the left periphery, Trinh (2011) proposes three possible structure-types of verb fronting (32).

(32) *Possible underlying structures of verb fronting* (Trinh 2011: 31)
    a.   Type 1   b.   Type 2   c.   Type 3

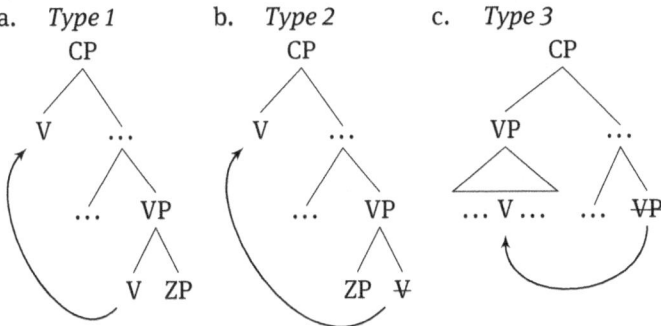

In type 1, the lower V copy does not end an XP and therefore will not be deleted as it does not satisfy the ECCD. This type is supposedly instantiated by Hebrew and Vietnamese. Intransitives are claimed to always be derived from transitives by incorporation of the head of a phonologically empty NP into the verb (cf. Hale & Keyser 1993, 2002). Consequently, a difference of copy realization is expected depending on whether the V or the VP is fronted. While both are phonologically indistinguishable, the former leaves a V copy that does not end a phrase and should therefore not be deleted (33-a) but the latter leaves a VP copy that ends the *v*P and thus is expected to be deleted in accordance with the ECCD (33-b).

(33) *Fronting of an intransitive verb*
   a.

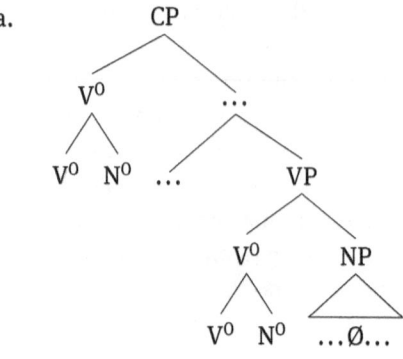

   b.

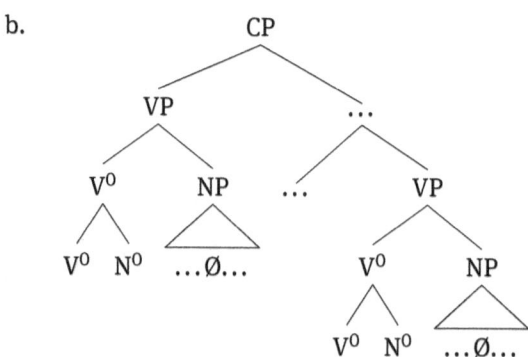

As both options, V and VP fronting are in principle available in Hebrew and Vietnamese, this predicts that there should be optionality because fronting of an intransitive is ambiguous between V and VP fronting. According to Trinh (2011: 39), this is in fact what can be observed (34).

(34) a. **Lalexet** Dan kiva **(lalexet)**.
    walk.INF Dan hoped walk.INF
    (without translation in source) (*Hebrew*, Trinh 2011: 39)
   b. **Ngu** thi no nen **(ngu)**.
    sleep TOP he should sleep
    (without translation in source) (*Vietnamese*, Trinh 2011: 39)

In type 2, the lower V copy is at the end of an XP, namely VP. The ECCD is fulfilled and the lower V copy is deleted. This structure is claimed to underly verb topicalization in German and Dutch. Finally, type 3 has been generated by remnant VP movement, and the lower VP copy is deleted in accordance with the ECCD as it ends the *v*P. This structure, Trinh argues, underlies verb topicalization in Swedish and Norwegian.

In summary, Trinh (2011) proposes that lower copies of a movement chain can only be deleted if they end a phrase. Under the assumption that (unergative) intransitive verbs always take a phonologically empty NP complement and that verb fronting is V-to-SpecCP movement, the Edge Condition on Copy Deletion predicts that SVO languages, like Hebrew and Vietnamese, show verb doubling in verb fronting, whereas SOV languages, like Dutch and German, exhibit a gap instead. Languages that are SVO but do not show verb doubling are argued to employ remnant verb phrase movement rather than V-to-SpecCP movement in verb fronting. Based on this, Trinh develops a typology where languages vary according to two parameters: (i) Whether they show verb doubling or not (±V doubling) and (ii) whether they allow bare verb movement into specifier position or not (±V topicalization).

(35)   *Trinh's typology* (Trinh 2011: 59)

	+V doubling	−V doubling
+V topicalization	Hebrew, Vietnamese	German, Dutch
−V topicalization	—	Swedish, Norwegian

Assuming the ±V doubling parameter as a basis, Trinh argues that the Edge Condition on Copy Deletion then straightforwardly derives the availability of V topicalization from the interaction of verb doubling and word order. SVO languages that are +V doubling need to have bare V-to-Spec movement because otherwise the verb could not be doubled. Hence, languages that are set to +V doubling but do not show V topicalization (in the sense of Ā-head movement) are predicted to be impossible. In SVO languages that are −V doubling this kind of movement would lead to verb doubling (due to the ECCD) which would contradict their −V doubling parameter. Therefore, they do not allow it. SOV languages are −V doubling but Ā-head movement of V to SpecCP does not lead to verb doubling anyway because the ECCD enforces deletion of the XP-final lower V copy. Thus, no parametrical conflict arises and the languages do allow V-to-Spec movement.

Although Trinh's (2011) idea of tying multiple copy pronunciation in verb fronting to the general word order of a language seems to have some cross-linguistic validity (see section 5.2.3) and in contrast to previous proposals does not rely on the empirically problematic condition that the verb moves twice there are a number of issues with its actual implementation. Several of these issues, both empirical and conceptual, have been raised in the various reply articles on a version of Trinh's proposal, which was published as a target article in Theoretical Linguistics (Trinh

2009). Here, I will discuss just a few empirical problems that have been pointed out.

The most obvious challenge for Trinh's account of verb doubling are languages, like Buli, Brazilian Portuguese, Dagaare, Russian, and many others that also exhibit verb doubling when the whole verb phrase is displaced into the left periphery. In fact, Hebrew is such a language (36).

(36)   **Liknot** et   ha-praxim hi **kanta**.
      buy.INF ACC the-flowers she buy.PST
      'As for buying the flowers, she bought (them).'

(Hebrew, Landau 2006: 37)

Although Trinh (2011) discusses Hebrew verb fronting in detail, an explanation of how verb phrase fronting would fit with his account is suspiciously absent from his thesis as Müller (2009a) notes. Indeed, it is not quite clear how verb doubling in verb phrase fronting should follow from the ECCD. As the lower copy of the VP movement chain ends an XP, we would expect it to be deleted. One might interject that V head-moves to v or T thereby creating a second movement chain of which it is the highest copy and therefore must be pronounced. However, this is exactly the solution that was presented in the previous proposal: The verb is actually part of the head of two separate movement chains, VP-to-SpecCP and V-to-T movement. Thus, the ECCD would have nothing to do with the multiple spell-out of V in verb phrase fronting. Consequently, there would be two distinct sources for verb doubling depending on whether the verb or the whole verb phrase undergoes fronting. In the former case, verb doubling is the result of the ECCD-induced failure to delete the lower V copy. In the latter, it is a consequence of the verbal head being (part of) the highest copy of two separate movement chains. I take this to be an undesirable result. In addition, Trinh (2011) explicitly argues that head movement takes place at PF and does not create any chains or leave any copies. Thus, he cannot appeal to parallel chains of $\bar{\text{A}}$-head movement and head(-to-head) movement to extend the analysis to verb phrase fronting.

In fact, verb doubling verb phrase fronting is not the only place where one needs to reintroduce a concept like parallel chains into Trinh's proposal in order to cover the data. His account undergenerates even if we restrict it to verb fronting only, where on the surface a single verb appears in the left periphery. If one considers the full cross-classification of the parameters word order, verb doubling and $\bar{\text{A}}$-head movement (Trinh's V-topicalization) (37), it turns out that the ECCD actually incorrectly rules out two combinations (shaded cells).

(37) Cross-classification of word order, verb doubling and $\bar{\text{A}}$-head movement

	SVO		SOV	
	+V doubling	−V doubling	+V doubling	−V doubling
+V topicalization	Hebrew, Vietnamese		Korean	Dutch, German
−V topicalization	Polish	Norwegian, Swedish		

Note that the distinction of ±$\bar{\text{A}}$-head movement does not lead to distinct surface structures in SOV languages because the lower copy is always XP-final be it a copy of V or VP. Hence, it is always deleted according to the ECCD. Therefore, German and Dutch could equally employ $\bar{\text{A}}$-head movement or remnant VP movement in verb fronting and the result would be a gap one way or another. For that very same reason, the ECCD predicts the inexistence of SOV languages with verb doubling. This prediction, as mentioned by Aboh (2009) and Müller (2009a), is falsified by Korean. Korean is an SOV language, where a verb can be preposed into the left periphery and a second copy is pronounced in the canonical sentence-final verb position (38).

(38) **Ilk**-ki-nun   Chelswu-ka   chayk-ul   **ilk**-ess-ta.
     read-NMLZ-TOP Chelswu-NOM book-ACC read-PST-DECL
     'Read the book, Chelswu does.'   (*Korean*, Hagstrom 1995: 32)

The second parametric combination that should never be instantiated is an SVO language that employs remnant VP movement in verb fronting and nonetheless displays verb doubling. In such a case, the low remnant VP copy is XP-final and conforming to the ECCD should therefore always undergo deletion. Yet, one languages that manifests this combination is Polish, where as Bondaruk (2009, 2012) argues verb fronting structures like (39) are actually derived by movement of a remnant verb phrase.

(39) **Wypić**   (to) Marek **wypije**   herbatę, ale nie wypije   kawy.
     drink.INF TO Marek will.drink tea   but not will.drink coffee
     'As for drinking, Marek will drink tea, but he will not drink coffee.'
                                                      (*Polish*, Bondaruk 2012: 55)

In order to account for the Polish data in Trinh's approach, one could again suggest that the verbal head of the low remnant VP copy undergoes a second movement, e.g. head movement to T. This would render the V in T the highest copy in a separate movement chain and prevent it from being affected by Copy Deletion.

Thus, it is necessary to reintroduce a parallel chains concept not only to account for languages that show VP fronting with verb doubling, but also to account for those like Polish that show verb doubling in verb fronting but arguably employ remnant movement instead of $\bar{\text{A}}$-head movement. In addition, head movement of the verb to T could in principle also explain why Korean allows verb doubling despite being an SOV language. As the TP is head-final, this movement would be string-vacuous, but would create the additional movement step in order for the verbal head to become the highest copy of a separate chain and thereby to not be targeted by Copy Deletion.[12] However, as mentioned above, Trinh (2011) explicitly takes head movement to be a PF operation that does not create chains or copies. It will therefore never be able to turn the low V copy into the head of a separate movement chain.

Despite the various empirical problems mentioned above, Trinh (2011) is the only account so far that if interpreted generously actually predicts asymmetric languages like Asante Twi and Limbum to exist. As SVO languages, $\bar{\text{A}}$-head movement of V into the focus position will always result in the lower V copy being pronounced as it is never the element that ends the VP. In contrast, verb phrase fronting is predicted to result in a gap because the lower VP copy actually is XP-final. Assuming that a dummy verb then is inserted to provide a host for inflectional affixes in Asp or T we end up with a pattern where verb doubling occurs in verb fronting and a dummy verb strategy is used in verb phrase fronting. However, this property of treating V and VP movement differently with regard to Copy Deletion is exactly what makes it difficult for Trinh (2011) to derive symmetric patterns of verb doubling such as Buli, Dagaare, Hebrew, and many other languages.

In conclusion, for Trinh (2011) double pronunciation of a verb in verb fronting is a consequence of the interaction of two factors: $\bar{\text{A}}$-head movement of the verb (rather than remnant verb phrase movement) and the VP-internal VO order. In this configuration, the lower copy of the V-chain cannot be deleted because not being XP-final it does not fulfill Trinh's Edge Condition on Copy Deletion. Although the account neatly derives the asymmetric pattern of Asante Twi and Limbum it does

---

12 Note that although the parallel chains solution might work for Korean it makes the wrong predictions for German. As a V2 language, German requires the verb to always head-move to C in non-embedded sentences. In a non-embedded verb fronting sentence we would therefore expect two copies of the verb to be pronounced, one being the head of the V-to-SpecCP chain and the other being the head of the V-to-C head-movement chain (see also Hein to appear). Such a sentence, however, is ungrammatical (i).

(i) *Essen isst Paul nur grünes Gemüse.
    eat.INF eats Paul only green vegetables
    Intended: 'As for eating, Paul only eats green vegetables.'

not straightforwardly explain why there is verb doubling in verb phrase fronting in many languages. Furthermore, it makes wrong empirical predictions concerning the existence of languages like Polish and Korean. These exhibit (a combination of) parameters that are not predicted to give rise to verb doubling, i.e. VO order and remnant VP movement in Polish and OV order in Korean. Nevertheless, verb doubling is attested in both verb and verb phrase fronting in these languages. Since the system undergenerates and modifying it appropriately would bereave it of any meaningful predictions, I conclude that it is not able to naturally derive the typology of verbal fronting in a simple and straightforward way.

3.5 Non-syntactic head movement

The most recent proposal, to my knowledge, that is concerned with verb doubling in verbal fronting constructions is LaCara (2016a). In contrast to Trinh (2011), he exclusively discusses cases of verb doubling that occur in verb phrase fronting. Based on his observation that verb doubling in verb phrase fronting occurs in languages that independently show V-to-T movement, LaCara (2016a) suggests that one can straightforwardly derive verb doubling if one abandons the idea that head movement is successive syntactic adjunction of a head to a higher head (see e.g. Travis 1984, Pollock 1989, Vikner 1995). Concretely, he adopts the view of head movement as Conflation (Hale & Keyser 2002, Harley 2004, 2013) where the features of a head that trigger lexical insertion come to be present on higher heads under certain conditions.[13] Due to economy considerations insertion of actual morphemes in the presence of more than one head with conflated features then only takes place in the highest head that contains the relevant features. Head movement is therefore not treated as actual displacement of a syntactic terminal but rather as a kind of feature propagation where all the features of a lower head are also present on any higher head within a certain domain.

As a consequence, there is only one syntactic movement that leads to the creation of verb copies, namely movement of the verb phrase to SpecCP, to which a copy deletion mechanism applies in a regular fashion deleting all but the highest copy. Crucially, in languages that show V-to-T movement, the verbs insertion-

---

13 The actual implementation is depicted in (i): When a head Y^0 with defective morpho-phonological features μ_y is merged with another head Z^0 with the features μ_z, μ_z is conflated with μ_y on Y^0. As the features of a head are shared by all its higher projections, YP also bears the conflated features $[\mu_y, \mu_z]$ (i-a). Upon merger of a higher head X^0 with defective features μ_x, YP's features are conflated with μ_x on X^0. The conflated feature set $[\mu_x, \mu_y, \mu_z]$ on X^0 contains all features of both lower heads Y^0 and Z^0 (i-b).

triggering features μ_V have been passed up to T by Conflation. Therefore, besides being spelled out as part of the verb phrase in SpecCP the verb will also be pronounced in T despite the fact that there is no actual V head in this position (40).

(40)

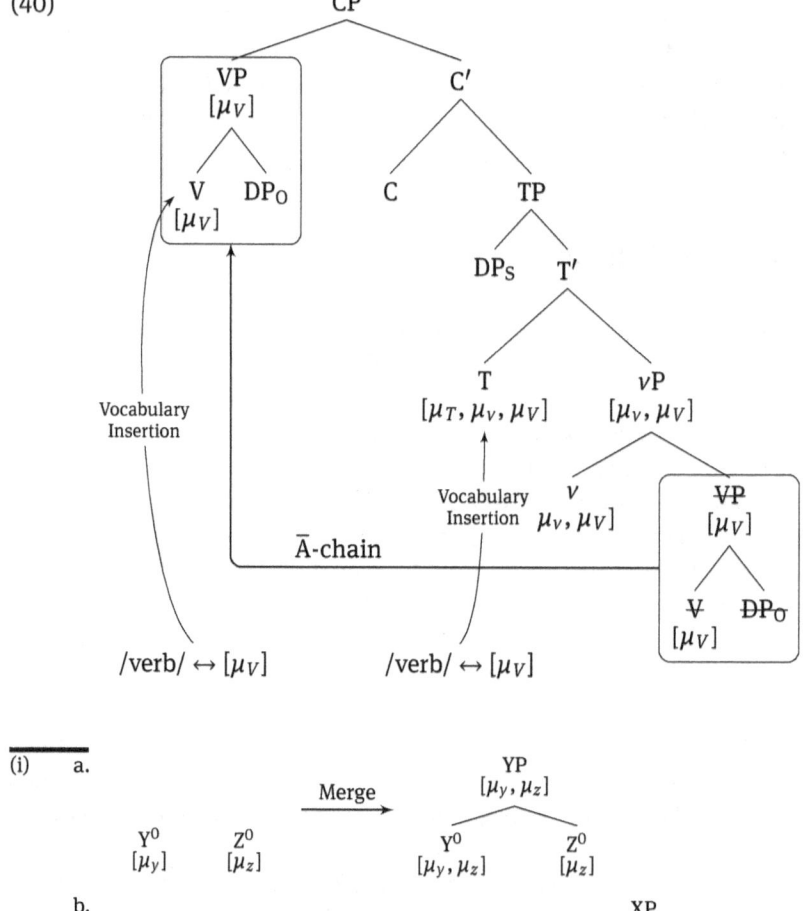

(i) a.

$Y^0\;[\mu_y]$ $Z^0\;[\mu_z]$ $\xrightarrow{\text{Merge}}$ $YP\;[\mu_y,\mu_z]$ dominating $Y^0\;[\mu_y,\mu_z]$ and $Z^0\;[\mu_z]$

b.

$X^0\;[\mu_x]$ dominating $YP\;[\mu_y,\mu_z]$ (which dominates $Y^0\;[\mu_y,\mu_z]$ and $Z^0\;[\mu_z]$) $\xrightarrow{\text{Merge}}$ $XP\;[\mu_x,\mu_y,\mu_z]$ dominating $X^0\;[\mu_x,\mu_y,\mu_z]$ and $YP\;[\mu_y,\mu_z]$ (which dominates $Y^0\;[\mu_y,\mu_z]$ and $Z^0\;[\mu_z]$)

Any head with defective features that is merged above XP will continue the conflation span and acquire all features of the lower heads. In effect, Conflation mimics the effects of head movement without actually displacing syntactic terminals. LaCara (2016a) claims that any implementation of head movement that does not derive it by actual syntactic displacement could in principle stand in for Conflation in his argumentation with the same results.

3.5 Non-syntactic head movement

Thus, LaCara (2016a) rejects an approach where distinct movements create a multitude of verb copies some of which have to be exempt from deletion due a special mechanism that he criticizes as more or less arbitrarily invoked when needed (like e.g. morphological reanalysis, Nunes 2004, or phonological content, Landau 2006). Rather, his proposal pursues the opposite direction where there is really just one verbal movement chain (i.e. VP-to-SpecCP) that can be reduced by an ordinary mechanism of chain resolution. The pronunciation of a second verb token is independent of any movement or resolution mechanism as it is the regular consequence of a distinct operation, Conflation, that has been designed as a replacement for syntactic head movement deriving the effects of the latter but avoiding the various problems associated with it.

Although LaCara's proposal is on the right track, I believe, concerning the abandonment of head movement as a syntactic movement operation it suffers from several empirical shortcomings. First, it is based on the empirically difficult claim that languages with verb doubling verb phrase fronting always exhibit V-to-T (or some funtional head outside the verb phrase) movement. The analysis requires that the verb's features are conflated onto T where they are spelled out even if the lower verb phrase copy has undergone deletion. In effect, this is a variant of the idea that is at the heart of parallel chains accounts (Aboh 2006, Aboh & Dyakonova 2009, Kandybowicz 2008) and to some extent Landau's (2006) P-recoverability approach: The verb undergoes two movements whose final landing sites are pronounced. LaCara (2016a) differs only in the implementation of the second (shorter) movement step thereby circumventing several open issues about copy deletion that were left unresolved in the other accounts. However, as he ties double pronunciation to V-to-v/T movement just as those did, he is unable to account for data like (41) where there seems to be no evidence for V-to-v/Asp/T movement since tense or agreement markers are free morphemes rather than bound affixes and nonetheless the verb is pronounced twice.

(41) a. [Bóɔ́ **dááó**] lá ká ń dà **dà**.
 goat buy.NMLZ FOC C 1SG PST buy
 'It is buying a goat that I did (as opposed to e.g. selling a hen).'
 (*Dagaare*, Hiraiwa & Bodomo 2008: 805)
 b. Ù-[**bán** wɔ́m] kɔ́ ḿbòm wɔ̀ **báŋ**-yè.
 NCM-build boat PRO.FOC Mbom 3SG build-STAT
 'It is building a boat Mbom built a boat.' (*Mani*, Childs 2011: 219)
 c. [**Doc** quyen sach nay] thi toi co **doc**, nhung khong hieu.
 read CL book this TOP I ASR read but not understand
 'As for reading this book, I read, but I don't understand.'
 (*Vietnamese*, Tran 2011: 60f.)

A further problem is presented by languages that do not exhibit verb doubling in verb phrase fronting although they are commonly assumed to have some type of V-to-higher head movement. Most Germanic languages, for instance, show V2 word order to some degree in at least a subset of sentences which is commonly analyzed as arising through V-to-C movement (see Koster 1975, Thiersch 1978, den Besten 1983, Haider 1986, Platzack 1986, Vikner 1995, among others).[14] According to LaCara (2016a), we would therefore expect the verb to be doubled if the verb phrase of a V2 sentence is topicalized with one token of the verb pronounced in the verb phrase in SpecCP and the other in C. However, when one considers verb phrase fronting in the relevant languages in (42) one observes, as LaCara (2016a: 12) himself acknowledges with regard to German, that "[t]his does not happen here; instead, the default verb *tun*, 'do', is inserted in C^0. Nonetheless, verb movement to C^0 is predicted to happen here rather than *do*-supprt regardless of whether one adopts Conflation [...]" (see also Hein to appear on verb phrase fronting in Germanic languages).

(42) a. [Haar **verraden**] **doet** hij niet.
her betray does he not
'He doesn't betray her.' (*Dutch*, Broekhuis & Corver 2015: 1043)

b. [Das Auto **waschen**] **tut** er nie.
the car wash.INF does he never
'Something that he never does is wash the car.'
(*German*, Diedrichsen 2008: 221)

c. Jasper lovede at vaske bilen og [**vaske** bilen] **gjorde**
Jasper promise.PST to wash car.DEF and wash car.DEF do.PST
han (så sandelig).
he so truly
'Jasper promised to wash the car and wash the car, he did (indeed).'
(*Danish*, Houser et al. 2006: 2)

d. [**Läser** boken] **gör** han nu.
reads book.DEF does he now
'Reading the book he is now.'
(*Swedish*, Källgren & Prince 1989: 47)

---

14 Some authors have also claimed that the verb does not (always) move all the way to C because some (or all) V2 clauses are actually TPs rather than CPs (see e.g. Travis 1984, 1991, Diesing 1990, Zwart 1991, 1997, Sells 2001, Mikkelsen 2010). Importantly, in all these approaches the verb still moves out of its base position to a higher functional head even if this head is not C but some head between C and V.

e. [Å **lese** bøk-er] **gjør** han hele dag-en.
   to read.INF book.PL-PL.INDEF does he whole day-DEF
   'Reading books he does all day.'

   (*Norwegian*, Siri M. Gjersøe p.c.)

Additionally, his analysis only explicitly targets verb phrase fronting. In attempting to extend it to verb fronting the prediction emerges that the left-peripheral movement of the verb cannot be head(-to-head) movement to C (or Foc/Top) because under the view of head movement adopted by LaCara this would result in the verbal features being conflated on C (/Foc/Top). As this head would be the uppermost host of the conflated set of features the verb should be exclusively pronounced in this position with no second pronunciation in T or v. Therefore, verb fronting must be V-to-SpecCP movement (or remnant verb phrase movement). Provided that this is indeed the case, the conflation account works fine for verb doubling verb fronting as long as there is V-to-higher functional head movement.

With regard to the asymmetric pattern of Asante Twi and Limbum, the problems of LaCara's (2016a) account manifest themselves in opposite ways. While the verb in Asante Twi arguably moves at least as high as Asp, it appears to remain *in situ* in Limbum. Hence, the Conflation approach predicts that the former should exhibit symmetric verb doubling as the verb's features will be available for pronunciation outside the lower copy of V(P) independent of whether V or VP have moved into the left periphery. The latter, however, should arguably show symmetric dummy verb insertion (or even symmetric gaps) as the verb's morpho-syntactic features remain inside the lower V(P) copy in both verb and verb phrase fronting and will therefore be deleted.

In conclusion, LaCara (2016a) provides a non-movement implementation of the idea of parallel chains. Thereby, he ties double pronunciation of a verb to independently available 'movement' of V to T (or another higher functional head). This dependency is falsified in both ways: There are languages that show verb doubling despite lacking evidence for V-to-T movement as well as languages where the verb obligatorily moves to a higher head and no verb doubling occurs. Furthermore, his account is unable to derive the asymmetric pattern instantiated in Asante Twi and Limbum. I therefore conclude that LaCara (2016a) is not able to derive the typology of verbal fronting as presented in section .

4 An analysis in terms of order of operations

In this chapter, I will propose a new analysis of verb doubling and dummy verb insertion in verbal fronting constructions which is able to derive the two symmetric patterns and the one attested asymmetric pattern. Crucially, the unattested second asymmetric pattern, namely dummy verb insertion in verb fronting and verb doubling in verb phrase fronting, cannot be derived by the system and is therefore correctly predicted to be inexistent. Generalization I thereby follows directly from the analysis. Further, Generalization IIa also naturally emerges as a consequence of the proposed system. In the following, I will first lay out the general idea behind the approach. Then, I will present some arguments from the literature in favour of syntactic Ā-head movement and post-syntactic head movement. Thereafter, I introduce the notion of copy deletion used here, the general syntactic system underlying the approach, and propose that languages have different orders of application of operations. I will then demonstrate how this account derives the two generalizations in detail.

4.1 The general idea and basic assumptions

The basic intuition that underlies this approach is a blend of various insights from previous approaches enriched with two important additional assumptions. Starting from the idea that verb doubling is the result of two distinct movements of the verbal head, one being Ā-movement into the left periphery and the other being head movement of the verb (Abels 2001, Aboh 2006, Landau 2006, Kandybowicz 2008, Aboh & Dyakonova 2009) the first question to be answered is why some languages show dummy verb insertion even though they usually exhibit movement of the verb to a higher functional head. Commonly, *do*-support phenomena are treated as Last Resort repair mechanisms for a high functional head like T/v/Asp in case the lexical verb is unable to combine with them (see among others Chomsky 1957, 1991, Lasnik 1981, 1995, Halle & Marantz 1993, Bobaljik 1995, Cowper 2010). Therefore, head movement of the verb in verbal fronting constructions must somehow be blocked in those languages where this construction shows dummy verb insertion. As head movement of the verb always takes place from the lower chain link of the left-peripheral Ā-movement, the blocking could be achieved if V-to-T/v/Asp movement applies too late, that is, only after the lower copy has already been deleted. That way, head movement would be bled by copy deletion. Since copy deletion is commonly presumed to apply in the PF-branch this entails that head movement in the relevant languages is a PF operation, too (as argued in e.g. Chomsky 1995b, 2001, Merchant

2002b, Platzack 2013, Boeckx & Stjepanović 2001, Schoorlemmer & Temmerman 2012, Zwart 2017). In fact, Houser et al. (2006) propose exactly that: Head movement can language-specifically apply either in the syntax or at PF. In the former case, it is counter-bled by copy deletion meaning that the verb moves out of the lower copy before it is deleted which then results in verb doubling. In the latter case, head movement is bled by copy deletion, that is, the verbal head is deleted as (part of) the lower copy of a syntactic movement chain and a dummy verb is inserted in T/v/Asp as a Last Resort. For conceptual reasons and reasons that have to do with copy deletion in remnant movement the division of head movement into a syntactic version and a post-syntactic version is unattractive (though see Harizanov & Gribanova 2019 for a proposal that different kinds of head movement take place in different modules of grammar). Concerning the former reason, it is in my view conceptually more attractive to encode cross-linguistic variation in the different interactions between grammatical operations rather than in the operations (like head movement) themselves. Concerning the latter reason, if head movement were syntactic in languages that show verb doubling, like Hebrew, one would have to make the copy deletion mechanism treat copies of heads and phrases differently to derive the fact that in remnant VP movement, the copy of the object in the fronted VP is not spelled out, whereas in the analogous verb fronting structures, the verb copy in the fronted VP is spelled out. However, the general idea that head movement and copy deletion can stand in a bleeding and counter-bleeding relation seems to capture the observations elegantly. I therefore propose that head movement takes place at PF in every language but that its order of application with regard to copy deletion is subject to language-specific choice. The proposal that there is a language-specific order of operations has already been made for various other syntactic and post-syntactic operations (Müller 2009a, Arregi & Nevins 2012, Schoorlemmer 2012, Georgi 2014, Assmann et al. 2015, Murphy & Puškar 2018, Puškar 2018).[1] In particular, Schoorlemmer (2012) shows that different definiteness marking strategies (i.e. double definiteness) in Germanic languages can be derived from language-specific orders of application between the two processes Chain Reduction (a copy deletion process) and Local Dislocation (a movement process) in the post-syntax. The claim then is that languages like Hebrew, which exhibit a symmetric pattern of verb doubling in verbal fronting, have the PF order of operations where head movement (HM) precedes copy deletion

---

[1] Müller (2016) even presents an analysis where the order between the two syntactic operations Merge and Copy derives all three attested patterns of Generalization I. As his approach abandons the Copy Theory of Movement as the source of an overt verb copy but rather assumes that a designated operation Copy that is also responsible for reduplication in morphology is active in syntax, I will not discuss it further here.

(CD) thereby allowing the verb to evade the deletion site and being pronounced in T (1-a). In contrast, languages that consistently show dummy verb insertion in verbal fronting contexts have chain reduction apply before head movement with the result that upon application of head movement the verb has already been deleted and hence cannot be moved to T. As a Last Resort repair, a dummy verb is inserted into T to enable spell out of T's features (1-b).

(1)   *PF operations applying to a VP fronting structure*

    a.   HM < CD: $[_{CP} [_{VP} \text{ V DP}] [_{C'} \text{ C} \ldots \text{V+}v\text{+T} \ldots \overline{\text{V+}v} \ldots \overline{[_{VP} \text{ V DP}]}]]$ (with CD over the last two constituents and HM arrows)

    b.   CD < HM: $[_{CP} [_{VP} \text{ V DP}] [_{C'} \text{ C} \ldots \text{T} \ldots v \ldots \overline{[_{VP} \text{ V DP}]}]]$ (with CD and HM marked x)

Table (2) nicely illustrates the relation between the order of operations and the repair. Depending on which order of application holds between the two PF operations head movement and copy deletion a language exhibits verb doubling or dummy verb insertion in both environments, verb fronting and verb phrase fronting.

(2)   *Repair in VP fronting depending on order of post-syntactic operations*

Order	Repair	Languages
CD < HM	dummy verb insertion	German, Dutch, Skou, …
HM < CD	verb doubling	Hebrew, Polish, Dagaare, …

The general derivation of symmetric verb doubling vs. symmetric dummy verb insertion being clear we can now turn to the question how the asymmetric pattern can arise in the current system. Variable choice of the PF order depending on the type of fronting is not an option as we would expect this to allow that a language chooses CD < HM in verb fronting, which results in dummy verb insertion, but opts for HM < CD in verb phrase fronting, which results in verb doubling. Thus, optional operation ordering does not exclude the unattested asymmetric pattern and is therefore not the solution we are looking for. Consequently, the languages that exhibit the asymmetric pattern also have to have a rigid order of PF operations. Apparently, then, the effect of this order on the repair in verbal fronting can be overridden or neutralized in one of the fronting types. Two options present themselves here: (i) The basic order is HM < CD, which usually gives rise to consistent verb doubling, but this effect is annihilated by a special property of verb phrase fronting in the relevant languages; (ii) the basic order is CD < HM, which usually results in

4.1 The general idea and basic assumptions — 119

consistent dummy verb insertion, but a special property of verb fronting overrides this effect and leads to exceptional verb doubling. I will pursue the latter approach here because there is an independently established dichotomy concerning verb fronting that the overriding can be attributed to whereas no such independent division is known to exist in verb phrase fronting. For verb fronting it has been argued that it can be brought about by two distinct kinds of movement, namely either movement of a remnant verb phrase, i.e. one that has been evacuated of all material apart from the verbal head itself (amongst others see den Besten & Webelhuth 1990, Grewendorf & Sabel 1994, Koopman 1997, Müller 1998, 2014, Takano 2000, Abels 2001, Hinterhölzl 2002, Aboh & Dyakonova 2009, Bondaruk 2012), or $\bar{A}$-head movement of the verb into the specifier position of CP/FocP/TopP (amongst others see Koopman 1984, van Riemsdijk 1989, Larson & Lefebvre 1991, Holmberg 1999, Fanselow 2002, Landau 2006, Vicente 2007, 2009, Harbour 2008, Bastos-Gee 2009, Trinh 2011). Since verb fronting by remnant verb phrase movement is in fact just a subcase of verb phrase fronting and is therefore affected by the order of operations in the same fashion as the latter it cannot lead to a repair that is different from the repair occurring in verb phrase fronting. In a nutshell, if verb fronting is remnant verb phrase movement, it always shows the same repair as verb phrase fronting. Consequently, it must be a particular property of $\bar{A}$-head movement that precludes it from resulting in dummy verb insertion despite the order CD < HM. I suggest that this property has to do with the particular phrase structural status of the element affected by this type of movement as a head. A verbal head in its base position projects a complete phrase by selecting a complement and assigning a structural Case. In place of Chomsky's (1995b) Chain Uniformity Condition that used to preclude this kind of movement completely (and therefore needs to be abandoned if $\bar{A}$-head movement exists, Vicente 2007, 2009), I propose that the copy deletion mechanism is such that it cannot delete projecting elements. Thus, $\bar{A}$-head movement, whose lowest copy will by definition always be a projecting head, remains unaffected by copy deletion.[2]

---

[2] This idea is very similar to the Uniformity Condition on Copy Deletion (UCCD) of Trinh (2011) (i) which he abandonded because it apparently was unable to account for the absence of verb doubling in German V topicalization.

(i) *Uniformity Condition on Copy Deletion* (Trinh 2011: 41)
 Copy Deletion cannot apply if the relevant chain is not uniform.

However, Trinh's argument only holds under the assumption that German verb fronting involves $\bar{A}$-head movement. If, instead, it is derived by remnant verb phrase fronting, which I take it to be following den Besten & Webelhuth (1990), Grewendorf & Sabel (1994), Müller (1998, 2014), Hinterhölzl (2002), his argument against the UCCD becomes invalid.

Therefore, a language might show verb doubling in verb fronting, despite it having the PF ordering CD < HM because although it applies first chain reduction will not delete the lower copy of the V-to-SpecCP Ā-head movement chain. Crucially, the logic does not work the other way around to derive the unattested pattern. In order for a language to exhibit dummy verb insertion in verb fronting it will have to derive it by remnant verb phrase movement and have the order CD < HM. With this order, however, it is not possible for verb phrase fronting to result in verb doubling, as the lower verb is always deleted before it can move outside the lower verb phrase copy and there is no special type of verb phrase movement that might exempt its copies from being deleted. The repair of a particular type of verbal fronting will thus be dependent on two factors: (i) the language's order of CD and HM in the post-syntax and (ii) the constituency of the moved element (3).

(3) *Repair strategy depending on order of operations and constituency*

Moved constituent	Order of post-syntactic operations		Surface
	HM < CD	CD < HM	
full VP	verb copy	dummy verb	verb phrase fronting
remnant VP	verb copy	dummy verb	verb fronting
bare V	verb copy	verb copy	verb fronting

With this in mind, I will now discuss data that have been taken as evidence for the existence of Ā-head movement. I will further show that this kind of movement follows naturally from the minimalist model of syntax that is assumed here. Subsequently, the operation copy deletion will be introduced and defined. Finally, I will present some of the arguments from the literature that are in favour of treating head movement as a post-syntactic operation and argue that it applies in a variable order with copy deletion, as has been argued to be the case for several other syntactic and post-syntactic operations.

4.1.1 Ā-head movement in syntax

Recently, Harizanov & Gribanova (2019) have proposed that head movement might not be as homogeneous an operation as has been assumed. Rather, it subsumes two very different movement operations, one being narrowly syntactic and exhibiting the same properties and restrictions as standard phrasal movement; the other, called *amalgamation*, taking place in the post-syntactic component, conforming to the Head Movement Constraint, and never showing any interpretive effects. I take it that the former type basically conforms to what has been called long head movement (as it can skip intervening heads, see amongst others Lema & Rivero 1990, 1991, Rivero 1991, 1993, Roberts 1994) or Ā-head movement (as it may cross clause boundaries, see amongst others Koopman 1984, Landau 2006, Vicente 2007, 2009, Harizanov 2019). Ā-head movement as movement of a head into a specifier position is commonly presumed to be precluded because it links a head position (which is minimal but not maximal since it projects) to a specifier position (which is minimal and maximal since it does not project and is itself not a projection of a lower head), an assumption that is encoded in Chomsky's (1995b) Chain Uniformity Condition (4).

(4) *Chain Uniformity Condition* (Chomsky 1995b: 253)
     A chain is uniform with regard to its phrase structure status.

This section is therefore dedicated to presenting empirical arguments for its necessity as well as conceptual reasoning that it naturally ensues from common views on syntax and movement.

The empirical evidence for the existence of Ā-head movement usually comes from verb fronting, where a bare verbal head has moved to the left periphery of a clause (i.e. SpecCP/SpecFocP/SpecTopP). In fact, Koopman (1984) was the first to suggest that this type of movement can straightforwardly account for cases of verb fronting. Provided that verb fronting can be shown to involve actual movement, one needs to exclude the possibility that the fronted verb is a remnant verb phrase in order to prove that it has undergone proper Ā-head movement. As remnant verb phrase movement requires independent VP-evacuating object movement (and movement of other VP-internal material; Landau 2007) it is sufficient to establish that such movement is not (as freely) available.

The most comprehensive argument along these lines is made by Vicente (2007, 2009) for Spanish which I will present here. First, VP-evacuating movement of the object, although it arguably exists in Spanish, is not general enough to create a remnant VP in all grammatical configurations which allow verb fronting.[3] As argued by Vicente (2009), object movement to a position above the subject's base position but below T (Ordóñez 1997, 1998) is the correct way to derive VOS word order as in (5-a). However, this movement must be restricted to VOS sentences in order to account for the ungrammaticality of (5-b).

---

[3] Actually, as Vicente (2007, 2009) shows (see section 8.2.12), the category of the fronted element is *v* rather than V. I will abstract away from this here as none of the arguments hinges on it.

(5) a. Hoy a traído [_Obj_ a cada_i_ niño] [_Subj_ Su_i_ madre].
today has brought   to each child   his mother
'His mother has brought each child today.'
b. *[_Subj_ Su_i_ madre] ha traído [_Obj_ a cada_i_ niño] hoy
his mother has brought   to each child today
'His mother has brought each child today.' (Vicente 2009: 174)

If object movement were generally available, we would expect (5-b) to be grammatical: The object could have moved above the subject's base position as in (5-a) before the subject moves to clause-initial position. On LF, the subject could then reconstruct into its base position under the moved object and binding should be possible, contrary to fact.[4] Hence, Vicente (2009) concludes, drawing on an insight from Zubizaretta (1998), that object movement is only available in order to focus the subject, i.e. to create VOS word order. If verb fronting were indeed remnant VP movement, we would therefore expect it to only be licensed with VOS order inside the comment part of the sentence. However, as we can see in the example in (6), SVO word order in verb fronting does not result in ungrammaticality (see section 8.2.12 for more examples of this kind).

(6) **Leer,** Juan ha **leído** un libro.
read.INF Juan has read a book
'As for reading, Juan has read a book.' (Vicente 2009: 159)

Furthermore, if object movement were to exceptionally apply in verb fronting, we would incorrectly predict the sentences in (7) to be grammatical for the same reasons that we expected (6) to be fine: The object would have moved above the base position of the subject into which the subject reconstructs on LF enabling the object to bind the subject.

(7) a. *Traer, [_Subj_ su_i_ madre] ha traído [_Obj_ a cada_i_ niño] hoy.
bring.INF   his mother has brought   to each child today
'As for bringing, his mother brought each child today.'
b. *Traer, hoy ha traído [_Subj_ su_i_ madre] [_Obj_ a cada_i_ niño].
bring.INF today has brought   his mother   to each child
'As for bringing, his mother brought each child today.'
(Vicente 2009: 176)

---

4 It does not matter whether subject movement is Ā- or A-movement for the latter has been shown to be able to reconstruct (Boeckx 2001, Legate 2003, Sauerland 2003; see Ordóñez 1997, 1998 for a Spanish-internal argument).

A further argument that the object has not undergone any movement in verb fronting sentences comes from an ambiguity in interpretation. Ordóñez (1997, 1998) shows that indefinite objects are ambiguous between a specific and non-specific reading when they appear in SVO and VSO clauses, where there is no object movement. Hence, in (8), *un ladrón* 'a thief' may either refer to some unspecified thief or to one certain thief in particular.

(8)   a.   Cada policía arrestó a un ladrón.
           each policeman arrested to a thief
           'Each policeman arrested a thief.'   (specific/non-specific)
     b.   Hoy arrestó cada policía a un ladrón.
           today arrested each policeman to a thief
           'Each policeman arrested a thief today.'   (specific/non-specific)
                                                                                                                                                    (Vicente 2009: 177)

In VOS clauses like (9), however, where object movement has taken place, only the specific reading is available.

(9)   Hoy arrestó a un ladrón cada policía.
      today arrested to a thief each polieman
      'Each policeman arrested a thief today.'   (specific/*non-specific)
                                                                                                                                                    (Vicente 2009: 177)

This asymmetry is not surprising in light of the standard view established by Diesing (1992) that indefinite objects obligatorily receive a specific reading when moving out of their thematic position. Now, consider verb fronting sentences with an indefinite object like those in (10). As Vicente (2009: 177) states, a non-specific reading of the objects is possible for them.

(10)   a.   Arrestar, cada policía arrestó a un ladrón.
            arrest.INF each policeman arrested.3SG to a thief
            'As for arresting, each policeman arrested a thief.' (non-specific thief)
      b.   Comprar, Juan quiere comprar un coche.
            buy.INF Juan wants.3SG buy.INF a car
            'As for buying, Juan wants to buy a car.'   (non-specific car)
                                                                                                                   (Vicente 2009: 177)

Therefore, the objects of these sentences cannot have undergone movement out of their thematic position because if they had, they would obligatorily be interpreted as specific like the moved object in (9). Consequently, the fronted verbs in (10) cannot be remnant VPs, as the creation of such a remnant VP requires the object to move out of it.

Another argument that Vicente (2009) puts forward rests on Freezing effects. As Müller (1998) observes, it is not possible to extract out of an already moved element. An effect that he calls Freezing. Torrego (1998) argues that it is this effect that underlies the impossibility to Ā-extract from objects headed by a definite/specific determiner in Spanish. Since overtly definite/specific objects are only licensed in a VP-external position (see Diesing 1992) they must have moved out of the VP which renders them opaque for further subextraction. Given that this analysis is correct, we can generalize that all moved objects in Spanish should be islands for further extraction. Following Vicente's (2009) reasoning, extraction out of objects stranded by verb fronting is predicted to be disallowed under an approach that treats verb fronting as remnant VP movement. This is because remnant-creation requires the object to move out of the VP. However, as shown in (11), extraction of the PP *sobre qué tema* 'about what topic' or the wh-phrase *qué equipo* 'what club' out of the stranded object is perfectly grammatical. Therefore, the object cannot have moved itself.

(11) a. Leer, [sobre qué tema]$_i$ has leído [varios libros ___$_i$].
 read.INF about what topic have.2SG read some books
 'As for reading, what topic have you read some books about?'
 b. Querer, [qué equipo]$_i$ quieres [que ___$_i$ gane la
 want.INF what club want.2SG that win.3SG the
 liga].
 championship
 'As for wanting, which club do you want to win the championship?'
 (Vicente 2009: 178)

A last argument against remnant movement comes from clitic doubling. For some ditransitive predicates, the goal argument is optionally doubled by a clitic (12).

(12) a. El profesor (*les*) entregó las notas a los alumnos.
 the teacher CL hand.3SG the grades to the students
 'The teacher handed the grades to the students.'
 b. Juan (*le*) ofreció vino a María.
 Juan CL offered.3SG wine to Maria
 'Juan offered Maria some wine.' (Vicente 2009: 178)

This optionality is lost when the argument leaves its canonical position. As evidenced by topicalization (13) and the marked goal-theme order (14), the doubling becomes obligatory in such a situation.

(13) a. A los alumnos, el profesor *(les) entregó las notas.
       to the students the teacher CL gave.3SG the grades
       'The students, the teacher handed them the grades.'
    b. A María, Juan *(le) ofreció vino.
       to Maria Juan CL offered.3SG wine
       'Maria, Juan offered the wine to her.' (Vicente 2009: 178)

(14) a. El profesor ??(les) entregó a los alumnos las notas.
       the profesor CL gave.3SG to the students the grades
       'The teacher handed the grades to the students.'
    b. Juan *(le) ofreció a María vino.
       Juan CL offered.3SG to Maria wine
       'Juan offered Maria some wine.' (Vicente 2009: 179)

In verb fronting sentences (15), however, clitic doubling remains optional which indicates that the argument has not moved out of the VP.

(15) a. Entregar, el profesor (les) entregó las notas a los alumnos.
       give.INF the teacher CL gave.3SG the grades to the students
       'As for handing, the teacher handed the grades to the students.'
    b. Ofrecer, Juan (le) ofreció vino a María.
       offer.INF Juan CL offered.3SG wine to Maria
       'Juan offered Maria some wine.' (Vicente 2009: 179)

In conclusion, although Spanish does have an operation of object movement it does not make use of this operation in verb fronting. Consequently, verb fronting cannot be remnant verb phrase movement but must be $\bar{\text{A}}$-movement of the verbal head.

A similar argument, though not as detailed, is presented for Hebrew in Landau (2007). He observes that while Hebrew freely allows verb fronting (16), partial VP fronting is only possible if the VP portion can also occur as a complete VP independently.[5]

(16) **Liknot** hi **kanta** et ha-praxim.
     buy.INF she bought ACC the-flowers
     'As for buying, she bought the flowers.' (Landau 2006: 37)

---

[5] Verbal fronting in Hebrew is $\bar{\text{A}}$-movement as it is unbounded and respects islands (see section 8.2.4).

(17) a. [**Le'hagis** et ha-ma'amar], hu **higiš** le-ktav-ha-et
submit.INF ACC the-article he submitted to-the-journal
lifney ha-dedlyne.
before the-deadline
'Submit the article to the journal, he did before the deadline.'
b. Gil raca [le'hagiš et ha-ma'amar].
Gil wanted submit.INF ACC the-article
'Gil wanted to submit the article.' (Landau 2007: 131, 133)

(18) a. *[**Le'hagis** le-ktav-ha-et], hu **higiš** et ha-ma'amar lifney
submit.INF to-the-journal he submitted ACC the-article before
ha-dedlyne.
the-deadline
b. *Gil raca [le'hagiš le-ktav-ha-et].
Gil wanted submit.INF to-the-journal
'Gil wanted to submit to the journal.' (Landau 2007: 131, 133)

Thus, fronting of the [V DP] portion [*le'hagiš et ha-ma'amar*] is possible in (17-a) because it may independently occur as a complete VP (17-b), while fronting of the [V PP] portion [*le'hagiš le-ktav-ha-et*] is ungrammatical (18-a) because it cannot act as a complete VP (18-b). This observation has been formulated as a condition on VP fronting (19).

(19) *Potential Complete VP Constraint (PCVC)* (Phillips 2003: 75)
The constraint on partial VP-fronting or VP-ellipsis is that the fronted or deleted constituent must be large enough to be a potential complete VP, with the consequence that strictly subcategorized VP material cannot be stranded.

Given this, Landau (2007: 143) points out that partial VP fronting in Hebrew (and English) cannot be remnant movement. If it were, the stranded portion of the VP would leave behind a trace or a copy when it evacuates the VP. As traces arguably are visible to θ-marking (and copies definitely are), the remnant VP would constitute a complete VP with all subcategorized arguments saturated. It would then remain unexplained why certain VP portions can undergo fronting while others cannot. The same logic also precludes an account in terms of selective deletion (see Fanselow & Ćavar 2002, Nunes 2004) as the VP would be complete at the point where it is moved to SpecCP. Since Hebrew does not show productive scrambling or Object Shift (Landau 2006: 51), Landau (2007) concludes that verb fronting must be $\bar{\text{A}}$-head movement.

On the conceptual side, the ban against $\bar{\text{A}}$-head movement goes back to Emonds (1970, 1976) Structure Preservation Principle, which was originally defined over transformations and ensured that constituents could only be displaced from positions of one kind into positions of the same kind thereby restricting the power of transformations. In X-bar theory it was reinterpreted so as to exclude movement of an element of a certain projection level, e.g. an X^0-level head, into a position of a different projection level, e.g. an XP-position. With the introduction of Bare Phrase Structure reference to distinct position types could no longer be made (cf. Carnie 1996, 2000, Harley 2004). The head vs. phrase opposition was then recast as a difference between elements that project, i.e. were dominated by a node of the same category and are therefore minimal, and those that do not, i.e. are not dominated by a node of the same category, and are therefore maximal (Chomsky 1995a). The Structure Preservation Principle thus took the form of the Chain Uniformity Condition (20) stating in effect that the links of a movement chain must either all be minimal or all be maximal.

(20) *Chain Uniformity Condition (CUC)* (Chomsky 1995b: 253)
A chain is uniform with regard to its phrase structure status.

As Vicente (2007, 2009) argues, in this form the CUC is both conceptually dubious and superfluous. First, certain syntactic elements, like e.g. clitics, are explicitly understood as being both minimal and maximal simultaneously. Those properties are apparently not in a complementary relation to one another. It is quite stipulative, then, to declare that movement chains cannot also concurrently contain elements of either specification.

Second, it is unclear why movement should be subject to a special condition that obviously does not hold for other elementary operations like Agree or Merge. Thus, the canonical situation with Merge is that it combines two objects that differ with respect to their phrase structure status, namely a head, which is minimal, and a phrase, which is maximal. If a restriction on Merge similar to the CUC existed, we would expect the syntactic combination of a head with its complement to be impossible. This difference between movement and Merge becomes even more disturbing once we adopt the idea that movement is actually just a version of Merge, namely Internal Merge (Chomsky 2001). Under this view, the CUC would have to hold for some applications of Merge (i.e. Internal Merge) while it must not hold for other applications of the same operation (i.e. External Merge). Equally, as Vicente (2009) points out, Agree between a minimal category and a maximal category must be licit to derive agreement patterns like the one in (21), where the verb agrees with a coordinate subject.

(21) Ayer   vinieron   [Pedro y   Juan].
yesterday came.3PL Pedro and Juan
'Pedro and Juan came yesterday.'   (Vicente 2009: 162)

Here, the verb is affixed with a plural agreement marker although each conjunct is singular in number. Thus, agreement must take place with the whole plural conjunct phrase, a maximal category. As subject agreement is standardly assumed to be located on T/Agr$_S$, a minimal category, Agree must have taken place between a minimal and a maximal category, indicating that a ban similar to the CUC does not hold for this operation.

Concerning the redundancy of the CUC, Vicente (2009) argues that the effects of the condition are already captured by other principles of syntax. One of these principles is the Extension Condition (Chomsky 1995b: 190) which states that Merge must always apply to the root of the current phrase marker. This derives the CUC effect that phrasal movement can only target specifier positions. The fact that a moved object does not project in its landing site, another consequence of the CUC, is accounted for by an often implicit cyclicity assumption that a new projecting head can only be introduced after the current head has saturated all its structure-building features. Hence, it is not possible to saturate only part of the selectional features of a head X, then merge a new selecting head Y, saturate Y's structure-building features, merge another head Z and saturate its features, and eventually move X to saturate its remaining features as depicted in (22).

(22)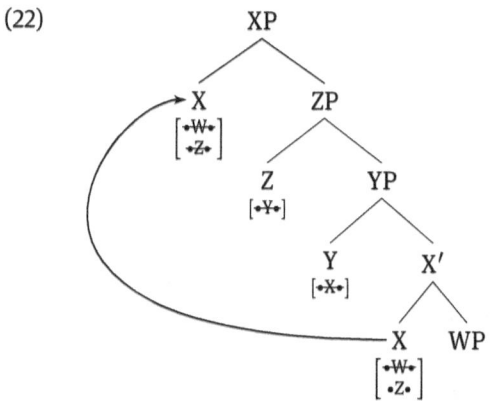

Again, the CUC is not necessary to ensure that a derivation like (22) is excluded. On the other side, the CUC arguably rules out standard syntactic head movement. In a traditional head movement structure the moved head X adjoins to the higher head Y creating a complex structure as in (23).

(23)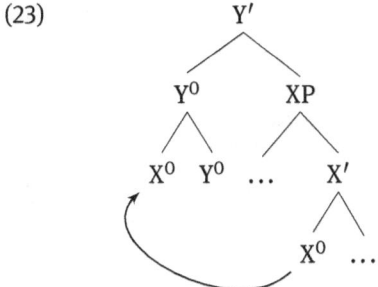

However, in this structure the X inside the Y is maximal, as it does not project any further, whereas the X inside XP is minimal, as it does project. This leads Chomsky (1995b: 322) to suggest that head-to-head movement is regulated by a distinct component, which he calls Word Interpretation. Crucially, this component is not subject to the CUC, which therefore does not apply to head movement. As Vicente (2009) correctly realizes, this is an odd result if one considers that the main purpose of the CUC was to enable an account of the structural properties of head movement chains.

I conclude from the empirical and conceptual arguments that $\bar{\text{A}}$-head movement is a necessary and theoretically unproblematic type of movement. In fact, under the approach to syntax adopted in this work, its existence emerges naturally. This approach will shortly be presented below.

The general framework that the analysis is couched in is the Minimalist Program introduced in Chomsky (1995b) based on the Y-model of grammar (24).

(24)   *The Y-model of grammar*

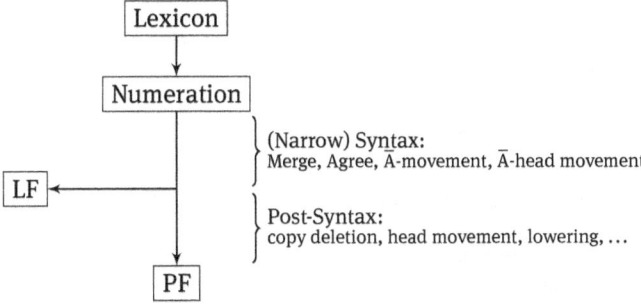

In contrast to the previous Government and Binding approach, Minimalism is a derivational model of syntax where syntactic structure is built incrementally. This is achieved by successive applications of the two basic operations Merge and Agree

(Chomsky 2000, 2001) to either lexical elements in the Numeration or structure that has already been built in previous stages of the derivation.

The operation Merge takes two items α and β creating a new item $[_\gamma \, \alpha \, \beta]$ (Chomsky 2000, 2001). It is triggered by structure-building features [•F•] on a lexical item, where F is the category label of the selected element (Heck & Müller 2007, Georgi 2014). A saturated [•F•] feature is marked inactive (indicated by striking through) but not completely deleted. The element that bears the structure-building feature determines the category of γ and obligatorily projects all unsaturated structure-building features onto γ. Projection of other features, in particular information-structurally relevant ones like [FOCUS] or [TOPIC] may optionally take place. I would like to point out that I understand the transfer of information-structural features here clearly as a property of Merge (i.e. projection) rather than percolation. The latter entails a number of problems, in particular, that it does not have a natural endpoint (see Heck 2008) and that, formulated as specifier-head agreement, it makes Minimalist Grammars more complex than context-sensitive grammars (see Kobele 2005). Following Chomsky (2004), Merge is further divided into external Merge and internal Merge. With the former, α and β are distinct from each other and both stem from the Numeration or another workspace. With the latter, α is contained within β. Thus, internal Merge is a reinterpretation of movement, which like external Merge, is triggered by structure-building features [•F•]. Working within the Copy Theory of Movement, I assume that when α undergoes internal Merge, a copy of it containing all and only the active features of α is merged with β.

The operation Agree is triggered by probe features [∗F:__∗] on an item α and copies the feature value for F on a goal β onto α if α and β are in a c-command configuration. Agree will not be of further interest in the analysis presented here.

The derivation proceeds bottom-up by sequentially saturating Merge and Agree features on the relevant syntactic items. In the process, it respects the Strict Cycle Condition (25) (Chomsky 1973, 1993) that prohibits operations from applying to a proper subpart of the created structure.

(25) *Strict Cycle Condition (SCC)* (as given in Heck 2016)
If Σ is the root of the current phrase marker, then no operation can take place exclusively within Ω, where Ω is properly dominated by Σ.

This also entails that Merge of a new head Y cannot apply until all structure-building features of the current head X have been saturated. Otherwise X's non-saturated features will cause a crash at the interfaces as there is no way in which they could be saturated without violating (25). Additionally, the traditional conception of head-to-head movement is ruled out as adjunction of a head to another head always takes place exclusively on that head (for discussion see Heck 2016).

Now note how Ā-head movement naturally emerges from such a system. When the verb enters the derivation equipped with a [FOCUS] feature. It first merges with the object DP triggered by its [•D•] feature that is then marked as saturated (indicated by striking through). The resulting syntactic object inherits the category feature and any unsaturated structure-building features from that one of its components which triggered the Merge operation, i.e. V in this case (26).

(26)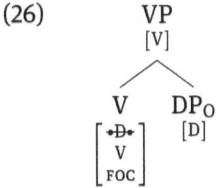

Crucially, although the option of projecting the [FOCUS] feature is available, it is not used here. Consequently, the feature remains located on the verb head. The derivation proceeds by merging *v*, the subject DP, and T as in (27).[6]

(27)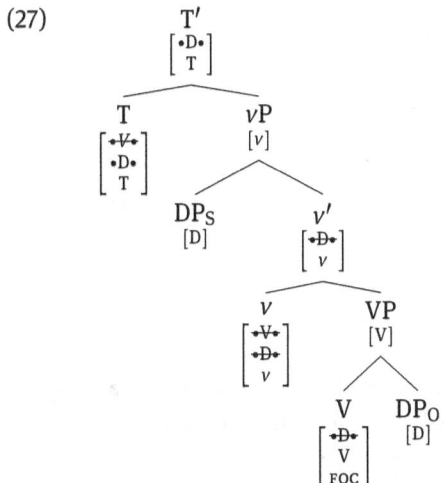

---

[6] I assume that the active [•D•] feature on T will be satured in tandem with its projected counterpart on T′ once the subject DP is internally merged with T′. This saturation on T does not violate the SCC as the operation does not exclusively target T, it also targets the current root node, which is T′. Alternatively, one could assume that projection of active structure-building features leads to them being absent on the head they originated from. This would result in them showing a different projection behaviour compared to category features like T, D, and V, which necessarily have to be present on their head of origin in order to identify its category. Nothing in this analysis hinges on that.

The T head's [•D•] feature then triggers internal Merge of a DP (assuming that the language shows this A-movement of the subject). According to the Minimal Link Condition (MLC, see Fanselow 1991, Ferguson 1993, Chomsky 1995b)[7] the closest DP is then moved to SpecTP, which entails that it is copied and merged with T'. Subsequently, the C head is merged which bears a structure-building feature that attracts a focus-marked element (28).

(28)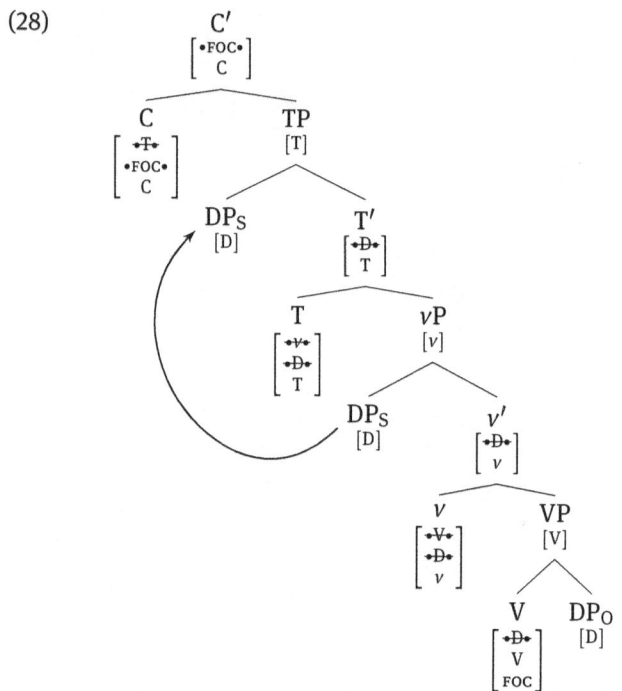

Now there is only one element in the structure that bears the relevant [FOCUS] feature to saturate the structure-building [•FOC•] feature on C, namely V.[8] Conse-

---

[7] The Minimal Link Condition states that only the closest element that bears the required feature will be accessible for an operation like Agree or Merge (i).

(i) *Minimal Link Condition* (as defined in Heck 2016: 16)
 If in a representation H...[...α...[...β...]...] both α and β are of the right type to establish a relation R with H, then H can establish R only with α (but not with β).

[8] In this system, the movement-triggering feature is a structure-building version of the information-structural FOCUS feature itself. Alternatively, one might pursue an approach to movement where internal Merge is the consequence of a preceding Agree relation between the attractor

quently, internal Merge applies, generating a copy which undergoes Merge with C′ (29) (to be refined below). Thus, Ā-head movement naturally emerges under this minimalist syntax, in contrast to head movement which is precluded by the SCC.

(29)
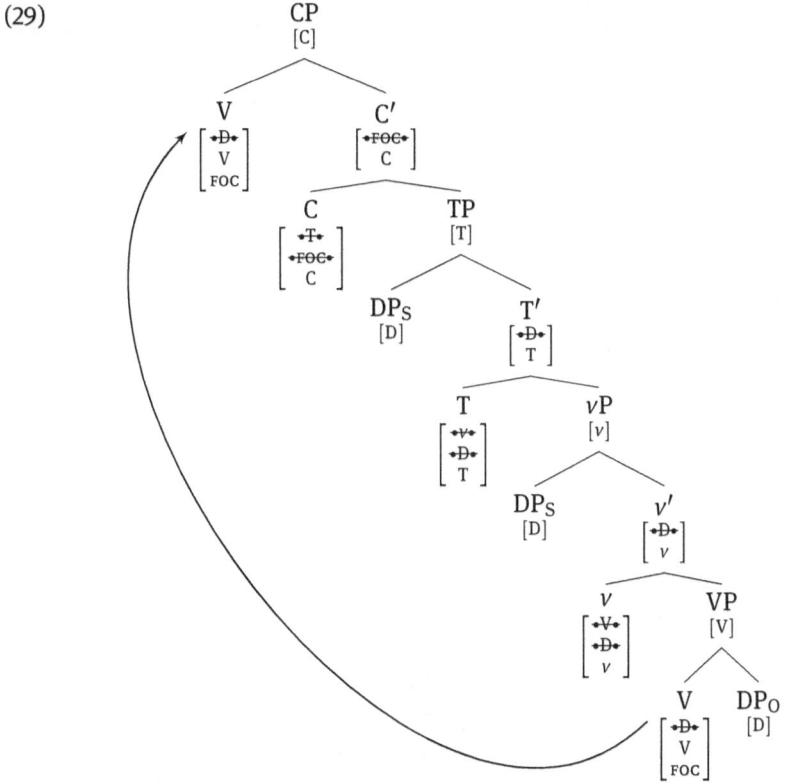

Thus, Ā-head movement is empirically necessary and theoretically unproblematic in a Minimalist syntax. The Chain Uniformity Condition must therefore be abandoned.

---

and the attractee (Chomsky 1995b, 2001). In this case, the movement-triggering feature would be an Agree-feature [∗Information Structure:__∗] that is valued by the verbs [∗Information Structure:FOCUS∗] feature and causes movement of V to SpecCP. It is only possible to trigger V movement by a structure-building feature [•V•] on C if the MLC is understood purely in terms of c-command. If it is understood in terms of c-command plus domination, the closest element with a corresponding category feature [V] is the VP in (28) and we would always expect the VP to be merged rendering Ā-head movement of V impossible (see Matushansky 2006, Preminger 2019, Harizanov 2019 who exploit this interpretation of the MLC to derive the Head Movement Constraint Travis 1984).

4.1.2 Head movement as a post-syntactic operation

Head movement, i.e. the displacement of a head onto another head, has traditionally been conceived of as being a narrow syntactic phenomenon that adjoins the head X of a phrase XP to the head Y of the next higher phrase YP (cf. Travis 1984, Chomsky 1986, Baker 1988, Pollock 1989) as in (30). As a process that takes place in the syntax, head movement is expected to have effects on LF.

(30)   *Traditional view of sytactic head movement*

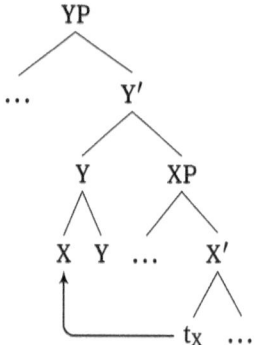

This view has been called into question as head movement standardly seems to have no semantic impact and is in conflict with several well-established syntactic principles like for instance the Extension Condition and the principle that the head of a movement chain c-commands its tail (see amongst others Chomsky 1995b, 2001, Brody 2000, 2003, Mahajan 2003, Müller 2004, Surányi 2005, Matushansky 2006).[9] As a consequence, many researchers have argued that head movement does not take place in syntax, but instead on the PF-branch of grammar, that is, in

---

[9] A very accessible example for the lack of semantic effects of head movement comes from idiomatic verb-object combinations. In German main clauses the verb usually has to appear in second position which is commonly analyzed as V-to-C head movement. When the verb is part of an idiom, as in (i-a), this movement does not cancel the idiomatic reading (i-b).

(i) a. Ist es wirklich wahr, dass er schon das Handtuch wirft?
        is it really true that he already the towel throws
        'Is it actually true that he already gives up?'
    b. Er wirft schon das Handtuch.
        he throws already the towel
        'He already gives up.'   (German)

Though see Lechner (2001, 2004, 2007), Iatridou & Zeijlstra (2010) and Roberts (2010) for arguments that some head movement does in fact show semantic effects.

the post-syntactic component (see e.g. Boeckx & Stjepanović 2001, Hale & Keyser 2002, Merchant 2002b, Schoorlemmer & Temmerman 2012, Platzack 2013, Zwart 2017). Here, I want to present a few of the most prominent empirically grounded arguments in favour of post-syntactic head movement.

The first one is from Boeckx & Stjepanović (2001) who argue that pseudogapping constructions like (31) receive a straightforward explanation if head movement applies after syntax.

(31)   Debbie ate the chocolate, and Kazuko did ⟨eat⟩ the cookies.
(Boeckx & Stjepanović 2001: 346)

According to Lasnik (1999) (following Jayaseelan 1990), (31) is derived by object movement and subsequent ellipsis of the remnant verb phrase (32).

(32)   Debbie ate the chocolate, and Kazuko did [$_{Agr_oP}$ the cookies$_i$ ⟨[$_{VP}$ eat t$_i$]⟩]
(Boeckx & Stjepanović 2001: 347)

An immediate question for this analysis is why the verb does not raise in (32) while it has to do exactly that in non-elliptical configurations (33) (given the assumption of obligatory overt object raising).

(33)   *Kazuko will the cookie$_i$ eat t$_i$ (vs. Kazuko will eat$_j$ the cookie$_i$ t$_j$ t$_i$)
(Boeckx & Stjepanović 2001: 347)

The solution presented by Lasnik is that verb movement is forced by a strong feature on the verb itself that according to the PF crash theory of strong features (Chomsky 1993) will cause the derivation to crash at PF if it remains unchecked. Consequently, either the verb moves to check its feature as in (33) or it is part of a deleted constituent as in (32) where the problematic feature is removed by ellipsis. In light of later developments, Boeckx & Stjepanović (2001) show that this account becomes problematic as it is not straightforwardly reformulatable in an Attract-based theory of movement that additionally has abandoned the notion of strong features. A fact that emerges as hard to capture is that object movement always has to take place obligatorily whereas the verb only obligatorily raises in non-elliptical construction and has to stay *in situ* in pseudogapping constructions. As Boeckx & Stjepanović (2001) argue, these problems can be avoided while retaining the arguably correct analysis of pseudogapping as remnant VP ellipsis if verb movement is a PF process. That way, object movement can be obligatorily triggered by a feature on the attracting head in the syntax. As a PF operation, head movement competes with the PF operation ellipsis the choice between them being determined by independent factors. Thus, whenever ellipsis applies head movement cannot take place and vice versa. Treating head movement as a PF process therefore provides an elegant solution to Lasnik's problem and with it a simple account of pseudogapping.

A second argument for post-syntactic head movement comes from Merchant (2001) and concerns sluicing in object wh-questions like (34).

(34) a. A: Max has invited someone.
B: Really? Who ⟨has he invited⟩? (English)
b. A: Max hat jemanden eingeladen.
B: Echt? Wen ⟨hat er eingeladen⟩? (German)
c. A: Max heeft iemand uitgenodigt.
B: Ja? Wie ⟨heeft hij uitgenodigt⟩? (Dutch)
d. A: Max har inviteret en eller anden.
B: Ja? Hvem ⟨har han inviteret⟩? (Danish)

As he convincingly argues, single wh-element questions are not simply echo questions but actually sluiced interrogative clauses (see Merchant 2001: 64–65). Given this, the E-feature that triggers deletion of all material except the wh-phrase, i.e. TP, must be located on the C head. This means that the C head itself is not elided in (34) and that languages with V2 word order in interrogative main clauses (like the ones in (34)), which is commonly analysed as head movement of the highest verb to C, should allow the finite verb to be pronounced in these sluices as they have the underlying structure in (35).

(35)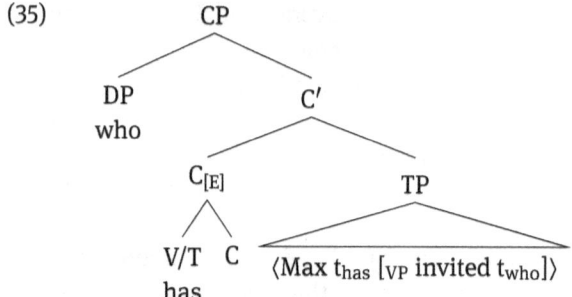

As demonstrated in (36) this prediction is not borne out.

(36) a. A: Max has invited someone.
B: Really? Who (*has)? (English)
b. A: Max hat jemanden eingeladen.
B: Echt? Wen (*hat)? (German)
c. A: Max heeft iemand uitgenodigt.
B: Ja? Wie (*heeft)? (Dutch)

d. A: Max har inviteret en eller anden.
    B: Ja? Hvem (*har)? (Danish)

Extending Lobeck's (1995) approach to the V2 cases above one could assume that the TP is simply an empty category combining with the C head and that the wh-item is base-generated in SpecCP. However, as Merchant (2001: 69–72) points out, it is not possible under this approach to preclude the verb from also being base generated in the C-domain which would predict the sentences in (36) to be grammatical. Instead, Merchant (2001: 72–74) proposes an ordering solution where ellipsis deletes the TP thereby bleeding late head movement to C. This is straightforwardly implemented if head movement is a post-syntactic process that may be preceded by the equally post-syntactic process of ellipsis.

Merchant (2002b) provides an additional argument for post-syntactic head movement based on swiping. Swiping[10] occurs when a wh-word complement of a preposition in a sluiced structure does not appear to the right of that preposition but to its left. Thus, (37-a) is an English sluice with the canonical word order *with who* whereas (37-b) instantiates swiping where the word order inside the PP is reversed to *who with*.

(37) a. Peter went to the movies, but I don't know with who.
      b. Peter went to the movies, but I don't know who with.

As Merchant (2002b) argues, sluices are best analyzed as regular wh-movement to SpecCP in a constituent question with subsequent ellipsis of the TP (38).

(38)

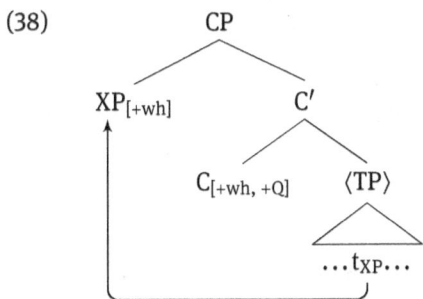

The strongest argument in favour of this analysis comes from the fact that preposition stranding under sluicing (i.e. the omission of the preposition) is only possible in languages that also allow the preposition to be stranded in regular wh-movement

---

10 Swiping is in fact an acronym for **s**luiced **w**h-word **i**nversion with **p**repositions (**in** Northern **G**ermanic) (Merchant 2002b: 289).

indicating that they involve the same underlying mechanism. Thus, for example, English (39) and Norwegian (40) allow for preposition stranding in regular wh-movement (b. examples) and may leave it unpronounced under sluicing (a. examples), German (41) and Yiddish (42) do not allow preposition stranding (b. examples) and have to pronounce the preposition in a sluice (a. examples).

(39) *English* (Merchant 2002b: 291)
    a. Peter was talking with someone, but I don't know (with) who.
    b. Who was he talking with?

(40) *Norwegian* (Merchant 2002b: 291)
    a. Per har snakket med en eller anden, men jeg vet ikke
        Peter has talked with one or another but I know not
        (med) hvem.
        with who
    b. Hvem har Per snakket med?

(41) *German* (Merchant 2002b: 292)
    a. Anna hat mit jemandem gesprochen, aber ich weiß nicht
        Anna has with someone spoken but I know not
        *(mit) wem
        with who
    b. *Wem hat sie mit gesprochen?

(42) *Yiddish* (Merchant 2002b: 292)
    a. Zi hot mit emetsn geredt, ober ikh veys nit *(mit) vemen.
        she has with someone spoken but I know not with who
    b. *Vemen hot zi mit geredt?

Now Merchant (2002b) observes that there are two conditions on swiping. First, only minimal wh-words like *who, what,* and *when* may undergo the inversion (43) but not polymorphemic or phrasal wh-elements like *which X, how rich, what time* (44).

(43)   a. Lois was talking, but I don't know who to.
      b. They were arguing; God only knows what about.
      c. He'll be at the Red Room, but I don't know when till.
                                              (Merchant 2002b: 294)

(44)   a. *This opera was written by an Italian composer in the 19th century, but we're not sure which (composer/one) by.
      b. *He's renting an apartment with a rich guy, and wait till you hear how rich (of a guy) with!

c. *He'll be held at the Red Room, but I don't know what time till.
(Merchant 2002b: 296)

Second, swiping, as the name suggests, only occurs under sluicing. Other environments where a preposition selects a wh-item do not allow the inversion (45).

(45) a. *I don't know [who to] Lois was talking.
b. *[Who to] was Lois talking?
c. *I finally met the guy [who about] she won't shut up.
(Merchant 2002b: 298)

These observations are formulated as conditions on swiping in (46) and (47), respectively.

(46) *The minimality condition* (Merchant 2002b: 297)
Only 'minimal' wh-operators occur in swiping.

(47) *The sluicing condition* (Merchant 2002b: 298)
Swiping only occurs in sluicing.

As Merchant (2002b) points out, previous accounts of swiping either fail to capture the minimality condition (Ross 1969, Rosen 1976, Richards 2001) or are unsuccessful in accounting for the sluicing condition (van Riemsdijk 1978, Lobeck 1995, Chung et al. 1995). Given this background, the argument for post-syntactic head movement is as follows: The minimality condition on swiping (46) can straightforwardly be accounted for if inversion is treated as head movement of the wh-marked D head into the prepositional head (*Incorporation*, see Baker 1988). Wh-elements that are polymorphic or phrasal are not heads and can therefore not be head-moved into P. Now as the sluicing condition shows, this head movement is only possible when all structure to the right of the wh-element (i.e. TP) has been deleted. It is thus fed by ellipsis which is itself a post-syntactic operation. Consequently, head movement must also be a post-syntactic operation.

A fourth argument comes from verb-stranding VP-ellipsis, the mirror image construction of pseudogapping. In this construction, a verb phrase is elided but the main verb is still overtly realized (48).

(48) *Irish verb-stranding VP-ellipsis* (McCloskey 1991: 274)
Ar cheannaigh siad teach? — Creidim gur
COMP.INTERR buy.PST they house believe.PRS.1SG COMP
cheannaigh.
buy.PST
'Did they buy a house?' — 'I believe they did.'

As verb-stranding VP-ellipsis and regular VP-ellipsis behave alike with regard to their distribution, discourse-function, and formal properties it has been argued that verb-stranding in VP-ellipsis is the result of prior head movement of V to a position outside the ellipsis site (i.e. VP) (McCloskey 1991, 2007, 2011, Goldberg 2005, Tucker 2011, Gribanova 2013; see Landau 2018, 2020 for a different analysis). It is also often claimed that the verb in verb-stranding VP-ellipsis has be identical to the verb in the antecedent VP (49) (cf. *verbal identity requirement*, Cyrino & Matos 2002, Goldberg 2005, McCloskey 2007, 2011, Gribanova 2013).

(49) *Irish verb-stranding VP-ellipsis with distinct verbs*
  a. *Níor **cheannaigh** siad ariamh teach ach **dhíol**.
     NEG buy.PST they ever house but sell.PST
     Intended: 'They never bought a house but they sold (a house).'
     (McCloskey 2007: 22)
  b. ***Cháin** sé é féin, ach ag an am chéanna **chosain**.
     criticize.PST he him REFL but at the time same defend.PST
     Intended: 'He criticized himself, but at the same time he defended (himself).'
     (McCloskey 2011: 22–23)

Goldberg (2005: chap. 4) demonstrates that this requirement can be traced back to the identification or recoverability condition on ellipsis, that states that the semantic content of an elided constituent has to be recoverable from its antecedent (see amongst others Hankamer & Sag 1976, Johnson 2001, Merchant 2001). Roughly speaking, antecedent and elided constituent have to be semantically identical. The stranded verb thus has to be the same as the one in the antecedent VP because it is interpreted as if it were still inside the VP and thus has to respect recoverability. Schoorlemmer & Temmerman (2012) argue, that this is because at LF the verb actually is still inside the VP as it has not undergone movement to T in the narrow syntax. Its overt realization on the surface is due to it raising to T before the VP is elided. As this movement has no effect on the semantic identity requirement it must apply in the PF component whose processes do not feed LF. This approach also correctly predicts two further properties of (verb-stranding) VP-ellipsis: First, inflectional material that originates outside the VP does not yield to the identity requirement (50).

(50) *Irish verb-stranding VP-ellipsis with distinct inflection*
  a. Dúirt mé go **gceannóinn** é agus **cheannaigh**.
     said I COMP buy.COND it and buy.PST
     'I said that I would buy it and I did.' (McCloskey 1991: 273)

b. **Gabh** ar mo dhroim anseo. **Chuaigh.**
go.IMP on my back here go.PST
'Get up here on my back. He did.' (McCloskey 2011: 24)

Second, as phrasal movement takes place in the syntax, it should not lead to an identity requirement. This prediction is borne out. The objects in the second clauses in (51) are not identical but the examples are grammatical.

(51) *English XP-movement out of VP-ellipsis*
    a. Abby took **Greek**, but I don't know **what language** Ben did.
(Merchant 2008: 147)
    b. **The pressure** should be monitored, and **the temperature** should be, too. (Schuyler 2001: 5)

Thus, the identity requirement on verbs in verb-stranding VP-ellipsis can be treated as a theorem following from the identity condition on ellipsis if head movement is a late process applying post-syntactically.

Yet another argument is presented in Zwart (2017). He argues, following recent research on morphology (see e.g. Börjars et al. 1997, Stump 2001, Ackerman & Stump 2004, Chumakina 2013, Spencer & Popova 2015), that periphrastic tense forms such as the Dutch periphrastic past (52) are not created in the syntax but occupy cells in a morphological paradigm created by intersection of grammatical features (53). From this they are chosen post-syntactically as realizations for syntactic terminals based on the latters' featural content.[11]

(52) *Inflection of Dutch verbs* (Zwart 2017: 29)

	Verb	Simple Past	Periphrastic Past	
a.	wandel-t	wandel-de	heeft	ge-wandel-d
	walk-3SG	walk-PST.3SG	AUX.3SG	GE-walk-PTCP
b.	loop-t	liep	heeft	ge-lop-en
	walk-3SG	walk.PST.3SG	AUX.3SG	GE-walk-PTCP
c.	gebeur-t	gebeur-de	is	ge-beur-d
	happen-3SG	happen-PST.3SG	AUX.3SG	GE-happen-PTCP
d.	kom-t	kwam	is	ge-kom-en
	happen-3SG	happen.PST.3SG	AUX.3SG	GE-happen-PTCP

---

11 Φ-features or tense features, which originate on syntactic heads different from the verb (the subject/object DP and T, respectively), come to be present on V by a feature sharing mechanism tied to Merge (as defined in Chomsky 2001; see also Koster 1987, Zwart 2005 for feature sharing).

(53) *Partial paradigm of* wandeln *'walk'* (Zwart 2017: 35)

TENSE	POV[12]	
	UNMARKED	ANTERIOR
PRESENT	wandelt	heeft gewandeld
PAST	wandelde	had gewandeld

Thus, auxiliaries do not realize functional heads like Asp or T, but are inserted into the verb node alongside the lexical verb. Hence, there is no head solely associated with the auxiliary in narrow syntax. Nonetheless, we observe that a (finite) auxiliary always moves to second position in Dutch main clauses (54). Consequently, this auxiliary movement cannot be syntactic. Rather, it must take place in the post-syntax once the verbal head has been realized by the periphrastic form. Zwart (2017: 45) then suggests that "[s]ince all finite verbs in main clauses are subject to the same linearization restriction, all of verb-second must be postsyntactic. And since verb-second represents a core case of head movement, a case can be made for the postsyntactic nature of head movement more generally."

One argument internal to Kwa languages for verb movement taking place post-syntactically is presented in Korsah (2017) based on the distribution of null object pronouns. He provides examples from Gã, a Kwa language of the Niger-Congo phylum, but claims that his account carries over to related languages with the same pattern like Akan (Stewart 1963, Boadi 1976, Saah 1992, 1994, Osam 1996, Korsah & Murphy 2019) of which Asante Twi is a dialect. In general, an object pronoun is null if it has an inanimate referent (54).

(54) Taki na (*lɛ).
      Taki see 3SG
      'Taki saw it.'   (*Gã*, Korsah 2017: 7)

However, overt pronouns (independent of their animacy) appear in the following four environments:
1. the pronoun's referent is animate (55-a)
2. the pronoun precedes an adverbial (55-b)
3. the pronoun is the object of a change of state predicate (55-c)
4. the pronoun is an argument of a depictive secondary predicate (55-d)

---

12 The POINT OF VIEW feature is responsible for relative tense interpretation (Wiltschko 2014: 75).

(55) a. Taki na *(lɛ).
Taki see 3SG
'Taki saw him/her'.
b. Taki na *(lɛ) oyá.
Taki see 3SG quickly
'Taki saw it quickly.'
c. Taki ku *(lɛ).
Taki break 3SG
'Taki broke it.'
d. Taki hɔɔ́ *(lɛ) ŋmɔ́ŋ.
Taki sell 3SG fresh
'Taki sold it fresh.' (Gã, Korsah 2017: 8)

Assuming that pronouns are bare φ heads and that the difference between animate and inanimate φ is the presence of a person feature on the former he argues that in all contexts where an overt pronoun is observed this pronouns has moved into a specifier position. Showing that contexts 2–4 above all independently involve movement of the object, he argues that *v* heads in Kwa languages come equipped with a person probe and a respective EPP-feature that attracts the probe's goal (i.e. an animate pronoun) into SpecvP. In doing so, he is able to capture all environments in which the object pronoun is overt as environments where the object pronoun has undergone movement. Concerning null pronouns in contexts like (54), Korsah (2017) argues that they are indeed syntactically present as they can control embedded subjects (56-a) and bind possessives (57-a) just like the corresponding overt DPs in (56-b) and (57-b).

(56) a. Taki kwɛ́ pro_i ni e_i-fɔ.
Taki watch COMP 3SG-wet
'Taki watched on for it to get wet.'
b. Taki kwɛ́ [woló lɛ́]$_i$ ni e_i-fɔ.
Taki watch book DEF COMP 3SG-wet
'Taki watched on for the book to get wet.' (Gã, Korsah 2017: 30)
(57) a. Taki kɛ pro_i wo e_i-susú adeká lɛ mli.
Taki take put 3SG.POSS-savings box DEF in(side)
'Taki put it in its savings box.'
b. Taki kɛ [shiká lɛ́]$_i$ wo e_i-susú-(a)déká lɛ́ mli.
Taki take money DEF put 3SG.POSS-savings-box DEF in(side)
'Taki put the money in its savings box.' (Gã, Korsah 2017: 31)

From this, he concludes that the null realization of inanimate object pronouns must be due to a late deletion operation at PF.

Inanimate object pronouns *in situ* must be deleted at PF because they pose a problem for linearization given that it requires asymmetric c-command (Kayne 1994). Unlike animate pronouns, which have moved to Spec*v*P due to their person feature (58-a), inanimate pronouns are still in the complement position of the verbal head at the point where linearization applies (58-b).

(58) a. b.

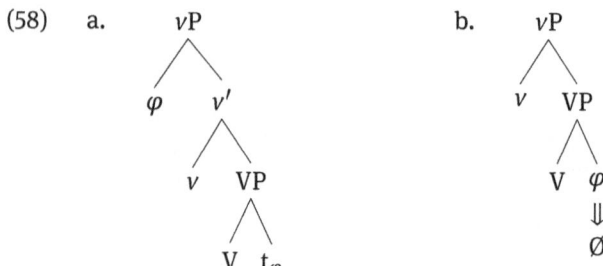

In this position there is a symmetric c-command relation between V and φ which is an unlinearizable configuration. Since the VP needs to be spelled out and movement of the pronoun is not an option (because movement is strictly feature-triggered), the only option to successfully linearize (58-b) is to delete the pronoun.

Now, crucially, there is also some evidence for V-to-T movement in Kwa languages. Tense (59-a) and negation (59-b) are usually marked as affixes on the lexical verb.

(59) a. Taki baá-hé adéká lɛ́.
       Taki FUT-buy box DEF
       'Taki will buy the box.'
    b. Taki hé-ŋ́   adéká lɛ́.
       Taki buy-NEG.FUT box DEF
       'Taki won't buy the box.' (Gã, Korsah 2017: 51)

However, when an auxiliary element like *nyɛ* 'can' is present, tense and negation are marked on this element rather than on the main verb (60).

(60) a. Taki baá-nyɛ́ɛ́-hé adéká   lɛ́.
       Taki FUT-can   3SG-buy box DEF
       'Taki will be able to buy the box.'
    b. Taki nyɛ́-ŋ́   é-hé   adéká lɛ́.
       Taki can-NEG.FUT 3SG-buy box   DEF
       'Taki won't be able to buy the box.' (Gã, Korsah 2017: 52)

This can be analyzed such that V-to-T movement takes place in (59) in order to provide a host for the affixal material in T. This movement is blocked in (60) by the auxiliary which is closer to T than V and therefore undergoes head movement to T.

This V-to-T movement would render the structure in (58-b) linearizable if it took place in syntax proper thereby obviating the need to delete φ. As we contrarily find that φ has undergone deletion, Korsah (2017: 53) concludes that head movement of V to T must take place only after the complement of the phase head v has undergone spellout, that is, it must take place post-syntactically.

As is common in the field of theoretical linguistics, these arguments have not gone unchallenged and various counter-proposals as well as independent arguments against head movement as a post-syntactic operation have been put forward (see Lechner 2001, 2004, 2007, Baltin 2002, Iatridou & Zeijlstra 2010, Roberts 2010, Gribanova 2013, 2017, Keine & Bhatt 2016, Sailor 2018). One recent proposal that might resolve the issue comes from Harizanov & Gribanova (2019) who suggest that the term head movement actually comprises two distinct movement operations, one being syntactic and the other post-syntactic. By adopting a post-syntactic account of some head movement phenomena and a syntactic account of others, this book, in successfully deriving the cross-linguistic patterns of verbal fronting repairs, might thus in itself be interpreted as an argument in favour of this view.

4.1.3 Heads, copies and copy deletion

Under the Copy Theory of Movement several copies of consituents are created during the derivation. At the interfaces to LF and PF, these copies are treated differently. At LF, lower copies are taken to account for so-called reconstruction phenomena (Chomsky 1977) where a moved element is interpreted as if it were still in its original position. A typical example are anaphors pied-piped under wh-movement as in (61) where *himself* can be bound by, and therefore coreferent, with *John* despite not being c-commanded by it.

(61)   Which book about himself$_i$ does John$_i$ never want to read *which book about himself$_i$*?

If at LF, a copy of the moved wh-phrase (in italics) is still in the c-command domain of *John*, this copy can be interpreted and account for the absence of a Principle A violation.

At PF, however, lower copies seem to be deleted as they do not receive an audible pronunciation, at least in the standard cases of movement.[13]

Several proposals have been made to account for this (Brody 1995, Bobaljik 1995, Groat & O'Neill 1996, Pesetsky 1997, 1998, Bobaljik 2002), the most recent one being Nunes (2004) who proposes an operation Chain Reduction that applies at PF and deletes lower elements as a consequence of a linearization paradox that they create (see section 3.1). In this book, I will adopt his approach insofar as I assume that there is an operation that applies post-syntactically and deletes copies, namely Copy Deletion. However, this operation is not triggered by a linearization conflict, but rather applies generally, identifying copies of an element and deleting them according to the definition in (62). For concreteness, I will postulate that copying of an element entails coindexing of the two resulting elements in order to mark them as copies of each other (these indices will be symbolized by superscripted lowercase letters).

(62) *Copy Deletion (CD)*
In a structure that contains multiple copies $X_1^i, X_2^i, \ldots, X_n^i$ of a constituent X (i.e. several elements 1–n that share the same movement-assigned index i) delete every X_m^i that does not fulfill a. or b.
  a. X_m^i c-commands X_b^i and there is no other X_c^i such that X_c^i c-commands X_m^i, or
  b. X_m^i is a head.

In this system, a head is an element that bears a saturated structure-building feature [•F•]. Considering the way in which syntactic structure is built in the present

---

[13] An often noted exception is the so-called copy construction exemplified in (i), where a long-distance wh-moved element is pronounced in all embedded complementizer positions (Chomsky 1977).

(i) a. **Wer** glaubst du, **wer** Recht hat?
   who believe you who right has
   'Who do you think is right?'
 b. **Wie** nimmt man an, **wie** der Prozess endet?
   how assumes one PRT how the trial ends
   'How do people think the trial will end?' (*German* Höhle 2000: 257)

This has apparently exceptionlessly (Boeckx 2008: 28) been analyzed as pronunciation of intermediate copies of the movement chain (see Thornton & Crain 1994, Bayer 1996, Fanselow & Mahajan 2000, Höhle 2000, Fanselow & Ćavar 2001, Nunes 2004, Felser 2004, Rett 2006, Bošković & Nunes 2007, Barbiers et al. 2009, Schippers 2012, Pankau 2009, 2013, Baier 2014 for analyses, and Murphy 2016 for recent criticism thereof).

system, namely by application of Merge which is triggered by structure-building features [•F•] that get saturated in the process, this notion of head ensures that the selecting element in a Merge operation is also the one that projects due to it being the head. It thus captures the fact that it is the X'-level constituent that acts as a head for the merging of a specifier. Crucially, saturated features are no longer visible for subsequent syntactic operations because one would otherwise expect them to trigger a second application of Merge. Therefore, the copying, which takes place during internal Merge does not duplicate them on the moved element.

Let us consider an example structure like the Ā-head movement of V to SpecCP in (29). According to the above assumptions it will actually look as in (63), where each movement has left its indices on both copies (*i* for the subject movement, *j* for the verb movement) and duplication of the V element has not copied the saturated [•D•] feature.

(63)

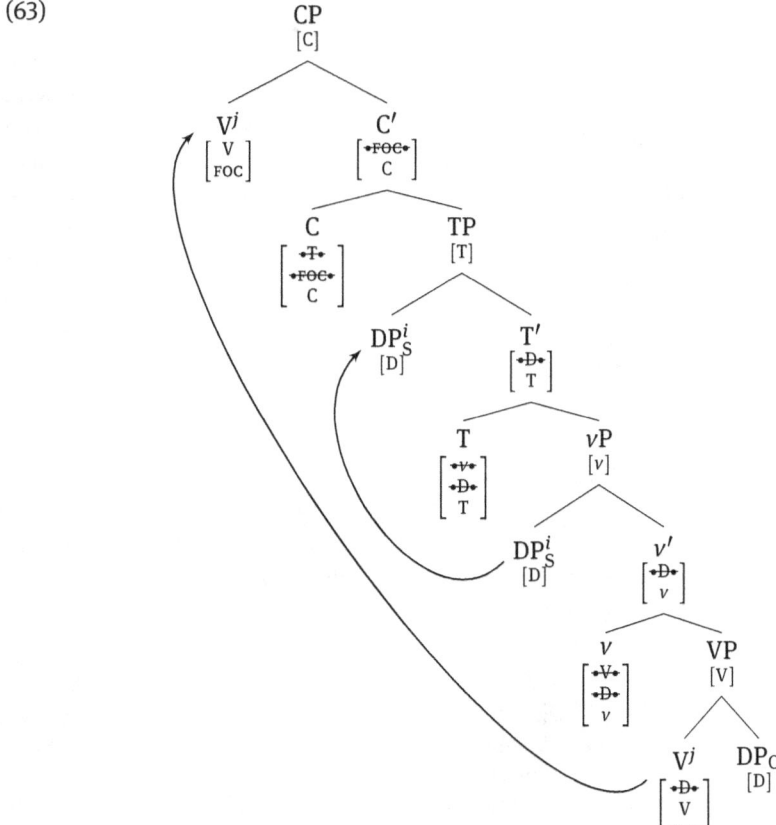

To this structure Copy Deletion will apply in the post-syntax. There are copies of two constituents here, namely the subject DP and the verb. Let us consider the subject first. The lower copy does not fulfill clause a. of (62) because it does not c-command another subject copy but is c-commanded by one. It also does not conform to clause b. as it is not a head, i.e. does not bear any saturated [•F•] features. Therefore, it will be deleted. The higher copy of the subject survives, as it c-commands the lower copy and is not itself c-commanded by a higher subject copy, thereby fulfilling clause a. of CD. Importantly, CD is evaluated simultaneously for all copies, not – as this description might have suggested – sequentially for each copy after the other.

Turning to the verb copies, the higher copy is not deleted because it c-commands the lower V copy and is not c-commanded by any higher V copy and thus complies with clause a. of (62). Crucially, the lower copy also evades deletion as it still bears the saturated [•D•] feature and therefore qualifies as a head.

At this point, it should be obvious how the proposed analysis accounts for the peculiarity of Ā-head movement with regard to triggering multiple pronunciation of copies. In contrast to lowest copies of phrasal movement chains, the lowest copy of an Ā-head movement chain inevitably has properties that define it as a head.[14] As such it is exempt from copy deletion by the definition in (62). Although this is very stipulative at the moment it will go a long way in accounting for the different patterns and generalizations found in the typology of verbal fronting. In section 4.2, I will show in detail how the present system derives these patterns and generalizations and how it fails to yield the unattested repair pattern. Before we turn to this issue, I will briefly present and discuss the idea of orders of application between (post-)syntactic operations.

4.1.4 Variable order of post-syntactic operations

The proposal that operations (have to) apply in a specific order goes back to at least Halle (1962: 57–58) who observed that the rules of Sanskrit vowel sandhi in Whitney (1889) could be significantly simplified by imposing an order of applica-

---

14 Under the definition of head presented here, this presupposes that intransitive (unergative) verbs also have to bear a structure-building feature [•D•] in order to qualify as a head. Since intransitives also undergo verb doubling in the relevant languages, they must be heads in the present approach, which entails that they always select a phonologically empty complement. In fact, this has been suggested for independent reasons (Hale & Keyser 1993, 2002, Bobaljik 1993: see among others). Alternatively, one could assume that unergatives enter the derivation with an already saturated [•D•] feature.

tion between them (the idea is taken up in SPE again, Chomsky & Halle 1968). The best known extension of this idea to syntax is probably Chomsky's (1995b, 2000) 'Merge-over-Move' principle that states that whenever a derivation encounters a situation where both operations can apply, Merge applies before Move.[15] With regard to the post-syntactic component (as understood in Halle & Marantz 1993, Harley & Noyer 2003, Embick & Noyer 2007), Embick & Noyer (2001) argue that displacement operations that make reference to hierarchical structure (i.e. *Lowering*) must apply before Vocabulary Insertion and linearization which in turn need to apply before displacement operations that refer to linear precedence (i.e. *Local Dislocation*). Later, based on Bizkaian Basque, Arregi & Nevins (2012) proposed that the ordering is even more fine-grained such that linearization has to precede Vocabulary Insertion. Thus, the idea that operations apply in a particular order is present across different grammatical modules.

However, all of the above proposals (apart from possibly the phonological one) share a common trait, namely, that the order is fixed across languages. Merge over Move is supposed to hold for German as well as for Ainu and Lowering has to precede Local Dislocation in Czech as well as in Warembori for the very reason that the former operates on hierarchical and the latter on linear structure. More recently, though, it has been argued that an approach to operation order that is cross-linguistically flexible is able to capture variation in an elegant manner. Thus, Müller (2009a) has argued that ergative vs. accusative argument encoding patterns can be derived by the order Merge over Agree vs. Agree over Merge, respectively. Assuming that accusative and ergative are different names for one and the same structural

---

15 The empirical argument for Merge-over-Move is based on the contrast in (i).

(i) a. There seems to be someone in the room.
　　b. *There seems someone to be in the room.

Suppose that at the point (ii) of the derivation, there is a choice between merging the expletive *there* from the numeration or moving the subject *someone*.

(ii) 　[$_{TP}$ to [$_{VP}$ be someone in the room]]

Merge-over-Move correctly predicts that *there* is merged which is subsequently raised into the subject position of *seem* (iii-a). Movement of *someone* would give rise to the ungrammatical derivation (iii-b).

(iii) a. 　[$_{CP}$ There [$_{VP}$ seems [$_{TP}$ t$_{there}$ to [$_{VP}$ be someone in the room]]]]

　　b. 　[$_{CP}$ There [$_{VP}$ seems [$_{TP}$ someone to [$_{VP}$ be t$_{someone}$ in the room]]]]

Hence, given applicability of both, Merge must precede Move to account of the pattern in (i).

case, called internal case, that is assigned by *v* (Murasugi 1992) and that Agree preferably takes place between a head and its specifier, he shows that when the external (with regard to *v*P) argument is merged first, subsequent case-assignment by Agree will target the external argument resulting in an ergative pattern (64). In contrast, if Agree takes place first, it will target the internal argument as the external argument has not been merged at this point, leading to an accusative pattern (65). The remaining argument will be assigned external case by T.

(64) *Merge before Agree: Ergative pattern*

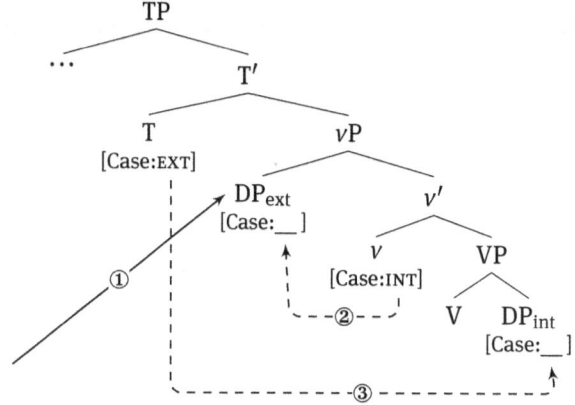

(65) *Agree before Merge: Accusative pattern*

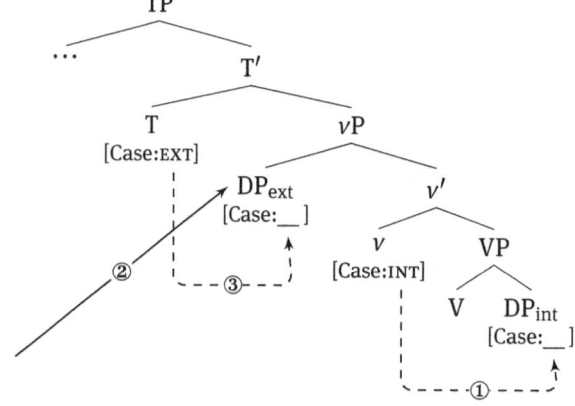

The proposal is extended by Lahne (2008a) and Assmann et al. (2015) who demonstrate that further distinctions between ergative and accusative languages follow if the order of Merge and Agree on T is the same as on *v*.

Similar proposals have been put forward by Georgi (2014) who derives different patterns of reflexes of successive-cyclic movement by means of variable orders of Merge and Agree; by Murphy & Puškar (2018) who derive patterns of conjunct agreement by varying orders of Merge and Agree inside the conjunct phrase; and by Puškar (2018) who derives the number-dependent gender agreement with hybrid nouns in Bosnian/Croation/Serbian by means of variable orders of Number-Agree and Gender-Agree operations.

With regard to post-syntactic operations, Schoorlemmer (2012) argues that a language-dependent variable order of application between Chain Reduction (Nunes 2004) and Local Dislocation (Embick & Noyer 2001) can account for the difference between Danish, which although it comprises of a definiteness-marking suffix does not exhibit double definiteness marking with modified nouns, and other Scandinavian languages, which exhibit this pattern. Thus, Swedish, Norwegian, and Faroese all use a definite suffix with unmodified nouns but both a suffix and a freestanding definite article with nouns that are modified by an adjective (66).

(66) *North Germanic definiteness-marking*
(a. Schoorlemmer 2012: 109; b., c. Julien 2005: 26–27)

a. hus-**et**
 house-DEF
 'the house'

a′. **det** stora hus-**et**
 DEF big house-DEF
 'the big house' (*Swedish*)

b. skjort-**a**
 shirt-DEF
 'the shirt'

b′. **den** gule skjort-**a**
 DEF yellow shirt-DEF
 'the yellow shirt' (*Norwegian*)

c. kettlingur-**in**
 kitten-DEF
 'the kitten'

c′. **tann** svarti kettlingur-**in**
 DEF black kitten-DEF
 'the black kitten' (*Faroese*)

By contrast, in Danish, unmodified nouns take a definite suffix (67-a) like in Swedish, Norwegian and Faroese, whereas this suffix is absent on modified nouns. Only a freestanding definite article occurs instead (67-b).

(67) a. hest-**en**
 horse-DEF
 'the horse'

b. **den** røde hest
 DEF red horse
 'the red horse'
 (*Danish*, Hankamer & Mikkelsen 2002)

Concerning the underlying structure of DPs containing an attributive adjective Schoorlemmer (2012) argues that they must provide two distinct D positions. First, in order for an adjective to show definiteness-sensitive inflection, that is, exhibit a strong vs. weak inflection distinction, it must c-command a D head that is specified for definiteness. Second, in order for an attributive adjective to be interpreted in the domain of a definite D (in contrast to a predicative adjective) it must be c-commanded by a definite D. Therefore, he argues, the D first selects an N(P) and, triggered by addition of an AP (either by adjunction, e.g. Ritter 1992, or as a specifier, e.g. Cinque 1999, Svenonius 2008), undergoes movement across the AP and reprojects above it (cf. Georgi & Müller 2010, Surányi 2005). The structure is depicted in (68).

(68)

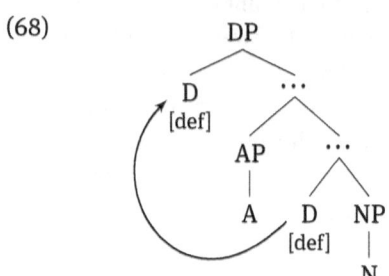

Given that these languages comprise of two Vocabulary Items for definite Ds, one that is a suffix (indicated by the hyphen before the marker) and is inserted under adjacency to an N(P) (69-a) while the other is a free morpheme and is freely inserted into any definite D (69-b), the observed patterns can, as Schoorlemmer (2012) argues, be derived by a variable order of application between Local Dislocation (Embick & Noyer 2001) and Chain Reduction (Nunes 2004).

(69) *Vocabulary Items for definite D in Swedish*
    a. /-et/ ↔ [D, def, sg, neuter]/__N
    b. /det/ ↔ [D, def, sg, neuter]

In Swedish, Norwegian, and Faroese, Local Dislocation, which has to follow Vocabulary Insertion and Linearization (see Embick & Noyer 2001), takes the suffixal definiteness marker and right adjoins it to the immediately adjacent noun, thereby creating a complex morphological unit headed by the noun (70).

(70) *Swedish: LD precedes CR*
    det stora -et hus $\xrightarrow{LD}$ det stora __ [hus+et] $\xrightarrow{CR}$ det stora huset

Subsequent Chain Reduction will then be unable to delete the lower instance of the definiteness marker as it has undergone morphological reanalysis (see also section 3.1) which results in the two definite Ds being pronounced.[16]

---

[16] This presupposes a view of Chain Reduction that diverges from Nunes' original proposal where CR applied in order to avoid conflicting linearization statements. As Linearization applies

In Danish, Chain Reduction applies before Local Dislocation, at a point where the suffix is still identifiable as a lower chain link. It therefore deletes it and bleeds subsequent right adjunction by Local Dislocation which gives rise to a surface structure that contains only one overt definiteness marker, namely the definite article *den* (71).

(71)   *Danish: CR precedes LD*
         den røde -en hest $\xrightarrow{CR}$ den røde -en hest $\xrightarrow{LD}$ den røde __ hest

As unmodified nouns do not involve a structure with two D positions because the AP which triggers D-movement is absent, no bleeding of Local Dislocation by Chain Reduction occurs and the suffix can be adjoined to its nominal host in Danish and the other languages alike. The patterns of definiteness marking in Scandinavian thus receive a simple analysis if the order of operations in the post-syntactic component is allowed to vary cross-linguistically.[17]

In my opinion, the abovementioned proposals all demonstrate that variable orders of operations in syntax and post-syntax are a simple and elegant means to capture parametric variation. Therefore, the analysis presented in this work

---

before CR in Schoorlemmer's approach, he takes the view that it repairs rather than avoids the conflicting linearization statements generated by Linearization. Further, Schoorlemmer's CR treats phonologically different Vocabulary Items such as *det* and *-et* above as identical, in case they realize exactly the same set of morphosyntactic and semantic features.

17 Schoorlemmer (2012) accounts for the West Germanic languages German, Dutch, and English that show no difference in definiteness marking between unmodified nouns and nouns modified by an adjective (i) by claiming that they simply lack a suffixal Vocabulary Item for definite Ds. They only dispose of the equivalent of b. in (69).

(i)   *West Germanic definiteness-marking* (Schoorlemmer 2012: 109)
    a.   **das** (große) Haus
         DEF   big   house
         'the (big) house'   (*German*)
    b.   **het** (grote) huis
         DEF   big   house
         'the (big) house'   (*Dutch*)
    c.   **the** (big) house   (*English*)

Icelandic, where both modified and unmodified nouns take a definite suffix while a definite article never appears (ii), is similarly analyzed as lacking a free morpheme Vocabulary Item for definite D. It therfore only comprises of the equivalent of a. in (69).

(ii)   (góði) maður-**inn**
         good man-DEF
         'the (good) man'   (*Icelandic*, Einarsson 1945)

will be based on a cross-linguistically flexible though language-internally rigid order of application between the operations copy deletion and head movement both of which are claimed to take place in the post-syntactic component before Linearization as they both make reference to hierarchical syntactic structure.

4.2 Deriving the typology

After having laid out the general framework, let me now demonstrate how the typology of verbal fronting can be derived by it. Recall that we established two generalizations in chapter 2 above. First, languages that have both verb and verb phrase fronting exhibit three out of four logically possible patterns (72). They either symmetrically show verb doubling or dummy verb insertion in both types of fronting, or asymmetrically exhibit verb doubling in verb fronting and dummy verb insertion in verb phrase fronting. The fourth pattern, namely dummy verb insertion in verb phrase fronting and verb doubling in verb fronting is unattested leading to a gap in the typology.

(72)   Attested patterns of repair mechanisms in verbal fronting

		V fronting	
		verb copy	dummy verb
VP fronting	dummy verb	Asante Twi, Limbum, …	German, Dutch, …
	verb copy	Hebrew, Polish, …	—

The generalization is given in (73)

(73)   *Generalization I*
If a language shows both verb and verb phrase fronting it either exhibits the same repair in both frontings (verb doubling or dummy verb insertion), or verb doubling in verb fronting and dummy verb insertion in verb phrase fronting. The reverse pattern is inexistent.

A second generalization that emerged from the data concerns languages that show only one type of verbal fronting, that is, either verb fronting or verb phrase fronting but not both. It is observed that languages that exclusively have verb fronting always use a repair of verb doubling, never one of dummy verb insertion. In contrast, languages that solely comprise of verb phrase fronting only ever exhibit dummy verb insertion. An overview of this patterning is given in (74). The respective generalization is formulated in two parts in (75).

(74) *Type of fronting and observed repair*

	Verb fronting only	Verb phrase fronting only
verb copy	Basaa, Berbice Dutch Creole, Edo, Ewe, Fongbe, Gungbe, Haitian Creole, Kisi, Leteh, Nupe, Nweh, Papiamentu, Pichi, Saramaccan, Tuki, Turkish, Vata	
dummy verb		Danish, Hausa, Japanese, Norwegian, Skou, Swedish, Welsh, Wolof

(75) *Generalization II*
   a. If a language allows only verb fronting it exclusively shows a verb doubling repair.
   b. If a language allows only verb phrase fronting it exclusively shows a dummy verb insertion repair.

In the following, I will discuss each generalization and each pattern in turn. The derivation of each of the patterns will be demonstrated based on one language that stands as a placeholder for all languages that show the same pattern. I will start with the attested asymmetric pattern of generalization I, continue with the symmetric verb doubling and symmetric dummy verb insertion patterns and conclude with the verb doubling pattern of generalization II. The pattern of dummy verb insertion in generalization IIb will be discussed in the next section as it currently does not directly follow from the framework.

4.2.1 Generalization I

4.2.1.1 The asymmetric pattern
The asymmetric pattern of generalization I is exemplified here by Asante Twi. As is evident from (76), verb fronting leads to verb doubling (76-a) whereas verb phrase fronting results in dummy verb insertion (76-b) in this language.

(76) a. **Sí**(-é)   na Kofí á-**sí**/*á-yɔ́   dán.
       build-NMLZ FOC Kofi PRF-build/PRF-do house
       'Kofi has BUILT a house.'
   b. [Dán **sí**]-é   na Kofí *á-sí/á-**yɔ́**.
       house build-NMLZ FOC Kofi PRF-build/PRF-do
       'Kofi has BUILT A HOUSE.'   (*Asante Twi*)

Let us first consider how verb phrase fronting is derived which, as argued in section 2.1.3.1, is Ā-movement of the VP. The clause structure of Asante Twi here is based on the one suggested in Kandybowicz (2015). In the narrow syntax, the subject and the VP move to SpecTP and SpecCP respectively, each leaving a copy in their base position (77-a). The fact that the word order inside the VP changes will be discussed in section 5.2.2.

(77)   *Asante Twi verb phrase fronting: Syntax*

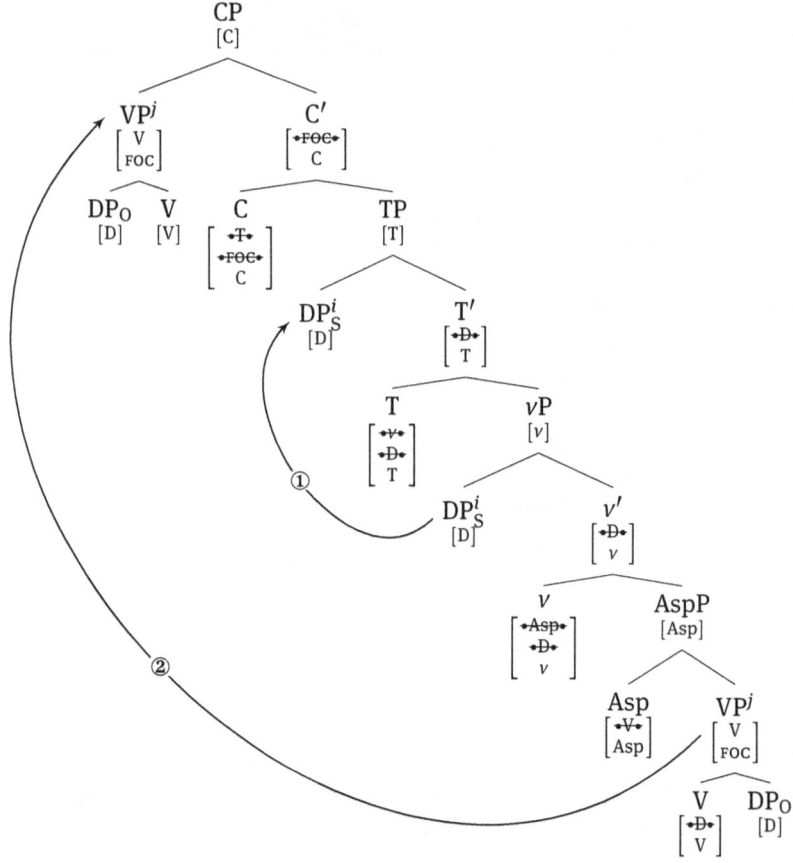

Since this is a case of verb phrase fronting, the movement-inducing FOCUS feature must reside on VP either because it has been projected there from the verbal head or because it has been added upon creation of the VP. Recall also that when an element is copied in order to be internally merged, its already saturated structure-building features will be ignored and remain uncopied and both copies will be assigned an index. Hence, the verb in the higher VP copy does not have the saturated [•D•]

feature of its counterpart in the lower VP copy but both share the same movement-index j.

Note that, in the tree in (77) and all following trees, I will always include subject-movement to SpecTP for two reasons: (i) Subject movement as an instance of regular phrasal movement will serve as a point of reference for the reader with which the treatment of verbal movements can be directly compared; (ii) By inspecting the treatment of subject movement it can be checked that the system does not in any way negatively affect regular phrasal movements..

The structure in (77) will then be sent off to the post-syntactic module, where according to our assumptions operations – including head-movement – apply in a strictly ordered fashion. As already mentioned in section 2.1.3.1, Kandybowicz (2015) argues that the verbal head moves to at least Asp, even higher up to T under the right circumstances (see also Kobele & Torrence 2006). Hence, we would expect V to head-move to Asp, thereby leaving the lower VP copy and evading subsequent deletion. But this is not what we observe in (76-b). Rather, the lower V does not occur anywhere in the sentence. Instead, a dummy verb yɔ takes its place. Consequently, copy deletion must apply before head movement in Asante Twi, and deletes the lower VP copy before the verb can move to Asp. The derivation in the post-syntax thus proceeds as depicted in (78): Copy deletion applies first and deletes the lower copies of DP_S and VP (step ①) as they fulfill neither clause a. nor clause b. of the definition of Copy Deletion (62), given again in (79). The higher copies both fulfill clause a., they each c-command another copy of the same element (i.e. with the same index) and are not c-commanded by another copy of the same element themselves. Deletion will be indicated by boxing. I adopt the most natural assumption that deletion of a phrasal level category entails deletion of all material contained in it.

(78) *Asante Twi verb phrase fronting: Post-syntax (CD ≺ HM)*

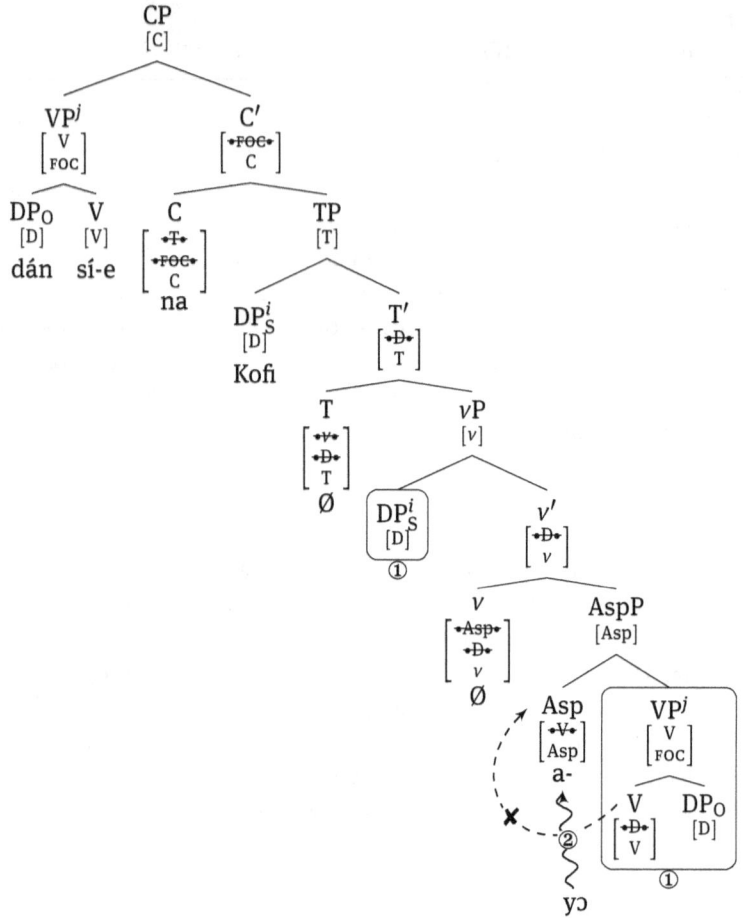

(79) *Copy Deletion (CD)*
In a structure that contains multiple copies $X_1^i, X_2^i, \ldots, X_n^i$ of a constituent X (i.e. several elements 1–n that share the same movement-assigned index i) delete every X_n^i that does not fulfill a. or b.
  a. X_m^i c-commands X_b^i and there is no other X_c^i such that X_c^i c-commands X_m^i, or
  b. X_m^i is a head.

Subsequent head movement of V is bled (step ✘) and insertion of the dummy verb yɔ 'do' takes place as a Last Resort to enable spell out of the aspectual affix a- (step ②).

Asante Twi's dummy verb insertion in verb phrase fronting is therefore a consequence of its applying of copy deletion before head movement in the post-syntactic component of the grammar. Let us now turn to the question, how the language's verb doubling is derived in verb fronting structures. In this case, as already suggested in section 2.1.3.1, it is not the verb phrase that undergoes Ā-movement, but rather the verbal head alone. The FOCUS feature thus must not have been projected up to the VP level. In the narrow syntax, the subject and the verbal head move to SpecTP and SpecCP respectively (80).

(80) *Asante Twi verb fronting: Syntax*

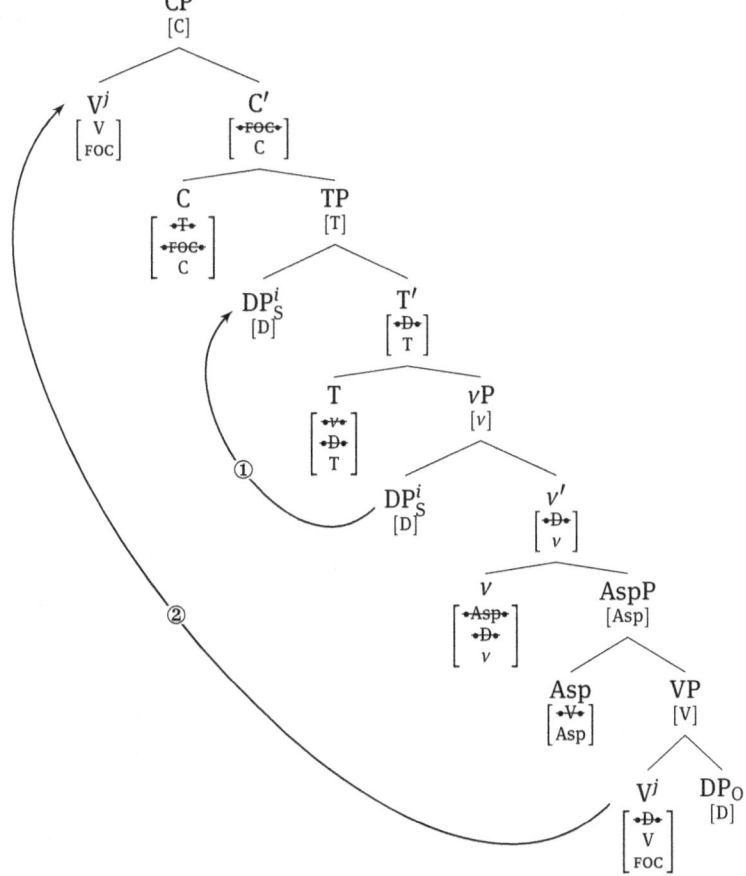

Crucially, again the saturated [•D•] feature of the verb is not copied alongside the FOCUS and category feature and therefore does not occur on the verb in SpecCP. The structure is then transferred to the post-syntactic component where copy deletion applies first (81). According to its definition (79), the lower subject copy is deleted while the higher one is retained. If the derivation proceeded analogous to the one for verb phrase fronting (78), we would expect the lower V copy to be deleted as well retaining only the one in SpecCP. However, this is not what happens. Consider first the high V copy. It c-commands the low V copy and is not itself c-commanded by another V copy with the same index thereby conforming to clause a. of (79) and being exempt from copy deletion as expected. The low V copy, on the other hand, does not c-command another V copy but is itself c-commanded by the high V copy. It thus does not fulfill clause a. of (79). However, as it still bears the saturated [•D•] feature, it qualifies as a head and is thereby excepted from copy deletion through clause b. of (79). Therefore, both copies of the verb stay in the structure until head movement applies.

(81)   *Asante Twi verb fronting: Post-syntax (CD ≺ HM)*

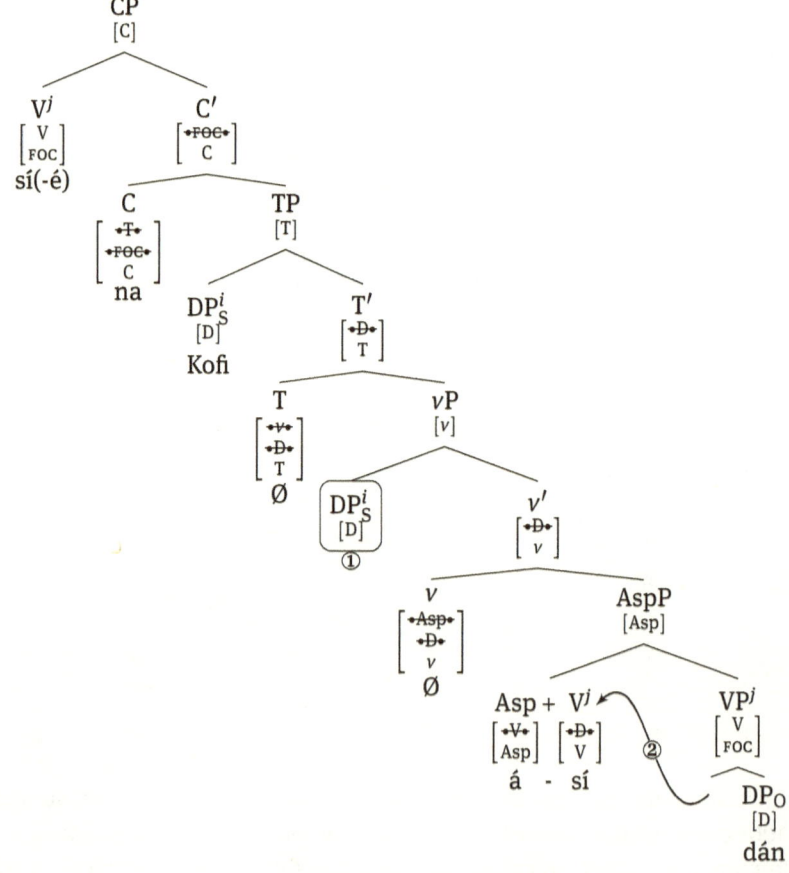

The lower V copy then head moves to Asp as an instance of regular V-to-Asp(-to-T) movement. Post-syntactic head movement does not leave any copies (cf. Boeckx & Stjepanović 2001, Sauerland & Elbourne 2002). The main motivation for the existence of copies came from the fact a displaced element may nonetheless be interpreted in its base position. However, if head movement takes place at PF and interpretation is located at LF then it makes no sense to postulate head movement copies as PF operations cannot influence LF operations. Furthermore, PF evidently comprises of a dedicated operation to rid itself of superfluous copies created in the narrow syntax. Copies thus seem to have a somewhat bothersome status at PF. The generation of additional copies in the post-syntax would be at odds with this general aversion against copies in this component. Thus, after head movement of V to Asp, there are still only two V copies in the structure both of which are overtly pronounced.

Despite the fact that copy deletion applies before head movement, which should give rise to consistent dummy verb insertion, verb doubling occurs in verb fronting in Asante Twi. This is due to the verb being Ā-head moved to SpecCP in the narrow syntax. This movement results in two copies of the verb the lower one of which still retains its head status. Therefore, none of the two copies can be affected by copy deletion because the higher one c-commands the lower one and is not itself c-commanded by an even higher V copy whereas the lower copy is a head. The fact that verb fronting involves Ā-head movement, which leads to the lowest copy having the special property of being a head, thus neutralizes the effect of the order of application between copy deletion and head movement in the post-syntactic module.

4.2.1.2 The symmetric verb doubling pattern

An example for a language that has a symmetric verb doubling pattern is Hebrew. Fronting of a verbal category in this languages gives rise to verb doubling independent of whether the fronted constituent is a verb or a verb phrase (82).

(82) a. **Liknot**, hi **kanta** et ha-praxim.
buy.INF she bought ACC the-flowers
'As for buying, she bought the flowers.'
b. [**Liknot** et ha-praxim], hi **kanta**.
buy.INF ACC the-flowers she bought
'As for buying the flowers, she bought (them).'

(*Hebrew*, Landau 2006: 37)

Beginning with the derivation of verb phrase fronting in (83), first, in narrow syntax, V merges with the object DP, the resulting VP is selected by and merged with *v*, which also introduces the subject DP. After merge of T, the subject DP moves to SpecTP, i.e. a copy of the DP is created and merged with T′ (step ①). Eventually, C is merged and triggers movement of the VP into SpecCP (step ②).

(83) *Hebrew verb phrase fronting: Syntax*

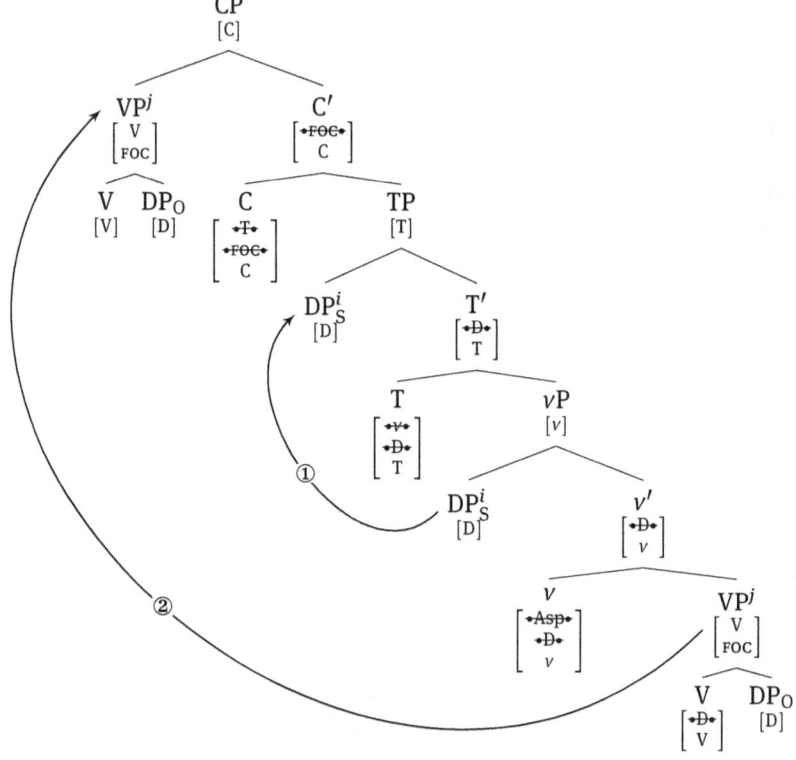

The FOCUS feature here, as in Asante Twi, is either projected to VP from V or is directly inserted on VP upon its creation. As mentioned before, two copies of the same item are marked as such by being assigned a movement-index, thus the subject DPs have the index *i* while the VP copies bear the index *j*.

This structure is then transferred to the post-syntactic component where head movement and copy deletion take place. Note that according to Landau (2006: 41) all verbs in Hebrew raise to T. Thus, the surface structure with two overt copies of the same verb indicates that head movement applies before copy deletion such that the verb can move from the lower VP copy up to T (step ①) before the former is deleted (step ②). This derivation is depicted in (84). As mentioned before, post-syntactic head movement does not leave any copies or traces.

(84) *Hebrew verb phrase fronting: Post-syntax (HM < CD)*[18]

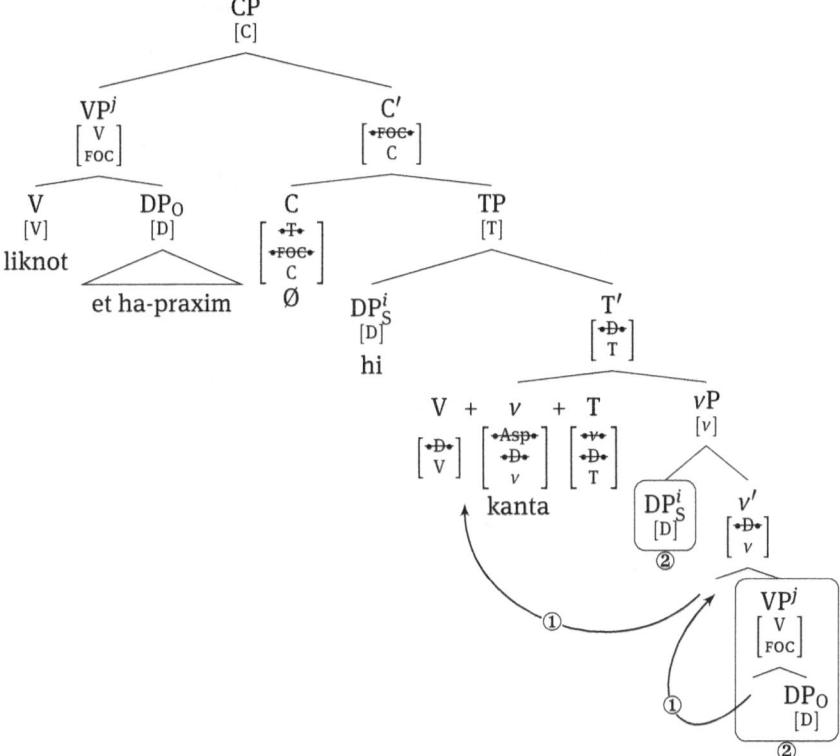

The two lower copies here, one of the subject and the other of the VP, are deleted because they do not fulfill either of the two clauses in the definition of copy deletion that would exempt them from deletion. The respective higher copies, however, both conform to clause a. by c-commanding but not themselves being c-commanded by a copy of the same element. Hence, they evade deletion. The fact that the verb copy originating inside the lower VP copy has left the VP does not disqualify it as a copy of VP because both the high and the low VP copy still bear the same index marking them as copies of each other and therefore subjecting them to closer inspection and possibly deletion by copy deletion. Equally, although the low V copy originated inside the to-be-deleted VP copy it is not itself subject to deletion.

---

18 There is a simplification here: Landau (2006) convincingly argues that the constituent that is fronted in Hebrew VP fronting is *v*P rather than VP. This does not affect the argumentation since V-to-T movement allows V to evacuate the *v*P as well as the VP and thus evade deletion. I treat the constituent as a VP here for reasons of simplicity, exposition, and comparability.

This is because elements contained inside a copy do not bear a movement-induced index unless they have themselves taken part in their own separate movement relation (a situation that will arise in remnant movement constructions as we will see later on). They are therefore not identifiable as (a part of) a copy and will not be affected by copy deletion. Consequently, Hebrew's order of head movement applying before copy deletion in the post-syntax enables the verb to vacate the lower VP copy before it is deleted which results in two V copies being pronounced on the surface, one in the VP in SpecCP and the other in the V+v+T complex.

The derivation of verb fronting is very similar. As argued by Landau (2006), Hebrew verb fronting is Ā-head movement rather than remnant movement. Thus, the only difference between the derivation of verb phrase fronting and that of verb fronting is the size of the moved constituent. This can be modelled as the difference between projecting the FOCUS feature up to the VP level or retaining it on the verbal head. In the latter case, when the C head is merged with TP, it attracts the verbal head with the FOCUS feature which is copied and merged in SpecCP as in (85).

(85)   *Hebrew verb fronting: Syntax*

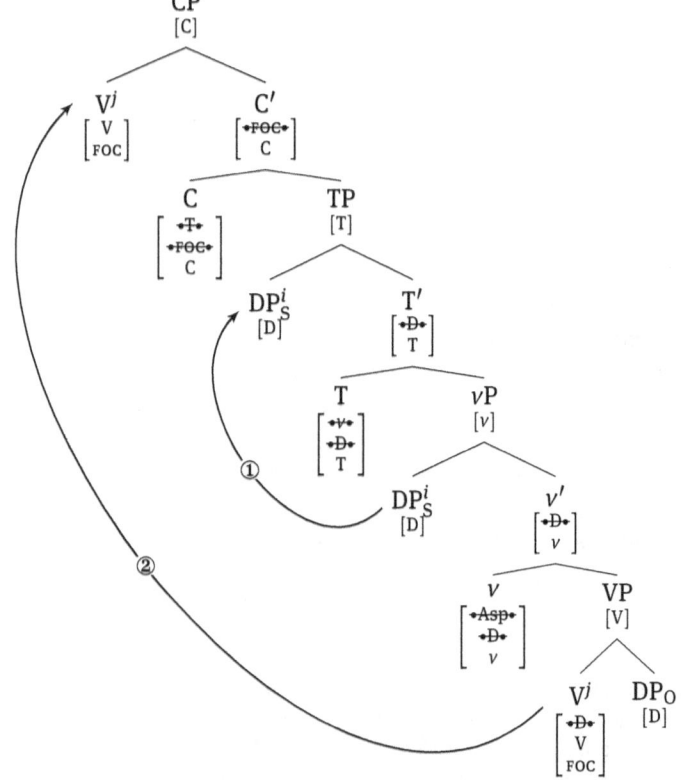

Once transferred to the post-syntactic module, this structure is first subjected to head movement, which displaces the lower V copy to v and T (step ①) as was the case in verb phrase fronting, too. Then, copy deletion applies (step ②). Of the two subject copies, the lower one is deleted as it is neither a head (clasue b.), nor does it c-command another subject copy while at the same time being not c-commanded by another subject copy (clause b.). The higher subject copy survives by clause a.; it c-commands the lower subject copy and is not itself c-commanded by any higher subject copy. With regard to the verb copies, we find that both of them are exempt from copy deletion. The higher one c-commands the lower one and there is no V copy that it is c-commanded by, while the lower one still carries the saturated structure-building [•D•] feature, thus qualifying as a head and as such evading copy deletion (86).[19]

---

[19] Again, Landau (2006) argues convincingly that what is fronted in Hebrew verb fronting is actually the V+v complex rather than the V alone. Since head movement in the present system takes place in the post-syntax, it counterfeeds syntactic $\bar{\text{A}}$-head movement of the V+v complex to SpecCP. One would thus have to assume that both V and v move to SpecCP independently in the syntax leaving a copy each as in (i).

(i) Syntax
     $[_{CP}\ v^k\ [_{C'}\ V^j\ [_{C'}\ C\ [_{TP}\ DP^i_S\ [_{T'}\ T\ [_{vP}\ DP^i_S\ [_{v'}\ v^k\ [_{VP}\ V^j\ DP_O\ ]]]]]]]]$

Post-syntactically, both the copy of V in base position and the one in SpecCP head-move to their respective copy of v resulting in a doubling of V+v on the surface (ii). Subsequent copy deletion could not delete the lower copies as they are both heads.

(ii) Post-syntax
     $[_{CP}\ V^j+v^k\ [_{C'}\ \ [_{C'}\ C\ [_{TP}\ DP^i_S\ [_{T'}\ T\ [_{vP}\ DP^i_S\ [_{v'}\ V^j+v^k\ [_{VP}\ \ DP_O\ ]]]]]]]]$

Alternatively, one could pursue a phase-based approach to spell-out, where head movement of V-to-v can feed further syntactic movement of the V+v complex to SpecCP. This is only possible if the entire phase is sent off to PF with its head and edge but not its domain accessible to further syntactic operations as argued for by Fox & Pesetsky (2003, 2005), Svenonius (2004, 2005), Fowlie (2010), Richards (2011) and Aelbrecht (2012). Under this premise, the entire vP phase would be transferred to PF upon completion. PF operations would apply and potentially alter the edge and head, e.g. creating a complex V+v head by head movement. This altered edge/head could then be affected by further syntactic operations like $\bar{\text{A}}$-head movement. Note that this approach is completely compatible with the present assumptions about syntax and the order of operations in the post-syntax. For now, I treat the fronted constituent as a bare V head for reasons of exposition and comprehensibility.

(86)   Hebrew verb fronting: Post-syntax (HM ≺ CD)

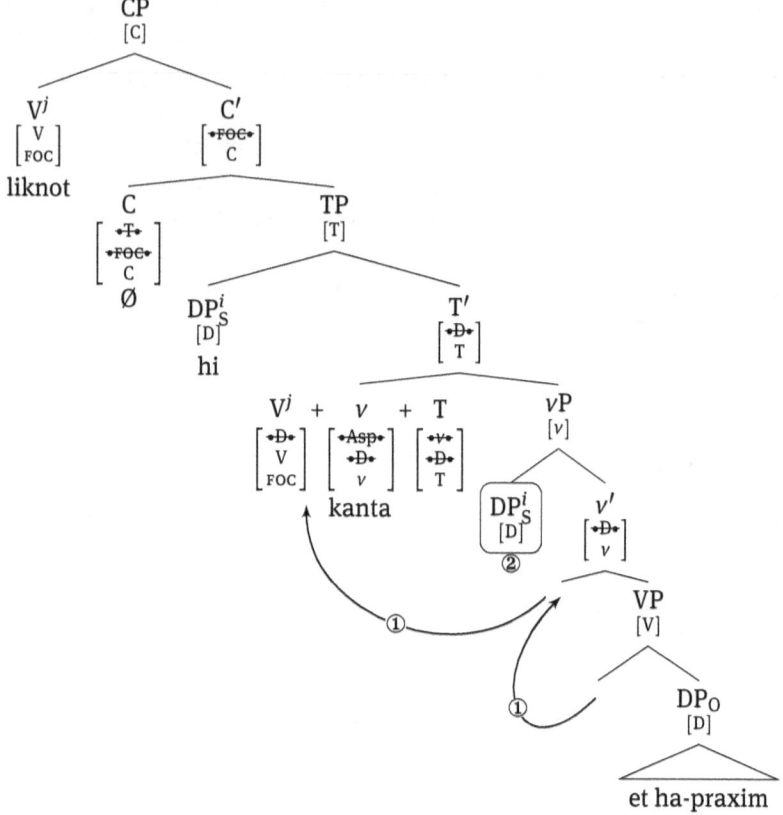

Thus, Hebrew exhibits symmetric verb doubling because it has an order of operations where head movement precedes copy deletion. In verb phrase fronting, the verb moves out of the deletion site before actual deletion takes place which results in two V copies being present in the structure. In verb fronting, the lower copy of the verb movement chain qualifies as a head and therefore evades deletion.

4.2.1.3 The symmetric dummy verb insertion pattern

Let us turn to the symmetric pattern of dummy verb insertion exemplified here by German. Examples of verb and verb phrase fronting are given again in (87).

(87)   a.   **Waschen tut** er das Auto nie.
            wash.INF does he the car   never
            'He never washes the car.'

b. [Das Auto **waschen**] **tut** er nie.
   the car wash.INF does he never
   'Something that he never does is wash the car.'

   (*German*, Diedrichsen 2008: 221)

German, a V2 language, requires the finite verb in main clauses to occupy the second position. In (87), though, the main verb is part of the (fronted) first constituent. Rather than solving this problem by copying the main verb, a semantically largely vacuous dummy verb *tun* 'do' is placed into the relevant position.

As show in section 4.2.1.1 for Asante Twi, a language showing dummy verb insertion with verb phrase fronting has to have the order of operations CD ≺ HM. In the derivation of German verb phrase fronting, the TP is derived as usual. Upon merge of C, the TOPIC-marked verb phrase is copied and merged in SpecCP (88).

(88)   *German verb phrase fronting: Syntax*

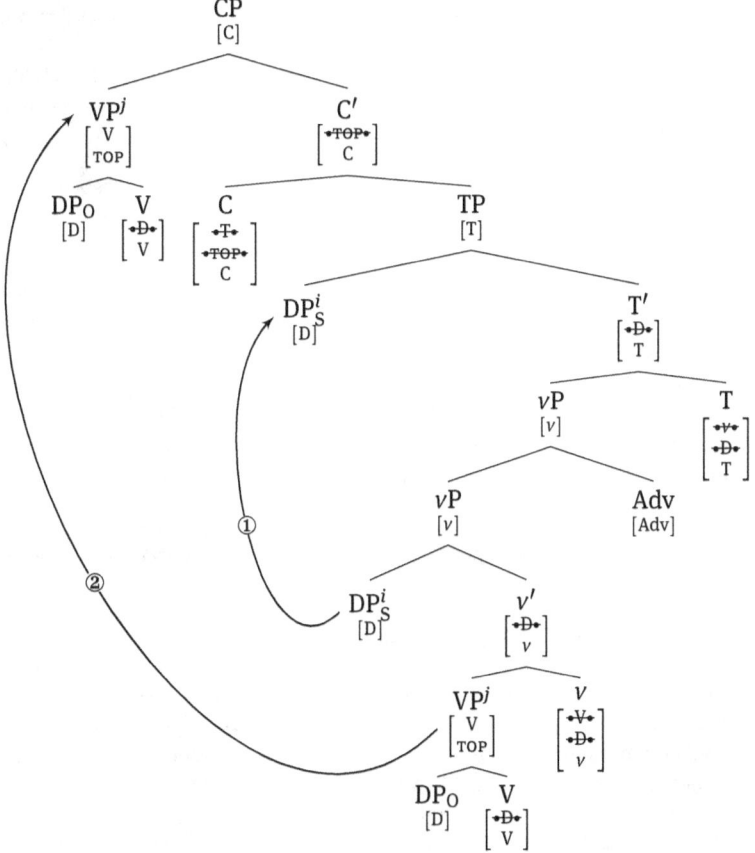

This structure is shipped to the post-syntactic component where copy deletion and head movement apply in this order (89).[20],[21] Even though there is no direct empirical evidence for V-to-T movement in German (or, in fact, for the existence of T at all, see Haider 2010), the status of V-to-C movement in verb second sentences is uncontroversial. As example (87-b) is a verb second sentence, V-to-C movement should in principle take place. However, this is obviously not the case. This is due to copy deletion applying before head movement. The lower copies of the subject and the VP are deleted (step ①) because they do not c-command but are themselves c-commanded by another copy of the subject and the VP respectively (clause a. in the definition of copy deletion). The higher copies are not affected as they c-command the lower copies but are not themselves c-commanded by any

---

20 I explicitly make no claim about the highly controversial issue of subject movement or the existence of T in German here (for discussion see e.g. Haider 2010). As mentioned on page 157, subject movement is included in the derivation solely as an example of regular phrasal movement to be compared with whichever verbal movement takes place.

21 A potential problem for this claim is so-called multiple fronting in German (i) (from Bildhauer & Cook 2010) where two DPs appear in the prefield (i.e. before the verb in a V2 sentence) that can usually only contain one constituent.

(i) [$_{DP}$ Dem   Saft] [$_{DP}$ eine   kräftigere   Farbe] geben
      DEF.M.SG.DAT juice   INDEF.F.SG.ACC strong.COMP.F.SG.ACC colour   give.3PL.PRES
     Blutorangen.
     blood.orange.PL
     'Blood oranges give the juice a stronger colour.'

One possible analysis of data like these is that a VP containing the trace of the verbal head has been moved to SpecCP (Müller 1998). Under the present assumptions, however, such headless VP fronting is underivable because post-syntactic head movement comes too late to create a headless VP that could be fronted in syntax. Instead, one would expect full VP fronting and dummy verb insertion as in (87-b), which is also a possible option (ii).

(ii) [$_{VP}$ Dem   Saft eine   kräftigere   Farbe geben   ] tun
      DEF.M.SG.DAT juice INDEF.F.SG.ACC strong.COMP.F.SG.ACC colour give.INF do.3PL.PRES
     Blutorangen.
     blood.orange.PL
     'Blood oranges give the juice a stronger colour.'

However, recent accounts of multiple fronting treat it either as involving movement of more than one constituent into SpecCP (Lötscher 1985, Speyer 2008) or as fronting of a VP that contains a silent verbal head rather than an actual trace of the overt verb (Fanselow 1993, St. Müller 2005, 2015). Both of these analyses are compatible with the assumptions in this book and under both analyses the absence of any kind of dummy verb insertion or verb doubling is the expected outcome because in both cases, the main verb would remain inside the TP domain in narrow syntax and can later undergo head movement to C in the post-syntax.

higher copies. Subsequent head movement of V-to-C cannot apply (step ✗) since the movee does not exist anymore. However, any movement of v-to-T-to-C (if it actually exists in German) may go forth unhindered.

(89) *German verb phrase fronting: Post-syntax (CD ≺ HM)*

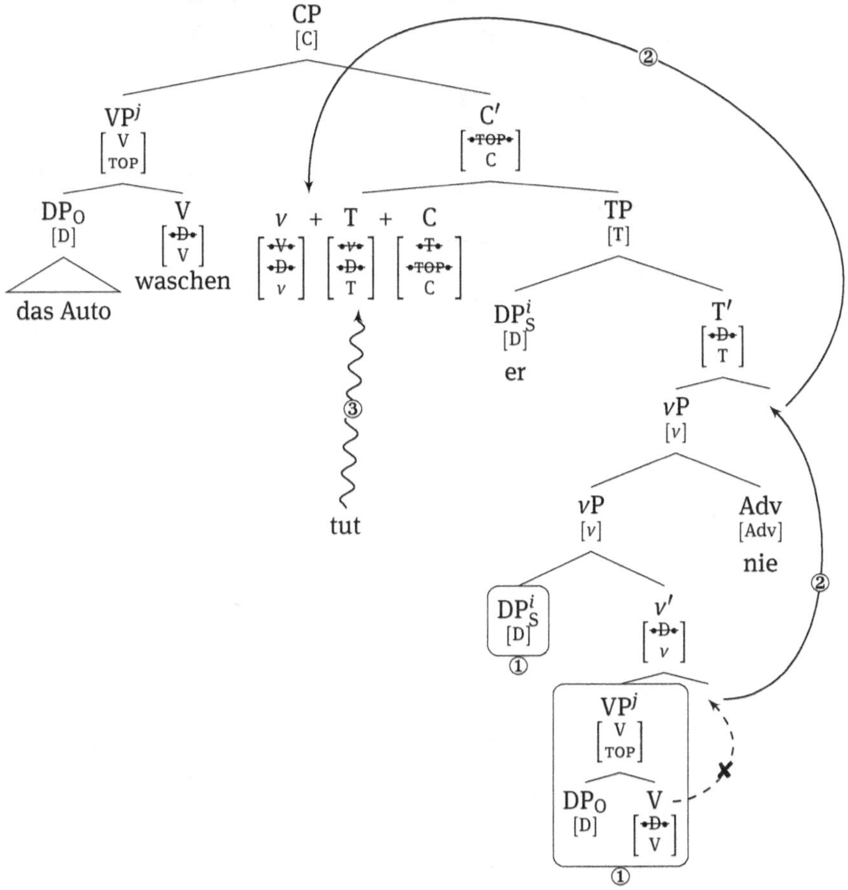

As a Last Resort to either satisfy the V2-requirement or provide a host for expression of finiteness or both, the dummy verb *tun* 'do' is inserted into the complex in C-position (step ③). Thus, copy deletion bleeds subsequent head movement of the main verb to C which leads to the dummy verb repair seen in verb phrase fronting. In this regard, German is like Asante Twi, where copy deletion also bleeds head movement of the main verb to a higher functional head. With respect to verb fronting, however, German differs from Asante Twi as it arguably makes use of remnant VP movement (see den Besten & Webelhuth 1990, Grewendorf & Sabel

1994, Koopman 1997, Müller 1998, 2014, Hinterhölzl 2002). As this movement is regular phrasal movement of a VP bereft of its object(s) we expect the order of post-syntactic operations to have exactly the same effect as in verb phrase fronting, namely copy deletion bleeding head movement which results in the insertion of a dummy verb. Consider the derivation of German verb fronting in (90). In order to create a remnant VP, the object has to scramble out of it. There is considerable disagreement in the field about what kind of movement (if at all) scrambling is and which position it targets (see Karimi 2005, for an overview). To be explicit, I assume scrambling to be movement to SpecvP here but nothing hinges on that. Thus, upon merge of v, the object moves to SpecvP (step ①) before the subject is introduced. The derivation continues by merger of T, subject movement to SpecTP (step ②), merger of C, and, eventually, movement of the remnant VP to SpecCP.

(90)   *German verb fronting: Syntax*

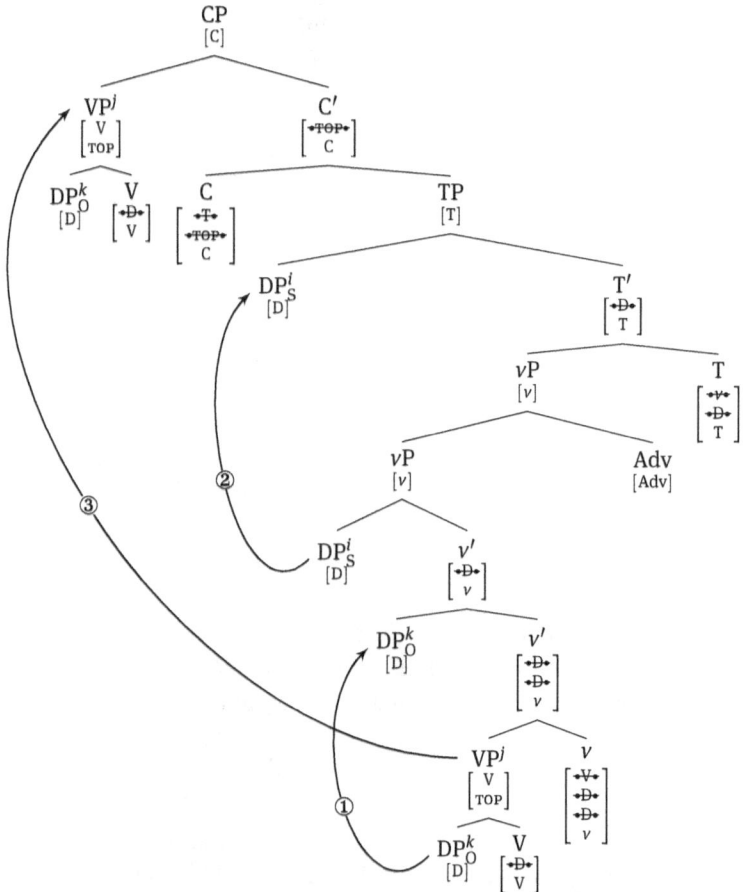

4.2 Deriving the typology

Note that since this analysis is couched in the copy theory, no actual remnant is created in syntax. Rather, compared to a derivation where no remnant-creating movement has taken place, there exists an additional copy of the object DP outside of the VP in (90). Moreover, all instances of the object DP bear the same movement-induced index k.

When this structure is transferred to the post-syntactic module, copy deletion applies before head movement as established above. Now, the crucial difference to regular verb phrase fronting is that there are three movements involved here, the object movement, the subject movement, and the VP movement, the copies of which are all evaluated by copy deletion simultaneously. Nonetheless, let me walk you through the evaluation in a stepwise fashion, to be clear about how the mechanism determines which copies are deleted and which ones are kept. For ease of comprehension, the definition of copy deletion is again provided in (91).

(91) *Copy Deletion (CD)*
In a structure that contains multiple copies $X_1^i, X_2^i, \ldots, X_n^i$ of a constituent X (i.e. several elements 1–n that share the same movement-assigned index i) delete every X_n^i that does not fulfill a. or b.
    a. X_m^i c-commands X_b^i and there is no other X_c^i such that X_c^i c-commands X_m^i, or
    b. X_m^i is a head.

First, consider the copies of the subject movement. The higher copy in SpecTP c-commands the lower copy in Spec$v$P. It is not itself c-commanded by some other copy of the subject DP, therefore, it conforms to clause a. of (91) and will not be deleted. The lower subject copy, however, does not c-command some other subject copy but is itself c-commanded by the higher subject copy. Since it is also not a head, it is eligible for deletion. Now let us turn to the three object copies, to which I will refer based on their position in the tree as the low, the middle, and the high object copy. The high object copy is not a head and also does not c-command any of the other object copies. Although it is not itself c-commanded by another object copy, it neither fulfills clause a. nor clause b. of (91) and is consequently deleted. Importantly, this step is the creation of the remnant VP in SpecCP. The middle object copy in Spec$v$P is not a head, but it c-commands the low object copy and is itself not inside the c-command domain of any other object copy. It is therefore exempt from deletion by clause a. of (91). The low object copy neither conforms to clause a., as it does not c-command but is c-commanded by the middle object copy, nor to clause b., as it is not a head. It will hence be deleted. This leaves us with the two copies of VP, of which the higher one evades deletion because it respects clause a.: It c-commands the lower VP copy and is not itself c-commanded by some higher VP copy. In contrast, the lower VP copy undergoes deletion because it shows the opposite properties of not c-commanding another VP copy but itself being c-commanded by the higher VP copy.

(92)   *German verb fronting: Post-syntax (CD ≺ HM)*

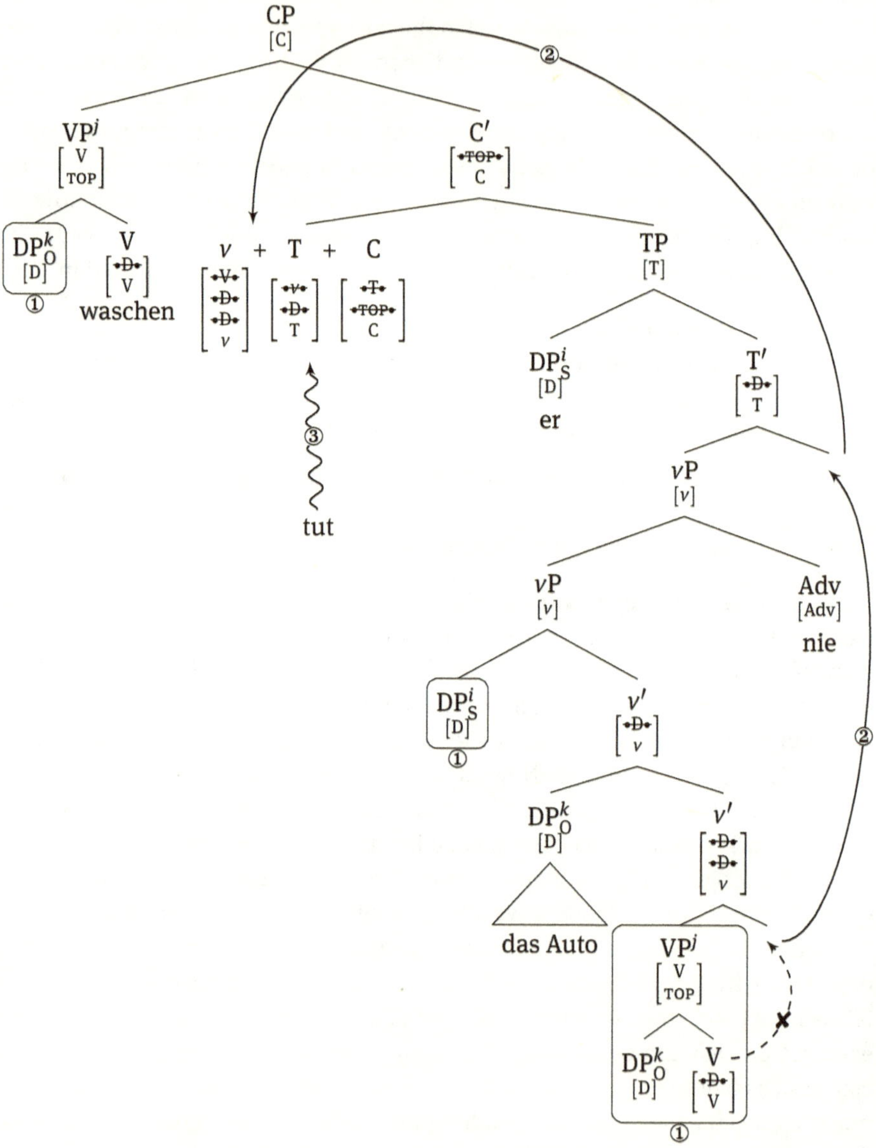

Together with the lower VP copy, of which it is a part the lower V has undergone deletion. Subsequent head movement can therefore not raise V up to *v* and T and C (step ✘). The non-deleted functional head *v*, however, as in verb phrase fronting may move to T and C (step ②). As the resulting complex in C-position lacks a main verb, the dummy *tun* 'do' is inserted to satisfy the V2-requirement and act as a host for expression of finiteness features such as tense and agreement.

The bleeding order of copy deletion before head movement, thus, inevitably leads to dummy verb insertion in case the lower verb copy is not itself marked with a movement-induced index which is the case if verb fronting is brought about by syntactic movement of a remnant verb phrase.

4.2.1.4 The gap and a second symmetric verb doubling pattern

So far, we have seen how the interaction of the different orders of post-syntactic operations (CD < HM vs. HM < CD) and the type of movement in verb fronting (Ā-head movement of V vs. remnant VP movement) derives the three attested repair patterns in verbal fronting constructions. The asymmetric pattern of Asante Twi is the result of an order where copy deletion precedes head movement and verb fronting involves Ā-head movement of the verb. If a language differs from this in having the reverse order of operations, i.e. head movement preceding copy deletion, like Hebrew does, the result is a symmetric pattern of verb doubling. On the other hand, if a language differs from Asante Twi in using remnant movement to front a verb, like German does, then its repair pattern is one of symmetric dummy verb insertion. The interplay of the two factors and the resulting patterns can be summarized as in (93).

(93)   *Interaction of order of operations and movement type (incomplete)*

	Ā-head movement	Remnant VP movement
CD < HM	asymmetric pattern (Asante Twi)	symmetric dummy verb insertion (German)
HM < CD	symmetric verb doubling (Hebrew)	???

Crucially, one interaction of the two factors has not yet featured in our discussion, namely the one where the order of operations is head movement before copy deletion as in Hebrew, but where verb fronting is brought about by remnant movement just like in German. This combination, however, does not give rise to the hitherto unattested asymmetric pattern, namely verb doubling in verb phrase fronting and dummy verb insertion in verb fronting, as one might have expected. Rather, it results in a symmetric pattern of verb doubling like the one instantiated in Hebrew. The reason for this is that the order of operations generally determines whether verb doubling occurs (HM ≺ CD) or not (CD ≺ HM) because copy deletion can bleed head movement which is necessary in order for verb doubling to occur. This is best visible in verb phrase fronting.

(94) Order of operations and effected repair in verb phrase fronting

Order	Repair	Languages
CD ≺ HM	dummy verb insertion	German, Asante Twi, ...
HM ≺ CD	verb doubling	Hebrew, Russian, ...

Now in verb fronting, this effect of the order of operations is retained if verb fronting is movement of a remnant verb phrase. In the copy theory, a remnant verb phrase is a full verb phrase in the syntax (see (90)), therefore verb fronting as remnant movement should behave exactly like verb phrase fronting. Ā-head movement, however, neutralizes the influence of the order of operations. Crucially, this neutralization works in one direction only, namely, it annihilates the bleeding relation between copy deletion and subsequent head movement. This is due to the head status of the lowest copy in an Ā-head movement chain, which renders that copy unable to undergo copy deletion. In a nutshell, Ā-head movement leads to exceptional non-deletion of a low verb copy (95).

(95) Neutralizing effects of movement types

Fronting	Movement type	Order of PF operations	
		HM ≺ CD	CD ≺ HM
verb phrase fronting	full VP	verb doubling	dummy verb
	Y	verb doubling	**verb doubling**
verb fronting	remnant VP	verb doubling	dummy verb
	V-head	verb doubling	**verb doubling**
	X	**dummy verb**	dummy verb

Importantly, there is no additional type of movement X in verbal fronting such that it can be used instead of remnant movement and Ā-head movement in verb fronting and exceptionally leads to dummy verb insertion despite the order HM ≺ CD. Equally, no type of movement Y for verb phrase fronting exists such that it exceptionally allows verb doubling despite the order CD ≺ HM. In order for a language with the order HM ≺ CD to show the unattested asymmetric pattern, it would have to use full VP movement in verb phrase fronting and the hypothetical movement X in verb fronting. A language with the order CD ≺ HM would be required to employ remnant VP movement in verb fronting and the hypothetical movement Y in verb phrase fronting. As those movements do not exist, the unattested asymmetrical pattern cannot be derived in the present analysis thereby correctly predicting it to be absent from the typology.

The full cross-classification of the available movement types with the orders of operations is given in (96). Of the four logically possible repair patterns in verbal fronting only three are generated by the grammatical system because two of the four combinations of movement type and order of operations converge on the same repair pattern.

(96) *Interaction of order of operations and movement type (complete)*

	Ā-head movement	remnant VP movement
CD ≺ HM	asymmetric pattern (Asante Twi)	symmetric dummy verb insertion (German)
HM ≺ CD	symmetric verb doubling (Hebrew)	symmetric verb doubling (Polish)

A language that instantiates the fourth combination of properties is Polish, where verbal fronting consistently leads to verb doubling as attested to in (97).

(97) a. **Wypić** (to) Marek **wypije** herbatę, ale nie wypije kawy.
    drink.INF TO Marek will-drink tea   but not will-drink coffee
    'As for drinking, Marek will drink tea, but he will not drink coffee.'
  b. [**Wypić** herbatę] (to) Marek **wypije,** ale nie wypije kawy.
    drink.INF tea   TO Marek will-drink but not will-drink coffee
    'As for drinking tea, Marek will drink it, but he will not drink coffee.'
                                                        (*Polish*, Bondaruk 2012: 55)

The derivation of (97-b) proceeds just like the derivation of Hebrew verb phrase fronting. First, the VP is built, which is selected by v, which then introduces the subject DP. According to Witkoś (1998), the vP is then merged with an Asp head. Upon merger of the T head with AspP, the subject moves to SpecTP. When C enters the derivation, it attracts the TOPIC-marked VP into its specifier, resulting in a structure like (98).[22]

---

[22] Like in Hebrew, the fronted constituent in verb phrase fronting is actually vP rather than VP (see Bondaruk 2009: 69, for arguments in favour of this). A more proper structure of verb phrase fronting would hence be (i).

(98) *Polish verb phrase fronting: Syntax*

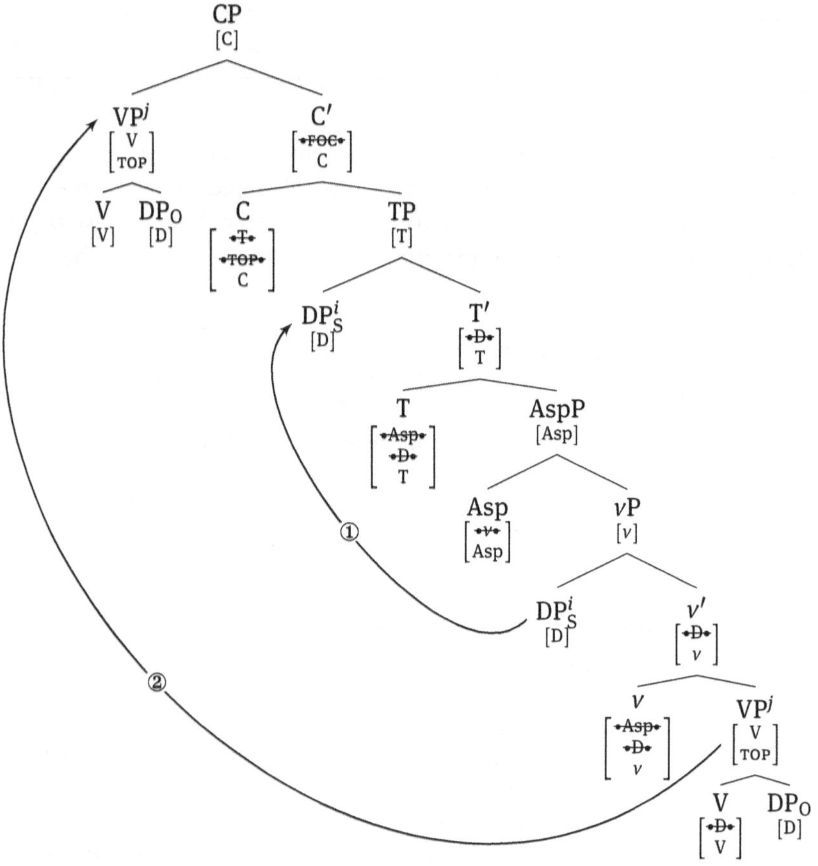

When this structure is delivered to the post-syntactic component, first, head movement applies (step ①). As Witkoś (1998) argues, the verb in Polish standardly raises up to Asp but not to T. Thus, the resulting V+v+Asp complex resides in Asp. Subse-

---

(i) [$_{CP}$ [$_{vP^j}$ DP^i_S [$_{v'}$ v [$_{VP}$ V DP$_O$]]] [$_{C'}$ C [$_{TP}$ DP^i_S [$_{T'}$ T [$_{AspP}$ Asp [$_{vP^j}$ DP^i_S [$_{v'}$ v [$_{VP}$ V DP$_O$]]]]]]]]

As already mentioned, this does not affect the argumentation here, because crucially, the verb head moves as high as Asp in the post-syntax. Since Asp is located higher than both VP and vP the verb leaves the lower copy of the fronted constituent before it is deleted independent of whether it is VP or vP. The additional copy of the subject inside the fronted vP will undergo deletion in the same way that the object copy does in a remnant VP movement structure because it does not c-command any of the lower subject copies thereby not conforming to clause a. of copy deletion. For reasons of consistency and ease of exposition, I simplify Polish verb phrase fronting to be movement of VP rather than vP.

quent copy deletion (step ②) then erases the lower subject copy and the lower VP copy as usual. The main verb, thus, evades deletion by virtue of having moved to outside of the lower VP copy giving rise to verb doubling on the surface (99).

(99) *Polish verb phrase fronting: Post-syntax (HM ≺ CD)*

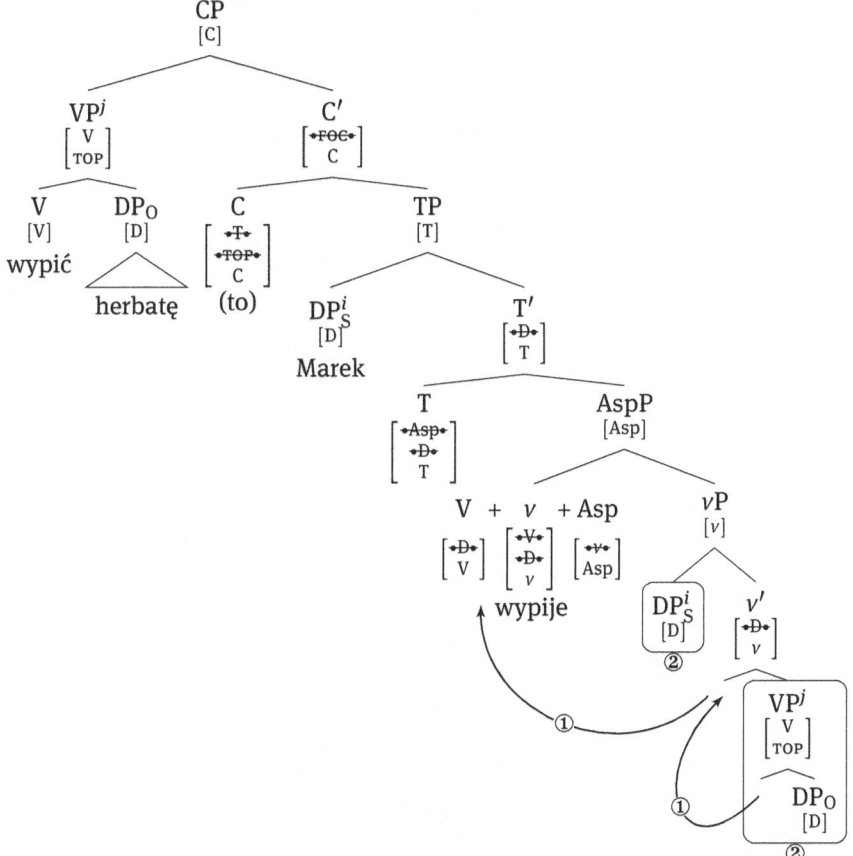

Verb fronting in Polish, in contrast to verb fronting in Hebrew, arguably involves remnant movement rather than Ā-head movement (Bondaruk 2009: 71–73). Thus, its derivation should be very similar to the one for verb phrase fronting with the difference that the object undergoes movement to a position higher than VP (which I will assume to be adjunction to SpecvP for concreteness' sake). In the narrow syntax, the object DP is adjoined to vP (step ①) resulting in the latter's completion. When T is merged, it attracts the subject DP which moves to SpecTP (step ②).

Eventually, C is merged and the FOCUS-marked VP is copied into the specifier position of C (step ③).[23]

(100) *Polish verb fronting: Syntax*

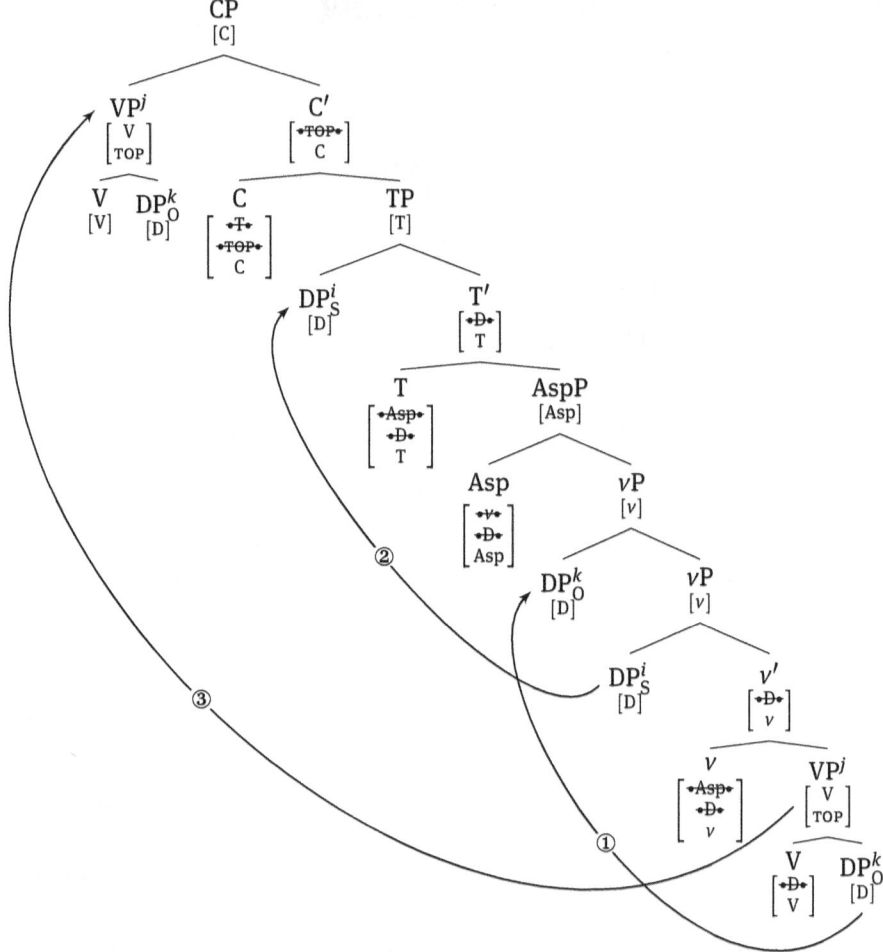

---

[23] At first glance, movement of the subject constitutes a violation of the Minimal Link Condition because there is an intervening DP, the object, between the movement-triggering head T and the moving DP. There are two possible solutions: (i) The movement-triggering features are relativized to a particular feature of the movee (i.e. case) such that the intervening DP does not bear that feature and therefore does not qualify as an intervener; or (ii) object scrambling is late adjunction that applies only after the subject has moved to SpecTP. Option (i) underlies the structures presented here, but nothing hinges on that. Also, I have simplified the structure again such that VP is moved to SpecCP while it is actually a remnant (the lower) *v*P (compare footnote 22).

4.2 Deriving the typology

This structure is transferred to the post-syntax, where head movement applies before copy deletion. The main verb raises to *v* and Asp, creating the V+*v*+Asp complex (step ①). Copy deletion then applies simultaneously to all copies (step ②). The high VP copy is exempt because it conforms to clause a. by c-commanding the low VP copy and not being c-commanded by any higher VP copy. The object copy contained inside it, however, is deleted. Although it is not c-commanded by any higher object copy it also does not c-command any of the two lower object copies. The high subject copy is not deleted due to clause a. The object copy adjoined to *v*P c-commands the low object copy and is not itself c-commanded by an object copy. Hence, it evades deletion. The low VP copy and the low object copy are deleted as they neither fulfill clause a. nor clause b.

(101) *Polish verb fronting: Post-syntax (HM ≺ CD)*

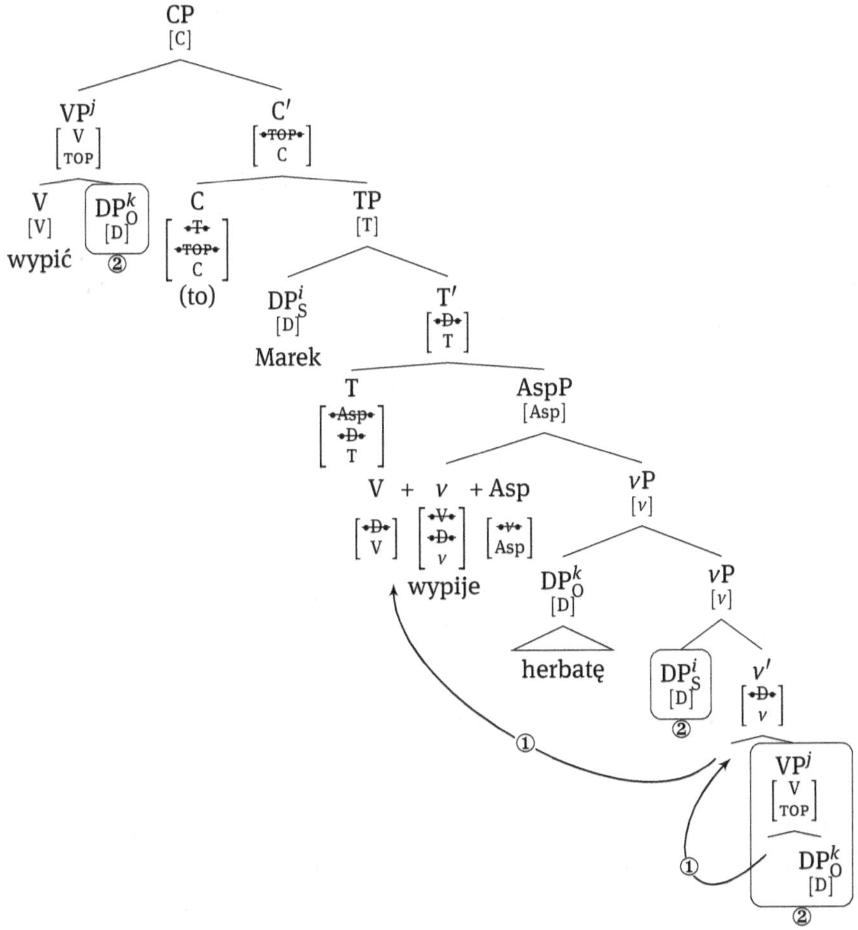

On the surface, the verb is then pronounced twice, once in the remnant VP in SpecCP and once in the complex in the Asp-position. The order of head movement before copy deletion in conjunction with remnant VP movement therefore leads to symmetric verb doubling because the verbal head is able to leave the lower VP copy before it is deleted in both verb and verb phrase fronting.

4.2.1.5 Interim summary

In this subsection, I have demonstrated how the interaction between the two language-specific properties order of operations and type of verb-preposing movement can account for the observed typological distribution of repairs in languages that allow both verb and verb phrase fronting (Generalization I). At the heart of the proposal is the bleeding relation between copy deletion and head movement: If copy deletion applies first, the low copy of the verb will be deleted and a dummy verb needs to be inserted as a Last Resort to express finiteness or to satisfy language-particular requirements like the V2-requirement in German. In case the order is inverted and head movement applies before copy deletion, the language will show consistent verb doubling provided that head movement of the verb targets a position outside of the deletion site. This relation between order of operations and observed repairs holds only if verb fronting is brought about by remnant verb phrase movement. The effect of the order of operations CD < HM can be neutralized in verb fronting, if a language allows syntactic $\bar{\text{A}}$-head movement of the verb into the left periphery. In this situation, the lower copy of the verb movement chain qualifies as a head and is thereby exempt from deletion giving rise to the asymmetric repair pattern. A similar neutralization in the other direction, i.e. annihilation of the effect of the order HM < CD such that exceptional deletion of the the head-moved V takes place, is not possible in the current system which accounts for the gap in the typology.

(102) *Interaction of order of operations and movement type (complete)*

	$\bar{\text{A}}$-head movement	Remnant VP movement
CD < HM	asymmetric pattern (Asante Twi)	symmetric dummy verb insertion (German)
HM < CD	symmetric verb doubling (Hebrew)	symmetric verb doubling (Polish)

As (102) shows, HM < CD consistently results in verb doubling in both verb and verb phrase fronting. The order CD < HM, however, only leads to symmetric dummy verb insertion if verb fronting is remnant verb phrase movement. Otherwise, only verb phrase fronting triggers dummy verb insertion whereas verb fronting gives rise to verb doubling.

4.2.2 Generalization II

The second generalization that could be drawn from the assessment of available data on verb doubling concerns languages that only allow for one of the two kinds of verbal fronting. It comes in two parts, which will be treated each on its own terms in the following. First, languages that solely exhibit verb fronting but no verb phrase fronting exclusively evince verb doubling. Second, if only verb phrase fronting is an option in a language but not verb fronting, the language exclusively displays dummy verb insertion. The generalization is formulated again in (103).

(103)   *Generalization II*
    a. If a language allows only verb fronting it exclusively shows a verb doubling repair.
    b. If a language allows only verb phrase fronting it exclusively shows a dummy verb insertion repair.

As we will see, part a. of the generalization straightforwardly follows from the current assumptions. In contrast, part b. escapes a direct derivation but might not be a very strong generalization after all.

4.2.2.1 Verb fronting and verb doubling (Generalization IIa)

A language that falls under the Generalization IIa is Nupe, where verb fronting is grammatical (104-a) but verb phrase fronting is not (104-b, c).

(104)   a. Bi-**ba**   Musa à   **ba** nakàn o.
              RED-cut Musa FUT cut meat   cut/RED-cut FOC
              'It is CUTTING that Musa will do to the meat (as opposed to say, *cooking*.)'   (Kandybowicz 2008: 79)
    b. *[Du-**du**   cènkafa] Musa à   **du** (cènkafa) o.
              RED-cook rice   Musa FUT cook rice   FOC
              'It is COOKING RICE that Musa will do.'
    c. *[Cènkafa du-**du**]   Musa à   **du** (cènkafa) o.
              rice   RED-cook Musa FUT cook rice   FOC
              'It is COOKING RICE that Musa will do.'   (Kandybowicz 2008: 86)

Verb phrase fronting is the surface result of syntactic movement of a VP or *v*P into the left periphery of the clause. For a language like Nupe, that lacks verb phrase fronting it must be the case that for some reason VP movement to SpecCP is not available as schematized in (105).

(105) *Unavailability of syntactic VP movement*
[$_{CP}$ [$_{VP}$ V DP$_O$] [$_{C'}$ C [$_{TP}$ DP$_S$ [$_{T'}$ T [$_{vP}$ v [$_{VP}$ V DP$_O$]]]]]]

Nonetheless, since verb fronting is evidently possible and arguably involves syntactic movement (see the movement diagnostics in section 7.1; and Kandybowicz 2008 for arguments for syntactic movement in Nupe in particular), the language must dispose of some kind of syntactic movement operation to displace the verb. This operation must be Ā-head movement (106) rather than remnant VP movement (107) because, as we have seen in section 4.2.1.3, in the copy theory of movement the latter actually is plain VP movement (preceded by movement of the object) which is not available in the languages under consideration here.

(106) *Ā-head movement of V*
[$_{CP}$ V [$_{C'}$ C [$_{TP}$ DP$_S$ [$_{T'}$ T [$_{vP}$ v [$_{VP}$ V DP$_O$]]]]]]

(107) *Remnant VP movement*
[$_{CP}$ [$_{VP}$ V DP$_O$] [$_{C'}$ C [$_{TP}$ DP$_S$ [$_{T'}$ T [$_{vP}$ DP$_O$ [$_{v'}$ v [$_{VP}$ V DP$_O$]]]]]]]

Having established that languages that exclusively show verb fronting lack syntactic left-peripheral VP movement but must allow Ā-head movement of the verb, it should be obvious why they consistently display verb doubling as a repair rather than dummy verb insertion independently of the order of post-syntactic operations they have.

The lower copy of Ā-head movement inevitably has head status and will as such always be exempt from copy deletion by clause b. The higher copy will always c-command the lower one but not be itself c-commanded by some higher copy of V and thereby evade deletion by clause a. There will, therefore, always be two copies of the verb in the structure that will receive an overt pronunciation.

In a nutshell, Generalization IIa emerges naturally from the present account because verb fronting in languages without verb phrase fronting must be Ā-head movement, which neutralizes the influence of the order of post-syntactic operations such that in addition to the highest copy the lowest one will also never be affected by deletion.

4.2.2.2 Verb phrase fronting and dummy verb insertion (Generalization IIb)

An example for a language that is subject to Generalization IIb is Norwegian. While verb phrase fronting is grammatical with a dummy verb in the canonical verb position (108-a), verb fronting is ungrammatical with both a dummy verb or a copy of the fronted verb (108-b).

(108) a. [(Å) **lese** bøk-er] **gjør**/*leser han hele dag-en.
 to read.INF book.PL-PL.INDEF does/reads he whole day-DEF
 'Reading books he does all day.'
 b. *(Å) lese gjør/leser han bøk-er hele dag-en.
 to read.INF does/reads he book.PL-PL.INDEF whole day-DEF
 'Reading he does to books all day.' (*Norwegian*)

Languages like Norwegian thus appear to allow syntactic verb phrase movement into the left periphery, which generates (108-a), but do not permit either of the two movement types that would bring about verb fronting, namely $\bar{\text{A}}$-head movement of V and remnant VP movement. In order for the latter to be excluded despite VP movement being obviously possible, the language needs to lack any type of remnant-creating movement.[24] By lacking both $\bar{\text{A}}$-head movement and remnant-VP-creating movement, a language is left with only one type of movement for verbal

---

[24] In Norwegian and other Scandinavian languages, this is arguably true for scrambling. However, there is another kind of object movement, namely Object Shift, which applies to pronominal objects and displaces them across an adverb or negation (i).

(i) Jon så den ikke ___den.
 Jon see.PST it NEG
 'John didn't see it.' (*Norwegian*, Anderssen & Bentzen 2012: 1)

A remnant VP created by Object Shift should then be able to undergo movement to SpecCP resulting in verb fronting. As example (ii-b) shows, verb fronting is curiously still ungrammatical despite Object Shift having taken place (as indicated by the pronoun *den* preceding the negation *ikke*).

(ii) a. Do you see his car?
 b. *(Å) **se** **gjør** jeg den ikke, men jeg hører den.
 to see.INF do I it not but I hear it
 'As for seeing, I don't see it but I hear it.' (*Norwegian*, Siri M. Gjersøe p.c.)

Taking into account Holmberg's Generalization (Holmberg 1986, Holmberg & Platzack 1995), which states that Object Shift cannot apply unless the verb has moved out of VP, it immediately becomes clear that Object Shift cannot feed verb fronting because the verb does not leave VP. If it did, thereby enabling Object Shift, the remnant VP would be empty. Object Shift is therefore not the kind of remnant VP-creating movement that could give rise to verb fronting in the relevant languages.

categories, namely full VP movement, which necessarily exclusively leads to full verb phrase fronting.

Syntactic full VP movement, however, is expected to give rise to both dummy verb insertion and verb doubling depending on the order of operations as pointed out in section 4.2.1.4. If copy deletion applies before head movement, the lower V is deleted as part of the lower VP copy before it can move resulting in dummy verb insertion. Conversely, if head movement applies before copy deletion, the lower V gets a chance to raise to a functional head outside of the lower VP copy prior to its deletion resulting in verb doubling. The emergence of Generalization IIb, therefore, comes as a surprise under the current approach.

Considering the very small number of eight languages in the sample that fall under the purported Generalization IIb and taking into account that three of them belong to the same sub-family of the Indo-European phylum, namely Germanic, which apparently has CD < HM as its family order (see German and Dutch), I would like to contend here that Generalization IIb has to be considered as a tendency rather than a true generalization. The fact that all relevant languages in the sample show dummy verb insertion is due partly to pure chance and partly to a bias rather than hard grammatical constraints against verb doubling. To exhibit verb doubling, a language that comprises only of full VP movement, has to have two properties: (i) An order of post-syntactic operations where head movement precedes copy deletion, and additionally (ii) V-to-Asp/v/T/C raising (a requirement that I will come back to in section 5.1). Without actually raising V to some higher functional head, head movement is unable to save the lower V copy from deletion even if the former takes place after the latter. Dummy verb insertion, on the contrary, only presupposes the order where copy deletion applies before head movement. The likelihood for a language with verb phrase fronting only to display dummy verb insertion is therefore higher than the likelihood to exhibit verb doubling. Consequently, in such a small sample of five languages (four from different families plus three Germanic languages) it is expected that most if not all of them show dummy verb insertion.

In a nutshell, Generalization IIb does not follow from the present approach as languages that exclusively display verb phrase fronting use phrasal VP movement, which variably leads to dummy verb insertion or verb doubling depending on the order of post-syntactic operations. However, the sample size is too small to make a strong claim and, in addition, the account predicts a bias in favour of dummy verb insertion for verb phrase fronting only languages. Therefore, Generalization IIb is weakened to be a tendency rather than a strict generalization.

4.2.3 Summary

In this section I have demonstrated how the proposed system derives the various patterns attested in verbal fronting constructions. At the core of the account is the interaction between the type of syntactic movement (or, in other words, the constituency of the moved element) and the order of application between the two post-syntactic operations head movement and copy deletion. There are three movement types, full VP movement, remnant VP movement, and Ā-head movement of V and two orders of operations, HM ≺ CD and CD ≺ HM. As head movement of V counterbleeds copy deletion, the former order consistently results in verb doubling. In the latter order, CD ≺ HM, copy deletion of the VP bleeds head movement of V and the result is dummy verb insertion. Exceptionally, Ā-head movement leads to verb doubling under either order because the lowest V copy is immune to copy deletion by virtue of being a head. The movement types, their associated repairs under the two orders, and their resulting surface configurations are given in (109).

(109) *Movement types, their repairs, and their surface configurations*

	Movement type	Order of PF operations		Surface configuration
		HM ≺ CD	CD ≺ HM	
1	full VP	verb doubling	dummy verb	verb phrase fronting
2	remnant VP	verb doubling	dummy verb	verb fronting
3	V-head	verb doubling	verb doubling	verb fronting

Now, different patterns of verbal fronting are the result of the types of syntactic movement that a particular language permits and the order of operations that it imposes in the post-syntax. The table in (110) shows which combination of movement types gives rise to which repairs in the two verbal fronting constructions (i.e. verb fronting, V-F, and verb phrase fronting, VP-F) under which order of operations.

(110) *Emergence of the typology*

Mvnt(s)	HM ≺ CD			CD ≺ HM		
	V-F	VP-F	Pattern	V-F	VP-F	Pattern
1	—	VV	VP-F only	—	dummy	VP-F only
3	VV	—	V-F only	VV	—	V-F only
1+2	VV	VV	sym. VV	dummy	dummy	sym. dummy
1+3	VV	VV	sym. VV	VV	dummy	asym.
1+2+3	VV	VV	sym. VV	VV/dummy	dummy	???

The first two rows represent languages that display either only verb phrase fronting (row 1) or only verb fronting (row 2). As we see, languages of the first row, that have only VP movement at their disposal and therefore only exhibit verb phrase fronting, may show verb doubling or dummy verb insertion depending on the order of operations. Row 1 thus corresponds to the tendency that formerly featured as Generalization IIb. Languages of the second row, that only comprise of $\bar{\text{A}}$-head movement and therefore only display verb fronting, uniformly employ a verb doubling repair independent of the order of operations. Row 2, hence, accounts for Generalization IIa.[25]

As soon as a language has a combination of two different types of movement (rows 3 and 4), it will feature both verb and verb phrase fronting. If verb fronting is brought about by remnant VP movement (row 3), then the repair, which is determined by the order of operations, will be the same for both kinds of fronting. Thus, row 3 derives symmetric verb doubling and symmetric dummy verb insertion patterns depending on the order operations. If verb fronting is achieved by $\bar{\text{A}}$-head movement (row 4), nothing changes if the order of operations is HM < CD. We still get symmetric verb doubling in this case. However, if the order is CD < HM, verb fronting will trigger verb doubling whereas verb phrase fronting is repaired by dummy verb insertion. This is the asymmetric pattern of Asante Twi and Limbum. Note that of the four different interactions of order and two-movement-combinations two result in the same repair pattern which accounts for the three attested patterns of Generalization I. The unattested asymmetric pattern, namely verb doubling in verb phrase fronting but dummy verb insertion in verb fronting, is therefore not derivable which correctly accounts for its absence.

The last combination of the three movement types is represented in row 5, where all of them are permitted. Under the order HM < CD this combination gives rise to symmetric verb doubling. Under the reverse order of CD < HM, however, it leads to a pattern where verb phrase fronting results in the expected repair of dummy verb insertion whereas verb fronting may optionally trigger either dummy verb insertion or verb doubling. Without further qualifications, like an *ad hoc* ban on combinations of more than two movement types, the present account predicts that there are languages in which such optionality in verb fronting can be oberved. This and other emergent predictions will be presented and examined in the following section.

---

25 The combinations where movement type 2, remnant VP movement, is permitted but movement type 3, full VP movement, is not are left out here because the remnant VP is in fact a full VP under the copy theory of movement and therefore presupposes full VP movement to be possible. Thus, movement type 2 should more accurately be labelled remnant-VP-creating movement.

5 Predictions and further issues

This chapter discusses two major predictions of the approach presented in the previous chapter and attempts to verify them. The first prediction is that there should be cases of gratuitous verb doubling with $\bar{\text{A}}$-head movement, that is verb doubling even below auxiliaries and modals. This predictions is borne out. The second prediction is that there should exist languages which exhibit optionality between verb doubling and dummy verb insertion in verb fronting contexts. Two possible candidate languages for supporting this claim, Basque and Breton, will be discussed and shown to not show the relevant optionality, leaving this prediction unconfirmed. The second section of this chapter is concerned with some further issues raised by the account, namely, how a language can be said to have a certain type of movement at its disposal or not, the relevance of nominalization of the fronted verbal constituent, and a possible explanation for the choice of repair based on the idea that it is conditioned by the need to avoid haplology.

5.1 Emergent predictions

The current system makes a number of interesting empirical predictions concerning the cooccurrence of verbal fronting patterns with certain grammatical processes such as scrambling or V-to-Asp/v/T movement, as well as implicational relations between patterns. In the following, I will introduce these predictions and, where possible, try to determine whether they are borne out or not. In many cases, the available descriptions of specific languages are not detailed enough to resolve this question satisfactorily, but as we will see, most of the predictions find at least some support in the data.

So far, I have given the impression that the interaction of just two factors, the type of movement in verb fronting and the order of post-syntactic operations, underlies the attested patterns of verbal fronting such that almost every pattern, with the exception of the symmetric verb doubling pattern and the verb fronting only pattern, is linked to just one single combination of features. Upon closer inspection, however, it turns out that almost all patterns may result from more than one combination of various independent factors.

As was mentioned several times already, languages where verb fronting involves remnant movement necessarily have to have some kind of remnant-creating movement. Commonly, this movement is assumed to be scrambling as in German. Scrambling, however, is logically independent of VP movement, that is, a language may very well have the option to scramble material out of a VP without having the option of moving that VP itself.

Equally, the general property of a language to head move the verb to some higher functional head like *v* or T, which I will refer to as V-raising, is independent of the order of application between head movement and copy deletion. Thus, a language might display dummy verb insertion in verbal fronting because it has the order CD < HM, but nonetheless exhibit V-to-T movement in clauses where the verbal head is not part of a lower VP copy and therefore not subject to copy deletion.

In fact, if remnant-creating movement and V-raising are treated as separate factors in the typology, the total number of factors that influence the patterns of verbal fronting cross-linguistically is five, where each factor can have two settings:
1. *Ā-head movement*: permitted (✓) vs. forbidden (–)
2. *VP movement* (into the left periphery): permitted (✓) vs. forbidden (–)
3. *Scrambling* (remnant-creating movement): permitted (✓) vs. forbidden (–)
4. *V-raising*: available (✓) vs. not available (–)
5. *Order of operations*: HM < CD vs. CD < HM

The possible combinations of these factors amount to $2^5 = 32$. However, the number of resulting surface patterns of verbal fronting is only 8:
1. absence of fronting of verbal categories
2. only verb fronting with verb doubling
3. only verb phrase fronting with verb doubling
4. only verb phrase fronting with dummy verb insertion
5. both verb and verb phrase fronting with symmetric verb doubling
6. both verb and verb phrase fronting with symmetric dummy verb insertion
7. both verb and verb phrase fronting, the former with verb doubling, the latter with dummy verb insertion
8. both verb and verb phrase fronting, the former with optionally verb doubling or dummy verb insertion, the latter with dummy verb insertion

This reduction from 32 to 8 is due to the fact that several combinations of factors result in the same verbal fronting pattern on the surface. The table in (1) gives an overview of the combinations without going into detail why the combinations lead to exactly these surface patterns.

(1) *Full typological interaction of relevant factors in verbal fronting*

	Factor					Pattern	
	Order	Ā-HM	VP Mov	Scr	V-Rais	V-F	VP-F
1	HM ≺ CD	✓	✓	✓	✓	VV	VV
2		✓	✓	✓	–	VV/dummy	dummy
3		✓	✓	–	✓	VV	VV
4		✓	✓	–	–	VV	dummy
5		✓	–	✓	✓	VV	–
6		✓	–	✓	–	VV	–
7		✓	–	–	✓	VV	–
8		✓	–	–	–	VV	–
9		–	✓	✓	✓	VV	VV
10		–	✓	✓	–	dummy	dummy
11		–	✓	–	✓	–	VV
12		–	✓	–	–	–	dummy
13		–	–	✓	✓	–	–
14		–	–	✓	–	–	–
15		–	–	–	✓	–	–
16		–	–	–	–	–	–
17	CD ≺ HM	✓	✓	✓	✓	VV/dummy	dummy
18		✓	✓	✓	–	VV/dummy	dummy
19		✓	✓	–	✓	VV	dummy
20		✓	✓	–	–	VV	dummy
21		✓	–	✓	✓	VV	–
22		✓	–	✓	–	VV	–
23		✓	–	–	✓	VV	–
24		✓	–	–	–	VV	–
25		–	✓	✓	✓	dummy	dummy
26		–	✓	✓	–	dummy	dummy
27		–	✓	–	✓	–	dummy
28		–	✓	–	–	–	dummy
29		–	–	✓	✓	–	–
30		–	–	✓	–	–	–
31		–	–	–	✓	–	–
32		–	–	–	–	–	–

As is evident from (1), it is not actually correct to say that the order HM ≺ CD uniformly results in verb doubling. It only does in case the language also has independent V-raising. Despite some minor inaccuracies, though, the general picture presented in the previous section is still valid. Languages that show both verb and verb phrase fronting fall into one of three patterns: (i) symmetric verb doubling (1, 3, 9); (ii) symmetric dummy verb insertion (10, 25, 26); and (iii) the asymmetric pattern (4, 19, 20), with some languages being a hybrid of patterns (ii) and (iii), which allows for a choice between verb doubling or dummy verb insertion in verb fronting (2, 17, 18). There is no combination of factors that corresponds to the unattested asymmetric pattern.

For languages that allow verb fronting to the exclusion of verb phrase fronting, we find that the only possible repair pattern is verb doubling (5–8, 21–24). For languages that contrarily exhibit verb phrase fronting to the exclusion of verb fronting, however, there are two options, either verb doubling (11) or dummy verb insertion (12, 27, 28). As pointed out in the discussion of Generalization IIb in section 4.2.2.2, there are two more combinations of properties that result in dummy verb insertion than that result in verb doubling, thereby probably making it more likely for some random verb phrase fronting only language to display the former repair.

Three further interesting predictions are easily observable in the table (1):
1. A language that displays dummy verb insertion in verb fronting necessarily shows verb phrase fronting (with dummy verb insertion).
2. A language that comprises of $\bar{\text{A}}$-head movement will always allow (if it also has remnant movement) or even force (if it lacks remnant movement) verb doubling in verb fronting, independent of whether it has V-raising.
3. There should be languages that allow both verb doubling and dummy verb insertion in verb fronting.

The first prediction is a variation of Generalization IIa. A language that shows dummy verb insertion in verb fronting must dispose of remnant VP movement. Remnant VP movement presupposes the availability of full VP movement. Since remnant-VP-creating scrambling is generally an optional process, we expect this language to necessarily also display verb phrase fronting generated by those derivations where scrambling has optionally not applied.

As far as I know, this prediction is borne out, at least in the sample investigated in this book. All languages that show dummy verb insertion in verb fronting (German, Dutch, Basque and Breton) (2) also show verb phrase fronting (3).

(2)   a.   **Waschen tut** er das Auto nie.
               wash.INF does he the car never
               'He never washes the car.'   (*German*, Diedrichsen 2008: 221)
     b.   **Verraden doet** hij haar niet.
               betray   does he her not
               'He doesn't betray her.'   (*Dutch*, Broekhuis & Corver 2015: 1045)

c. **Erosi** esan didate [**egi**-n zenue-la etxe-a].
buy say AUX do-PERF AUX-C house-DET
'They have told me that you BOUGHT the house.' (as opposed to, say, rent it) (*Basque* Elordieta & Haddican 2016: 237)

d. **Debriñ** a **raio** Yannig krampouezh e Kemper hiziv.
eating PRT will.do Johnny crêpes in Quimper today
'Johnny will eat crêpes in Quimper today.'
(*Breton*, Anderson 1981: 34)

(3) a. [Das Auto **waschen**] **tut** er nie.
the car wash.INF does he never
'Something that he never does is wash the car.'
(*German*, Diedrichsen 2008: 221)

b. [Haar **verraden**] **doet** hij niet.
her betray does he not
'He doesn't betray her.' (*Dutch*, Broekhuis & Corver 2015: 1043)

c. [Torrea **ikus**-i] **egin** d-u-t.
tower-ABS see-INF do 3SG(ABS)-have-1SG(ERG)
'I have SEEN the tower.' (*Basque*, Haddican 2007: 753)

d. [**Debriñ** krampouezh] a **raio** Yannig e Kemper hiziv.
eat crêpes PRT will.do Johnny in Quimper today
'Johnny will eat crêpes in Quimper today.'
(*Breton*, Anderson 1981: 30)

However, as Generalization IIa, to which the prediction is closely related, has been extracted from exactly this sample its validation by this same sample is probably not very informative. Nonetheless, the prediction formulated here is simple and clear. It should therefore be easily testable once new data on the issue are available. I will discuss the other two predictions in turn in separate sections below.

5.1.1 Gratuitous verb doubling under $\bar{\text{A}}$-head movement

One very interesting property of $\bar{\text{A}}$-head movement is that it will always give rise to verb doubling. This is independent of the order of operations and, crucially, also independent of V-raising. As the highest copy c-commands but is not itself c-commanded by another copy of the same element, it will be exempt from copy deletion by clause a. The lowest copy, on the other hand, will always be a head and, thus, evade copy deletion by clause b. Consequently, whenever $\bar{\text{A}}$-head movement applies, we expect it to lead to verb doubling.

This leads to two predictions concerning the interaction of verb doubling with auxiliaries/modals. In the absence of $\bar{\text{A}}$-head movement, verb doubling requires two things in order to occur: (i) the order of operations HM ≺ CD and (ii) V-raising such that the lower V copy actually head-moves out of the deletion site. The presence of auxiliaries or modals in Asp or T usually blocks head movement of the verb with the consequence that the verb will undergo deletion as part of the lower VP copy. Equally, when T is non-finite, as is the case when embedded under a restructuring or control verb, V-to-T movement is not necessary to express finiteness in T. Therefore, verb doubling as a consequence of HM ≺ CD and V-raising should not occur when the main verb is embedded under an auxiliary, a modal, or another infinitive-embedding verb. Indeed, this prediction seems to be borne out. Consider, for instance, Russian, which arguably does not comprise of Ā-head movement and where, therefore, verb doubling in (4) must be a consequence of HM ≺ CD and V-raising.

(4) **Čitat'** (-to) Ivan eë **čitaet,** no ničego ne ponimaet.
 read.INF TO Ivan it.FEM.ACC reads but nothing not understands
 'Ivan does read it, but he doesn't understand a thing.'
(Russian, Abels 2001: 1)

Now, if the lexical verb is embedded under an auxiliary, like the future auxiliary in (5-a), fronting does not result in verb doubling (5-b). Rather, we find a gap instead of a pronounced low V copy (5-c).

(5) a. On budet čitat'.
 he will read.INF
 b. ***Čitat'** (-to) on budet **čitat'**.
 read.INF TO he will read.INF
 c. Čitat' (-to) on budet ___v.
 read.INF TO he will
 'He will read.' (<i>Russian</i>, Abels 2001: 4f.)

Similar data can be observed in Polish, where it has been argued that verb fronting like (6) is remnant *v*P movement (Bondaruk 2012) and that the verb moves to Asp (outside of *v*P, Witkoś 1998) before deletion takes place thereby giving rise to verb doubling.

(6) **[Wypić]** (to) Marek **wypije** herbatę, ale nie wypije kawy.
 drink.INF TO Marek will-drink tea but not will-drink coffee
 'As for drinking, Marek will drink tea, but he will not drink coffee.'
(Polish, Bondaruk 2012: 55)

When verb fronting takes place from under an auxiliary (7-a) or a restructuring verb (7-b), however, verb doubling is ungrammatical.

(7) a. **Pracować** to Marek będzie nad tym (***pracować**), ale czy mu
work.INF TO Marek will on this work.INF but if him
się to uda skończyć.
REFL this manage finish
'As for working, Marek will work on this, but will he manage to finish?'
b. [**Pisać** list] to Maria zaczęła (***pisać**), ale go nie skończyła.
write.INF letter TO Maria started write.INF but it not finished
'As for writing a letter, Maria started to do this, but she didn't finish it.'
(*Polish*, Bondaruk 2012: 63)

In general, verb doubling in verb phrase fronting, which necessarily arises by means of V-raising before copy deletion, should be impossible under an auxiliary. Thus, even in languages like Hebrew, Brazilian Portuguese, Dagaare, and others, where verb fronting arguably involves $\bar{\text{A}}$-head movement, verb phrase fronting should nevertheless lack verb doubling under auxiliaries or modals. Unfortunately, most of the literature and data sources do not provide examples of verb (phrase) fronting from a position embedded under an auxiliary or modal. One example comes from Spanish, where the perfect auxiliary *haber* 'have' embeds the lexical verb *leer* 'read' (8-a). However, contrary to our expectations, when the verb phrase is fronted, the resulting sentence shows verb doubling (8-b).

(8) a. Juan ha leído el libro.
Juan has read.PTCP the book
'Juan has read the book.'
b. [**Leer** el libro], Juan lo ha **leído**.
read.INF the book Juan CL has read
'As for reading the book, Juan has indeed read it.'
(*Spanish*, Vicente 2009: 167)

Nonetheless, this is no proper counter-example to the prediction that verb doubling under an auxiliary should not be possible in verb phrase fronting. In the Spanish case, the low V copy appears in participial form whereas the higher V copy is an infinitive. This suggests that the low copy has head-moved to some functional head associated with participial morphology. As no copy of this head appears in the fronted VP as evidenced by the absence of any participial morphology there, it must be positioned higher in the structure than VP, otherwise it would have been copied and fronted together with the verb phrase. This functional head is not occupied by the auxiliary (if it were, the auxiliary should show participle morphology, contrary to fact) and the low V copy can thus head-move to it before the lower VP copy is deleted (9) thereby giving rise to verb doubling under an auxiliary.

(9) [CP [VP Leer el libro] [TP Juan lo ha [PartP leído [VP ~~leer el libro~~②]]]].
                                                              ↖____①____↗

A proper counter-example to the abovementioned claim would have to have the lower, sentence-internal verb copy be morphologically identical to the higher, sentence-initial one like in the pseudo-Spanish example (10).

(10) [**Leer** el libro], Juan lo ha **leer**.
       read.INF the book Juan it has read.INF

Here, head-movement to some higher morphology-bearing head not occupied by the auxiliary can be excluded.

Interestingly, in Polish, the future auxiliary (i.e. a future form of *być* 'be') may optionally embed a participial rather than an infinitive form of the lexical verb. In exactly this case, doubling of the main verb under an auxiliary, as in Spanish, becomes possible as well (11).

(11) **Pracować** to Marek będzie nad tym **pracował,** ale czy mu się to
       work.INF TO Marek will on this work but if him REFL this
       uda skończyć.
       manage finish
       'As for working, Marek will work on this, but will he manage to finish?'
       (*Polish*, Bondaruk 2012: 63)

This receives a straightforward explanation if participial morphology, like in Spanish, is hosted by a higher functional head (possibly between AspP and *v*P) that the main verb moves to.

To summarize, in all cases of movement that are not $\bar{\text{A}}$-head movement, verb doubling in verbal fronting from under an auxiliary or modal is expected to be impossible unless there is some higher functional head not occupied by the auxiliary (like a participle head) that the low V copy can head-move to in order to evade deletion as part of the lower VP copy.

A second, opposite prediction pertains to verb fronting that involves $\bar{\text{A}}$-head movement. Due to the property of this type of movement to lead to verb doubling independently of V-raising, we predict that the presence or absence of auxiliaries and modals should have no effect.

This prediction is of particular interest, because it contradicts the common intuition that the lower copy of the verb has to serve some grammatical purpose in the sentence in order to be pronounced. Usually, this purpose is the hosting of inflectional affixes in Asp, *v* and/or T, i.e. the expression of finiteness, or some other language-specific requirement like, for instance, the V2-requirement. The tight connection between V-raising and verb doubling above nicely captures this intuition because V-raising takes place to link inflectional affixes to V (or achieve a V2 word order) and V-raising is a *sine qua non* for verb doubling, hence verb doubling occurs when the verb fulfills some requirement inside the clause. If an auxiliary or modal is present, it takes over whatever task the lexical verb had to fulfill and thereby renders pronunciation of the low copy superfluous. Thus, if there exists a language that displays verb doubling in verb fronting from under an auxiliary or modal, this strongly supports the proposed implementation of Ā-head movement and its immunity to copy deletion. Indeed, there are (at least) two languages for which the prediction is borne out, Vietnamese and Hebrew. First, consider the Vietnamese example of verb fronting in (12).

(12) **Doc** thi no nen *(**doc**) sach.
 read TOP he should read book
 'As for reading, he should read books.' (*Vietnamese*, Trinh 2009: 38)

Here, the verb *doc* 'read' is embedded under the modal *nen* 'should' and has undergone verb fronting via Ā-head movement. Despite their morphological identity, which indicates that the lower copy has not moved to some higher inflectional head, both copies of *doc* are pronounced. In contrast, when the whole verb phrase *doc sach* 'read books' is fronted, no verb doubling occurs (13).

(13) [Doc sach] thi no nen.
 read book TOP he should
 'As for reading books, he should do that.' (*Vietnamese*, Trinh 2011: 37)

This is expected, as in this case, the verb would have to head-move out of the lower VP copy before it gets deleted which due to the blocking of V-raising by the modal is not possible even under the order where head movement precedes copy deletion.

Consequently, for fronting of intransitive verbs from under an auxiliary/modal, we expect verb doubling to be optional because this fronting may either be Ā-head movement of V, in which case the low copy is pronounced, or simple VP movement, in which case the low copy is deleted. As is demonstrated in (14), verb doubling of intransitive verbs is indeed optional in such a situation.

(14) a. **Ngu** thi no nen (**ngu**).
 sleep TOP he should sleep
 'As for sleeping, he should sleep.'
 b. **Den** thi no se (**den**).
 come TOP he will come
 'As for coming, he will come.'

 (*Vietnamese*, Trinh 2011: 39, 195 fn. 18)

A similar pattern can be observed for verbal fronting with the control verb *kiva* 'hoped' in the following examples from Hebrew (15).

(15) a. **Liknot** Dan kiva **liknot** et ha-sefer.
buy.INF Dan hoped buy.INF ACC the-book
'As for buying, Dan hoped to buy the book.'
b. [Liknot et ha-sefer] Dan kiva.
buy.INF ACC the-book Dan hoped
'As for buying the book, Dan hoped to (do it).'
c. **Lalexet** Dan kiva (**lalexet**).
walk.INF Dan hoped walk.INF
'As for walking, Dan hoped to walk.' (*Hebrew*, Trinh 2011: 32, 39)

In (15-a), verb doubling is obligatory because verb fronting in Hebrew involves Ā-head movement of V to SpecCP (Landau 2006). In verb phrase fronting (15-b), which usually also gives rise to verb doubling in Hebrew, movement of V to T does not take place because T is non-finite and therefore does not require V as a host to express finiteness. Consequently, despite the order HM < CD, the low V copy is deleted as part of the low VP copy. For intransitive verbs, both types of movement, Ā-head movement and phrasal VP movement, are an option when moving into the left periphery and, hence, verb doubling is optional (15-c).

Importantly, the fact that verb doubling under an auxiliary or modal is attested does not prove that the abovementioned intuition is wrong. There are languages where verb fronting from a position under an auxiliary or modal apparently does not entail verb doubling despite arguably arising by Ā-head movement. Consider, for instance, the examples from Kisi in (16).

(16) À wé cèé lé **pìsúltáŋ** ndá wà ⎯⎯pìsúltáŋ ní.
they AUX fight NEG play they AUX FOC
'They weren't fighting, it's playing they were doing.'
(*Kisi*, Childs 1995: 272)

As a language that only displays verb fronting, not verb phrase fronting, it must dispose of Ā-head movement. Fronting of the verb *pìsúltáŋ* 'play' across the auxiliary *wà* should therefore necessarily lead to verb doubling, which it obviously does not in (16).

In these languages, contrary to Vietnamese, there must, thus, be active an additional redundancy filter that prevents the pronunciation of low V copies unaffected by copy deletion just in case these copies do not serve some particular purpose in the clause.

Unfortunately, the literature hardly provides the relevant data to evaluate the prediction further. Particularly for languages that show only verb fronting either the behaviour of auxiliaries is hardly reported or they lack auxiliaries at all.

5.1.2 Optionality of repairs in verb fronting

Recall from the overview of interactions between relevant factors of verbal fronting in (1) that we expect there to be languages that show symmetric dummy verb insertion but optionally allow verb doubling in verb fronting. The relevant rows of the table are given again in (17).

(17) *Symmetric dummy verb insertion with optional verb doubling in verb fronting*

	Factor					Pattern	
	Order	Ā-HM	VP Mov	Scr	V-Rais	V	VP
2	HM < CD	✓	✓	✓	–	VV/dummy	dummy
17	CD < HM	✓	✓	✓	✓	VV/dummy	dummy
18		✓	✓	✓	–	VV/dummy	dummy

In fact, in the sample under investigation in this book there are two possible candidates that might instantiate such a pattern, namely Basque and Breton. Both of them generally show symmetric dummy verb insertion with a restricted set of verbs also displaying the possibility of verb doubling in verb fronting. I will discuss both of them in turn and show that Breton displays proper optionality (for a restricted set of verbs) while in Basque the verb doubling is restricted to the imperfective where, if it occurs, it occurs obligatorily. Nonetheless, both languages do not represent fully convincing examples of the predicted pattern.

In (Central and Western dialects of) Basque, verbal fronting for focus is standardly repaired by insertion of the dummy verb *egin* 'do' (18), which takes the place of the lexical verb and is inflected like the lexical verb would be in a non-focus sentence (see section 8.1.1 for more details).

(18) a. **Erosi** esan didate [**egi**-n zenue-la etxe-a].
        buy say AUX do-PERF AUX-C house-DET
        'They have told me that you BOUGHT the house.' (as opposed to, say, rent it)   (Elordieta & Haddican 2016: 237)
     b. [Torrea **ikus**-i] **egin** d-u-t.
        tower-ABS see-INF do 3SG(ABS)-have-1SG(ERG)
        'I have SEEN the tower.'   (*Basque*, Haddican 2007: 753)

In addition to the focus strategy with a dummy verb *egin* Western dialects show the option to have a verb copy in the clause (19) (Elordieta & Haddican 2016: 222).

(19) a. Mi-k j-**aki**-n d-**aki**-t egia.
I-ERG VM-know-INF 3SG-know-1SG truth
'I know the truth.' (as opposed to 'think' or 'believe' it)

b. J-**ue**-n d-**oie**, ala e-torr-i dator, ba.
VM-go-INF 3SG-go or VM-come-INF come.3SG then
'Well, is he leaving (right now), or is he coming?'

c. I-**bil**-i d-**abil** beti kale-a-n.
VM-walk-INF 3SG-walk always street-DET-LOC
'She is always WALKING in the street./She IS always walking in the street.' (*Basque*, Elordieta & Haddican 2016: 221f.)

This strategy, however, is restricted to a small closed class of verbs and is not productive. These special verbs exhibit synthetic morphology in imperfective finite contexts, that is, tense and agreement appear on the main verb (20-a) rather than on an auxiliary, as they usually do (20-b). In non-imperfective environments the affixes occur on the auxiliary independent of whether the verb is special (20-c) or not (20-d). The inventory of such special verbs varies from dialect to dialect.

(20) a. Jon dator.
Jon come.3SG
'Jon is coming.' (special verb in imperfective)

b. Jon bazkal-tzen ari da.
Jon lunch-IMPERF PROG AUX.3SG
'Jon is eating lunch.' (regular verb in imperfective)

c. Jon etorr-i da.
Jon come-PERF AUX.3SG
'Jon has come.' (special verb in perfective)

d. Jon-ek bazkal-du du.
Jon-ERG lunch-PERF AUX.3SG
'Jon has eaten lunch.' (regular verb in perfective)
(*Basque*, Elordieta & Haddican 2016: 223)

Verb doubling with special verbs is only possible in contexts in which they take a synthetic form, i.e. in the imperfective. If a doublet occurs in a perfective context the sentence is ungrammatical. Hence, example (21-a) is not felicitous because the special verb *ibil* 'to walk' is doubled in a perfective sentence. Regular verbs, like *bazkal* 'to lunch' never undergo doubling, not even in imperfective contexts (21-b).

(21) a. ***Ibil**-i **ibil**-i da.
 walk-INF walk-PERF AUX
 'She has WALKED.'
 b. ***Bazkal**-du **bazkal**-tzen ari da.
 lunch-INF lunch-IMPERF PROG AUX.3SG
 'Jon is EATING LUNCH.' (*Basque*, Elordieta & Haddican 2016: 224)

Furthermore, it seems to be the case that only verb fronting can display verb doubling. Attempts to front more than the bare verbal head and have verb doubling lead to ungrammaticality (22).

(22) a. *[Kalean **ibil**-i] **dabil**.
 street.in walk-INF walk.3SG
 'She is WALKING IN THE STREET.'
 b. *[Ingeles eta frantses **jakin**] **daki**.
 English and French know-INF know.3SG
 '(S)he KNOWS ENGLISH AND FRENCH.'
 (*Basque*, Elordieta & Haddican 2016: 224)

The data above indicate that verb doubling with a specific set of verbs is the result of exceptional V-to-T head movement of these special verbs. Verb doubling is only available when the verb takes a synthetic form, i.e. when an auxiliary that expresses tense and agreement features in T is absent and the V therefore moves to T to provide a means to express the finiteness features. Regular verbs that cooccur with an auxiliary in the imperfective do not allow verb doubling because they cannot move to T to evade copy deletion. Equally, special verbs in the perfective, where they cooccur with an auxiliary and V-to-T movement is blocked, also do not show verb doubling.

In light of the unproductive nature of this verb doubling, its confinement to particular grammatically defined environments (i.e. imperfective), and the fact that there is no free variation with a corresponding dummy verb alternative, it is most probably not the kind of optional verb doubling in verb fronting that is predicted by the typology. Rather, it is an artifact of the idiosyncratic property of a few verbs to exceptionally undergo V-to-T movement in the imperfective.

The Breton data, on the other hand, allow for a different analysis. Similar to Basque, Breton shows symmetric insertion of the dummy verb *ober* 'do' in verbal fronting constructions (23).

(23) a. **Debriñ** a **raio** Yannig krampouezh e Kemper hiziv.
 eating PRT will.do Johnny crêpes in Quimper today
 'Johnny will eat crêpes in Quimper today.'

b. [**Debriñ** krampouezh] a **raio** Yannig e Kemper hiziv.
   eat   crêpes   PRT will.do Johnny in Quimper today
   'Johnny will eat crêpes in Quimper today.'

(*Breton*, Anderson 1981: 34, 30)

In addition, Breton has fairly recently innovated verb doubling as in (24) with a small restricted class of verbs, including *ober* 'do', *bezañ* 'be', *rankout* 'must', *dleout* 'must', *gallout* 'can', *dont* 'come', *mont* 'go', *gouzout* 'know', *kerzhout* 'walk', *redek* 'run', and *lenn* 'read' (Jouitteau 2011: 127).

(24) a. **Rencout** a **rencan** da vont.
        must.INF PRT must.1SG P go
        'I have to go.'
     b. **Dleout** a **zlean** ober ma gwele.
        must.INF PRT must.1SG do my bed
        'I have to make my bed.'
     c. **Gallout** a **c'hallfen** lako ma avaloù en douar.
        can.INF PRT can   put POSS apple/potato P.DET soil
        'I can plant my potatoes.' (*Breton*, Jouitteau 2011: 127)

This doubling is restricted to verb fronting. Verb phrase fronting with a copy of the verb clause-internally is ungrammatical (25-a). Internal arguments have to be stranded unless they are cliticized to the verb (25-b).

(25) a. *[**Gouzout** an doare da vont] a **ouzez**.
         know   DET reason P go   PRT know.2SG
     b. [Hen **gouzout**] a **ouzez**.
        CL.3SG know   PRT know.1SG
        'I know it (well).' (*Breton*, Jouitteau 2011: 128f.)

Crucially, those verb doubling constructions all still have a corresponding counterpart with the dummy verb *ober* 'do' (Jouitteau 2011: 127). Within the lexically restricted set of verbs that can be doubled, Breton thus shows full optionality between verb doubling and dummy verb insertion.

However, if verb doubling in Breton is indeed a consequence of $\bar{\text{A}}$-head movement, one would have to assume that this type of movement is restricted to a particular set of verbs that, as Jouitteau (2011: 130) puts it, "fail to form a class at the syntactic level". Furthermore, although verb doubling verb fronting (26) behaves parallel to verb fronting with dummy verb insertion (27) in that it is clause bound (a. examples) and incompatible with negation (b. examples), both differ from verb phrase fronting, which is unbounded (28-a) and may cooccur with negation (28-b).

(26) a. *__Gouzout__ ne gredan ket a __ouzez__ ken.
       know NEG know.1SG NEG PRT know.2SG anymore
       Intended: 'I don't think you know anymore.'
    b. (*N') __gouzout__ (*n') __ouzon__ ket.
       NEG know NEG know.1SG NEG

(*Breton*, Jouitteau 2011: 130)

(27) a. *[$_V$ __Debrin__] a ouian [$_{CP}$ e __rae__ Yann krampouezh
       eat PRT know.1SG PRT did Yann pancakes
       ed-du].
       buckwheat
    b. *[$_V$ __Debrin__] ne ra ket Yann krampouezh ed-du.
       eat NEG do NEG Yann pancakes buckwheat

(*Breton*, Borsley et al. 1996: 69)

(28) a. [$_{VP}$ __Debrin__ krampouezh ed-du] a ouian [$_{CP}$ e __rae__
       eat pancakes buckwheat PRT know.1SG PRT did
       Yann].
       Yann
       'I know that Yann ate buckwheat pancakes.'
    b. [$_{VP}$ __Debrin__ krampouezh ed-du] ne ra ket Yann.
       eat pancakes buckwheat NEG do NEG Yann
       'Yann does not eat buckwheat pancakes.'

(*Breton*, Borsley et al. 1996: 69)

Thus, one would have to claim that $\bar{\text{A}}$-head movement in Breton is prevented from displacing a verbal head across a clause-boundary, thereby accounting for (26-a). This would, however, leave unexplained why remnant VP movement (leading to verb doubling with dummy verb insertion) is also clause-bound (27), while full VP movement is not; a fact that is particularly puzzling under the current approach, where remnant VP movement is full VP movement preceded by object movement and the two should therefore behave alike. All this points to the conclusion that Breton verb fronting in general involves a mechanism that is different from both $\bar{\text{A}}$-head movement and remnant VP movement. If this is true, the optionality between the two repairs in verb fronting in Breton is not an instance of the predicted pattern. Rather, it must be due to some idiosyncratic property of whatever operation underlies surface verb fronting.

Thus, there is no language in the present sample that manifests the symmetric dummy verb insertion pattern with optional verb doubling in verb fronting. However, this does not necessarily mean that such a language does not exist. This pattern is actually expected to be rare. For economical reasons it is unlikely that a language retains two distinct movement types, $\bar{\text{A}}$-head movement and remnant VP movement, that result in the same surface structure of verb fronting and lead to the same interpretation of verb focus/topic. In such a case, one would expect that language users prefer one option which would quickly lead to the loss of the other. The absence of a language instantiating the optional pattern from the sample is therefore not surprising.

5.1.3 Summary

In this section, I have identified and discussed three main predictions of the proposed account of verbal fronting:

1. A language that displays dummy verb insertion in verb fronting necessarily shows verb phrase fronting (with dummy verb insertion).
2. A language that comprises of Ā-head movement will always allow (if it also has remnant movement) or even force (if it lacks remnant movement) verb doubling in verb fronting, independent of whether it has V-raising.
3. There should be languages that allow both verb doubling and dummy verb insertion in verb fronting.

Prediction one is the mirror image of Generalization IIa, which was extracted from the present sample. The fact that it is borne out in this sample is, therefore, not very meaningful. A full evaluation of it requires more data.

Prediction two is probably the most interesting one. While the presence of auxiliaries, modals, or infinitive-embedding verbs should block verb doubling in verb phrase fronting, it should not block it in verb fronting, if the language has Ā-head movement. Hebrew and Vietnamese behave exactly as predicted. Verb phrase fronting from under an auxiliary results in a gap (29) while verb fronting from the same position obligatorily leads to verb doubling (30).

(29) a. [$_{VP}$ Doc sach] thi no nen ___VP.
 read book TOP he should
 'As for reading books, he should do that.'

 (*Vietnamese*, Trinh 2011: 37)

 b. [$_{VP}$ Liknot et ha-sefer] Dan kiva ___VP.
 buy.INF ACC the-book Dan hoped
 'As for buying the book, Dan hoped to (do it).'

 (*Hebrew*, Trinh 2011: 32)

(30) a. [_V **Doc**] thi no nen *(**doc**) sach.
 read TOP he should read book
 'As for reading, he should read books.'

(Vietnamese, Trinh 2009: 38)

b. [_V **Liknot**] Dan kiva **liknot** et ha-sefer.
 buy.INF Dan hoped buy.INF ACC the-book
 'As for buying, Dan hoped to buy the book.'

(Hebrew, Trinh 2011: 32)

The prediction is thus far borne out. However, the behaviour of verbal fronting in the presence of auxiliaries, modals, or infinitive-embedding verbs is poorly documented for the majority of (in particular the verb fronting only) languages. A more robust evaluation would require more and also more detailed data.

Prediction three, although apparently instantiated in Breton and Basque, does not find confirmation in the sample upon closer investigation. The Basque exceptional doubling for a small set of particular verbs is not optional but confined to the specific environment of the imperfective. Breton verb doubling in verb fronting shows full optionality, however, it is also restricted to a small class of verbs and most plausibly does not involve $\bar{\text{A}}$-head movement. Thus, prediction three still awaits confirmation. A language that displays the required pattern, however, might be hard to come by because a state where there are two ways ($\bar{\text{A}}$-head movement and remnant VP movement) to achieve verb fronting with the same interpretation of verbal focus/topic is uneconomical and should therefore be lost relatively quickly in language change.

To conclude, two of the three predictions are borne out in the sample with no direct counter-evidence while the third one still remains to be validated.

5.2 Further issues

In this section, I will discuss some of the issues that are raised either by the data themselves or by the theoretical account of it, and have been left unaccounted for. Those issues concern the implementation of a movement type's availability in a language, the nominalization of the fronted constituent that can be observed predominantly in the African languages in the sample, as well as the VP-internal word order change in Asante Twi verb phrase fronting and the question whether word order in general might play a role in determining which repair a languages chooses in verbal fronting constructions.

5.2.1 Availability of Ā-head movement

One crucial assumption of the current approach is that languages can vary with regard to whether they comprise of Ā-head movement or not. Thus, there must be some way to implement this language-specific choice. Similarly, it must be possible to formulate the ban against phrasal movement of verbal categories in those languages that only display verb fronting but not verb phrase fronting.

I would like to suggest that this optionality is tied to the projection behaviour of the information-structural feature that is responsible for the movement. Recall that when a head is merged with its complement, its merge-triggering structure-building feature is saturated (indicated by strikethrough) and its category feature as well as any unsaturated structure-building features are projected to the newly created syntactic object (31).

(31)
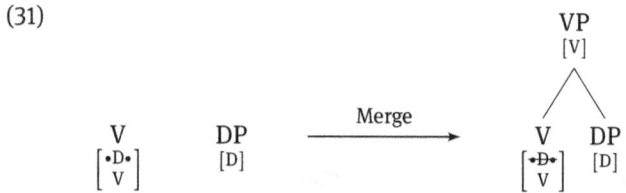

Equally, movement of some verbal constituent to SpecCP is dependent on some information-structural feature like [FOC(US)] or [TOP(IC)] being present on that constituent. This is because the C head bears a structure-building feature [•FOC/TOP•] that explicitly selects for the FOCUS/TOPIC-marked element to be internally merged. Since internal merge is subject to the Minimal Link Condition (Fanselow 1991, Ferguson 1993, Chomsky 1995b), it will always be the closest focus/topic element that is displaced into SpecCP. In this respect, Ā-head movement is no different from phrasal movement. With the former, the relevant feature is located only on a head X (32-a), whereas with the latter it is also located on a phrase-level constituent XP (32-b). Consequently, in the first case, it is only the head X that undergoes copying and merge with C′, whereas in the second case, it is the whole XP that is copied and merged in SpecCP.

(32) Ā-head movement vs. phrasal movement

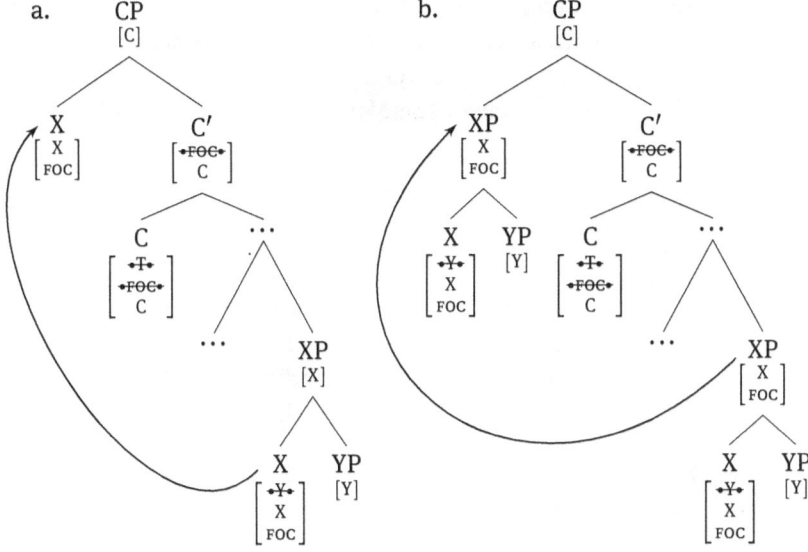

Now, assume that information-structural features are special in the sense that their projection behaviour may be restricted on a language-specific basis. In some languages, projection of these features is illicit, in other languages, it is obligatory, and in yet another set of languages, it is optional. It is easy to see that if applied to the FOCUS/TOPIC feature on a verbal head, the three language types correspond to, in this order, languages that allow only Ā-head movement of a verb, languages that allow only verb phrase movement and remnant verb phrase movement (if they have a remnant-creating movement), and languages that allow both Ā-head movement of the verb and verb phrase movement (plus possibly remnant verb phrase movement).

Therefore, there is no actual ban on verb phrase movement (or phrasal movement in general) in languages that only allow verb fronting. Rather, the verb phrase just never gets to bear the feature that, together with a corresponding structure-building feature on C, triggers movement of the verb phrase. Ā-head movement then is a natural consequence of the general assumptions about movement and its triggers and is therefore implemented in the exact same fashion as phrasal movement is, namely, as a two step operation where the moving element is first copied and the copy is then merged with the attractor.

On the other hand, languages that do not comprise of Ā-head movement do not need to have a dedicated constraint prohibiting it. Its unavailability follows from the obligatory projection of FOCUS/TOPIC. A head has been defined in section 4.1.3

as a syntactic element that bears at least one structure-building feature. Heads therefore always select and necessarily project at least once in the derivation. Since the information-structural feature is obligatorily projected to the next higher level, there will always be an XP that is closer to the attracting head and bears the attracted feature. Phrasal movement therefore always bleeds Ā-head movement in this scenario.

5.2.2 Nominalization of the fronted constituent

In a number of predominantly African languages, the fronted verbal constituent must be or may be nominalized.[1] For example, in Nupe, the fronted verb is obligatorily reduplicated with a CV prefix pattern that indicates nominalization (33-a). In the absence of this nominalization, verb fronting becomes ungrammatical (33-b).

(33) a. Yi-**yà** Musa **yà** etsu èwò o.
    RED-give Musa give chief garment FOC
    'Musa GAVE the chief a garment.'
   b. ***Yà** Musa **yà** etsu èwò o.
    give Musa give chief garment FOC

(*Nupe*, Kandybowicz 2008: 87)

Equally, in Buli, the fronted verbal constituent, be it a bare verb (34-a) or a verb phrase (34-b), has to be overtly marked by the nominalizing suffix *-kā* (singular) or *-tā* (plural).

(34) a. (Ká) **dē**-kā àlī/àtì Àtìm *(**dè**) máŋgò-kǔ dīēm.
    FOC eat-NMLZ C Àtìm ate mango-DEF yesterday
    'It is eating that Àtìm ate the mango yesterday. (not e.g. throwing it away)'
   b. (Ká) [máŋgò-kú **dē**]-kā àlī/àtì Àtìm *(**dè**) dīēm.
    FOC mango-DEF eat-NMLZ C Àtìm ate yesterday
    'It is eating the mango that Àtìm ate yesterday. (not e.g. buying a banana)' (*Buli*, Hiraiwa 2005a: 262)

Asante Twi is slightly different because overt marking of nominalization with an affix is only optional and actually dispreferred (35).

---

[1] These languages are: Asante Twi (section 2.1.3.1), Basaa (section 7.1.1), Buli (section 8.2.2), Dagaare (section 8.2.3), Edo (section 7.1.3), Ewe (section 7.1.4), Fongbe (section 7.1.5), Haitian Creole (section 7.1.7), Hausa (section 7.2.2), Kisi (section 7.1.8), Krachi (section 8.2.7), Leteh (section 7.1.9), Mani (section 8.2.9), Nupe (section 7.1.10), Nweh (section 7.1.11), and Yoruba (section 8.2.16).

(35) a. **Sí**(-é)   na Kofí á-**sí**/*á-yɔ́   dán.
          build-NMLZ FOC Kofi PRF-build/PRF-do house
          'Kofi has BUILT a house. (not e.g. bought one)'
      b. [Dán **sí**](-é)   na Kofí *á-sí/á-**yɔ́**.
          house build-NMLZ FOC Kofi PRF-build/PRF-do
          'Kofi has BUILT A HOUSE. (not e.g. bought a boat)'   (*Asante Twi*)

However, with verb phrase fronting there is a conspicuous change in word order from VO (36-a) to OV (36-b) (that can also be observed in verb phrase fronting in Buli and a number of other languages).

(36) a. Kofí [$_{VP}$ á-si   dán].
          Kofi   PRF-build house
          'Kofi has built a house.'
      b. [$_{VP}$ Dán **sí**   ](-é) na Kofí *á-sí/á-**yɔ́**.
          house build NMLZ FOC Kofi PRF-build/PRF-do
          'Kofi has BUILT A HOUSE. (not e.g. bought a boat)'   (*Asante Twi*)

As the verbal domain in the language is head-initial whereas the nominal domain is head-final, this switch can be interpreted as a consequence or (additional) exponent of nominalization. I will therefore treat the fronted verbal constituent as obligatorily nominalized with the option of marking this nominalization with a zero affix.

Commonly, all these languages also display fronting of regular nominal elements such as object DPs. Concerning the three languages above, examples are given in (37).

(37) a. Nakàn sasi Musa à   ba   èsun   làzi   yin o.
          meat some Musa FUT cut tomorrow morning PRT FOC
          'Musa will cut SOME MEAT tomorrow morning.'
                                              (*Nupe*, Kandybowicz 2008: 83)
      b. (Ká) mángò-kú-lá   àlī/àtì Àtìm dè (*mángò-kú-lá/*kù)
          FOC mango-DEF-DEM C   Àtìm ate mango-DEF-DEM/3SG)
          dīēm.
          yesterday
          'It is that mango that Àtìm ate yesterday.'   (*Buli*, Hiraiwa 2005b: 548)
      c. Dán   na Kofí á-sí.
          house FOC Kofi PRF-build
          'It is a house that Kofi has built.'   (*Asante Twi*)

However, a reanalysis of verbal fronting as regular nominal fronting applied to an independently available structure that contains a nominalized verbal constituent *in situ*, i.e. a cognate object construction, is implausible, at least in the three example languages considered here. I will show this for each language in turn.

In Nupe, cognate object formation is not productive (see also Kandybowicz 2008: § 4.3.1.2.1). There is thus no independent structure where a nominalized verb (apart from a handful of exceptions) appears in a position embedded under a non-nominalized version of the same verb (38).

(38)   a.   *Musa ba nakàn è-ba.
             Musa cut meat   NMLZ-cut
       b.   *Musa ba nakàn bi-ba.
             Musa cut meat   RED-cut   (*Nupe*, Kandybowicz 2008: 99)

Buli disposes of a somewhat productive cognate object construction. The cognate object is usually a root with a plural nominalizing suffix (39-a–d) but may also be a proper noun (39-d). Hiraiwa (2005a: 266) points out that the cognate object may be singular only when no corresponding plural form exists (39-d). The presence of the thematic object of the cognate is dispreferred in many cases (39-a, c).

(39)   a.   Àtìm **nàyì** ($^{??}$Àmɔ̀ak) **nāyī**-$^{??}$kā/tā.
             Atim hit   Amoak hit-NMLZ.SG/NMLZ.PL
             'Atim hit (Amoak). Lit.: Atim hit (Amoak) hittings.'
       b.   Àtìm **lè**   (Àmɔ̀ak) **lē**:-$^{??}$kā/tā.
             Atim insulted   Amoak insult-NMLZ.SG/NMLZ.PL
             'Atim insulted (Amoak). Lit.: Atim insulted (Amoak) insults.'
       c.   Àtìm **pù:sì**   ($^{?}$Àmɔ̀ak) **pū:sī**-$^{??}$kā/sā/$^{??}$k.
             Atim greeted   Amoak greet-NMLZ.SG/NMLZ.PL/SG
             'Atim greeted (Amoak). Lit.: Atim greeted (Amoak) greetings.'
       d.   wà **zù**   **zùm/zū**-kā/$^{??}$tā.
             3SG stole theft(ID.SG)/steal-NMLZ.SG/NMLZ.PL
             'He carried out a theft.'   (*Buli*, Hiraiwa 2005a: 266)

However, verbal fronting cannot be derived from these constructions. First, besides the option of fronting the cognate object like a normal NP (40-b) it is possible to have verb fronting with a cognate object appearing in its regular position (40-c). We would expect this to be blocked if verbal fronting were indeed movement of the cognate object.

(40)   a.   Àtìm pù:sì   pū:s-ā.
             Atim greeted greeting-ID.PL
             'Atim greeted greetings.'

b. (ká) **pū:s**-ā   àlī/àtì Àtìm **pù:sì**.
   FOC greeting-ID.PL C   Atim greeted
   'It is greetings that Atim greeted.'
c. (ká) **pū:sī**-kā   àlī/àtì Àtìm **pù:sì** **pū:s**-ā.
   FOC greet-NMLZ.SG C   Atim greeted greeting-ID.PL
   'It is greeting that Atim greeted.'

(*Buli*, Hiraiwa 2005a: 267)

Second, as mentioned above, cognate objects strongly prefer to be plural marked independently of whether they are interpreted as singular or plural (41-a). Their morphological marking thus does not depend on their semantics. Fronted verbs or verb phrases, in contrast, may take either singular or plural marking based on the interpretation that they receive (41-b). If verbal fronting constructions were derived by movement of cognate objects, we would expect the fronted constituent to be plural marked no matter whether it is semantically singular or plural, contrary to fact.

(41) a. Àtìm **nàyì** nāyī-[??]**kā**/**tā**.
        Atim hit   hit-NMLZ.SG/NMLZ.PL
        'Atim hit. Lit.: Atim hit hittings.'
     b. (Ká) nāyī-**kā**/**tā**   àlī/àtì Àtìm nāyī Àmɔ̀ak.
        FOC hit-NMLZ.SG/NMLZ.PL C   Atim hit Amoak
        'It is hitting/hittings that Atim hit Amoak.'

(*Buli*, Hiraiwa 2005a: 268)

Finally, while thematic direct objects in cognate object constructions usually show quite a low acceptability that varies with different verbs (42-a), their presence in verbal fronting constructions is perfectly grammatical (42-b, c). If verbal fronting were derived from cognate object constructions we would expect direct objects to be equally marginal in the former as they are in the latter.

(42) a. Àtìm **nàyì** ([?/??]*Àmɔ̀ak*) **nāyī**-[??]kā/tā.
        Atim hit   Amoak hit-NMLZ.SG/NMLZ.PL
        'Atim hit (Amoak). Lit.: Atim hit (Amoak) hittings.'
     b. (Ká) [*Àmɔ̀ak* **nāyī**]-kā/tā   àlī/àtì Àtìm **nàyī**.
        FOC Amoak hit-NMLZ.SG/NMLZ.PL C   Atim hit
        'It is hitting Amoak that Atim hit.'
     c. (Ká) **nāyī**-kā/tā   àlī/àtì Àtìm **nāyī** *Àmɔ̀ak*.
        FOC hit-NMLZ.SG/NMLZ.PL C   Atim hit Amoak
        'It is hitting that Atim hit Amoak.'   (*Buli*, Hiraiwa 2005a: 268)

For Asante Twi, we find that undoing the purported movement of a cognate object in verbal fronting results in an ungrammatical structure as well (43). This is independent of whether the main verb of the sentence is the dummy yɔ 'do' or the same verb as the one that is nominalized.

(43) a. *Kofí á-yɔ/á-si [dán sí](-é).
Kofi PFV-do/PFV-build house build-NMLZ
b. *Kofí á-yɔ/á-si dán sí(-é).
Kofi PFV-do/PFV-build house build-NMLZ (Asante Twi)

In conclusion, nominalization and verbal fronting must go hand in hand in these languages such that either nominalization necessarily triggers verbal fronting or, conversely, that verbal fronting enforces nominalization. However, in contrast to verb fronting, where the fronted constituent is always nominalized, deverbal nominal constituents may occur in environments where they have not undergone verbal (focus) fronting. Thus, the following grammatical examples (44), (45), and (46) each contain a nominalized verbal element that is not in a fronting configuration.

(44) a. Musa sundàn [bi-bé nyá Gana].
Musa fear RED-come POSS Gana
'Musa feared Gana's coming.'
b. [Bi-ba na u: ba nakàn na] tan Musa.
RED-cut COMP 3SG cut meat PRT pain Musa
'His cutting the meat pained Musa.'
(Nupe, Kandybowicz 2008: 88f.)

(45) Àtìm nāyī-kā/-tā àn nālā.
Atim hit-NMLZ.SG/-NMLZ.PL NEG good
'Hitting(s) Atim is not good.'
'Atim's hitting(s) is not good.' (Buli, Hiraiwa 2005b: 555)

(46) a. Ghánàní bíárá pɛ̀ [ǹsúó nóḿ].
Ghanaian every like water drink
'Every Ghanaian likes to drink water.'
b. Me kyiri [nám dí].
1SG hate fish eat
'I hate to eat fish.' (Asante Twi)

Therefore, nominalization of a verbal constituent does not enforce fronting movement of the same constituent. From this I conclude that nominalization must be a consequence of verbal fronting, rather than the reverse. Presumably, only nominal elements are licensed in the left periphery, such that a (late) nominalization process applies to verbal elements in this position in order to avoid a violation of this constraint. To be concrete, this nominalization could be implemented as late insertion of a nominalizing *n* head in the post-syntax before Vocabulary Insertion.[2] The resulting structure of SpecCP would then look like (47).

(47)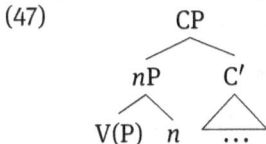

Upon Vocabulary Insertion, the *n* head is then realized by the nominalizing prefix RED$_{CV}$- in Nupe (48-a) or by one of the nominalizing suffixes -*é* and -*Ø* in Asante Twi (48-b) depending on its position with respect to V(P).

(48) a. **Yi-yà** Musa **yà** etsu èwò o.
RED-give Musa give chief garment FOC
'Musa GAVE the chief a garment.' (*Nupe*, Kandybowicz 2008: 87)

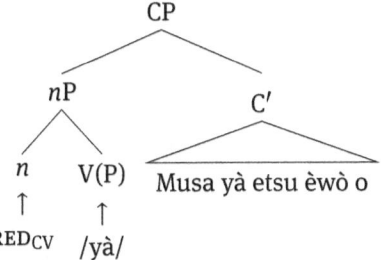

b. **Sí**(-é) na Kofi **á-sí** dán.
build-NMLZ FOC Kofi PRF-build house
'Kofi has BUILT a house. (not e.g. bought one)' (*Asante Twi*)

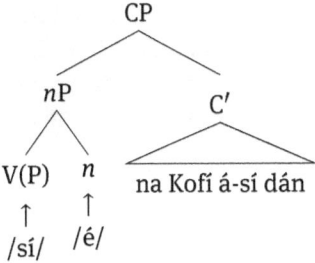

---

2 This is similar to the concept of dissociated morphemes (Embick 1997, Embick & Noyer 2007, Embick 2015), although a dissociated morpheme is taken to be adjoined to the existing structure while the late addition of *n* here must result in the creation of an *n*P rather than an *n*-adjoined VP.

This structure also provides a neat account for the switch of word order in verb phrase fronting from VO to OV in Asante Twi, Buli, and some other SVO languages (for a detailed implementation of this idea, see Hein & Murphy to appear). After the addition of the suffixal *n* head, the resulting *n*P is head-final but immediately dominates a head-initial VP, a configuration which violates the Final-over-Final Condition (Biberauer et al. 2007, 2008, 2014) given in (49).

(49) *Final-over-Final Condition (FOFC)* (Biberauer et al. 2014: 171)
A head-final phrase αP cannot dominate a head-initial phrase βP, where α and β are heads in the same extended projection.

As a gerund-like structure, the nominalized VP can be classified as a mixed extended projection (a term coined by Grimshaw 1991) where "a verb is associated with one or more nominal functional categories" (Borsley & Kornfilt 2000: 102) and therefore falls into the domain of the FOFC. In order to repair the structure (50-a), either the V head incorporates into *n* (50-b) or the VP exceptionally becomes head-final (50-c). In any case, the result is a change in surface word order of the fronted verb phrase from VO to OV.

(50)

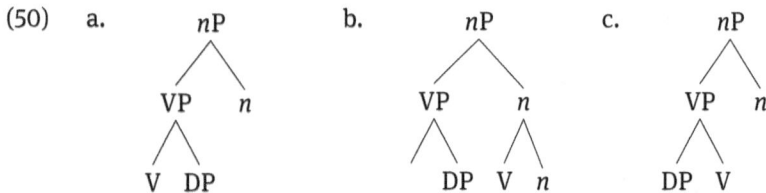

One prediction that this account makes is that languages with suffixal nominalizers and VO word order switch to OV order in fronted verb phrases while those with OV order should retain it. For languages with prefixal nominalizers such a word order switch is not necessary but also not prohibited should it arise for other independent reasons. Indeed, this is what we find in the data. Asante Twi (51), Buli (52), and Dagaare (53), which are all VO languages and exhibit suffixal nominalizers, consistently display OV order in fronted verb phrases.

(51) a. Kofí á-si   dán.
         Kofi PRF-build house
         'Kofi has built a house.'
      b. [Dán **sí**](-é)   na Kofí á-yɔ́.
         house build-NMLZ FOC Kofi PRF-do
         'Kofi has BUILT A HOUSE. (not e.g. bought a boat)'   (*Asante Twi*)

(52) a. Àtìm dè̩ máŋgò-kú-lá dīēm.
Àtìm ate mango-DEF-DEM yesterday
'Àtìm ate that mango yesterday.' (Hiraiwa 2005b: 546)
b. (Ká) [máŋgò-kú **dē̩**]-kā àlī/àtì Àtìm *(**dè̩**) dīēm.
FOC mango-DEF eat-NMLZ C Àtìm ate yesterday
'It is eating the mango that Àtìm ate yesterday. (not e.g. buying a banana)' (*Buli*, Hiraiwa 2005a: 262)

(53) a. Ǹ dà dá lá bɔ́ɔ́.
1SG PST buy FOC goat
'I bought a goat.'
b. [Bɔ́ɔ́ **dááó**] lá ká ń dà **dà** (*ò/*bɔ́ɔ́).
goat buy.NMLZ FOC C 1SG PST buy it/goat
'It is buying a goat that I did (as opposed to e.g. selling a hen).'
(*Dagaare*, Hiraiwa & Bodomo 2008: 802, 805)

With the OV language Korean, which also has a suffixal nominalizer, the word order as expected does not change in verb phrase fronting (54).

(54) a. John-i Mary-lul manna-ss-ta.
John-NOM Mary-ACC meet-PST-DECL
'John met Mary.' (Choi 2000: 333)
b. [Sakwa-lul **mek**]-ki-nun John-i **mek**-ess-ta.
apple-ACC eat-NMLZ-TOP John-NOM eat-PST-DECL
'As for eating apples, John did.' (*Korean*, Cho & Kim 2002: 679)

Contrarily, Mani (55) and Yoruba (56), both VO languages with a prefixal nominalizer (or prefixal nominal class marker), do not exhibit any word order change in fronted verb phrases.

(55) a. Ù̩ ká tɔk dòmɔ́ mì.
1SG PST wash shirt 1SG
'I washed my shirt.'
b. Ù̩-[**bán** wɔ́m] kɔ́ ḿbɔ̀m wɔ̀ **báŋ**-yè̩.
NCM-build boat PRO.FOC Mbom 3SG build-STAT
'It is building a boat Mbom built a boat.'
(*Mani*, Childs 2011: 148, 219)

(56) a. Ajé ra ìwé.
Aje buy paper
'Aje {is buying/bought} {a book/books}.'

b. Rí-[**rà** ìwé] ni Ajé **ra** ìwé.
   NMLZ-buy paper FOC Aje buy paper
   'It is book-buying that Aje {is doing/did}.' [i.e. he didn't go yam-selling]

(*Yoruba*, Manfredi 1993: 19f.)

However, as the example (57) from the VO language Krachi demonstrates, prefixal nominalizers do not preclude a change in word order, if it occurs independently. In this case, as Kandybowicz & Torrence (2016) argue, it is associated with a contrastive focus reading whereas the base order VO expresses exhaustive focus.

(57) a. ɔkyı wʊ ɛ-dıkɛ i-gyo.
        woman the PST-cook PL-yam
        'The woman cooked yams.'
     b. Kɛ-[**dıkɛ** i-gyo] yı ɔkyı wʊ ɛ-**dıkɛ**.
        NMLZ-cook PL-yam FOC woman the PST-cook
        'The woman only cooked yams (i.e. she did nothing else).'
     c. Kɛ-[i-gyo **dıkɛ**] yı ɔkyı wʊ ɛ-**dıkɛ**.
        NMLZ-PL-yam cook FOC woman the PST-cook
        'It was COOKING YAMS that the woman did (not, say, eating rice).'

(*Krachi*, Kandybowicz & Torrence 2016: 227f.)

These observations lend further support to an analysis where word order change is restricted by the Final-over-Final Condition.

To conclude, the nominalization of the fronted verbal constituent in some predominantly African languages is a consequence of rather than a prerequisite for verbal fronting. It is required by a licensing constraint that only allows nominal elements in the left periphery and can be modelled as late addition of a nominalizing *n* head inducing a violation of the Final-over-Final Condition in VO languages. This violation is then repaired by switching the word order of the fronted VP.

5.2.3 Order as a consequence of haplology avoidance

One part of this book is the proposal that the order of application between the two post-syntactic operations copy deletion and head movement can vary across languages. One might wonder whether the choice between the orders is arbitrary for each language or whether there are other properties of a language's grammar to which the choice can be linked. An indication towards the latter approach comes from an observation concerning German and Yiddish both being V2 languages but differing in their word order, one being OV and the other VO. If German as an OV language had the order HM < CD, fronting of a verb phrase would give rise to a configuration in which two identical verbs occur adjacent to each other, one on the right boundary of the fronted verb phrase, the other in V2 position in C. In order to avoid this haplology or "Obligatory Contour Principle"-like violation, the order of post-syntactic operations in German is set to CD < HM, which leads to the verb in V2 position being a dummy rather than a full lexical verb. In the VO language Yiddish, on the other hand, the object in the fronted verb phrase intervenes between the two identical verbs. Therefore, no haplology arises and there is no need to switch from the order HM < CD, which might be treated as the neutral/default order, to CD < HM.[3]

Looking at the languages in the present sample that display verb phrase fronting listed in sections 7.2 and 8 with the naked eye, there indeed seems to be a slight tendency such that those with an OV order in the fronted verb phrase tend to exhibit dummy verb insertion. As shown in the table in (58), of the ten OV languages six display dummy verb insertion while four exhibit verb doubling. There is also a slight bias for VO languages to display verb doubling. Of the 19 VO languages only six show dummy verb insertion while the majority of 13 languages displays verb doubling.

(58) *Distribution of repair mechanism depending on VP word order*

Language	fronted VP word order	repair	probable order of operations	V2
Asante Twi	OV	dummy verb	CD < HM	no
Basque	OV	dummy verb	CD < HM	no
Danish	OV	dummy verb	CD < HM	yes
Dutch	OV	dummy verb	CD < HM	yes
German	OV	dummy verb	CD < HM	yes
Japanese	OV	dummy verb	CD < HM	no
Skou	OV	dummy verb	CD < HM	no
Buli	OV	verb doubling	HM < CD	no
Dagaare	OV	verb doubling	HM < CD	no
Korean	OV	verb doubling	HM < CD	no
Krachi[4]	VO/OV	verb doubling	HM < CD	no
Br. Portuguese	VO	verb doubling	HM < CD	no
Hebrew	VO	verb doubling	HM < CD	no

---

3 The intriguing observation about the link between OV and CD < HM and VO and HM < CD as well as the idea to treat it as the result of an OCP-like effect are due to an anonymous Glossa reviewer to whom I am very grateful for bringing this to my attention.

4 Due to its variable word order in the fronted verb phrase Krachi is considered to be both a VO and an OV language.

(58) *Distribution of repair mechanism depending on VP word order (continued)*

Language	fronted VP word order	repair	probable order of operations	V2
Hungarian	VO	verb doubling	HM < CD	no
Mandarin	VO	verb doubling	HM < CD	no
Mani	VO	verb doubling	HM < CD	no
Polish	VO	verb doubling	HM < CD	no
Russian	VO	verb doubling	HM < CD	no
Spanish	VO	verb doubling	HM < CD	no
Tiv	VO	verb doubling	HM < CD	no
Vietnamese	VO	verb doubling	HM < CD	no
Yiddish	VO	verb doubling	HM < CD	yes
Yoruba	VO	verb doubling	HM < CD	no
Breton	VO	dummy verb	CD < HM	no
Hausa	VO	dummy verb	CD < HM	no
Norwegian	VO	dummy verb	CD < HM	yes
Swedish	VO	dummy verb	CD < HM	yes
Welsh	VO	dummy verb	CD < HM	no
Wolof	VO	dummy verb	CD < HM	no

Althought a proper assessment of the purported biases requires a solid statistical analysis of the distributions (which I will not undertake here), we can already determine that even if they turn out to be real they cannot be explained solely by some kind of haplology or OCP-effect.

On the one hand, it is true that all languages where the fronted verb phrase has OV word order and is immediately followed by the inflected verb, i.e. verb-second languages, display dummy verb insertion which indicates that the order of operations is CD < HM. Those languages are Danish, Dutch, and German. It is also true that there is no language that is expected to have CD < HM, i.e. dummy verb insertion, as the consequence of haplology but does not do so.

On the other hand, however, there is a considerable number of languages that have a fronted OV word order and dummy verb insertion but where the finite verb does not immediately follow the fronted constituent because the subject or a focus marker or both intervene. Examples of this are Asante Twi, Basque, Japanese, Skou, and Korean. In these languages the choice of the order CD < HM cannot be reduced to haplology avoidance unless one comes up with a very sophisticated understanding of haplology that ignores subjects and focus/topic markers.

An argument against the order of operations being determined by some haplology avoidance principle comes from verb fronting. A language like Yiddish, where verb phrase fronting does not lead to haplology due to the VO word order (59-a), still exhibits haplology in verb fronting constructions like (59-b).

(59) a. [**Essen** fish] **est** Maks.
 eat.INF fish eats Max
 'As for eating fish, Max eats them.'
 b. **Essen est** Maks fish.
 eat.INF eats Max fish
 'As for eating, Max eats fish.' (*Yiddish*, Cable 2004: 2)

This haplology does not cause Yiddish to have the order CD < HM which would result in dummy verb insertion. Apparently, the ban on adjacent identical verbs is not active here. But if it is not active, it cannot serve as a means to derive the difference between Yiddish and German/Dutch from their independently different word orders. One could of course restrict the ban to verb phrase fronting only. However, this seems to me to be quite an *ad hoc* restriction which also undermines the general idea that the choice of order of operations is meant to reduce the overall occurrence of adjacent identical verbs in a language, not just their occurrence in verb phrase fronting.

To conclude this section, although there seems to be a tendency that OV word order correlates with dummy verb insertion and VO word order with verb doubling, there is by no means a direct one-to-one correlation. Although basing the choice of the order of operations on the avoidance of haplology might explain some of the distribution in table (58), it cannot be the only factor that contributes to the issue. Thus, for now, I will assume that this choice is made on a language-by-language basis. However, I do think that, ultimately, it is desirable to connect the order of post-syntactic operations to other independent properties of a language.

6 Conclusion

This monograph investigated the behaviour and various properties of verbal fronting constructions such as (1) and (2) cross-linguistically, focussing in particular on the patterns of repairs that can be observed in the absence of stranded auxiliary or modal elements.

(1)   a.   **Liknot** hi **kanta** et ha-praxim.
            to.buy she bought ACC the-flowers
            'As for buying, she bought the flowers.'
    b.   [**Liknot** et ha-praxim], hi **kanta**.
            buy.INF ACC the-flowers she bought
            'As for buying the flowers, she bought (them).'
                                          (*Hebrew*, Landau 2006: 37)

(2)   a.   **Verraden doet** hij haar niet.
            betray does he her not
            'He doesn't betray her.'
    b.   [Haar **verraden**] **doet** hij niet.
            her betray does he not
            'He doesn't betray her.'
                                (*Dutch*, Broekhuis & Corver 2015: 1045, 1043)

It was observed that there are two possible repairs in these situations, namely verb doubling as in (1) or dummy verb insertion as in (2). Further, a distinction was established between languages that allow both verb fronting and verb phrase fronting (like Hebrew and Dutch above) and those that permit either only verb fronting like Nupe (3) or only verb phrase fronting like Norwegian (4).

(3)   a.   Bi-**ba** Musa à **ba** nakàn o.
            RED-cut Musa FUT cut meat cut/RED-cut FOC
            'It is CUTTING that Musa will do to the meat (as opposed to say, *cooking*.)'
    b.   *[Du-**du** cènkafa] Musa à **du** (cènkafa) o.
            RED-cook rice Musa FUT cook rice FOC
            'It is COOKING RICE that Musa will do.'
    c.   *[Cènkafa du-**du**] Musa à **du** (cènkafa) o.
            rice RED-cook Musa FUT cook rice FOC
            'It is COOKING RICE that Musa will do.'
                                        (*Nupe*, Kandybowicz 2008: 79, 86)

(4) a. [(Å) **lese** bøk-er] **gjør**/*leser han hele dag-en.
 to read.INF book.PL-PL.INDEF does/reads he whole day-DEF
 'Reading books he does all day.'
 b. *(Å) **lese** **gjør/leser** han bøk-er hele dag-en.
 to read.INF does/reads he book.PL-PL.INDEF whole day-DEF
 'Reading he does to books all day.'

(*Norwegian*, Siri M. Gjersøe p.c.)

Concerning the former type of languages, it seemed to be the case that no matter which type of repair a given language displays it symmetrically displays it in both verb and verb phrase fronting. This monograph introduced new verbal fronting data from Asante Twi (Kwa, Niger-Congo) and Limbum (Grassfields, Niger-Congo) attesting that this is not true. Both languages allow verb fronting as well as verb phrase fronting as shown in (5) and (6). However, they exhibit different repairs, namely verb doubling in verb fronting (a. examples) but dummy verb insertion in verb phrase fronting (b. examples).

(5) a. **Sí**(-é) na Kofí **á-sí**/*á-yɔ́ dán.
 build-NMLZ FOC Kofi PRF-build/PRF-do house
 'Kofi has BUILT a house. (not e.g. bought one)'
 b. [Dán **sí**](-é) na Kofí *á-sí/**á-yɔ́**.
 house build-NMLZ FOC Kofi PRF-build/PRF-do
 'Kofi has BUILT A HOUSE. (not e.g. bought a boat)' (*Asante Twi*)

(6) a. Á r-**yū** (cí) njíŋwè fɔ́ bí **yū**/*gī msāŋ.
 FOC 5-buy (COMP) woman DET FUT1 buy/do rice
 'The woman will BUY rice.'
 b. Á r-[**yū** msāŋ] (cí) njíŋwè fɔ́ bí *yū/**gī**.
 FOC 5-buy rice (COMP) woman DET FUT1 buy/do
 'The woman will BUY RICE.' (*Limbum*)

In a sample of another 45 languages (22 of which permit both kinds of verbal fronting) the mirror image pattern, namely dummy verb insertion in verb fronting but verb doubling in verb phrase fronting, is unattested. I therefore contend that there is a systematic typological gap in the distribution of repair patterns of verbal fronting such that of the four logically possible combinations only three are attested in the world's languages as depicted in table (7). The ensuing generalization is given in (8).

(7) *Possible repair patterns in languages with both kinds of verbal fronting*

	verb fronting	verb phrase fronting	languages
I	verb copy	verb copy	Hebrew, Buli, ...
II	dummy verb	dummy verb	Dutch, German, ...
III	verb copy	dummy verb	Asante Twi, Limbum, ...
IV	dummy verb	verb copy	—

(8) *Generalization I*
If a language shows both verb and verb phrase fronting it either exhibits the same repair strategy in both frontings (verb doubling or dummy verb insertion), or verb doubling in verb fronting and dummy verb insertion in verb phrase fronting. The reverse pattern is inexistent.

Concerning the other type of languages where only one kind of verbal fronting is licit, it was found that languages like Nupe, that only allow verb fronting, always display verb doubling as a repair, whereas languages like Norwegian, which exclusively permit verb phrase fronting, consistently show dummy verb insertion. This is summarized in table (9). The ensuing generalization is given in (10).

(9) *Possible repair patterns in languages with only one kind of verbal fronting*

	verb fronting	verb phrase fronting	languages
A	verb copy	—	Nupe, Tuki, ...
B	dummy verb	—	—
C	—	verb copy	—
D	—	dummy verb	Norwegian, Wolof, ...

(10) *Generalization II*
  a. If a language allows only verb fronting it exclusively shows verb doubling as repair.
  b. If a language allows only verb phrase fronting it exclusively shows dummy verb insertion as repair.

This book developed and proposed an analysis of verbal fronting repairs within the Copy Theory of Movement that accounts for Generalization I by means of a language-specific order of application between the operations head movement and copy deletion, both of which are taken to apply post-syntactically, and its interaction with two types of movement, syntactic Ā-head movement and syntactic remnant VP movement. With verb phrase fronting which can only be effected by syntactic phrasal movement of a complete VP, the order of operations directly affects the type of repair in the following way: If HM (11-a) applies before CD (11-b), the verb inside the lower VP copy can evade deletion by moving to some functional head outside the deletion site (counter-bleeding) where it will be phonologically realized resulting in verb doubling.

(11) *Verb doubling in verb phrase fronting: HM ≺ CD*
    a.   [$_{CP}$ [$_{VP}$ V DP] [$_{C'}$ C [$_{TP}$ T ... [$_{VP}$ V DP]]]]
    b.   [$_{CP}$ [$_{VP}$ V DP] [$_{C'}$ C [$_{TP}$ V+T ... [$_{VP}$ V DP]]]]

If CD (12-a) applies before HM (12-b), however, the verb will be deleted as part of the lower VP copy before it can leave the deletion site (bleeding). A semantically largely vacuous dummy verb is inserted into T (or Asp or *v*) as a Last Resort to provide a host for affixes or the expression of finiteness.

(12) *Dummy verb insertion in verb phrase fronting: CD ≺ HM*
    a.   [$_{CP}$ [$_{VP}$ V DP] [$_{C'}$ C [$_{TP}$ T ... [$_{VP}$ V DP]]]]
    b.   [$_{CP}$ [$_{VP}$ V DP] [$_{C'}$ C [$_{TP}$ *do*+T ... [$_{VP}$ V DP]]]]

With verb fronting, the effect of the order of operations is the same as in verb phrase fronting as long as verb fronting is the result of underlying remnant VP movement. Thus, HM applying before CD results in verb doubling (13) while CD applying before HM leads to dummy verb insertion (14).

(13) *Verb doubling in verb fronting via remnant movement: HM ≺ CD*
    a.   HM: [$_{CP}$ [$_{VP}$ V DP] [$_{C'}$ C [$_{TP}$ T ... DP [$_{VP}$ V DP]]]]
    b.   CD: [$_{CP}$ [$_{VP}$ V DP] [$_{C'}$ C [$_{TP}$ V+T ... DP [$_{VP}$ V DP]]]]

(14) *Dummy verb insertion in verb fronting via remnant movement: CD ≺ HM*
    a.   [$_{CP}$ [$_{VP}$ V DP] [$_{C'}$ C [$_{TP}$ T ... DP [$_{VP}$ V DP]]]]
    b.   [$_{CP}$ [$_{VP}$ V DP] [$_{C'}$ C [$_{TP}$ *do*+T ... DP [$_{VP}$ V DP]]]]

If, however, verb fronting involves Ā-head movement of the verb into the left periphery, the low copy of this movement is a projecting head and as such by assumption immune to copy deletion. As a result, Ā-head movement consistently gives rise to verb doubling. Therefore, the effect of the order CD ≺ HM, which leads to dummy verb insertion, is overwritten in Ā-head movement contexts (15).

(15) *Effect of order of operations in verbal fronting*

	Order of post-syntactic operations		Surface
Moved item	HM ≺ CD	CD ≺ HM	
full VP	verb doubling	dummy verb insertion	verb phrase fronting
remnant VP	verb doubling	dummy verb insertion	verb fronting
bare V	verb doubling	**verb doubling**	verb fronting

Given that languages have to employ full VP movement in order to show verb phrase fronting on the surface but may differ in whether they use Ā-head movement or remnant VP movement to achieve verb fronting, the account yields four combinations of properties (2 types of verb fronting movement × 2 orders of operations). Crucially, due to the lower copy of Ā-head movement being exempt from copy deletion only the three attested repair patterns can be generated (16).

(16) *Interaction of order of operations and movement type*

	Ā-head movement	remnant VP movement
CD ≺ HM	asymmetric pattern (Asante Twi)	symmetric dummy verb insertion (German)
HM ≺ CD	symmetric verb doubling (Hebrew)	symmetric verb doubling (Polish)

The unattested pattern IV is underivable under the current set of syntactic movement types (phrasal movement, remnant phrasal movement, Ā-head movement).

With regard to Generalization II, the proposed account was shown to naturally account for why languages that only allow verb fronting must necessarily exhibit a verb doubling repair. As these do not show verb phrase fronting they can be assumed to lack the relevant phrasal VP movement. Being a subtype of phrasal VP movement, remnant VP cannot underly verb fronting in these languages. Therefore, it must involve Ā-head movement, which exceptionlessly results in verb doubling.

The observation that languages that only permit verb phrase fronting consistently show dummy verb insertion, however, does not follow from the present system. As I pointed out in section 4.2.2.2, this language type is the least represented in the sample and the lack of verb doubling might thus simply be a result of the relatively small number of exemplars. Additionally, under the present account, verb doubling with this type of language only emerges under a specific combination of properties whereas dummy verb insertion is yielded by various different combinations.[1] Eventually, further research is needed in order to determine whether Generalization IIb is real and, if it is, whether there are additional factors at work besides order of operations and type of movement.

There are, of course, many other things that warrant future research. On the empirical side, it is clear that for many languages the available data is not detailed enough to allow for well-grounded substantial claims about properties of verbal fronting. I hope that by trying to evaluate all 47 languages of my sample against the properties in table 2.1 I have made obvious that what we do not know outweighs what we do know for a lot of languages. One main goal of future endeavours in the realm of verbal fronting would therefore be to get rid of the questionmarks in table 2.1 and fill the many gaps.

A second empirical issue concerns the second prediction in section 5.1.2 that there should be languages that show symmetric dummy verb insertion but optionally also allow verb doubling in verb fronting. Now that this expectation has been made explicit, one needs to determine whether these languages do exist or not. Similarly, having suggested that Generalization IIb is not real, I definitely expect there to be languages in which only verb phrase fronting is available but the corresponding repair is verb doubling rather than dummy verb insertion.

On the theoretical side, various issues have remained unexplored and undiscussed here. Concerning the claim that there is an order of application between copy deletion and head movement, it is hitherto unclear where this order comes from. I have treated it as extrinsically imposed but ideally it would be linked to other independent properties of a language such that it naturally falls out from them or their interaction with one another. The idea that the VP-internal word order might play a role (see section 5.2.3) was a proposal along these lines, although it turned out to be untenable. On the other hand, the order of operations is probably

---

1 The relevant combinations and their respective repair pattern are given again in (i). There are three combinations that yield dummy verb insertion versus one combination that results in verb doubling.

(i)   Possible combinations of properties in verb phrase fronting only languages

Factor					Pattern	
Order	Ā-HM	VP Mov	Scr	V-Rais	V-F	VP-F
HM < CD	–	✓	–	✓	–	VV
	–	✓	–	–	–	dummy
CD < HM	–	✓	–	✓	–	dummy
	–	✓	–	–	–	dummy

expected to have effects beyond the repairs in verbal fronting in other areas where syntactic movement, head movement and deletion interact.

One area in which deletion and head movement interact prominently and where the same two types of repairs can be observed as in verbal fronting is VP ellipsis. In languages like English, the main verb of the clause in which elision occurs is elided with the VP and a dummy verb appears instead (17-a). Overt expression of the main verb is ungrammatical (17-b).

(17) Arthur [_{VP} brought a present to Hall],
    a.   and Julia *did* [bring a present to Hall] too.
    b.   *and Julia *brought* too; *and Julia *will bring* too.

(*English*, Goldberg 2005: 1)

In other languages, like Hebrew, however, the main verb of the clause containing the elided VP surfaces overtly (18). This phenomenon has been termed verb-stranding VP-ellipsis (for discussion, see Goldberg 2005, Gribanova 2013) and seems to be very similar to the verb doubling repair in verbal fronting.

(18) Q: Šalaxt   etmol   et   ha-yeladim   le-beit-ha-sefer?
          send.PST.2SG.FEM yesterday ACC the-children to-house-the-book
          '(Did you) send the children to school yesterday?'
     A: Šalaxti.
          send.PST.1SG
          '(I) sent [the children to school yesterday]'

(*Hebrew*, Doron 1999: 129)

The current analysis of ellipsis takes it to be an operation that applies post-syntactically and leads to the non-pronunciation of the elided material (see among others Fox 2000, Johnson 2001, Merchant 2001, 2002a, 2003). The observation that Hebrew allows verb-stranding VP-ellipsis while English does not can then straightforwardly be reduced to the fact that Hebrew shows (syntactic) V-to-T head movement while English does not (Goldberg 2005, though see Landau 2018, 2020 for a different view). In the former case, V moves out of the ellipsis site before it is elided whereas in the latter case it has to remain inside the ellipsis site and gets elided as part of the VP. However, as it stands, this does not account for the fact that the mainland Scandinavian languages Danish, Norwegian, and Swedish, which arguably comprise of some kind of VP-evacuating head movement, do not allow verb-stranding VP ellipsis but show insertion of a dummy verb instead (19)–(21).

(19) a. *Mona og Jasper **vaskede** bilen, eller rettere Mona **vaskede**.
Mona and Jasper wash.PST car.DEF or rather Mona wash.PST
Intended: 'Mona and Jasper washed the car, or rather Mona did.'
b. Mona og Jasper **vaskede** bilen, eller rettere Mona **gjorde**.
Mona and Jasper wash.PST car.DEF or rather Mona do.PST
'Mona and Jasper washed the car, or rather Mona did.'
(*Danish*, Houser et al. 2011: 249)

(20) a. *Johan **leste** ikke *Lolita*, men Marie **leste**.
Johan read.PST not *Lolita* but Marie read.PST
Intended: 'Johan didn't read *Lolita*, but Marie did.'
b. Johan **leste** ikke *Lolita*, men Marie **gjorde**.[2]
Johan read.PST not *Lolita* but Marie do.PST
Intended: 'Johan didn't read *Lolita*, but Marie did.'
(*Norwegian*, Thoms 2012: 7)

(21) a. *Johan **läste** inte *Lolita*, men Kalle **läste**.
Johan read.PST not *Lolita* but Kalle read.PST
Intended: 'Johan didn't read *Lolita*, but Kalle did'.
b. Maria **körde** inte bilen, men Johan **gjorde** det.
Maria drive.PST not car.DEF but Johan do.PST it
'Maria didn't drive the car, but Johan did.'
(*Swedish*, Sailor 2018: 856)

As Sailor (2018: 856f.) argues the lack of verb-stranding VP ellipsis in Scandinavian can be attributed to a bleeding relation between ellipsis and VP-evacuating verb movement. He proposes, *pace* the common PF-deletion account of ellipsis, that both ellipsis and head movement are operations that take place or are effected in syntax and that the trigger for verb movement on C enters the derivation too late to save the verb from being elided by T's [E]-feature. However, there is also another way to account for the facts, namely treating both operations as taking place post-syntactically. In Scandinavian, ellipsis would precede head movement while it follows it in Hebrew-type languages. Curiously, this order parallels the order of copy

---

2 Note that the Norwegain example in this form is only accepted by some speakers. For others, the pronoun *det* necessarily has to follow the dummy verb as in (i).

(i) Johan leste ikke *Lolita*, men Marie gjorde det.
Johan read.PST not Lolita but Marie do.PST it
'Johan didn't read *Lolita*, but Marie did.'

For those speakers that allow the pronoun-less version, a version with the pronoun present is optionally possible.

deletion with respect to head movement in these languages. This, taken together with the fact that copy deletion and ellipsis are types of non-pronunciation, could be taken as an indication that they are not differentiated for the purposes of the order of application (i.e. their order with respect to each other never matters) and therefore always exhibit the same order with regard to head movement. That way a link between the choice of repair in verbal fronting and the availability of verb-stranding in VP-ellipsis is established. The interesting prediction that this makes is that languages which show verb doubling in verb phrase fronting should exhibit verb-stranding VP ellipsis (provided that they allow VP ellipsis in the first place), while languages that show dummy verb insertion in verb phrase fronting are expected to lack verb-stranding VP ellipsis. A very coarse survey of the literature seems to be in accordance with this: Hebrew, Russian, and Brazilian Portuguese all arguably allow verb-stranding VP ellipsis (see Doron 1999, Gribanova 2013, Sailor 2014) and show verb doubling in verb phrase fronting, while English, Danish, Norwegian, and Swedish all lack the verb-stranding type of VP ellipsis (see Sailor 2018) and show dummy verb insertion in verb phrase fronting. A case of debate are Japanese and Korean which have been claimed to both display verb-stranding VP ellipsis (Otani & Whitman 1991) and not display it (Goldberg 2005). In any case, research in this direction might provide insights into the nature of head movement, ellipsis and their place in the theory of grammar.

Part II: **Language data**

In this part, I will provide data on verbal fronting for each of the additional 45 languages of the sample (for Asante Twi and Limbum, see sections 2.1.3.1 and 2.1.3.2, respectively). I will first establish what kind of fronting can be found in the language, i.e. whether an object cannot, or must, or may be fronted alongside the verb. Then, if available, data in favour of verbal fronting being $\bar{\text{A}}$-movement will be presented, followed by data that can be used to conclude what the size of the fronted constituent is. Subsequently, if applicable, I will discuss any possible base constructions from which verbal fronting could be said to be derived and which independently show verb doubling or the presence of a dummy verb. Each language section conludes with a short summary giving the relevant properties that the investigated language has, the pattern that it instantiates (i.e. pattern I, II, III, A, or D), and a table providing an overview over these properties. As mentioned before, unfortunately, there is not enough data available for all languages to determine their behaviour with regard to all relevant features beyond doubt. The tables will therefore oftentimes remain incomplete. The first chapter will present data for languages that I have classified as exhibiting one kind of verbal fronting only. First, languages that exclusively show (bare) verb fronting are discussed. Then, languages that conversely only exhibit verb phrase fronting will be investigated. The subsequent chapter gives data on languages that allow both verb and verb phrase fronting, beginning with those that show symmetric dummy verb insertion and concluding with the ones that show symmetric verb doubling. The few data on Afrikaans, which is a language that very likely also exhibits the asymmetric pattern, can be found in section 2.1.3.3 in part I.

7 Languages with only one kind of verbal fronting

7.1 Languages with verb fronting only

7.1.1 Basaa

Basaa (pronounced ɓasàá by the native speakers) is a Bantu language spoken by an estimate of up to one million speakers (Bassong 2014: 60) in the central and coastal regions of Cameroon.

Verbal displacement may be to the left (1-a) or alternatively to the right (1-b) and triggers a contrastive (exhaustive) focus interpretation of the verb or, if appropriate, of the whole verb phrase (Bassong 2014: 146). While the displaced verb is always nominalised, as is the case in many (West) African languages, there is a fully inflected copy of the verb in its base position.

(1) Q: Did the boy LEARN MATHEMATICS or PLAY FOOTBALL?
    Q: Did the boy LEARN or TEACH mathematics?
  a. N-**nígl**-ak   wɔ́-n hí-bí-**nígíl**   mínsɔngí.
      3.NMLZ-learn-NMLZ 3-FOC 19.SM-PST2-learn 4.mathematics
      'The boy LEARNED MATHEMATICS (he did not teach it/play football).'
  b. Hí-bí-**nígíl**   mínsɔngí   n-**nígl**-ak.
      19.SM-PST2-learn 4.mathematics NMLZ-learn-NMLZ
      'He LEARNED MATHEMATICS (he did not teach it/play football).'
                                                    (Bassong 2014: 146)

According to Bassong (2014), both types of displacement have the exact same interpretation of contrastive (exhaustive) focus.

(2) a. Mɛ bí-**ɓám**   ɓáúdú   m-**ɓám**-ây.
         I PST2-blame.PERF 2.students 3.NMLZ-blame-NMLZ
         'I BLAMED (e.g. as opposed to BEAT) the students.'
    b. M-**ɓám**-ây   wɔ́-n mɛ bí-**ɓám**   ɓáúdú.
         3.NMLZ-blame-NMLZ 3-FOC I PST2-blame.PERF 2.students
         'I BLAMED (e.g. as opposed to BEAT) the students.'
                                                      (Bassong 2014: 281)

As shown in (3), fronting the internal argument with the verb is ungrammatical.

(3) *N-[**nígl**-ak   mínsɔngí]   wɔ́-n hí-bí-**nígíl**.
      3.NMLZ-learn-NMLZ 4.mathematics 3-FOC 19.SM-PST2-learn
                                                     (Bassong 2014: 146)

Fronting of the internal argument(s) together with the verb is possible only when both are the complement of modal (4) or control (5) predicates. In this construction, in contrast to the one in (2), no doublet of the displaced verb occurs, rather there is a gap in its original position.

(4) a. N-[lúy-á   mátówa í   ŋgwa nɔ̂y] wɔ́-n Ewas
       NMLZ-drive-NMLZ 6.cars   LOC 3.day 9.rest 3-FOC 1.Ewas
       a-ń-la   (*lúy (*mátówa í   ŋgwa nɔ̂y)).
       1.SM-PRS-can   drive   6.cars   LOC 3.day 9.rest
       'DRIVING A CAR ON SUNDAY is what Ewas can do.'
   b. [Li-lúy   mátówa í   ŋgwa nɔ̂y] jɔ́-n Ewas a-ń-la
       INF-drive 6.cars   LOC 3.day 9.rest 3-FOC 1.Ewas 1.SM-PRS-can
       (*lúy (*mátówa í   ŋgwa nɔ̂y)).
       drive   6.cars   LOC 3.day 9.rest
       'DRIVING A CAR ON SUNDAY is what Ewas can do.' (Bassong 2014: 243)

(5) Q: What does the boy want to do?
    A: [Li-nígíl   mínsɔngí]   jɔ́-n hilɔ́gá hí-ŋ-gwês   kií ka
       3.INF-learn 4.mathematics 5-FOC 19.boy 19.SM-PRS-want as such
       hega   ... ndí íbálê yak lijowa   bipân lí   yê
       19.example ... but if   also 5.INF-wash 8.plates 5.SM be
       hi-gá-ɓɔŋ   hála.
       19.SM-FUT2-do so
       'The boy wants to STUDY MATHEMATICS, for example, but if washing the plates is also required, he will do that.' (Bassong 2014: 147)

Note that the verb in the fronted verb phrase may either be nominalized (4-a) as in verb fronting or alternatively bear an infinitive prefix *li-* (4-b) with no difference in meaning. Whether this optionality also extends to verb fronting remains an open issue. Bassong (2014), however, does not provide an example of verb fronting with the infinitive marker, which might be taken as an indication that *li-* is restricted to verb phrase fronting.

As indicated by the continuation '...for example' in (5), with verb phrase fronting contexts the focus is not necessarily contrastive. Although a contrastive reading can be obtained as evidenced by (6).

(6) [Li-nígíl   mínsɔngí]   jɔ́-n hilɔ́gá hí-ŋ-gwês
    3.INF-learn 4.mathematics 5-FOC 19.boy 19.SM-PRS-want
    hí-ŋ-gwês   ɓéé sál.
    19.SM-PRS-want NEG work
    'The boy wants to LEARN MATHEMATICS (he does not want *to work*).'

(Bassong 2014: 147)

Having established that Basaa shows verb but not verb phrase displacement with a copy of the verb appearing in the canonical verb position, I will present some more properties of both leftwards and rightwards displacement in turn.

Leftwards displacement
First, leftwards displacement exhibits properties of $\bar{\text{A}}$-movement. The dependency between the displaced verb and its clause-internal copy can cross finite clause boundaries (7) and is sensitive to islands such as the Complex NP Island (8), the Wh-Island (9), the Subject Island (10), the Adjunct Island (11), and the Coordinate Structure Constraint (12).

(7) a. M-**ɓɔŋ**-ɔ́k wɔ́-n mɛ n-nɔy [lɛ́ mut wɨβ
NMLZ-do-NMLZ 3-FOC I PST1-hear that 1.man 3.theft
a-m-**ɓɔ̂ŋ** múdaá].
1.SM-PST1-do 1.woman
'I heard that the thief DID (it to) the woman.'
b. Ŋ-**hól**-ga wɔ́-n mɛ ŋ́-hɔ́ŋɔ̂l [lɛ́ mudaá a-bí-kăl
NMLZ-help-NMLZ 3-FOC I PRS-think that 1.woman 1.SM-PST2-say
lɛ́ ɓɔɔŋɛ́ ɓá-bí-**hólá** málêt].
that 2.children 2.SM-PST2-help 1.teacher
'I think that the woman said that the children HELPED the teacher.'
(Bassong 2014: 249f.)

(8) *Complex NP Island*
a. *Ŋ-**hól**-ga wɔ́-n mɛ bí-ɓɔmá [í ɓɔɔŋɛ́
NMLZ-help-NMLZ 3-FOC I PST2-meet DEF 2.children
ɓá-bí-**hólá** málêt].
2.SM-PST2-help 1.teacher
'HELPING I met the children who helped the teacher.'
b. *M-**ɓát**-ga wɔ́-n mudaá a-n-nɔ̂y [ɲáŋ lɛ́
NMLZ-collect-NMLZ 3-FOC 1.woman 1.SM-PST1-heard 3.story that
maaŋɛ́ a-bí-**ɓátá** bítuyû].
1.child 1.SM-PST2-collect 8.toys
'COLLECT the woman heard the story that the children collected the toys.' (Bassong 2014: 250)

(9) *Wh-Island*
a. *M-**ɓát**-ga wɔ́-n mudaá a-bí-ɓat [lɛ́ kɛ́lkíí
NMLT-collect-NMLZ 3-FOC 1.woman 1.SM-PST2-ask that 1.when
ɓɔɔŋɛ́ ɓá-bí-**ɓátá** mákúβé].
2.children 2.SM-PST2-collect 6.bananas
'COLLECT the woman asked when the children collected the bananas.'

b. *N-**tìl**-ga wɔ́-n malet a-ḿ-ɓat [lɛ́ hɛ́ɛ́
   NMLZ-write-NMLZ 3-FOC 1.teacher 1.SM-PRS-ask that 1.where
   ɓaúdú ɓá-bí-**tìl**-APPL bíkaat].
   2.children 2.SM-PST2-write-LOC 8.letters
   'WRITE the teacher is asking where the students wrote the letters.'
   (Bassong 2014: 250f.)

(10) *Subject Island*
   a. *N-**nɛd**-êk wɔ́-n [lɛ́ ɓaúdú ɓá-n-**nêd** mákeksɛ]
      NMLZ-pass-NMLZ 3-FOC that 2.children 2.SM-PST1-pass 6.exams
      (hala) a-ŋ́-kosná máséé.
      that 1.SM-PRS-make 6.joy
      'PASS that the students passed the exams makes happy.'
   b. *M-**ɓííbá**-yá wɔ́-n [lɛ́ Ewas a-m-**ɓííɓa**]
      NMLZ-get.married-NMLZ 3-FOC that Ewas 1.SM-PST1-get.married
      (hala) a-ye lɔ́ŋ↓gɛ́.
      that 1.SM-be good
      'GET MARRIED that Ewas got married is good.' (Bassong 2014: 251)

(11) *Adjunct Island*
   a. *M-**ɓát**-ga wɔ́-n mɛ bí-ɓɔmá maaŋgɛ́ [ilɔlɛ́
      NMLZ-collect-NMLZ 3-FOC I PST2-meet 1.child before
      a-ḿ-**bátá** bítúyûl].
      1.SM-PST-collect 8.toys
      'COLLECTING I met the child before collecting the toys.'
   b. *M-**ɓom**-ôy wɔ́-n ɓɔɔŋgɛ́ ɓá-yé máséé [ínyuúlɛ́
      NMLZ-roast-NMLZ 3-FOC 2.children 2.SM-be joy because
      mudaá a-m-**ɓôm** kóp].
      1.woman 1.SM-PST1-roast 9.chicken
      'ROAST the children are happy because the woman roasted chicken.'
      (Bassong 2014: 250)

(12) *Coordinate Structure Constraint*
   a. *N-**lamb**-âk wɔ́-n hiŋgɔnda [hi-bí-**lâmb** bíjêk ni
      NMLZ-cook-NMLZ 3-FOC 19.girl 19.SM-PST2-cook 8.food and
      jowa ɓipân].
      wash 8.clothes
      'COOK the girl cooked food and washed the clothes.'
   b. *N-**jê**-k wɔ́-n maaŋgɛ́ [a-bí-**jɛ́** líkúβé ni ɲɔ́
      NMLZ-eat-NMLZ 3-FOC 1.child 1.SM-PST2-eat 5.banana and drink
      malép].
      6.water
      'EAT the child ate a banana and drank water.' (Bassong 2014: 250)

A further indication that verbal fronting involves movement is the lack of genus-species effects, where the two copies of the displaced material show a lexical mismatch such that one of them semantically entails the other (Cable 2004). As shown in (13) such effect is indeed not found in Basaa.

(13)   a. *N-**jé**-ɛk   wɔ́-n maaŋgé a-bí-**ɲámbáá**   líkúβé.
           NMLZ-eat-NMLZ 3-FOC 1.child   1.SM-PST2-chew 5.banana
           'EATING the child chewed a banana.'
    b. *N-**lámb**-âk   wɔ̂-n mudaá a-m-**ɓôm**   kóp.
           NMLZ-cook-NMLZ 3-FOC 1.woman 1.SM-PST1-roast 9.chicken
           'COOKING the woman roasted chicken.'
    c. *N-[**lámb**-âk   hínuní] wɔ́-n mudaá a-bí-**lámb**
           NMLZ-cook-NMLZ 19.bird 3-FOC 1.woman 1.SM-PST2-cook
           híβɛŋ.
           19.pigeon
           'COOKING A BIRD the woman cooked a pigeon.'   (Bassong 2014: 249)

The fronted verb also cannot support any tense or aspectual affixes (14-a) and must not be negated (14-b).

(14)   a. *Bi-**téédá** mudaá a-bí-**téédá**   βítúgûl bí   ɓɔ́ɔ́ŋgé.
           PST2-keep 1.woman 1.SM-PST2-keep 8.toys 8.GEN 2.children
           Intended: 'The woman KEPT the toys of the children.'
    b. *****Téédá**-yá ɓéé mudaá a-**téédá**-yá   ɓéé βítúgûl bí
           keep-PROG NEG 1.woman 1.SM-keep-PROG NEG 8.toys 8.GEN
           ɓɔ́ɔ́ŋgé.
           2.children
           Intended: 'The woman was not KEEPING the toys of the children.'
                                                       (Bassong 2014: 251f.)

Rightwards displacement
Rightwards displacement of the verb displays the same properties as its leftwards counterpart. It can cross finite clause boundaries with bridge verbs (15) but cannot cross island boundaries as shown for the Complex NP Island (16), the Coordinate Structure Constraint (17) and embedding under factive/non-bridge verbs (18).

(15)   Mɛ ŋ́-hɔ́ŋɔ́l   [lɛ́ ɓagwâl ɓá-bíkǎl   [lɛ́ malêt
        I   PRS-think that 2.parents 2.SM-PST2-say that 1.teacher
        a-bí-**ɓám**   ɓáúdú]] m-**ɓám**-ây.
        1.SM-PST2-blame 2.students NMLZ-blame-NMLZ
        'I think that the parents said that the teacher BLAMED the students.'
                                                                  (Bassong 2014: 281)

(16) *Complex NP Island*
??Mɛ bí-ɓɔmá [ɓáúdú (ɓá) ɓá-bí-**sɔ́mb** bikaat]
I PST2-meet 2.students 2.REL 2.SM-PST2-buy 4.books
n-**sɔ́mb**-ɔ̂y.
NMLZ-buy-NMLZ
'I met the students who BOUGHT the books.' (Bassong 2014: 281)

(17) *Coordinate Structure Constraint*
*ɓɔɔŋgɛ́ [ɓá-ń-tčy no **jɛ́**] n-**jɛ́**-ɛy.
2.children 2.SM-PRS-play and eat NMLZ-eat-NMLZ
'The children play and EAT.' (Bassong 2014: 282)

(18) *Factive/Non-bridge Island*
*Malêt a-bí-tâm [lɛ́ mɛ bí-**sɔ́ŋgɔ́l** bíkaat yaaní]
1.teacher 1.SM-PST2-regret that I PST2-read 8.books 1.yesterday
n-**sɔ́ŋ**-l-ak.
NMLZ-read-EPTH-NMLZ
'The teacher regretted that I read the books yesterday READ.'
(Bassong 2014: 282)

Inherent complement verbs

For verbs that take an inherent complement it is possible to displace either the (nominalized) verb alone (19-a, b) leaving a copy in the base position or its inherent complement (19-c) leaving a gap. Both strategies have the same focus interpretation. Fronting of both the verb and its inherent complement together leaving a copy of the verb is ungrammatical (19-d).

(19) a. Di ń-**nɔ́k** masée n-**nɔ́y**-ɔ̂k.
we PRS-feel.IPFV 6.happiness 3.NMLZ-feel-NMLZ

b. N-**nɔ́y**-ɔ̂k wɔ́-n di ń-**nɔ́k** masée.
3.NMLZ-feel-NMLZ 3-FOC we PRS-feel.IPFV 6.happiness

c. Masée mɔ́-n di ń-nɔ́k.
6.happiness 6-FOC we PRS-feel.IPFV
'We ARE HAPPY.'

d. *N-[**nɔ́y-ɔ̂k** masée] wɔ́-n di ń-**nɔ́k**.
3.NMLZ-feel-NMLZ 6.happiness 3-FOC we PRS-feel.IPFV
(Bassong 2014: 284f.)

Summary

As we have seen, Basaa shows verb displacement with verb doubling while verb phrase displacement is only possible if the verb phrase is the complement of an infinitive embedding predicate. Displacement may happen to the left or to the right periphery of the clause, it may cross finite clause boundaries and is sensitive to islands. Additionally, the displaced element and its copy do not exhibit genus-species effects. These diagnostics indicate that the dependency between the displaced verb and its copy in base position is of an $\bar{\text{A}}$-nature. In clause-peripheral position, the verb may not be accompanied by tense or aspectual affixes or negation. Instead, it must be nominalized. The findings are summarized in table 7.1. To conclude, Basaa instantiates pattern A of Generalization IIa.

Tab. 7.1: Properties of verbal fronting in Basaa

	Copy	Dummy	Unbound	Islands	GS	TAM	L-Adv	H-Adv	Neg	L/R	Top/Foc
V	✓	–	✓	✓	–	–	n.d.	n.d.	–	L & R	Foc
VP	–	–									

7.1.2 Berbice Dutch Creole

Berbice Dutch Creole, as the name says, is a Dutch-lexicon based Creole which is spoken in Guyana alongside the Berbice River between the two towns Kwakwani and New Amsterdam. For Berbice Dutch Creole (BDC) verbal fronting constructions there is only limited data available. As Kouwenberg (1994: 438) states: "cleft constructions are not frequent [...] and it is hard to elicit cleft constructions or interpretations for cleft constructions." She distinguishes three types of verb fronting constructions all of which exhibit a copy of the verb in its canonical position. I present and discuss every type in turn.

Type one
In type one the verb is optionally flanked by *da* and *sa* (often shortened to *s* when followed by the subject pronoun *o*). No article or relative pronoun appears with it (20).

(20)   **Nun**=o   **nun**-t=o.
       pull=3SG pull-PF=3SG
       'It pulled it real hard.' (referring to fish pulling the bait).
                                                                      (Kouwenberg 1994: 437)

This fronting receives what Kouwenberg refers to as the "really" interpretation, that is, the reality of the activity or event denoted by the verb is emphasized. I understand this to indicate a verum focus interpretation. TAM-marking or adverbal modifiers do not occur on the fronted verb in spontaneous speech (21).

(21) a. En=a bi dat, **lap**=s=o **lap**-t=o ka?
 3PL=not say that cuff=FOC=3SG cuff-PF=3SG NEG
 'Well didn't they say that he had really hit him?'
 b. Da **mu**=s=o wa **mu**-te.
 BE go=FOC=3SG PAST go-PF
 'He had really gone.' (Kouwenberg 1994: 438)

But aspectual suffixes can be elicited, as shown in (22) in contrast to preverbal particles (23-a), adverbs (23-b) or arguments (23-c).

(22) **Korj**-a so o **korj**-a.
 work-IPF FOC 3SG work-IPF
 'He is working.' (Kouwenberg 1994: 439)

(23) a. *[Wa **kori**] ɛk wa **kori**-a.
 PAST work 1SG PAST work-IPF
 Intended: 'I was really working.'
 b. *[Mu gau-gau] o mu-tɛ gau-gau.
 run quick-quick 3SG run-PF quick-quick
 Intended: 'He really went quickly.'
 c. *[**Skrifu** brifu] ɛkɛ wa **skrif**-a brifu hɛl daka.
 write letter 1SG PAST write-IPF letter whole day
 Intended: 'I was writing letters all day long.'
 (Kouwenberg 1994: 439)

Extraction from non-finite complements of verb-embedding verbs is possible (24).

(24) An ju nin-tɛ, die potman da. **Blɛnd**=s=o bigin-tɛ **blɛndɛ**.
 and 2SG know-PF the old.man BE blind=FOC=3SG begin-PF blind
 'And you know, the father, he started to really get blind.'
 (Kouwenberg 1994: 439)

Also, fronting the matrix verb, i.e. *suku* 'want' in (25) and (26) is equally grammatical as fronting the embedded verb, i.e. *kori* 'work' in (25) and (26), where (25) is an ECM construction and (26) a control construction.

(25) a. Da **kori** s=o sukw-a di toko **kori**.
 BE work FOC=3SG want-IPF the child work
 b. Da **suk**=so o **sukw**-a di toko kori.
 BE want=FOC 3SG want-IPF the child work
 'He really wants the child to work.' (Kouwenberg 1994: 439)

(26) a. Da **kor**=so ori sukw-a **kori**.
       BE work=FOC 3SG want-IPF work
    b. Da **suk**=so o **sukw**-a kori.
       BE want=FOC 3SG want-IPF work
       'He really wants to work.' (Kouwenberg 1994: 439)

Further, in serial verb constructions both verbs of the verbal complex may be fronted, if they serve as content verbs, that is, if their meaning in some way contributes to the overall meaning of the sentence (27).

(27) a. Da **mu**=s=o mu-t **mu** pɛlɛ.
       BE go=FOC=3SG go-PF go play
       'He has gone to play.'
    b. Da **pɛlɛ**=s=o mut mu **pɛlɛ**.
       BE play=FOC=3SG go-PF go play
       'It is playing he has gone to do.' (Kouwenberg 1994: 440)

If the verb only serves as a modifying verb, fronting is ungrammatical (28).

(28) *Da **mu** ɛk wa manggi-tɛ **mu**-tɛ.
     BE go 1SG PST run-PF go-PF
     Intended: 'I really ran there.' (Kouwenberg 1994: 440)

Type two
In type two the fronted verb is preceded by the definite article *di* and optionally followed by a relative pronoun *wati* 'what'. The fronted verb may be preceded by *da* but is never followed by the focus marker *sa*. This construction gives rise to an interpretation of temporal simultaneity or immediate precession (29) and (30).

(29) Di **drai** wat ju **drai**-tɛ di, o ku-tɛ ju.
     the turn what 2SG turn-PF the 3SG catch-PF 2SG
     'As soon as you turn aroune, (the), it catches you.'
     (Kouwenberg 1994: 437)

(30) Di **drai** ɛkɛ **drai** fan di obokwar fi kum iʃi wari? Di
     the turn 2SG turn from the hen.house for come 1PL house? the
     pak=ɛkɛ paka fan di rum ben? ɛkɛ kiki di kɛna
     come.out=1SG come.out from the room inside? 1SG see the person-PL
     latopara bringi.
     lift.IPF.3SG bring
     'As I turned from the henhouse to come to our house, as I came out of the room, I saw them carrying him here.' (Kouwenberg 1994: 441)

The categorial status of the fronted element is somewhat ambiguous between verb and noun. For some fronted verbs, e.g. *kori* 'work', verbal inflection is acceptable (31-a), while it is ungrammatical for other verbs, e.g. *tiri* 'send'.

(31) a. Di **kor**-tɛ wat=jo **kor**-tɛ, ...
 the work-PF what=3SG work-PF, ...
 'The work he has finished...(...was too much for him).'
 b. Di **tiri**(*-tɛ) wat-ɛk **tir**-t=o o brɛkɛ-tɛ.
 the send(-PF) what=1SG send-PF=3SG 3SG break-PF
 'As I sent it, it broke.' (Kouwenberg 1994: 441f.)

On the other hand, the fronted element is accompanied by the definite article and adjectival modification is also accepted sometimes (32).

(32) Di kali **manggi** o **manggi**-tɛ...
 the small run 3SG run-PF...
 'When he had just run off a little way.' (Kouwenberg 1994: 442)

Verbs may be extracted from embedded clauses as shown in (33).

(33) Di **flor** wat=o bi çnapan **flor**-t...
 the lose what=3SG say 3POSS.gun lose-PF...
 'Rather than having lost his gun, as he claims, ...'(Kouwenberg 1994: 442)

Also, in the following serial verb construction, both the matrix verb *mu* 'go' and the embedded verb *twa* 'put' may be fronted.

(34) a. Di **mu** o **mu**-tɛ tw=o,...
 the go 3SG go-PF put=3SG...
 'When he went to put it away, ...'
 b. Di **twa** o mu-tɛ **twa** dangga,...
 the put 3SG go-PF put there...
 'When he went to put (it) away there, ...(he broke it).'
 (Kouwenberg 1994: 442)

This, however, as was the case for type one fronting, is only possible if both verbs are contentful. In the following example (35), *bi(fi)* 'say' has no impact on the meaning of the sentence. It only serves to introduce a complement clause. Consequently, it is only grammatical to front *pama* 'tell' (35-a) but not *bi(fi)* 'tell' (35-b).

(35) a. Di **pama** en **pam**-tɛ=kɛ bi o ʃiki, ek mu-t mu lur=o.
 the tell 3PL tell-PF=3SG say 3SG ill 1SG go-PF PURP look=3SG
 'As soon as they told me that he was ill, I went to see him.'

b. *Di **bifi** en pam-tɛ=kɛ **bifi** o ʃiki, ...
   the say 3PL tell-PF=3SG say 3SG ill   (Kouwenberg 1994: 443)

Based on the fact that the definite article is obligatory, that there is an (optional) relative pronoun, and that the focus marker *sa* is impossible, I am inclined to regard type two constructions as relative constructions with a deverbal head noun rather than monoclausal constructions with a verbal element moved to the left periphery.

Type three
In type three the verb may be flanked by *da* and *sa* and always takes the indefinite article *en*. In all three types there is a copy of the fronted verb in the canonical verb position.

(36) En **kuma** ɛkɛ **kuma**-tɛ tutu nau, ɛkɛ na mu ababa tu R.
     one remain 1SG remain-PF until now 1SG not go anymore to R.
     'I remained until now, I did not go back to R. any more.'
                                                    (Kouwenberg 1994: 437)

The interpretation is one of uninterrupted activity or irreversibility.

(37) En **mu** o **mu**-tɛ.
     one go 3SG go-PF
     a. 'He went all the way without resting.'
     b. 'He has gone for good.'   (Kouwenberg 1994: 444)

As with type two fronting, it is not possible to front and double a verb that serves as a modifying verb in a serial verb construction, rather than as a contentful verb (38).

(38) *En **mu** iç wenggi-tɛ **mu**-tɛ.
     one go 1PL walk-PF go-PF
     Int.: 'We walked all the way (without resting).'   (Kouwenberg 1994: 444)

No further information for this type of fronting is provided in Kouwenberg (1994).

Summary
In Berbice Dutch Creole, fronting of a verb is possible, whereas fronting of a whole verb phrase is not. In case the verb is displaced to the left periphery, a copy of it occurs in base position. Kouwenberg (1994) distinguished three types of verbal fronting constructions, the latter two of which seem to instantiate relative construc-

tions with a deverbal noun as head. This is suggested by the obligatory presence of an article (definite in type two, indefinite in type three) and the optionally occuring relative marker *wati* 'what'. They therefore do not fall under the kind of verbal fronting constructions that this thesis is concerned with and will be disregarded. In contrast, the fronting branded as type one seems to be genuine verb fronting since the fronted element does not exhibit any nominal modification, only verbal affixes are grammatical to a certain extent. The impossibility of fronting preverbal particles and adverbs may be due to them being independent morphemes which do not lose their host when the bare verb is displaced and therefore can be stranded. Furthermore, instead of being optionally followed by a relative marker the fronted verb may be followed by a focus marker indicating that it is located in a designated (left-peripheral) focus position of the clause. Unfortunately, Kouwenberg (1994) does not provide any examples that could be used to diagnose the kind of dependency between the two verb copies, like binding or island examples. Hence, we can summarize the properties of type one verbal fronting in Berbice Dutch Creole in table 7.2. Berbice Dutch Creole thus instantiates pattern A, as it shows only verb fronting and the associated repair is verb doubling.

Tab. 7.2: Properties of verbal fronting (type one) in Berbice Dutch Creole

	copy	dummy	Unbound	Islands	GS	TAM	L-Adv	H-Adv	NEG	L/R	Top/Foc
V	✓	–	(✓)[1]	–	n.d.	n.d.	(✓)[2]	n.d.	n.d.	L	Foc
VP	–	–									

7.1.3 Edo

Edo, a Kwa language of the Niger-Congo family, is spoken in the midwestern part of Nigeria. Based on a 1991 census there are more than one and a half million speakers of the language, which is also called Benin or Bini in older literature.

Edo shows a verbal fronting construction in which a nominalized verb occupies the sentence-initial position while a copy of the verb occurs in the canonical verb

---

[1] Fronting of embedded infinive verbs and contentful serial verbs is possible. No data for fronting out of embedded finite clauses is available.
[2] TAM-suffixes may appear on the fronted verb. Free TAM morphemes cannot be fronted with the verb.

position (39-b). This construction conveys the interpretation of contrastive focus. The basic word order of Edo is SVO as shown in (39-a).

(39) a. Òzó khiɛ́n èbé.
 Ozo sell book
 'Ozo sold the book.'
 b. Ù-**khiɛ́n**-mwèn ɔ́ré Òzó *(**khiɛ́n**) èbé.
 NMLZ-sell-NMLZ FOC Ozo sell book
 'It is selling that Ozo did to the book (not say give as a gift).'
 (Stewart 2001: 92)

This kind of fronting is also attested with unergatives (40) and unaccusatives (41).

(40) a. Òzó só.
 Ozo shouted
 b. Ù-**só**-mwèn ɔ́ré Òzó *(**só**).
 NMLZ-shout-NMLZ FOC Ozo shout
 'It is shouting that Ozo did (not say wail).' (Stewart 2001: 92)

(41) a. Òzó dé.
 Ozo fell
 b. Ù-**dé**-mwèn ɔ́ré Òzó *(**dé**).
 NMLZ-fall-NMLZ FOC Ozo fall
 'It is falling that Ozo did (not say rolling).' (Stewart 1998: 106)

Fronting of the verb with its internal object is grammatical only for some older speakers as Stewart (2001: 114, en. 7) states. Two examples of such verb phrase fronting are given in (42).

(42) a. Ù-[**khiɛ́n**-bé]-mwèn ɔ́ré Òzó *(**khiɛ́n**) èbé.
 NMLZ-sell-book-NMLZ FOC Ozo sell book
 'It is book-selling that Ozo did, (not say give as gift).'
 b. Ù-[**lé**-vbáré]-mwèn ɔ́ré Òzó **lé** èvbàré.
 NMLZ-cook-food-NMLZ FOC Ozo cook food
 'It is food-cooking that Ozo did, not throw the food away.'
 (Stewart 2001: 114, en. 7)

As Stewart (1998, 2001) argues, these constructions are not genuine verbal fronting constructions. Rather they are derived by fronting a deverbal cognate object of the main verb. Verbal fronting which leaves a copy of the verb behind would thus be reduced to standard NP focalization with the difference that the NP is actually a cognate object derived from the main verb. Evidence for this approach comes from the fact that what acts as the sentence-initial constituent in presumed verb fronting can also appear *in situ* (43).

(43) a. Òzó **gbé** èkhù ù-**gbé**-mwèn.
Ozo hit door NMLZ-hit-NMLZ
'Ozo hit the door a hitting.'
b. Òzó **rrí** èvbàré ù-**ré**-mwèn.
Ozo eat food NMLZ-eat-NMLZ
'Ozo ate the food a eating.' (Stewart 2001: 95f.)

Additionally, there are verbs whose cognate object is not derived using the *ù-mwèn* nominalizer but some vowel prefix (44-a). Among those are verbs like *hiɔ́* 'urinate, *kpá* 'vomit', *khián* 'walk', *wén* 'breast feed', and *tué* 'greet'. When constructing a fronting sentence with such a verb, the fronted constituent also shows the irregular nominalization (44-b).

(44) a. Òzó **tué** úyì ò-**tué**.
Ozo greet Uyi NMLZ-greet
'Ozo greeted Uyi a greeting.'
b. Ò-**tué** ɔ́ré Òzó **tué**.
NMLZ-greet FOC Ozo greet
'It is greeting that Ozo greeted, not (say) a sneer.'
(Stewart 1998: 94, 96)

According to Stewart (1998), if the nominalization of the sentence-initial constituent were a property or consequence of the fronting itself, we would expect all verbs to show the same nominalization. However, as evidenced by (45), the regular nominalization is not available for the relevant verbs.

(45) *Ù-**tué**-mwèn ɔ́ré Òzó **tué**.
NMLZ-greet-NMLZ FOC Ozo greet (Stewart 2001: 95)

I do not see why this is supposed to be an argument against an approach that treats verbal fronting as being derived from actual verb movement. In my opinion, there is no reason to assume that the lexically conditioned allomorphy of the nominalizer cannot also be active when a verb is nominalized in the left periphery. As its name indicates it is lexically rather than position conditioned.

Anticipating a possible counter-argument to his proposal, Stewart points out that, as we have already seen in (44-a), a cognate object can cooccur with the thematic direct object of a transitive verb. Hence, transitive sentences in which the main verb seems to be copied and fronted in a nominalized form pose no problem for the anaylsis of fronting as cognate object focalization.

A last argument in favour of his approach comes from the fact that a fronted cognate object cannot cooccur with one *in situ* (46).

(46) *Ù-**tuɛ́**-mwèn ɔ́ré Òzó **tuɛ́** ò-**tuɛ́**.
 NMLZ-greet-NMLZ FOC Ozo greet NMLZ-greet

(Stewart 2001: 98)

Although one cannot be sure that the ungrammaticality of (46) is due to the presence of the cognate object or due to the fact that the nominalizer on the fronted verb is *ù-mwèn*, which we know from (45) to be independently ungrammatical, this is probably Stewart's strongest argument. Given that nominalized verbs serving as cognate objects are available *in situ*, if the fronting constructions were derived by genuinely fronting a verb (nominalizing it during the process) nothing would preclude a derivation in which the verb *tuɛ́* 'greet' in (46) underwent fronting, thereby turning into a deverbal noun, while its cognate object *òtuɛ́* 'greeting' remained in place.

Summary
To summarize, verbal fronting in Edo is argued to not be actual fronting of a verb. Rather, it is suggested to be NP fronting of an independently available deverbal cognate object. Stewart (1998, 2001) does not provide any data concerning the possibility of verbal morphology, negation or adverbs on the fronted element nor does he discuss genus-species effects or island restrictions. The overview over the properties of Edo verbal fronting in table 7.3 is therefore quite short.

Tab. 7.3: Properties of verbal fronting in Edo

	Copy	Dummy	Unbound	Islands	GS	TAM	L-Adv	H-Adv	Neg	L/R	Top/Foc
V	✓	–	n.d.	n.d.	n.d.	n.d.	n.d.	n.d.	n.d.	L	Foc
VP	(✓)[3]	–								L	Foc

Setting aside Stewart's arguments in favour of cognate object movement for the moment, we can classify Edo as falling under pattern A, as a language that exhibits only verb fronting with verb doubling, or, alternatively, under pattern I for the older speakers who still allow verb phrase fronting with verb doubling.

---

[3] VP fronting is only possible for older speakers. If it is accepted, it shows verb doubling rather than dummy verb insertion.

7.1.4 Ewe

Ewe is a Kwa language (Niger-Congo) spoken by more than three million people in Ghana, Southern Togo, and Benin. Its basic word order is SVO (Collins 1993: 16).

(47) ɖèví lá ɖù àkɔ́ɖú.
child DET eat banana
'The child ate a banana.' (Buell 2012: 3)

In some dialects of Ewe (Aŋlɔ, Kpele, Waci; see Ameka 1992: 12), though not in Standard Ewe, there is a verb focus construction in which the verb shows up in sentence-initial position while a copy of the verb appears in the canonical verb position (48-b).

(48) a. Kofi sí.
Kofi escape
'Kofi escaped.'
b. **Sí** Kofi **sí**.
escape Kofi escape
'Escape Kofi did.' (Ameka 1991: 44f.)

This construction is also available for transitive verbs as exemplified in (49).

(49) **ɖu** me **ɖu** nǔ
eat 1SG eat thing
'Eat I did.' (Ameka 1992: 12)

Note that there is no overt indication that the fronted verb is nominalized in (49). However, in other examples, like those in (50) and (51), the verb is overtly nominalized and optionally marked with the focus particle *(y)é* which also shows up in regular nominal focus.

(50) φo-**φo**-é wò-**φo**-é.
RED-hit-FOC 3SG-hit-3SG
'Beating s/he beat him/her.' (Ameka 1992: 12)

(51) ƒò-**ƒò**-é wò-**ƒò** ɖèví-á.
RED-hit-FOC 3SG-hit child-DEF
'He gave the child a rough beating.'
Lit.: 'Beating, he beat the child.' (Ameka 2010: 159)

Apparently, different dialects use different strategies in verbal fronting constructions. Examples with a fronted verb phrase, however, are only documented with the aspectual auxiliary *lè* 'be at' present (52).

(52)   [Mɔ́lì ɖù gé]₁   mè-lè   ___₁.
       rice eat PROSP 1SG-be.at
       'I'm about to EAT SOME RICE.'   (Buell 2012: 4)

This situation is analogous to Gungbe (see section 7.1.6) where verb phrase fronting can also only be observed if a progressive aspect auxiliary is stranded in the clause. In both languages no repair is triggered by this kind of verb phrase fronting. I thus conclude that Ewe does not allow verb phrase fronting in the sense of this book.

Concerning the syntactic properties of the construction, I was unable to find any data in the literature showing which elements may be fronted together with the verb (e.g. TAM-markers, negation, adverbs, etc.). Equally absent are examples that might help to reveal whether there is an Ā-dependency between the verb copies or not (e.g. island sentences, genus-species effects, etc.). Collins (1993: 178) remarks, though without providing evidence, that "[t]he copy cleft construction evidently involves movement of a nominalization of the verb". Thus, at this point, I have to remain agnostic about most of the properties of verbal fronting in Ewe.

Summary

What we can take as a fact is that Ewe disposes of a verb fronting construction and that in this construction two copies of the verb are present, one sentence-initially and another in the canonical position. Only bare verbs seem to be licit clause-initially with a clause-internal repair but not whole verb phrases. Whether the fronted verb is nominalized or not is probably subject to dialectal variation. Thus, we can summarize what we know in table 7.4. Showing only verb fronting with a verb doubling repair Ewe thus instantiates pattern A.

Tab. 7.4: Properties of verbal fronting in Ewe

	Copy	Dummy	Unbound	Islands	GS	TAM	L-Adv	H-Adv	NEG	L/R	Top/Foc
V	✓	–	n.d.	n.d.	n.d.	n.d.	n.d.	n.d.	n.d.	L	Foc
VP	–	–									

7.1.5 Fongbe

Fongbe, another Kwa language of the Niger-Congo family, is spoken by more than two million people most of which live in Benin. Smaller groups of speakers can be found in Togo and Nigeria. The basic word order is SVO in non-nominalized clauses and SOV in nominalized clauses (Lefebvre & Brousseau 2002).

Fongbe makes use of (slightly different) verb fronting constructions to express a variety of meanings. Example (53-a) shows a temporal adverbial clause, example (53-b) a causal adverbial clause. In both of them the verb is fronted and a copy of the verb is left in the base position. Factive clauses also contain two copies of the verb (53-c), as do predicate cleft constructions (53-d), where the fronted verb receives a contrastive focus interpretation (Lefebvre 1992, Lefebvre & Brousseau 2002).

(53) a. **Wá** Kɔ̀kú **wá** (tlóló) bɔ̀ Bàyí yì.
arrive Koku arrive as.soon.as and Bayi leave
'As soon as Koku arrived, Bayi left.'
b. **Wá** Kɔ̀kú **wá** útú Bàyí yì.
arrive Koku arrive cause Bayi leave
'Because Koku arrived, Bayi left.'
c. **Wá** ɖé-è Kɔ̀kú **wá** ɔ́ víví nú nɔ̀ tɔ̀n.
arrive OP-RES Koku arrive DEF please for mother GEN
'The fact that Koku arrived pleased his mother.'
d. **Wá** wɛ̀ Kɔ̀kú **wá**.
arrive FOC[4] Koku arrive
'It is arrived that Koku has.' (not, e.g., leave)

(Lefebvre & Brousseau 2002: 503)

In what follows, I will focus on the predicate cleft construction (53-d) to make verb fronting and verb doubling in Fongbe easily comparable with the other languages of the sample, in which verb fronting with doubling/dummy verb insertion most often serves to express a similar (contrastive) focus or topic meaning rather than temporal/causal adverbials. For the most part, though, adverbial verb doubling constructions show the same properties as their respective contrastive focus counterparts (see Lefebvre & Brousseau 2002 for detailed discussion of the properties of the adverbial and factive construction).

First, it is not possible to front the internal argument together with the verb as evidenced by the ungrammaticality of (54). Thus, Fongbe only allows verb fronting but not verb phrase fronting.

(54) *[Gbà xwé ɔ́] wɛ̀ é gbà (xwé) ɔ́.
destroy house DEF FOC 3SG destroy house DEF

(Lefebvre & Brousseau 2002: 507)

---

[4] Lefebvre & Brousseau (2002) gloss wɛ̀ as 'it.is'. However, I follow Ndayiragije (1992) who argues that subject and object clefts involve movement to SpecCP, thus are monoclausal, and that wɛ̀, which also shows up in these contexts, is therefore actually a focus marker rather than a copula.

However, fronting of the verb may trigger both a contrastive interpretation on the verb (55-a) or on the whole verb phrase (55-b).

(55) a. **Xò** wὲ Àsíbá **xò** Kɔ̀kú. e hù è   ǎ.
       hit FOC Asiba hit Koku he kill him NEG
       'It's HIT that Asiba did to Koku. He did not kill him.'
    b. **Xò** wὲ Àsíbá **xò** Kɔ̀kú. e hù Sika ǎ.
       hit FOC Asiba hit Koku he kill Sika NEG
       'It's HIT KOKU that Asiba did. He did not kill Sika.'
       (Law & Lefebvre 1995: 35)

The fronting of a verb whose delimiting internal argument is indefinite, where a delimiting argument is "the argument which imposes an end point to the event denoted by the verb" (Lefebvre 1992: 55, fn. 5) is ungrammatical. Thus, of the following example (56-a, b) only the one with a definite internal argument is licit in Fongbe. This also holds for arguments of unaccusative verbs (56-c, d).

(56) a. **ɖù** wὲ Kɔ̀kú **ɖù** àsòn ɔ́.
       eat FOC Koku eat crab DET
    b. *****ɖù** wὲ Kɔ̀kú **ɖù** àsɔ́n.
       eat FOC Koku eat crab
       'It is eat that Koku did to the/a crab (not e.g. throw it away).'
    c. **Yì** wὲ Kɔ̀kú **yì**.
       leave FOC Koku leave
    d. *****Yì** wὲ súnù **yì**.
       leave FOC man leave
       'It is leave that Koku/some man did (not e.g. arrive).'
       (Lefebvre 1992: 58)

With verbs like *sé* 'know' or *kpé* 'accompany', which never show a delimiting argument, verb fronting is impossible (57).

(57) a. *****Sé** wὲ Kɔ̀kú **sé**   fongbe.
       know FOC Koku know Fon
       'It is know that Koku knows Fon.'
    b. *****Kpé**   wὲ Kɔ̀ku **kpé**   Àsíbá.
       accompany FOC Koku accompany Asiba
       'It is accompany that Koku accompanied Asiba.'   (Lefebvre 1992: 58)

Verb fronting shows properties of Ā-movement. The dependency between the two verb copies may cross finite clause boundaries (58). Verbs may also be fronted when they are embedded under an infinitive-embedding verb (59).

(58) **Xò** wè Sìká lìn [ɖɔ̀ Kɔ̀fí ɖɔ̀ [ɖɔ̀ Àsíbá **xò** Kɔ̀kú]].
hit FOC Sika think C Kofi say C Asiba hit Koku
'It is hit that Sika thinks that Kofi said that Asiba did to Koku.'
(Law & Lefebvre 1995: 32)

(59) **Wá** wè Kɔ̀kú jló ná **wá**.
come FOC Koku want DEF.FUT come
'It is come that Koku wants to do.' (Lefebvre & Brousseau 2002: 155)

In such long-distance dependencies, subjacency effects occur (60) indicating that verb fronting involves Ā-movement.

(60) *ɖù wè kɔ̀kú kànbyɔ̀ Àsíbá [ɖɔ̀ mè wè ɖù àsɔ́n ɔ́ à-jí].
eat FOC Koku ask Asiba C person FOC eat crab DEF Q-on
Lit.: 'It is eat that Koku asked Asiba who did to the crab.'
(Law & Lefebvre 1995: 16)

Furthermore, the construction is sensitive to islands such as the Complex NP Island (61-a) and the Wh-Island (61-b)

(61) a. *Gbà (wè) ùn tùn [súnû ɖé-è **gbà** xwé ɔ́].
destroy FOC 1SG know man OP-RES destroy house DEF
b. *Bló (wè) Bàyí kànbyɔ̀ [ɖɔ̀ étè₁ (wè) Kɔ̀kú **bló** ___₁].
do FOC Bayi ask C what FOC Koku do
(Ndayiragije 1993: 107f.)

In addition, the cooccurrence of verb fronting with other Ā-movements, like Wh-extraction (62-a), NP cleft (62-b), and relative clauses (62-c) is ungrammatical in the same clause.

(62) a. *Été₁ wè, **ɖù** wè Kɔ̀kú **ɖù** ___₁.
what FOC eat FOC Koku eat
b. *[Àsɔ́n ɔ́]₁ wè, **ɖù** wè Kɔ̀kú **ɖù** ___₁.
crab DEF FOC eat FOC Koku eat
c. *[Àsɔ́n ɔ́]₁, **ɖù** wè, ɖé-è Kɔ̀kú **ɖù** ___₁ ɔ́.
crab DEF eat FOC OP-RES Koku eat DEF
(Law & Lefebvre 1995: 16)

We can therefore safely conclude that Ā-movement is involved in the verb fronting construction.

Further restrictions concern the size, categorial status, and semantic type of the fronted verb and the kind of material that may cooccur with it. There is no overt nominal morphology on the fronted verb, even though such morphology exists in the language, and its tone pattern and segmental make-up is exactly the same as for the verb in canonical position (Lefebvre & Brousseau 2002: 504). However, with underlyingly disyllabic verbs, the fronted verb may either occur as the full disyllabic verb or, at least for some speakers, as a truncated monosyllabic form (63). Collins (1994) interprets this truncation as a kind of nominal morphology.

(63) **Sísɔ́/sí/*sɔ́** wɛ̀ Kɔ̀kú **sísɔ́**.
       tremble   FOC Koku tremble
       'It is tremble that Koku did.'   (Lefebvre & Brousseau 2002: 504)

Another piece of evidence in favour of the nominal category of the fronted verb comes from the fact that definite and demonstrative determiners may appear with it (64).

(64) **Yì** ɔ́ wɛ̀ Kɔ̀kú **yì**.
       leave DEF FOC Koku leave
       'It is leave (as expected) that Koku did (not e.g. stay home)'
                                              (Lefebvre & Brousseau 2002: 506)

Besides the determiner, however, nothing may accompany the fronted verb, neither TAM-markers (65) nor negation (66) nor adverbs (67) nor adjuncts (68). Although all of these can occur clause-internally, as expected.

(65) a. *Ná   **yì** wɛ̀ Kɔ̀kú ná   **yì**.
          DEF.FUT leave FOC Koku DEF.FUT leave
      b. **Yì** wɛ̀ Kɔ̀kú ná   **yì**.
         leave FOC Koku DEF.FUT leave
         'It is leave that Koku will leave.' (Lefebvre & Brousseau 2002: 507)

(66) a. ***Yì** ǎ wɛ̀ Kɔ̀kú **yì**.
          leave Neg FOC Koku leave
      b. *Mà **yì** wɛ̀ Kɔ̀kú **yì**.
         NEG leave FOC Koku leave
      c. **Yì** wɛ̀ Kɔ̀kú **yì** ǎ.
         leave FOC Koku leave Neg
         'It is not the case that Koku left.' (he did something else)
                                              (Lefebvre & Brousseau 2002: 507)

(67) a. ***dù** gànjí wɛ̀ Kɔ̀kú **dù** nú.
          eat well   FOC Koku eat thing
      b. **dù** wɛ̀ Kɔ̀kú **dù** gànjí.
         eat FOC Koku eat well
         'As for eating, Koku ate well.'   (Lefebvre & Brousseau 2002: 508)

(68) a. *Xò kpó bá kpó wè Kɔ̀kú **xò** Àsíbá.
hit with stick with FOC Koku hit Asiba
b. **Xò** wè Kɔ̀kú **xò** Àsíbá kpó bá kpó.
hit FOC Koku hit Asiba with stick with
'It is hit that Koku hit Asiba with a stick.'

(Lefebvre & Brousseau 2002: 508)

Not all types of verbs may be fronted in a contrastive focus construction. The relevant distinction is between individual-level and stage-level predicates (for a discussion of the distinction see Carlson 1977, Kratzer 1995). Individual-level predicates denote permanent properties of individuals whereas stage-level predicates denote actions or temporary properties of individuals. The former include verbs like *sé* 'know' and *ɖì* 'resemble'. These cannot be used in a verb fronting construction (69).

(69) a. ***Sé** wè Kɔ̀kú **sé** fɔ̀ngbè.
know FOC Koku know Fongbe
b. ***Túùn** wè Kɔ̀kú **túùn** Bàyí.
know FOC Koku know Bayi
c. ***ɖì** wè Kɔ̀kú **ɖì** tɔ́ tɔ̀n.
resemble FOC Koku resemble father GEN

(Lefebvre & Brousseau 2002: 510)

Inherent complement verbs and cognate object verbs

Cognate object verbs do not show the verb doubling effect found with other kinds of verbs. Rather, the cognate object is fronted to achieve the same interpretation that verb doubling would yield with normal predicates (70).

(70) a. nɔ́ ànɔ́
suck breast
'to suck'
b. *****Nɔ́** wè ví ɔ́ **nɔ́** ànɔ́.[5]
suck FOC child DEF suck breast
'It is suck that the child did.'
c. Ànɔ́ wè ví ɔ́ nɔ́___.
breast FOC child DEF suck
'It is suck breast that the child did (not e.g. suck from a bottle/not e.g. cry).' (Lefebvre & Brousseau 2002: 512f.)

---

5 Note that some speakers also accept this example as grammatical in addition to c.

With inherent complement verbs the situation is slightly different. In addition to the possibility of fronting the verb leaving a copy in base position (71-a) there is the option to front the inherent complement leaving a gap clause-internally (71-b). Both options give rise to the same contrastive focus reading.

(71) a. **Kùn** wὲ Kɔ̀kú **kùn** hún.
 drive FOC Koku drive vehicle
 'It is drive that Koku did (not e.g. ride a horse).'
 b. Hún wὲ Kɔ̀kú kùn ___.
 vehicle FOC Koku drive
 'It is drive that Koku did (not e.g. ride a horse).'

(Lefebvre & Brousseau 2002: 515)

Light verb constructions (72) show the same behaviour as inherent complement verbs.

(72) a. **Jì** wὲ Kɔ̀kú **jì** hàn.
 produce FOC Koku produce song
 'It is sing that Koku did (not e.g. dance).'
 b. Hàn wὲ Kɔ̀kú jì ___.
 song FOC Koku produce
 'It is sing that Koku did (not e.g. dance).'

(Lefebvre & Brousseau 2002: 515f.)

Summary

As we have seen in the previous sections, Fongbe shows verb fronting with a copy of the verb occurring in the base position, which gives rise to a contrastive focus interpretation on the verb or the verb phrase. This fronting is restricted to stage-level predicates and verbs with a definite delimiting internal object. In contrast, fronting of a whole verb phrase is not possible. Definite and demonstrative determiners can accompany the verb whereas TAM-markers, negation, adverbs and adjuncts are not allowed to be part of the fronted constituent. This indicates that the fronted verb is actually nominalized. Concerning the nature of the dependency between the fronted verb and the one in base position, there are three diagnostics showing that it involves $\bar{A}$-movement. First, the fronting may take place across clause boundaries, finite as well as infinite ones. Second, fronting from islands results in ungrammaticality. And, third, fronting of a verb is impossible if there is another $\bar{A}$-dependency from the same clause. The properties are summarized in table 7.5. In conclusion, Fongbe constitutes a prime example for a language with pattern A, namely only exhibiting verb fronting with the associated repair of verb doubling.

Tab. 7.5: Properties of verbal fronting in Fongbe

	Copy	Dummy	Unbound	Islands	GS	TAM	L-Adv	H-Adv	Neg	L/R	Top/Foc
V	✓	–	✓	✓	n.d.	–	–	n.d.	–	L	Foc
VP	–	–									

7.1.6 Gungbe

Gungbe, like Ewe and Fongbe, is a Kwa language of the Niger-Congo family. It is spoken by about 600 000 speakers in Benin and Nigeria. Its basic word order is quite strictly SVO(IO) and SAuxVO with auxiliary constructions (Aboh 1998).

Both, fronting of the verb and fronting of the verb phrase are attested in Gungbe giving rise to a focus interpretation which is not specified any further in Aboh (1998). However, while verb fronting is relatively freely applicable, fronting of the verb phrase is restricted to progressive constructions with the auxiliary *tè*. Also, the former leaves a copy of the fronted verb in the base position (73-a) in contrast to the latter which leaves a gap when fronted (73-b).

(73)   a.   **Gbá** (wè) Séná **gbá** xwé lɔ́.
            build FOC Sena build.PERF house the
            'Sena BUILT the house.'
   b.   [Xwé lɔ́ gbá]$_1$ (wè) Séná tè ____$_1$
            house the build FOC Sena PROG
            'Sena is BUILDING THE HOUSE.'   (Aboh 1998: 16)

Example (74) shows that verb phrase fronting with a copy of the verb in its canonical position results in ungrammaticality.

(74)   *[Wémà lɔ́ **xìá**] Rèmí **xìá**.
      book the read Remi read.PERF   (Aboh 1998: 37)

For some speakers, the focus marker is optional while it must be absent for others. When present, the former group of speakers assigns some kind of heavy focus interpretation to the construction (Aboh 1998). As the verb phrase fronting in (73-b) is not the kind of verbal fronting this book is concerned with because it does not trigger verb doubling or dummy verb insertion, I will only briefly outline some of its properties here.

Verb phrase fronting is possible with only one special type of progressive where an auxiliary *tò* occurs and the object appears in a preverbal position despite the general SAuxVO order (75).

(75) Séná tò   mótò lɔ́ dǐn.
      Sena PROG car   the search
      'Sena is looking for the car.'   (Aboh 1998: 25)

When a verb phrase is fronted in such a progressive construction, it is impossible to strand the object (76-a) or to revert the OV order (76-b).

(76) a. *Dín   Séná tò   Kòfí.
             search Sena PROG Kofi
      b. *Dín   mì Séná tè.
             search 1SG Sena PROG   (Aboh 1998: 26)

Also, the auxiliary *tò* must change to *tè* when crossed over by the verb phrase (77).

(77) [Nyɛ̀   dín]₁ (wɛ̀) Séná tè/*tò __₁.
      1SG[STRONG] search FOC Sena PROG
      'Sena is LOOKING FOR ME.'   (Aboh 1998: 26)

Since aspectual material is stranded clause-internally, the fronted constituent must be smaller than the aspect phrase.

Turning to the bare verb fronting construction, we find that the valency pattern of the verb has no influence on its frontability. Intransitive unergative verbs (78-a), unaccusative verbs (78-b), as well as transitive (78-c) and ditransitive verbs (78-d) may appear in sentence-initial position.

(78) a. **Fɔ́n** yé **fɔ́n**   bléblé.
             stand 3PL stand.PERF quickly
             'They STOOD UP quickly.'
      b. **Wá** yé **wá**.
             arrive 3PL arrive
             'They ARRIVED.'
      c. **ɖù** Séná **ɖù**   blédì lɔ́.
             eat Sena eat.PERF bread the
             'Sena ATE the bread.'
      d. **Kplɔ́n** Séná **kplɔ́n** hàn vǐ lé.
             teach Sena teach.PERF song child PL
             'Sena TAUGHT the children a song.'   (Aboh 1998: 36)

In contrast to Fongbe, where verb fronting is linked to the definiteness of the delimiting argument (see section 7.1.5), Gungbe shows no such definiteness constraint. Verb fronting is grammatical even if the delimiting argument is indefinite/unspecific as shown in (79).

(79) a. **Hù** yé **hù** dàwè ḍɛ́ ḍó àlìò jí.
kill 3PL kill.PERF man a PREP road on
'They KILLED a man on the road.'
b. **Gbà** kpònɔ̀ lɛ̀ **gbà** xwé ḍé.
break soldier PL break.PERF house a
'The soldiers DESTROYED a house.' (Aboh 1998: 37)

A further difference between Fongbe and Gungbe lies in the fact that while verb fronting across clause boundaries is possible in the former it is not possible in the latter (80). If the fronting happens within the embedded clause, however, the sentence is perfectly grammatical (81).

(80) a. *__ḍù__ ún sè [ḍɔ̀ yé **ḍù** blɛ́ḍì lɔ́].
eat 1SG hear.PERF C 3PL eat.PERF bread the
b. *__ḍù__ ún ḍɔ̀ [ḍɔ̀ yé **ḍù** blɛ́ḍì lɔ́].
eat 1SG say.PERF C 3PL eat.PERF bread the (Aboh 1998: 38)

(81) Ùn sè [ḍɔ̀ **xɔ̀** Súrù **xɔ̀** wémá].
1SG hear C buy Suru buy book
'I heard that Suru BOUGHT a book.' (Aboh & Dyakonova 2009: 1046)

This piece of data might be taken as an indication that the dependency between the fronted verb and its copy in base position is not Ā-movement.

It is equally ungrammatical to front the verb affixed with TAM-markers, as evidenced by (82). Due to the scarcity of the data, it has to remain open whether this restriction extends to negation and adverbs.

(82) a. *__ḍù__-ná-nɔ̀ yé **ḍù** blɛ́ḍì lɔ́.
eat-FUT-HAB 3PL eat bread the
b. *__ḍù__-nɔ̀-ná yé **ḍù** blɛ́ḍì lɔ́.
eat-HAB-FUT 3PL eat bread the
c. *__ḍù__ yé ná nɔ̀ **ḍù** blɛ́ḍì lɔ́.
eat 3PL FUT HAB eat bread the (Aboh 1998: 38)

With inherent complement verbs, verbal fronting is ungrammatical (83-a). In order to achieve a focus interpretation analogous to fronting of regular verbs, the inherent complement can be placed in clause-initial position (83-b). As is the case with regular verbs, fronting of the whole verb phrase leaving a copy of the verb in the base position results in ungrammaticality (83-c). Example (83-d) serves to show that the combination of *dó* and *wèzùn* acts as a semantic unit where neither of the two parts can be left out without affecting the grammaticality of the sentence.

(83) a. Wézùn₁ (wè) Kòfí dó ___₁ sɔ́n xwégbè.
race FOC Kofi plant from house
'Kofi RUN out from the house.'
b. *Dó Kòfí dó wèzùn sɔ́n xwégbè.
plant Kofi plant race from house
c. *Dó wézùn (wè) Kòfí dó sɔ́n xwégbè.
plant race FOC Kofi plant from house
d. Kòfí *(dó) *(wèzùn) sɔ́n xwégbè.
Kofi plant race from house
'Kofi ran out from the house.' (Aboh & Dyakonova 2009: 1059)

Summary
To summarize this section, Gungbe shows verb fronting with verb doubling, but not verb phrase fronting. The latter is only allowed in a specific progressive construction and does not require a verb copy or dummy verb clause-internally. The interpretation associated with verbal displacement is focalization of the displaced constituent. Verb fronting is not restricted by the valency of the verb or the definiteness of the internal argument. However, it is clause-bound, it may take place in embedded clauses and it disallows TAM-marked verbs in sentence-initial position. Lastly, inherent complement verbs cannot undergo fronting, instead, their inherent complement may be placed in the left-peripheral focus position. Taken together, the important properties are summarized in table 7.6. Judging from the available data, Gungbe instantiates pattern A by displaying verb fronting only with a corresponding repair of verb doubling.

Tab. 7.6: Properties of verbal fronting in Gungbe

	Copy	Dummy	Unbound	Islands	GS	TAM	L-Adv	H-Adv	Neg	L/R	Top/Foc
V	✓	–	–	–	n.d.	–	n.d.	n.d.	n.d.	L	Foc
VP	–	–									

7.1.7 Haitian Creole

Haitian Creole is a French-based creole language spoken by ten to twelve million speakers the largest part of which live in Haiti itself.

There is a verb fronting construction in Haitian Creole where the verb is displaced to the sentence-initial position preceded by *se* and a copy of the verb occurs in the base position (84). The construction triggers a contrastive focus interpretation of the fronted verb.

(84) a. Se **kouri** Jan **kouri**.
 SE run John run
 'It is running that John did.' (not walking)
 b. Se te **manje** li tre di Jan t' ap **manje** pen an.
 SE TNS eat he TNS say John TNS ASP eat bread DET
 'It was eating the bread he said that John did.' (not drinking the water)
 (Lefebvre 1987: 169)

The internal argument of the verb cannot occur in the fronted position with the verb (85).

(85) a. *Se [**manje** pen an] Jan **manje** pen an.
 SE eat bread DET John eat bread DET
 (Larson & Lefebvre 1991: 248)
 b. *Se [**manje** yon pòm] Jan **manje** (yon pòm).
 SE eat an apple John eat an apple
 Intended: 'John ATE AN APPLE.' (Harbour 2008: 856)

The particle *se* which is homophonous with the copula obligatorily appears in verb fronting (86-a, b) while it is optional in regular NP fronting (86-c, d).[6]

(86) a. *(Se) **kontan** li **kontan**.
 'That's HAPPY he is happy.'
 b. *(Se) **pati** li **pati**.
 'That's LEAVE that he left.'
 c. (Se) ki mun ki vini?
 'It's who who came?'
 d. (Se) Jan ki vini.
 'It's John who came.'
 (Lumsden & Lefebvre 1990: 771, no gloss in source)

Regarding the interpretation, the scope of the contrastive focalization usually comprises the verb alone. However, it can be shifted to include the whole verb phrase or even the object to the exclusion of the verb if an aspectually delimiting complement (cf. Tenny 1987) or certain aspectual verbs are present (Larson &

---

6 I gloss *se* as SE and remain agnostic as to whether it actually is a copula in the verb fronting construction or a focus marker which arose through grammaticalization of the copula in this construction.

Lefebvre 1991: 251f.). In other words, an endpoint of the event or action denoted by the verb must be implied. Thus, in (87), the delimiting phrase *al lekol* 'to school' is present and implies an endpoint of the action of walking denoted by the verb *mache* 'walk'. In this case, the three interpretational options in (87-a–c) are available.

(87)   Se **mache** Jan   **mache** al lekol.
       SE walk   John walk   to school
   a.   'It is walk that John did to school (not, e.g., run).'
   b.   'It is walk to school that John did (not, e.g., run home).'
   c.   'It is to school that John walked (not, e.g., to the park).'
                                                  (Larson & Lefebvre 1991: 251)

However, when replacing the goal phrase *al lekol* 'to school' with a non-delimiting locative phrase like *nan lari a* 'in the street', no endpoint of the walking action is implied anymore (88). Consequently, only the interpretation with the contrastive focus falling on the verb alone (88-a) is possible. Verb phrase or object contrastive focalization (88-b, c) are precluded.

(88)   Se **mache** Jan   **mache** nan lari   a.
       SE walk   John walk   in   street DET
   a.   'It is walk that John did in the street (not, e.g., run).'
   b.   *'It is walk in the street that John did (not, e.g., run home).'
   c.   *'It is in the street that John walked (not, e.g., in the park).'
                                                  (Larson & Lefebvre 1991: 251)

The same pattern is shown in (89) and (90), this time it is the aspect of the clause-internal verb copy that allows all three interpretations (89) whereas the absence of this aspect restricts the possible interpretations to default narrow verb focus (90).

(89)   Se **fè**   Jan   fèk **fè**   tab.
       SE make John ASP make table
   a.   'It is making that John is just finished doing with a table (not, e.g., painting).'
   b.   'It is making a table that John is just finished doing (not, e.g., painting walls).'
   c.   'It is just finished that John is with respect ti making a table (not, e.g., just starting).'   (Larson & Lefebvre 1991: 252)

(90)   Se **fè**   Jan   fè   tab.
       SE make John make table
   a.   'It is making that John did with tables (not, e.g., painting).'

b. *'It is making a table that John did (not, e.g., painting walls).'
c. *'It is a table that John made (not, e.g., a chair).'

(Larson & Lefebvre 1991: 252)

Turning to the evidence for the Ā-nature of the dependency between the fronted verb and the copy in the base position, we find that fronting is grammatical across clause-boundaries with bridge-verbs and control verbs (91).

(91) a. Se **malad** m kwè [yo di [Mari **malad**]].
SE sick I believe they say Mary sick
'I believe they said Mary is SICK.' (Piou 1982: 123)
b. Li di [li vle [se **ale** pou Jan **ale** avè li]].
3SG say 3SG want SE go COMP John go with 3SG
'He said she wants John to GO with her.'
c. Li di [se **ale** li vle [pou Jan **ale** avè li]].
3SG say SE go 3SG want COMP John go with 3SG
'He said she wants John to GO with her.'
d. Se **ale** li di [li vle [pou Jan **ale** avè li]].
SE go 3SG say 3SG want COMP John go with 3SG
'He said she wants John to GO with her.' (Piou 1982: 130–133)

Additionally, verb fronting is island-sensitive. A verb cannot be fronted out of a Complex NP Island (92), a Wh-Island (93), a Subject Island (94) (which is also at the same time a Relative Clause island), or an Adjunct Island (95).

(92) *Se **mouri** mwen kwè [istwa ke ou te **mouri** a].
SE die 1SG believe story that 2SG ANT die the
Intended: 'I believed the rumour that you had DIED.'

(Harbour 2008: 856)

(93) *Se **kuit** m ap mande m [ki sa pou m **kuit** pou li].
SE cook 1SG PROG ask 1SG what COMP 1SG cook for 3SG
Intended: 'I'm wondering what to COOK for him.'

(Harbour 2008: 856)

(94) a. *Se **vann** [madanm ki te konn **vann** mwen akasan an] mouri.
SE sell woman REL ANT HAB sell me akassan the die
Intended: 'The woman who used to SELL me akassan died.'
b. *Se **kraze** y ap rebati [kay ki te kraze nan tanpèt la].
SE destroy 3PL PROG rebuild house REL ANT destroy in storm the
Intended: 'They're rebuilding the house that was DESTROYED in the storm.' (Harbour 2008: 856)

(95) a. M an reta [paske se **ede** mwen t ap **ede** yon
1SG late because SE help 1SG ANT PROG help a
granmoun]
old.person
'I'm late because I was HELPING an old person.'
b. *Se **ede** m an reta [paske mwen t ap **ede** yon
SE help 1SG late because 1SG ANT PROG help a
granmoun].
old.person
Intended: 'I'm late because I was HELPING an old person.'
(Harbour 2008: 856)

Thus, verb fronting shows properties that are generally associated with Ā-dependencies.

Concerning restrictions on the type of verbs that can be fronted and the material that may accompany them, we find that only stage-level predicates, which denote an action or a transitory property of an individual, are licensed in the construction (96). It is ungrammatical to front individual-level predicates (97), which denote permanent properties of individuals.

(96) a. Se **kouri** Jan **kouri**.
SE run John run
'It is run that John did.' (not walk)
b. Se **domi** Jan **domi** (pandan inèdtan).
SE sleep Joh sleep (fo an.hour)
'It is sleep (not sit) that John did (for an hour).'
c. Se **manje** Jan **manje** pen.
SE eat John eat bread
'It is eat bread that John did.' (not bake)
d. Se **fè** Jan **fè** tab.
SE make John make table
'It is make tables that John did.' (not paint)
e. Se **achte** Jan **achte** flè.
SE buy John buy flower
'It is buy flowers that John did.' (not steal)
f. Se **gade** Jan **gade** television an.
SE watch John watch television DET
'It is watch television that John did.' (not fix)
g. Se **tande** Jan **tande** volè a.
SE hear John hear thief DET
'It is hear the thief that John did.' (not see) (Lefebvre 1987: 171f.)

(97) a. *Se **entèlijan** Jan **entèlijan**.
 SE intelligent John intelligent
 b. *Se **konnè** Jan **konnè** lang sa a.
 SE know John know language this DET
 c. *Se **renmen** Jan **renmen** Mari.
 SE love John love Mary
 d. *Se **sanble** Jan **sanble** ak papa-l.
 SE resemble John resemble with father-his

(Lefebvre 1987: 172)

That the split is really between stage-level and individual-level, and not between stative and non-stative verbs is evidenced by the fact that transitory property denoting statives are grammatical in the focus position (98).

(98) a. Se **chita** Jan **chita**.
 SE sit John sit
 'It is sit that John did (not, e.g., stand).'
 b. Se **kanpe** Jan **kanpe**.
 SE stand John stand
 'It is stand that John did (not, e.g., sit).'
 c. Se **tande/wè** Jan **tande/wè** vòlè a.
 SE hear/see John hear/see thief DET
 'It is hear/see the thief that John did (not, e.g., see/hear).'

(Larson & Lefebvre 1991: 250)

The material that can be fronted with the verb includes aspectual auxiliaries (99). As with main verbs, a copy of the auxiliary remains in its clause-internal position.

(99) Se [fèk/sot **achte**] li fèk/sot **achte** flè yo.
 SE just buy he just buy flower DET
 'It is just buying flowers that he did.' (Lefebvre 1987: 175)

These auxiliaries may also occur in the focus position on their own without the main verb, leaving a copy in the base position (100).

(100) a. Se **pral** li **pral** achte flè yo.
 SE about.to he about.to buy flower DET
 'It is about to buy flowers that he is about to do.'
 b. Se **fèk/sòt** li **fèk/sòt** achte flè yo.
 SE just he just buy flower
 'It is just buying flowers that he did.' (Lefebvre 1987: 175)

It is equally grammatical to pied-pipe low adverbs like *vit* 'quickly' and *byen* 'well' with the fronted verb while a copy of the adverb stays in its base position (101).

(101) a. Se [**mache** vit] l' ap **mache** vit.
SE walk quickly 3SG ASP walk quickly
'It is walk quickly that he/she did (not, e.g., run).'
b. Se [byen **domi**] Mari te byen **domi**.
SE well sleep Marie TNS well sleep
'It is sleep really well that Mary did (not, e.g., run well).'
(Larson & Lefebvre 1991: 248)

However, Harbour (2008) provides the counter-example (102) to this claim. These different judgements could be due to dialectal or inter-speaker variation. In any case, more research is required to clarify the situation.

(102) *Se **pale** vit Jan te **pale** (vit).
SE speak fast John ANT speak (fast)
Intended: 'John SPOKE FAST.' (Harbour 2008: 857)

The following example (103) shows that not just auxiliaries and adverbs but also tense markers may accompany the fronted verb. As with the former, a copy of the fronted element appears in its base position.

(103) Se [te **vini**] Mari te di m Jan te **vini** ak Pol.
SE TNS come Marie TNS say me John TNS come with Paul
'That was come Marie said to me that John came with Paul.'
(Lumsden 1990: 746)

Harbour (2008) draws attention to the fact that there exists an independent low verb doubling construction in Haitian Creole in which the verb is replicated *in situ* giving rise to an emphatic or continuative kind of interpretation of the action denoted by the verb (104).

(104) a. Men, nèg la yo pito ap kontinye mande mande
but man the the.PL instead PROG continue ask ask
"blan, eske n mouri?"
white Q 1PL die
'But the men preferred to keep asking, "White guy, are we dead?"'
b. Ou mèt ekri ekri poèm wi.
you put write write poen yes
'You can keep on writing poems.'

c. Yo touye Janmari Vensan pou dan ri, militè ak
   they kill Janmari Vensan for teeth grin soldiers and
   atache touye touye Janmari Vensan.
   militia.men kill kill Janmari Vensan
   'They killed Janmari Vensan for no reason whatsoever, the soldiers and militia men really killed Janmari Vensan.'
d. Bondye gran mèt tande tande priyè m.
   god big master hear hear prayer 1SG
   'Lord God, truly hear my prayer.' (Harbour 2008: 858)

He argues that this construction might be the base for verb fronting. The verb fronting structure would simply be the low verb doubling construction with one of the two verbs appearing clause-initially. The advantage of this view is that it explains without further complications why when the verb is fronted there are two tokens of it whereas with normal NP fronting there is a gap clause-internally. This approach is supported by the fact that low verb doubling and verb fronting cannot cooccur (105), a restriction that is expected if the latter construction is derived from the former, tearing the two verb copies apart in the process (see Harbour 2008 for detailed argumentation).

(105) a. ?*Se kouri kouri Jan ap kouri kouri.
         SE run run John PROG run run
      b. *Se kouri kouri Jan ap kouri.
      c. *Se kouri Jan ap kouri kouri. (Harbour 2008: 861)

Whether this approach to verb fronting is correct or not, Haitian Creole disposes of a verb fronting construction where a copy of the verb occurs in base position and therefore bears on the Generalizations presented in this book.

There are two other constructions exhibiting verb fronting and doubling in Haitian Creole: temporal and causal adverbial clauses (106-a, b) and factive clauses (106-b).

(106) a. **Rive** Jan **rive** (a), Mari pati.
         arrive John arrive DET Mary leave
         'As soon as John arrived, Mary left.'
      b. **Rive** Jan **rive** (a), Mari pati.
         arrive John arrive DET Mary leave
         'Because John arrived, Mary left.'
      c. **Tann** fok Jan **tann** Mari a fè li pa kap soti.
         wait COMP John wait Mary DET make him not able leave
         'The fact that John has to wait for Mary makes him unable to leave.'
         (Lefebvre & Ritter 1993: 65f.)

In contrast to the verb focalization, the adverbial and factive constructions show somewhat distinct properties, which I will not discuss in detail here. Instead, the interested reader is referred to Lefebvre & Ritter (1993). What is important to note with regard to their relevance for the classification of Haitian Creole with regard to the repair patterns is that they do not allow to front the internal argument(s) together with the verb (107).

(107) a. *[**Fini** travay] la ou **fini** (travay la), ou ava al wè Mari.
 finish work DET you finish work DET you FUT go see Mary
 Intended: 'As soon as you have finished this work, you will go see Mary' (Lefebvre & Ritter 1993: 67)
 b. *[**Achte** flè yo] Jan **achte** (flè yo), Mari kontan.
 buy flower DET John buy flower DET Mary happy
 Intended: 'Since John bought flowers, Mary is happy.' (Lefebvre & Ritter 1993: 72)
 c. *[**Fini** travay la] ou **fini** (travay la) fè ou gen kont
 finish work DET you finish work DET make you have enough
 tan pou ou repose ou.
 time for you rest you
 Intended: 'The fact that you have finished this work makes you have enough time to rest.' (Lefebvre & Ritter 1993: 82)

Therefore, just like the verb focalization, these three constructions fall under the Generalization IIa, which states that languages that only show verb fronting but no verb phrase fronting always employ verb doubling as a repair.

In addition, there is also a verb fronting construction where a dummy verb appears in the base position of the verb. This constructions is restricted to intransitive verbs. As argued in section 2.1.3.3, this could be analyzed as verb phrase fronting with verb doubling turning Haitian Creole into a third example of the asymmetric pattern III. Unfortunately, no further properties of this construction could be investigated due to lack of data.

Summary

To summarize, we have found that Haitian Creole disposes of several verb fronting constructions where a copy of the verb occurs in base position. Concentrating on the one that by having a contrastive focus interpretation is similar to verb fronting verb doubling constructions in other languages its properties are displayed in table 7.7. The fronting may cross finite clause-boundaries and is sensitive to islands. Only stage-level predicates, not individual-level predicates, can undergo fronting and doubling. Tense and aspect markers may pied-pipe along with the verb, while the data on adverbs is not conclusive.

In conclusion, Haitian Creole at first glance seems to exhibit patternI. However, if my analysis in section 2.1.3.3 is correct, it might turn out to be an additional instantiation of the asymmetric pattern III of Generalization I.

Tab. 7.7: Properties of verbal fronting in Haitian Creole

	Copy	Dummy	Unbound	Islands	GS	TAM	L-Adv	H-Adv	NEG	L/R	Top/Foc
V	✓[7]	–	✓	✓	n.d.	✓	?[8]	n.d.	n.d.	L	Foc
VP	–	(✓)[9]	n.d.	n.d.	n.d.	n.d.	n.d.	n.d.	n.d.	L	Foc

7.1.8 Kisi

Kisi, a Mel language of the Niger-Congo family, is spoken by about half a million speakers in Guinea, Sierra Leone, and Liberia (Childs 1997). The basic word order is SVO but with auxiliaries this order changes to SAuxOV.

Verb focalization in Kisi involves the fronting of a nominalized copy of the verb while another copy appears in the canonical verb position. Sentence-finally, there is an obligatory focus marker *ní* (108).

(108) a. **Pùéŋ**-ndáŋyá **púéŋ** ní.
        forget-NMLZ I forget FOC
        'It's forgetting that I did.'
     b. **Yòù**-wó   yá **yóú** ndú ní.
        lend-NMLZ I   lend him FOC
        'It's lending to him I did.'
     c. **Kpùwà**-á ò **kpúwá** yá ndú ó   bà   ní.
        grab-NMLZ he grab   me him PREP hand FOC
        'It's grabbing he did to me.'   (Childs 1997: 50)

When focussing a periphrastic verb, the auxiliary is stranded and instead of a copy of the verb there is a gap in the base position (109).

---

[7] This verb fronting is restricted to stage-level predicates.
[8] The data on adverb fronting are not conclusive. Some sources provide examples where it is possible while other provide examples where it is explicitly ungrammatical.
[9] This verb phrase fronting is restricted to intransitive verbs (see section 2.1.3.3).

(109) a. À wé cèé lé pìsúltáŋ₁ ndá wà ___₁ ní.
they AUX fight NEG play they AUX FOC
'They weren't fighting, it's playing they were doing.'

b. Fàfálá₁ sùkúùwó yá có ___₁ ní léláŋ mɛ̀ɛ́ mí
struggle school I AUX FOC therefore MOD CONJ.1SG
dííkŭŋ.
submit
'I'm really struggling to get educated, so I have to be submissive.'
(Childs 1995: 272)

Childs (1995), providing the example in (110), states that arguments may not be fronted together with the verb. Unfortunately, he does not list any ungrammatical examples with fronted arguments. However, taking his statement together with the absence of any grammatical examples of this sort, I will proceed on the assumption that verb phrase fronting does not exist in Kisi.

(110) Fèfèlìáá₁ ó có ___₁ bùŋgàŋ mùŋ ní.
staying he AUX portions these FOC
'He's sticking around for those portions.' (Childs 1995: 272)

Summary

As this is all the relevant data that I could find in the literature, we conclude that Kisi has a verb fronting construction, in which the fronted verb is nominalized and leaves a copy in the base position but no parallel verb phrase fronting construction (see table 7.8). Kisi therefore provides an instance of pattern A of Generalization II.

Tab. 7.8: Properties of verbal fronting in Kisi

	Copy	Dummy	Unbound	Islands	GS	TAM	L-Adv	H-Adv	Neg	L/R	Top/Foc
V	✓	–	n.d.	n.d.	n.d.	n.d.	n.d.	n.d.	n.d.	L	Foc
VP	–	–									

7.1.9 Leteh (Larteh)

Leteh (also referred to as Larteh) is a Kwa language (Niger-Congo) with about 8 300 speakers in the town of Larteh in southeastern Ghana (Ansah 2010). Its basic word order is SVO as exemplified in (111).

(111) Ananse dɔ̀ fɔ́ a ntente.
Ananse PST.climb barn DEF quickly
'Ananse climbed the barn quickly.' (Ansah 2014: 164)

Verbal focus in Leteh is expressed by fronting the main verb while a copy of it appears in the base position (112). The fronted copy is nominalized which is marked by a change in the tone pattern (Ansah 2009).

(112) a. Ama fòkyè daa.
Ama PRS.sweep everyday
'Ama sweeps everyday.'
b. **Fókyè** né Ama **fòkyè** daa a.
sweep.NMLZ FOC Ama PRS.sweep everyday DEF
'Ama SWEEPS everyday.' (Ansah 2014: 174)

The focus marker *né* is identical to the one which is used in argument focus constructions (113). It has to cooccur with the clausal determiner *a* in both constructions.

(113) a. Sika né Ananse bè-wúrì a.
money FOC Ananse FUT-steal DEF
'Ananse will steal MONEY.'
b. Ananse wùrí sika a.
Ananse PST.steal money DEF
'ANANSE stole money.' (Ansah 2014: 167f.)

Due to the paucity of available data nothing more can be said about verbal fronting in Leteh at the moment.

Summary

The scarce information on Leteh verb focus is summarized in table 7.9. I will assume that the absence of any data showing verb phrase fronting indicates its non-existence until evidence to the contrary is presented. In conclusion, Leteh provides a further example of pattern A of Generalization II.

Tab. 7.9: Properties of verbal fronting in Leteh (Larteh)

	Copy	Dummy	Unbound	Islands	GS	TAM	L-Adv	H-Adv	NEG	L/R	Top/Foc
V	✓	–	n.d.	n.d.	n.d.	n.d.	n.d.	n.d.	n.d.	L	Foc
VP	–	–									

7.1.10 Nupe

Nupe, the main Nupoid language of the Niger-Congo family, is spoken by approximately one million people in Nigeria. Its principal word order is SVO as shown in the neutral declarative sentence (114)

(114) Musa à ba nakàn sasi èsun làzì yin.
Musa FUT cut meat some tomorrow morning PRT
'Musa will cut some meat tomorrow morning.' (Kandybowicz 2008: 83)

The verbal fronting construction in Nupe is associated with a contrastive focus interpretation on the verb. The left-peripheral copy of the verb is nominalized by reduplication with a CV prefix, another copy of the verb appears in the canonical verb position (115). The focus marker *o* occupies the sentence-final position.

(115) Bi-**ba** Musa à *(**ba**) nakàn (*ba/*bi-ba) o.
RED-cut Musa FUT cut meat cut/RED-cut FOC
'It is CUTTING that Musa will do to the meat (as opposed to say, *cooking*.)'
(Kandybowicz 2008: 79)

This fronting is restricted to verbs. If the verb and its object are placed in sentence-initial position, the result is ungrammatical (116).

(116) a. *Du-**du** cènkafa Musa à **du** (cènkafa) o.
RED-cook rice Musa FUT cook rice FOC
'It is COOKING RICE that Musa will do.'
b. *[Cènkafa du-**du**] Musa à **du** (cènkafa) o.
rice RED-cook Musa FUT cook rice FOC
'It is COOKING RICE that Musa will do.' (Kandybowicz 2008: 86)

The fronted verb obligatorily has to be nominalized while the clause-internal copy must not be nominalized (117).

(117) a. Yi-**yà** Musa **yà** etsu èwò o.
RED-give Musa give chief garment FOC
'Musa GAVE the chief a garment.'
b. ***Yà** Musa **yà** etsu èwò o.
give Musa give chief garment FOC
c. *Yi-**yà** Musa yi-**yà** etsu èwò o.
RED-give Musa RED-give chief garment FOC
d. ***Yà** Musa yi-**yà** etsu èwò o.
give Musa RED-give chief garment FOC
(Kandybowicz 2008: 87)

There are two other nominalization strategies in the language, object-verb inversion and prefixation with è. However, only reduplication is acceptable in verb fronting while object-verb inversion (118-a) and è-prefixation (118-b) are ungrammatical.

(118)   a.   *[Nakàn **ba**] Musa (nakàn) **ba** (nakàn) o.
               meat   cut Musa meat   cut   meat   FOC
               Intended: 'It is MEAT-CUTTING that Musa did.'
       b.   *È̀-**fá**   Musa **fá**   tsúwó   o.
               NMLZ-rest Musa rest yesterday FOC
               Intended: 'It was RESTING that Musa did yesterday.'
                                                     (Kandybowicz 2008: 89f.)

While the inapplicability of OV-inversion is expected here because fronting the object with the verb is disallowed, there is *a priori* no reason for the ungrammaticality of è-prefixation. However, note that è-prefixation is an irregular unproductive strategy restricted to a subset of verbs (Kandybowicz 2008: 90). Since irregular processes are usually located in the lexicon while productive regular ones take place in syntax, the unavailability of è-prefixation straightforwardly follows if verb fronting and doubling involve syntactic processes (i.e. movement and copying), which trigger the nominalization of the affected syntactic element. Under this assumption, only a regular productive process, like reduplication but unlike è-prefixation, can apply to the moved element. Hence, example (118-b) is grammatical if reduplication instead of è-prefixation is used (119).

(119)   Fi-**fá**   Musa **fá**   tsúwó   o.
        RED-rest Musa rest yesterday FOC
        'It was RESTING that Musa did yesterday.'   (Kandybowicz 2008: 90)

Further (and stronger) arguments for treating verb fronting as (Ā-)movement come from the fact that it shows typical properties thereof. It is able to cross finite clause boundaries with bridge verbs (120-a) but not with non-bridge verbs (120-b), and it is sensitive to islands such as the Complex NP Island (121), the Wh-Island (122), the Subject Island (123), the Adjunct Island (124), and the Coordinate Structure Constraint (125).

(120)   a.   Si-**si**   Musa gàn gànán Nànă kpe   gànán Gana **si**   eci   o.
               RED-buy Musa say COMP Nana know COMP Gana buy yam FOC
               'It was BUYING that Musa said that Nana knows that Gana did to a yam.'
       b.   *Si-**si**   u: tán   Musa gànán mi: **si**   doko o.
               RED-buy 3SG pain Musa COMP 1SG buy horse FOC
               'It pained Musa that I BOUGHT a horse.'   (Kandybowicz 2008: 84)

(121) *Complex NP Island*
 *Gi-**gi** Musa si [bise na **gi** eyì na] o.
 RED-eat Musa buy hen COMP eat corn PRT FOC
 'Musa bought the hen that ATE the corn.' (Kandybowicz 2008: 84)

(122) *Wh-Island*
 *Si-**si** Musa gbíngàn [ké Gana **si** o] o.
 RED-buy Musa ask what Gana buy FOC FOC
 'Musa asked what Gana BOUGHT' (Kandybowicz 2008: 84)

(123) *Subject Island*
 *Si-**si** [gànán etsu **si** doko] tán Musa o.
 RED-buy COMP chief buy horse pain Musa FOC
 'That the chief BOUGHT a horse pained Musa.' (Kandybowicz 2008: 84)

(124) *Adjunct Island*
 *Bi-**ba** [Musa gá è **ba** nakàn] o, Gana à pa eci.
 RED-cut Musa COND PRS cut meat FOC Gana FUT pound yam
 'If Musa is CUTTING the meat, then Gana will pound yam.'
  (Kandybowicz 2008: 85)

(125) *Coordinate Structure Constraint*
 a. *Bi-**ba** [Musa$_i$ à **ba** nakàn] u:$_i$ ma à du cènkafa o.
   RED-cut Musa FUT cut meat 3SG and FUT cook rice FOC
   'It is CUTTING that Musa$_i$ will do to the meat and he$_i$ will cook the rice.'
 b. *Du-**du** Musa$_i$ à ba nakàn [u:$_i$ ma à **du** cènkafa] o.
   RED-cook Musa FUT cut meat 3SG and FUT cook rice FOC
   'Musa$_i$ will cut the meat and it is COOKING that he$_i$ will do to the rice.'
   (Kandybowicz 2008: 85)

It is also possible to displace a verb within an embedded clause, as exemplified in (126).

(126) Musa gàn [gànán du-**du** u: **du** eci o].
 Musa say COMP RED-cook 3SG cook yam FOC
 'Musa said that it was COOKING that he did to a yam.'
  (Kandybowicz 2008: 102)

The interaction of wh-questions and verb doubling provides another argument for the Ā-nature of the latter. It is not possible to front a wh-expression and a verb in the same clause (127) which receives a straightforward explanation if both involve the same kind of movement targeting the same single position (i.e. SpecCP).

As wh-movement is the prototypical case of Ā-movement verb fronting must be Ā-movement, too.

(127) a. *Ké bi-**ba** Musa **ba** o?
what RED-cut Musa cut FOC
'What did Musa CUT?'
b. *Bi-**ba** ké Musa **ba** o.
RED-cut what Musa cut FOC   (Kandybowicz 2008: 85)

Besides the verb no further material may appear in the fronted position, neither TAM-markers (128-a, b) or low adverbs (128-c), nor nominal modifiers (128-d, e).

(128) a. *[(À) du-du (à) Musa à] **du** cènkafa o.
FUT RED-cook FUT Musa FUT cook rice FOC
'It is COOKING that Musa will do to the rice.'
b. *[(À) du-**du** (à)] Musa à cènkafa **du** o.
FUT RED-cook FUT Musa FUT rice cook FOC
'It is COOKING that Musa will do to the rice.'
c. *(Dàdà) du-**du** (sanyín) Musa à **du** cènkafa o.
quickly RED-cook quietly Musa FUT cook rice FOC
'It is QUICK/QUIET COOKING that Musa will do to the rice.'
d. *[Wu-**wu** gútá] Gana **wu** Musa o.
RED-hit three Gana hit Musa FOC
'It was HITTING THREE TIMES that Gana did to Musa.'
e. *[Wu-**wu** wangi] Gana **wu** Musa o.
RED-hit good Gana hit Musa FOC
'It was A GOOD HITTING that Gana gave to Musa.'

(Kandybowicz 2008: 86f.)

A restriction of verb fronting to stage-level predicates like in Fongbe (see section 7.1.5) or Haitian Creole (see section 7.1.7) is not attested in Nupe. Individual-level predicates may front and double freely as shown in (129).

(129) a. Bi-**bè** Musa **bè** Gana o.
RED-resemble Musa resemble Gana FOC
'Mus RESEMBLES Gana.'
b. Kpi-**kpe** Musa **kpe** làbárì o.
RED-know Musa know story FOC
'Musa KNOWS/IS AWARE OF the story.'   (Kandybowicz 2008: 93)

Further, fronting of auxiliary verbs, as found in Haitian Creole (see section 7.1.7), is illicit.

(130) *Yi-**yá** Musa **yá** eci yin du o.
 RED-begin Musa begin yam PRT cook FOC
 Intended: 'Musa STARTED to cook the yam.' (Kandybowicz 2008: 103)

However, similar to Haitian Creole, Nupe has a low verb doubling construction with an intensive emphatic meaning (131) which verb fronting has been argued to be derived from (Kandybowicz 2004).

(131) Musa **ba** nakàn **ba**.
 Musa cut meat cut
 'Musa DID IN FACT cut the meat.' (Kandybowicz 2008: 101)

In fact, as pointed out by Kandybowicz (2008) this construction's distribution is parallel to that of verb fronting. In serial verb constructions (SVC), the first verb may both low copy (132-a) and front (132-b) while the following verb in the SVC may not (132-c, d).

(132) a. Musa **du** eci **du** kún.
 Musa cook yam cook sell
 'Musa DID IN FACT cook a yam and (then) sell it.'
 b. Du-**du** Musa **du** exi kún o.
 RED-cook Musa cook yam sell FOC
 'It was COOKING that Musa did to a yam before selling.'
 c. *Musa du eci **kún kún**.
 Musa cook yam sell sell
 'Musa cooked a yam and (then) DID IN FACT sell it.'
 d. *Ku-**kún** Musa du exi **kún** o.
 RED-sell Musa cook yam sell FOC
 'Musa cooked a yam and (then) SOLD it.' (Kandybowicz 2008: 101f.)

Also, both constructions do not allow wh-fronting from the same clause (133) but are licit in embedded contexts (134).

(133) a. Ké Musa du o?
 what Musa cook FOC
 'What did Musa cook?'
 b. *Ké Musa **du du** o?
 what Musa cook cook FOC
 'What DID IN FACT Musa cook?'
 c. *[Ké du-**du**] / [du-**du** ké] Musa **du** o?
 what RED-cook RED-cook what Musa cook FOC
 'What did Musa COOK?' (Kandybowicz 2008: 102)

(134) a. Musa gàn [gànán u: **du** eci **du**].
Musa say COMP 3SG cook yam cook
'Musa said that he DID IN FACT cook a yam.'
b. Musa gàn [gànán du-**du** u: **du** eci o].
Musa say COMP RED-cook 3SG cook yam FOC
'Musa said that it was COOKING that he did to a yam.'

(Kandybowicz 2008: 102)

And, finally, low verb doubling and verb fronting cannot cooccur (135).

(135) *Du-**du** Musa **du** eci **du** o.
RED-cook Musa cook yam cook FOC
'It was COOKING that Musa DID IN FACT do to a yam.'

(Kandybowicz 2008: 102)

Nevertheless, Kandybowicz (2008) argues that low verb doubling is not the input to verb fronting. First, he points out that the distributional parallels can be predicted from independent factors including pronunciational economy, Relativized Minimality, and the availability of only one focus position (for detailed argumentation see Kandybowicz 2008: 102–103). Second, he provides two examples for contexts where low verb doubling is possible but verb fronting is not. One concerns the behaviour of modal-auxiliaries (136) and the other relative clause-internal predicates (137).

(136) a. Musa **yá** eci yin **yá** du.
Musa begin yam PRT begin cook
'Musa DID IN FACT start to cook the yam.'
b. *Yi-**yá** Musa **yá** eci yin du o.
RED-begin Musa begin yam PRT cook FOC
'Musa STARTED to cook the yam.' (Kandybowicz 2008: 103)

(137) a. Musa si [bise na **gí** eyì **gí** na].
Musa buy hen COMP eat corn eat PRT
'Musa bought the hen that DID IN FACT eat the corn.'
b. *Musa si [bise na gi-**gí** **gí** eyì o na].
Musa buy hen COMP RED-eat eat corn FOC PRT
'Musa bought the hen that ATE the corn.'

(Kandybowicz 2008: 103)

The argument would be stronger if grammaticality judgements were reversed, that is, if fronting were grammatical but the purported low verb doubling base were not, because there might be independent factors that preclude the formation of verb fronting from the available low verb doubling construcions. However, as long as no such factors have been identified, I will follow Kandybowicz (2008: 103) in treating the two constructions as derived independently of each other.

Summary
Summarising, Nupe disposes of a verbal fronting construction with a copy of the verb occurring in the canonical verb position clause-internally. The fronted verb is obligatorily nominalized by reduplication. Fronting of arguments, TAM-markers, low adverbs, or nominal modifiers together with the verb leads to ungrammaticality. Moreover, verb fronting exhibits $\bar{\text{A}}$-properties: It may cross finite clause boundaries, it is sensitive to islands, and it is in complementary distribution to wh-fronting, another $\bar{\text{A}}$-dependency, in the same clause. Table 7.10 gives an overview over the relevant properties. In conclusion, Nupe verb fronting behaves just as in pattern A of Generalization II.

Tab. 7.10: Properties of verbal fronting in Nupe

	Copy	Dummy	Unbound	Islands	GS	TAM	L-Adv	H-Adv	Neg	L/R	Top/Foc
V	✓	–	✓	✓	n.d.	–	–	n.d.	n.d.	L	Foc
VP	–	–									

7.1.11 Nweh

Nweh, a Narrow Grassfields Bantu language (Niger-Congo), is spoken by approximately 85 000 native speakers in the southwestern region of Cameroon (Nkemnji 1995: 5).

It is the sole language discussed in this book which exclusively shows rightwards displacement of the verb. However, as this construction involves displacement to the periphery (although the right one) and receives the contrastive focus interpretation associated with verbal fronting in many languages, I will briefly present its properties here, as far as data are available.[10]

---

[10] There are theoretical approaches to this kind of right dislocation deriving it either as displacement into the left periphery of the identical second clause of a biclausal base with subsequent deletion of this clause (see Ott & de Vries 2016) or by leftward displacement and subsequent displacement of the remnant material across the first element in a Kayne (1994)-style syntax (see e.g. Nkemnji 1995, Koopman 1997). If these are on the right track, Nweh verbal right dislocation is underlyingly fronting and therefore falls in the domain of this monograph.

An example of the construction in a declarative sentence is given in (138-a) while (138-b) shows an interrogative version.

(138) a. À kɛ̀ʔ n-**cù** ká **cǔ**.
s/he P N-boil crab boil
'She BOILED the crab (as opposed to frying it).'
b. À kɛ̀ʔ n-**cù** ká **cǔ** lɛ̌?
s/he P N-boil crab boil Q
'Did she BOIL the crab (as opposed to frying it).' (Koopman 1997: 71)

An interesting cross-linguistic observation is that NP focus in Nweh is expressed quite differently from verb focus. In contrast to verb focus, it is signalled by leftwards displacement. The focussed NP is followed by a designated focus marker *mə̂* and, in addition, a relative marker appears in the clause (139-b).

(139) a. Atem a kɛ̀ʔ nčúū akendɔ̀ŋ.
Atem AGR P-1 boil plantains
'Atem boiled plantains.'
b. Akendɔ̀ŋ mə̂ a zàā Atem a kɛ̀ʔ nčúū.
plantains FOC AGR REL Atem AGR P-1 boiled
'It is plantains (and not something else) that Atem boiled.'
Lit.: 'Plantains is what Atem boiled.' (Nkemnji 1995: 198)

Coming back to verbal displacement, it is also licit with intransitive (140-a) and NP-PP-complement verbs (140-b).

(140) a. Ŋúa a kɛ̀ʔ ase n-**déē léē**.
child AGR P1 ASP N-sleep sleep
'The child was (only) SLEEPING.'
b. Njikem a kɛ́ʔ ǹ-**fóō** ǹkāp anbó Zinkeng **fóō**.
Njikem AGR P1 N-borrow money from Zinkeng borrow
'Njikem BORROWED money from Zinkeng.' (Nkemnji 1995: 200)

In all these examples, the displaced verb occurs in its bare unprefixed form. Unfortunately, it has to remain undetermined whether this lack of prefixation is interpreted as a nominalization or whether it is more similar to infinitivization found with verb fronting in many Indo-European languages.

Concerning the dependency between the two verb copies, no data are available on its island-sensitivity or its behaviour across clause boundaries. We do find examples showing cooccurrence of verb displacement and wh-questions. However, these are not very instructive with regard to the question whether the latter instantiates an Ā-dependency as wh-questions themselves do not exhibit any signs of Ā-displacement because the wh-elements stay *in situ*. Nonetheless, it shall be mentioned that cooccurrence of verb fronting and wh-questions is licit only if the questioned element is the subject (141-a). If the wh-element is the object, the sentence is ungrammatical (141-b).

(141)   a.   Àwɔ́ kɛ̀? ǹ-**juɔ̀** bɛ́   **jùɔ́** lɛ́.
          who P1 n-buy fufu buy Q
          'Who BOUGHT the fufu?' (as opposed to who sold the fufu)
    b.   *Àtɛ̀m kɛ̀? ǹ-**juɔ̀** kɔ́   **jùɔ́** lɛ́.
          Atem P1 n-buy what buy Q
          'What did Atem BUY?' (as opposed to sell)   (Koopman 1997: 72)

Summary

Due to the scarcity of data we conclude here that Nweh shows a construction in which the verb is displaced into the right periphery while a copy of it occurs in the base position. The two tokens of the verb are morphologically distinct as, in contrast to the clause-internal one, the peripheral one does not bear a prefix. Table 7.11 summarizes our knowledge. Interpreting the absence of any rightwards displaced full verb phrases as indicative of their non-existence, Nweh verb displacement instantiates the repair pattern A of Generalization II.

Tab. 7.11: Properties of verbal fronting in Nweh

	Copy	Dummy	Unbound	Islands	GS	TAM	L-Adv	H-Adv	NEG	L/R	Top/Foc
V	✓	–	n.d.	n.d.	n.d.	n.d.	n.d.	n.d.	n.d.	R	Foc
VP	–	–									

7.1.12 Papiamentu

Papiamentu is a Spanish/Portuguese-lexicon creole language spoken on the Carribean islands Aruba, Bonaire, and Curaçao (Muysken 1978: 65).

The language shows a verb fronting construction where the verb appears clause-initially, optionally preceded only by the particle *ta*[11], while a copy of the

---

[11] The particle *ta* is homophonous with the copula. However, I treat it as a distinct element and consequently gloss it as FOC because they behave differently. As Römer (1977) points out, the copula undergoes contextual tone assignment while the focus particle always bears a low tone, and, additionally, there exists an anterior form *tabata* of the copula but no such form is attested for the focus marker.

verb occupies the canonical verb position (142). Without providing data, Kouwenberg & Murray (1994: 36) state that in this construction "the element which appears in focus is a lexical head, not a phrase, [and] cannot be accompanied by particles or complements".

(142) Ta **pòst** mi no a **pòst** e karta.
 FOC mail 1SG not ASP mail the letter
 'It's just that I hadn't mailed the letter.'

(Kouwenberg & Murray 1994: 36)

In contrast to wh-dependencies, which may cross finite clause boundaries (as evidenced for subjects (143-a), objects (143-b), and adjuncts (143-c)), the data on verb fronting is contradictory (144).

(143) a. Ta Wanchu b'a bisa [ku a bai kas].
  FOC John you.ASP say that ASP go home
  'It's John that you said has gone home.'
 b. Ta e buki b'a bisa [(ku) Wanchu ta lesa].
  FOC the book you.ASP say that John ASP read
  'It's the book that you said John is reading.' (Muysken 1977: 92)
 c. Ki dia bo ta kere [bo ta haya bo outo bèk]?
  which day 2SG ASP believe 2SG ASP get 2SG car back
  'When do you think you are getting your car back?'

(Kouwenberg & Murray 1994: 36)

(144) a. *Ta **lesa** b'a bisa [(ku) Wanchu ta **lesa** e buki].
  FOC read you.ASP say that John ASP read the book
  'It certainly is some reading that you said that John is doing with the book.' (Muysken 1977: 92)
 b. Ta **lesa** b'a bisa [(ku) Wanchu ta **lesa** e buki].
  FOC read you.ASP say that John ASP read the book
  'It certainly is some reading that you said that John is doing with the book.' (Muysken 1978: 69)

The sentence in (144-a) is completely identical to the sentence in (144-b). However, while (144-a) is presented as an argument for the ungrammaticality of long verb fronting in Muysken (1977), the identical (144-b) is put forth as evidence for its unboundedness by Muysken (1978). *A priori* it is unclear what motivated this change in judgements and hence we have to remain agnostic with regard to the grammaticality of verb fronting across clause boundaries. Genus-species effects are unattested in Papiamentu (145).

(145) *Ta **kore** Wanchu a **bay** kas.
 FOC run John ASP go home
 'John went running home.' (Muysken 1978: 76)

Turning to the material that may accompany the fronted verb, we find that Kouwenberg & Murray's (1994) statement can be supplemented with an example showing the ungrammaticality of a fronted aspectual particle (146-a).

(146) a. *Ta a **traha** e a **traha**.
 FOC ASP work he ASP work
 b. Ta **traha** e a **traha**.
 FOC work he ASP work
 'He certainly did some work.' (Muysken 1977: 93)

Summary

As no further informative data are available, the attested properties of Papiamentu verbal fronting are summarized in table 7.12. The language disposes of a verb fronting construction where a copy of the verb appears in the base position. Besides the verb, only the focus marker *ta* optionally occurs in the fronted position. TAM-particles or verbal complements are illicit in this position. Genus-species effects are not attested for the construction. Based on these properties, verbal fronting in Papiamentu falls under pattern A of Generalization II.

Tab. 7.12: Properties of verbal fronting in Papiamentu

	Copy	Dummy	Unbound	Islands	GS	TAM	L-Adv	H-Adv	NEG	L/R	Top/Foc
V	✓	–	?[12]	n.d.	–	–	n.d.	n.d.	n.d.	L	Foc
VP	–	–									

7.1.13 Pichi

Pichi, an Atlantic English-lexicon based creole language, is spoken as a primary or secondary language by about 70 000 people on the island of Bioko (Equatorial Guinea), which lies off the coast of Cameroon (Yakpo 2009: 1).

---

[12] The data on unboundedness are contradictory. One and the same sentence is judged grammatical in one but ungrammatical in another publication.

The language comprises of a verbal fronting construction in which a verb/predicate preceded by the focus marker *nà*, is fronted while a copy of it appears in the canonical verb position (147). The associated meaning is one of emphasis or affirmation that the action denoted by the verb really took place.

(147) Nà **go** à dè **go** ò.
FOC go 1SG.SBJ IPFV go SP
'[Mind you] I'm going.' (Yakpo 2009: 297)

Object clitics may be fronted together with the verb (148). Whether this is also true for arguments cannot be determined from the available data.

(148) Nà [**krach**=àn] yù dè **skrach**.
FOC scratch=3SG.OBJ 2SG IPFV scratch
'You're actually scratching it.' (Yakpo 2009: 298)

The fronting of subjects or adverbial modifiers, however, is not allowed, as stated by Yakpo (2009). He unforutnately only provides an ungrammatical example with a fronted adverbial (149), none with a fronted subject.

(149) *Nà [**luk** fayn] yù **luk**.
FOC look fine 2SG look
'You looked really well.' (Yakpo 2009: 298)

According to Yakpo (2009), but again without negative examples, it is equally ungrammatical to mark the fronted verb with tense, aspect, or mood particles. As shown in (150), the tense and aspect markers *bìn* and *dè* stay with the clause-internal copy of the verb. Negated verb fronting with the negative focus marker *nɔ* is also not possible.

(150) Nà **waka** wì bìn dè **waka** go de.
FOC walk 1PL PST IPFV walk go there
'We actually walked there.' (Yakpo 2009: 298)

In serial verb constructions (SVC), it is the major or highest verb that undergoes fronting, while the other verb(s) stay(s) in the canonical position. This is shown in (151-a) for a motion-direction SVC and in (151-b) for a modal SVC.

(151) a. Nà **waka** wì **waka** go de.
FOC walk 1PL walk go there
'We walked there.'

b. Nà **waka** è   want **waka** so.
   FOC walk 3SG.SBJ want walk like.this
   'He really wants to walk right now.'   (Yakpo 2009: 298)

Relative marking of the out-of-focus part is ungrammatical (152-b)

(152) a. Chico, nà **big** è   **big**.
         boy   FOC big 3SG.SBJ big
         'Oh boy, it's really big.'
      b. *Nà **big** we è   **big**.
         FOC big SUB 3SG.SBJ big
         'It's really big.'   (Yakpo 2009: 297)

Based on the available data, this is all we can say about verbal fronting in Pichi.

Summary

In summary, Pichi disposes of a verb fronting construction where the verb is doubled. The fronted verb may be accompanied by an object clitic but never by a subject, by TAM-markers or by negation. Examples of fronting of a full object with the verb are not attested which will be interpreted as the absence of full verb phrase fronting in the language. Unfortunately, data that might shed light on the nature of the dependency between the two verb copies is unavailable. The known properties of Pichi verbal fronting are presented in table 7.13. As it stands, Pichi verb fronting instantiates pattern A of Generalization II.

Tab. 7.13: Properties of verbal fronting in Pichi

	Copy	Dummy	Unbound	Islands	GS	TAM	L-Adv	H-Adv	NEG	L/R	Top/Foc
V	✓	–	n.d.	n.d.	n.d.	–	–	n.d.	–	L	Foc
VP	–	–									

7.1.14 Saramaccan

Saramaccan is an English and Portuguese-based creole language spoken by 20 000 people in the jungle interior of Suriname (Byrne 1987: xi, 1).

The language shows verb fronting with verb doubling as evidenced by (153). The construction receives a focus interpretation that is not further specified by Byrne (1987).

(153) **Sì** Kòfi **sì** dì mujée bi-tà-woòkò a dì kéiki.
see Kofi see the woman TNS-ASP-work LOC the church
'Kofi SAW the woman working at the church.' (Byrne 1987: 58)

Objects cannot be fronted alongside the verb (154-b) indicating that verb phrase fronting is unavailable in Saramaccan.

(154) a. **Sùku** a **sùku** en.
look.for he look.for him
'He LOOKED FOR him.'
b. *[**Sùku** en] a sùku.
look.for him he look.for (Byrne 1987: 97)

Concerning the Ā-nature of the dependency between the verb copies, the data showing cross-clausal fronting (155) do not receive uniform judgements by all speakers. Two of the four speakers consulted by Byrne accept extraction from embedded clauses whereas the other two judge it ungrammatical. Hence, the examples (155) are marked by an asterisk in parentheses.

(155) a. (*)**Woòkò** Kòfi sì [dì mujée bi-tà-**woòkò** a dì kéiki].
work Kofi see the woman TNS-ASP-work LOC the church
'Kofi saw the woman WORKING at the church.'
b. (*)**Lùku** a méni [tàà dì wòmi mìi **lùku** dì wòsu].
look.at he thinks say/that the man child look.at the house
'He thinks that the little boy LOOKED AT the house.'
c. (*)**Njàn** a ke [fu di mìi **njàn** dì muungà].
eat he want for the child eat the porridge
'He wants the child to EAT the porridge.' (Byrne 1987: 59f.)

However, fronting inside the embedded CP is deemed grammatical by all four speakers (156).

(156) a. A méni [tàà **lùku** dì wòmi mìi **lùku** dì wosu].
he think that look.at the man child look.at the house
'He thinks that the little boy LOOKED AT the house.'
b. A ke [fu **njàn** dì mìi **njàn** dì muungà].
he want for eat the child eat the porridge
'He wants the child to EAT the porridge.' (Byrne 1987: 60)

An argument in favour of verb fronting involving an Ā-dependency comes from the ungrammaticality of sentences in which wh-movement has taken place in the embedded clause (157-a). In these sentences verb fronting across the wh-element, i.e. out of a wh-island, behaves like NP fronting (157-b) in that it is ungrammatical even for those speakers which usually allow long verb fronting (157-c).

(157) a. Kòfi sì [naàse dì mujée bi-tà-woòkò].
           Kofi see where the woman TNS-ASP-work
           'Kofi saw where the woman was working.'
       b. *[Dì mujée]₁ Kòfi sì [naàse ___₁ bi-tà-woòkò].
            the woman Kofi see where   TNS-ASP-work
       c. *Woòkò Kòfi sì [naàse dì mujée bi-tà-woòko].
            work   Kofi see where the woman TNS-ASP-work
                                                                (Byrne 1987: 102)

Unfortunately, other islands have not been tested by Byrne (1987). However, the data that are available can cautiously be interpreted as evidence for the Ā-nature of the dependency between the two verb copies in the verb fronting construction.

Summary

Table 7.14 summarizes the properties of verb fronting in Saramaccan. The language shows verb fronting, but not verb phrase fronting, where a copy of the verb appears in the base position. The construction shows Ā-properties insofar as it is unbounded (at least for a subset of speakers) and respects Wh-Islands. Thus, Saramaccan shows pattern A of Generalization II.

Tab. 7.14: Properties of verbal fronting in Saramaccan

	Copy	Dummy	Unbound	Islands	GS	TAM	L-Adv	H-Adv	Neg	L/R	Top/Foc
V	✓	–	✓[13]	✓[14]	n.d.	n.d.	n.d.	n.d.	n.d.	L	Foc
VP	–	–									

7.1.15 Tuki

Tuki, a Southern Bantoid language of the Niger-Congo family, is spoken by 26 000 native speakers in central Cameroon (Biloa 2013: 35).

---

[13] Half of the consulted speakers (2/4) allow verb fronting from embedded clauses while the other half deems it ungrammatical.
[14] This statement only holds for Wh-Islands. Data on other islands was not available.

In Tuki, it is possible to place the verb in sentence-initial position with a copy of it appearing in the canonical verb position (158). The fronted verb has to be an infinitive. This construction expresses a contrastive focus meaning or syntactic prominence of the fronted element (Biloa 2013: 84).

(158)   a.   O-**nyá** ówú vítsu tu-**nyám** cwí.
             INF-eat FOC we   SM-eat   fish
             'We ATE fish.'
        b.   O-**nyá** ówú mámú o-nú **nyám** ndzámbu.
             INF-eat FOC you SM-F1 eat   meat
             'You will EAT meat.' (Biloa 2013: 75f.)

The object of the verb may not accompany it in sentence-initial position, otherwise, ungrammaticality results (159-b).

(159)   a.   O-**nyá** ówú nŭ ngu-nú-**nyám** cwí.
             INF-eat FOC I SM-F1-eat   fish
             'I will EAT fish.'
        b.   *[O-**nyá** cwí] ówú nŭ ngu-nú-**nyám** cwí.
             INF-eat fish FOC I SM-F1-eat   fish   (Biloa 2013: 76)

Although the construction differs from XP fronting in the sense that in contrast to a gap it leaves a copy of the fronted element, the focus marker *ówú* is the same that occurs with adverb or adjunct fronting (160-a, b). The focus markers in argument fronting, however, are different (160-c, d).

(160)   a.   Námbárí ówú Putá o-endám n(a) adongo.
             tomorrow FOC Puta SM-goes to village
             'It is tomorrow that Puta will go to the village.'
        b.   Na wúcó wa átóki ówú Putá a-m(á)-iba mŏni.
             in front of throat FOC Puta SM-P2-steal money
             'It is out of greed that Puta stole money.'
        c.   Abongo ódzú a-má-kós-én-a   agéé wáá yĕndze ídzó.
             Abongo FOC SM-P2-buy-APPL-FV wife his house yesterday
             'It is Abongo who bought his wife a house yesterday.'
        d.   Yĕndze aye Abongo a-má-kós-én-a   agéé wáá ídzó.
             house FOC Abongo SM-P2-buy-APPL-FV wife his yesterday
             'It is a house that Abongo bought for his wife yesterday.'
             (Biloa 2013: 408, 410)

Basically any verb can be fronted, even morphologically modified ones. The following examples show this for an unergative verb (161-a), an unaccusative verb

(161-b), a ditransitive verb (161-c), an idiomatic verb (161-d), a causative verb (161-e), a reciprocal verb (161-f), and an applicative verb (161-g).

(161) a. O-**biná**   ówú Putá a-kutu-**biná**.
 INF-dance FOC Puta SM-PROG-dance
 'Puta is DANCING.'
 b. **Wárá** (=o+árá)   ówú vădzu   va-m(á)-**árá**.
 come INF+come FOC children SM-P2-come
 'The children CAME.'
 c. O-**fá**   ówú Ndumá a-mu-**fá** ísa wáá moní.
 INF-give FOC Nduma SM-P1-give father her money
 'Nduma GAVE her father money.'
 d. O-**súwa** ówú nubúra nu-má-**súwa** ídzo.
 INF-wash FOC rain   SM-P2-wash yesterday
 'It RAINED yesterday.'
 e. O-**bang**-éy-a   ówú Putá a-má-**bang**-éy-a mwaná wáá.
 INF-cry-CAUS-FV FOC Puta SM-P2-cry-CAUS-FV child   her
 'Puta made her child CRY.'
 f. O-**dínga**-na ówú Díma na Kunu vá-**dingá**-ná-ḿ.
 INF-love-REC FOC Dima and Kunu SM-love-REC-ASP
 'Dima and Kunu LOVE each other.'
 g. O-**námb**-en-a   ówú Putá a-má-**námb**-en-a anémé wáa
 INF-cook-APPL-FV FOC Puta SM-P2-cook-APPL-FV husband her
 vibúfa.
 vegetable
 'Puta COOKED vegetables for her husband.'   (Biloa 2013: 501f.)

The constructions shows a number of properties typically associated with Ā-dependencies. First, it is able to cross finite clause boundaries (162).

(162) a. **Wénda** ówú Mbárá a-bunganám [ée o-nu-**éndám** ná Púrási].
 go   FOC Mbara SM-think   that SM-F1-go   to Paris
 'Mbara thinks that you will GO to Paris.'
 b. O-**bánga** ówú Mbárá a-b   [ée nŏsi   wáá a-nu-**bangám**].
 INF-cry FOC Mbara SM-say that mother her SM-F1-cry
 'Mbara says that his mother will CRY.'   (Biloa 2013: 502f.)

Second, it is sensitive to islands such as the Complex NP Island (163) or the Wh-Island (164).

(163) *Complex NP Island*
    *O-**fendá** ówú Isomo a-m(u)-úba [marú ama ée Díma a-má-**fendá**
    INF-repair FOC Isomo SM-P1-hear story this that Dima SM-P2-repair
    matúwa wáá].
    car   his
    'Isomo heard the story that Dima REPAIRED his car.'   (Biloa 2013: 503)

(164) *Wh-Island*
    ***Wénda** ówú tu-t-ídzima [táne t-**éndam**].
    go   FOC SM-NEG-know where SM-go
    'We do not know where we are GOING.'   (Biloa 2013: 503)

Third, cooccurrence of wh-fronting and verb focus results in ungrammaticality (165) which is expected if both involve the same kind of movement targeting the same structural position.

(165) a. O-**nyá** ówú Isomo a-**nyám** cwí.
       INF-eat FOC Isomo SM-eat fish
       'Isomo EATS fish.'
   b. *O-**nyá** ówú ate Isomo a-**nyám**.
       INF-eat FOC what Isomo SM-eats
   c. *Ate o-**nyá** ówú Isomo a-**nyám**.
       what INF-eat FOC Isomo SM-eats   (Biloa 2013: 502f.)

Additionally, verb fronting behaves like wh-fronting with regard to embedded contexts. Both may occur in subordinate clauses (166)

(166) a. Mbárá a-b-[ée o-**nyá** ówú Isomo a-**nyám** cwí].
       Mbara SM-say-that INF-eat FOC Isomo SM-eat fish
       'Mbara says that Isomo EATS fish.'
   b. Mbárá a-sesám [ée ate áyé Isomo a-nyám].
       Mbara SM-ask that what FOC Isomo SM-eat
       'Mbara asks what Isomo eats.'   (Biloa 2013: 512)

Besides the infinitive marker, only (low) adverbs may be fronted together with the verb (167).

(167) [O-**numá** ifúndu] ówú ongúna o-má-**numá** (*ifúndu) ídzo.
      INF-shine much FOC sun SM-P2-shine much yesterday
     'The sun SHINED a lot yesterday.'   (Biloa 2013: 500)

Among the material excluded from fronting are TAM-markers (168-b, d) and negation (169).

(168) a. O-**námba** ówú vakútu vá-má-**námba** víbufa idzó.
      INF-cook FOC women SM-P2-cook vegetables yesterday
      'Women COOKED vegetables yesterday.'
   b. *Vá-má-**námba** ówú vakútu va-má-**námba** víbufa ídzo.
      SM-P2-cook FOC women SM-P2-cook vegetables yesterday
   c. O-**vánga** ówú Putá a-kutu-**vánga** cwí.
      INF-fry FOC Puta SM-PROG-fry fish
      'Puta is FRYING fish.'
   d. *O-kutu-**vánga** ówú Putá a-kutu-**vánga** cwí.
      INF-PROG-fry FOC Puta SM-PROG-fry fish (Biloa 2013: 76, 499)

(169) O-(*a-tá-má-kutu-)**nambá** ówú Putá a-tá-má-kutu-**nambá** súbu a
      INF-SM-NEG-P2-PROG-cook FOC Puta SM-NEG-P2-PROG-cook sauce of
      ngó.
      chicken
      'Puta was not COOKING chicken soup.' (Biloa 2013: 500)

In contrast to Fongbe (see section 7.1.5) and Haitian Creole (see section 7.1.7) we do not find a restriction of verb fronting to stage-level predicates. Individual-level predicates may freely undergo fronting and doubling.

(170) a. O-**dínga** ówú Isomo a-má-**dingá** Tsimi.
      INF-love FOC Isomo SM-P2-love Tsimi
      'Isomo LOVED Tsimi.'
   b. O-**fwánena** ówú Isomo a-**fwánenám** ísa wáá.
      INF-resemble FOC Isomo SM-resemble father his
      'Isomo RESEMBLES his father.'
   c. **Wídzima** (=o+ídzima) ówú Isomo **ídzimám** agee wáá.
      know INF+know FOC Isomo know wife his
      'Isomo KNOWS his wife.' (Biloa 2013: 516)

Contrary to what is the case in many other (West) African languages, there is no evidence that the fronted verb is nominalized. The infinitive form of the fronted verb does not behave like a nominal, that is, modification with e.g. a possessive pronoun is ungrammatical (171-b).

(171) a. **Wénda** ówú Putá a-m-**énda** ná mbóo.
      go FOC Puta SM-P1-go to market
      'Puta WENT to the market.'
   b. *wénda wáme
      go my (Biloa 2013: 513f.)

There is another form of the verb similar to English gerundives which allows nominal modification e.g. with a possessive pronoun (172). However, this form never occurs in the verb fronting construction (Biloa 2013: 514)

(172) a. mbíníno ráme
   dancing my
   'my dancing'
  b. ndíngíno ráme
   loving my
   'my loving'
  c. ngéndéno ráme
   going my
   'my going' (Biloa 2013: 514)

Hence, it cannot be the case that the fronted verb is just a deverbal noun and verb fronting is eventually only NP fronting in disguise.

Summary

To conclude the discussion of Tuki, verb fronting for focus is available and leaves a copy of the verb in the canonical clause-internal position. Complements as well as TAM-markers and negation may not accompany the fronted verb, but adverbs can do so. The construction plausibly involves an $\bar{\text{A}}$-dependency since it can cross finite clause boundaries, is sensitive to islands and is in complementary distribution with wh-extraction. A restriction to stage-level predicates as found in Fongbe or Haitian Creole is not attested in Tuki. Also, there is no evidence for nominalization of the fronted verb. The properties of verb fronting are assembled in table 7.15. Therefore, Tuki verb fronting manifests pattern A of Generalization II.

Tab. 7.15: Properties of verbal fronting in Tuki

	Copy	Dummy	Unbound	Islands	GS	TAM	L-Adv	H-Adv	NEG	L/R	Top/Foc
V	✓	–	✓	✓	n.d.	–	✓	n.d.	–	L	Foc
VP	–	–									

7.1.16 Turkish

Turkish, a language of the Turkic family, is spoken by about 70 million people, mainly in Turkey but also by Turkish populations in other countries.

Turkish shows a particular construction in which the verb is placed in sentence-initial position affixed with the morpheme *mAsInA* and a copy of it occurs in the canonical verb position (173). The meaning of the construction is identified by Lee

(2002) as contrastive topic, indicated by the adversative continuation that follows it (the part in parentheses in (173)).

(173) **Gel**-mesine **gel**-di (ama sahne-ye çık-ma-dı).
come-CONTR.TOP come-PST but stage-to go.on-NEG-PST
'She did come but she didn't go on the stage.' (Lee 2002: 361)

Apart from this example, I was able to find only two other (unglossed) sentences in the literature (174).

(174) a. **Git**miş **git**mesine, ama doktor gelmemiş.
'I gather he did go, but the doctor didn't come.'
b. **Konuş**masına **konuş**acağ ım da, bakalım o dinleyecek mi.
'Yes, I'm going to talk to her, but let's see if she'll listen.'
(Göksel & Kerslake 2005: 410)

Oddly enough, the construction does not seem to figure prominently in the discussion on verb doubling even though Turkish is by no means an underresearched language. As it stands, however, due to this disinterest I am not able to provide further details about the construction than those presented in table 7.16. In Turkish, a single verb is displaced and a copy of it is left in base position which is exactly the pattern A of Generalization II.

Tab. 7.16: Properties of verbal fronting in Turkish

	Copy	Dummy	Unbound	Islands	GS	TAM	L-Adv	H-Adv	Neg	L/R	Top/Foc
V	✓	–	n.d.	n.d.	n.d.	n.d.	n.d.	n.d.	n.d.	L	Top
VP											

7.1.17 Vata

Vata, a Kru language of the Niger-Congo family, is spoken by an estimated 10 000 people in the Ivory Coast (Koopman 1984).

The language disposes of a verb fronting construction in which the verb is focussed and leaves a copy in its base position (175). The fronted verb always receives a mid tone as a consequence of its underlyingly being unmarked for tone (Koopman 1984: 38).

(175) a. **Lē à lē** sáká.
eat we eat rice
'We are really EATING rice.'
'We are EATING rice.'
b. **Lī ɔ́** dā sáká lī.
eat s/he PERF rice eat
'S/he has EATEN rice.'
c. **Lī ɔ́** lì sáká.
eat s/he ate rice
'S/he ATE rice.' (Koopman 1984: 38)

Fronting the object together with the verb results in ungrammaticality independent of whether the object is a full NP (176-a) or a pronoun (176-b).

(176) a. *[Lī sáká] à lì sáká.
eat rice we ate rice
b. [(*Ma) lī] ń ká má lí.
it eat I FUT-A it eat (Koopman 1984: 38,155)

There is also another construction which exhibits verb doubling (177). However, in contrast to the verb fronting mentioned before, in this construction the fronted verb obligatorily occurs with a genitive-marked 'subject' and the copy in base position is affixed with the relative clause marker *bɔ́*. It serves as a temporal adverbial construction with the respective meaning of contemporaneity.

(177) a. Kòfí nî̀ **yī** ɔ́ **yi**-wá-bɔ́ jàà, wá lā kɔ́ jlɔ́.
Kofi GEN arrive he arrive-PT-REL just they PERF-A PART stand
'Hardly did Kofi arrive, or they were standing up.'
b. Nání **fītɔ̄lē** ń **fītɔ̄lè**-wá-bɔ́ jàà, wá nà gúguè.
my appear I appear-PT-REL hardly they with flight
'As soon as I arrived, they fled.' (Koopman 1984: 156)

The properties of this construction have not been described yet but Koopman (1984: 156) conjectures that it "represents the equivalent of a 'verbal' relative". I will therefore focus on the construction with a focus meaning because its properties are known and well described in Koopman (1984).

Fronting is not restricted to any particular type of verb. Any verb that has a base form (i.e. can undergo morphological processes affecting verbs) may be focussed. This includes unergatives (178-a), transitives (175-c), unaccusatives (178-b), ditransitives (178-c), particle verbs (178-d), idiomatic verbs (178-e), 'adjectival' verbs (178-f), causatives (178-g), reciprocals (178-h), applicatives (178-i), and passives (178-j).

(178) a. **Ngɔ̄nɔ̄** n̄ **ngɔ̄nɔ̄**-ɔ̄?
sleep you sleep-Q
'Are you sleeping?' (Koopman 1984: 154)
b. **Mlī** wá **mlì**.
leave they leave
'They LEFT.'
c. **Nyē** à **nyɛ́**` à nɔ́ dàlá`.
give we give our mother money
'We GAVE money to our mother.'
d. **Gā** wá **gá**` mlí.
shout they shout PRT
'They SHOUTED.'
e. **Pā** wá **pà** wī nā...
throw they throw voice NA...
'They ANNOUNCED that...'
f. **Zālē** ɛ́ **zàlè** dùùù.
red it red 'like blood'
'It is very RED.'
g. **Zālīà** n̄ **zàlıà** zàmú.
redden I redden sauce
'I really REDDENED the sauce.'
h. **Lā-lɛ̄-lā-lɛ̄** wà **lá-lɛ̄-lā-lɛ̄**-ɛ̄.
call-LE-call-LE they call-LE-call-LE-Q
'Do they CALL each other.'
i. **Bīdōlē** n̄ ká sàmàná` mlí **bīdōlē**.
wash.APPL you FUT-A soap in wash.APPL
'You are going to WASH yourself with SOAP.'
j. **Dlālɔ̄** wá **dlálɔ̄**.
beat.PASS they beat.PASS
'They have been KILLED.' (Koopman 1984: 157)

Turning to the syntactic behaviour of verb fronting, we find that just like wh/NP-fronting it can take place out of embedded contexts. This is shown for three different embedding constructions in (179-a–c), where the primed examples display a wh/NP-extraction corresponding to the verb fronting in the unprimed examples.

(179) a. **Lā** n̄ dā [yué-é **lá** kā mlī ā`]?
go you PERF-A children-DEF call KA go Q
'Have you gone to call the children?'
a'. Àlɔ́ nī` yúe n̄ lā [lá kā mlī lá]?
who GEN children you PERF-A call KA go WH
'Whose children did you go call?'

b. **Yē** ǹ gūgū [nā Àbà pá` wī [nā ǹ **yɛ́`** ngʋá yé é]]?
see you think NA Aba throw voice NA you saw them PRT Q
'Do you think that Aba announced that you SAW them?'

b'. Àlɔ́ ǹ gūgū [nā Àbà pà wī [nā ǹ yɛ̀` yé lá]]?
who you think NA Aba throw voice NA you see PRT WH
'Who do you think that Aba announced that you saw?'

c. **Zʋ̄** ǹ bò kʋ́ [lé ǹ nɪ́ mí kàfɛ́` mlí **zʋ́** à`]?
put you forgot PRT and you NEG-A it coffee in put Q
'Did you forget to PUT it in your coffee?'

c'. Yī ǹ bò kʋ́ [lé ǹ nɪ́ kàfɛ́ mlí zʋ̀ lá]?
what you forgot PRT and you NEG-A coffee in put WH
'What did you forget to put in the coffee?' (Koopman 1984: 158f.)

The parallelism with wh/NP-movement, however, is not complete. Consider the examples in (180) where, again, the primed ones present a wh/NP-movement sentence corresponding to the verb fronting sentence in the unprimed ones.

(180) a. *****Yē** Kòfí sálɛ̀ ngʋá dʋ̀dʋ̀kʋ́ dí [nā ɔ́ **yɛ́`** mɔ́ yé].
see Kofi told them softly PRT NA he saw you PRT
'Kofi told them softly that he SAW you.'

a'. Àlɔ́ Kòfí sálɛ̀ mɔ́ dʋ̀dʋ̀kʋ́ dí [nā ǹ yɛ̀` yé lá]?
who Kofi tell you softly PRT NA you saw PRT WH
'Who did Kofi tell you softly that he saw?'

b. *****Yē** Kòfí pé mlí [nā wá **yɛ́`** mɔ́ yé].
see Kofi shout PRT NA they saw him PRT
'Kofi shouted that they SAW him.'

b' Àlɔ́ Kòfí pɛ́` mlí [nā ǹ yɛ̀` yé lá]?
who Kofi shout PRT NA you saw PRT WH
'Who did Kofi shout that you saw?' (Koopman 1984: 160f.)

While the matrix verb in each sentence seems to be a bridge verb for wh/NP-extraction it acts like a non-bridge verb for verb fronting rendering the unprimed example sentences ungrammatical.

With regard to islands the parallelism between verb fronting and wh/NP-extraction is equally flawed. Whereas both constructions are sensitive to Complex NP Islands (181) only verb fronting respects Wh-Islands (182-a, b). Wh/NP-extraction out of a Wh-Island, on the other hand, is grammatical (182-c, d).

(181) *Complex NP Island*
 a. *Tākā ǹ wà [fòtó` mūmʋ` ǹ tàkà ɓɔ́ Àbà].
    show you like picture ITIT   you showed REL Aba
 b. *Àbà mɔ́₁ ǹ wà [fòtó` mūmʋ` ǹ tàkà ɓɔ́ ___₁].
    Aba HER you like picture ITIT   you show REL
                                            (Koopman 1984: 159)

(182) *Wh-Island*[15]
 a. ***Nyɛ̄** à nɪ́ [zɛ̄ à ká ɓɔ́ Kòfí **nyɛ́**] yì.
    give we NEG-A thing we FUT-A REL Kofi give know
    'We don't know what to GIVE to Kofi.'
 b. ***Nū** à nɪ́ [zɛ̄ à nɪ̄-tà **nū**] yì.
    do we NEG thing we FUT-A-FT do know
    'We don't know what to DO.'   (Koopman 1984: 160)
 c. Àlɔ́ ǹ nɪ́ [zɛ̄ à nyɛ́`-ɓɔ́] yì là.
    who you NEG-A thing we gave-REL know WH
    'To whom don't you know what we have given?'
 d. Kɔ̀` mɔ̄-mɔ̀` ǹ nɪ́-ɓɔ́ [zɛ̄ à nyɛ́`-ɓɔ́] yì.
    man.DEF HIM-HIM you NEG-A-REL thing we gave-REL know
    'The man to whom you don't know what we have given.'
                                            (Koopman 1984: 36f.)

Nonetheless, verb fronting and wh-extraction cannot cooccur in the same clause (183) independently of the order that the fronted verb and the fronted wh-element/NP take with respect to each other.

(183) a. *Sáká má **lī** Kòfí ká **lī**.
      rice IT eat Kofi FUT-A eat
   b. ***Lī** sák` má Kòfí ká **lī**.
      eat rice IT Kofi FUT-A eat
   c. *Àlɔ́ **lē** ɔ̀ lē **lá**?
      who eat he.R eat WH   (Koopman 1984: 158)

Despite the difference between wh/NP-extraction and verb fronting with regard to Wh-Islands and bridge verbs, the latter still shows properties of $\bar{\text{A}}$-movement and, judging by the ungrammaticality of (183), seems to target the same structural position as the former.

---

[15] Despite exhibiting a relative clause surface structure the Wh-Island sentences syntactically behave like indirect questions indicating an underlying syntactic stucture that is different from relative clauses (Koopman 1984: 185, en. 5).

Concerning the material that can accompany the verb in sentence-initial position, this is restricted to some adverbs (184).

(184) [Yē kpē`] lágɔ̀ **yē**.
come really rain comes
'It is really RAINING, isn't it.' (Koopman 1984: 156)

TAM-markers and negation, in contrast, are not licit in this position (185).

(185) a. *Lī-dā à lī-dā zué sáká.
eat-PST we eat-PST yesterday rice
b. (*Ná`) **lē** wá ná`-lē-kā.
NEG eat they NEG-eat-FT
'They will not EAT.' (Koopman 1984: 38,156)

There is one exception, namely the imperfective aspect, which is marked by lowering of a high vowel (e.g. $li \rightarrow le$). This may show up on the fronted verb (186) indicating that the ban on TAM-markers in sentence-initial position only holds for concatenative or free morphemes but not for morphemes that are realized as phonological changes of the verb stem.

(186) **Lē** ǹ lē ē?
eat you eat Q
'Are you eating?' (Koopman 1984: 155)

Concerning the categorial status of the fronted verb, there are no overt signs of nominalization. In contrast, if a nominalized verb occurs in fronted position the sentence takes the form associated with regular NP fronting. There is a gap in the base position of the nominalized verb and a resumptive pronoun immediately follows the fronted verb. The contrast between verb fronting and deverbal nominal fronting is illustrated in (187-a) vs. (187-b)

(187) a. **Ngɔ̄nū** ǹ wà nā ǹ ká **ngɔ́nú** á?
sleep you want NA you FUT-A sleep Q
'Do you want to SLEEP?'
b. [**Ngɔ́nú**]$_1$-lì mí ǹ wà ___$_1$ à?
sleep-NMLZ it you want Q
'Is it sleeping you want?' (Koopman 1984: 154)

Summary
In summary, Vata shows verb fronting only where the verb leaves a copy in clause-internal position. The fronted verb is neither nominalized nor marked for negation,

tense or aspect, with the exception of imperfective aspect. There are no restrictions on the type of verbs that can occur in this construction. Fronting shows properties of Ā-dependencies in being unbounded, respecting the Complex NP Island and the Wh-Island, and leading to ungrammaticality when cooccurring with other Ā-extractions in the same clause. However, its behaviour is not entirely parallel to wh-movement, which is insensitive to Wh-Islands and may take place across matrix verbs that do not act as bridge verbs for verb fronting. The properties of Vata verb fronting are presented in table 7.17. Thus far, Vata verbal fronting exhibits pattern A of Generalization II.

Tab. 7.17: Properties of verbal fronting in Vata

	Copy	Dummy	Unbound	Islands	GS	TAM	L-Adv	H-Adv	NEG	L/R	Top/Foc
V	✓	–	✓[16]	✓[17]	n.d.	–[18]	✓	n.d.	–	L	Foc
VP	–	–									

7.2 Languages with verb phrase fronting only

7.2.1 Danish

Danish, a Germanic language of the Indo-European family, is spoken by about five million people principally in Denmark and by small populations in neighbouring countries. Like many Germanic languages, e.g. Swedish, German, and Dutch, it is a V2 language.

Like Swedish and Norwegian, Danish shows a verb phrase fronting construction where a dummy verb occurs in the canonical verb position inside the clause. Consider the second conjunct in example (188). The fronted verb phrase is either discourse-old or stands in a contrastive set relation to an already evoked VP (Houser et al. 2006).

---

[16] The number of bridge verbs for verb fronting is a subset of those available for wh-extraction.
[17] Verb fronting is not possible from Wh-islands whereas wh-extraction is.
[18] The fronted verb may be marked for imperfective aspect which is realized non-concatenatively.

(188) Jasper lovede   at vaske bilen   og [**vaske** bilen] **gjorde** han
      Jasper promise.PST to wash car.DEF and wash car.DEF do.PST he
      (så sandelig).
      so truly
      'Jasper promised to wash the car and wash the car, he did (indeed).'

      (Houser et al. 2006: 2)

Verb fronting is only attested with intransitive verbs (189) or transitive verbs without an overtly realized object (190). It is thus plausible to conclude that fronting of a transitive verb while stranding its objects is ungrammatical, as it is in the closely related mainland Scandinavian languages.

(189) [**Venter**] **gør** han ikke.
      wait.PRS does he not
      'He doesn't wait.'   (Ørsnes 2011: 410)

(190) Nej, [**pynter**]   **gør** de   ikke.
      no   decorate.PRS do they not
      'No, they are not actually decorating.'   (Ørsnes 2011: 412)

Like in the other mainland Scandinavian languages, the fronted verb may be finite or non-finite (191) (see section 1.3 for an explanation). In contrast to Swedish (see section 7.2.6) but like in Norwegian (see section 7.2.4), the non-finite option is the preferred one (Lødrup 1990: 8).

(191) ...og [**kørde/køre**   bilen] **gjorde** han.
          and drive.PST/drive.INF car.DEF did   he
      '...and drive the car, he did.'   (Platzack 2008: 280)

At first glance, it might look like verb phrase fronting can occur in embedded clauses (192).

(192) Jeg vil   sige, at [**købe** den] ville   jeg aldrig **gøre**.
      I   would say   that buy   it   would I   never do
      'Buy it, I don't think I would ever do that.'   (Ørsnes 2011: 415)

It should be noted, however, that the embedded clause in (192) is an embedded V2 clause (i.e. has matrix/root clause properties) as evidenced by the fact that the finite verb *ville* 'would' precedes the adverb *aldrig*. It is therefore likely that verb phrase fronting is restricted to root clauses in Danish as it is in Norwegian and Swedish.

Notably, *gøre* 'do' does not appear when verb phrase fronting strands an auxiliary (193-a) or a modal (193-b) indicating that dummy verb insertion in Danish takes place to provide a host for finiteness marking otherwise stranded by verb phrase fronting. Insertion of *gøre* is thus not necessary in case an auxiliary or modal can take on this marking.

(193) a. [Forsøgt] har man selvfølgelig...
 attempted has one of.course
 'Though people have tried of course...'
 b. [Undersøge noget] kan man jo altid...
 investigate something can one ADV always
 'One can always investigate something...' (Houser et al. 2006: 5)

Concerning the $\bar{\text{A}}$-properties of the construction, I was unable to find any examples of verb phrase fronting with dummy verb insertion crossing finite clause boundaries or leaving an island. The only example of grammatical 'long-distance' verb fronting is out of the infinitive complement of the raising verb *syntes* 'seemed' (194).

(194) [**See** paa hende] syntes han ikke [at **goere**].
 look.INF at her seemed he not to do
 'He didn't seem to be looking at her.' (Ørsnes 2011: 415)

However, judging from the unboundedness and island-sensitivity of the corresponding construction in the closely related languages Swedish (see section 7.2.6) and Norwegian (see section 7.2.4) it would be unexpected if the Danish verb phrase fronting were clause-bound and insensitive to islands. In fact, there are examples showing that Danish verb phrase fronting respects islands like the Wh-Island (195), the Subject Island (196), the Adjunct Island (197), and the Coordinate Structure Constraint (198), but all of them contain an auxiliary or a modal, which as mentioned above precludes the occurrence of the dummy verb *gøre*.

(195) *Wh-Island*
 *[Drukket kaffe]$_1$ spørger de altid [hvornår man sidst har
 drink.PTCP coffee ask.PRS they always when one last have.PRS
 ___$_1$]

 Intended: 'They always ask when you last had a cup of coffee.'
 (Houser et al. 2011: 285)

(196) *Subject Island*
 *[Lave mad]$_1$ overrasker [at han godt kan ___$_1$] mig ikke.
 make.INF food surprises that he well can me not
 Intended: 'That he can cook doesn't surprise me.'
 (Houser et al. 2011: 284)

(197) *Adjunct Island*
 *[Lave   mad]₁ går   de tit   ud og spiser [selvom
  make.INF food go.PRS they often out and eat.PRS even.though
  han kan ___₁]
  he can
  Intended: 'They often go out to eat, even though he can cook.'
(Houser et al. 2011: 285)

(198) *Coordinate Structure Constraint*
 a. *[Lave   mad]₁ kan de ___₁ og vaske   op.
    make.INF food can they   and wash.INF up
    Intended: 'They can cook and do laundry.'
 b. *[Vaske   tøj]₁ kan de lave   mad og ___₁.
    wash.INF clothes can they make.INF food and
    Intended: 'They can cook and do laundry.'
(Houser et al. 2011: 285f.)

Due to the close interrelatedness of the mainland Scandinavian languages, I suspect that many of the key results presented in the sections on Swedish (see section 7.2.6) and Norwegian (see section 7.2.4) carry over to Danish straightforwardly.

Summary
In conclusion, Danish shows verb phrase fronting, but not verb fronting, where a dummy verb *gøre* 'do' occupies the canonical verb position in the clause. The verb in the fronted phrase is preferably an infinitive but may also optionally occur in finite form. The construction most probably involves movement, although this could not be demonstrated with clear examples and thus must remain a strong conjecture at this point. However, just like in Swedish, the dummy verb does not appear when the verb phrase strands an auxiliary or a modal. Table 7.18 provides an overview over some properties of the construction in Danish. Thus, Danish verb phrase fronting instantiates pattern D of Generalization II.

Tab. 7.18: Properties of verbal fronting in Danish

	Copy	Dummy	Unbound	Islands	GS	TAM	L-Adv	H-Adv	Neg	L/R	Top/Foc
V	–	–									
VP	–	✓	(✓)[19]	(✓)[20]	n.d.	(✓)[21]	n.d.	n.d.	n.d.	L	Top

7.2.2 Hausa

Hausa, a Chadic language of the Afro-Asiatic phylum, is spoken by more than 35 million people in Hausaland, a region covering the North-Western part of Nigeria and the South-Western part of Niger (Newman 2000: 1).

Verbal focus, that is both new information and contrastive focus (Jaggar 2001: 493), can be expressed by displacing the verb phrase into the left periphery of the clause while the base position of the verb phrase is occupied by a form of the dummy verb *yi* 'do' (199).

(199) a. [**Tàmbayàr̃tà**] mukà   **yi**.
           ask.VN.of.3F   1PL.FOC.PF do
           '(It's) asking her we did = we asked her.'
       b. [**Tsarè** fur̃sùnàn]   nē   akà   **yi** (bà har̃bè
           jail   prisoner.DD(m) FOC.COP(m) 4PL.FOC.PF do NEG shoot
           shi ba).
           3M NEG
           '(It's) jail(ing) the prisoner one did = the prisoner has been jailed (not shot).'   (Jaggar 2001: 502)

The fronted verb either occurs as a nominalized verbal noun phrase (199-a) or a verbal infinitival phrase (199-b). The difference between these two lies mainly in their internal composition. While the former do not necessarily have to contain an overtly expressed object, the latter always consist of a finite verb plus its direct or indirect object (Jaggar 2001: 286ff.).

According to Hartmann (2006), however, only verbal noun phrases, but not infinitive phrases, may be fronted. Apparently, speakers' judgements vary on these constructions.

(200) a. [**Shân/*sha**   taabàà] ya-kèè   **yi**.
           drink.VN/drink tobacco 3SG-REL.CONT do
           'It is smoking that he is doing.'
       b. [**Cîn/*ci**   àbinci] ta-kèè   **yi**.
           eatVN/eat food   3SG.FEM-REL.CONT do
           'It is eating food that she is doing.'   (Hartmann 2006: 585)

The focus marker *nee* (glossed as a post-focus copula in Jaggar 2001) that occurs after the fronted verb phrase is optional.

---

19 This is conjectured based on parallel behaviour in Swedish and Norwegian.
20 See footnote 19.
21 The verb in the fronted phrase may be finite, i.e. marked for tense/aspect.

(201) a. [**D'aurè** ʃàraawòò] (nee) su-kà **yi.**
tie.up thief FOC 3PL-REL.PERF do
'To tie up the thief is what they did.'
b. [**Ginà** masallaacii] (nèè) su-kèè sô sù **yi.**
build mosque FOC 3PL-REL.CONT want 3PL.SUBJ do
'It is building a mosque that they want to do.'

(Hartmann 2006: 585)

In this construction, it is not possible to front the verb alone and strand its complement (202).

(202) a. *[**Karanta**] suka **yi** littaafii.
read.VN(Pr) 3P.REL do book
'Reading they did the book.'
b. *[**Araawaa**] na **yi** masc (ga/da) littaafii.
lend.VN(Pr) 2S.REL do to.him at/with book
'Lending I did him with a book.' (Tuller 1986: 428f.)

An exception to this pattern are PP- and TP-complements which can be stranded by verb fronting (203). However, Tuller (1986: 429) remarks that these can plausibly be argued to undergo extraposition out of VP rendering the examples in (203) instantiations of remnant verb phrase fronting.

(203) a. **Soo** akee **yii** [_TP_ a saami daliilin da ya saa ...].
want.VN indef do indef get reason.the that 3SM make
'Wanting one does to find out why...'
b. [**Kai** kaayaa] sukee **yi** wa Muusa.
take.VN loads 3P do to Musa
'Taking the loads they are doing to Musa.' (Tuller 1986: 429)

A copy of the fronted verb which instead of the dummy verb _yi_ 'do' occupies the canonical verb position leads to ungrammaticality (204).

(204) a. [**Karanta** ƙur'aanii] suka **yi/*karanta** (*shi) da saahe.
read.VN Koran 3P do/read it at morning
'Reading the Koran they did/read (it) in the morning.'
b. [**Araa** masa littaafii] na **yi/*araa** (*shi).
lend.VN to.him book 1S do/lend it
'Lending him a book I did/lent (it).'
c. [**Cin** abinci da saurii] suka **yi/*ci** (*shi).
eat.VN food with haste 3P do/eat it
'Eating food in a ahurry they did/ate (it).' (Tuller 1986: 430)

As shown in (204), it is also ungrammatical to take up the object of the fronted verb with a resumptive pronoun following *yi*. As Tuller (1982, 1986) argues, these facts fall out easily under an analysis of the construction as involving movement of the verb phrase (rather than the verb and the object separately).

There is more evidence to the claim that verb phrase fronting involves Ā-movement. First, verb phrase fronting may cross finite clause boundaries (205) and is sensitive to (at least) Wh-Islands (206).[22]

(205) [**Karanta** ƙuraanii] Ali ya cee [yaaraa sunaa **yii** da
 read.VN Koran Ali 3SM.PERF say children 3P.CONT do at
 saahe].
 morning
 'Reading the Koran Ali said the children do in the morning.'

 (Tuller 1986: 432)

(206) *[**Karanta** ƙuraanii] Ali ya cee [waa yakee **yii**].
 read.VN Koran Ali 3SM.PERF say who 3SM.REL.CONT do
 'Reading the Koran Ali said who does.' (Tuller 1986: 432)

Second, continuous and perfective aspect markers in the matrix clause that provides the final landing site of verb phrase fronting must occur in the relative form (207).

(207) a. [**Gyaara** mootaa-taa] suka **yi**.
 repair.VN(Pr) car-my 3P.REL.PERF do
 'Repairing my car they did.'
 b. [**Cin** abincii da saurii] aka cee sun/suka **yi**. shii ya
 eat.VN food with speed indef say 3P.PERF/3P.REL do it 3SM
 saa sukee rashin laafiyaa.
 make 3P lack.of health
 'Eating food in a hurry one said they did. This is why they are sick.'
 c. [**Karanta** ƙur'aanii] ya cee maalaamai sunaa/sukee
 read.VN Koran 3SM.REL say imams 3P.CONT/3P.REL
 soo mu **yi**.
 want 1P.SUB do
 'Reading the Koran he said the imams want us to do.'

 (Tuller 1986: 428)

---

22 Unfortunately, Tuller (1986) does not gloss these examples properly. The glosses here were inferred by me from glossing of parts occurring in other glossed examples. However, she explicitly cites them as examples of Wh-Islands.

This form is also required in wh-contexts (208-a), regular NP fronting (208-b), and relativization (208-c), all of which typically involve Ā-movement (Tuller 1986: 109ff.). Clauses inbetween the final landing site and the origin of the verb phrase may optionally also show relative aspect marking.

(208) a. Mee sukee/*sunaa tsammaanii yaaraa sun yi?
what 3P.REL/3P.CONT think children 3P.COMPL do
'What do they think the children did?'

b. Yaaran da sukee/*sunaa tsammaanii sun tafi
children.the that 3P.REL/3P.CONT think 3P.COMPL go
daajii.
bush
'the children (that) they think went to the bush'

c. Yan Muusaa sukee/*sunaa tsammaanii sun tafi daajii.
kids.of Musa 3P.REL/3P.CONT think 3P.COMPL go bush
'They think MUSA'S KIDS went to the bush.' (Tuller 1986: 109)

As expected, VP-adjoined adverbs like *da saurii* 'with speed/haste' may be fronted with the verb phrase (209).

(209) a. [**Cin** abinci da saurii] suka **yi**.
eat.VN food with haste 3P.REL.PERF do
'Eating food in a hurry they did.'

b. [**Tafiyaa** Kanoo] muka **yi**.
go.VN to.Kano 1P.REL.PERF do
'Going to Kano we did.' (Tuller 1986: 430)

The fronting of TAM-markers together with the verb, however, is not possible (210).

(210) a. *[kan **Fitaa**], ai, mu (kan) **fitaa/yi** (ta) wani lookacii.
HAB go.out.VN PRT 1P HAB go.out/do it some time

b. *[Sukan **fitaa**], ai, yaaraa sukan **yi** (ta) wani lookacii.
3P.HAB go.out.VN PRT children 3P.HAB do it some time
(Tuller 1986: 427)

Left dislocation vs. verb phrase fronting
There is another construction in Hause where a verb phrase, or more accurately a verbal noun phrase, is placed in sentence-initial position, receiving a topic interpretation, and a dummy verb is inserted in the base position within the part that is interpreted as the comment (211-a). In contrast to verb phrase fronting, however, a copy of the verb in the comment instead of the dummy verb is licit as well (211-b). A gap, on the other hand, is not licensed (211-c).

(211) a. [**Rubuutaa** wa sarkii waasiiƙaa] ai, zan **rubuutaa** goobe.
 write.VN(Pr) to emir letter PRT 1S write tomorrow
 'Writing the emir a letter, I'll write tomorrow.'
 b. [**Rubuutaa** wa sarkii waasiiƙaa] ai, zan **yi** goobe.
 write.VN(Pr) to emir letter PRT 1S do tomorrow
 'Writing the emir a letter, I'll do tomorrow.'
 c. *[**Rubuutaa** wa sarkii waasiiƙaa]₁ ai, zan ___₁ goobe.

(Tuller 1986: 424)

At first sight, this construction seems to contradict Generalization IIb which states that in languages that only show verb phrase fronting it triggers dummy verb insertion, not verb doubling. The situation is aggravated when examples like (212) are taken into account, where apparently the verb *gyārā* 'fix' alone has been fronted stranding its object *mōtàř* 'car' and dummy verb insertion has taken place. An example like this additionally contradicts Generalization IIa. Taken together, both examples could even disprove Generalization I because they instantiate exactly the pattern where verb fronting triggers dummy verb insertion and verb phrase fronting results in verb doubling.

(212) [**Gyārā**], sâ **yi** wà mōtàř gòbe.
 fix.VN 3PL.POT do IOM car.DD(f) tomorrow
 'Fixing, they'll probably do (it) to the car tomorrow.' (Jaggar 2001: 542)

However, several properties of this topicalization show that it is more similar to Germanic-style left dislocation than to the focalization mentioned above and therefore does not serve as a counter-example to any of the abovementioned generalizations.

First, as pointed out by Jaggar (2001: 542), example (212) includes the indirect object marker *wà* which indicates that the stranded object is actually an applicative indirect object. As such, it might be introduced by a high applicative head which attaches above the verb phrase (Pylkkänen 2008). Thus, the fronted verb in (212) might actually be a whole intransitive verb phrase that strands the applicative phrase containing the indirect object *mōtàř* 'car'.

Second, topicalization (213-a), in contrast to focalization (213-b), is not sensitive to islands which indicates that the topicalized constituent is base generated in its surface position rather than being moved there from a clause-internal base position.[23]

---

[23] The examples in (213) are unglossed in Tuller (1986). The glosses here were inferred by me from glossing of parts occurring in other glossed examples. However, they are explicitly cited as examples of Wh-Islands.

(213) a. [**Karanta** ƙuraanii], ai, Ali yaa san waa yakee
 read.VN Koran PRT Ali 3SM.PERF know who 3SM.REL.CONT
 yii.
 do
 'Reading the Koran, well, Ali knows who does.' (Tuller 1986: 432)
 b. *[**Karanta** ƙuraanii] Ali ya cee waa yakee **yii**.
 read.VN Koran Ali 3SM.REL.PERF say who 3SM.REL.CONT do
 'Reading the Koran Ali said who does.' (Tuller 1986: 432)

This is further corroborated by the fact that the matrix clause in a topic construction like (213-a) is not marked for relative aspect, which is obligatory in verb focalization and other contexts that commonly involve Ā-movement, like wh-extraction, NP fronting, and relativization. The respective relative form of *yaa* in (213-a) would be *ya* with a short vowel (Tuller 1986: 55).

The treatment of topics as being base-generated in a position external to the main clause is furthermore in line with an observation about the prosody of the construction. While focalization is monoclausal, the preposed topic constituent is "external to the clause proper and is *typically segregated from the comment by a prosodic (often comma-marked) pause*." (Jaggar 2001: 538, my emphasis). This prosodic break indicates that the connection between the topic and the comment clause is rather loose. Additionally, exclamatory particles, like *ai* 'well', can intervene between topic and comment (Jaggar 2001: 539).

A last piece of evidence against Ā-movement of the topic is provided by the distribution of pronouns which refer back to the topicalized constituent. As we have seen in the focalization example (204), repeated below as (214), it is not possible to focalize a verb phrase and refer to it with a clause-internal pronoun.

(214) a. [**Karanta** ƙur'aanii] suka **yi/*karanta** (*shi) da saahe.
 read.VN Koran 3P do/read it at morning
 'Reading the Koran they did/read (it) in the morning.'
 b. [**Araa** masa littaafii] na **yi/*araa** (*shi).
 lend.VN to.him book 1S do/lend it
 'Lending him a book I did/lent (it).'
 c. [**Cin** abinci da saurii] suka **yi/*ci** (*shi).
 eat.VN food with haste 3P do/eat it
 'Eating food in a ahurry they did/ate (it).' (Tuller 1986: 430)

As focalization involves syntactic movement of the verb phrase this state of affairs is expected because the moved constituent leaves a trace that is pronounced as *yi* 'do' (cf. Tuller 1986: 430) and can therefore not be pronounced by a second element, i.e. the pronoun.

In the topicalization construction, a very different picture emerges. A pronoun may optionally occur when the comment part contains the dummy verb *yi* 'do' (215-a) and also when it contains a copy of the (di/mono-transitive) verb (215-b).

(215) a. [**Rubuutaa** wa sarkii waasiiƙaa], ai, zan **yi** shi
 write.VN(Pr) to emir letter(f) PRT 1S.FUT do it(m)
 goobe.
 tomorrow
 'Writing a letter to the emir, well I'll do it tomorrow.'
 b. [**Rubuutaa** wa sarkii waasiiƙaa], ai, zan **rubuutaa** ta
 write.VN(Pr) to emir letter(f) PRT 1S.FUT write it(f)
 goobe.
 tomorrow
 'Writing a letter to the emir, well I'll write it tomorrow.'
 (Tuller 1986: 424)

The pronoun in (215-a) refers to the whole topicalized verb phrase as can be told from its default masculine form whereas the one in (215-b) exclusively refers to the direct object *waasiiƙaa* 'letter' as indicated by the feminine gender agreement between the two. Upon closer scrutiny, the direct object pronoun turns out to be obligatory when the direct object denotes a human (216-a, b) while this is not the case for the verb phrase pronoun (216-c).

(216) a. [**Ganin** sarkii], ai, mun **gan** shi da saahe.
 see.VN emir PRT 1P see him at morning
 'Seeing the emir, well, we saw him in the morning.'
 b. *[**Ganin** sarkii], ai, mun **ganii** ∅ da saahe.
 'Seeing the emir, well, we saw in the morning.'
 c. [**Ganin** sarkii], ai, mun **yii** (shi) da saahe.
 'Seeing the emir, well, we did (it) in the morning.' (Tuller 1986: 425)

In fact, the optionality of pronouns in (215) and (216-c) might have nothing to do with the topicalization construction. It is an independent fact in Hausa that "only non-human pronouns may be null" (Tuller 1986: 425). Hence it is plausible to assume that pronouns are obligatorily present with verb phrase topicalization and their optional absence is conditioned by the independently available option of pro-drop of non-human pronouns. Since a verb phrase is never human the pronoun following the dummy verb *yi* is always optional, while direct object pronouns can only be dropped if the direct object is human.

Now, if the topicalized constituent or a part of it is always correlated with a pronoun in the comment part of the sentence, this indicates that the connection between the topic and the presumed base position is one of semantic reference rather than one of syntactic movement which in turn favours a base generation approach of topicalization.

Based on the arguments presented above, I conclude that topicalization does not involve syntactic movement and consequently does not fall under any of the verbal fronting generalizations. Therefore, examples such as (217), where a fronted verb phrase goes along with verb doubling (217-a) while verb fronting seems to trigger dummy verb insertion (217-b) do not disprove the Generalizations I and II.

(217) a. [**Rubuutaa** wa sarkii waasiiƙaa] ai, zan **rubuutaa** goobe.
write.VN(Pr) to emir letter PRT 1S write tomorrow
'Writing the emir a letter, I'll write tomorrow.' (Tuller 1986: 424)
b. [**Gyārā**], sâ **yi** wà mōtàr̃ gòbe.
fix.VN 3PL.POT do IOM car.DD(f) tomorrow
'Fixing, they'll probably do (it) to the car tomorrow.'
(Jaggar 2001: 542)

Summary

Hausa comprises of a verb phrase fronting focus construction in which a dummy verb appears in the base position of the verb phrase. It is not possible to front a verb and strand its argument and it is equally ungrammatical to front the verb phrase and have a copy of the verb appear clause-internally. The fronted verb phrase is either a verbal noun phrase or an infinitive phrase, though with regard to the latter the sources are not in agreement. A focus marker *nee* may optionally follow the constituent in focus position. The construction shows properties of Ā-movement since it can cross finite clause boundaries, is sensitive to Wh-Islands, and triggers relative aspect marking obligatorily in the matrix clause and optionally in intermediate clauses, a phenomenon that also emerges with other construction that commonly involve Ā-movement, like wh-extraction, regular NP focalization, and relativization. While VP-adverbs may appear with the fronted verb phrase, TAM-markers are precluded. An overview is given in table 7.19. Having argued that verbal left dislocation structures expressing a topic meaning do not involve movement and thus do not fall under the generalizations, we can conclude that Hausa instantiates only one verbal fronting pattern in the sense of this book, namely pattern D of Generalization II.

Tab. 7.19: Properties of verbal fronting in Hausa

	Copy	Dummy	Unbound	Islands	GS	TAM	L-Adv	H-Adv	NEG	L/R	Top/Foc
V	–	–									
VP	–	✓	✓	✓[24]	n.d.	–	✓	n.d.	n.d.	L	Foc

7.2.3 Japanese

Japanese, a member of the Japonic family, is spoken by approximately 128 million speakers predominantly in Japan with some larger groups of speakers in the United States, Canada, China, and Korea. Its basic word order is SOV (218).

(218) Yeonghee-ga   sushi-o   tabe-ta.
       Yeonghee-NOM sushi-ACC eat-PST
       'Yeonghee ate sushi.'   (Aoyagi 2006: 1)

The language shows verb phrase fronting with a form of the dummy verb *suru* 'do' appearing in sentence-final position (219-a). The fronted constituent receives a focus interpretation. Substituting a verb copy for the dummy verb results in ungrammaticality (219-b) as does verb fronting (219-c).

(219) a. [Sushi-o   **tabe**-sae] John-ga   **si**-ta.
          sushi-ACC eat-even   John-NOM do-PST
          'Even eat sushi, John did.'
                                (Nishiyama & Cho 1998: 467, citing Hoji et al. 1989)
      b. *[Computer-o   **kai**-wa/sae]   John-ga   **kat**-ta.
          computer-ACC   buy-CON/even   John-NOM buy-PST-but
          Intended: '(Even) buy a computer, John bought.'
                                                (Nishiyama & Cho 1998: 467)
      c. ***Tabe**-sae John-ga   sushi-o   **si**-ta.
          eat-even   John-NOM sushi-ACC do-PST
          Intended: 'Even eat, John did sushi.'
                                (Nishiyama & Cho 1998: 467, citing Whitman 1987)

Although (219-a) is the more obvious example of verb phrase fronting, there is another variant of it which also shows the dummy verb but has the word order SOV-dummy (220). In fact, this SOV-dummy order is the unmarked order.

---

24 The data only show Wh-islands.

(220) [John-ga computer-o **kai**-wa] **si**-ta.
John-NOM computer-ACC buy-CON do-TNS
'Indeed, John bought a computer, (but...)'

(Nishiyama & Cho 1998: 464)

Nishiyama & Cho (1998) argue that this construction involves verb phrase fronting as well. In contrast to the obvious examples in (219), however, it is the *v*P including the subject that moves in (220). This entails that the subject may optionally stay in the Spec*v*P position where it is first merged and does not move to SpecTP. Depending on whether the subject moves to SpecTP or not, verb phrase fronting either results in the marked OVS-dummy order or in the SOV-dummy order.

There is yet another construction similar to (220), in which instead of a dummy verb a copy of the lexical verb appears sentence-finally (221-a). In addition to the contrastive particle *wa* one of the three particles *koto, ni, no* and a tense marking obligatorily appear on the non-final verb while the final verb copy is also marked for tense. In this construction, dummy verb insertion is ungrammatical (221-b) in the same way that verb doubling is ungrammatical if the non-final verb is only marked with the contrastive particle *wa* (221-c). The full pattern is given in (221).

(221) a. John-ga computer-o **kat**-ta-koto-wa **kat**-ta.
John-NOM computer-ACC buy-TNS-KOTO-CON buy-TNS
b. *John-ga computer-o **kat**-ta-koto-wa **si**-ta.
John-NOM computer-ACC buy-TNS-KOTO-CON do-TNS
c. *John-ga computer-o **kai**-wa **kat**-ta.
John-NOM computer-ACC buy-CON buy-TNS
d. John-ga computer-o **kai**-wa **si**-ta.
John-NOM computer-ACC buy-CON do-TNS
'Indeed, John bought a computer, (but...)'

(Nishiyama & Cho 1998: 463f.)

As Nishiyama & Cho (1998) show, the verb doubling construction involves TP rather than verb phrase fronting. First, the non-final verb bears tense-marking indicating that the T head is part of the constituent and, second, it is not possible to have verb doubling when the object and the verb precede the subject. If the SOV-constituent of example (221-a) were indeed a verb phrase, one would expect the same options as with dummy verb insertion, i.e. fronting should be possible without the subject as part of the fronted constituent (222-a). However, as (222-b) attests, this option is not available with verb doubling.

(222) a. [Computer-o **kai**-wa/sae] John-ga **si**-ta.
computer-ACC buy-CON/even John-NOM do-TNS

b. *[Computer-o **kat**-ta-koto-wa] John-ga **kat**-ta.
computer-ACC buy-TNS-KOTO-CON John-NOM buy-TNS
(Nishiyama & Cho 1998: 467)

According to Ishihara (2010: 57f.) the two constructions also differ with regard to their interpretation. The verb phrase fronting construction receives a verb or verb phrase focus reading (223-a) whereas the TP fronting construction is interpreted as a verum focus (223-b).

(223) a. Taro-wa ringo-o **muki**-wa **si**-ta (ga tabe-na-katta).
Taro-TOP apple-ACC peel-FOC do-PST but eat-NEG-PST
'Peel the apple, Taro did, (but he didn't eat it).'
b. Taro-wa ringo-o **mui**-ta ni/koto/no-wa **mui**-ta (ga tabe-na-katta).
Taro-TOP apple-ACC peel-PST ni/koto/no-TOP peel-PST but eat-NEG-PST
'As for Taro's peeling the apple, he did peel it, (but he didn't eat it).'
(Ishihara 2010: 57f.)

I will not be particularly concerned with the TP fronting construction in what follows and have nothing to say about why and how a copy of the verb arises in this construction. The interested reader is referred to Ishihara (2010).

A copy of the fronted object cannot appear alongside the dummy verb in cases of verb phrase fronting (224-a). However, there is inter-speaker variation for examples of TP fronting (224-b) where some speakers accept an object copy while others reject it.

(224) a. *Boku-ga [*gohan*-o **tabe**-wa] *gohan*-o **si**-ta.
I-NOM rice-ACC eat-CON rice-ACC do-TNS
b. Boku-ga *gohan*-o **tabe**-ta-koto-wa (%*gohan*-o) **tabe**-ta.
I-NOM rice-ACC eat-TNS-KOTO-COM rice-ACC eat-TNS
'Indeed, I ate rice, (but...)' (Nishiyama & Cho 1998: 477)

There is also a difference between TP and verb phrase fronting with regard to the placement of negation. It only appears on the dummy verb in verb phrase fronting (225) whereas it obligatorily occurs on each of the verb copies in TP fronting (226).

(225) John-ga [computer-o **kai**-wa] **si**-*nakat*-ta.
John-NOM computer-ACC buy-CON do-NEG-TNS
'Indeed, John did not buy a computer, (but...)'
(Nishiyama & Cho 1998: 469)

(226) a. Taro-wa tabako-o **suwa**-*na*-i ni/koto/no-wa
Taro-TOP cigarette-ACC smoke-NEG-NONPST ni/koto/no-CON
suwa-*na*-i (ga tabako-ga kiraide-mo na-i).
smoke-NEG-NONPST but cigarette-NOM dislike-also NEG-NONPST
'As for Taro's not smoking, he does not smoke, (but it is not that he does not like cigarettes).'
b. *Taro-wa hon-o **ka**-u ni/koto/no-wa **ka**-u
Taro-TOP book-ACC buy-NONPST ni/koto/no-CON buy-NONPST
ga **yom**-u ni/koto/no-wa **yoma**-*na*-i.
but read-NONPST ni/koto/no-TOP read-NEG-NONPST
Intended: 'As for buying books, Taro does buy books, but as for reading them, he does not read them.'
c. *Taro-wa hon-o **yoma**-*na*-i ni/koto/no-wa
Taro-TOP book-ACC read-NEG-NONPST ni/koto/no-CON
yom-u.
read-NONPST (Ishihara 2010: 46)

Turning to the evidence for Ā-movement, Nishiyama & Cho (1998) provide the following example of verb phrase fronting across a finite clause boundary (227).

(227) [Computer-o **kai**-wa/sae] boku-wa [$_{CP}$ John-ga **si**-ta-to]
computer-ACC buy-CON/even I-TOP John-NOM do-TNS-C
omou.
think
'Buy a computer, I think John did.' (Nishiyama & Cho 1998: 466)

Furthermore, verb phrase fronting is not possible from inside an island like the Relative Clause Island (228).

(228) *Relative Clause Island*
*[Computer-o **kai**-wa] boku-ga [**si**-ta hito-o] sitteiru.
computer-ACC buy-CON I-NOM do-TNS person-ACC know
'Buy a computer, I know a person who did.'
(Nishiyama & Cho 1998: 466)

We can therefore conclude that verb phrase fronting in Japanese involves Ā-movement of the verb phrase to some position above the TP.

The status of the dummy verb *suru* 'do' in the above construction is different from that which can be found in light verb constructions. Its presence is dependent on the presence of focus particles like *wa* (cf. Tateishi 1991) indicating that it is a true repair triggered by movement of the verb phrase into a focus position. In the absence of such particles, a dummy verb is not licensed (229).

(229) John-ga computer-o **kai***(-wa/mo/sae) **si**-ta.
John-NOM computer-ACC buy-CON/also/even do-TNS
'(Also/even) buy a computer, John did.'
(Nishiyama & Cho 1998: 466, fn. 3)

Summary
As we have seen in the previous section, Japanese comprises of a verb phrase fronting construction where the canonical sentence-final position of the verb is occupied by a dummy verb inflected for tense and negation. Verb fronting is not attested with this type of dummy verb. A related construction in which a copy of the lexical verb appears involves TP fronting rather than verb phrase fronting and therefore has no impact on the validity of the Generalizations I and II. The fronted verb phrase cannot contain negation or any tense marking but it may include the subject. Nishiyama & Cho (1998) argue that this suggests that what is fronted is a *v*P in whose specifier the subject is base-merged and that this subject does not necessarily have to move to SpecTP. As a consequence, at the point when the verb phrase is moved the subject is still contained in it and is therefore fronted along with the verb and the object. The dependency between the lexical verb and the dummy verb is unbounded and respects islands indicating that it involves Ā-movement. The properties of verb phrase fronting are again listed in table 7.20. In conclusion, Japanese verbal fronting exhibits pattern D of Generalization II, as it only shows verb phrase fronting and employs dummy verb insertion as a repair. The verb doubling construction mentioned above involves TP fronting and therefore does not fall under the generalizations.

Tab. 7.20: Properties of verbal fronting in Japanese

	Copy	Dummy	Unbound	Islands	GS	TAM	L-Adv	H-Adv	Neg	L/R	Top/Foc
V	–	–									
VP	–	✓	✓	✓	n.d.	–	n.d.	n.d.	–	L	Foc

7.2.4 Norwegian

Norwegian[25], a Germanic language of the Indo-European family, is spoken by approximately five million speakers predominantly in Norway. Like many of its

---

25 I am indebted and grateful to Siri M. Gjersøe for providing her judgements on the examples in this section which unless marked otherwise are due to her. All errors are my own.

Germanic relatives it is a V2 language meaning that in main clauses the verb always appears in second position (230).

(230) Han leser bøk-er hele dag-en.
he reads book.PL-PL.INDEF whole day-DEF
'He is reading books all day.'

The language comprises of a verb phrase fronting construction where a form of the dummy verb *gjøre* 'do' occupies the canonical verb position inside the clause (231-b). It is, however, not possible to front a transitive verb alone while stranding its object (231-b).

(231) a. [Å **lese** bøk-er] **gjør** han hele dag-en.
to read.INF book.PL-PL.INDEF does he whole day-DEF
'Reading books he does all day.'
b. *Å **lese** **gjør** han bøk-er hele dag-en.
to read.INF does he book.PL-PL.INDEF whole day-DEF
'Reading he does to books all day.'

This type of verbal fronting is commonly called VP-topicalization as the fronted verb phrase is interpreted as a topic.

If a modal is present in the clause, fronting of the verb phrase may optionally trigger the presence of a dummy verb (232-a). In contrast, the dummy is obligatory when verb phrase fronting strands an auxiliary (232-b).

(232) a. [Å **lese** bok-en] vil han (**gjøre**) i dag.
to read.INF book-DEF wants he do.INF in day
'Read the book, he wants to do today.'
b. [**Lest**/Å **lese** bok-en] har han *(**gjort**) på ferie.
read.PTCP/to read.INF book-DEF has he done on holidays
'Read the book, he's done on holidays.'

Fronting the verb phrase including the modal/auxiliary to force the presence of *gjøre* is ungrammatical (233).

(233) a. *[(Å) **ville** **lese** bok-en] **gjør** han i dag.
to want.INF read.INF book-DEF does he in day
Intended: 'Wanting to read the book, he does today.'
b. *[(Å) **ha** **lest** bok-en] **gjør** han på ferie.
to have.INF read.PTCP book-DEF does he on holidays
Intended: 'Having read the book, he does on holidays.'

Turning to the diagnostics for Ā-movement, we find that verb phrase fronting can cross finite clause boundaries (234).

(234) a. [(Å) **vaske** bil-en] vet jeg ikke [om hun vil [at
to wash.INF car-DEF know I not whether she wants that
han **gjør** i dag]].
he does in day
'Wash the car I don't know whether she wants that he does today.'
b. [(Å) **vaske** bil-en] tror jeg ikke [at hun vil [at han
to wash.INF car-DEF believe I not that she wants that he
gjør i dag]].
does in day
'Wash the car I don't believe that she wants that he does today.'

In addition, the dependency respects island conditions such as the Complex NP Island (236), the Subject Island (236), the Adjunct Island (237), the Relative Clause Island (238), and the Coordinate Structure Constraint (239).

(235) *Complex NP Island*
*[(Å) **vaske** bil-en] hørte jeg [rykte om at han **gjør** i dag].
to wash.INF car-DEF heard I rumour about that he does in day
'Wash the car did I hear a rumour that he does today.'

(236) *Subject Island*
??[(Å) **vaske** bil-en] er ergerlig [at han **gjør** akkurat i dag].
to wash.INF car-DEF is annoying that he does exactly in day
'Wash the car it is annoying that he does today of all days.'

(237) *Adjunct Island*
*[(Å) **vaske** bil-en] kan Helge ikke komme [fordi han **gjør**].
to wash.INF car-DEF can Helge not come.INF because he does
'Wash the car Helge cannot come because he does.'

(238) *Relative Clause Island*
*[(Å) **vaske** bil-en] møtte jeg mannen [som **gjorde** i dag].
to wash.INF car-DEF met I man.DEF REL.PRON does in day
'Wash the car I met the man who does (wash the car) today.'

(239) *Coordinate Structure Constraint*
*[(Å) **vaske** bil-en] [**gjør** han og rydder opp hus-et] i dag.
to wash.INF car-DEF does he and tidies up house-DEF in day
'Wash the car he does and tidy up the house today.'

Verbal fronting out of a Wh-Island, in contrast, is grammatical (240), or at least not as degraded as in the examples above.

(240) *Wh-Island*
[(Å) **vaske** bil-en] spurte jeg henne [hvorfor han **gjør** akkurat nå].
to wash.INF car-DEF asked I her why he does exactly now
'Wash the car I asked her why he does right now.'

In this respect, verbal fronting patterns with wh-extraction, which as reported in Maling & Zaenen (1982), Kush & Lohndal (2017), Kush et al. (2018) does not give rise to ungrammaticality when taking place from a Wh-Island (241).[26]

(241) Hvilke bøker spurte Jon [hvem som hadde skrevet]?
which books asked Jon who C had written
'What books did Jon ask who had written?'
(Kush et al. 2018: 3, adapted from Maling & Zaenen 1982: 231)

We also find reconstruction effects, which are typical for $\bar{\text{A}}$-movement, for both Principle C and Principle A in verb phrase fronting. In example (242), the fronted verb phrase contains the proper name *Helge* which is coindexed with a personal pronoun *han* 'he' inside the clause. However, the sentence is ungrammatical despite the fact that on the surface the proper name is not bound by the coindexed pronoun. This ungrammaticality easily falls out if the verb phrase reconstructs into its base position within the c-command domain of the pronoun thereby triggering a violation of Principle C.

(242) *[(Å) **se** på et bilde av *Helge$_i$*] **gjør** *han$_i$* nesten aldri.
to look.INF at a photo of Helge does he almost never
'Look at a photo of Helge$_i$, he$_i$ almost never does.'

If the preposed verb phrase contains the anaphor *seg selv* 'his-/herself' coindexed with a binding element *han* 'he' inside the clause as in (243), however, the sentence is grammatical. On the surface, the anaphor appears to be unbound as it is not c-commanded by the coindexed pronoun but if the verb phrase reconstructs into its base position c-command between the pronoun and the anaphor holds.

---

26 Maling & Zaenen (1982) claim that wh-extraction is licit from Complex NP Islands and Relative Clause Islands in addition to Wh-Islands. However, Kush & Lohndal (2017) and Kush et al. (2018) experimentally verified that wh-extraction from CNP-Islands and RC-Islands is just as unacceptable as from Subject or Adjunct Islands, whereas a majority of speakers judged it to be fine from Wh-Islands.

(243) [(Å) **hate** seg selv_i] **gjør** han_i bare når han er full.
to hate.INF REFL self does he only when he is full
'Hate himself_i, he_i only does when he's drunk.'

We may thus conclude, that verb phrase fronting involves proper Ā-movement, not base generation, as it shows typical Ā-properties like island sensitivity and reconstruction effects.

With regard to the size/category of the fronted constituent it is worth noting that neither negation (244-a) nor sentential adverbs (244-b) may be part of it. Equally, the occurence of auxiliaries (244-c) or modals (244-d) is ungrammatical.

(244) a. [(*Ikke) **lese** (*ikke) boken (*ikke)] **gjør** han bare i dag.
           NEG read.INF NEG book.DEF NEG does he only in day
           'As for reading the book, he only does it today.'
       b. *[(Å) **lese** sannsynligvis boken] **gjør** han bare i dag.
           to read.INF probably book.DEF does he only in day
           Intended: 'As for probably reading the book, he only does it today.'
       c. *[(Å) **ha** lest boken] **gjør/gjorde** han på ferie.
           to have.INF read.PTCP book.DEF does/did he on holidays
           Intended: 'As for having read the book, he does/did it on holidays.'
       d. *[(Å) **vil(le)** lese boken] **gjør** han bare i dag.
           to want.INF read.INF book.DEF does he only in day
           Intended: 'As for wanting to read the book, he only does it today.'

Since negation, sentential adverbs and auxiliaries as well as modals are all located higher in the clause structure than *v*P, the data in (244) indicate that what is fronted is maximally as big as *v*P but not bigger. Evidence that it is in fact even smaller, namely a VP, comes from different readings with the adverb *igjen* 'again'. As is the case with the German cognate *wieder* 'again' (von Stechow 1996, Rapp & von Stechow 1999), Dobler (2008) argues that *igjen* receives a different interpretation depending on whether it is adjoined to *v*P or VP. In the former case, the reading is a repetitive one while in the latter case it is restitutive. A neutral declarative sentence is therefore ambiguous between the two readings (245).

(245) Terje åpnet døra igjen.
       Terje opened door.DEF again
       'Terje opened the door again.'
       Repetitive: Terje has opened it before.
       Restitutive: The door has been open before and was closed in the meantime.

Under verb phrase fronting, the ambiguity disappears. Depending on whether *igjen* is part of the fronted constituent (246-a) or stranded inside the clause (246-b) either only the restitutive or only the repetitive reading is available.

(246) a. [(Å) **åpne** døra igjen] **gjorde** faktisk Terje.
to open.INF door.DEF again did actually Terje
'As for opening the door again, Terje did in fact do it.'
*Repetitive: Terje has opened it before.
Restitutive: The door has been open before and was closed in the meantime.
b. [(Å) **åpne** døra] **gjorde** Terje igjen.
to open.INF door.DEF did Terje again
'As for opening the door, Terje did it again.'
Repetitive: Terje has opened it before.
*Restitutive: The door has been open before and was closed in the meantime.

Since the restitutive reading is associated with VP-adjunction of the adverb and this reading is only available if the adverb is part of the fronted constituent, we can conclude that the fronted constituent is in fact a VP.

There is, however, one issue with this analysis. According to Lødrup (1990), just as in Danish (see section 7.2.1) and Swedish (see section 7.2.6) it is optionally possible for the fronted verb to bear tense and agreement marking (247).[27]

(247) [**Spille/Spiller** golf] **gjør** jeg aldri.
play.INF/play.PRS golf do.PRS I never
'Play golf, I never do.' (Lødrup 1990: 3)

For an explanation of the possibility to have an inflected verb in the fronted verb phrase, see section 1.3.

Concerning the dummy verb's status as a repair, I would like to point out that no independent construction similar to the German *tun*-periphrase (see section 8.1.4) exists from which verb phrase fronting could be derived by simple VP preposing (248).

(248) *Jeg **gjør** aldri **spille** golf.
I do never play golf
Intended: 'I never play golf.' (Lødrup 1990: 9)

---

[27] In fact, my informant said she would never use an inflected form of a fronted verb, but accepts them from other speakers.

The dummy verb can also not be a verbal proform in a left dislocation structure. First, as a V2 language, the position before the verb in a matrix clause has to be occupied by exactly one constituent. If the topicalized verb phrase were left-dislocated, it should not be part of the following sentence (Zaenen 1997, Ott 2014) and thus not serve as the single preverbal constituent. In turn, a verb phrase fronting construction as (249-a) should be ungrammatical just like any other declarative matrix clause without a preverbal constituent (249-b), contrary to fact.

(249) a. [(Å) **lese** boken] [$_{CP}$ **gjør** han i dag].
to read.INF book.DEF does he in day
'As for reading the book, he does it today.'
b. *Leser han boken i dag.
reads he book.DEF in day
Intended: 'He reads the book today.'

Equally, one would expect that it is possible to have some constituent occupy the position between the left-dislocated verb phrase and the finite verb, contrary to fact (250).

(250) *[(Å) **lese** boken] [$_{CP}$ i dag **gjør** han].
to read.INF book.DEF in day does he

Second, the VP-proform in Norwegian is usually not just the verb *gjøre* but a combination of this verb with the neuter singular pronoun *det* (251) (see Bentzen et al. 2013, and references therein).

(251) Liker du jordbær? Ja, jeg gjør det.
likes you strawberries yes I do it
'Do you like strawberries? Yes, I do.' (Lødrup 1990: 4)

In fact, in a proper VP left dislocation structure, the pronoun *det* has to show up in between the dislocated VP and the dummy verb (252).

(252) [(Å) **lese** boken] det **gjør** han i dag.
to read.INF book.DEF it does he in day
'Read the book, that's what he does today.'

I thus conclude that verb phrase fronting in Norwegian is not left dislocation with a verbal proform.

Summary

To summarize, Norwegian disposes of a verb phrase fronting construction in which a dummy verb is inserted in the base position of the verb. The fronted verb phrase is interpreted as a topic. When the verb phrase originates from under a modal dummy verb insertion is optional whereas it is obligatory under an auxiliary. The construction shows movement properties: it is unbounded, sensitive to islands, and shows reconstruction for Principle A and Principle C. What is fronted is not *v*P but the smaller VP with the consequence that high (sentential) adverbs, negation or auxiliaries, may not occur with the fronted verb phrase. However, the displaced verb may appear in a finite form instead of in the infinitive. The properties are given in table 7.21. As it stands, Norwegian thus shows pattern D of Generalization II.

Tab. 7.21: Properties of verbal fronting in Norwegian

	Copy	Dummy	Unbound	Islands	GS	TAM	L-Adv	H-Adv	Neg	L/R	Top/Foc
V	–	–									
VP	–	✓	✓	✓	n.d.	(✓)[28]	n.d.	–	–	L	Top

7.2.5 Skou

Skou is a member of the small Skou family and is spoken in three villages (Skou Yambe, Skou Mabo, and Skou Sai) located centrally on the north coast of New Guinea (Donohue 2004: 1). Its basic word order is SOV (Donohue 2004: 105).

There is a verb phrase fronting construction in the language, where the verb phrase is displaced to sentence-initial position while the dummy verb *li* 'do' appears in the canonical verb position (253-b). The fronted constituent is interpreted as a topic. A neutral baseline sentence is given in (253-a).

(253) a. Bàng moerító ke=k-ang.
 yesterday fish(sp.) 3SG.NF=3SG.NF-eat
 'He ate some Yellowtail scad yesterday.'
 b. [Moerító ke=k-**ang**=inga], bàng ke=**li**.
 fish(sp.) 3SG.NF=3SG.NF-eat=the yesterday 3SG.NF=do
 'Eating Yellowtail scad, he did (it) yesterday.' (Donohue 2004: 126f.)

---

[28] The verb in the fronted phrase is optionally finite, i.e. shows tense morphology.

As shown in (254), the dummy verb's presence in this topic construction is obligatory. Its omission results in ungrammaticality.

(254) a. *[Moerító ke=k-ang=inga], bàng.
 fish(sp.) 3SG.NF=3SG.NF-eat=the yesterday
 b. *[Moerító ke=k-ang=inga], bàng ke=baléng.
 fish(sp.) 3SG.NF=3SG.NF-eat=the yesterday 3SG.NF=man
 (Donohue 2004: 127)

The fronted constituent is always marked by the clitic =*inga* 'the' which can be split into the two constituent parts *ing*, signalling very general deictic reference, and *a*, which marks discourse givenness. Donohue (2004: 132f.) remarks that, taken together, the two fulfill a similar function like a definiteness marker in English.

Donohue (2004: 127) states that fronting of the verb alone while stranding its object is ungrammatical. He provides the example in (255) as evidence. However, in this example there is no verb in the base position, neither the dummy verb *li* nor a copy of the displaced verb. As shown in (254), it is ungrammatical to have a verbal gap in the clause. Therefore, (255) does not unambiguously demonstrate the impossibility of verb fronting, because its ungrammaticality might be caused by the verbal gap rather than by the stranded object.

(255) *[Ke=k-ang=inga], bàng ke=baléng moerító.
 3SG.NF=3SG.NF-eat=the yesterday 3SG.NF=man fish(sp.)
 (Donohue 2004: 127)

However, there are data that show that what is fronted in this topicalization structure has to be a complete verb phrase. Based on the behaviour of goals and locatives with respect to auxiliary placement, Donohue (2004) argues that the former, but not the latter, are contained within the verb phrase. Consequently, if topicalization only allows full verb phrases to be fronted, the expectation would be that goals obligatorily accompany the fronted constituent because they are part of it, whereas locatives cannot do so as they are located outside the verb phrase. This expectation is indeed confirmed by the data. Consider example (256-a), where the VP includes a goal *bàng* 'the beach' (italicized). In (256-b), this goal is fronted together with the verb and the example is grammatical. In (256-c), however, stranding the goal renders the example ungrammatical.

(256) a. Fetànghapa te=angku nawò te=y-atà
 morning 3PL=child many 3PL=3PL-walk.running
 t-o te *bàng*.
 3PL-seaward 3PL.go beach
 'This morning a lot of children ran to the beach.'

b. [Te=y-**atà** t-o te *bàng*=inga],
   3PL=3PL-walk.running 3PL-seaward 3PL.go beach=the
   fetànghapa te=angku nawò te=**ti**.
   morning 3PL=child many 3PL=do
   'Running to the beach, a lot of children did this morning.'

c. *[Te=y-**atà** t-o te=inga], fetànghapa
   3PL=3PL-walk.running 3PL-seaward 3PL.go=the morning
   te=angku nawò te=**ti** *bàng*.
   3PL=child many 3PL=do beach   (Donohue 2004: 127)

In contrast, the locative expression *pá* 'house' is used in (257-a) (italicized). Again, this expression is fronted with the verb in (257-b) which, unlike what is the case with goals, results in ungrammaticality. When the locative is stranded as in (257-c), however, the sentence becomes grammatical.[29]

(257) a. È-ke-ké=ke hòe pe=tue
       wife-3SG.NF.DAT-3SG.NF.GEN=3SG.NF.DAT sago 3SG.F=3SG.F.do
       pá.
       house
       'His wife is making sago jelly at home.'

   b. *[Hòe pe=**tue** *pá*=inga],
       sago 3SG.F=3SG.F.do home=the
       è-ke-ké=ke pe=**tue**.
       wife-3SG.NF.DAT-3SG.NF.GEN=3SG.NF.DAT 3SG.F=3SG.F.do

   c. [Hòe pe=**tue**=inga],
       sago 3SG.F=3SG.F.do=the
       è-ke-ké=ke pe=**tue** *pá*.
       wife-3SG.NF.DAT-3SG.NF.GEN=3SG.NF.DAT 3SG.F=3SG.F.do home
       'Making sago jelly, his wife is doing (it) at home.'
       (Donohue 2004: 127)

This data show that the fronted constituent has to be a full verb phrase and thus support Donohue's (2004) claim that object-stranding verb fronting is not possible.

Concerning the dummy verb's status in the topic construction one might wonder whether it is just an auxiliary stranded by verb phrase displacement rather than a repair element that is inserted to avoid a gap. If this were true, we would expect there to be a construction in which the verb phrase is placed *in situ* followed by a form of *li*. The topicalization would then be derived from this construction

---

29 Examples (257-b) and (257-c) only superficially look like they involve verb doubling because the main verb *tue* 'do' used here is by chance the same verb that serves as the dummy verb in Skou.

by leftwards displacement of the verb phrase. Indeed, example (258) shows a potential candidate for such a construction.

(258) a. Nì ró à nì=**hù**-hù **li**.
    1SG clothes thread 1SG=sew-RED do
    'I want to sew (some) clothes.' (Donohue 2004: 269)

However, (258) may not serve as a base construction for topicalization for one simple reason, besides the fact that it always expresses a desiderative meaning which is not found in the purported corresponding topic structure: The main verb in (258) is reduplicated while this is not the case for the main verb in topicalization. In fact, this auxiliary construction obligatorily exhibits reduplication which, in positive sentences, might also occur on the auxiliary instead of the main verb (259-b)

(259) a. Pa ke=k-**ung**-kung **li**.
    water 3SG.NF=3SG.NF-drink-RED do
    'He wants to drink some water.'
  b. Pa ke=k-**ung** **li**-li.
    water 3SG.NF=3SG.NF-drink do-RED
    'He wants to drink some water.' (Donohue 2004: 265)

Hence, the dummy verb in topicalization cannot plausibly be a stranded auxiliary but must be regarded as a repair element which is inserted into the structure to avoid a verbal gap.

Unfortunately, Donohue (2004) does not discuss the properties of verbal fronting with regard to islands and other $\bar{\text{A}}$-diagnostics. However, it should be mentioned that an intonational break occurs between the constituent in topic position and the rest of the clause, indicated by a comma in the examples. In the discussion of Hausa 7.2.2, an intonational break was interpreted as favouring a base generation over a movement approach to topicalization. However, in Hausa it was just one of several clues against movement while hitherto it is the only one in Skou. As the question whether topics are base generated or moved is not as relevant in Skou as it was in Hausa, because Skou topicalization is not in conflict with any of the generalizations presented in this thesis, I will leave this issue for future research here.

Summary

In conclusion, Skou shows verb phrase fronting with a dummy verb occupying the canonical verb position. Verb fronting which strands the object (or other material contained in the VP like goals) is ungrammatical. Fronting marks the verb phrase as discourse-old information, i.e. a topic, which is emphasised by the appearance of the 'definite' clitic *inga*. The relevant properties are summed up in table 7.22. Whether Skou topicalization involves movement or not is not crucial here. If it does, then Skou verbal fronting instantiates pattern D of Generalization II. If it does not, then it does not bear on any of the generalizations established in this monograph.

Tab. 7.22: Properties of verbal fronting in Skou

	Copy	Dummy	Unbound	Islands	GS	TAM	L-Adv	H-Adv	Neg	L/R	Top/Foc
V	–	–									
VP	–	✓	n.d.	n.d.	n.d.	n.d.	n.d.	n.d.	n.d.	L	Top

7.2.6 Swedish

Swedish is a Germanic language of the Indo-European phylum. It is the official language of Sweden spoken by approximately nine million people as a first language. It is a V2 language, that is, the verb always occurs in the second position in neutral main clauses.

Swedish shows a verb phrase fronting construction in which the canonical verb position is occupied by a form of the dummy verb *göra* 'do' (260-b) (with (260-a) as a baseline example instantiating the neutral word order). The fronted constituent is interpreted as a topic. A comparable example with a transitive verb in sentence-initial position and overt stranded objects is judged ungrammatical indicating that verb fronting is unavailable (260-c).

(260) a. Han läser boken nu.
he reads book.DEF now
'He is reading the book now.'

b. [**Läser** boken] **gör** han nu.
reads book.DEF does he now
'Reading the book he is now.' (Källgren & Prince 1989: 47)

c. *****Säljer gör** han den inte, men han kanske lånar ut den ibland.
sell.PRS does he it no but he perhaps lend out it sometimes (Holmberg 1999: 12)

There is disagreement on whether the verb in the fronted verb phrase has to be finite as in (260-b) or whether it can also optionally be an infinitive with the finite version being more natural. The former view is taken by Platzack (2012) while the latter is held by Lødrup (1990) and Teleman et al. (1999). An explanation for how the fronted verb can show finiteness is provided in section 1.3.

Verb fronting shows Ā-movement properties. It may cross finite clause boundaries (261) and is impossible out of islands such as the Complex NP Island (262), or a free relative clause island (263)

(261) [**Läste** boken] sa John [att han **gjorde**].
 read book.DEF said John that he did
 'Read the book, John said that he did.' (Platzack 2012: 280)

(262) *Complex NP island*
 *[**läste** boken] tillbakavisade John [påståendet att hand
 read.PST book.DEF rejected John claim.DEF that he
 gjorde].
 did
 Intended: 'Read the book, John rejected the claim that he did.'
 (Platzack 2012: 280)

(263) *Free Relative Clause Island*
 *[**läser** boken] är det lugnt [där han **gör**].
 reads book.DEF is it quiet where he does
 Intended: 'Read the book, it is quiet where he does.'
 (Källgren & Prince 1989: 51)

It also behaves parallel to nominal Ā-topicalization (in Swedish and several other Germanic languages) in that it is impossible in embedded clauses.

(264) *Det är bra att [**läser** boken] **gör** han.
 it is good that reads book.DEF does he
 (Källgren & Prince 1989: 51f.)

It seems clear from the above that verb phrase fronting in Swedish is Ā-movement.

Turning to the size of the fronted constituent we find that neither negation (265-a) nor sentential adverbs (265-b) may occur in it. This also holds for auxiliaries like *hade* 'had' (265-c).

(265) a. [(*Inte) **läste** (*inte) boken (*inte)] **gjorde** han.
 NEG read.PST NEG book.DEF NEG did he
 b. *[**Läste** troligen boken] **gjorde** han.
 read.PST probably book.DEF did he
 c. *[**Hade läst** boken] **hade/gjorde** han.
 had read.PST.PTCP book.DEF had/did he
 (Platzack 2012: 290)

All of the abovementioned elements are usually taken to be generated above *v*P indicating that what is fronted is not bigger than a *v*P. This is further corroborated by the fact that adverbs like *trots hennes protester* 'despite her protests' in (266) and *ofta* 'often' in (267) which according to Teleman et al. (1999: III:410) c-command *v*P may not be fronted together with the verb and its object(s). Adverbs that are adjoined to VP on the other hand, like *i kyrkan* 'in the church', can occur in this position (267-d).

(266) a. Han la henne i sängen *trots hennes protester*.
       he put.PST her in bed.DEF in.spite.of her protests
       'He put her to bed despite all her protests.'
   b. [**La** henne i sängen] **gjorde** han *trots hennes*
      put.PST her in bed.DEF did he in.spite.of her
      protester.
      protests
      'Put her to bed he did, despite all her protests.'
   c. ??[**La** henne i sängen *trots hennes protester*] **gjorde**
      put.PST her in bed.DEF in.spite.of her protests did
      han.
      he
      Intended: 'Put her to bed despite all her protests, he did.'

(Platzack 2012: 291f.)

(267) a. Vi sjunger *ofta* i kyrkan.
       we sing.PST often in church.DEF
       'We often sing in church.'
   b. [**Sjunger**] **gör** vi *ofta* i kyrkan.
      sing.PST do we often in church.DEF
      'Sing we often do in church.'
   c. *[**Sjunger** *ofta*] **gör** vi i kyrkan.
      sing.PST often do we in church.DEF
      Intended: 'Often sing, we do in church.'
   d. [**Sjunger** i kyrkan] **gör** vi *ofta*.
      sing.PST in church.DEF do we often
      'Sing in church, we often do.'   (Platzack 2012: 292)

The fronted constituent thus cannot be bigger than *v*P. Evidence that it is in fact even smaller, i.e. VP instead of *v*P, is provided by the variably placeable adverb *igen* 'again'. This adverb has two different readings depending on whether it is adjoined to *v*P or to VP. In the former case *igen* receives a repetitive interpretation while in the latter case it has a restitutive reading (von Stechow 1996, Rapp & von

Stechow 1999, Dobler 2008). A neutral sentence is therefore ambiguous between the two readings (268).

(268) John öppnade dören *igen*.
John opened door.DEF again
'John opened the door again.'
Repetitive: John has opened it before.
Restitutive: The door has been open before. (Platzack 2012: 292)

If *igen* occurs in the topic part of a verb phrase fronting construction, however, only the restitutive reading is available (269).

(269) [**Öppnade** dören *igen*] **gjorde** John.
opened door.DEF again did John
'Open the door again, John did.'
*Repetitive: John has opened it before.
Restitutive: The door has been open before. (Platzack 2012: 293)

If the topic constituent in (269) were a *v*P we would expect the sentence to show the same ambiguity as the neutral sentence in (268) since *igen* could be adjoined to either *v*P or VP. As this is not the case and the reading associated with *v*P-adjunction is not whereas the VP-adjunction reading is available, the fronted constituent must be a VP rather than a *v*P.

When verb phrase fronting strands an inflected verbal element, such as a modal or an auxiliary (270), dummy verb insertion does not take place.

(270) Kysst henne har jag inte __ (bara hållit henne i handen).
kissed her have I not only held her in hand.DEF
'Kissed her I haven't (only held her by the hand).'
(Holmberg 1999: 7)

This indicates that the dummy verb's purpose in verb phrase fronting is to express finiteness of the clause. Whenever there is another verbal element that can fulfill this task, insertion of *göra* is not necessary. Interestingly, there exists a version of the sentence in (270) where a transitive verb is fronted stranding its direct object although verb fronting is supposedly impossible in Swedish (271).

(271) Kysst$_1$ har jag henne inte ___$_1$ (bara hållit henne i handen).
kissed have I her not only held her in hand.DEF
'Kissed have I her not (only held her by the hand).'
(Holmberg 1999: 7)

As pointed out in section 1.3 already, it seems to be the case that the exceptional fronting of a transitive verb in (271) is tied to its participial form. Comparable structures where an infinitive-embedding verb is stranded, like the modal *ska* 'shall' in (272), do not allow verb fronting.

(272) *?Träffa₁ ska jag henne inte ___₁, men vi ska hålla kontakt per
meet.INF shall I her not but we shall keep contact by
e-mail.
e-mail (Holmberg 1999: 12)

As (271) does not show an overt repair, I will leave it aside here and with it the issue of whether it might constitute an exceptional case of verb fronting or rather be regular verb phrase fronting of a participle phrase.

Verb phrase fronting vs. left dislocation

There is another construction in Swedish, left dislocation, in which a verb phrase seems to have undergone fronting while a dummy verb is inserted into the canonical verb position. It differs from the verb phrase fronting above in that it conatins an additional pronoun *det* 'that' that acts as an internal argument of the dummy verb *göra* 'do' and refers to the topicalized constituent (273).

(273) [**Läser** boken], det **gör** han.
reads book.DEF it does he
'Read the book, that he does.' (Källgren & Prince 1989: 48)

As this construction also involves dummy verb insertion it might not serve as a potential counter-example to Generalizations I or II, in contrast to left dislocation in Hausa (cf. section 7.2.2). However, it is worth comparing it with verb phrase fronting to show that it is structurally distinct and to indicate that it does not make use of the same mechanisms that underly verb phrase fronting, i.e. Ā-movement.

First, according to Källgren & Prince (1989), certain stative verbs, like *kan* 'know', cannot undergo verb phrase fronting (274-a) while they are licit in left dislocation structures (274-b).

(274) a. *[**Kan** svenksa] **gör** Kari.
knows Swedish does Kari
b. [**Kan** svenska], det **gör** Kari.
knows Swedish it does Kari
'Know Swedish, Kari does that.' (Källgren & Prince 1989: 49)

Whether there is a similar restriction for stative verbs in Swedish as there is for individual-level predicates in Fongbe (see section 7.1.5) or Haitian Creole (see section 7.1.7) I cannot determine due to paucity of data in the available literature. If this is indeed the case, one might suspect that the underlying reason for this is similar across these languages. However, at this point, I leave this question for future research.

Second, as a V2 language, Swedish only allows one constituent to precede the finite verb of a clause, e.g. in a nominal topicalization construction (275-a). Whenever more than one constituent appear in pre-verbal position, the sentence is ungrammatical (275-b, c).

(275)   a.   Boken   läser han nu.
              book.DEF reads he   now
              'The book he is reading now.'
      b.   *Boken nu läser han.
      c.   *Nu boken läser han.   (Källgren & Prince 1989: 50)

This constraint does not apply to left-dislocation structures where two distinct constituents easily cooccur pre-verbally (276-a–c). In fact, it is ungrammatical if only a single constituent precedes the finite verb (276-d).

(276)   a.   Boken,   han läser den nu.
              book.DEF he reads it   now
              'The book, he's reading it now.'
      b.   Boken, den läser han nu.
      c.   Boken, nu läser han den.
      d.   *Boken, läser han den nu.   (Källgren & Prince 1989: 50)

This suggests that the left-dislocated element is located in a position external to the following clause while the constituent immediately preceding the finite verb occupies the single structural position in the clausal left-periphery (i.e. SpecCP). The ungrammaticality of (276-d) then follows because the element *boken* 'the book' is located outside the clause and no element occupies the clause-initial position before the finite verb in violation of the otherwise quite robust V2 constraint.

In a verb phrase fronting structure, it is ungrammatical when a second constituent besides the verb phrase precedes the finite dummy verb (277).

(277)   a.   *[**Läser** boken],   han **gör** nu.
              reads book.DEF he does now
      b.   *[**Läser** boken],   nu **gör** han.
              reads book.DEF now does he   (Källgren & Prince 1989: 50)

This shows that verb phrase fronting and left dislocation are superficially similar constructions which have a quite distinct underlying syntactic structure.

Summary

To summarize, Swedish disposes of a verb phrase fronting construction in which a dummy verb is inserted in the base position of the verb. The fronted verb phrase is interpreted as a topic. The construction shows movement properties; it is unbounded, sensitive to islands, and like nominal topicalization it is impossible in embedded clauses. What is fronted is not vP but the smaller VP with the consequence that only low adverbs but not high (sentential) adverbs, negation or auxiliaries, may occur with the fronted verb phrase. The displaced verb is preferred to be finite while (at least according to some sources) it may optionally also be an infinitive. The properties are displayed in table 7.23. As it stands, Swedish provides a further example of pattern D of Generalization II as it shows verb phrase fronting only with dummy verb insertion.

Tab. 7.23: Properties of verbal fronting in Swedish

	Copy	Dummy	Unbound	Islands	GS	TAM	L-Adv	H-Adv	Neg	L/R	Top/Foc
V	–	–									
VP	–	✓	✓	✓[30]	n.d.	(✓)[31]	✓	–	–	L	Top

7.2.7 Welsh

Welsh, a Celtic language of the Indo-European phylum, is spoken by approximately 500 000 speakers predominantly in Wales and other parts of the United Kingdom and Ireland. As is common for Celtic languages its basic (neutral) word order is VSO.

Despite its verb-initial clause structure, Welsh shows a verb phrase fronting construction in which the position following the fronted constituent is occupied by a dummy verb *gwneud* 'do' (278). The fronted constituent usually receives a contrastive focus interpretation (Tallerman 1996: 98).

---

[30] Examples show only the Complex NP Island and the Relative Clause Island.
[31] The verb in the fronted phrase is preferably finite, i.e. shows tense morphology. However, if the tense is marked with an analytical form, the auxiliary is not licit in the clause-initial position.

(278) [**Pori'r** comin a'r cloddiau] a **wnaeth** Ifas am y
browse.the common and.the hedges PRT did.3SG Ifas for the
lleill.
others
'Ifas BROWSED THE COMMON AND THE HEDGES for the others.'
(Tallerman 1996: 100)

A parallel verb fronting construction is not reported in the literature, neither with verb doubling nor with dummy verb insertion.

The abovementioned verb phrase fronting is called 'mixed' construction in much of the literature on Welsh. In addition, there exists a quite similar construction named the 'abnormal' construction which shows fronting of a phrasal constituent. As I was not able to find an example of an 'abnormal' verb phrase fronting construction, an NP example is given instead in (279).

(279) Myfi a gefais anrheg.
me PRT got.1SG gift
'I got a gift' (Tallerman 1996: 98)

Though superficially similar, the two constructions show a range of distinct properties. While the 'mixed' construction has a contrastive focus reading, allows only one constituent in the pre-verbal slot, and is productive in Modern Welsh, the 'abnormal' construction is more naturally interpreted as a topic-comment structure, has been found with up to five constituents in pre-verbal position, and was only productive in Middle Welsh, to mention only a few differences (for details see Fife & King 1991, Tallerman 1996). Tallerman (1996) argues that 'abnormal' sentences involve adjunction to CP, whereas the fronted constituent in 'mixed' sentences is located in the specifier of CP. I will therefore only discuss the 'mixed' type in what follows.

As is the case with verb phrase fronting constructions in Swedish (see section 7.2.6) and Danish (see section 7.2.1), dummy verb insertion is absent if an auxiliary like *mae* 'be' is stranded by the fronted verb phrase (280-b).

(280) a. Y mae'r dyn wedi gweld y ci.
PRT be.3SG.PRS.the man PERF.PRT see the dog
'The man has seen the dog.'
b. [Wedi gweld y ci]$_1$ y mae'r dyn ___$_1$.
PERF.PRT see the dog PRT is.3SG.PRS.the man
'It's having seen the dog that the man is.' (Sproat 1985: 178)

Verb phrase fronting may not only occur in root clauses but also in embedded clauses (281).

(281) Dywedodd mai [[**gadael** y ddinas] a **wnaeth** y rhai eraill].
said.3SG PRT leave the city PRT did.3SG the ones other
'He said that it was leave the city that those others did.'

(Tallerman 1996: 101)

Furthermore, it may take place across an infinitive embedding verb (282).

(282) [**Canu** 'r anthem] y mae Gwyn yn ceisio ei
sing.INF the anthem PRT be.PRS.3SG Gwyn PROG try.INF 3MS
wneud.
do.INF
'Singing the anthem is what Gwyn is trying to do.'

(Borsley et al. 2007: 42)

Unfortunately, I could not find any data concerning the behaviour of verb phrase fronting with regard to islands, finite clause boundaries, or other $\bar{\text{A}}$-diagnostics. It is therefore not possible to determine whether it involves $\bar{\text{A}}$-movement or not.

Turning to the status of *gwneud* 'do' as a repair, it seems to be a consensus in the literature that verb phrase fronting can and should be derived from the periphrastic verb construction. In Welsh, a sentence may either contain a synthetic main verb (283-a) or a periphrastic verb form (283-b).

(283) a. **Gwelodd** Siôn ddraig.
see.3SG.PST John dragon
'John saw a dragon.'
b. **Gwnaeth** Siôn **weld** draig.
do.3SG.PST John see dragon
'John saw a dragon.' (Sproat 1985: 176)

According to Sproat (1985) and Borsley et al. (2007) there is no difference in meaning between both options and they are both equally likely to occur, at least in colloquial use. Rouveret (2012: 917), however, argues that there is a difference in that "with lexically telic verbs [...] the *gwneud*-construction puts the emphasis on the acting on the part of the subject, whereas the simple verb construction denotes a simple event. With other predicate classes, it seems that the periphrastic construction carries an aspectual interpretation which can be characterized in terms of a shift in the nature of the event denoted by the predicate. For example, for stems denoting an activity consisting of repeated smaller events, the presence of *gwneud* induces a semelfactive interpretation."

An argument in support of *gwneud*-support being derived from the periphrastic construction comes from the a restriction that applies to both structures. As Rouveret (2012) notes, the periphrastic *gwneud*-construction is only available for stage-level predicates (284-a) but not for individual-level predicates (284-b).

(284) a. Mi **wnaeth** Siôn **brynu** y llyfr hwn.
 PRT did Siôn buy the book this
 'Siôn bought this book.'
 b. *Mi **wnâi ddeall** Cymraeg Canol yn berffaith.
 PRT did know Welsh Middle PRED perfect
 (Rouveret 2012: 918)

The same pattern emerges with verb phrase fronting. While fronting of stage-level predicates is grammatical with a form of *gwneud* clause-internally (285-a), with individual-level predicates, a form of *bod* 'be' has to be used instead of *gwneud* 'do' (285-b).

(285) a. [**Cau** y glwyd] y **gwnaeth** y ffermwr.
 shut the gate C did the farmer
 'Shut the gate, the farmer did.'
 b. [**Deall** Cymraeg Canol] yr **oedd** yn berffaith.
 know Welsh Middle C was PRED perfect
 'He knew Middle Welsh perfectly.' (Rouveret 2012: 918)

This split is reminiscent of the split found with verb fronting in Fongbe (see section 7.1.5) and Haitian Creole (see section 7.1.7), where verb fronting is licit with stage-level predicates but ungrammatical with individual-level predicates. The difference between these languages and Welsh (apart from the verb vs. verb phrase and verb doubling vs. dummy verb distinction) then lies in the possibility to nonetheless front individual-level verb phrases but with a different kind of replacement verb in the clause.

The parallel behaviour of the periphrastic construction and verb phrase fronting receives a straightforward explanation if the latter is built upon the former. In this case, the Generalization IIb would not apply to Welsh verb phrase fronting because the dummy verb in this construction is not inserted as a repair but present independently of the fronting.

An argument in favour of treating *gwneud* as a repair despite the aforementioned parallel behaviour to the periphrastic construction is based on data from infinitive-embedding (286).

(286) a. [**Canu** 'r anthem] y mae Gwyn yn ceisio ei
sing.INF the anthem PRT be.PRS.3SG Gwyn PROG try.INF 3MS
wneud.
do.INF
'Singing the anthem is what Gwyn is trying to do.'
b. Mae Gwyn yn ceisio (***gwneud**) **canu** 'r anthem.
be.PRS.3SG Gwyn PROG try.INF do.INF sing.INF the anthem
'Gwyn is trying to sing the anthem.'

(Borsley et al. 2007: 42)

In (286-a), the fronted verb phrase *canu 'r anthem* 'sing the anthem' originates from a position embedded under the control verb *mae ceisio* 's/he is trying'. As expected, the infinitive form of *gwneud* (modulo mutation) appears in this position, since *mae ceision* requires its complement to be infinitive. However, the presumed base construction (286-b) where the verb phrase *canu 'r anthem* occurs *in situ* does not allow the periphrastic form *gwneud canu* 'do sing'. This indicates that *wneud* 'do' in the verb phrase fronting construction (286-a) is not the periphrastic *gwneud* but rather a repair form inserted to avoid a verbal gap.

Summary

Welsh disposes of a verb phrase fronting construction in which the verbal gap is occupied by a form of the dummy verb *gwneud* 'do'. Examples of a similar verb fronting construction are not reported. The fronting may take place in embedded clauses. Whether it is also possible from inside an island and across a finite clause boundary is unclear as no such examples have been found in the literature. Equally debatable is the status of the dummy verb in the construction. It may be identical to the *gwneud* found in the periphrastic construction indicating that verb phrase fronting might derive from the latter. However, not every verb phrase fronting has a grammatical periphrastic counterpart which supports a repair-type understanding of *gwneud*. I will take the latter view here. The properties of verbal fronting in Welsh are summarized in tabel 7.24. In conclusion, Welsh, showing verb phrase fronting with dummy verb insertion, instantiates pattern D of Generalization II.

Tab. 7.24: Properties of verbal fronting in Welsh

	Copy	Dummy	Unbound	Islands	GS	TAM	L-Adv	H-Adv	NEG	L/R	Top/Foc
V	–	–									
VP	–	✓	n.d.	n.d.	n.d.	n.d.	n.d.	n.d.	n.d.	L	Foc

7.2.8 Wolof

Wolof, an Atlantic language of the Niger-Congo family, is spoken as a first language by approximately four million people mainly in Senegal and The Gambia (Torrence 2013a: 7). Its neutral word order is SVO (Martinović 2017: 210).

The language allows verb phrase fronting where the fronted constituent receives an exhaustive/identificational focus interpretation and a dummy verb *def* 'do' appears in the canonical verb position (287-a). It does not allow verb fronting with verb doubling, as shown in (287-b).

(287) a. [**Suub** simis b-i]   l-a-a   *(**def**).[32]
       dye shirt CL-DEF.PROX *l*-C-1SG do
       'Dye the shirt is what I did.'
   b. *****Suub** l-a-a **suub** simis b-i.
       dye *l*-C-1SG dye shirt CL-DEF.PROX
       Intended: 'I DYED the shirt.'   (Torrence 2013a: 68)

However, Torrence (2013a,b) does not provide an example showing the ungrammaticality of verb fronting with dummy verb insertion. What he does show is that it is possible to front strings of verbs as shown in (288-b) where like in (287) a dummy verb occupies the clause-internal verb position. Example (288-a) instantiates the corresponding neutral sentence.

(288) a. Door-na-a   jéém ë   suub simis b-i.
       begin-FIN-1SG try a_{INF} dye shirt CL-DEF.PROX
       'I began to try to dye the shirt.'
   b. [**Door a   jéém ë   suub**] l-a-a **def** simis b-i.
       begin a_{INF} try a_{INF} dye *l*-C-1SG do shirt CL-DEF.PROX
       'Begin to try to dye the shirts is what I did.'
                                              (Torrence 2013a: 68)

Depending on further data it might thus be the case that Wolof actually disposes of verb and verb phrase fronting. For the time being, though, I will treat it as a VP fronting only language.

Turning to the arguments for ($\bar{\text{A}}$-)movement, we find that verb phrase fronting may cross finite clause boundaries (289).

---

[32] The form *l-a* is glossed as XPL-COP in Torrence (2013a). However, I follow Martinović (2017: 211) who argues that the sentence particle *a* is an allomorph of the complementizer and consequently gloss it as C. Under this view the *l*, interpreted as an expletive by Torrence, is a prefixal element that occurs when a non-subject instead of a subject crosses the C-position.

(289) [**Jox**-leen-ko] l-a-ñu wax ne l-a-a **def.**
give-3PL-3SG *l*-C-3PL say that *l*-C-1SG do
'Give it to them is what they said that I did.' (Torrence 2013b: 197, fn. 24)

Unfortunately, there are no examples that attest to the behaviour of verb phrase fronting with regard to islands. However, Torrence (2005: 233–235) and Torrence (2013b: §3.1) shows that the corresponding process of DP fronting is sensitive to them. In addition, DP fronting exhibits reconstruction effects (for details, see Torrence 2013b: §4). Since he treats fronting as a more or less independent operation that can apply to various categories in Wolof (e.g. DP, PP, AdvP, etc., Torrence 2013b: 182) the findings for DP fronting may be taken to carry over to VP fronting with the only difference being the dummy verb that shows up in the original position of the verb phrase.

There are two more arguments in favour of verb phrase fronting involving $\bar{\text{A}}$-movement. The first comes from the form of the complementizer. As Torrence (2005) shows, the complementizer *(l)a* is associated with $\bar{\text{A}}$-movement.[33] It is obligatory in long-distance dependencies where it occurs in the matrix clause and in every intermediate clause and it mimicks the *that*-trace effect by showing a subject/non-subject asymmetry, taking the form *a* with subject extraction but *la* with all other extracted elements (Klecha & Martinović 2015). Constructions in which it occurs are sensitive to islands, show reconstruction effects and pass a Wolof-specific $\bar{\text{A}}$-movement test, which involves the distribution of the applicative suffix *al* (see Torrence 2013a: §4.3.3 for details). The fact that *la* appears in verb phrase fronting constructions then shows that they involve $\bar{\text{A}}$-movement.

The second argument as presented by Torrence (2013b: §4.5.2) is based on the interaction of non-subject clitics and verb phrase fronting. Consider the two examples in (290), which both express the exact same meaning.

(290) a. Jox-*leen-ko* l-a-a def.
give-3PL-3SG *l*-C-1SG do
'Give it to them is what I did.'
b. Jox l-a-a-*leen-ko* def.
give *l*-C-1SG-3PL-3SG do
'Give it to them is what I did.' (Torrence 2013b: 197)

While the non-subject clitics *leen* '3PL' and *ko* '3SG' have been fronted together with the verb phrase in (290-a), they are stranded behind in (290-b). This data is

---

[33] There is also another $\bar{\text{A}}$-complementizer, consisting of a class marker and the vowel *u*. For the most part, both forms are in complementary distribution, except in *wh*-questions where both forms are possible. I refer the interested reader to Martinović (2017) for a detailed discussion.

easily accounted for, if the clitics originate inside the verb phrase and may either be moved as its constituents when the verb phrase is fronted (290-a) or alternatively climb out of the verb phrase before it is moved (290-b). That clitic climbing is possible (and even obligatory out of nonfinite clauses) in Wolof is shown in (291) where they occur on the finite verb even though they are arguments of the applied verb *togg-al* 'cook-BEN'.

(291) a. Door-na-a-*leen-fa*   [a jéém [a togg-al   ceeb]].
           begin-FIN-1SG-3PL-LOC *A* try   *A* cook-BEN rice
           'I began to try to cook rice for them there.'
       b. *Door-na-a   [a jéém [a togg-al-*leen-fa*   ceeb]].
           begin-FIN-1SG *A* try   *A* cook-BEN-3PL-LOC rice

(Torrence 2013b: 196)

As is evidenced by (292), climbing clitics cannot be split.

(292) *Door-na-a-*leen*   a jéém a togg-al-*fa*.
       begin-FIN-1SG-3PL *A* try   *A* cook-BEN-LOC

(Torrence 2013b: 196)

Now, with this in mind we would expect that non-subject clitics in verb phrase fronting also cannot be split. Under the assumption that verb phrase fronting involves movement, in order to achieve a split one of the two clitics would have to climb out of the verb phrase before it moves while the other clitic remains *in situ* and is moved as part of the verb phrase later on. As we have seen in (292), however, selective climbing of only one non-subject clitic is not possible. Indeed, this expectation is confirmed by the data (293), where only one of the clitics (*ko* in (293-a) and *leen* in (293-b)) would have to have climbed out of the verb phrase while the other has not.

(293) a. *[**Jox**-*leen*] l-a-a-*ko*   **def.**
           give-3PL *l*-C-1SG-3SG do
       b. *[**Jox**-*ko*] l-a-a-*leen*   **def.**
           give-3SG *l*-C-1SG-3PL do

(Torrence 2013b: 197)

If verb phrase fronting did not involve movement, the verb phrase would have to be base generated in sentence-initial position. The clitics, on the other hand, would need to be generatable either inside this verb phrase or in the position following the subject marker in order to capture the data in (290). It would then remain obscure why one cannot generate one clitic in one position and the other one in the other position. It seems clear from these arguments that Wolof verb phrase fronting is in fact $\bar{\text{A}}$-movement.

With regard to the status of the dummy verb in verb phrase fronting one might argue that it is just a stranded auxiliary. This view gains further strength when one takes into account that akin to emphatic *do* in English *def* 'do' in Wolof can occur inpendent of verb phrase fronting and triggers a similar verb or verb phrase focus interpretation (294). As verb phrase fronting involves Ā-movement one could suggest that it is derived from the construction in (294) by moving the verb phrase across *def*.

(294)   Xale yi   **d(ef)**-a-ñu (>dañu) **gis** golo.
        child DEF.PL do-C-3SG   see monkey
        'The children SAW a monkey.'/'It's that the children saw a monkey.'
                                                    (Martinović 2017: 269)

However, there are arguments against treating the form *def* in emphatic constructions and the *def* in verb phrase fronting as the same element. Consider first that in neutral clauses the main verb (or the imperfective auxiliary *di*) raises to the position of the sentence particle, which as Martinović (2017) (following arguments by Dunigan 1994) argues occupies C. It carries along any functional morphology associated with it (295).

(295)   a. Xale yi   lekk-na-ñu ceeb.
            child DEF.PL eat-C-3PL rice
            'The children ate rice.'
        b. Xale yi   lekk-oon-na-ñu ceeb bi.
            child DEF.PL eat-PERF-C-3PL rice DEF.SG
            'The children ate the rice (a long time ago).'
        c. Xale yi   di-na-ñu   lekk ceeb bi.
            child DEF.PL IMPF-C-3PL eat rice DEF.SG
            'The children will eat the rice.'
        d. Xale yi   d(i)-oon-na-ñu   lekk ceeb bi.
            child DEF.SG IMPF-PERF-C-3PL eat rice DEF.PL
            'The children were eating the rice.'   (Martinović 2015: 29)

In emphatic *def* constructions, the dummy verb *def* 'do' appears in C together with the sentence particle and neither the main verb nor the imperfective auxiliary raise. However, following Martinović (2015: 30), the absence of any functional morphology on *def* in (296) (where *dañu* can be decomposed into *d(ef)-a-ñu* 'do-C-3PL') indicates that it is inserted directly into its surface position rather than raising there from some unspecified lower position.

(296) a. Xale yi   da-ñu   lekk ceeb.
        child DEF.PL do.C-3PL eat rice
        'It's that the children ate rice.'
    b. Xale yi   da-ñu   di   (>dañuy) lekk ceeb.
        child DEF.PL do.C-3PL IMPF   eat rice
        'It's that the children are eating rice.'
    c. Xale yi   da-ñu   lekk-oon ceeb.
        child DEF.PL do.C-3PL eat-PERF rice
        'It's that the children ate rice (a long time ago).'
    d. Xale yi   da-ñu   d(i)-oon   lekk ceeb.
        child DEF.PL do.C-3PL IMPF-PERF eat rice
        'It's that the children were eating rice.'   (Martinović 2015: 29f.)

Having established that *def* in emphatic constructions is located in C and does not originate from a lower position, we would expect it to also occupy this position (or a higher one) in verb phrase fronting constructions if the latter were in fact derived from the former. As we have seen in example (287-a) at the beginning of this section (repeated below as (297)), this is not the case. The dummy verb occurs below the sentence particle, that is, below the complementizer position and therefore cannot be the same kind of dummy verb that shows up in emphatic constructions.

(297) [**Suub** simis b-i]   l-a-a   *(**def**).
      dye shirt CL-DEF.PROX l-C-1SG do
      'Dye the shirt is what I did.'   (Torrence 2013a: 68)

Therefore, verb phrase fronting cannot be derived from the emphatic construction even though the dummy verb *def* is present in both of them.

Summary

To conclude this section, we can state that Wolof shows verb phrase fronting, where the canonical position of the verb is filled with a dummy verb *def* 'do'. Verb fronting with verb doubling is ungrammatical, but it is unclear whether it is possible with a dummy verb. Awaiting further data on this, I will assume that it is not available in Wolof. Verb phrase fronting may cross finite clause boundaries and triggers the use of the complementizer *(l)a* which is associated with Ā-movement. In conjunction with data from its interaction with clitic placement this shows that verb phrase fronting involves Ā-movement. Furthermore, it cannot be derived from the emphatic construction which also makes us of the dummy verb *def* 'do' because the two *def*s occupy different structural positions. This supports *def*'s status as a repair element in verb phrase fronting. Table 7.25 provides an overview.

In conclusion, Wolof instantiates pattern D of Generalization II by allowing only verb phrase fronting and using a dummy verb as a repair.

Tab. 7.25: Properties of verbal fronting in Wolof

	Copy	Dummy	Unbound	Islands	GS	TAM	L-Adv	H-Adv	Neg	L/R	Top/Foc
V	–	?[34]									
VP	–	✓	✓	n.d.	n.d.	n.d.	n.d.	n.d.	n.d.	L	Foc

---

[34] It is unclear whether verb fronting is possible with dummy verb insertion. As example (288-b) shows, a string of verbs may be preposed without the object of one of the verbs involved, but no such example can be found with only a single transitive verb fronted.

8 Languages with both kinds of verbal fronting

8.1 Languages with symmetric dummy verb insertion

8.1.1 Basque

Basque is a language isolate spoken by ca. 700 000 speakers in the Basque Country between Spain and France (Hualde 2003: 3). Its neutral word order is SOV (1).

(1) Jon-ek ardoa   ekarri du.
     Jon-ERG wine.DET.ABS bring AUX
     'Jon brought the wine.'   (Etxepare 2003: 364)

There is considerable dialectal variation in the language. This section focusses on the Central and Western dialects described in Haddican (2007) and Elordieta & Haddican (2016). These show a construction where the main verb appears together with a semantically empty verb *egin* 'do' (2-a). This construction triggers a (contrastive) focus interpretation of the verb which is not available in the absence of the dummy verb *egin* (2-b).

(2) a. Ines **etorri egin** da.
         Ines come do   AUX
         'Ines has COME.'
     b. Ines etorri da.
         Ines come AUX
         'Ines has come.' / *'Ines has COME.'   (Haddican 2007: 736)

Although the main verb does not seem to be fronted here, the dummy verb behaves as if it has taken the place of the main verb. It bears one of the aspectual markers *-Ø, -t(z)en, -ko* (perfective, imperfective, future) and (if applicable) agreement marking usually realized on the main verb, whereas the main verb itself occurs in an infinitival citation form (3).

(3) a. **Eror**-i (**egin**-go/**egi**-ten) da etxea.
         fall-INF do-FUT/do-IMPERF AUX house
         'The house i going to FALL./The house is FALLING.'
     b. Etxea (erori-ko/eror-tzen) da.
         house fall-FUT/fall-IMPERF AUX
         'The house is going to fall./The house is falling.' (Haddican 2007: 748)

Egin further behaves parallel to the main verb in non verb-focus sentences with regard to word order. It appears immediately left-adjacent to the auxiliary in affirmative sentences (4) and to the right of the auxiliary in negative sentences (possibly separated by arguments or other material) (4-b).

(4) a. **Hil**-Ø **egin**-Ø da aurten gure aita.
die-INF do-PERF AUX this.year our father
'Our father has DIED this year.'
b. (?)**Etor(r)**-i ez da **egin**-Ø (Jon).
come-INF NEG AUX do-PERF Jon
'Jon hasn't COME.' (Haddican 2007: 745)

The lexical verbs in this focus construction bear one of four affixes *-tu, -i, -n, -Ø* where *-tu* is the open class affix. Classically, these affixes are analysed as perfective markers (Laka 1990, Ortiz de Urbina 1989, Zabala & Odriozola 1996). Haddican (2007), however, argues that they are infinitive markers. First, they cooccur with other aspect markers on *egin* in the same clause which can be specified for distinct aspect values.

(5) a. **Eror**-i **egin**-Ø da etxea.
fall-i do-PERF AUX house
'The house has FALLEN.'
b. **Eror**-i **egi**-ten da etxea.
fall-i do-IMPERF AUX house
'The house FALLS.'
c. **Eror**-i **egin**-go da etxea.
fall-i do-FUT AUX house
'The house is going to FALL.' (Haddican 2007: 741)

Second, verbs selected by modals like *ahal* 'can', *nahi* 'want', and *behar* 'need' obligatorily bear one of the affixes regardless of the perfectiveness of the action (6).

(6) Egun har-tan esan zidan, egunero *etor(r)-i* nahi zu-ela.
day that.on say AUX everyday come-INF want AUX-COMP
'That day she told me she wanted to come everyday.' (want > every)
(Haddican 2007: 742)

Third, besides serving as the citation form of the verb they behave similar to infinitives cross-linguistically in two further ways. Certain prepositions and postpositions specifically select for a verb affixed with *-tu/i/n/Ø* (7).

(7) a. nahiz gaztea *iza-n*
despite young be-INF
'despite being young'

b. *ikus-i* gabe
   see-INF without
   'without seeing' (Haddican 2007: 742)

And verbs affixed with one of those affixes participate in short wh-movement (8).

(8) Ez dakit zer *abes-tu*.
    not know what sing-INF
    'I don't know what to sing.' (Haddican 2007: 742)

Following Rebuschi's (1983) and Haddican's (2005, 2007) argumentation, the Basque verb focus construction looks suspiciously similar to verb focus constructions in other languages, e.g. Hausa (see section 7.2.2) or Welsh (see section 7.2.7), in that the lexical verb appears as a non-finite form outside of its base position in which a fully inflected dummy verb occurs instead. As the dummy verb takes on the inflection it seems like it is present because the lexical verb cannot be inflected. Haddican (2005, 2007) argues that the reason for this is that the lexical verb has moved to a designated structural focus position in the specifier of a focus phrase. Evidence for this can be found in the parallel behaviour of focalized verbs and regular non-verbal foci. The canonical position of foci is left-adjacent to the aspect-bearing verb in affirmative clauses (9-a) and left-adjacent to the negative morpheme *ez* in negative clauses (9-b).

(9) a. Nor-k/JON-EK   ikus-i du Miren?
       who-ERG/Jon-ERG see-PERF AUX Miren
       'Who/JON has seen Miren.'
    b. Nor-k/JON-EK   ez du (Miren) ikus-i   (Miren)?
       who-ERG/Jon-ERG not AUX Miren see-PERF Miren
       'Who/JON hasn't seen Miren.' (Haddican 2007: 744)

Non-focussed material cannot appear between the focus and the aspect-bearing verb (10-a) or between the focus and the negative morpheme *ez* (10-b).

(10) a. Nor-k/JON-EK   (*Miren) ikus-i   du (Miren)?
        who-ERG/Jon-ERG Miren see-PERF AUX Miren
        'Who/JON has seen Miren?'
     b. Nor-k/JON-EK   (*Miren) ez du (Miren) ikus-i   (Miren)?
        who-ERG/Jon-ERG Miren not AUX Miren see-PERF Miren
        'Who/JON hasn't seen Miren?' (Haddican 2007: 744)

Now consider focalized verbs which show the exact same word order and intervention restriction observed for non-verbal foci (11).

(11) a. **Hil**-Ø (*aurten/*gure aita) **egin**-Ø da aurten gure aita.
die-INF this.year/our father do-PERF AUX this.year our father
'Our father has DIED this year.'
b. (?)**Etor(r)**-i (*Jon) ez da **egin**-Ø (Jon).
come-INF Jon NEG AUX do-PERF Jon
'Jon hasn't COME.' (Haddican 2007: 745)

A further parallel between verbal and non-verbal foci is the fact that, at least for some speakers, they can both undergo extraction from embedded clauses, particularly under verbs of saying (12). This indicates that focalization involves $\bar{\text{A}}$-movement.

(12) a. Hor(r)-ela uste dut [egin behar-ko litzateke-ela aukeramena].
this-way think AUX make need-FUT AUX-COMP choice
'IN THIS WAY do I think the choice should be made.'
(Etxepare & de Urbina 2003, as cited in Haddican 2007: 746)
b. %**Etor(r)**-i esan didate [**egin** zine-la].
come-INF say AUX do AUX-COMP
'They have told me that you CAME.' (Haddican 2007: 746)
c. **Erosi** esan didate [**egi**-n zenue-la etxe-a].
buy say AUX do-PERF AUX-C house-DET
'They have told me that you BOUGHT the house.' (as opposed to, say, rent it) (Elordieta & Haddican 2016: 237)

Recall that we cannot decide whether a language shows verb or verb phrase fronting based solely on examples involving intransitive verbs because these are ambiguous between a verb and a verb phrase. As is evident from (12-c), it is possible to focalize a transitive verb while stranding its objects, which means that Basque indeed shows verb fronting. That it also comprises of verb phrase fronting is shown in (13).

(13) a. [Torrea **ikus**-i] **egin** d-u-t.
tower-ABS see-INF do 3SG(ABS)-have-1SG(ERG)
'I have SEEN the tower.'
b. [Joni liburua **ema**-n] **egin**
Jon-DAT book.ABS give-INF do
d-i-o-t.
3SG(ABS)-have-3SG(DAT)-1SG(ERG)
'I have GIVEN Jon the book.' (Haddican 2007: 753)

Note that the scope of the focus lies on the verb alone in both verb phrase fronting (13) and in verb fronting (14-a).[1] Focus of the whole verb phrase, as Elordieta & Haddican (2016) argue, requires movement of the verb (phrase) into focus position with subsequent movement of the remnant material across the focussed verb (14-b) which gives the impression of right-peripheral focus on the surface.

(14) a. Mirenek [den-denak **jan**] **egin** ditu.
       Miren   all-all   eat   do.PERF AUX
       'Miren has EATEN them all./*Miren has EATEN THEM ALL.'
     b. Mirenek **egin** ditu [den-denak **jan**].
        Miren   do-PERF AUX all-all   eat
        'Miren has EATEN THEM ALL.'   (Elordieta & Haddican 2016: 236f.)

Concerning the question of whether verb fronting involves a bare head or a remnant verb phrase, I follow Haddican (2005, 2007) and Elordieta & Haddican (2016) who treat all verbal fronting as phrasal movement. However, they never explicitly argue against a bare head movement approach to verb fronting.

The focussed constituent may not contain negation (15). Concerning the appearance of adverbs, I was not able to find conclusive examples.

(15) *Ez **etorr**-i **egin** da.
      not come-INF do   AUX
      'He has NOT COME.'   (Haddican 2007: 753)

However, there is evidence that infinitives behave like nominals. For example, they can take an overt determiner as in (16).

(16) Sentitzen dut Miren berandu etorri iza-n-*a*.
     regret   AUX Miren late   come   have-INF-the
     'I regret Miren having come late.'   (Zabala & Odriozola 1996: 239, fn. 3)

A closed class of infinitives also allows adjectival modification (17-a) and/or a genitive modificator (17-b).

---

1 As suggested by Elordieta & Haddican (2016: 237, fn. 6), the fact that verb phrase fronting, too, receives a narrow verb focus interpretation might be related to the availability of *in situ* verb phrase focus without any movement or *egin*-insertion in Basque. Involving less structure or fewer derivational steps the *in situ* option is preferred over the verb phrase movement option by principles like the *Minimal Structure Principle* (Bošković 1997) or *Economy of Derivation* (Emonds 1994). The use of the more complex verb phrase movement violates this principle and thereby triggers a pragmatic inference that the speaker does not want to express the verb phrase focus interpretation. Therefore, the meaning is corrected to narrow verb focus.

(17) a. Guk irabaz-i *handi-ak* atera ditugu.
we gain-INF big-PL take.out AUX
'We've had big gains.'
b. *Aitonaren* esa-n *zahar(r)-ak.*
grandpa's say-INF old-PL
'Grandpa's old sayings.' (Artiagoitia 1995: 433, 437)

That focalized infinitives behave in a similar nominal fashion is indicated by the fact that (for some speakers) they can trigger object agreement. In (18), the auxiliary *du* is marked with transitive agreement even though the (rightward) focussed verb phrase *bertara joan* 'go there' is intransitive. This leaves the infinitivized verb phrase as the sole source for the agreement (Haddican 2007: 752).

(18) Jon-ek egi-ten **du** astero-astero [bertara joa-n].
Jon-ERG do-IPFV AUX.TR weekly-weekly there go-INF
'What Jon does is go there every week.' (Haddican 2007: 752)

Verb doubling

In addition to the focus strategy with the dummy verb *egin* Western dialects show the possibility to have a doublet of the verb in the clause (19). The associated interpretation is either contrastive verb focus or positive polarity focus (Elordieta & Haddican 2016: 222).

(19) a. Mi-k j-**aki**-n d-**aki**-t egia.
I-ERG VM-know-INF 3SG-know-1SG truth
'I know the truth.' (as opposed to 'think' or 'believe' it)
b. J-ue-n d-oie, ala e-**torr**-i **dator**, ba.
VM-go-INF 3SG-go or VM-come-INF come.3SG then
'Well, is he leaving (right now), or is he coming?'
c. I-**bil**-i d-**abil** beti kale-a-n.
VM-walk-INF 3SG-walk always street-DET-LOC
'She is always WALKING in the street./She IS always walking in the street.' (Elordieta & Haddican 2016: 221f.)

This strategy, however, is restricted to a small closed class of verbs and is not productive. These special verbs exhibit synthetic morphology in imperfective finite contexts, that is, tense and agreement appear on the main verb (20-a) rather than on an auxiliary, as they usually do (20-b). In non-imperfective environments the affixes occur on the auxiliary independent of whether the verb is special (20-c) or not (20-d). The inventory of such special verbs varies from dialect to dialect.

(20) a. Jon dator.
Jon come.3SG
'Jon is coming.' (special verb in imperfective)
b. Jon bazkal-tzen ari da.
Jon lunch-IMPERF PROG AUX.3SG
'Jon is eating lunch.' (regular verb in imperfective)
c. Jon etorr-i da.
Jon come-PERF AUX.3SG
'Jon has come.' (special verb in perfective)
d. Jon-ek bazkal-du du.
Jon-ERG lunch-PERF AUX.3SG
'Jon has eaten lunch.' (regular verb in perfective)
(Elordieta & Haddican 2016: 223)

Verb doubling with special verbs is only possible in contexts in which they take a synthetic form, i.e. in the imperfective. If a doublet occurs in a perfective context the sentence is ungrammatical. Hence, example (21-a) is not felicitous because the special verb *ibil* 'to walk' is doubled in a perfective sentence. Regular verbs, like *bazkal* 'to lunch' never undergo doubling, not even in imperfective contexts (21-b).

(21) a. ***Ibil**-i **ibil**-i da.
walk-INF walk-PERF AUX
'She has WALKED.'
b. ***Bazkal**-du **bazkal**-tzen ari da.
lunch-INF lunch-IMPERF PROG AUX.3SG
'Jon is EATING LUNCH.' (Elordieta & Haddican 2016: 224)

Furthermore, it seems to be the case that only bare verbal heads can undergo focus movement with doubling. Attempts to focus-move more than the bare verb lead to ungrammaticality (22).

(22) a. *[Kalean **ibil**-i] **dabil**.
street.in walk-INF walk.3SG
'She is WALKING IN THE STREET.'
b. *[Ingeles eta frantses **jakin**] **daki**.
English and French know-INF know.3SG
'(S)he KNOWS ENGLISH AND FRENCH.'
(Elordieta & Haddican 2016: 224)

In general, the kind of movement involved in verb doubling seems to be more restricted than the one found in verbal focalization with *egin*-insertion. First, although verb doubling may occur in embedded clauses (23-a) it cannot cross the clause-boundary (23-b).

(23) a. Ez takkitt j-[**oa**-n **six-oi-an** ala **etorri etorren**].
       NEG know VM-go-INF go.PAST-C or come come.PAST-C
       'I don't know whether he was COMING or GOING.'
    b. *****Etorri**₁ esan dute [___₁ **datorr**-ela].
       come say AUX comes-C
       'They said she is COMING.' (Elordieta & Haddican 2016: 226)

Additionally, the target position of the movement is different from that of regular verbal and non-verbal foci. Note that in the latter nothing except for the negative morpheme *ez* (24-a) and the class of evidential and speech act particles, including *ei* 'allegedly' (24-b), may intervene between the focus and the aspect-bearing verb. In verb doubling constructions, however, even these are precluded from occuring between the focussed verb and its inflected copy (24-c)

(24) a. Jon ez dator.
       Jon NEG come.3SG
       'JON isn't coming.'
    b. Jon ei dator.
       Jon EVID come.3SG
       'JON is allegedly coming.'
    c. *****Jakin** ez/ei **dakizu** zuk hori.
       know NEG/EVID know.2SG you that
       'You don't/allegedly KNOW that.' (Elordieta & Haddican 2016: 225)

The movement involved in the verb doubling focus construction is thus different from the $\bar{\text{A}}$-movement found in other foci. Rather, it seems to be a kind very local head movement that leaves a copy for some reason. As it is, in addition, a severely idiosyncratic and non-productive phenomenon I leave it aside here. For the purposes of the typology developed in this book, Basque only disposes of verbal fronting which triggers dummy verb insertion not verb doubling.

Summary
Basque exhibits a verbal focalization operation that displaces verbs or verb phrases and inserts a dummy verb in their stead which takes on all the inflection markers usually associated with the lexical verb. The displaced verbs are infinitives which in certain respects behave parallel to nominals. The dependency between the focalized verb (phrase) and the dummy verb shows $\bar{\text{A}}$-properties in being able to cross finite clause boundaries. Negation may not appear inside the displaced

constituent. These properties are summarized in table 8.1. Thus, although Basque shows a verb doubling pattern of focussed bare verbal heads with a restricted set of verbs in a restricted set of contexts it manifests pattern II of Generalization I.

Tab. 8.1: Properties of verbal fronting in Basque

	Copy	Dummy	Unbound	Islands	GS	TAM	L-Adv	H-Adv	Neg	L/R	Top/Foc
V	–	✓	✓	n.d.	n.d.	–	n.d.	n.d.	–	L	Foc
VP	–	✓	✓	n.d.	n.d.	–	n.d.	n.d.	–	L	Foc

8.1.2 Breton

Breton, a Celtic language of the Indo-European family, is spoken by an estimate of 100 000–200 000 people (Press 1986: 1) in the region of Brittany in France and in some exiles around the world. Despite its typological classification, Breton has been argued to be a V2 language like German or Dutch (see, e.g. Schafer 1995, Borsley & Kathol 2000, Jouitteau 2005, 2008) because, on the surface, the verb is always preceded by one constituent (25).

(25) a. [Perig] a to o klask e vreur er c'hoad.
        Peter PRT is at looking.for his brother in.the woods
        'Peter is looking for his brother in the woods.'
    b. [E vreur] a zo Perig o klask er c'hoad.
        his brother PRT is Peter at looking.for in.the woods
        'As for his brother, Peter is looking for him in the woods.'
    c. [Er c'hoad] emañ Perig o klask e vreur.
        in.the woods is Peter at looking.for his brother
        'In the woods, Peter is looking for his brother.' (Anderson 1981: 28)

The language exhibits a construction in which the position before the inflected verb is occupied by a non-finite verbal constituent, either a verb (26-a) or a verb phrase (26-b). In these verbal frontings a form of the dummy verb *ober* 'do' is placed in the second position, which is fully inflected.

(26) a. **Debriñ** a **raio** Yannig krampouezh e Kemper hiziv.
        eating PRT will.do Johnny crêpes in Quimper today
        'Johnny will eat crêpes in Quimper today.'
    b. [**Debriñ** krampouezh] a **raio** Yannig e Kemper hiziv.
        eat crêpes PRT will.do Johnny in Quimper today
        'Johnny will eat crêpes in Quimper today.' (Anderson 1981: 34, 30)

Anderson (1981) claims that the fronted constituent is a topic whereas Jouitteau (2011) attributes a focus reading to a fronted verb phrase (27), while verb fronting has no influence on information packaging and is claimed to be due to the *Late Expletive Insertion Trigger* (LEIT) which requires the position before the finite verb to be filled.

(27) [**Dimeziñ** gant ma merc'h] ne **ri** ket.
 marry with my daughter NEG do.FUT.2SG NEG
 'You won't MARRY MY DAUGHTER.'
 (Jouitteau 2011, 125, citing Gléau 1973: 45, citing Le Lay 1925)

As the interpretation of the fronting constructions is not the main concern of this investigation and because dummy verb insertion rather than verb doubling occurs under both approaches, I will remain agnostic about this issue here.

The verbs *bezañ/bout* 'to be' and *kaout* 'to have' (28) are systematically excluded from fronting. Other stative (or individual-level) predicates like *seblantout* 'to seem' on the other hand are perfectly able to undergo fronting.

(28) a. ***Kaout** a **ran** un oto.
 have PRT do.1SG a car
 'I have a car.' (Jouitteau 2011: 122)

In case the lexical verb that is to be fronted is an analytical auxiliary-verb complex (29-a), occurrence of a dummy verb is optional (29-b). This indicates that dummy verb insertion is not necessarily triggered by the need to express finiteness in the absence of the lexical verb.

(29) a. Ma hent am-eus kollet. b. **Koll** am-eus (**graet**) ma hent.
 my road I-have lost lose I-have done my road
 'I have lost my way.' 'I have lost my way.'
 (Anderson 1981: 30)

Although the above presentation gives the impression that verb and verb phrase fronting are two sides of the same coin there are notable differences in syntactic behaviour. First, while verb phrase fronting may cross finite clause boundaries (30-a), indicating that it involves $\bar{\text{A}}$-movement, verb fronting is clause-bound (30-b).

(30) a. [**Debrin** krampouezh ed-du] a ouian [e **rae** Yann].
 eat pancakes buckwheat PRT know.1SG PRT did Yann
 'I know that Yann ate buckwheat pancakes.'
 b. ***Debrin** a ouian [e **rae** Yann krampouezh ed-du].
 eat PRT know.1SG PRT did Yann pancakes buckwheat
 (Borsley et al. 1996: 69)

In addition, verb phrase fronting obeys island conditions which is another typical property of an Ā-dependency. It may thus not take place from inside a Wh-Island (31) or a Relative Clause Island (32).

(31) *Wh-Island*
 *[**lenn** al levr] e sonjen [piv **reas**]
 read the book PRT wondered.1SG who did
 (Borsley et al. 1996: 73, en. 2)

(32) *Relative Clause Island*
 *[**lenn** al levr] a ouian an den [a **reas**]
 read the book PRT know.1SG the man PRT did
 (Borsley et al. 1996: 73, en. 2)

Second, verb phrase fronting is compatible with negation in the same clause (33-a) whereas negation with verb fronting leads to ungrammaticality (33-b).

(33) a. [**Debrin** krampouezh ed-du] ne **ra** ket Yann.
 eat pancakes buckwheat NEG do NEG Yann
 'Yann does not eat buckwheat pancakes.'
 b. ***Debrin** ne **ra** ket Yann krampouezh ed-du.
 eat NEG do NEG Yann pancakes buckwheat
 (Borsley et al. 1996: 69)

Third, when embedded under a modal or auxiliary, according to Borsley et al. (1996), verb fronting is not allowed (34-a, b). In contrast, the same sentence is grammatical if the fronted constituent is a whole verb phrase (34-c, d).[2]

(34) a. ***Lenn** en deus **graet** Yann al levr.
 read 3SG.M have done Yann the book
 b. ***Lenn** a c'hellan **ober** al levr.
 read PRT may.1SG do the book

---

[2] Note that the judgements are the reverse when the fronted constituent contains a participle instead of a verbal noun. With participle fronting dummy verb insertion is not required. Thus, fronting of a participle plus direct object is ungrammatical (i-a) whereas fronting of a participle on its own stranding the direct object is fine (i-b).

(i) a. *[Kollet ma hent] am-eus.
  lost my road I-have
  'I have lost my road.' (Anderson 1981: 34)
 b. Kollet am-eus ma hent.
  lost I-have my road
  'I have lost my way.' (Anderson 1981: 30)

c. [**Lenn** al levr] en deus **graet** Yann.
   read the book 3SG.M have done Yann
   'Yann has read the book.'
d. [**Lenn** al levr] a c'hellan **ober**.
   read the book PRT may.1SG do
   'I may read the book.' (Borsley et al. 1996: 69)

However, Anderson (1981) provides an example, already given in (29-b) above, that clearly shows that a verb may appear clause-initially in its verbal-noun form while stranding its direct object even when embedded under an auxiliary (35).

(35) **Koll** am-eus **graet** ma hent.
     lose I-have done my road
     'I have lost my way.' (Anderson 1981: 30)

I am not sure whether these contradictory judgements are due to dialectal/idiolectal variation or to restrictions on the specific lexical items involved.

However, the abovementioned divergences regarding syntactic behaviour strongly suggest that only verb phrase fronting is comparable to regular nominal fronting whereas verb fronting involves a distinct operation that underlies more restrictions than the former. In that sense, Breton might actually be classified as only showing $\bar{\text{A}}$-fronting of verb phrases. I have sorted it with the languages that allow both verb and verb phrase fronting because the two are superficially very similar and because both occur with dummy verb insertion. In that sense, Breton does not challenge the two Generalizations: If we accept it as a verb and verb phrase fronting languages, then it fits pattern II of Generalization I. If it is classified as a verb phrase fronting only language, then it instantiates pattern D of Generalization IIb. Admittedly, though, its classification influences the numbers of the different language types and thereby the strength of the respective generalization.

Material that may accompany the fronted constituent includes low adverbs like *mad* 'well' or *a-walc'h* 'gladly' (36) but excludes the subject (37).

(36) a. [**Kousked** *mad*] a **rez**.
        sleep well PRT you.did
        'Did you sleep well?'
     b. [**Kredi** *a-walc'h*] a **rafen**.
        believe gladly PRT I.would.do
        'I'd be glad to believe (it).' (Anderson 1981: 30)
(37) *[**Debriñ** *Yannig*] a **raio** krampouezh e Kemper hiziv.
     eat Johnny PRT will.do crêpes in Quimper today
     'Johnny will eat crêpes in Quimper today.' (Anderson 1981: 30)

The fact that the preverbal particle that occurs in verbal fronting constructions in *a* suggests that the fronted constituent is nominalized. In contrast to the particle *e* that occurs when adjectives, adverbials, or prepositional phrases are fronted, *a* usually only appear when a noun is sentence-initial (Anderson 1981: 31; see also Weisser 2019 for a recent analysis of this alternation).

Additionally, the verb in verbal fronting takes the form of a so-called verbal noun. This form generally allows a verb to take nominal modifiers like articles (38), prepositional phrases (39), and possessives (40). The a. and c. examples show a regular noun while the b. and d. examples present a verbal noun (in bold).

(38) a. *ar* mor
   the sea
   'the sea'
   b. *al* **laboured** douar
   the working land
   'the fact of working the land.'
   c. *eul* levr
   a book
   'a book'
   d. en *eur* **gerzet**
   in a walk
   'while walking'
   (Anderson 1981: 32)

(39) a. eul louzou *ouzh ar remm*
   a remedy for the rheumatism
   'a remedy for rheumatism'
   b. **sellout** *ouzh an den*
   to.look at the man
   'looking at the man'
   (Anderson 1981: 32)

(40) a. doriou *an ti*
   doors the house
   'the doors of the house'
   b. **sevel** *an ti*
   building the house
   'to build the house'
   (Anderson 1981: 32)

Verbs in their verbal noun form may appear in every position in which a normal NP can appear including subject position (41-a), direct object position (41-b), and as the object of a preposition (41-c).

(41) a. Pegoulz vo an **dornañ**?
   when will.be the to.thresh
   'When will the threshing be?'
   b. Ne garan ket **kleved** kurunou.
   NEG I.like not hearing thunder
   'I don't like to hear the thunder.'

c. Staotad a   rae ar gigerez en he dilhad gand ar **c'hoarzin**
   pissed PRT did the butcher in her clothes by   the laughing
   a   rae.
   PRT did
   'The butcher(ess) pissed in her pants with the laughing she did.'
   (Anderson 1981: 32f.)

If the fronted verb phrase as a verbal noun actually behaves like an NP, one might be tempted to suggest that verbal fronting is derived from a construction in which *ober* selects a verbal noun complement which is subsequently moved to the left periphery. *Ober* would then not be a (Last Resort) repair but an expected auxiliary-like head. Indeed, such a construction exists in Breton, although with a quite distinct meaning (42).

(42) Me a **raio   sevel**   eun ti.
     I PRT I.will.do building a   house
     'I'm going to have a house built.' (Anderson 1981: 34)

However, this structure cannot serve as the base for deriving verbal fronting for various reasons. First, the meaning difference between (42) and its corresponding verbal fronting structure (43) would remain unaccounted for, if the latter were derived from the former.

(43) [**Sevel**   eun ti]   a   **rin**.
     building a house PRT I.will
     'I'm going to build a house.' (Anderson 1981: 34)

Second, the approach would predict that fronting of a verbal noun without its object should not be possible because the verbal noun and its object together form the direct object of *ober*. In order to allow verb fronting, *ober* would have to select two direct objects. However, there are no Breton verbs that show this configuration on the surface, *ober* would be unique. Furthermore, if this were the right structure, we would expect the second direct object (i.e. the object of the verbal noun) to be displacable to the front, contrary to fact (44).

(44) *Krampouezh a   **rai**   Yannig **debriñ** e Kemper hiziv.
     crêpes   PRT will.do Johnny to.eat   in Quimper today
     (Anderson 1981: 34)

In light of recent arguments for syntactic $\bar{\text{A}}$-head movement (see e.g. Vicente 2007, 2009, Harizanov 2019), the last two examples could be explained, if Breton showed phrasal movement of the VP but $\bar{\text{A}}$-head movement of the verbal noun. However, as will be argued in section 4, Ā-head movement always results in verb doubling, which is not observed in (43). Hence, this approach seems implausible.

Third, topicalized object NPs can in general be represented by a resumptive pronoun. If the fronted verb is actually a nominal object of *ober*, it should be resumable by such a pronoun. However, this strategy is not available for fronted verbal nouns (45).

(45) *[**Lenn** eul levr brezhoneg] a   **ra**   Yannig *anezhañ* bemdez.
     reads a book Breton   PRT does Johnny of.it   everyday
     'Johnny reads a Breton book everyday.'   (Anderson 1981: 34)

Verbal fronting structures can therefore not be derived from a structure in which *ober* selects a verbal noun and its object as a complement.

On the other hand, there is an argument against treating *ober* as a repair insertion. Some intransitives show 'have' as the perfect auxiliary while others take 'be'. In verbal fronting, only 'have' is grammatical (as required by transitive *ober*). In case the particle is fronted instead of a verbal noun, the auxiliary that is appropriate for the respective verb appears. Hence in (46), the auxiliary in the first part of the conjunct is 'have' because the fronted verbal element is the verbal noun *menel* while the auxiliary in the second conjunct is 'be' because the fronted verbal element is a participle and the verb 'stay' requires 'be' as its perfect auxiliary.

(46)   **Menel** d'eureuji   am-*oa* **graet**, hag **manet** *on*   abaoe.
     stay   at.unmarried I-had   done   and stayed I.am since
     'I remained unmarried, and I have stayed (that way) since.'
                                                                    (Anderson 1981: 35)

Anderson (1981) argues that if *ober* is indeed a repair that is inserted late (after the verb(al noun) has been moved to the left periphery), it is not expected to influence the choice of the auxiliary. However, if one adopts a late insertion approach to morphology (e.g. Distributed Morphology, Halle & Marantz 1993, 1994, Halle 1997) this observation can be explained. Syntax operates on morpho-syntactic features exclusively while the phonolgical features of the elements are only inserted post-syntactically via a process of Vocabulary Insertion. Assume, thus, that all movements have taken place and all superfluous copies have been deleted. Insertion starts from the most deeply embedded nodes. Therefore, *ober* is inserted before the auxiliary in the Perf or T head. Subsequent insertion of phonological features into the head hosting the auxiliary then takes into account the information of the already inserted *ober* which leads to insertion of 'have'.

In conclusion, it is evidently not possible to derive verb fronting constructions from *ober* plus verbal noun complement constructions. However, *ober* can plausibly be treated as a (Last Resort) repair, despite the argument to the contrary presented in Anderson (1981).

Verb doubling

Breton has fairly recently innovated verb doubling with a small restricted class of verbs, including *ober* 'do', *bezañ* 'be', *rankout* 'must', *dleout* 'must', *gallout* 'can', *dont* 'come', *mont* 'go', *gouzout* 'know', *kerzhout* 'walk', *redek* 'run', *lenn* 'read' (Jouitteau 2011: 127) Those constructions still always have a corresponding counterpart with the dummy verb *ober* 'do'.

(47) a. **Rencout** a   **rencan**   da vont.
         must.INF PRT must.1SG P go
         'I have to go.'
    b. **Dleout** a   **zlean**   ober ma gwele.
         must.INF PRT must.1SG do my bed
         'I have to make my bed.'
    c. **Gallout** a   **c'hallfen** lako ma avaloù   en   douar.
         can.INF PRT can   put POSS apple/potato P.DET soil
         'I can plant my potatoes.'   (Jouitteau 2011: 127)

This doubling is also restricted to verb fronting (48-a). Internal arguments have to be stranded unless they are cliticized to the verb (48-b).

(48) a. *[**Gouzout** an doare da vont] a   **ouzez**.
         know   DET reason P go   PRT know.2SG
    b. [Hen   **gouzout**] a   **ouzez**.
         CL.3SG know   PRT know.1SG
         'I know it (well).'   (Jouitteau 2011: 128f.)

It behaves parallel to verb fronting with dummy verb insertion in that it is clause bound (49-a) and incompatible with negation (49-b)

(49) a. *****Gouzout** ne   gredan   ket a   **ouzez**   ken.
         know   NEG know.1SG NEG PRT know.2SG anymore
         Intended: 'I don't think you know anymore.'
    b. (*N') **gouzout** (*n') **ouzon**   ket.
         NEG know   NEG know.1SG NEG   (Jouitteau 2011: 128, 130)

Verb-doubling verb fronting and verb fronting with dummy verb insertion thus pattern together. They are both distinct from verb phrase fronting particularly with regard to their syntactic properties. While verb phrase fronting is available across clause boundaries, respects islands, and is not restricted in its cooccurrence options, both kinds of verb fronting are bounded inside the clause and may not cooccur with negation in the same clause. I therefore think it is reasonable to conclude that they involve a different operation from Ā-movement.

Summary

Breton disposes of verb and verb phrase fronting with dummy verb insertion. Whether this fronting gives rise to a topic or focus reading is not clear from the literature. When the fronted verb was embedded under an auxiliary, the presence of a dummy verb is optional. Additionally, there is verb doubling in verb fronting with a limited set of verbs. With regard to their syntactic behaviour verb and verb phrase fronting differ considerably. While the former is clause-bound and may not cooccur with negation in the same clause, the latter is undbounded, sensitive to islands, and free to occur with negation. Inside the fronted verb phrase, low adverbs may appear. Although there exists an independent construction with the dummy verb embedding a verb(al noun) phrase as its complement, this construction cannot serve as the base for verbal fronting as argued above. It therefore remains plausible that the dummy verb is indeed a repair element. An overview is provided in table 8.2. If classified as a language that allows both verb and verb phrase fronting, Breton thus instantiates pattern II, symmetric dummy verb insertion, of Generalization I, if one ignores the very restricted and idiosyncratic verb doubling verb fronting. It could, however, in principle also be regarded as a language that onyl allows verb phrase fronting, because verb fronting seems to involve a quite distinct operation, i.e. not Ā-movement. In that case the language would manifest pattern D of Generalization II.

Tab. 8.2: Properties of verbal fronting in Breton

	Copy	Dummy	Unbound	Islands	GS	TAM	L-Adv	H-Adv	NEG	L/R	Top/Foc
V	✓[3]	✓	–	–	n.d.	–	n.d.	n.d.	–[4]	L	?[5]
VP	–	✓	✓	✓[6]	n.d.	–	✓	n.d.	n.d.	L	?

---

[3] Verb doubling is only available for a limited set of verbs, each of which also allows the regular dummy verb insertion.
[4] Verb fronting may not cooccur with negation in the same clause.
[5] The literature is not consistent with regard to whether fronting is topicalization or focalization.
[6] Examples for Wh-Islands and Relative Clause Islands are attested.

8.1.3 Dutch

Dutch, a Germanic language of the Indo-European family, is spoken by around 22 million speakers in the Netherlands, Belgium and Luxembourg. It is a V2 language meaning that in main clauses the verb always occupies the second position. In embedded clauses, however, the word order is SOV.

The language comprises of verb (50-a) and verb phrase fronting (50-b), in which a form of the dummy verb *doen* 'to do' appears in the base position of the displaced verb. The fronted constituent receives a topic interpretation.

(50) a. **Verraden doet** hij haar niet.
betray does he her not
'He doesn't betray her.'
b. [Haar **verraden**] **doet** hij niet.
her betray does he not
'He doesn't betray her.' (Broekhuis & Corver 2015: 1045, 1043)

In case the fronted verb (phrase) was embedded by an auxiliary or a modal, dummy verb insertion is ungrammatical (51-a). Instead, a gap appears (51-b, c).

(51) a. *[Haar **verraden**] **doet** hij niet kunnen.
her betray.INF does he not be.able.INF
b. [Haar **verraden**] kan hij niet.
her betray.INF is.able he not
'He can't betray her.' (Broekhuis & Corver 2015: 1043)
c. **Verraden** wil hij haar niet.
betray.INF wants he her not
'He doesn't want to betray her.' (Broekhuis & Corver 2015: 1045)

With regard to $\bar{A}$-diagnostics, verbal fronting behaves like an $\bar{A}$-dependency. It may take place across finite clause boundaries (52) in the presence of a bridge verb but not when embedded under a non-bridge verb (53).

(52) a. **Geloven** denk ik [dat dit verhaal allen Jan **doet**].
believe.INF think I that this story only Jan does
'As for believing, I think that only Jan believes this story.'
b. [Het boek **lezen**] denk ik [dat Jan alleen 's avonds **doet**].
the book read.INF think I that Jan only in.the evening does
'Read the book, I think Jan only does in the evening.'
(Cora Pots p.c.)

(53) a. ?**Lezen** betreur/fluister ik [dat Jan een boek **doet**].
     read.INF regret/whisper I that Jan a book does
     Intended: 'As for reading, I regret/whisper that Jan reads a book.'
  b. *[Een boek **lezen**] betreuer/fluister ik [dat Jan **doet**].
     a book read.INF regret/whisper I that Jan does
     Intended: 'As for reading a book, I regret/whisper that Jan reads a book.' (Hedde Zeijlstra p.c.)

The crossing of finite clause-boundaries is also observed when the subordinate clause is a V2-clause as in (54).

(54) a. **Geloven** denk ik [**doet** dit verhaal alleen Jan].
     believe.INF think I does this story only Jan
     'As for believing, I think only Jan believes this story.'
  b. [Het boek **lezen**] denk ik [**doet** Jan alleen 's avonds].
     the book read.INF think I does Jan only in.the evening
     'Read the book, I think Jan only does in the evening.'
     (Cora Pots p.c.)

Furthermore, the dependency is sensitive to island conditions such as the Complex NP Island (55), the Subject Island (56), and the Adjunct Island (57).

(55) *Complex NP Island*
  a. ***Lezen** geloof ik [dat verhaal dat Jan een boek **doet**].
     read.INF believe I the story that Jan a book does
     Intended: 'As for reading, I believe the story that Jan reads a book.'
  b. *[Een boek **lezen**] geloof ik [dat verhaal dat Jan **doet**].
     a book read.INF believe I the story that Jan does
     Intended: 'As for reading a book, I believe the story that Jan does it.'
     (Hedde Zeijlstra p.c.)

(56) *Subject Island*
  a. ***Lezen** is [dat Jan een boek **doet**] totaal verrassend.
     read.INF is that Jan a book does totally surprising
     Intended: 'As for reading, that Jan reads a book is totally surprising.'
  b. *[Een boek **lezen**] is [dat Jan **doet**] totaal verrassend.
     a book read.INF is that Jan does totally surprising
     Intended: 'As for reading a book, that Jan reads a book is totally surprising.' (Hedde Zeijlstra p.c.)

(57) Adjunct Island
  a. ***Lezen** ben ik gelukkig [omdat Jan een boek **doet**].
     read.INF am I happy because Jan a book does
     Intended: 'As for reading, I am happy because Jan reads a book.'
  b. *[Een boek **lezen**] ben ik gelukkig [omdat Jan **doet**].
     a book read.INF am I happy because Jan does
     Intended: 'As for reading a book, I am happy because Jan reads a book.'

(Hedde Zeijlstra p.c.)

Therefore, the construction seems to involve $\bar{\text{A}}$-movement.

Low adverbs may be fronted together with the verb in both verb (58-a) and verb phrase fronting (58-b). Whether this also holds for negation remains to be investigated. As verbal fronting presumably involves phrasal movement of a (possibly remnant) VP or vP, it would be unexpected to find that negation, which is usually assumed to attach above vP, may occur in the sentence-initial constituent.

(58) a. *Zeker* **weten** doet Els het antwoord niet.
        certain know.INF does Els the answer not
        'Els does not know the answer for sure.'
     b. [Het antwoord *zeker* **weten**] doet Els niet.
        the answer certain know.INF does Els not
        'Els does not know the answer for sure.'

(Broekhuis & Corver 2015: 1047)

Concerning the dummy verb's status as a repair element, it is worth pointing out that Dutch, like German (see section 8.1.4) and Welsh (see section 7.2.7) does permit a periphrastic use of *doen* like in (59).

(59) Hij doet werken.
     He does work.INF
     'He is working/works.' (Broekhuis & Corver 2015: 1042)

This periphrastic construction shows no meaning difference in comparison with the synthetic form of the verb and it particularly does not trigger an emphatic reading like the corresponding English construction. Even though *doen*-periphrasis is stigmatized as non-standard Dutch or highly dialectal it is very vitally used in at least Netherlandic Dutch (Kersten 2015). It is therefore possible that verbal fronting is derived from it by moving the lexical verb (phrase) into the topic position stranding the auxiliary *doen*. If this is indeed the correct analysis, *doen* would not be a (Last Resort) repair element that is inserted whenever a proper verb goes missing from a clause. Rather, *doen* would be independently present in the sentence. As I have argued in section 1.4, however, if dummy verb insertion is treated as a proper repair, this allows us to capture a wider variety of languages with a unified analysis.

Summary
Dutch shows verb and verb phrase fronting, both of which cooccur with an inflected dummy verb in clause-internal position. The verb in the fronted constituent always occurs in its infinitival form and the whole constituent is interpreted as a topic. When embedded under an auxiliary or a modal, the displaced verb does not leaves a gap rather than a copy in its base position. Verbal fronting shows properties of an $\bar{\text{A}}$-dependency: It can cross finite clause boundaries and is sensitive to islands. Fronting of low adverbs together with the verbal constituent is possible but whether this is also holds for high adverbs and negation is not apparent from the available data. The relevant properties of Dutch verbal fronting are given again in table 8.3. In conclusion, Dutch verbal fronting instantiates pattern II of Generalization I showing verb phrase fronting with dummy verb insertion.

Tab. 8.3: Properties of verbal fronting in Dutch

	Copy	Dummy	Unbound	Islands	GS	TAM	L-Adv	H-Adv	Neg	L/R	Top/Foc
V	–	✓	✓	✓	n.d.	–	✓	n.d.	n.d.	L	Top
VP	–	✓	✓	✓	n.d.	–	✓	n.d.	n.d.	L	Top

8.1.4 German

German[7], a Germanic language of the Indo-European family, is spoken by approximately 100 million people predominantly in Germany, Austria, and Switzerland. It is a V2 language meaning that the verb always occupies the second position in main clauses. The word order in embedded clauses disregarding a few exceptions is SOV.

The language comprises of verb (60-a) and verb phrase fronting (60-b) both of which trigger a topic interpretation. The verb position inside the clause is occupied by a form of the dummy verb *tun* 'do' in both constructions. Although substandard, verbal fronting with dummy verb insertion seems to be available to many speakers and is used to a considerable degree in colloquiual German.

---

[7] Unless noted otherwise, the judgements in this section are my own.

(60) a. **Waschen tut** er das Auto nie.
 wash.INF does he the car never
 'He never washes the car.'
 b. [Das Auto **waschen**] **tut** er nie.
 the car wash.INF does he never
 'Something that he never does is wash the car.'

(Diedrichsen 2008: 221)

Some varieties of German also show verb doubling in verbal fronting (Fleischer 2008, Bayer 2008). These are mostly Northern or North Eastern dialects (what Bayer calls peripheral Prussian) and some heritage German varieties in the former Soviet Union. A few examples (as cited in Bayer 2008 with year of documentation where available) are given in (61).

(61) a. **Schaden schadet** ihm das nichts.
 harm.INF harms him that nothing
 'This does not harm him.' (*Prussian, 1967*)
 b. ... aber ihr redet bloß und **geben gebt** ihr nichts.
 but you talk only and give.INF give you nothing
 '... you only talk and talk but never give anything.' (*Prussian, 1964*)
 c. [Schniffke **schnûwe**] **schnöfft** hei nich, man [Branntwîn
 snuff snuff.INF snuffs he not but brandy
 sûpe] **söppt** hei sêr.
 guzzle.INF guzzles he very
 'He does not snuff tobacco but he guzzles a lot of brandy.'

(*Prussian, 1876*)
 d. **Syn bischt** schoon albig der glych verdamt Schelm!
 be.INF are.you still always the same damned rogue
 'You are still the same old rogue!' (*Alemannic (Splügen, Davos), 1939*)
 e. **Weerchu weerchut**=er weenig.
 work.INF works=he little
 'He works little.' (*Alemannic (Aosta Valley)*)

As I do not have any data on these dialects, I will not further discuss them here. However, it should be noted that, at first glance, many attestations of this verb doubling seem to contain only a single verb in the left periphery (i.e. (61-a, b, d)). The only example of verb phrase fronting with verb doubling is (61-c) which in addition is considerably older than the others, possibly indicating that verb phrase fronting with verb doubling is not as readily available in more modern stages of the dialects. If this turns out to be a more general pattern, I would tend to claim that the dialects in question comprise of Ā-head movement in addition to or instead of the Standard German remnant VP-movement for verb fronting. As the lowest copy of

Ā-head movement never undergoes copy deletion, this gives rise to verb doubling. For (diachronic stages of) dialects which also exhibit verb doubling with verb phrase fronting, the analysis would be that the order of operations compared to Modern Standard German is HM < CD, rather than CD < HM. Of course, this entails that these varieties, in contrast to Standard German, should not allow any dummy verb insertion in verbal fronting. I will have to leave it at that for the time being. The expectations concerning the behaviour of verbal fronting in the respective dialects are clear and await confirmation or falsification by empirical evidence.

Returning to Standard German, the verb in the fronted constituent always has to appear in the infinitive. An inflected form is not licit in this position (62).

(62) a. ***Wäscht tut** er das Auto nie.
        washes does he the car   never
     b. *[Das Auto **wäscht**] tut er nie.
         the car   washes   does he never

There are no restrictions on the semantic class of verbs that may undergo fronting. Individual-level predicates like *lieben* 'love' (63) or *ähneln* 'resemble' (64) may be fronted just like the stage-level predicate *waschen* 'wash' above.

(63) a. **Mögen tut** Heike Kaninchen noch nicht so lange.
        like.INF does Heike bunnies   yet not   so long
        'As for liking, Heike hasn't been liking bunnies for that long yet.'
     b. [Kaninchen **mögen**] tut Heike noch nicht so lange.
         bunnies   like.INF does Heike yet not   so long
        'Liking bunnies Heike hasn't been doing for that long yet.'

(64) a. **Ähneln**   tut Stephan seinem Opa,   aber seinem Vater
        resemble.INF does Stephan his   grandpa but his   father
        nicht so sehr.
        not   so very
        'As for resembling, Stephan resembles his grandpa, but his father not so much.'
     b. [Seinem Opa   **ähneln**]   tut Stephan, aber seinem Vater
         his   grandpa resemble.INF does Stephan but his   father
        nicht so sehr.
        not   so very
        'Resemble his grandpa Stephan does, but his father not so much.'

The only exception to this are verbs in idiomatic verb-complement constructions. When a verb is fronted without its internal argument, the idiomatic reading is lost or hard to obtain and a pragmatically odd literal reading is predominant. Hence, example (65-a) is not a faithful translation of the corresponding English sentence, even though the idiomatic expression *den Vogel abschießen* 'to shoot the bird' can be translated as 'to be the most entertaining, to entertain best'. If the whole verb phrase is fronted, however, the idiomatic reading remains intact (65-b).

(65) a. #**Abschießen tut** Felix den Vogel aber immer mit seiner
 shoot.INF does Felix the bird but always with his
 Tanzeinlage.
 dance.interlude
 'As for entertaining, Felix always entertains best when he performs his dance.'
 Lit.: 'Shoot, Felix always shoots the bird with his dance interlude.'
 b. [Den Vogel **abschießen**] **tut** Felix aber immer mit seiner
 the bird shoot.INF does Felix but always with his
 Tanzeinlage.
 dance.interlude
 'Entertain best, Felix always does when he performs his dance.'

Equally, verbal fronting is not restricted to a certain morpho-syntactically defined set of verbs. On the contrary, the set of frontable verbs (and verb phrases) includes unaccusatives (66-a), undergatives (66-b), ditransitives (66-c, d), particle verbs (66-e, f), and reciprocals (66-g).

(66) a. **Hinfallen tut** Franz mittlerweile leider häufig.
 tumble.INF does Franz by.now unfortunately frequently
 'As for tumbling, Franz tumbles quite frequently nowadays.'
 b. **Tanzen tut** Christoph fast nie.
 dance.INF does Christoph almost never
 'As for dancing, Christoph hardly ever dances.'
 c. **Schicken tut** Brigitte ihrem Enkel lustige Nachrichten
 send.INF does Brigitte her grandson funny messages
 neuerdings mit WhatsApp.
 latterly with WhatsApp
 'As for sending, Brigitte latterly sends her grandson funny messages via WhatsApp.'
 d. [Ihrem Enkel lustige Nachrichten **schicken**] **tut** Brigitte
 her grandson funny messages send.INF does Brigitte
 neuerdings mit WhatsApp.
 latterly with WhatsApp
 'Sending her grandson funny messages Brigitte latterly does via WhatsApp.'

e. **Anbraten tut** Maria den Rotkohl immer mit Schmalz.
   fry.INF does Maria the red.cabbage always with lard
   'As for frying, Maria always fries the red cabbage with lard.'
f. [Den Rotkohl **anbraten] tut** Maria immer mit Schmalz.
   the red.cabbage fry.INF does Maria always with lard
   'Frying the red cabbage Maria always does with lard.'
g. **Aufregen tut** sich Uwe nur selten.
   get.into.a.fuss does REFL Uwe only rarely
   'As for getting into a fuss, Uwe only rarely gets into a fuss.'

With regard to ditransitives, we find that it is possible to front partial verb phrases containing only one of the two arguments. Hence in the example (66-d), it is possible to front the verb with the direct object *lustige Nachrichten* 'funny messages' (67-a). However, it is not possible to front the verb together with the indirect object *ihrem Enkel* 'her grandson' only (67-b).

(67) a. [*Lustige Nachrichten* **schicken] tut** Brigitte ihrem Enkel
       funny messages send.INF does Brigitte her grandson
       neuerdings mit WhatsApp.
       latterly with WhatsApp
       'As for sending funny messages, Brigitte latterly sends (them to) her grandson via WhatsApp.'
   b. ??[*Ihrem Enkel* **schicken] tut** Brigitte lustige Nachrichten
       her grandson send.INF does Brigitte funny messages
       neuerdings mit WhatsApp.
       latterly with WhatsApp
       'As for sending (to) her grandson, Brigitte latterly sends funny messages (to him) with WhatsApp.'

This is in accordance with Landau's (2007) condition on partial VP-fronting given in (68). As is evident from (69), the indirect object can be dropped independently (69-a) and therefore can be stranded by partial VP-fronting whereas leaving out the direct object (69-b) leads to ungrammaticality, which in turn means that the direct object cannot be stranded by partial VP-fronting.

(68) *Condition on fronted VP-portions* (Landau 2007: 134)
     [[V Arg$_1$]... Subject... Arg$_2$] is grammatical iff [Subject... [$_{VP}$ V Arg$_1$]...] is grammatical (i.e., if Arg$_2$ may be dropped independently).

(69) a. Brigitte versucht [*lustige Nachrichten* mit WhatsApp zu
        Brigitte tries   funny   messages   with WhatsApp to
        schicken].
        send.INF
        'Brigitte tries to send funny messages with WhatsApp.'
    b. *Brigitte versucht [*ihrem Enkel* mit WhatsApp zu schicken].
        Brigitte tries   her grandson with WhatsApp to send.INF
        'Brigitte tries to send (to) her grandson with WahtsApp.'

When embedded under a modal or an auxiliary, fronting of the lexical verb (phrase) does not trigger dummy verb insertion. Rather, the modal (70) or auxiliary (71) occupies the second position that would otherwise be realized by the dummy verb.

(70) a. Programmieren₁ kann Raymond seit dem Studium alles
        program.INF   can Raymond since the study   all
        Mögliche   ___₁.
        possible.NMLZ
        'As for programming, Raymond can programm all sorts of things since completing his studies.'
    b. [Alles Mögliche   programmieren]₁ kann Raymond seit
        all   possible.NMLZ program.INF   can Raymond since
        dem Studium ___₁.
        the study
        'Programming all sorts of things can Raymond since completing his studies.'

(71) a. Waschen₁ wird   Thekla die Wäsche der Kinder noch ein
        wash.INF AUX.FUT Thekla the laundry the children still a
        paar Jahre lang ___₁.
        few years long
        'As for washing, Thekla will wash the children's laundry for a few more years still.'
    b. [Die Wäsche der Kinder   waschen]₁ wird   Thekla noch ein
        the laundry the children wash.INF AUX.FUT Thekla still a
        paar Jahre lang ___₁.
        few years long
        'Washing the children's laundry Thekla will do for a few more years still.'

However, fronting of the auxiliary itself with a dummy verb occupying the second position is ungrammatical (72-a). The same holds for examples in which the auxiliary and the main verb have been displaced together (72-b) and for those where the constituent including the auxiliary, the verb and its object(s) have undergone fronting (72-c).

(72) a. *Werden tut Markus erst in ein paar Monaten ein Eigenheim
AUX.FUT does Markus first in a few months a house
besitzen.
own.INF
'As for going to, Markus is going to own a house but only in a few months time.'
b. *[Besitzen werden] tut Markus erst in ein paar Monaten ein
own.INF AUX.FUT does Markus first in a few months a
Eigenheim.
house
'As for going to own, Markus is going to own a house but only in a few months time.'
c. *[Ein Eigenheim besitzen werden] tut Markus erst in ein paar
a house own.INF AUX.FUT does Markus first in a few
Monaten.
months
'Going to own a house Markus is but only in a few months time.'

The situation is slightly different with modals since they contribute somewhat more meaning (i.e. obligation, permission, volition, etc.) to the sentence. In contrast to auxiliaries, fronting of a modal is not completely out (73-a). The more material is fronted together with the modal the more the sentence improves. Hence, example (73-b) is better than (73-a) because the modal is accompanied by the lexical verb. When the whole verb phrase including the modal is displaced to the left periphery as in (73-c), the sentence becomes perfectly grammatical, at least to my ears.

(73) a. ??Müssen tut Sarah dieses Lied schon heute singen, aber
must does Sarah this song already today sing.INF but
wollen tut sie es erst in einer Woche.
want.INF does she it first in a week
'As for being obliged, Sarah is obliged to sing this song today already but, as for wanting, she only wants to sing it in a weeks time.'
b. ?[Singen müssen] tut Sarah dieses Lied schon heute, aber
sing.INF must.INF does Sarah this song already today but
aufnehmen wollen tut sie es erst morgen.
record.INF want.INF does she it first tomorrow
'As for having to sing, Sarah has to sing this song today already but, as for wanting to record, she only wants to record it tomorrow.'

c. [Dieses Lied singen müssen] tut Sarah schon heute.
   this song sing.INF must.INF does Sarah already today
   'Having to sing this song Sarah does today already.'

Concerning the Ā-properties of the dependency, we find that it behaves parallel to other Ā-dependencies like wh-movement or regular non-verbal topicalization. As is well-known, long extraction from *dass*-clauses is subject to considerable variation: In some (dialect) regions and for some speakers it is perfectly grammatical while it is just impossible in others (see among many others Reis & Rosengren 1992, Haider 2010). Hence, it is not surprising that the examples in (74) also receive mixed judgements from prompt acceptance to outright rejection (which I indicate by double question marks). An additional factor that might influence the assessment of (74) is the substandard nature of the construction and prescriptive rules against its usage.

(74) a. ??**Trinken** denke ich [dass Elise zur Zeit gern Kakao **tut**].
        drink think I believes no-one that Elise to.the time gladly cocoa does
        'As for drinking, I think that Elise currently likes to drink cocoa.'
     b. ??[Kakao **trinken**] denke ich [dass Elise zur Zeit gern **tut**].
        cocoa drink.INF denke I that Elise to.the time gladly does
        'Drinking cocoa Elise currently likes to do.'

In contrast to *dass*-clauses, verb second complement clauses are more permissive with regard to Ā-extraction of wh-elements or non-verbal topics.[8] Consequently, verbal fronting also considerably improves if it takes place from an embedded V2 sentence (75).

(75) a. **Trinken** denke ich [**tut** Elise zur Zeit gern Kakao].
        drink.INF think I does Elise to.the time gladly cocoa
        'As for drinking, I think Elise currently likes to drink cocoa.'
     b. [Kakao **trinken**] denke ich [**tut** Elise zur Zeit gern].
        cocoa drink.INF think I does Elise to.the time gladly
        'Drinking cocoa Elise currently likes to do.'

The same pattern is found when trying to front a verbal constituent inside the embedded clause. In case it is a *dass*-clause, ungrammaticality results (76).

---

[8] Though see (Reis 1996) for arguments against a movement approach of extraction from embedded V2 and in favour of an analysis as parentheticals.

(76) a. *Ich glaube [dass **studieren** Ulrich Computervisualistik
I believe that study.INF Ulrich computational.visualistics
schon seit Jahren **tut**].
already since years does
'I believe that, as for studying, Ulrich has been studying computational visualistics for years.'

b. ?*Ich glaube [dass [Computervisualistik **studieren**] Ulrich
I believe that computational.visualistics study.INF Ulrich
schon seit Jahren **tut**].
already since years does
'I believe that, study computational visualistics Ulrich has been doing for years.'

However, verbal fronting inside an embedded verb-second clause is grammatical (77).

(77) a. Ich glaube [**studieren tut** Ulrich Computervisualistik
I believe study does Ulrich computational.visualistics
schon seit Jahren].
already since years
'I believe (that), as for studying, Ulrich has been studying computational visualistics for years.'

b. Ich glaube [[Computervisualistik **studieren**] **tut** Ulrich
I believe computational.visualistics study.INF does Ulrich
schon seit Jahren].
already since years
'I believe (that) study computational visualistics Ulrich has been doing for years.'

Thus, verbal fronting patterns with wh-movement and topicalization with respect to extractability. Further, both verb and verb phrase fronting are sensitive to islands such as the Complex NP Island (78), the Subject Island (79), the Adjunct Island (80), and the Relative Clause Island (81).

(78) *Complex NP Island*

a. *****Backen** verbreitet jemand [das Gerücht dass Isa einen
bake.INF spreads someone the rumour that Isa a
Käsekuchen **tut**].
cheesecake does
'As for baking, someone is spreading the rumour that Isa is baking a cheesecake.'

b. *[Einen Käsekuchen **backen**] verbreitet jemand [das Gerücht
    a   cheesecake bake.INF spreads   someone the rumour
dass Isa **tut**].
that Isa does
'Baking a cheesecake someone is spreading the rumour that Isa does.'

(79) *Subject Island*

a. ***Verletzen** ist [dass Klaus sein Knie wieder **tut**] sehr ärgerlich.
   injure.INF is that Klaus his knee again does very annoying
'As for injuring, it is very annoying that Klaus injures his knee again.'

b. *[Sein Knie **verletzen**] ist [dass Klaus wieder **tut**] sehr ärgerlich.
    his knee injure.INF is that Klaus again does very annoying
'As for injuring his knee, it is very annoying that Klaus does it again.'

(80) *Adjunct Island*

a. ***Füttern** kann Maria nicht ausschlafen [weil   sie Leoni jeden
   feed.INF can Maria not   sleep.in   because she Leoni every
Tag um sieben **tut**].
day at seven does
'As for feeding, Maria cannot sleep in because she feeds Leoni at seven every day.'

b. *[Leoni **füttern**] kann Maria nicht ausschlafen [weil   sie jeden
    Leoni feed.INF can Maria not   sleep.in   because she every
Tag um sieben **tut**].
day at seven does
'As for feeding Leoni, Maria cannot sleep in because she feeds her at seven every day.'

(81) *Relative Clause Island*

a. ***Trinken** habe ich Martin lange nicht gesehen [der
   drink.INF have I   Martin long not   seen   REL.PRON
besonders gern Espresso **tut**].
particularly gladly espresso does
'As for drinking, I haven't seen Martin for a long time who particularly likes to drink espresso.'

b. *[Espresso **trinken**] habe ich Martin lange nicht gesehen [der
    espresso drink.INF have I   Martin long not   seen   who
besonders gern **tut**].
particularly gladly does
'As for drinking espresso, I haven't seen Martin for a long time who particularly likes to do it.'

Fronting out of a Wh-Island, however, does not trigger ungrammaticality (82).

(82) *Wh-Island*
  a. ?**Spielen** weiß ich genau [was Leo gerade **tut**].
       play.INF know I exactly what Leo right.now does
       'As for playing, I know exactly what Leo is playing right now.'
  b. ?[Minecraft **spielen**] weiß ich nicht [wie lange Leo schon **tut**].
       Minecraft play.INF know I not how long Leo already does
       'Playing Minecraft I don't know for how long Leo has done already.'

This is, however, not unexpected. As Fanselow (1987) shows, regular NP-topicalization of objects (in contrast to subjects) is not hindered by Wh-Islands (83).

(83) a. Radios₁ weiß ich nicht [wer ___₁ repariert].
       radios know I not who repairs
       'As for radios, I don't know who repairs them.'
  b. *Linguisten₁ weiß ich nicht [was ___₁ reparieren].
       linguistis know I not what repair
       'As for linguists, I don't know what they repair.' (Fanselow 1987: 57f.)

A verbs and verb phrases behave parallel to objects in this regard, we may conclude that they involve the same kind of movement, i.e. $\bar{\text{A}}$-movement. The difference in extractability between the subject and the object/verb/verb phrase is linked by Fanselow (1987) to the fact that the former occupies a structural position outside the verb phrase. How the influence of this structural difference on extractability could be implemented in the current theory will be left to future research.

Although all island tests seem to indicate that verbal fronting is $\bar{\text{A}}$-movement, one might argue that a base generation approach is not completely excluded yet. As the sentences above are all biclausal it is imaginable that the fronted verb (phrase) is base generated in the left periphery of the embedded clause and moves to the matrix clause. The islands diagnose this movement step while the dummy verb is not due to movement but to the base generation of the constituent in the embedded left periphery. The coordination examples in (84), which each contain only one CP, show that this cannot be the case. Fronting of each one of the two conjoined verbs or verb phrases seperately leads to ungrammaticality.

(84) *Coordinate Structure Constraint*[9]
  a. *ced**Trinken** [$_{C'}$ **tut** Linda gern Sekt] und [$_{C'}$ isst Michael
       drink.INF does Linda gladly champagne and eats Michael
       am liebsten Rind].
       at.the dearest beef
       'As for drinking, Linda likes to drink champagne and Michael preferably eats beef.'

b. ***Essen** [$_{C'}$ trinkt Linda gern Sekt] und [$_{C'}$ **tut** Michael
 eat.INF drinks Linda gladly champagne and does Michael
 am liebsten Rind].
 at.the dearest beef
 'As for eating, Linda likes to drink champagne and Michael preferably eats beef.'

c. *[Sekt **trinken**] [$_{C'}$ **tut** Linda gern] und [$_{C'}$ isst Michael
 champagne drink.INF does Linda gladly and eats Michael
 am liebsten Rind].
 at.the dearest beef
 'As for drinking champagne, Linda likes to do it and Michael preferably eats beef.'

d. *[Rind **essen**] [$_{C'}$ trinkt Linda gern Sekt] und [$_{C'}$ **tut**
 beef eat.INF drinks Linda gladly champagne and does
 Michael am liebsten].
 Michael at.the dearest
 'As for eating beef, Linda likes to drink champagne and Michael preferably does it.'

---

9 Note that in contrast to the corresponding Brazilian Portuguese examples (see section 8.2.1) the subject in the second conjunct must be overtly distinct from the one in the first conjunct. Otherwise, the sentence could receive a structural analysis as an SLF construction (*Subjectlücke in finiten Sätzen*, Höhle 1983, 1990, 1991). This construction, together with a few others from various languages, has been subsumed under the term *asymmetric coordination* because superficially they all look like proper coordination but crucially do not show the same syntactic behaviour. Most importantly, they seem to be able to violate the Coordinate Structure Constraint. This also holds for the SLF construction, where for instance an NP can be topicalized from one of the two conjuncts without rendering the sentence ungrammatical (i-a). Equally, verbal fronting out of one conjunct in such an SLF construction results in a grammatical sentence (i-b, c).

(i) a. Sekt trinkt Linda gern und isst dazu am liebsten Rind.
 champagne drinks Linda gladly and eats there.to at.the dearest beef
 'Champagne, Linda likes to drink and preferably eats beef with it.'
 b. Trinken tut Linda gern Sekt und isst dazu am liebsten Rind.
 drink.INF does Linda gladly champagne and eats there.to at.the dearest beef
 'As for drinking, Linda likes to drink champagne and preferably eats beef with it.'
 c. [Sekt trinken] tut Linda gern und isst dazu am liebsten Rind.
 champagne drink.INF does Linda gladly and eats there.to at.the dearest beef
 'Drinking champagne Linda likes to do and preferably eats beef with it.'

Asymmetric coordinations have been analyzed as underlying subordinations that become superficial coordinations in the course of the derivation (see Weisser 2015). For an analysis of SLF constructions along these lines see Barnickel (2017).

Further evidence for the Ā-nature of the dependency between the fronted verbal constituent and the dummy verb in clause-internal position comes from reconstruction effects that occur with these constructions.

There is reconstruction for Principle A and for Principle C. Thus, the anaphor in the fronted verb phrase in (85) can be coreferent with the subject of the clause despite not being located in its c-command domain on the surface. Likewise, the NP inside the fronted verb phrase in (86) cannot be coreferent with the subject pronoun although the latter falls within the c-command domain of the former.

(85) [Sich selbst$_i$ **loben**] tut Anja$_i$ normalerweise nicht.
  REFL self praise does Anja normally not
  'Praise herself$_i$, Anja$_i$ usually doesn't.'

(86) *[Fotos von Anja$_i$ **mögen**] tut sie$_i$ oft nicht
  photos of Anja like does she often not
  'Like photos of Anja$_i$, she$_i$ often doesn't.'

Lastly, there is one more piece of evidence in favour of verbal fronting involving Ā-movement: It targets the same position as wh-movement and regular non-verbal topicalization with the consequence that these cannot cooccur with verbal fronting in the same clause (87).

(87) a. ***Singen** wer **tut** Bachs Kantaten am Sonntag?
   sing.INF who does Bach's cantatas on.the sunday
   'As for singing, who will sing Bach's cantatats on sunday?'
  b. *[Bachs Kantaten **singen**] wer **tut** am Sonntag?
   Bach's cantatas sing.INF who does on.the sunday
   'As for singing Bach's cantatas, who does it on sunday?'

Judging from the presented data it is plausible to conclude that verbal fronting in German is an Ā-dependency.

Let us now turn to the question which material can accompany the verb (phrase) into the left periphery. As shown in (62), repeated here as (88), it is not possible to front any TAM-marking together with the verb (phrase).

(88) a. ***Wäscht tut** er das Auto nie.
   washes does he the car never
  b. *[Das Auto **wäscht**] **tut** er nie.
   the car washes does he never

Negation inside the fronted constituent, in contrast, is acceptable in the proper context (89).

(89) Context: Rüdiger has bad hearing. However, he usually understands everything that is said to him.
    a. *Nicht* **verstehen** tut er ein Gespräch nur wenn es in
        not understand.INF does he a conversations only when it in
        der Umgebung sehr laut ist.
        the environment very loud is
        'As for not understanding, he only doesn't understand a conversation if it is very loud around him.'
    b. [Ein Gespräch *nicht* **verstehen**] tut er nur wenn es in
        a conversation not understand.INF does he only when it in
        der Umgebung sehr laut ist.
        the environment very loud is
        'Not understand a conversation he only does if it is very loud around him.'

Equally, low adverbs of manner like *aufmerksam* 'attentively' may be fronted as part of the verbal constituent (90).

(90) a. [*Aufmerksam* **lesen**] tut Andy einen Aufsatz nur im Büro,
        attentively read.INF does Andy a paper only in.the office
        nirgendwo sonst.
        nowhere else
        'As for attentively reading, Andy only attentively reads a paper in the office but nowhere else.'
    b. [(*Aufmerksam*) einen Aufsatz (*aufmerksam*) lesen] tut Andy
        attentively a paper attentively read.INF does Andy
        nur im Büro, nirgendwo sonst.
        only in.the office, nowhere else
        'Read a paper attentively, Andy only does in the office but nowhere else.'

This option is not available for high sentential adverbs like *hoffentlich* 'hopefully' (91).

(91) a. *[*Hoffentlich* **einreichen**] tut Zoka die Dissertation noch vor
        hopefully submit does Zoka the dissertation still before
        Juli.
        July
        'As for submitting, hopefully Zoka submits the dissertation before July.'

b. *[(*Hoffentlich*) die Dissertation (*hoffentlich*) **einreichen**] **tut**
hopefully the dissertation hopefully submit does
Zoka noch vor Juli.
Zoka still before July
'Hopefully submit the dissertation Zoka does before July.'

Coming to the question of the size of the fronted constituent, we have seen that negation can be part of it but sentential adverbs cannot. As the former is usually assumed to be merged above *v*P while the latter are adjoined to TP, one can conclude that the fronted part must at least be as large as *v*P (or NegP in case negation is included) but cannot be larger than that (i.e. cannot be TP). Whether verb fronting involves remnant movement or Ā-head movement has been a matter of debate in the research on German syntax. While the former position seems to be dominant (den Besten & Webelhuth 1990, Grewendorf & Sabel 1994, Müller 1998, Müller 2002, Takano 2000, Abels 2001, Hinterhölzl 2002) it has not gone unchallenged (Kuthy & Meurers 2001, Fanselow 2002). Nonetheless, I follow Müller (2014: 99–121), who countering the arguments raised by the critics makes a convincing case in favour of verb fronting being remnant movement.

Let us now focus on the dummy verb's status as a repair. While it seems clear that *tun* 'do' has to appear in verbal fronting sentences in order to provide a locus for the expression of tense/finiteness one might wonder whether it can also optionally occur in run-of-the-mill declarative clauses to serve the same purpose. Indeed, such sentences are possible (92) but only in substandard or dialectal German (for an overview, see e.g. Abraham & Fischer 1998, Schwarz 2009, Weber 2017).

(92) a. Joanna tut schon eine ganze Weile an ihrer Dissertation
Joanna does already a whole while at her dissertation
schreiben.
write.INF
'Joanna has been writing her dissertation for quite a while now.'
b. Ich vermute dass Joanna schon eine ganze Weile an ihrer
I suspect that Joanna already a whole while at her
Dissertation schreiben tut.
dissertation write.INF does
'I suspect that Joanna has been writing her dissertation for quite a while now.'

Can these constructions serve as the basis from which the verbal fronting examples are derived by moving into the left periphery the consituent consisting of the lexical verb and its internal argument? Under this approach, *tun* 'do' would not be a repair that shows up whenever the verb is unable to host tense or other finiteness features (e.g. when it has been displaced). Rather, it would independently be present as a lexical item in the derivation from the start and therefore not fall under the categorization of repair. However, there are two issues with this. First, not all speakers who accept examples of verbal fronting with *tun* also accept *tun*-periphrasis *in situ*. For these speakers, the *tun* that appears when the lexical verb is moved to the left periphery cannot be the same element as the one that occurs in *tun*-periphrases like (92) simply because their grammar does not contain the latter. Second, according to Bayer (2008) (see also Freitag 2019, Bayer & Freitag to appear), the declarative *tun*-periphrase is not available for individual-level predicates like *besitzen* 'to own' (93-a) or *ähneln* 'to resemble' (93-b).[10]

(93)   a.   *Der Klaus **tut** einen guten Charakter **besitzen**.
           the Klaus does a   good character own
           'Klaus has good character.'
      b.   *Der Klaus **tut** seinem Vater **ähneln**.
           the Klaus does his   father resemble
           'Klaus resembles his father.'   (Bayer 2008: 4)

Nonetheless, the respective verb and verb fronting counterparts of (93) are fine.

(94)   a.   **Besitzen tut** der Klaus einen guten Charakter nicht erst seit
           own.INF does the Klaus a   good character not   first since
           er im   Internat   war, aber man bemerkt ihn seitdem
           he in.the boarding.school was but one notices him since
           sicherlich noch deutlicher.
           certainly   more obviously
           'As for having, Klaus doesn't just have good character since he went to a boarding school but one surely notices it more obviously since then.'
      b.   [Einen guten Charakter **besitzen**] **tut**   der Klaus nicht erst seit
           a   good character own   does the Klaus not   first since
           er im   Internat   war.
           he in.the boarding.school was
           'As for having good character, Klaus does not only have it since he went to bearding school.'

(95)   a.   **Ähneln tut** der Klaus seinem Vater nur äußerlich.
           resemble does the Klaus his   father only externally
           'As for resembling, Klaus only resembles his father in the looks.'

---

10 To me these examples are not necessarily ungrammatical. However, they are definitely degraded compared to those in (92).

b. [Seinem Vater **ähneln**] **tut** der Klaus nur äußerlich.
his father resemble does the Klaus only externally
'As for resembling his father, Klaus only resembles him in the looks.'

This divergence of judgements is unexpected under the approach where verbal fronting is derived from *tun*-periphrase.

A further alternative to treating the dummy verb as a repair is to analyze it as a verbal anaphor in a left dislocation structure. Under this view, the base construction for verbal fronting is a left dislocation structure where the verbal anaphor *das tun* 'do it/do so' shows up as in (96).

(96) [Ein Buch **lesen**], das **tut** er nur wenn er Urlaub hat.
the car wash.INF that does he only when he holidays has
'As for reading a book, he only does it when he's on holidays.'

From this, verbal fronting could be derived by topic drop of *das*. This analysis, however, is untenable because it is not applicable to verb fronting.[11] As demonstrated in (97), left dislocation of a single verb is ungrammatical.

(97) *****Lesen**, das tut er ein Buch nur wenn er Urlaub hat.
read.INF that does he a book only when he holidays has
Intended: 'As for reading, he only reads a book when he's on holidays.'

In conclusion, the appearance of a dummy verb in verbal fronting in German cannot be attributed to its independent presence in a purported base construction. It must therefore be a proper repair that is triggered by verbal displacement and takes place in order to avoid a situation in which tense and other finiteness features are left unpronounced.

Summary
German verbal fronting consists of verb and verb phrase fronting, both of which trigger the presence of a dummy verb inside the clause. Usually, the fronted constituent receives an interpretation as a contrastive topic. The verb in the fronted portion is always infinite and can be any semantic and syntactic type of verb. For partial verb phrase fronting, Landau's (2007) condition on fronted VP-portions holds. No dummy verb appears when fronting strands an auxiliay or a modals. While fronting of auxiliaries on their own or as part of a larger unit including the lexical verb is ungrammatical, fronting of a modal is possible although marked and improves when the lexical verb or the whole verb phrase is fronted along with it.

---

[11] I am grateful to Klaus Abels for pointing this out to me.

Verbal fronting shows the same behaviour as other Ā-dependencies: It is marginally able to cross a *dass*-clause boundary but perfectly fine out of a verb-second complement clause; it respects island conditions (except for the notoriously permissible Wh-island) and it shows reconstruction effects for Principle A and Principle C. Although TAM-marking inside the fronted constituent is ungrammatical, negation may accompany the verb. Equally acceptable are low adverbs, whereas sentential adverbs lead to ungrammaticality. The relevant properties are summarized in table 8.4. German verbal fronting thus instantiates Pattern II of Generalization I, namely symmetric dummy verb insertion.

Tab. 8.4: Properties of verbal fronting in German

	Copy	Dummy	Unbound	Islands	GS	TAM	L-Adv	H-Adv	Neg	L/R	Top/Foc
V	–	✓	✓[12]	✓[13]	–	✓	–	✓	–	L	Top
VP	–	✓	✓	✓	–	✓	–	✓	–	L	Top

8.2 Languages with symmetric verb doubling

8.2.1 Brazilian Portuguese

Brazilian Portuguese, like its European sister language, is a Romance language of the Indo-European family. It is the official language of Brazil spoken by about 200 million people. The basic word order of the language is SVO (98).

(98)　O　veterinario　vaccinou　cachorro de rua.
　　　the veterinarian vaccinated dog　　of street
　　　'The veterinarian vaccinated a stray dog.'　　　　(Bastos-Gee 2009: 169)

The language comprises of verb (99-a) and verb phrase fronting (99-b, c), in which a copy of the displaced verb appears in the clause-internal base position. As Bastos-

---

[12] While verb fronting from a V2 complement clause is uniformly judged grammatical, verb fronting out of a *dass*-clause is subject to inter-speaker variation. This also holds for verb phrase fronting.

[13] Respected conditions include the Complex NP Island, the Subject Island, the Adjunct Island, the Relative Clause Island, and the Coordinate Structure Constraint. Violation of the Wh-Island, which is known to be more permissible in German, does not necessarily trigger ungrammaticality. This also holds for verb phrase fronting.

Gee (2009: 171ff.) shows, the fronted constituent may only contain discourse-old information and is thus interpreted as a topic.

(99) a. **Temperar** o cozinheiro **temperou** o peixe (não a carne).
 season.INF the cook seasoned the fish not the meat
 'As for seasoning something, the cook seasoned the fish (not the meat).'
 b. [**Temperar** aquele peixe] o cozinheiro **temperou** (mas...)
 season.INF that fish the cook seasoned but
 'As for seasoning that fish, the cook seasoned it (but...)'
 c. [**Temperar** peixe] o cozinheiro sempre **tempera** nos fins
 season.INF fish.SG the cook always seasons on.the ends
 de semana.
 of week
 'As for seasoning fish, the cook always seasons it on weekends.'
 (Bastos-Gee 2009: 162)

The difference between the two types of verb phrase fronting (99-b) and (99-c) is that the former (type 1) only allows non-generic (i.e. specific) readings of the internal argument whereas the latter (type 2) only allows generic ones. As will be demonstrated in what follows, the two verb phrase frontings also exhibit distinct syntactic properties, while type 1 patterns with the verb fronting in (99-a) with regard to syntactic behaviour, type 2 seems to have a different structure.

Although verb fronting and both types of verb phrase fronting may take place from finite clauses as shown in (100), their sensitivity to islands varies.

(100) a. **Temperar**, eu acho [que o cozinheiro temperou o peixe
 season.INF I think that the cook seasoned the fish
 (não a carne)].
 not the meat
 'As for seasoning something, I think the cook seasoned the fish (not the meat).'
 b. [**Temperar** aquele peixe], eu acho [que o cozinheiro
 season.INF that fish I think that the cook
 temperou] (mas...)
 seasoned but
 'As for seasoning that fish, I think the cook seasoned it (but...)'
 c. [**Temperar** peixe], eu acho [que o cozinheiro (só) tempera
 season.INF fish I think that the cook only seasons
 nos fins de semana].
 on.the ends of week
 'As for seasoning fish, I think the cook (only) seasons it on weekends.'
 (Bastos-Gee 2009: 164–166)

While verb fronting and type 1 verb phrase fronting both respect island conditions, type 2 verb phrase fronting does not. It is therefore possible to front a verb phrase out of an island, if the object inside that phrase is non-specific. The behaviour of verb and verb phrase fronting with regard to islands is exemplified for the Complex NP Island (101), the Adjunct Island (102), and the Coordinate Structure Constraint (103).

(101) *Complex NP Island*
    a. *****Temperar**, eu conheci [o cozinheiro que **temperou** o
        season.INF I met the cook that seasoned the
        peixe] (não a carne).
        fish not the meat
        'As for seasoning something, I met the cook that seasoned the fish (not the meat).'
    b. *[**Temperar** aquele peixe], eu conheci [o cozinheiro que
        season.INF that fish I met the cook that
        temperou] (mas...)
        seasoned but
        'As for seasoning that fish, I met the cook that seasoned it (but...)'
    c. [**Temperar** peixe], eu conheço [um cozinheiro que (só)
        season.INF fish I met a cook that only
        tempera nos fins de semana].
        seasons on.the ends of week
        'As for seasoning fish, I met a cook that (only) seasons it on weekends.'
                                                    (Bastos-Gee 2009: 164–166)

(102) *Adjunct Island*
    a. *****Temperar**, o cozinheiro comprou o sal [antes de
        season.INF the cook bought the salt before of
        temperar o peixe] (não a carne).
        season.INF the fish not the meat
        'As for seasoning something, the cook bought salt before seasoning the fish (not the meat).'
    b. *[**Temperar** aquele peixe], o cozinheiro comprou o sal
        season.INF that fish the cook bought the salt
        [antes de **temperar**] (mas...)
        before of season.INF but
        'As for seasoning that fish, the cook bought salt before seasoning it (but...)'

c. [**Temperar** peixe], o   cozinheiro (só)   compra sal [antes de
      season.INF fish the cook   only buys   salt before of
      temperar].
      season.INF
      'As for seasoning fish, the cook (only) buys salt before seasoning.'

      (Bastos-Gee 2009: 164–166)

(103)   *Coordinate Structure Constraint*
   a. *****Temperar**, o   cozinheiro [comprou o   sal e   **temperou** o
      season.INF the cook   bought the salt and seasoned   the
      peixe] (não a   carne).
      fish   not the meat
      'As for seasoning something, the cook bought the salt and seasone
      the fish (not the meat).'
   b. *[**Temperar** aquele peixe], o   cozinheiro [comprou o   sal e
      season.INF that fish   the cook   bought the salt and
      temperou] (mas...)
      seasoned   but
      'As for seasoning that fish, the cook bought salt and seasoned it
      (but...)'
   c. [**Temperar** peixe], o   cozinheiro [compra sal e   **tempera**
      season.INF fish   the cook   buys salt and seasons
      nos   fins de semana].
      on.the ends of week
      'As for seasoning fish, the cook buys salt and seasons it on weekends.'

      (Bastos-Gee 2009: 164–166)

As mentioned above, the two types of verb phrase fronting also differ with regard to the specificity of the object inside the fronted verb phrase. Following the argumentation in Bastos-Gee (2009), I will show that there is indeed a one-to-one correspondence between the specificity of the object and the sensitivity to islands. Consequentially, the internal argument's specificity may serve as a diagnostic for Ā-movement.

First, note that some objects are ambiguous between a specific and generic reading depending on the tense/aspect of the clause. Thus, in (104-a), where the aspectual marking is perfective, the definite DP *o jornal* 'the newspaper' has a specific reading only. A given newspaper has been read at a certain time in the past and the reading action is completed. In contrast, (104-b) and (104-c), exhibit a present and imperfective marking respectively. In these examples, a habitual meaning is conveyed, where someone usually reads or used to read the newspaper. The definite DP *o jornal* 'the newspaper' most naturally refers to different newspapers of the same brand or to a group of newspapers. It may also refer to a specific newspaper but in that case the interpretation of the sentences is pragmatically odd because someone would have to usually read or used to read one and the same single newspaper again and again.

(104)   a. [**Ler**   o   jornal],   eu acho que ele **leu**   (mas…)
             read.INF the newspaper I   think that he read.PST.PFV but
             'As for reading the newspaper, I think that he read it (but…)'
        b. [**Ler**   o   jornal],   eu acho que ele **lê**   (mas…)
             read.INF the newspaper I   think that he read.PRS   but
             'As for reading the newspaper, I think that he reads it (but…)'
        c. [**Ler**   o   jornal],   eu acho que ele **lia**   (mas…)
             read.INF the newspaper I   think that he read.PST.IPFV but
             'As for reading the newspaper, I think that he used to read it (but…)'
             (Bastos-Gee 2009: 167)

With regard to the movement-diagnosing island tests, the sentences in (104) show the pattern in (105). Example (105-a), where the object has a specific reading, obeys the Complex NP Island, whereas examples (105-b, c) with a non-specific object are grammatical. Here, the specificity of the object and the island diagnostic for movement pattern alike and single out example a. as the one instantiating type 1 verb phrase fronting.

(105)   a. *[**Ler**   o   jornal],   eu tenho/tive [um amigo que
             read.INF the newspaper I   have/had   a   friend that
             leu]   (mas…)
             read.PST.PFV but
             'As for reading the newspaper, I have/had a friend that read it (but…)'
        b. [**Ler**   o   jornal],   eu tenho [um amigo que **lê**]
             read.INF the newspaper I   have   a   friend that read.PRS
             (mas…)
             but
             'As for reading the newspaper, I have a friend that reads it (but…)'
        c. [**Ler**   o   jornal],   eu tenho/tinha [um amigo que
             read.INF the newspaper I   have/had   a   friend that
             lia]   (mas…)
             read.PST.IPFV but
             'As for reading the newspaper, I have/had a friend that used to read it (but…)'   (Bastos-Gee 2009: 167f.)

A non-specific reading of the object in example (105-a) can be forced by adverbs like *diariamente durante dez anos* 'daily for ten years'. If there is indeed a one-to-one correspondence between the specificity of the object and Ā-movement we would expect (105-a) to become grammatical when adding this adverb. As evidenced by (106), this is the case.

(106)   [**Ler**   o   jornal],   eu tenho [um irmão que **leu**
        read.INF the newspaper I   have   a   brother that read.PST.PFV
        diariamente durante dez anos].
        daily   during ten years
        'As for reading newspaper, I have a brother who read it daily for ten years.'
                                                  (Bastos-Gee 2009: 168)

A further argument comes from the behaviour of inherently specific objects, like proper names, vs. inherently generic ones, like bare singular NPs. While with the former the verb phrase containing them may not be fronted out of an island (107-a), this is perfectly possible with the latter (107-b).

(107)   a.   *[**Vacinar**   o   Rex], eu briguei com [o   veterinário que
               vaccinate.INF the Rex I   fought with   the veterinarian that
               vacinou] (mas...)
               vaccinated but
               'As for vaccinating the Rex, I fought with the veterinarian that vaccinated.'
   b.   [**Vacinar**   cachorro de rua], eu conheço [um veterinário
              vaccinate.INF dog   of street I   met   a   veterinarian
              que **vacina**].
              that vaccinates
              'As for vaccinating stray dogs, I met a veterinarian that vaccinates.'
                                                  (Bastos-Gee 2009: 169)

We can therefore conclude, that there are two distinct types of verb phrase fronting, one involving Ā-movement and the other probably involving base generation of the constituent in sentence-initial position. In the absence of any movement diagnostics, one would expect a verb phrase fronting example to be ambiguous between the two underlying structures. However, as we have shown above, the specificity of the object inside the fronted verb phrase can be exploited to diagnose these structures. Specific objects are only allowed in a movement structure while non-specific objects can only occur in a base generation structure.

Having established this correspondence, we can discuss an additional difference between verb fronting and type 1 verb phrase fronting on the one hand, and type 2 verb phrase fronting on the other. The latter optionally license a resumptive phrase *fazer isso* 'do this' instead of a copy of the verb clause-internally (108).

(108) a. [**Vacinar** cachorro], eu conheço [um veterinárion que
vaccinate.INF dog I know a veterinarian that
faz isso].
does it
'As for vaccinating dog, I know a veterinarian that does it.'
b. [**Vacinar** cachorro], eu conheço [um veterinário que
vaccinate.INF dog I know a veterinarian that
vacina].
vaccinates
'As for vaccinating dog, I know a veterinarian that does it.'

(Bastos-Gee 2009: 170)

This kind of resumption, however, is not available in fronting structures that involve Ā-movement, like verb fronting (109) or type 1 verb phrase fronting (110). With these, only verb doubling is licit.

(109) a. *****Vacinar,** o veterinário *fez isso* com o cachorro.
vaccinat.INF the veterinarian did this with the dog
'As for vaccinating, the veterinarian did it with the dog.'
b. **Vacinar,** o veterinário **vacinou** o cachorro.
vaccinate.INF the veterinarian vaccinated the dog
'As for vaccinating, the veterinarian vaccinated the dog.'

(Bastos-Gee 2009: 170)

(110) a. *[**Vacinar** o Rex], o veterinário *fez isso* (mas...)
vaccinate.INF the Rex the veterinarian did this but
'As for vaccinating the Rex, the veterinarian did it.'
b. [**Vacinar** o Rex], o veterinário **vacinou** (mas...)
vaccinate.INF the Rex the veterinarian vaccinated but
'As for vaccinating the Rex, the veterinarian did it.'

(Bastos-Gee 2009: 170)

The situation here is somewhat reminiscent of the Germanic languages. These also show the option of having a resumptive phrase containing a dummy verb 'do, make' (SWE: *göra det*, DAN/NOR: *gjøre det*, GER: *das tun*, all meaning 'do this') in the base position of the displaced verb (phrase). And similar to Brazilian Portuguese, the presence of this resumption is indicative of a construction that superficially looks similar to movement-generated verb (phrase) fronting but is most probably generated by other means like base-generation. The crucial difference between Brazilian Portuguese and the Germanic languages is that the former shows verb doubling in verbal movement constructions while the latter show dummy verb insertion which makes it harder to tease the two constructions apart.

Cable (2004) reports that Brazilian Portuguese verb phrase fronting exhibits genus-species effects, where the denotation of the fronted constituent is a superset of the denotation of the copy in base position (111).

(111) **[Comer peixe]**, a Maria acha que eu **como salmão**.
 eat.INF fish the Mary thinks that I eat salmon
 'As for eating fish, Mary thinks I eat salmon.' (Cable 2004: 11)

Those are unexpected if the construction involves movement. We would therefore expect (111) to be a type 2 verb phrase fronting and, indeed, in this case the object in the sentence-initial verb phrase has a generic reading indicative of that type of construction.[14]

Concerning the size of the fronted constituent, the data suggest that it is no larger than vP because negation (112-a) and high sentential adverbs (112-b) may not be fronted together with the verb phrase.

(112) a. *[*Não* **terminar** a tese], a Maria (não) **terminou**...
 not finish the thesis, the Mary not finished
 'As for not finishing the thesis, Mary did (not) ...'
 b. *[*Certamente* **terminar** a tese], a Maria (certamente)
 certainly finish the thesis the Mary certainly
 terminou...
 finished
 'As for certainly finishing the thesis, Mary (certainly) did.'
 (Bastos-Gee 2009: 178)

On the other hand, the word order in the clause-initial verb phrase indicates that it is no smaller than vP either. The basic word order in ditransitive verb phrases is V DP PP, which is most probably derived by V-to-v movement. Since this is also the order in the fronted constituent (113-a), the verb must have moved to v there too,

---

14 The prediction that genus-species effects should only be found with type 2 verb phrase fronting could be tested with a sentence like (i), where a specific reading of the object is forced by the perfective aspect on the verb and the presence of the adverb *ontem* 'yesterday'. According to what was argued above, this example must be generated by movement since the fronted object receives a specific interpretation. Therefore, the genus-species effect should be ungrammatical.

(i) [**Ler** o **jornal**], eu acho que ele **leu** **The Times** ontem (mas...)
 read.INF the newspaper I think that he read.PST.PFV the times yesterday but
 'As for reading the newspaper, I think that he read the Times yesterday.'

Unfortunately, I was not able to test this with a native speaker.

which implies that the constituent contains *v*. The presumed word order before V-to-*v* movement is ungrammatical in the fronted verb phrase (113-b).

(113) a. [**Emprestar** o livro para a Maria], o João **emprestou**
lend.INF the book to the Mary the John lent
(mas…)
but
'As for lending the book to Mary, John did it, but…'

b. *[O livro **emprestar** para a Maria], o João **emprestou**
the book lend.INF to the Mary the John lent
(mas…)
but
'As for lending the book to Mary, John did it, but…'

(Bastos-Gee 2009: 178)

The behaviour of low adverbs is not discussed by Bastos-Gee (2009). This is particularly unfortunate with regard to determination of the size of the fronted constituent in verb fronting. If low adverbs are allowed to accompany the verb, it is plausible that the initial constituent is a remnant verb phrase. In case low adverbs are precluded from that position, a bare head analysis is more feasible. Also, there is no data on partial verb phrase fronting of ditransitives, which if possible, would favour a remnant movement approach.

Summary

In summary, Brazilian Portuguese disposes of verb and verb phrase topicalization fronting with verb doubling. Two types of verb phrase fronting can be distinguished: One that like verb fronting is unbounded, respects islands, and disallows replacing the verb copy with the phrase *fazer isso* 'do this', and another one that although equally unbounded is not sensitive to islands and can exhibit the resumptive phrase instead of a copy of the verb. Therefore, the former type, like verb fronting, is generated by Ā-movement while the latter type probably involves base generation of some sort. In the former, only specific objects occur whereas in the latter only non-specific objects are allowed. A conjecture about the genus-species effects attested for the language is that they exclusively occur with the base-generation type of verb phrase fronting and therefore never appear with a specific object. The topicalized constituent cannot be larger than a *v*P since both negation and sentential adverb, that are usually assumed to adjoin above *v*P, are precluded from it. Word order facts indicate that it is also not smaller than *v*P. The main properties of verbal fronting in Brazilian Portuguese are presented in table 8.5. Taken together, Brazilian Portuguese verbal fronting follows pattern I of Generalization I. Both verb fronting and the relevant verb phrase fronting that involves movement show verb doubling consistently as expected.

Tab. 8.5: Properties of verbal fronting in Brazilian Portuguese

	Copy	Dummy	Unbound	Islands	GS	TAM	L-Adv	H-Adv	Neg	L/R	Top/Foc
V	✓	–	✓	✓	–	–	n.d.	–	–	L	Top
VP	✓	–	✓	✓	✓	–	n.d.	–	–	L	Top

8.2.2 Buli

Buli, a Gur language of the Niger-Congo family, is spoken by about 160 000 speakers in Northern Ghana. Its basic word order is SVO (114) (Hiraiwa 2003: 45).

(114) Àtìm dè mángò-kú-lá dīēm.
  Àtìm ate mango-DEF-DEM yesterday
  'Àtìm ate that mango yesterday.' (Hiraiwa 2005b: 546)

The language allows verb (115-a) and verb phrase fronting (115-b) both of which exhibit a copy of the moved verb in the canonical verb position. The constituent in focus position is nominalized in both cases and receives a (contrastive) focus interpretation with the contrast scoping over the verb in verb fronting and over the whole verb phrase in verb phrase fronting (Hiraiwa 2005a: 250). The focus marker *ká* is optional and the word order in the fronted verb phrase deviates from the neutral VO found in verb phrases *in situ*.

(115) a. (Ká) **dḕ**-kā àlī/àtì Àtìm *(**dè**) mángò-kŭ dīēm.
   FOC eat-NMLZ C   Àtìm ate mango-DEF yesterday
   'It is eating that Àtìm ate the mango yesterday. (not e.g. throwing it away)'
 b. (Ká) [mángò-kú **dḕ**]-kā àlī/àtì Àtìm *(**dè**) dīēm.
   FOC mango-DEF eat-NMLZ C   Àtìm ate yesterday
   'It is eating the mango that Àtìm ate yesterday. (not e.g. buying a banana)' (Hiraiwa 2005a: 262)

Like in regular subject focus but in contrast to object focus, movement in verb (phrase) focus is obligatory (116).

(116) *Àtìm **dè** (ká) **dē**-(kā) máŋgò dīēm.
Àtìm ate FOC eat-NMLZ mango(ID) yesterday
'It is eating that Àtìm ate a mango yesterday.' (Hiraiwa 2005b: 552)

Verb (phrase) fronting is not a root phenomenon. It is also available in embedded clauses (117).

(117) Àtìm wèːnì àyīn (ká) **dē**-kā àlī/àtì Àmɔ̀àk *(**dè**) máŋgò
Àtìm said C FOC eat-NMLZ C Àmɔ̀àk ate mango(ID)
dīēm.
yesterday
'Àtìm said that it is eating that Àmɔ̀àk ate a mango yesterday.'
'It is eating that Àtìm said that Àmɔ̀àk ate a mango yesterday.'
(Hiraiwa 2005b: 551)

Since the focus marker *ká* is homophonous with the copula (118), it is worth pointing out that it does not function as a copula in verb (phrase) fronting and that the latter therefore does not involve a bi-clausal structure where *ká* is the copula of the matrix sentence and the matrix subject is a null pronoun or null expletive.

(118) Àtìm ká kpārōā.
Àtìm CPL farmer(ID)
'Àtìm is a farmer.' (Hiraiwa 2005b: 547)

First, *ká* as a focus marker is always optional (shown for regular object focus in (119-a)), while *ká* in its function as a copula can never be omitted (119-b).

(119) a. *(Ká)* máŋgò-kú-lá àlī/àtì Àtìm dè (*máŋgò-kú-lá/*kù)
FOC mango-DEF-DEM C Àtìm ate mango-DEF-DEM/3SG
dīēm.
yesterday
'It is that mango that Àtìm ate yesterday.'
b. Àtìm *(ká)* kpārōā.
Àtìm CPL farmer(ID)
'Àtìm is a farmer.' (Hiraiwa 2005b: 548)

Second, Buli does not allow null pronouns (120). Hence, the missing subject in the presumed matrix clause in verb (phrase) fronting cannot be a null pronoun.

(120) *(Wà) (kǎ) kpārōā.
3SG CPL farmer(ID)
'He is a farmer.' (Hiraiwa 2005b: 548)

It can also not be a null expletive. Although Buli has an expletive element *kù* this is obligatory when used (121-a). If it is omitted or dropped, the embedded subject must raise into matrix subject position (leaving a resumptive pronoun) (121-b).

(121) a. *(Kù) à ɲē sī   Àmɔ̀àk à: dē gbāŋ-ká (lá).
       it   PRS do as.if Àmɔ̀àk PRS win game-DEF DEM
       'It seems that Àmɔ̀àk is winning the game.'
   b. Àmɔ̀àk à ɲē sī wà lì dē gbāŋ-ká (lá).
       Àmɔ̀àk PRS do as.if he FUT win game-DEF DEM
       'It seems that Àmɔ̀àk is winning the game.'
       (Hiraiwa 2005b: 549, citing Norris 2003)

A further argument against a bi-clausal treatment brought forth in Hiraiwa (2005b: 549) concerns the absence of a resumptive pronoun in local subject focus, which is unexpected if the subject is extracted from a lower clause. Hence, it is more feasible to regard the focus construction, including verb (phrase) focus, as having a monoclausal structure.

Evidence to the fact that fronting involves Ā-movement is fourfold. First, verb (phrase) fronting can cross finite clause boundaries (122) (but only without intermediate copies), in which case only the base position and the final landing site exhibit an overt realization of the verb. Fronting out of an island like the Complex NP Island (123) or the Wh-Island (124), however, results in ungrammaticality.

(122) (Ká) **dē**-kā   àlī/àtì Àtìm wè:nì [àyīn (ká) (***dē**-kā) àlī/àtì Àmɔ̀àk
       FOC eat-NMLZ C Àtìm said C   FOC   eat-NMLZ C   Àmɔ̀àk
       *(**dè**) mángò   dīēm].
       ate mango(ID) yesterday
       'Àtìm said that it is eating that Àmɔ̀àk ate a mango yesterday.'
       (Hiraiwa 2005b: 551)

(123) *Complex NP Island*
       * (Ká) **dē**-kā   àlī/àtì Àtìm ɲà [núrú-wā:ȳ àlī **dè** mángò].
       FOC eat-NMLZ C   Àtìm saw man-REL C ate mango(ID)
       'It is eating that Àtìm saw the man who ate a mango.'
       (Hiraiwa 2005b: 551)

(124) *Wh-Island*
       * (Ká) **dē**-kā   àlī/àtì Àtìm bègì àyìn [wànà àlī **dè** mángò].
       FOC eat-NMLZ C   Àtìm asked C who C ate mango(ID)
       Lit.: 'It is eating that Àtìm asked if who ate mango.' (Hiraiwa 2005b: 551)

Second, in verb phrase fronting where the object is a pronoun or an anaphor, there are reconstruction effects for condition A (125-a) and condition B (125-b).

(125) a. (Ká) [wà-dĕk$_i$ nāyī]-kā àlī/àtì Àtìm$_i$ nàyì.
 FOC 3SG-self hit-NMLZ C Àtìm hit
 'It is hitting himself$_i$ that Àtìm$_i$ hit.'
 b. * (Ká) [wà$_i$ nāyī]-kā àlī/àtì Àtìm$_i$ nàyì.
 FOC 3SG hit-NMLZ C Àtìm hit
 'It is hitting him$_i$ that Àtìm$_i$ hit.' (Hiraiwa 2005b: 552)

Third, the complementizers *àlī* and *àtì* appearing with verb (phrase) fronting are strongly associated with Ā-movement as they only occur in typical Ā-dependencies, e.g. wh-questions, relativization, and factives (see Hiraiwa 2005a: chap. 7).

And fourth, it is not possible that verb fronting and wh-questioning cooccur in the same clause (126-a) indicating that they both target the same position or involve the same kind of movement, i.e. Ā-movement. Interestingly, this also holds for *in situ* wh-questions where it is usually assumed that an operator undergoes Ā-movement (126-b). The only exception to this is a case where the wh-object is contained within the moved verb phrase (126-c)

(126) a. * (Ká) [dḕ]-kā àlī/àtì Àtìm dè̀ bwà dīem?
 FOC eat-NMLZ C Atim ate what yesterday
 Intended: 'It is eating that Atim ate what yesterday?'
 b. * (Ká) [bwà] àlī/àtì [dḕ]-kā àlī/àtì Àtìm dè̀ dīem?
 FOC what C eat-NMLZ C Atim ate yesterday
 Intended: 'What, it is eating that Atim ate yesterday?'
 c. (Ká) [bwà dḕ]-kā àlī/àtì Àtìm dè̀ dīem?
 FOC what eat-NMLZ C Atim ate yesterday
 'It is eating what that Atim ate yesterday?'
 (Hiraiwa 2005a: 260, fn. 11)

It is therefore safe to conclude that verb (phrase) fronting in Buli involves Ā-movement.

Material that is allowed to appear inside the fronted verb phrase includes objects only (127-a). Adverbials (127-b), subjects (127-c), and prepositional phrases (127-d) are ungrammatical in this position.

(127) a. (Ká) [mángò(-kŭ) dḕ]-kā àlī/àtì Àtìm dè̀ (*mángò-kŭ)
 FOC mango-D eat-NMLZ C Atim ate mango-D
 dīem.
 yesterday
 'It is eating the/a mango that Atim ate yesterday.'

b. * (Ká) [dīem/nwūlī **dɛ̄**]-kā àlī/àtì Àtìm **dè** máng ò-kǔ.
   FOC yesterday/quickly eat-NMLZ C   Atim ate mango-D
   Intended: 'It is eating yesterday/quickly that Atim ate the mango.'
c. * (Ká) [Àtìm **dɛ̄**]-kā àlī/àtì (wà) **dè** máng ò-kǔ dīem.
   FOC Atim eat-NMLZ C   3SG ate mango-D yesterday
   Intended: 'It is Atim's eating that he ate the mango yesterday.'
d. * (Ká) [àlì Àtìm **chēŋ**]-kā àlī/àtì Àmɔ̀ak **chēŋ** Accra dīem.
   FOC with Atim go-NMLZ C   Amoak went Accra yesterday
   Intended: 'It is going with Atim that Amoak went to Accra yesterday.'

(Hiraiwa 2005a: 259f.)

It is equally ungrammatical to front the negation marker *àn* or the progressive aspect auxiliary *bòròa* together with the verb.

(128) a. (Ká) [(*bòrò-à*) **dɛ̄**]-kā àlī/àtì Àtìm bòrò-à **dè** máng ò,
   FOC PROG-PROG eat-NMLZ C   Àtìm PROG-PROG ate mango
   àtì ǹ jàm lǎ.
   C 1SG came DEM
   'When I came, it was eating that Àtìm was eating a mango.'
b. (Ká) [(*àn*) **dɛ̄**]-kā àlī/àtì Àtìm àn **dè** máng ò dīēm.
   FOC NEG eat-NMLZ C   Àtìm NEG ate mango(ID) yesterday
   'It is not eating that Àtìm didn't eat a mango yesterday.'

(Hiraiwa 2005b: 556)

It is difficult to decide whether the fronted verb (phrase) is a VP or a *v*P and if verb fronting actually involves a phrasal rather than a bare head constituent at all. Judging from the fact that PPs, which are usually assumed to adjoin to VP, are not licit in the fronted constituent (127-d) we might assume that what is fronted is even smaller than VP. Furthermore, looking at (127-b), it seems that verb fronting involves just the V head, not a remnant VP, because the low VP-adjoined adverb *nwūlī* 'quickly' cannot accompany the verb. However, there might be an independent constraint underlying the observed restriction here.

Let us consider the nominalization that is obligatory in verbal fronting constructions.[15] There are two things to note about this: The regular VO word order inside a verb phrase is turned into OV and, importantly, the object seems to receive

---

15 As a side remark, it is interesting to note that the nominalizing suffix obligatorily bears a mid tone and varies with the number value of the nominalized element (i).

(i) a. (Ká) nāyī-**kā** àlī/àtì Àtìm nàyì Àmɔ̀ak.
      FOC hit-NMLZ.INDEF.SG C   Atim hit Amoak
      'It is hitting (once) that Atim hit Amoak.'

nominative/genitive instead of accusative case. This becomes apparent when the object is a pronoun like ǹ/mə̄ '1SG' in (129), where it occurs in its accusative form mə̄ when the verb phrase is *in situ* (129-a) whereas its nominative/genitive form ǹ is used when the verb phrase has undergone nominalization (129-b).

(129)   a.   Àtìm pù:sì   *ǹ/mə̄.
              Atim greeted   1SG.NOM,GEN/1SG.ACC
              'Atim greeted me.'
      b.   (Ká) ǹ/*mə̄   pū:sī-tā   àlī/àtì Àtìm pù:sì.
            FOC 1SG.NOM,GEN/1SG.ACC greet-NMLZ.PL C   Atim greeted
            'It is greeting me that Atim greeted.'

(Hiraiwa 2005a: 261, fn. 14)

The object in the fronted verb phrase thus behaves like a nominal that is embedded under another nominal, which also explains the reverse order as the nominal domain in contrast to the clausal/verbal domain in Buli is head-final (Hiraiwa 2005a: 262). The reason for the ungrammaticality of adverbs and prepositional phrases with the fronted verb (phrase) might thus be due to their inability to bear genitive case. If this is on the right track, the behaviour of non-object material in verb (phrase) fronting does not tell as anything about the size of the fronted constituent because this material is independently excluded. We therefore have to remain agnostic as to whether the fronted verb phrase is a VP or a *v*P and whether verb fronting involves a bare head or a remnant verb phrase.

---

      b.   (Ká) nāyī-tā   àlī/àtì Àtìm nàyì Àmɔ̀ak.
            FOC hit-NMLZ.INDEF.PL C   Atim hit   Amoak
            'It is hitting more than once that Atim hit Amoak.'   (Hiraiwa 2005a: 264)

The two nominalizers *ká* and *tá* are segmentally identical to the class III singular marker and the class IV plural marker. However, in contrast to those they cannot mark definiteness since that would require them to be high-toned which is ungrammatical in a fronting construction (ii).

(ii)   a.   (Ká) nāyī-kā/*ká   àlī/àtì Àtìm nàyì Àmɔ̀ak.
            FOC hit-NMLZ.INDEF.SG/NMLZ.DEF.SG C   Atim hit   Amoak
            'It is hitting (once) that Atim hit Amoak.'
      b.   (Ká) nāyī-tā/*tá   àlī/àtì Àtìm nàyì Àmɔ̀ak.
            FOC hit-NMLZ.INDEF.PL/NMLZ.DEF.PL C   Atim hit   Amoak
            'It is hitting more than once that Atim hit Amoak.'   (Hiraiwa 2005a: 265)

Cognate objects

For some languages, like Edo (see section 7.1.3) and Yoruba (see section 8.2.16), it has been argued that verbal fronting constructions derive from underlying cognate object constructions. This neatly explains both the nominal status of the fronted constituent and the fact that there are two tokens of the verb. Buli also disposes of a somewhat productive cognate object construction. The cognate object is usually a root with a plural nominalizing suffix (130-a–d) but may also be a proper noun (130-d). Hiraiwa (2005a: 266) points out that the cognate object may be singular only when no corresponding plural form exists (130-d). The presence of the thematic object of the cognate is dispreferred in many cases (130-a, c).

(130) a. Àtìm **nàyì** (²²Àmɔ̀ak) **nāyī**-²²kā/tā.
Atim hit   Amoak hit-NMLZ.SG/NMLZ.PL
'Atim hit (Amoak). Lit.: Atim hit (Amoak) hittings.'
b. Àtìm **lè**   (Àmɔ̀ak) **lē**:-²²kā/tā.
Atim insulted Amoak insult-NMLZ.SG/NMLZ.PL
'Atim insulted (Amoak). Lit.: Atim insulted (Amoak) insults.'
c. Àtìm **pùːsì**   (²Àmɔ̀ak) **pūːsī**-²²kā/sā/²²k.
Atim greeted   Amoak greet-NMLZ.SG/NMLZ.PL/SG
'Atim greeted (Amoak). Lit.: Atim greeted (Amoak) greetings.'
d. Wà **zù**   **zùm/zū**-kā/²²tā.
3SG stole theft(ID.SG)/steal-NMLZ.SG/NMLZ.PL
'He carried out a theft.'   (Hiraiwa 2005a: 266)

One might propose to derive verbal fronting from the constructions in (130) by simply moving the cognate object into the left periphery (i.e. SpecCP). This, however, cannot be the case for four main reasons. First, besides the option of fronting the cognate object like a normal NP (131-b) it is possible to have verb fronting while a cognate object appears in its regular position (131-c). We would expect this to be blocked if verbal fronting were indeed movement of the cognate object.

(131) a. Àtìm pùːsì   pūːs-ā.
Atim greeted greeting-ID.PL
'Atim greeted greetings.'
b. (Ká) **pūːs**-ā   àlī/àtì Àtìm **pùːsì**.
FOC greeting-ID.PL C   Atim greeted
'It is greetings that Atim greeted.'
c. (Ká) **pūːsī**-kā   àlī/àtì Àtìm **pùːsì**   pūːs-ā.
FOC greet-NMLZ.SG C   Atim greeted greeting-ID.PL
'It is greeting that Atim greeted.'   (Hiraiwa 2005a: 267)

Second, objects in Buli do not have to move for focus as in (132-a). It is also possible to mark them with a focus particle *in situ* (132-b). The interpretation remains the same.

(132) a. (Ká) *mángò-kú-lá* àlī/àtì Àtìm dɛ̀ (*mángò-kú-lá/*kù) dīēm.
 FOC mango-DEF-DEM C Àtìm ate mango-DEF-DEM/3SG
 yesterday
 'It is that mango that Àtìm ate yesterday.'
 b. Àtìm dɛ̀ *ká mángò-kú-lá* dīēm.
 Àtìm ate FOC mango-DEF-DEM yesterday
 'It is that mango that Àtìm ate yesterday.' (Hiraiwa 2005b: 546)

Hiraiwa (2005a: 267) mentions that this is not the case for verb fronting and cognate object constructions, that is, the purported cognate object base construction and the derived verb fronting construction cannot have the same interpretation when a focus marker appears on both. While in (133-b) the contrast is between an eating event and some other event, it is between 'eat eating' and 'eat X-ing' in (133-a) which is therefore ungrammatical.

(133) a. *Àtìm **dɛ̀** ká **dē**-kā/tā.
 Atim ate FOC eat-NMLZ.SG/NMLZ.PL
 'Atim ate.'
 b. (Ká) **dē**-kā/tā àlī/àtì Àtìm **dɛ̀**.
 FOC eat-NMLZ.SG/NMLZ.PL C Atim ate
 'It is eating/eatings that Atim ate.' (Hiraiwa 2005a: 268)

Third, as mentioned above, cognate objects strongly prefer to be plural marked independently of whether they are interpreted as singular or plural (134-a). Their morphological marking thus does not depend on their semantics. Fronted verbs or verb phrases, in contrast, may take either singular or plural marking based on the interpretation that they receive (134-b). If verbal fronting constructions were derived by movement of cognate objects, we would expect the fronted constituent to be plural marked no matter whether it is semantically singular or plural, contrary to fact.

(134) a. Àtìm nàɣì nāɣī-??**kā/tā**.
 Atim hit hit-NMLZ.SG/NMLZ.PL
 'Atim hit. Lit.: Atim hit hittings.'
 b. (Ká) nāɣī-**kā/tā** àlī/àtì Àtìm nāɣī Àmɔ̀ak.
 FOC hit-NMLZ.SG/NMLZ.PL C Atim hit Amoak
 'It is hitting/hittings that Atim hit Amoak.' (Hiraiwa 2005a: 268)

Finally, while thematic direct objects in cognate object constructions usually show quite a low acceptability that varies with different verbs (135-a), their presence in verbal fronting constructions is perfectly grammatical (135-b, c). If verbal fronting were derived from cognate object constructions we would expect direct objects to be equally marginal in the former as they are in the latter.

(135)   a.   Àtìm **nàyì** (?/?? *Àmɔak*) **nāyī**-?? kā/tā.
            Atim hit   Amoak hit-NMLZ.SG/NMLZ.PL
            'Atim hit (Amoak). Lit.: Atim hit (Amoak) hittings.'
       b.   (Ká) [*Àmɔak* **nāyī**-kā/tā]   àlī/àtì Àtìm **nāyī**.
            FOC Amoak hit-NMLZ.SG/NMLZ.PL C   Atim hit
            'It is hitting Amoak that Atim hit.'
       c.   (Ká) **nāyī**-kā/tā   àlī/àtì Àtìm **nāyī** *Àmɔak*.
            FOC hit-NMLZ.SG/NMLZ.PL C   Atim hit   Amoak
            'It is hitting that Atim hit Amoak.'   (Hiraiwa 2005a: 268)

In conclusion, it is implausible that verbal fronting in Buli is the result of moving the cognate object into sentence-initial position.

Summary

Buli shows both verb and verb phrase fronting for contrastive focus with a dummy verb occurring in the clause-internal verb position. It has been demonstrated that these constructions are monoclausal despite the fact that the initial focus marker is homophonous with the copula. Verbal fronting may cross finite clause boundaries and is sensitive to islands. In addition, a special complementizer *àlī/àtì* that is associated with Ā-movement is used. Only objects may appear inside the fronted constituent, other material like adverbials, PPs, negation, or TAM-markers are precluded from this position. The fronted constituent is obligatorily nominalized but cannot be a cognate object that has simply been moved to the left periphery. The relevant properties are listed in table 8.6. In total, Buli verbal fronting fits pattern I of Generalization I, as it shows verb and verb phrase fronting with a symmetric verb doubling repair.

Tab. 8.6: Properties of verbal fronting in Buli

	Copy	Dummy	Unbound	Islands	GS	TAM	L-Adv	H-Adv	Neg	L/R	Top/Foc
V	✓	–	✓	✓	n.d.	–	–	–	–	L	Foc
VP	✓	–	✓	✓	n.d.	–	–	–	–	L	Foc

8.2.3 Dagaare

Dagaare, a Gur language of the Niger-Congo phylum, is spoken by about 900 000 speakers in Northwestern Ghana. Its basic neutral word order is SVO (136).

(136)   Ǹ dà dá lá bóɔ́.
        1SG PST buy FOC goat
        'I bought a goat.'   (Hiraiwa & Bodomo 2008: 802)

The particle *lá* glossed as FOC in (136) is multi-functional but its exact functions are still unclear. It predominantly indicates focus and assertion and is obligatory in matrix declarative clauses (Hiraiwa & Bodomo 2008: 802). Furthermore, a clause may only contain one instance of it. As it disappears under negation (137), Hiraiwa & Bodomo (2008) assume that it occupies a low focus head inside the *v*P.

(137)   Ǹ dà bá dà (*lá) bóɔ́.
        1SG PST NEG buy FOC goat
        'I did not buy a goat.'   (Hiraiwa & Bodomo 2008: 802)

It must also be absent from its low position in Ā-construction (Hiraiwa & Bodomo 2008: 800, fn. 2) where a higher focus head that follows the moved constituent instead of a *v*P-internal one is realized by *lá* (138).

(138)   Bòng lá ká fó dà dà (*lá)?
        what FOC C 2SG PST buy FOC
        'What did you buy?'   (Hiraiwa & Bodomo 2008: 802)

In (138) and similar constructions, *lá* cannot have moved from its base position into the higher position. First, as evidenced by (139), it also occurs in nominal focus (139-b) and wh-constructions (139-c) even when the underlying sentence is negative (139-a) and therefore does not contain a lower instance of *lá*.

(139)   a. Ǹ dà bá dà (*lá) bóɔ́.
            1SG PST NEG buy FOC goat
            'I did not buy a goat.'
        b. Bóɔ́ lá ká ǹ dà bá dà (*lá).
            goat FOC C 1SG PST NEG buy FOC
            'It is a goat that I did not buy.'
        c. Bòng lá ká fó dà bá dà (*lá)?
            what FOC C 2SG PST NEG buy FOC
            'What did you not buy?'   (Hiraiwa & Bodomo 2008: 802f.)

Second, the higher *lá* is ungrammatical in relative clauses (unlike in wh/focus constructions) even though the lower *lá* has disappeared (140-b).

(140) a. Dàkóráá sέ   lá   nɛ́nὲ.
           Dàkóráá roast FOC meat
           'Dàkóráá roasted meat.'
       b. À   nɛ́nὲ (*lá) Dàkóráá náng sέ   (*lá).
           DEF meat FOC Dàkóráá C   roast FOC
           'the meat that Dàkóráá roasted.'   (Hiraiwa & Bodomo 2008: 803)

In Dagaare, it is possible to contrastively focus a verb (141-a) or a verb phrase (141-b) by placing it in the sentence-initial position followed by the focus marker *lá*. A copy of the displaced verb then occurs in the clause-internal verb position. The contrast falls on the verb only in (141-a) while it comprises the verb and its object in (141-b).

(141) a. **Dááó**   lá   ká ń   dà **dà** bóɔ́.
           buy.NMLZ FOC C   1SG PST buy goat
           'It is buying that I did to a goat (as opposed to e.g. selling it).'
                                                  (Hiraiwa & Bodomo 2008: 803)
       b. [Bóɔ́ **dááó**]   lá   ká ń   dà **dà**   (*ò/*bóɔ́).
           goat buy.NMLZ FOC C   1SG PST buy   it/goat
           'It is buying a goat that I did (as opposed to e.g. selling a hen).'
                                                  (Hiraiwa & Bodomo 2008: 805)

The fronted verb phrase in (141-b) shows the reverse word order OV compared to the order VO in which it occurs *in situ*. This reversal cannot be due to incorporation of the object into the verb. Although only noun phrases may accompany the verb inside the fronted verb phrase (Hiraiwa & Bodomo 2008: 804, fn. 4) these show properties that are not attested in proper incorporation structures. There is no size restriction on the object noun phrase and modification with determiners and demonstratives is allowed (142) (Hiraiwa & Bodomo 2008: 805).

(142) [À   bóɔ́/bó-vèlàà   ná **dááó**]   lá   ká ń   (dà) **dà**.
       DEF goat/goat-good DEM buy.NMLZ FOC C   1SG   PST buy
       'It is buying that (good) goat that I did.'
                                                  (Hiraiwa & Bodomo 2008: 805)

Moreover, verb phrase fronting cannot be treated as multiple focalisation either. As shown in (143), the two constituents *sòɔ́* 'knife' and *nɛ́nὲ* 'meat' are not tolerated in the focus position. It may only contain one constituent, meaning that the fronted verb and object in verb phrase fronting are actually a single phrasal constituent.

(143) *[À sòɔ́]₁ [nɛ́nɛ̀]₂ lá ká ó dé ___₁ ___₂ ngmàà.
      DEF knife meat FOC C 3SG take.PFV cut
      'It is the knife, meat that he took and cut.'
                                              (Hiraiwa & Bodomo 2008: 805)

Turning to the Ā-properties of verb fronting we find that it may cross finite clause boundaries (144).

(144) **Dááó** lá kà Dàkóráá bɔ̀ng [ká ń dà **dá** lá bóɔ́].
      buy.NMLZ FOC C Dàkóráá know C 1SG PST buy FOC goat
      'It is buying that Dàkóráá knows that I did to a goat (as opposed to e.g. selling it).'   (Hiraiwa & Bodomo 2008: 804)

With regard to islands, Hiraiwa & Bodomo (2008: 804) mention that verbal fronting "out of an island shows strong ungrammaticality". They do not, however, provide examples that demonstrate this.

In contrast to Fongbe (see section 7.1.5) and Haitian Creole (see section 7.1.7), it is possible to front individual-level predicates in addition to stage-level predicates, as shown for the two individual-level verbs *nɔ̌ng* 'like' and *bɔ̌ng* 'know' in (145).

(145) a. **Nɔ́ngóó** lá kà Dàkóráá **nɔ̀ng** ò bâ.
         like.NMLZ FOC C Dakoraa like 3SG father
         'It is liking that Dakoraa does to his father (as opposed to e.g. being afraid of him).'
      b. **Bɔ́ngóó** lá kà ń **bɔ̀ng** Dàkóráá.
         know.NMLZ FOC C 1SG know Dakoraa
         'It is knowing that I do to Dakoraa (as opposed to e.g. hearing about him before).'   (Hiraiwa & Bodomo 2008: 804)

Summary

Dagaare exhibits both verb and verb phrase fronting which cause a verb copy to appear in the clause-internal verb position. In verb phrase fronting the word order inside the VP is reversed with no indication of incorporation or multiple fronting. The fronted constituent is nominalized and may be modified like other nominals, i.e. by determiners and adjectives. Verbal fronting shows Ā-properties in being unbounded but illicit out of an island. There is no restriction on the semantic class of the verbs that can appear in fronted position, both stage-level and individual-level predicates are allowed. Table 8.7 provides an overview. In conclusion, Dagaare verb and verb phrase fronting show pattern I of Generalization I, namely symmetric verb doubling.

Tab. 8.7: Properties of verbal fronting in Dagaare

	Copy	Dummy	Unbound	Islands	GS	TAM	L-Adv	H-Adv	Neg	L/R	Top/Foc
V	✓	–	✓	✓	n.d.	n.d.	n.d.	n.d.	n.d.	L	Foc
VP	✓	–	✓	✓	n.d.	n.d.	n.d.	n.d.	n.d.	L	Foc

8.2.4 Hebrew

Hebrew, a Semitic language of the Nilo-Saharan phylum, is spoken by approximately five million speakers predominantly in Israel. Its basic word order is SVO (Berman 1980: 1).

The language disposes of both verb (146-a) and verb phrase fronting (146-b). In both cases, a copy of the verb occupies the base position inside the clause. The fronted constituent is usually interpreted as a topic or a contrastive focus (see Ziv 1997). According to Landau (2006, 2007), both interpretations involve a meaning of the fronted constituent that is already present in the discourse: either the meaning of the constituent itself or some set of alternative meanings with which a contrast is established.

(146) a. **Liknot** hi **kanta** et ha-praxim.
         buy.INF she bought ACC the-flowers
         'As for buying, she bought the flowers.'
    b. [**Liknot** et ha-praxim] hi **kanta**.
         buy.INF ACC the-flowers she bought
         'As for buying the flowers, she bought.' (Landau 2006: 37)

The verb in the fronted constituent appears in the infinitive while the verb copy inside the clause is fully inflected.

The verb *lihyot* 'to be' is used as an auxiliary and as the copula in Hebrew. In its use as an auxiliary, it may not undergo verb fronting (147-a) (but note that verb phrase fronting is fine (147-b)) while verb fronting is grammatical in its use as a locative copula (148).

(147) a. *****Lihyot**, Gil lo tamid **haya** zamin.
         be.INF Gil not always was available
         'As for being, Gil wasn't always available.'
    b. [**Lihyot** zamin], Gil lo tamid **haya**.
         be.INF available Gil not always was
         'As for being available, Gil wasn't always.' (Landau 2006: 41)

(148) **Lihyot**, Gil **haya** be-nyu york (aval rak xaci yom).
be.INF Gil was in-New York but only half day
'As for being, Gil *was* in New York, but only for half a day.'

(Landau 2006: 41)

When trying to front a verb phrase from a position under an infinitive embedding verb like *kiva* 'hoped' there is no verb doubling or dummy verb insertion observed (149). In this regard, Hebrew behaves like many other languages such as Polish (see section 8.2.10) or German (see section 8.1.4).

(149) [**Liknot** et ha-sefer]$_1$ Dan kiva ___$_1$.
buy.INF ACC the-book Dan hoped
'As for buying the book, Dan hoped to (do it).' (Trinh 2011: 32)

In contrast to Polish and German, however, verb fronting from the same position results in verb doubling rather than a gap (150).

(150) **Liknot** Dan kiva **liknot** et ha-sefer.
buy.INF Dan hoped buy.INF ACC the-book
'As for buying, Dan hoped to buy the book.' (Trinh 2011: 32)

This behaviour is predicted under the system developed in this book. Contrary to verb fronting in German and Polish, Hebrew verb fronting does not involve remnant movement but $\bar{\text{A}}$-head movement. As the lowest copy of this latter type of movement never undergoes copy deletion it does not matter that V-to-T movement for finiteness cannot take place in (150) (either because *kiva* occupies T or because *kiva* embeds a non-finite TP). The lowest copy of V will be pronounced anyway thereby giving rise to verb doubling. With intransitive verbs, this analysis predicts that we should find optional verb doubling because intransitive verb fronting is ambiguous between $\bar{\text{A}}$-head movement (which results in verb doubling) or phrasal movement of a complete VP (which leads to a gap). Indeed, Hebrew shows such an optionality (151).

(151) **Lalexet** Dan kiva (**lalexet**).
walk.INF Dan hoped walk.INF
'As for walking, Dan hoped to walk.' (Trinh 2011: 39)

The Hebrew data thus support the analysis presented in chapter 4.
There does not seem to be a restriction on the semantic class of verbs that can undergo fronting. However, as in Yiddish (see section 8.2.15) and Polish (see section 8.2.10), a condition on partial verb phrase fronting holds on double-object verbs. Take DP-PP verbs as an illustration. For a subset of these verbs including

le'hagis 'to submit', it is possible to front [V-DP] stranding PP (152-a) but impossible to do the reverse, i.e. front [V-PP] stranding DP (152-b).

(152) a. [**Le'hagis** et ha-ma'amar], hu **higiš** le-ktav-ha-et
 submit.INF ACC the-article he submitted to-the-journal
 lifney ha-dedlyne.
 before the-deadline
 'Submit the article to the journal, he did before the deadline.'
 b. *[**Le'hagis** le-ktav-ha-et], hu **higiš** et ha-ma'amar lifney
 submit.INF to-the-journal he submitted ACC the-article before
 ha-dedlyne.
 the-deadline (Landau 2007: 131)

For another subset of DP-PP verbs including *lixtov* 'to write', however, both options are grammatical (153).

(153) a. [**Lixtov** mixtavim xosfaniyim], hi **katva** le-Gil.
 write.INF letters revealing she wrote to-Gil
 b. [**Lixtov** le-Gil], hi **katva** mixtavim xosfaniyim.
 write.INF to-Gil she wrote letters revealing
 'Write revealing letters to Gil, she did.' (Landau 2007: 132)

As Landau (2007: 133) observes, the property of individual verbs to allow partial verb phrase fronting with only one or both of its arguments correlates with another property. Under the right circumstances, one of the two arguments of a double-object verb may be dropped. While for one set of verbs this option is only available for one argument (154), with another set of verbs both arguments may be dropped (154).

(154) a. Gil raca [le'hagiš et ha-ma'amar].
 Gil wanted submit.INF ACC the-article
 'Gil wanted to submit the article.'
 b. *Gil raca [le'hagiš le-ktav-ha-et].
 Gil wanted submit.INF to-the-journal
 'Gil wanted to submit to the journal.' (Landau 2007: 133)

(155) a. Hi nista [lixtov mixtavim xosfaniyim].
 she tried write.INF letter revealing
 'She tried to write revealing letters.'
 b. Hi nista [lixtov le-Gil].
 she tried write.INF to-Gil
 'She tried to write to Gil.' (Landau 2007: 134)

Crucially, those verb-argument combinations which are not allowed to appear without the second argument (154-b) are also those which are not allowed to occupy the sentence-initial position in a fronting construction (152-b). The condition as formulated by Landau (2007) is given in (156).

(156) *Condition on fronted VP-portions* (Landau 2007: 134)
[[V Arg$_1$]...Subject...Arg$_2$] is grammatical iff [Subject...[$_{VP}$ V Arg$_1$]...] is grammatical (i.e., if Arg$_2$ may be dropped independently).

A further restriction concerns the fronting of idiomatic verb-argument combinations such as *litfos taxat* 'to act arrogantly' (lit. 'to grab ass'). While the idiomatic interpretation is generally retained with verb phrase fronting (157-a), verb fronting, which splits the verb from its internal argument, destroys the idiomatic reading and coerces a literal interpretation (157-b), which might lead to ungrammaticality of the sentence.

(157) a. Gil omnam xadaš po, aval [**litfos** *taxat*] hu kvar
   Gil although new here but grab.INF ass he already
   tafas.
   grabbed
   'Although new here, Gil already acted arrogantly.'
   b. *Gil omnam xadaš po, aval **litfos** hu kvar **tafas**
   Gil although new here but grab.INF he already grabbed
   taxat.
   ass   (Landau 2006: 41)

Turning to the evidence for Ā-movement, we find that Hebrew verbal fronting is able to cross finite clause boundaries with bridge verbs (158), (159) but not with non-bridge verbs (160).

(158) a. **La'azor,** eyn li safek [še-Gil hivtiax [še-hu
   help.INF there.isn't to.me doubt that-Gil promised that-he
   ya'azor le-Rina]].
   will.help to-Rina
   'As for helping, I have no doubt that Gil promised he would help Rina.'
   b. [**La'azor** le-Rina], eyn li safek [še-Gil hivtiax
   help.INF to-Rina there.isn't to.me doubt that-Gil promised
   [še-hu **ya'azor**]].
   that-he will.help
   'As for helping Rina, I have no doubt that Gil promised he would help.'
                                                    (Landau 2006: 42)

(159) a. **Le-nakot,** nidme li   [še-Rina amra [še-Gil kvar
            clean.INF seems to.me that-Rina said   that-Gil already
            nika   et   ha-xacer]].
            cleaned ACC the-yard
            'As for cleaning, it seems to me that Rina said that Gil had already cleaned the yard.'
       b. [**Le-nakot** et   ha-xacer], nidme li   [še-Rina amra [še-Gil
            clean.INF ACC the-yard   seems to.me that-Rina said   that-Gil
            kvar   **nika**]].
            already cleaned
            'As for cleaning the yard, it seems to me that Rina said that Gil had already cleaned.' (Landau 2006: 42)

(160) a. ***Le'hacbia,** Gil laxaš/hitcta'er   [še-Rina   kvar   **hicbia**
            vote.INF   Gil whipsered/regretted that-Rina already voted
            la-avoda].
            to-the-Labor
            'As for voting, Gil whispered/regretted that Rin ahad already voted to the Labor party.'
       b. *[**Le'hacbia** la-avoda], Gil laxaš/hitcta'er   [še-Rina
            vote.INF   to-the-Labor Gil whispered/regretted that-Rina
            kvar   **hicbia**].
            already voted
            'As for voting to the Labor part, Gil whispered/regretted that Rina had already voted.' (Landau 2006: 44)

Furthermore, it is sensitive to islands like the Complex NP Island (161), the Wh-Island (162), the Subject Island (163), or the Adjunct Island (164).

(161) *Complex NP Island*
       a. ***Likro** Gil daxa   [et ha-te'ana še-hu kvar   **kara** et
            read.INF Gil rejected ACC the-claim that-he already read ACC
            ha-sefer].
            the-book
            'As for reading, Gil rejected the claim that he had already read the book.'
       b. *[**Likro**   et   ha-sefer] Gil daxa   [et ha-te'ana še-hu
            read.INF ACC the-book Gil rejected ACC the-claim that-he
            kvar   **kara**].
            already read
            'As for reading the book, Gil rejected the claim that he had already read.' (Landau 2006: 43)

(162) *Wh-Island*
    a. ??**Likro** ša'alti [matay Gil kvar **kara** et ha-sefer].
        read.INF asked.1SG when Gil already read ACC the-book
        'As for reading, I asked when Gil had already read the book.'
    b. ??[**Likro** et ha-sefer] ša'alti [matay Gil kvar **kara**].
        read.INF ACC the-book asked.1SG when Gil already read
        'As for reading the book, I asked when Gil had already read.'
                                            (Landau 2006: 43)

(163) *Subject Island*
    a. *****Likro** [še-yevakšu me-Gil še-**yikra** et
        read.INF that-will-ask.3PL from-Gil that-will-read.3SG ACC
        ha-sefer] ze ma'aliv.
        the-book it insulting
        'As for reading, that they would ask Gil to read the book is insulting.'
    b. *[**Likro** et ha-sefer] [še-yevakšu me-Gil
        read.INF ACC the-book that-will-ask.3PL from-Gil
        še-**yikra**] ze ma'aliv.
        that-will-read.3SG it insulting
        'As for reading the book, that they would ask Gil to is insulting.'
                                            (Landau 2006: 43)

(164) *Adjunct Island*
    a. *****Likro** nifgašnu [axarey še-kulam **kar'u** et
        read.INF met.1PL after that-everybody read.3PL ACC
        ha-sefer].
        the-book
        'As for reading, we have met after everybody read the book.'
    b. *[**Likro** et ha-sefer] nifgašnu [axarey še-kulam
        read.INF ACC the-book met.1PL after that-everybody
        kar'u].
        read.3PL
        'As for reading the book, we have met after everybody read.'
                                            (Landau 2006: 44)

An additional indication that verbal fronting indeed involves movement rather than base generation is presented by the absence of any genus-species effects (165).

(165)   a. *[**Le'exol** *dagim*] Rina xoševet še'ani **oxel** *salmon*.
            eat.INF fish Rina thinks that-I eat salmon
            'As for eating fish, Rina thinks that I eat salmon.'

b. *[**Letayel** *le-amerika*] **tasti** *le-nyu york.*
   travel.INF to-America I-flew to-New York
   'As for travelling to America, I have flown to New York.'

(Landau 2006: 45)

Let us now consider which kind of elements may accompany the verb (phrase) in the clause-initial position. We find that negation and sentential adverbs like *tamid* 'always' lead to ungrammaticality when fronted together with a verb phrase (166-b).

(166) a. [**Le'horid** et ha-maym] Gil *lo tamid* **morid**.
         flush.INF ACC the-water Gil not always flushes
         'As for flushing the toilet, Gil doesn't always flush.'
      b. [(*Lo*) (*tamid*) **le'horid** et ha-maym] Gil **morid**.
         not always) flush.INF ACC the-water Gil flushes

(Landau 2006: 38)

They may only occur in this position if the constituent that is fronted is a whole clause which was embedded under a control predicate, for example (167). In those cases, however, no doubling is involved.

(167) [(Lo) (tamid) le'horid et ha-maym]₁ Gil hištadel ___₁.
      not always flush.INF ACC the-water Gil tried
      'To (not) (always) flush the toilet, Gil tried.' (Landau 2006: 38)

The data above indicate that the constituent that is fronted in verb phrase fronting is not bigger than a *v*P. Landau (2006) argues that it is also not smaller than a *v*P. The Hebrew verb system, as in many Semitic languages, derives verb froms by combining a usually triconsonantal root with a specific vowel pattern called *binyan*. While the root is assumed to be hosted in V, the vowel pattern has been argued to reside in *v* such that a full verb form is created by movement of V to *v* (Arad 1999, Doron 2003). Infinitives, as they occur in the verbal fronting constructions, are formed by adding the prefix *li-/le-/la-* to a verb form that already appears in a specific *binyan*. The list in (168) shows a few such infinitives derived from the root [s,r,k] plus different *binyans*.

(168) *Infinitival verbs from the root [s,r,k]* (Landau 2006: 47)

a.	*li-srok*	'to scan'
b.	*le-hisarek*	'to be scanned'
c.	*le-sarek*	'to comb'
d.	*le-histarek*	'to comb oneself'

Thus, as the fronted verb occurs in such an infinitive form and therefore has been combined with a *binyan*, the *v* head needs to be included in the fronted constituent.

With regard to the question whether what is fronted in verb fronting is a remnant *v*P or a bare (complex V+*v*) head, Landau (2006: 51) argues that the former is not plausible in Hebrew. There is no independent evidence for any kind of verb phrase evacuating movement like scrambling or Object Shift. Moreover, if such a movement were involved in verb fronting, we would possibly expect restrictions on the kind of element that this movement can apply to and, therefore, on the kind of element that can be stranded by verb fronting. However, even PPs (169-a) and secondary predicates (169-b) can be stranded, which are commonly precluded from scrambling.

(169) a. **Le'hitxabe** Gil **hitxabe** *me'axorey ha-aron*.
hide.INF Gil hid behind the-closet
'As for hiding, Gil hid behind the closet.'
b. **Lecalem** et Gil Rina **cilma** *be-erom*.
photograph.INF ACC Gil Rina photographed in-nude
'As for photographing Gil, Rina photographed in nude.' (Gil or Rina is nude.) (Landau 2006: 51)

The fronted constituent in verb fronting constructions, as Landau (2006) follows, must hence be a complex V+*v* head. In turn, this means that Hebrew comprises of a type of Ā-head movement.

Summary

To summarize, Hebrew exhibits verb and verb phrase fronting, both of which trigger the presence of a copy of the displaced verb in its canonical position. The fronted constituent is interpreted as a topic or a contrastive focus and needs to contain the infinitive form of the verb. Verb phrase fronting further adheres to the condition on partial VP-fronting (Landau 2007: 134). Verbal fronting exhibits typical Ā-properties as it crosses finite clause boundaries and is sensitive to islands. Genus-species effects are unattested. The fronted constituent must be a *v*P because negation and sentential adverbs may not accompany the verb (phrase) in clause-initial position but the verb appears in a specific vowel pattern which associated with *v*. Verb fronting most plausibly involves Ā-head movement rather than remnant verb phrase movement since there is no evidence for remnant-creating movements. Table 8.8 gives an overview over the relevant findings. Thus, Hebrew verbal fronting instantiates pattern I of Generalization I, that is, symmetric verb doubling.

Tab. 8.8: Properties of verbal fronting in Hebrew

	Copy	Dummy	Unbound	Islands	GS	TAM	L-Adv	H-Adv	Neg	L/R	Top/Foc
V	✓	–	✓	✓	–	–	n.d.	–	–	L	Top/Foc
VP	✓	–	✓	✓	–	–	n.d.	–	–	L	Top/Foc

8.2.5 Hungarian

Hungarian, a Uralic language, is spoken by about 13 million people in Hungary and neighbouring countries.

The language shows verb fronting as in (170), where an infinitival form of the verb occurs sentence-initially while its base position inside the clause is realized by a finite copy of the same verb. As we see comparing (170-a) to (170-b), the position of the finite verb with respect to the subject may vary. The same construction is shown in (171) with a transitive verb.

(170) a. **Énekelni énekelt** Mari.
         sing.INF sang   Mari
     b. **Énekelni** Mari **énekelt**.
         sing.INF Mari sang
         'As far as singing is concerned, Mari did sing yesterday (...but she did not play the piano, for example).'

         (Lipták & Vicente 2009: 652)

(171) **Elolvasni elolvasta** a Hamletet Kristóf.
      PV-read-INF PV-read the Hamlet-ACC Kristóf
      'As far as reading is concerned, Kristóf did read Hamlet (...but he did not write a review about it).'   (Lipták & Vicente 2009: 652)

Commonly, the fronted constituent is interpreted as a contrastve topic and triggers an adversative continuation.

The situation with verb phrase fronting is somewhat difficult. According to Ürögdi (2006: 297), post-head modifiers are not allowed inside the fronted constituent (172-a), but pre-head modifiers are (172-b). There is always a copy of the pre-head modifier inside the clause and the word order is the same in both the fronted constituent and its copy inside the clause. Since OV is not the basic word order in Hungarian, Ürögdi (2006) concludes that the object has moved into a predicate-modifier position immediately left-adjacent to the predicate.

(172) a. *[**Venni** virágot] (virágot) **vett** (virágot)...
         buy.INF flower.ACC (flower.ACC) bought (flower.ACC)

b. [Virágot **venni**] virágot **vett**...
    flower.ACC buy.INF flower.ACC bought
    'As for buying flowers, that's what he did (but I don't know where he did that).' (Ürögdi 2006: 317)

This position may also be filled by adverbs (173-a, b). As evidenced by (173-c), whenever the predicate-modifier position is filled, the relevant element occupying it must be fronted with the verb. Fronting of the verb alone leads to ungrammaticality.

(173) a. [*Haza* **men-ni**] *haza* **ment** (de nem tudott auldni).
         home go-INF home went but not could sleep
         'He did go home but he couldn't fall asleep.'
      b. [*Jól* **ír-ni**] *jól* **ír** (de nincs benne
         well write-INF well he.writes but there.isn't in.him
         önfegyelem).
         dicipline
         'He does write well, but he doesn't have any discipline.'
         (Ürögdi 2006: 298)
      c. *****Men-ni** haza-**mentem** (de már nem maradt időm
         go-INF home-I.went but already not remained time.mine
         pihenni).
         rest.INF
         'I did go home, but I didn't have any time left to rest.'
         (Ürögdi 2006: 316)

In contrast, Lipták & Vicente (2009: 652) state that no material may front together with the verb independent of whether it precedes or follows the verb in base position (174).

(174) a. *[Moziba **menni**], moziba **ment** tegnap Péter.
         cinema.INTO go.INF cinema.INTO went yesterday Peter
      b. *[Moziba **menni**], **ment** moziba tegnap Péter.
         cinema.INTO go.INF went cinema.INTO yesterday Peter
         Intended: 'As far as going to the cinema is concerned, Peter went to the cinema yesterday.' (Lipták & Vicente 2009: 652, fn. 2)

The data are therefore inconclusive with regard to the question whether Hungarian does or does not comprise of verb phrase fronting and further research needs to be done.

Turning to the $\bar{\text{A}}$-properties of the construction, it is evident from (175-a) that predicate fronting may cross finite clause boundaries embedded under a bridge verb. This is not possible when the embedding predicate forms a factive island

(175-b). Unfortunately, Ürögdi (2006) does not provide examples with a fronted verb, only with fronted adjectival predicates. However, I assume that the underlying fronting construction is the same for both verbal and adjectival predicates and that they therefore show the same restrictions.

(175) a. **Bátor**-nak azt   hiszem/tudom   [hogy **bátor** volt].
        brave-DAT that-ACC I.believe/I.know COMP brave was
        'As for brave, I believe/know he was. (But he still didn't become a good soldier.)'
    b. *__Beteg__-nek sajnálom [hogy **beteg** volt].
        sick-DAT I.regret COMP sick was
        'I do regret that he was sick. (But I'm still not sorry he didn't come to the party.)'   (Ürögdi 2006: 314)

Further, the fronting seems to respect at least the Wh-Island (176) and the Coordinate Structure Constraint (177). I was unable to find any data for other islands in the literature.

(176) *Wh-Island*
    ??**Beteg-nek** meg-kérdeztem [hogy mikor volt **beteg** utoljára].
    sick-DAT I-asked COMP when was sick last
    'As for being sick, I asked him when he was last sick. (But I forgot to ask whether he took sick leave that time.)'   (Ürögdi 2006: 314)

(177) *Coordinate Structure Constraint*
    *__Szép-nek__ [**szép** és okos] volt (de...).
    pretty-DAT pretty and smart was but
    'As for being pretty, she was pretty and smart (but...)' (Ürögdi 2006: 314)

More evidence in favour of Ā-movement over base-generation is the absence of any genus-species effects (178).

(178) *__Szép-nek gyönyörű__ volt nekem mégsem tetszett.
    pretty-DAT beautiful was me still.not appealed
    'As for being pretty, she was beautifull, but I still didn't like her.'
                                (Ürögdi 2006: 315)

Summary

At this point, all that can be said is that Hungarian has verb fronting and possibly also verb phrase fronting, both of which trigger the presence of a copy of the displaced verb (and of the displaced object) in base position. The fronted verb appears in the infinitive and is interpreted as a contrastive topic. (Low) adverbs may be fronted together with the verb. The dependency between the sentence-initial verbal constituent and its clause-internal copy shows properties of an Ā-dependency: It is unbounded and is sensitive to island conditions. Further, there are no genus-species effects, which would favour a base-generation approach. The relevant properties are given in table 8.9. Thus far, Hungarian verbal fronting presents a case of the symmetric verb doubling pattern I of Generalization I, given that verb phrase fronting is in fact consistently available.

Tab. 8.9: Properties of verbal fronting in Hungarian

	Copy	Dummy	Unbound	Islands	GS	TAM	L-Adv	H-Adv	NEG	L/R	Top/Foc
V	✓	–	✓	✓[16]	–	n.d.	✓	n.d.	n.d.	L	Top
VP	(✓)[17]	–	n.d.	n.d.	n.d.	n.d.	n.d.	n.d.	n.d.	L	Top

8.2.6 Korean

Korean, a member of the Koreanic language family, is spoken by between 50 and 70 millions people in the Korean peninsula and neighbouring parts of China. Its basic word order is SOV (179).

(179) John-i Mary-lul manna-ss-ta.
John-NOM Mary-ACC meet-PST-DECL
'John met Mary.' (Choi 2000: 333)

The language shows both verb (180-a, b)[18] and verb phrase fronting (180-c, d) both of which result in a copy of the displaced verb in sentence-final position.

---

16 Attested islands include the Wh-Island and the Coordinate Structure Constraint.
17 It is unclear whether Hungarian consistently allows verb phrase fronting. Data are inconclusive on that matter. However, if it is possible, it also exhibits verb doubling, not dummy verb insertion.
18 Cho & Kim (2002) judge verb fronting to be ungrammatical (i).

(i) *(Cacwu) manna-ki-nun John-i Tom-ul manna-ass-ta.
often meet-NMLZ-TOP John-NOM Tom-ACC meet-PST-DECL (Cho & Kim 2002: 665)

The above example differs from those given by Hagstrom (1995) and Jo (2000) only in the animacy of the direct object. It might be the case that verb fronting is somehow influenced by this property of the object. A more likely explanation, in my opinion, is that the availability of verb fronting is simply subject to dialectal variation and/or peer pressure as to what is considered proper Korean.

(180) a. **Ilk**-ki-nun Chelswu-ka chayk-ul **ilk**-ess-ta.
 read-NMLZ-TOP Chelswu-NOM book-ACC read-PST-DECL
 'Read the book, Chelswu does.' (Hagstrom 1995: 32)
 b. **Masi**-ki-nun Chelsu-ka mayckwu-lul **masi**-ess-ta.
 drink-NMLZ-TOP Chelsu-NOM beer-ACC drink-PST-DECL
 'As for drinking, Chelswu drank beer.' (Jo 2000: 97, en. 4)
 c. [Computer-lul **sa**-ki-nun] John-i **sa**-ss-ta.
 computer-ACC buy-NMLZ-TOP John-NOM buy-PST-DECL
 'Indeed, the fact is that John bought a computer, (but he did not pay).'
 (Cho 1997: 40)
 d. [Sakwa-lul **mek**-ki-nun] John-i **mek**-ess-ta.
 apple-ACC eat-NMLZ-TOP John-NOM eat-PST-DECL
 'As for eating apples, John did.' (Cho & Kim 2002: 679)

Commonly, the displaced verb is marked with a suffix -*ki* that can be glossed as a nominalizer and the suffix -*nun* that is usually glossed as a (contrastive) topic marker. Consequently, the fronted constituent is most often referred to as a topic, although some researchers (e.g. Hagstrom 1995, Choi 2000, Aoyagi 2006) also treat it as a focus. As argued by Büring (1997) and Krifka (2007), contrastive topics might actually be a subtype of focus, which explains the construction's variable interpretation in the literature. As this book is about the syntax of these constructions, I will leave the exact semantic designation open here.

The same verb doubling can be found with the nominalized and topic-marked constituent following rather than preceding the subject of the sentence (181). In these examples it is not possible to distinguish between verb and verb phrase topicalization both lead to the same surface string.

(181) a. Chelswu-ka chayk-ul **ilk**-ki-nun **ilk**-ess-ta.
 Chelswu-NOM book-ACC read-KI-TOPIC read-PST-DECL
 'Read the book, Chelswu does.' (Hagstrom 1995: 32)
 b. Chelsu-ka maykcwu-lul **masi**-ki-nun **masi**-ess-ta.
 Chelsu-NOM beer-ACC drink-NMLZ-TOP drink-PST-DECL
 'As for drinking, it is the case that Chelsu drank beer.'
 (Jo 2000: 97, en. 4)
 c. John-i computer-lul **sa**-ki-nun **sa**-ss-ta.
 John-NOM computer-ACC buy-KI-CON buy-TNS-MOOD
 'Indeed, John bought a computer, (but...)'
 (Nishiyama & Cho 1998: 464)
 d. John-i sakwa-lul **mek**-ki-nun **mek**-ess-ta.
 John-NOM apple-ACC eat-NMLZ-TOP eat-PST-DECL
 'John ate apples, but...' (Cho & Kim 2002: 662)

Despite their different surface word order, both (181) and (180) appear to exhibit no interpretational differences. Although Cho & Kim (2002) claim that the constructions are semantically distinct in that (181-d) triggers an adversative implicature which is absent in (180-d) this is not corroborated by the data found elsewhere in the literature. Consider, for instance, the other three pairs of examples, where the different constructions either both lack an adversative implicature (181-a, b) vs. (180-a, b), or both exhibit it (181-c) vs. (180-c). In the absence of further evidence I will therefore assume that both constructions are equivalent and that their sole difference is the surface position of the subject. Further, judging from the fact that verb fronting is apparently not generally available (see footnote 18) while the low doubling is unanimously accepted, I suggest that the latter is less marked than the former and probably the more basic construction.

The presence of a verb copy is suggestive of movement because it receives a straightforward explanation as either arising through movement itself (Copy Theory) or being the spell-out of a movement trace. Hence, many analyses involve some type of movement (e.g. Hagstrom 1995, Nishiyama & Cho 1998, Choi 2003, Jo 2013). For actual pre-subject verbal fronting, $\bar{\text{A}}$-movement diagnostics like unboundedness (182)[19] and islands (183) show that it involves $\bar{\text{A}}$-movement.

(182) [Computer-lul sa-ki-nun] [na-nun [John-i sa-ss-ta-ko]
computer-ACC buy-KI-CON I-TOP John-NOM buy-TNS-MOOD-C
saegkakhassta].
think
'Buy a computer, I think John did.' (Nishiyama & Cho 1998: 466)

(183) *Relative Clause Island*
a. ***Ssu**-ki-nun Chelswu-ka [ku chayk-ul ssu-n]
write-NMLZ-TOP Chelswu-NOM this book-ACC write-REL
ceca-lul manna-ass-ta.
author-ACC meet-PST-DECL
Intended: 'It is WRITE that Chelswu met the author who wrote this book.' (Hagstrom 1995: 38)
b. *[Computer-lul **sa**-ki-nun] nae-ga [**san**] saram-ul
computer-ACC buy-NMLZ-TOP I-NOM buy person-ACC
alkoissta.
know
Intended: 'Buy a computer, I know a person who did/bought.'
(Nishiyama & Cho 1998: 466)

---

[19] An example of (bare) verb fronting across a clause boundary could not be found in the consulted literature.

Unfortunately, such diagnostics do not apply to sentence-internal movement. As a working hypothesis for now, I will assume that low doubling involves short movement of either the verb or the verb phrase into a topic position below the subject position. It may then optionally undergo a second movement step into the left periphery.

Korean also shows a very similar verbal fronting construction, which at first glance only deviates from the above-mentioned verb doubling constructions in that instead of a copy of the displaced verb there is a dummy verb *ha* 'do' in the canonical verb position. This dummy verb construction shows variability as to whether the verb phrase precedes (184-a, b) or follows the subject (184-c, d). In contrast to the verb doubling construction, fronting of a single verb without its object is not possible (185).

(184) a. [Ku chayk-ul **ilk**-ki-nun] John-i **ha**-ess-ta.
 the book-ACC read-NMLZ-TOP John-NOM do-PST-DECL
 'As for reading the book, John did.' (Jo 2000: 78)
 b. [Computer-lul **sa**-ki-nun] John-i **hae**-ss-ta.
 computer-ACC buy-KI-CON John-NOM do-TNS-MOOD
 'Indeed, the fact is that John bought a computer, (but he did not pay).'
 (Cho 1997: 46)
 c. John-i ku chayk-ul **ilk**-ki-nun **ha**-ess-ta.
 John-NOM the book-ACC read-NMLZ-TOP do-PST-DECL
 'It is the case that John read the book.' ('John DID read the book.')
 (Jo 2000: 78)
 d. John-i computer-lul **sa**-ki-nun **hae**-ss-ta.
 John-NOM computer-ACC buy-KI-CON do-TNS-MOOD
 'Indeed, John bought a computer, (but...)'
 (Nishiyama & Cho 1998: 463f.)

(185) ***Mek**-ki-nun Chelswu-ka ppang-ul **ha**-ess-ta.
 eat-NMLZ-TOP Chelswu-NOM bread-ACC do-PST-DECL
 (Hagstrom 1995: 33)

As the dummy verb construction also triggers a (contrastive) topic interpretation, it appears to be equivalent to the verb phrase fronting verb doubling construction. Concerning the generalizations established in part I Korean thus might pose a challenge because it comprises of both verb and verb phrase fronting but does not unambiguously show one of the three mentioned patterns. Rather, it seems to allow optionality in verb phrase fronting (186) and therefore gives the impression of an amalgam of the symmetric verb doubling pattern of Hebrew and the asymmetric pattern of Asante Twi.

(186) [Pap-ul **mek**-ki-nun] John-i **mek**-ess-ta/**hay**-ess-ta.
meal-ACC eat-NMLZ-TOP John-NOM eat-PST-DECL/do-PST-DECL
'As for eating a meal, John did it.' (Cho & Kim 2002: 667, fn. 1)

However, the two constructions differ with regard to a number of properties which, as I will argue following Jo (2000) and Cho & Kim (2002), indicates that only the verb doubling construction falls under the scope of the generalizations on verbal fronting whereas the dummy verb *ha* is not actually a repair but a light verb that selects a nominalized verb phrase as its complement. In the following, I will thus refer to the construction containing *ha* as the *ha* verb construction. The data that exemplify the differences between the constructions are predominantly given in the form where the subject is sentence-initial. As already pointed out above, the hypothesis is that both subject-initial and verb (phrase)-initial word order are equivalent for our purposes.

Word order is also the first dimension along which verb doubling and *ha* verb constructions differ. As Hagstrom (1995) notes the topic-marked verb may be freely reordered in the verb doubling construction (187)[20], whereas the *ha* verb construction requires it to be adjacent to the inflected *ha* verb (188) with the one exception of pre-subject order (186-a). Even adverbs like *ecey* 'yesterday' are precluded from intervening between lexical verb and *ha* (188-d).[21]

---

[20] Though consider Cho & Kim's (2002) judgements of (i) which are parallel to (187) but with an animate object.

(i) a. *John-i [(cacwu) manna-ki-nun]₁ Tom-ul ___₁ manna-ass-ta.
John-NOM often meet-NMLZ-TOP Tom-ACC meet-PST-DECL
b. *[(Cacwu) manna-ki-nun]₁ John-i Tom-ul ___₁ manna-ass-ta.
often meet-NMLZ-TOP John-NOM Tom-ACC meet-PST-DECL
(Cho & Kim 2002: 665)

The data on this issue are therefore not decisive.

[21] In contrast to the *ha* verb construction (i-a), adverbs intervening between the two verb copies in the verb doubling construction are fine though (i-b).

(i) a. */??John-i Tom-ul silheha-ki-nun cengmal ha-yess-ta.
John-NOM Tom-ACC dislike-NMLZ-TOP really do-PST-DECL
'John really disliked Tom, but…'
b. John-i Tom-ul silheha-ki-nun cengmal silhehanta.
John-NOM Tom-ACC dislike-NMLZ-TOP really dislike
'John really dislikes Tom, but…' (Cho & Kim 2002: 666)

(187) a. Chelswu-ka   chayk-ul **ilk**-ki-nun   **ilk**-ess-ta.
       Chelswu-NOM book-ACC read-KI-TOPIC read-PST-DECL
       'Read the book, Chelswu does.'
   b. Chelswu-ka **ilk**-ki-nun chayk-ul **ilk**-ess-ta.
   c. **Ilk**-ki-nun Chelswu-ka chayk-ul **ilk**-ess-ta.   (Hagstrom 1995: 32)

(188) a. Chelswu-ka   ppang-ul **mek**-ki-nun **ha**-ess-ta.
       Chelswu-NOM bread-ACC eat-KI-TOPIC do-PST-DECL
       'Eat bread, Chelswu did.'
   b. *Chelsw-uka **mek**-ki-nun ppang-ul **ha**-ess-ta.
   c. ***Mek**-ki-nun Chelswu-ka ppang-ul. **ha**-ess-ta
   d. *Chelswu-ka   ppang-ul **mek**-ki-nun ecey   **ha**-ess-ta.
       Chelswu-NOM bread-ACC eat-KI-TOPIC yesterday do-PST-DECL
       Intended: 'Eat bread, Chelswu did yesterday.'   (Hagstrom 1995: 33)

Second, the accusative marker *-lul* instead of the topic marker *-nun* may be attached to the nominalized verb in the *ha* verb construction (189-a). This option is not available in the verb doubling construction (189-b). This indicates that the nominalized verb phrase in the latter is actually selected by the verb *ha* and behaves like a proper object complement of it whilst the verb phrase is not a complement in the verb doubling construction where the inflected verb copy serves as a repair rather than as a standard accusative-assigning transitive verb.

(189) a. John-i   sakwa-lul **mek**-ki-lul   **ha**-ss-ta.
       John-NOM apple-ACC eat-NMLZ-ACC do-PST-DECL
       (without translation in source)
   b. *John-i   sakwa-lul **mek**-ki-lul   **mek**-ess-ta.
       John-NOM apple-ACC eat-NMLZ-ACC eat-PST-DECL
                                              (Cho & Kim 2002: 666)

Third, the short negation prefix *an-*, which occurs on verbs, has to occur on both verb copies in the verb doubling construction (190-a), but cannot be prefixed to both the lexical verb and the dummy verb in the *ha* verb construction (190-b). This again, hints towards an analysis where the verb doubling construction involves proper movement and actual copying whereas the *ha* verb construction is just a standard transitive construction with only one negation.

(190) a. John-i   Tom-ul an-**manna**-ki-nun   an-**manna**-ass-ta.
       John-NOM Tom-ACC NEG-meet-NMLZ-TOP NEG-meet-PST-DECL
       'John didn't meet Tom, but...'
   b. *John-i   Tom-ul an-**manna**-ki-nun   an-**ha**-yess-ta.
       John-NOM Tom-ACC NEG-meet-NMLZ-TOP NEG-do-PST-DECL
                                              (Cho & Kim 2002: 666)

Related to this is the observation that the long-form negation *ani* is only available in *ha* verb construction (191-b) while it is ungrammatical in the verb doubling construction (191-a).

(191) a. *Chelswu-ka chayk-ul **ilk**-ci ani **ilk**-ess-ta.
Chelswu-NOM book-ACC read-CI NEG read-PST-DECL
b. Chelswu-ka chayk-ul **ilk**-ci ani **ha**-ess-ta.
Chelswu-NOM book-ACC read-CI NEG do-PST-DECL
'Chelswu did not read the book.' (Hagstrom 1995: 33)

Fourth, the set of delimiters that can be attached to the nominalized verb is different for both constructions. While both of them allow attachment of *-nun* and *-man* 'only', *-cocha* 'even' can exclusively occur on the lexical verb in the *ha* verb construction (192-b) but not in the verb doubling construction (192-a).

(192) a. John-i sakwa-lul **mek**-ki-nun/man/*cocha **mek**-ess-ta.
John-NOM apple-ACC eat-NMLZ-TOP/only/even eat-PST-DECL
(without translation in source)
b. John-i sakwa-lul **mek**-ki-nun/man/cocha **hay**-ess-ta.
John-NOM apple-ACC eat-NMLZ-TOP/only/even do-PST-DECL
(without translation in source) (Cho & Kim 2002: 663, 666)

Fifth, while temporal and locative adverbials can occur inbetween the two verb copies in the verb doubling construction (193-a) their presence in this position in the *ha* verb construction leads to ungrammaticality (193-b). This indicates that the connection between *ha* and the nominalized verb phrase is tighter than that between the two verb copies. A possible explanation could be that *ha* must directly select the nominalized verb phrase and therefore does not allow any material to intervene while the nominalized verb phrase in the doubling construction actually has to move to create the verb copy and thereby may move across the adverbial material.

(193) a. John-i **o**-ki-nun (hankwuk-eye)/(ilnyon-ceneye)
John-NOM come-NMLZ-TOP Korea-LOC/one.year-before
o-ass-ta.
come-PST-DECL
(without translation in source)
b. *John-i **o**-ki-nun (hankwuk-eye)/(ilnyon-ceneye)
John-NOM come-NMLZ-TOP Korea-LOC/one.year-before
ha-yess-ta.
do-PST-DECL (Cho & Kim 2002: 666f.)

Sixth, in a complex predicate construction like *manna cwu* 'meet give' the first verb *manna* 'meet' may optionally be doubled together with the second verb *cwu* 'give' in the verb doubling construction (194-a). In the *ha* verb construction, this doubling is precluded (194-b). This difference receives a simple explanation: If *ha* selects the nominalized verb phrase which includes the complex verb, there is no reason to copy a part of it.

(194) a. John-un Tom-ul manna cwu-ki-nun (manna) cwuessta.
John-TOP Tom-ACC meet give-NMLZ-TOP meet gave
(without translation in source)
b. John-un Tom-ul manna cwu-ki-nun (*manna) hayessta.
John-TOP Tom-ACC meet give-NMLZ-TOP meet did
(without translation in source) (Cho & Kim 2002: 667)

In total, these differences between the *ha* verb construction and the verb doubling construction provide a clear case against treating them as two versions of the same underlying structure. Even if an approach to the *ha* verb construction in terms of simple transitive selection turns out to be on the wrong track it is clear that it is structurally/syntactically different from the verb doubling construction. Also, although both appear to have the same semantics there are apparently some fine distinctions. As Hyunjung Lee (p.c.) confirms, the *ha* verb construction conveys the semantics of a simple topicalization independent of whether the verb phrase is fronted or appears after the subject. The verb doubling construction, on the other hand, is perceived as a contrastive/exhaustive topicalization. Therefore, I conclude that Korean does not challenge any of our generalizations: Verb and verb phrase topicalization symmetrically trigger verb doubling and the dummy verb *ha* that may occur in verb phrase fronting is not a repair to avoid a gap created by verb phrase movement but rather a standard transitive verb that selects for a nominalized verb phrase complement and may also assign accusative to it.

Since Korean has optional (195-a) and sometimes even obligatory cognate objects (195-b), one might be tempted to analyse the nominalized verb as a cognate object that has been moved elsewhere.

(195) a. Sunhi-ka *(kkum-ul) kku-ess-ta.
Sunhi-NOM dream(N)-ACC dream-PST-DECL
'Sunhi dreamed.'
b. Sunhi-ka (cam-ul) ca-ess-ta.
Sunhi-NOM sleep(N)-ACC sleep-PST-DECL
'Sunhi slept/took a nap.' (Hagstrom 1995: 37)

However, this cannot be the basis for verb (phrase) fronting for two reasons. First, the cognate objects are marked with the accusative marker *-(l)ul*. If verb doubling were indeed derived by moving the cognate object into some topic position, we would expect it to also be accusative marked there contrary to fact (see example (189-b), repeated below as (196)).

(196) *John-i sakwa-lul **mek**-ki-lul **mek**-ess-ta.
John-NOM apple-ACC eat-NMLZ-ACC eat-PST-DECL
(Cho & Kim 2002: 666)

Second, cognate objects and verb doubling can cooccur which would be unexpected if the nominalized verb were in fact a cognate object.

(197) a. **Kku**-ki-nun Yenghi-ka *(hengpokham) **kkum**-al
dream-NMLZ-TOP Yenghi-NOM happy dream(N)-ACC
kku-ess-ta.
dream-PST-DECL
'It is DREAM that Yenghi dreamed a happy dream.'
b. **Ca**-ki-nun Sunhi-ka *(nat) **cam**-ul **ca**-ess-ta.
sleep-NMLZ-TOP Sunhi-NOM nap sleep(N)-ACC sleep-PST-DECL
'It is NAP that Sunhi took a nap.' (Hagstrom 1995: 37)

This again supports the view that verb doubling is a proper repair rather than derived from some independently available construction with two verb-like elements.

For completeness' sake, I would like to mention that there is yet another type of verb doubling construction in which both the nominalized verb and the inflected verb bear tense marking. Thus, in (198-a) the tense marker *-ss-* appears in the nominalized verb form *manna-ss-ki-nun* and also in the inflected verb *manna-ss-ta*. The same pattern can be observed in (198-b, c) with the verbs *sa* and *mek*.

(198) a. John-i Mary-lul **manna**-ss-ki-nun **manna**-ss-ta.
John-NOM Mary-ACC meet-PST-NOM-CONT meet-PST-DECL
(without translation in source) (Choi 2000: 337)
b. John-i computer-lul **sa**-ss-ki-nun **sa**-ss-ta.
John-NOM computer-ACC buy-TNS-KI-CON buy-TNS-MOOD
'Indeed, John bought a computer, (but...)'
(Nishiyama & Cho 1998: 463)
c. Yeonghee-ka chopap-ul **mek**-ess-ki-nun **mek**-ess-ta.
Yeonghee-NOM sushi-ACC eat-PST-KI-FOC eat-PST-DECL
without translation in source (Aoyagi 2006: 359)

Whether this double tense marking is also available with the *ha* verb construction is not entirely evident from the data. While Choi (2000) rejects it (199-a) Nishiyama & Cho (1998) and Aoyagi (2006) accept it as grammatical (199-b, c).

(199) a. *John-i   Mary-lul   **manna**-ss-ki-nun   **hay**-ss-ta.
           John-NOM Mary-ACC meet-PST-NOM-CONT do-PST-DECL
                                                        (Choi 2000: 337)
     b. John-i   computer-lul   **sa**-ss-ki-nun   **hae**-ss-ta.
        John-NOM computer-ACC buy-TNS-KI-CON do-TNS-MOOD
        'Indeed, John bought a computer, (but...)'
                                              (Nishiyama & Cho 1998: 464)
     c. Yeonghee-ka   chopap-ul **mek**-ess-ki-nun **ha**-ess-ta.
        Yeonghee-NOM sushi-ACC eat-PST-KI-FOC   do-PST-DECL
        (without translation in source)   (Aoyagi 2006: 359)

In any case, the bilocational tense marking indicates that whatever has been moved in this construction must comprise the T head and hence does not fall under our concept of verbal fronting. Indeed, Nishiyama & Cho (1998) analyse this construction as derived by TP movement. A further argument that it is not the verb phrase that is moved in this construction comes from the fact that it does not allow preposing of the verb phrase (200).

(200) *[Computer-lul **sa**-ss-ki-nun]   John-i   **sa**-ss-ta.
       computer-ACC buy-TNS-KI-CON John-NOM buy-TNS-MOOD
                                  (TP-movement, Nishiyama & Cho 1998: 467)

Consequently, I agree with Nishiyama & Cho (1998) in regarding this construction as involving movement of a TP rather than a verb phrase and hence ignore it in this investigation on verbal fronting.

Summary

In summary, Korean shows both verb and verb phrase fronting both with the option of occurring before or after the subject of the sentence. Its interpretation is that of a simple topic. The fronted verb (phrase) is nominalized and a copy of the verb appears in the canonical verb position at the end of the sentence. Both verb and verb phrase fronting show sensitivity to $\bar{\text{A}}$-diagnostics when they occur in pre-subject position. The verb phrase fronting construction in which an apparent dummy verb *ha* occupies the sentence-final position is argued to be a product of direct selection of the verb phrase by the *ha* verb. It is therefore not a repair but a basic construction of the language and thus does not have any impact on the generalizations. The properties of the verb doubling construction, as far as I was able to determine them, are listed in table 8.10. Consequently, Korean does not challenge any of the abovementioned generalization but rather instantiates a symmetric verb doubling pattern, i.e. pattern I of Generalization I.

Tab. 8.10: Properties of verbal fronting in Korean

	Copy	Dummy	Unbound	Islands	GS	TAM	H-Adv	L-Adv	Neg	L/R	Top/Foc
V	✓	–	✓	✓	n.d.	–	n.d.	n.d.	n.d.	L	Top
VP	✓	–	✓	✓	n.d.	–²²	n.d.	n.d.	✓²³	L	Top

8.2.7 Krachi

Krachi, a Kwa language of the Niger-Congo family, is spoken by about 50 000 people in and around the town Kete-Krachi in Eastern Ghana (Kandybowicz & Torrence 2016: 227). Its basic word order is SVO (201).

(201) ɔkyı wʊ ɛ-dıkɛ i-gyo.
woman the PST-cook PL-yam
'The woman cooked yams.' (Kandybowicz & Torrence 2016: 227)

The language shows both verb fronting (202-a) and verb phrase fronting with the latter further subdivided with regard to whether the word order inside the fronted verb phrase is VO (202-b) or OV (202-c). While verb fronting is ambiguous between exhaustive and contrastive focus the interpretation of verb phrase fronting depends on the word order. VO verb phrases trigger an exhaustive focus reading and OV phrases a contrastive one. In all cases, however, a copy of the verb appears inside the clause.

(202) a. Kɛ-[dıkɛ] yı ɔkyı wʊ ɛ-**dıkɛ** i-gyo.
NMLZ-cook FOC woman the PST-cook PL-yam
'It was COOKING that the woman did to yams (not, say, eating).'
'It was only cooking that the woman did to the yams.'
b. Kɛ-[**dıkɛ** i-gyo] yı ɔkyı wʊ ɛ-**dıkɛ**.
NMLZ-cook PL-yam FOC woman the PST-cook
'The woman only cooked yams (i.e. she did nothing else).'
c. Kɛ-[i-gyo **dıkɛ**] yı ɔkyı wʊ ɛ-**dıkɛ**.
NMLZ-PL-yam cook FOC woman the PST-cook
'It was COOKING YAMS that the woman did (not, say, eating rice).'
(Kandybowicz & Torrence 2016: 227f.)

---

23 If the fronted verb shows tense-marking, the construction involves TP fronting rather than verb phrase fronting.
23 This holds for the short negation prefix *an-* which occurs on both copies of the verb. The free morpheme negation *ani* is illicit in verbal fronting constructions.

Moreover, the fronted constituent is always nominalized with the proclitic *kɛ* and may be modified by nominal modifiers, for example by the adjective *tıma* 'good' in (203).

(203) Kɛ-**watı** tıma yı ɔkyı wʊ ɛ-**watı** i-gyo.
 NMLZ-pound good FOC woman the PST-pound PL-yam
 'It was a GOOD POUNDING that the woman did to yams.'
 (Kandybowicz & Torrence 2016: 230)

With regard to Ā-properties, Kandybowicz & Torrence (2016) provide examples that show that verb fronting can cross finite clause boundaries (204) and is sensitive to islands like the Complex NP Island (205), the Wh-Island (206), or the Adjunct Island (207). As corresponding examples for verb phrase fronting are not provided but it is also not explicitly pointed out that it behaves differently, I assume that verb phrase fronting shows the same unboundedness and island sensitivity as verb fronting.

(204) Kɛ-watı yı Gifty ɛ-gyɛnı [fɛɛ Kofi e-nu [fɛɛ Ama
 NMLZ-pound FOC Gifty PST-think COMP Kofi PST-hear COMP Ama
 ɛ-watı i-gyo]].
 PST-pound PL-yam
 'It was POUNDING that Gifty thought that Kofi heard that Ama did to yams.'
 (Kandybowicz & Torrence 2016: 230)

(205) *Complex NP Island*
 *Kɛ-**watı** yı Kofi e-gyi [i-gyo kɛ Ama ɛ-**watı**].
 NMLZ-pound FOC Kofi PST-eat PL-yam REL Ama PST-pound
 Intended: 'Kofi ate the yams that Ama POUNDED.'
 (Kandybowicz & Torrence 2016: 230)

(206) *Wh-Island*
 *Kɛ-**watı** yı mı e-bise [fɛɛ nsɛ yı ɔ-**watı** i-gyo].
 NMLZ-pound FOC 1SG PST-ask COMP who FOC 3SG-pound.PST PL-yam
 Intended: 'I asked who POUNDED yams.'
 (Kandybowicz & Torrence 2016: 230)

(207) *Adjunct Island*
 *Kɛ-**dıkɛ** yı Kofi ɛ-dı [ansaŋ Ama ɛ-**dıkɛ** mwe].
 NMLZ-cook FOC Kofi PST-sleep before Ama PST-cook rice
 Intended: 'Kofi slept before Ama COOKED rice.'
 (Kandybowicz & Torrence 2016: 230)

With regard to the size of the fronted constituent in verb fronting, Kandybowicz & Torrence (2016) argue that it is a verb phrase, more specifically a *v*P, because stranded object quantifiers like *kpatii* 'few' (208-b) as well as low manner adverbs like *bireŋ* 'quickly' (208-c) may accompany the fronted verb.

(208) a. Ama ɛ-fɛ a-kyʊŋ kpatii.
　　　　Ama PST-sell PL-fowl few
　　　　'Ama sold few fowls.'
　　b. Kɛ-[**fɛ** kpatii] yı Ama ɛ-**fɛ** a-kyʊŋ.
　　　　NMLZ-sell few FOC Ama PST-sell PL-fowl
　　　　'It was SELLING that Ama did to FEW fowls.'
　　　　NOT: 'It was FEW SELLINGS that Ama did to fowls.'
　　c. Kɛ-[**mɔ** bireŋ/damrase] yı Kofi ɛ-**mɔ** a-kyʊŋ.
　　　　NMLZ-kill quickly/well FOC Kofi PST-kill PL-fowl
　　　　'It was SLAUGHTERING QUICKLY/WELL that Kofi did to fowls.'
　　　　　　　　　　　　　　　　(Kandybowicz & Torrence 2016: 231)

Tense morphology or negation, in contrast, cannot appear on the fronted verb (209). These are assumed to reside in functional heads outside the VP, i.e. T or Neg.

(209) *Kɛ-[ɛ/kɛ-n-**dıkɛ**] yı ɔkyı wʊ ɛ/kɛ-n-**dıkɛ** i-gyo.
　　　　NMLZ-PST/FUT-NEG-cook FOC woman the PST/FUT-NEG-cook PL-yam
　　　　　　　　　　　　　　　　(Kandybowicz & Torrence 2016: 231)

Consequently, sentence adverbials like *kɛsıŋtıŋ* 'truly', that are adjoined in a position above the VP or *v*P, should be equally ungrammatical inside the fronted constituent. This is indeed the case as evidenced by (210).

(210) *Kɛ-[**mɔ** kɛsıŋtıŋ] yı Kofi ɛ-**mɔ** a-kyʊŋ.
　　　　NMLZ-kill truly FOC Kofi PST-kill PL-fowl
　　　　'It was TRULY SLAUGHTERING that Kofi did to fowls.'
　　　　　　　　　　　　　　　　(Kandybowicz & Torrence 2016: 231)

The same properties hold of verb phrase fronting with VO word order. All constituents internal to the *v*P, like indirect objects (211-a), object and instrumental PPs (211-b), complement CPs (211-c), and low manner adverbs (211-d)

(211) a. Kɛ-[**kyʊŋɛ** Kofi owore] yı Ama ɛ-**kyʊŋɛ**.
　　　　NMLZ-send Kofi book FOC Ama PST-send
　　　　'Ama only sent Kofi a book.'
　　b. Kɛ-[**tıŋ** i-gyo yɛ ɔsıkan] yı Ama ɛ-**tıŋ** (*i-gyo) (*yɛ
　　　　NMLZ-cut PL-yam with knife FOC Ama PST-cut PL-yam with
　　　　ɔsıkan).
　　　　knife
　　　　'Ama only cut yams with a knife.'

c. Kɛ-[**bise** fɛɛ nsɛ yı ɔ-dıke i-gyo] yı Kofi e-**bise**.
   NMLZ-ask COMP who FOC 3SG-cook PL-yam FOC Kofi PST-ask
   'Kofi only asked who cooked yams.'
d. Kɛ-[**dıkɛ** i-gyo bireŋ/damrase] yı ɔkyı wʊ ɛ-**dıkɛ**.
   NMLZ-cook PL-yam quickly/well FOC woman the PST-cook
   'The woman only cooked yams quickly/well.'

(Kandybowicz & Torrence 2016: 233)

Tense (212-a) and negation (212-b) may not occur on the verb inside the fronted verb phrase.

(212) a. *Kɛ-[ɛ/kɛ-**dıkɛ** i-gyo] yı ɔkyı wʊ ɛ/kɛ-**dıkɛ**.
        NMLZ-PST/FUT-cook PL-yam FOC woman the PST/FUT-cook
     b. *Kɛ-[m-**mɔ** a-kyʊŋ] yı Kofi ɛ-(m-)**mɔ**.
        NMLZ-NEG-kill PL-fowl FOC Kofi PST-NEG-kill

(Kandybowicz & Torrence 2016: 233)

And like verb fronting, verb phrase fronting does not permit high sentential adverbs like *paa* 'certainly' to accompany the fronted constituent (213).

(213) *Kɛ-[**dıkɛ** i-gyo *paa*] yı ɔkyı wʊ ɛ-**dıkɛ**.
      NMLZ-cook PL-yam certainly FOC woman the PST-cook

(Kandybowicz & Torrence 2016: 233)

Whether verb phrase fronting with OV word order shows the same behaviour as well remains unclear at this point. Kandybowicz & Torrence (2016) do not provide any examples or discussion of its properties. On the one hand, it is possible that the object simply shifts across the verb while verb phrase fronting proceeds as usual and therefore shows the same structural possibilities and restrictions as VO verb phrase fronting. On the other hand, OV word order might involve object incorporation and thus lead to a limitation of the material in the left-peripheral focus position to the object and the verb alone. As Hein & Murphy (to appear) suggest, OV word order might also result from flexible (re-)linearization inside the VP. Without further data, this issue cannot be resolved.

Summary
In summary, Krachi disposes of a verb fronting and a verb phrase fronting construction in which a copy of the verb occupies the clause-internal verb position. The fronted verb is nominalised and the dependency between it and the clause-internal copy shows $\bar{\text{A}}$-properties in being unbounded and sensitive to islands. Verb fronting may underlyingly be remnant verb phrase fronting, as it exhibits the

same properties as (VO) verb phrase fronting, that is, low adverbs and stranded object quantifiers may occur in the left periphery but high adverbs, negation and tense markers may not do so. Whether OV verb phrase fronting patterns with its VO correspondent cannot be determined from the available data. The properties of verb and verb phrase fronting are collectively presented in table 8.11. Krachi, thus, exhibits pattern I of Generalization I, namely symmetric verb doubling.

Tab. 8.11: Properties of verbal fronting in Krachi

	Copy	Dummy	Unbound	Islands	GS	TAM	L-Adv	H-Adv	Neg	L/R	Top/Foc
V	✓	–	✓	✓	n.d.	–	✓	–	–	L	Foc
VP	✓	–	✓	✓	n.d.	–	✓	–	–	L	Foc

8.2.8 Mandarin Chinese

Mandarin, a Sino-Tibetan language, is spoken by roughly one billion people in China and some neighbouring countries. Its basic word order is SVO (214).

(214) Ta da-guo   liangci na-xie   huaidan.
       he beat-ASP twice   those-CL bad.guy
       'He beat those bad guys twice.'   (Hsieh 2009: 496)

Mandarin in fact shows two constructions with verbal fronting. The first one is called the cleft-construction while the other is termed the *lian...dou* construction (Cheng & Vicente 2013). I will present and discuss each one in turn.

The cleft construction
Examples of regular NP versions of this construction are given in (215). One or more non-verbal elements are displaced into the left periphery of the clause where they are interpreted as topics with the constituent immediately to the right of the copula/topic marker *shì* receiving a (contrastive) focus reading (Cheng 2008).

(215) a. [_T Zhāngsān] shì [_F zuótiān   ] kàndào Wáng xiǎojiě (bú shì
              Zhangsan   COP   yesterday   see   Wang Ms.   not COP
           qiántiān).
           day.before.yesterday
           'It is yesterday that Zhangsan saw Ms. Wang.'

b. [T Zhāngsān] [T zuótiān] shì [F kàndào] Wáng xiǎojiě (bú
   Zhangsan   yesterday   COP   see   Wang Ms.   not
   shì gēn tā shuō-guò huà).
   COP with her talk.EXP word
   'It is seeing Ms. Wang that Zhangsan did yesterday (and not talking
   to her).'   (Cheng & Vicente 2013: 4)

It is also possible to front a verb into the position to the left of *shì*. However, in these cases a copy of the verb obligatorily appears in the remainder of the sentence, usually right-adjacent to *shì*, thus as a focussed element (216-A). In contrast to the NP cleft example (215-b), the focussed verb in (216-A) is not interpreted as a contrastive focus but as expressing a verum focus meaning, i.e. affirmation of the truth of the proposition (Höhle 1992, Krifka 2007).

(216) Q: Nǐ chī-guò fàn měiyǒu?
         you eat-EXP rice not.have
         'Have you eaten already?'
      A: [T **Chī**], [T wō] shì [F **chī**-guò], búguò...
            eat   I   COP   eat-EXP   but
         'As for eating, I have indeed eaten, but...'
                                                 (Cheng & Vicente 2013: 5)

The construction does not seem to allow verb phrase fronting. Although it is possible to have what appears to be a verb phrase in sentence-initial position (217), this has been analyzed as an instance of multiple topicalization of an NP and a verb (Cheng & Vicente 2013) rather than verb phrase topicalization.

(217) Fan, **chi** shi   **chi** guo le, dan shi mei you chi bao.
      rice eat COP/TOP eat PERF PF but COP not   eat enough/full
      'Rice, I ate, but I didn't eat enough.'   (Lee 2002: 17)

Independent of whether this analysis is correct, example (217) shows the same repair as verb fronting and therefore does not contradict the generalizations.

Following Cheng (2008), Cheng & Vicente (2013) analyze the copula/topic marker *shì* as taking a small clause complement containing a *pro* predicate which moves to the left of the copula (218).

(218)   *pro*$_1$ shì [SC [Subject XP] ___$_1$]

They argue that the subject of the small clause in verum focus readings (i.e. in verb fronting examples) has to be a *v*P based on the fact that low adverbs like *tiāntiān* 'daily' can intervene between *shì* and the lower verb copy without affecting the verum focus interpretation (219-a). Elements that usually attach higher than *v*P, like subjects (219-b) or speaker-oriented adverbs like *xiǎnrán* 'obviously' (219-c), are not allowed in this position indicating that the constituent cannot be larger than *v*P.

(219) a. Chī, wǒ shì tiāntiān chī, ...
           eat I COP daily eat
           'As for eating, I do eat every day; but...'
       b. *Chī, shì wǒ chī-guò, búguò...
            eat COP I eat-EXP but
       c. *Chī, ta shì yiǎnrán chī-guò, búguò...
            eat he COP obviously eat-EXP but (Cheng & Vicente 2013: 6)

There is evidence that the two verb copies are connected by Ā-movement. First, verb fronting may span an arbitrary number of intervening clauses (220-A), a hallmark property of Ā-dependencies.

(220) Q: Zhāngsān kàn-guò zhè-bù diànyǐng ma.
           Zhangsan see-EXP this-CL movie   Q
           'Has Zhangsan seen this movie?'
       A: **Kàn**, wǒ xiāngxìn [tā shì **kàn**-guò], búguò...
           see I believe he COP see-EXP but
           'As for seeing, I believe he has indeed seen it, but...'
                                                    (Cheng & Vicente 2013: 7)

Second, this long-distance dependency is blocked by islands like the Complex NP Island (221) and the Adjunct Island (222).

(221) *Complex NP Island*
       ***Kàn**, wǒ tóngyì [nèi-ge tā shì **kàn**-guò (yícì) de kànfǎ], búguò...
        see I agree that-CL he COP see-EXP once DE opinion but
        Intended: 'As for seeing, I agree with the opinion that he has indeed seen it once, but...'   (Cheng & Vicente 2013: 8)

(222) *Adjunct Island*
       ***Chī**, [tā shì yǐjīng **chī**-le yǐhòu], wǒ cái huídào jiā,
        eat he COP already eat-PERF after I then return home
        búguò...
        but
        Intended: 'As for eating, I returned home after he has indeed already eaten, but...'   (Cheng & Vicente 2013: 8)

A third indication that verb fronting involves Ā-movement rather than base generation or operator movement is the absence of genus-species effects, where the lower copy is lexically different from although taxonomically related to the higher copy (223).

(223)   a.   ***Lǚxíng**, wǒ shì [F **zuò**-guò] fēijī.
             travel   I   COP   sit-EXP   airplane
             Intended: 'As for travelling, I have taken a plane.'
        b.   ***Zhǔ**-cài, wǒ shì [F **kǎo**-guò] jī.
             cook-meal I   COP   roast-EXP   chicken
             Intended: 'As for cooking a meal, I have indeed roasted a chicken.'
                                              (Cheng & Vicente 2013: 9)

This is particularly unexpected as Mandarin allows so-called aboutness topics where the denotation of a topicalized noun phrase *yiě-shēng dòng-wù* 'wild animal' is further specified and narrowed down by a lexically different noun phrase *shīzi* 'lion' inside the clause (224).

(224)   Yiě-shēng dòng-wù, wǒ zuì xǐ-huān shīzi.
        wild   animal   I   most like   lion
        'As for wild animals, I like lions the best.'   (Cheng & Vicente 2013: 9)

Hence, Cheng & Vicente (2013: 8) propose a structure as in (225) for verb doubling cleft constructions in Mandarin. The verb $\bar{\text{A}}$-moves from the subject *v*P inside the small clause complement of *shì* into the specifier position of the CP leaving a copy that is pronounced in addition to the verb in SpecCP.[24]

(225)   [CP Verb$_1$ [XP pro$_{PRED}$ shì [SC [$_{vP}$ ... Verb$_1$ ...] ──PRED]]]
                        $\bar{\text{A}}$

We can thus summarize that the cleft-construction only allows verb fronting with a copy of the verb occupying the canonical verb position and that the two copies are related by $\bar{\text{A}}$-movement.

---

24 Note that movement of the verb out of the subject of the small clause should not be possible as the whole construction is an inverse predication which is known to not allow $\bar{\text{A}}$-extraction of a post-copular subject (Heycock 1994, Moro 1997, den Dikken 2006). It is not possible to treat the lower verb copy as a resumptive element circumventing island conditions because we would then predict (221) and (222) to be grammatical contrary to fact. Cheng & Vicente (2013) argue that the seemingly general ban on extraction is due to the edge of the small clause's subject usually being occupied which prevents successive-cyclic movement of material out of the subject. However, as the subject in verb fronting is a *v*P (not a CP like in the other cases) its edge is empty and movement of the verb to the matrix CP via the edge of the small clause *v*P is possible (for details, see Cheng & Vicente 2013: §2.3).

The *lian...dou* construction

The second construction that can be treated as a kind of verbal fronting is the *lian...dou* construction. An example of a regular NP version of the construction is given in (226). The constituent immediately to the right of *lián* is focussed and always precedes *dōu*. Further, the presence of *lián*, which is usually treated as a focus particle (Gao 1994, Shyu 2004, Badan 2007, among others), is optional and may – in conjunction with the focussed constituent – also be place before the subject of the clause (226-b).

(226)   a.   Tā lián [F zhè-běn shū] dōu kàn-wán-le.
             he LIAN   this-CL   book   DOU read-finish-PERF
             'He finished reading even this book.'
        b.   (Lián) [F zhè-běn shū], tā dōu kàn-wán-le.
             LIAN   this-CL   book   he DOU read-finish-PERF
             'He finished reading even this book.'   (Cheng & Vicente 2013: 14)

When the focus-constituent appears sentence-initially, the topic marker *a* and a resumptive pronoun may optionally occur in the sentence (227-a) which must be absent if it is in post-subject position (227-b).

(227)   a.   (Lián) [F kàn] (a)   tā dōu méi   kàn.
             LIAN   look   TOP he DOU not.have look
             'He didn't even look.'
        b.   Tā (lián) [F kàn] (*a)   dōu méi   kàn.
             he LIAN   look   TOP DOU not.have look
             'He didn't even look.'   (Cheng & Vicente 2013: 15)

As Shyu (1995) and Badan (2007) argue, the sentence-initial *lián*-constituent acts as a contrastive topic which licenses the occurrence of the topic marker, while clause-internally, the constituent is a simple focus. Cheng & Vicente (2013) refer to Büring (1997) and Krifka (2007) for the assumption that the former is a subtype of the latter, which explains why the supposed focus marker *lián* can cooccur with the topic marker *a*. A further difference between the two options is that the pre-subject *lián* allows long-distance displacement (228-a) while the post-subject one does not (228-b). This indicates that displacement of the *lian*-constituent into the post-subject position is A-movement whereas sentence-initial *lian* involves $\bar{\text{A}}$-movement (Shyu 1995).

(228)   a.   (Lián) zhè-běn shū   wǒ yǐwéi [tā dōu kàn-le].
             LIAN this-CL book I   think   he DOU read-PERF
             'Even this book, I thought that he has read.'

b. *Wǒ lián zhè-běn yǐwéi tā dōu kàn-le.
   I LIAN this-CL book think he DOU read-PERF
   Intended: 'I thought that he has even read this book.'

(Cheng & Vicente 2013: 16)

Interestingly, the *lián*-constituent can also contain a verb. In that case, a copy of the focussed verb appears in the canonical verb position inside the clause (229). For the most part, the construction shows the same behaviour as regular NP focussing with *lián*, that is, the *lián* particle is generally optional (229-a), the focus constituent can appear sentence-initially before the subject (229-b), in which case the topic marker *a* can optionally be used (a resumptive pronoun for verbal elements does not exist in Mandarin, Cheng & Vicente 2013: 15), and initial *lian* allows long-distance extraction (229-c) while post-subject *lian* does not (229-d).

(229) a. Tā (lián) [F **kàn**] (*a) dōu méi **kàn**.
         he LIAN look TOP DOU not.have look
         'He didn't even look.'
      b. (Lián) [F **kàn**] (a) tā dōu méi **kàn**.
         LIAN look TOP he DOU not.have look
         'He didn't even look.'
      c. (Lián) **kàn** wǒ xiāngxìn [tā dōu méi **kàn**].
         LIAN look I believe he DOU not.have look
         'As for looking, I believe that he didn't even look.'
      d. *Wǒ lián **kàn** xiāngxìn tā dōu méi **kàn**.
         I LIAN look believe he DOU not.have look
         Intended: 'I believe that he didn't even look.'

(Cheng & Vicente 2013: 15f.)

There is, however, one difference between regular and verbal *lian…dou* constructions: In contrast to the former, the latter always require the presence of either overt sentential negation (230-a) or a superlative (230-b, c).

(230) a. Tā (lián) [F **kàn**] dōu *(bú) **kàn**.
         he LIAN look DOU not look
         'He didn't even look.'
      b. (Lián) [F **chuān**] tā dōu yào **chuān** *(zuì-hǎo de).
         LIAN wear he DOU want wear SUP-good DE
         'Even when it comes to clothes, he wants to wear the best.'
      c. Tā (lián) [F **chī**] DOU **chī** *(zuì-guì de).
         he LIAN eat DOU eat SUP-expensive DE
         'He even has to eat the most expensive (thing).'

(Cheng & Vicente 2013: 16)

This requirement is presumably related to the fact that the semantics of the *lian...dou* construction always involves scalarity connected to the focussed constituent (Cheng & Vicente 2013). That is, in the regular NP focus examples above, the focussed book is on one extreme end of a scale and the fact that he has finished reading even this book, which was a very unlikey event, triggers an implicature that he has also finished reading books lower on the scale. For the verbal examples above, the focussed verb needs to be on such an extreme end of a scale but, as Cheng & Vicente (2013) speculate, such a scale might only be construable by polarity or superlatives.

So far we have only encountered verb fronting in this *lian...dou* construction and although most examples contained an intransitive verb and are therefore not decisive between verb and verb phrase fronting, examples (230-b, c) clearly show that the transitive verbs *chuān* 'wear' and *chī* 'eat' can be focussed with *lián* while their respective complements are stranded. Hence, it seems plausible to speak of the *lian...dou* construction as allowing verb fronting. This immediately raises the question whether it is also possible to focus a whole verb phrase. Indeed, there are examples where it appears that a full verb phrase is moved between *lian* and *dou*. Consider example (231), where the phrasal constituent *peng jirou* 'touch the chicken' is focussed. However, unlike with verb fronting there is no doublet of the verb, in fact, such a doublet is ungrammatical. Instead, a dummy verb *zuo* 'do' occupies the canonical position of the verb in the sentence.

(231) Zhangsan lian [F peng jirou] dou mei zuo/*peng
 Zhangsan LIAN touch chicken DOU not do/touch
 'Zhangsan did not even touch the chicken.' (Hsieh 2009: 495)

Thus, verb fronting with *lian...dou* gives rise to verb doubling whereas verb phrase fronting with *lian...dou* leads to the insertion of a dummy verb. This is exactly the asymmetric pattern that we also find in Asante Twi (see section 2.1.3.1) and Limbum (see section 2.1.3.2). Hence, at least one verbal fronting construction in Mandarin Chinese constitutes a further example of this pattern.

Interestingly, when the verb phrase is fronted from below a modal verb such as *gan* 'dare' instead of a dummy verb there is a gap.

(232) Zhangsan lian [F peng jirou] dou bu gan (*zuo)
 Zhangsan even touch chicken all NEG dare do
 'Zhangsan dare not even touch the chicken. (Hsieh 2009: 503)

Concerning the diagnostics for $\bar{\text{A}}$-movement, the *lian...dou* construction behaves like the cleft construction at least with respect to verb fronting. Examples where a whole verb phrase is fronted have not been available in the literature. In verb fronting, the *lian*-constituent may be extracted from a finite clause (233).

(233)   (Lián) [F kàn] wǒ xiāngxìn tā dōu méi   kàn.
       LIAN   look I believe he DOU not.have look
       'I believe that he didn't even look.'   (Cheng & Vicente 2013: 18)

Moreover, fronting from inside an island like the Wh-Island (234) or the Adjunct Island (235) leads to ungrammaticality.

(234)   *Wh-Island*
      * (Lián) [F kàn] wǒ zhīdào tā wèishěnme dōu méi   kàn.
        LIAN   look I know he why   DOU not.have look
        'I know why he didn't even look.'   (Cheng & Vicente 2013: 18)

(235)   *Adjunct island*
      * (Lián) [F kàn] tā bèi chē zhuàng-le yīnwèi tā dōu méi   kàn.
        LIAN   look he by car hit-PERF   because he DOU not.have look
        'He was hit by a car because he didn't even look.'
                                                   (Cheng & Vicente 2013: 18)

Another indication that verb(al) fronting in the *lian…dou* construction is movement rather than base generation is the absence of any genus-species effects (236).

(236)   a. * (Lián) [F zhǔ (cài)], Zhāngsān dōu méi   kǎo jī.
          LIAN   cook meal Zhangsan DOU not.have roast chicken
          Intended: 'Zhangsan didn't even cook by roasting chicken.'
      b. * (Lián) [F liàn-shēn   ], Zhāngsān dōu méi   yóu yǒng.
          LIAN   practice-body Zhangsan DOU not.have swim swim
          Intended: 'Zhangsan didn't even train (his body) by swimming.'
                                                   (Cheng & Vicente 2013: 19)

In conclusion, verb(al) fronting with *lian…dou* involves $\bar{\text{A}}$-movement of the *lian*-constituent.

Against remnant verb phrase movement
Concerning verb fronting, the fronted verb is ambiguous between a bare verbal head and a remnant verb phrase. As we have seen, at least in the *lian…dou* construction, verb phrase movement is possible and the fronted verb could therefore be a verb phrase whose objects have been scrambled out. Indeed, there is scrambling in Mandarin. Example (237-a) is derived from (237-b) by scrambling the object *nàge rén* 'that person' across the adverbial *liǎng cì* 'twice'.

(237) a. Wǒ qǐng-guò nà-ge rén liǎng cì.
         I   invite-EXP that-CL person two time
         'I invited that person twice.'
     b. Wǒ qǐng-guò liǎng cì nà-ge rén.
         I   invite-EXP two time that-CL person
         'I invited that person twice.'   (Cheng & Vicente 2013: 24)

As argued by Soh (1998), the [adverb-object] order is the base order, because it only allows for direct scope (238-a), while the derived order [object-adverb] can have both direct and inverse scope (238-b). This pattern is the same in German and Dutch, which uncontroversially comprise of object scrambling.

(238) a. Wǒ qǐng-guò liǎng cì quánbù de xuéshēng.
         I   invite-EXP two time all   DE student
         'I have invited every student twice.'   ($\forall > 2, *2 > \forall$)
     b. Wǒ qǐng-guò quánbù de xuéshēng liǎng cì.
         I   invite-EXP all   DE student two time
         'I have invited every student twice.'   ($\forall > 2, 2 > \forall$)
                                                 (Cheng & Vicente 2013: 24)

However, this scrambling is not productive enough in order to create the remnant verb phrase necessary for verb fronting. The object usually does not scramble across the verb. If it does, as in (239), it is interpreted as a contrastive topic (Badan 2007).

(239) Zhāngsān [nà-běn shū] hái méi kàn-wán.
      Zhangsan that-CL book still not.have read-finish
      'Zhangsan has not finished reading that book (but has finished some other book(s)).'   (Cheng & Vicente 2013: 25)

A remnant movement derivation of a *lian...dou* sentence would probably have to proceed as in (240). Starting with the base sentence (240-b), first, the adverb *jǐ-kǒ* has to scramble out of the verb phrase, presumably into the contrastive topic position between the subject and the verb (240-c). Then, the remnant verb phrase *lián chī* with the focus marker *lián* has to move to the left periphery leaving a copy of the verb (240-d). In order to arrive at the correct word order of a *lian...dou* sentence (240-a) all material that follows the scrambled adverb *jǐ-kǒ* has to move across it (240-e).

(240) a. Lián chī, tā dōu méi chī jǐ-kǒ.
         LIAN eat he DOU not.have eat several-mouth
         'As for eating, he didn't even eat much.'

b. tā dōu méi [lián chī] jǐ-kǒ (Base order)
c. tā jǐ-kǒ$_1$ dōu méi [lián chī] ___$_1$ (Object movement)
d. [lián chī]$_2$, tā jǐ-kǒ$_1$ dōu méi chī$_2$ ___$_1$ ([lian-V] movement)
e. [lián chī]$_2$, tā [dōu méi chī2]$_3$ jǐ-kǒ$_1$ ___$_3$ ___$_1$
(Movement of post-*jǐkǒ* material)
(Cheng & Vicente 2013: 25)

There are basically two issues with this derivation. First, an additional movement step of the material following the scrambled elements is necessary to derive the correct word order. This movement step has no independent motivation. Second, since the verb phrase-internal material scrambles into a contrastive topic position, we would expect it to be interpreted as a contrastive topic. It is, however, not the case that all post-verbal material receives such an interpretation, neither in *lian…dou* constructions nor in verb doubling cleft constructions. Cheng & Vicente (2013: 26–27) therefore conclude that Mandarin verb fronting does not involve remnant verb phrase movement but rather $\bar{\text{A}}$-head movement.

Summary

To summarize, Mandarin comprises of two different verbal fronting constructions: The cleft construction that presumably only allows verb fronting, and the *lian…dou* construction that allows both verb and verb phrase fronting. The former shows verb doubling and allows fronting across finite clause boundaries. It also respects islands and does not exhibit genus-species effects, indicating that the two verb copies are related by $\bar{\text{A}}$-movement. The latter construction shows verb doubling with verb fronting and dummy verb insertion with verb phrase fronting, the same asymmetric pattern found in Asante Twi and Limbum. This construction also shows positive $\bar{\text{A}}$-diagnostics, it can cross clause boundaries and is sensitive to islands. Since scrambling, although available in Mandarin, is not able to create remnant verb phrases as needed, verb fronting cannot be remnant verb phrase movement. Rather, Cheng & Vicente (2013) suggest that it involves $\bar{\text{A}}$-head movement of the verbal head. The properties of both fronting constructions are summarized again in table 8.12. In conclusion, Mandarin instantiates two distinct patterns in the two constructions. The cleft construction allows verb fronting only and shows verb doubling as predicted for pattern A of Generalization II. The *lian…dou* construction behaves like Asante Twi and Limbum in allowing both verb and verb phrase fronting with the former triggering verb doubling but the latter showing dummy verb insertion. This pattern conforms to the single asymmetric pattern, namely pattern III, that is allowed by Generalization I. Therefore, Mandarin verbal fronting supports the claim that this asymmetric pattern is a proper pattern in the world's languages, not just a quirk of Asante Twi and Limbum.

Tab. 8.12: Properties of verbal fronting in Mandarin

	Copy	Dummy	Unbound	Islands	GS	TAM	H-Adv	L-Adv	NEG	L/R	Top/Foc
cleft construction											
V	✓	–	✓	✓	–	n.d.	n.d.	n.d.	n.d.	L	Top
VP	–	–									
lian...dou construction											
V	✓	–	✓	✓	–	n.d.	n.d.	n.d.	n.d.	L	Foc
VP	–	✓	n.d.	n.d.	–	n.d.	n.d.	n.d.	n.d.	L	Foc

8.2.9 Mani

Mani, a Mel language of the Niger-Congo family, is spoken by not more than a few hundred people along the coastal border region between Guinea and Sierra Leone (Childs 2011: 1ff.). Its basic word order is SVO (Childs 2011: 19).

(241) Ù ká tɔ̀k dòmɔ̀ mì.
       1SG PST wash shirt 1SG
       'I washed my shirt.' (Childs 2011: 148)

The language shows both verb (242-a) and verb phrase (242-b) fronting with a copy of the verb appearing in the clause-internal verb position. The fronted constituent is nominalized and receives a focus interpretation. Independent of whether the verb phrase or just the verb is fronted the focus domain seems to be the verb phrase including the object.

(242) a. Ù-**bán** kɔ́ m̀bòm wɔ̀ **bán** wɔ́m-yè.
         NCM-build PRO.FOC Mbom 3SG build boat-STAT
         'It is building a boat that Mbom did (build a boat).'
      b. Ù-[**bán** wɔ́m] kɔ́ m̀bòm wɔ̀ **bán**-yè.
         NCM-build boat PRO.FOC Mbom 3SG build-STAT
         'It is building a boat Mbom did (build a boat).' (Childs 2011: 219)

The focus marker *kɔ́* is used for inanimate and indefinite foci whereas animates usually require the focus marker *ŋɔ́* (243).

(243) Póténɔ ŋɔ́ yà lɛ́.
European PRO.FOC 1SG COP
'It is a European I am.' (Childs 2011: 220)

Generally, the focus marker varies depending on the animacy and the noun class of the fronted element, as shown in (244) for NP fronting.

(244) a. [Càmɔ̀ cɛ́] wɔ̀ yó ǹ-dé ǹ-cɛ̀.
boy DEF PRO.FOC eat NCM$_{ma}$-food NCM$_{ma}$-DEF
'It is the boy [who] ate the rice.'
b. [Kìl tì-cɛ́] tá ŋá sìnì-yɛ́.
house NCM$_{ta}$-DEF PRO.FOC 3PL destroy-STAT
'It is the houses they (the rebels) destroyed.'
c. [Mɛ́n ǹ-cɛ́] má ŋá pèrì-yɛ́.
water NCM$_{ma}$-DEF PRO.FOC 3PL spill-STAT
'It is water they spilled.' (Childs 2011: 217f.)

Even though the focus markers are glossed as focal pronouns by Childs and vary according to properties of the focussed item, the above constructions are distinct from relative constructions in Mani. The latter involve a class-marked demonstrative (distinct from the focal pronouns) at the beginning of the relative clause and a relative marker yɔ̀ (sometimes reduced to -ɔ̀) at the end (245).

(245) a. À ké mɛ́n ǹ-cɛ̀ [mànà kɔ̀cí wɔ̀ tɔ̀r-í yɔ̀].
1SG see water NMC$_{ma}$-DEF DEM$_{ma}$ Kochi 3SG pour-CS REL
'I saw the water that Kochi spilled. (Lit.: I saw the water this Kochi made pour.)'
b. Kùfànà tí-wé cɛ̀ [wɔ̀nɛ̀ kɔ́ tékól yɔ̀] tá
wing NCM$_{ta}$-bird DEF DEM$_{wɔ}$ PRO.INDEF there REL PRO$_{ta}$
tì-yɔ̀rún.
NCM$_{ta}$-red
'The wings of the bird over there are red. (Lit.: The wings of the bird it it [is] over.there REL they are red.)' (Childs 2011: 228f.)

Unfortunately, no further data are provided that might reveal whether verbal fronting involves Ā-movement or not and which elements may accompany the fronted verbal category.

Summary
We can conclude that Mani comprises of verb and verb phrase fronting for focus where a copy of the displaced verb occurs in the base position. A focus marker

has to be present which agrees with the fronted element for animacy and noun class. The verbal fronting construction is different from relativization. Table 8.13 presents an overview. Unless evidence to the contrary is presented, I will assume that the fronted element has Ā-moved into the sentence-initial position. Since it shows the same verb doubling repair in both verb and verb phrase fronting, Mani is understood to manifest pattern I of Generalization I.

Tab. 8.13: Properties of verbal fronting in Mani

	Copy	Dummy	Unbound	Islands	GS	TAM	L-Adv	H-Adv	Neg	L/R	Top/Foc
V	✓	–	n.d.	n.d.	n.d.	n.d.	n.d.	n.d.	n.d.	L	Foc
VP	✓	–	n.d.	n.d.	n.d.	n.d.	n.d.	n.d.	n.d.	L	Foc

8.2.10 Polish

Polish, a Slavic language of the Indo-European phylum, is spoken by approximately 40 million speakers in Poland and neighbouring regions.

The language exhibits both verb and verb phrase fronting where a copy of the displaced verb appears in the clause-internal canonical verb position (246). The fronted constituent is optionally followed by the particle *to* and is usually interpreted as a contrastive topic, which triggers the presence of an adversative clause with opposite polarity (Bondaruk 2009: 66).

(246) a. [**Wypić**] (to) Marek **wypije** herbatę, ale nie wypije
 drink.INF TO Marek will-drink tea but not will-drink
 kawy.
 coffee
 'As for drinking, Marek will drink tea, but he will not drink coffee.'
 b. [**Wypić** herbatę] (to) Marek **wypije**, ale nie wypije
 drink.INF tea TO Marek will-drink but not will-drink
 kawy.
 coffee
 'As for drinking tea, Marek will drink it, but he will not drink coffee.'
 (Bondaruk 2012: 55)

The verb in sentence-initial position is morphologically distinct from the copy in base position as it has to be an infinitive. A finite form that is identical to the lower copy leads to ungrammaticality (247).

(247) *Złamała to ona się złamała, ale się nie
break.PST.3SG.FEM TO she REFL break.PST.3SG.FEM but REFL not
rozpadła.
disintegrated
'As for breaking, it did break, but it didn't disintegrate.'
(Bondaruk 2012: 61)

However, the two copies have to bear the same aspect (248-a). If this is not the case, as in (248-b), the sentence becomes ungrammatical.

(248) a. **Zjeść** śniadanie to oni **zjedli,** ale nie zjedli obiadu.
eat.INF.PFV breakfast TO they ate.PFV but not ate dinner
'As for eating breakfast, they did eat it, but they didn't eat dinner.'
b. ***Jeść** śniadanie to oni **zjedli,** ale nie zjedli obiadu.
eat.INF.IPFV breakfast TO they ate.PFV but not ate dinner
'As for eating breakfast, they did eat it, but they didn't eat dinner.'
(Bondaruk 2012: 59)

Verb fronting may also occur in embedded clauses (249). The same restrictions with regard to the morphological form of the two copies hold as above.

(249) Mama powiedziała, [że **wiedzieć** Marka to **widziała**], ale z
mother said that see.INF Marek TO she.saw but with
nim nie rozmawiała.
him not talked
'Mother said that as for seeing Marek, she did see him, but she did not talk to him.'
(Bondaruk 2012: 61)

There is no verb doubling if the fronted verb (phrase) originates from a position under an infinitive-embedding verb, like a restructuring verb (250-a) or a control verb (250-b). Presumably, in these cases finiteness in the embedded clause is expressed on the restructuring/control verb instead of the lexical verb. Therefore, movement of the latter does not deprive the finiteness marking of its host and hence does not trigger the need for a copy of the displaced verb to appear in this position.

(250) a. [**Pisać** list] to Maria zaczęła (***pisać**), ale go nie
write.INF letter TO Maria started write.INF but it not
skończyła.
finished
'As for writing a letter, Maria started to do this, but she didn't finish it.'

b. **Czytać** to Marek lubi (***czytać**).
   read.INF TO Marek likes read.INF
   'As for reading, Marek likes doing it.' (Bondaruk 2012: 63f.)

The same reasoning applies to verb fronting from under auxiliaries. However, there is a slight difference to other infinitive-embedding environments. In Polish, there is optionality with regard to the form that the lexical verb takes if it occurs together with an auxiliary. It may either be an infinitive or a participial form. As we have seen above, the fronted verb is always an infinitive. Now what we find with verb fronting from auxiliary constructions is that there is a copy in the base position only if that copy is morphologically distinct from the fronted verb, i.e. when it appears in the participial form (251-a). In this form it expresses a (formal morphological) feature that is not expressed by the auxiliary and hence would be stranded under verb fronting. To avoid this, a copy of the verb is left behind to serve as a host for this feature. If, on the other hand, the lexical verb in the auxiliary construction appears in its infinitival form, fronting obligatorily leads to a gap in the base position (251-b).

(251) a. **Pracować** to Marek będzie nad tym **pracował**, ale czy mu
   work.INF TO Marek will on this work but if him
   się to uda skończyć.
   REFL this manage finish
   'As for working, Marek will work on this, but will he manage to finish?'
b. **Pracować** to Marek będzie nad tym (***pracować**), ale czy mu
   work.INF TO Marek will on this work.INF but if him
   się to uda skończyć.
   REFL this manage finish
   'As for working, Marek will work on this, but will he manage to finish?'
   (Bondaruk 2012: 63)

Besides the monotransitives that we have already seen in (246), fronting can also take place with unergatives (252-a) and unaccusatives (252-b).

(252) a. **Narzekać** (to) Marek stale **narzeka**, ale nic nie
   complain.INF TO Marek constantly complains but nothing not
   robi.
   does
   'As for complaining, Marek constantly complains, but does nothing.'
b. **Rosnąć** (to) dziecko szybko **rośnie**, ale często choruje.
   grow.INF TO child quickly grows but often is.ill
   'As for growing, the child grows fast, but is often ill.'
   (Bondaruk 2009: 66)

With ditransitive verbs, we find that verb fronting (253-a) as well as full verb phrase fronting (253-b) is possible. In addition, there can be partial verb phrase fronting where the verb and its direct object are fronted while the indirect object is stranded (253-c). Fronting of the verb and its indirect object to the exclusion of the direct object, however, is ungrammatical (253-d).[25]

(253) a. **Dać** (to) **dał** jej kwiaty, ale prezentu nie kupił.
 give.INF TO he.gave her flowers but present not bought
 'As for giving, he gave her flowers, but he didn't buy a present.'
 b. [**Dać** jej kwiaty] (to) **dał**, ale prezentu nie kupił.
 give.INF her flowers TO he.gave but present not bought
 'As for giving her flowers, he did (give her flowers), but he didn't buy a present.'
 c. [**Dać** kwiaty] (to) jej **dał**, ale prezentu nie kupił.
 give.INF flowers TO her he.gave but present not bought
 'As for giving flowers, he gave her (flowers), but he didn't buy a present.'
 d. *[**Dać** jej] (to) **dał** kwiaty, ale prezentu nie kupił.
 give.INF her TO gave flowers but present not bought
 'As for giving her, he gave (her) flowers, but he didn't buy a present.'
 (Bondaruk 2009: 67)

Turning to the Ā-properties of the construction we find that it behaves on a par with other Ā-structures like e.g. wh-extraction. It is unbounded from subjunctive *żeby* clauses (254-a) and infinitive clauses (254-b).

(254) a. **Kupić** (to) Marek chciał, [żebym **kupił** kwiaty], ale nie dał
 buy.INF TO Marek wanted so.that buy flowers but not gave
 mi pieniędzy.
 me money
 'As for buying, Mark wanted me to buy flowers, but he didn't give me money.'
 b. [**Kupić** kwiaty] (to) Marek chciał, [żebym **kupił**], ale nie dał
 buy.INF flowers TO Marek wanted so.that buy but not gave
 mi pieniędzy.
 me money
 'As for buying flowers, Mark wanted me to buy them, but he didn't give me money.' (Bondaruk 2009: 69f.)

---

[25] This does not hold for all speakers of Polish. Some accept partial verb phrase fronting of a ditransitive with a stranded direct object as in (253-d) as perfectly grammatical.

But (like wh-movement) verbal fronting from embedded finite clauses with *że* complementizer is ungrammatical.

(255) *?[**Kupić** kwiaty] (to) Maria powiedziała mi, [że Marek **kupił**], ale
   buy.INF flowers TO Maria told me that Marek bought but
   nie kupił prezentu.
   not bought present
   'As for buying flowers, Maria told me that Marek did buy them, but he
   didn't buy a present.' (Bondaruk 2012: 61)

Furthermore, verbal fronting is sensitive to islands like the Wh-Island (256), the Relative Clause Island (257), and the Subject Island (258). The examples only show verb fronting but as Bondaruk (2009: 70, fn. 5) asserts the island constraints are also obeyed by verb phrase fronting.

(256) *Wh-Island*
   ?***Kupić** (to) spytałam ją [gdzie **kupiła** kwiaty], ale nie
   buy.INF TO I.asked her where she.bought flowers but not
   spytałam jakie.
   I.asked which
   'As for buying, I asked her where she bought flowers, but I didn't ask which ones.' (Bondaruk 2009: 70)

(257) *Relative Clause Island*
   ***Kupić** (to) spotkałam mężczyznę, [który kupił kwiaty], ale nie
   buy.INF TO I.met man who bought flowers but not
   spotkałam tego, który nie kupił.
   I.met this who not bought
   'As for buying, I met a man who had bought flowers, but I didn't meet the one who hadn't.' (Bondaruk 2009: 70)

(258) *Subject Island*
   ***Zdać** (to) [żeby Marek **zdał** egzamin] jest konieczne, ale
   pass.INF TO so.that Marek would.pass exam is necessary but
   nie jest konieczne, żeby nadal studiował.
   not is necessary so.that still would.study
   'As for passing, it is necessary for Marek to pass the exam, but it isn't necessary for him to continue his studies.' (Bondaruk 2009: 70)

In addition, there are reconstruction effects for condition A. The fronted constituent may contain an anaphoric expression like *siebie* 'himself' in object position which can be coreferential with the subject of the clause (259).

(259) [Dbać o siebie$_i$] (to) Marek$_i$ **dbał**.
look.INF after himself TO Marek looked.after
'As for looking after himself, Marek did (look after himself).'
(Bondaruk 2009: 69)

An apparent argument against verbal fronting being Ā-movement comes from the fact that it can cooccur with wh-movement (260).

(260) a. **Kupić** (to) *komu* **kupił** kwiaty, a nie kupił prezentu?
buy.INF TO for.who bought flowers but not bought present
'As for buying, who did he buy flowers for, but didn't buy a present?'
b. [**Kupić** kwiaty] (to) *komu* **kupił**, a nie kupił prezentu?
buy.INF flowers TO for.who bought but not bought present
'As for buying flowers, who did he buy them for, but didn't buy a present?'
(Bondaruk 2009: 75)

However, Polish as a multiple wh-fronting language allows more than one Ā-dependency to target the left periphery of the clause as demonstrated in (261) for multiple wh-movement.

(261) a. Kto co robił?
who what did
'Who did what?' (Rudin 1988: 449)
b. Kto komu co dał?
who.NOM who.DAT what.ACC gave
'Who gave whom what?' (Cichocki 1983: 53)

The common explanation is that while the leftmost element occupies SpecCP all other extracted items are adjoined to TP/IP (Rudin 1988). Evidence in favour of this view is presented by the possibility of material like parenthetical expressions or adverbs to split the wh-word sequence between the leftmost and the other extracted elements (262).

(262) a. Kto według ciebie komu co dał?
who according.to you whom what gave
'Who in your opinion gave what to whom?' (Cichocki 1983: 469)
b. Kto naprawdę komu co dał?
who really whom what gave
'Who really gave what to whom?' (Joanna Zaleska p.c.)

Therefore, the cooccurrence of verbal fronting and wh-extraction is no counter-argument against the former's Ā-nature *per se*.

There is no restriction on the class of verbs that may undergo fronting. In contrast to Fongbe (see section 7.1.5) and Haitian Creole (see section 7.1.7), both stage-level predicates (262) and individual-level predicates (263) can be topicalized.

(263) a. **Kochać** to on mnie **kocha**, ale mnie nie szanuje.
love.INF TO he.NOM me.DAT love.3SG but me.DAT not respect.3SG
'As for loving, he loves me, but doesn't respect me.'
b. [**Kochać** mnie] to on **kocha**, ale mnie nie
love.INF me.DAT TO he.NOM love.3SG but me.DAT not
szanuje.
respect.3SG
'As for loving me, he loves (me), but doesn't respect me.'
c. **Przypominać** nowy samochód **przypomina** BMW, ale
resemble.INF new.NOM car.NOM resemble.3SG BMW but
silnik ma jak w trabancie.
engine have.3SG like in trabant.LOC
'As for resembling, the new car resembles a BMW, but has an engine like a Trabant.'
d. [**Przypominać** BMW] nowy samochód **przypomina**, ale
resemble.INF BMW new.NOM car.NOM resemble.3SG but
silnik ma jak w trabancie.
engine have.3SG like in trabant.LOC
'As for resembling a BMW, the new car resembles (a BMW), but has an engine like a Trabant.' (Joanna Zaleska p.c.)

However, there is a restriction concerning the fronting of the copula *być*. It can never be topicalized on its own (264-a) but only together with a complement which must be a stage-level predicate (264-b) rather than an individual-level predicate (264-c). If the copula has a locative function this restriction does not apply (264-d, e).

(264) a. ?***Być** (to) **był** sławny/dyrektorem, ale już nie
be.INF TO he.was famous/a director but no.longer
jest.
not is
'As for being, he was famous/a director but he no longer is.'
b. [**Być** sławny/dyrektorem] (to) **był**, ale już nie jest.
be.INF famous/director TO he.was but no.longer not is
'As for being famous/a director, he was (famous/a director), but he no longer is.'
c. *[**Być** wściekła na niego] jeszcze nie **była**, ale będzie.
be.INF angry with him yet not was but will.be
'As for being angry with him, she still has not been, but she will be.'

d. **Być** (to) ona może **była** w Nowym Yorku, ale niewiele
   be.INF TO she maybe was in New York but little
   widziała.
   saw
   'As for being, maybe she was in New York, but she saw little.'

e. [**Być** w Nowym Yorku] (to) ona może **była**, ale niewiele
   be.INF in New York TO she maybe was but little
   widziała.
   saw
   'As for being in New York, maybe she was (there), but she saw little.'
   (Bondaruk 2009: 67f.)

Concerning the size of the fronted constituent, Bondaruk (2009, 2012) argues that it is a (remnant) *v*P rather than a VP. First, note that elements that usually attach outside of the verbal domain, like negation (265-a) and sentential adverbs (265-b), are not licit in the sentence-initial constituent.

(265) a. *[*Nie* **pić** (alkoholu)] (to) Marek raczej nie **pił**, ale dużo
       not drink.INF alcohol TO Marek rather not drank but a.lot
       jadł.
       ate
       'As for not drinking, Marek didn't (drink), but he ate a lot.'
    b. *[*Przypuszczalnie* **upić** się] (to) się **upił**, ale nie
       probably get.drunk.INF REFL TO REFL got.drunk but not
       robił awantury.
       made row
       'As for probably getting drunk, he did so, but he didn't make a row.'
       (Bondaruk 2009: 68)

In contrast, elements that adjoin to VP, like low adverbs (266-a) and prepositional phrases (266-b) may accompany the fronted verb (phrase).

(266) a. [**Pisać** artykuły *szybko*] (to) Marek **pisze**, ale wolno je
       write.INF papers quickly TO Marek writes but slowly them
       poprawia.
       revises
       'As for wrtiting papers quickly, Marek writes them quickly, but he revises them slowly.' (Bondaruk 2009: 69)

b. [**Pracować** z   dużym zaangażowaniem] (to) Marek **pracuje**,
    work.INF with great involvement   TO Marek works
    ale nie osiąga zbyt dobrych wyników.
    but not get   too good   results
    'As for working with great involvement, Marek does so, but he does
    not get particularly good results.'   (Bondaruk 2012: 55)

The fronted constituent therefore has to be at least as small as *v*P but no smaller than VP. That it is in fact a *v*P can, as Bondaruk (2009: 69) argues, be seen from the fact that adverbs like *celowo* 'deliberately' and *świadomie* 'voluntarily', which require the presence of an agent argument and therefore must adjoin at the *v*P rather than VP level, can occur in the topic constituent.

(267)   [**Kłamać** *celowe/świadomie*]   (to) Marek nie **kłamie**, ale
        lie.INF deliberately/voluntarily TO Marek not lies   but
        czasami   kłamie bezwiednie.
        sometimes lies   involuntarily
        'As for lying deliberately/voluntarily, Marek doesn't do so, but sometimes lies involuntarily.'   (Bondaruk 2009: 69)

We can now turn to the question whether the fronted verb is a bare head or rather a remnant verb phrase. First, if it were indeed a bare head, this would presuppose that head-to-spec movement is available in Polish because as has been shown above verb fronting involves $\bar{\text{A}}$-movement. If such a movement were available, one would assume that any kind of verb could be affected, including auxiliaries. However, as demonstrated in (268), fronting the auxiliary results in ungrammaticality.

(268)   *****Być**   (to) Marek **będzie** nad tym pracował, ale czy mu się to
        will.INF TO Marek will   on this work   but if him REFL this
        uda   skończyć.
        manage finish   (Joanna Zaleska p.c.)

A prerequisite for remnant movement is the (independent) existence of remnant-creating movement. In our case, all elements contained within the verb phrase except for the verb itself would have to scramble out of it. Example (269) serves as evidence that scrambling of direct objects (269-a), prepositional objects (269-b) and secondary predicates (269-c) is attested in Polish.

(269)   a. Marek *książkę*$_1$ [$_{vP}$ położył ___$_1$ na stole].
            Marek book   put   on table
            'Mark put a book on the table.'

b. Marek *na stole*₁ [vP położył książkę ___₁].
   Marek on table   put   book
   'Amrek put a book on the table.'
c. Marek *na surowo*₁ [vP jadł rybę ___₁] , ale nie mięso.
   Marek raw   ate fish   but not meat
   'Marek ate the fish raw, but he didn't eat meat.'
   (Bondaruk 2009: 71)

Crucially, the remnant vPs created in (269) can be fronted resulting in (270).

(270) a. [**Położyć** książkę] (to) Marek **położył** na stole, a   zeszyt
         put.INF   book   TO Marek put   on table but notebook
         położył na biurku.
         put   on desk
         'As for putting a book, Marek put it on the table, but he put a notebook on the desk.'
   b. [**Położyć** na stole] (to) Marek **położył** książkę, a   zeszytu
         put.INF on table TO Marek put   book   but notebook
         nie położył na stole.
         not put   on table
         'As for putting on the table, Marek put a book there, but he didn't put a notebook on the table.' (Bondaruk 2009: 72)
   c. [**Jeść**] (to) Marek **jadł** rybę na surowo, ale nigdy nie jadł
         eat.INF TO Marek ate   fish raw   but never not ate
         mięsa.
         meat
         'As for eating, Mark ate the fish raw, but he never ate meat.'
         (Bondaruk 2009: 71)

A further indication that the object is scrambled in verb fronting contexts is the freezing effect. Moved elements in their final landing site become islands for further subextraction. In example (271), it is not possible for the wh-element *jaki* 'what' to undergo left-branch extraction out of the object *jaki samochód* 'what car' which indicates that this phrase itself has already been moved via scrambling.

(271) *****Kupić** (to) *jaki*₁ Marek **kupił** [___₁ *samochód*], a   nie zamierzał.
       buy.INF TO what Marek bought   car   but not intended
       'As for buying, what car did Mark buy but he didn't intend to?'
       (Bondaruk 2009: 72)

Idiomatic readings provide another diagnostic for remnant versus bare head movement. In Spanish (see section 8.2.12) and Hebrew (see section 8.2.4), verb fronting is argued to involve bare head movement while verb phrase fronting is regular phrasal movement. Crucially, if in one of these languages verb fronting applies to a verb that is part of a verb-complement idiomatic expression, the sentence loses the idiomatic reading whereas it retains it in verb phrase fronting. In Polish, however, the idiomatic reading is available under both verb and verb phrase fronting (272).

(272) a. **Wyciągnąć** (to) on **wyciągnął** nogi, ale nikt tego nie
stretch.INF TO he stretched legs but nobody this not
zauważył.
noticed
'As for dying, he died, but nobody noticed this.'

b. [**Wyciągnąć** nogi] (to) on **wyciągnął**, ale nikt tego nie
stretch.INF legs TO he stretched but nobody this not
zauważył.
noticed
'As for dying, he died, but nobody noticed it.' (Bondaruk 2009: 74)

If verb fronting were achieved by bare head movement, we would expect the idiomatic reading to be unavailable analogous to Spanish and Hebrew. That this is not the case strongly suggests that verb fronting in Polish is not bare head but rather remnant verb phrase movement.

A problem for the remnant movement treatment of verb fronting is presented by ditransitive verbs. As we have seen in example (253), repeated as (273-a, b) below, it is possible to front a ditransitive verb with its direct object only (273-a) but not with its indirect object only (273-b).

(273) a. [**Dać** kwiaty] (to) jej **dał**, ale prezentu nie kupił.
give.INF flowers TO her he.gave but present not bought
'As for giving flowers, he gave her (flowers), but he didn't buy a present.'

b. *[**Dać** jej] (to) **dał** kwiaty, ale prezentu nie kupił.
give.INF her TO gave flowers but present not bought
'As for giving her, he gave (her) flowers, but he didn't buy a present.'
(Bondaruk 2009: 72)

Under a remnant movement approach, this contrast is unexpected because it is possible to scramble each object individually (Bondaruk 2009: 73). However, the ungrammaticality of (273-b) can be accounted for by Landau's (2007) condition on partial VP fronting. This condition states that a partial verb phrase is only licit in fronted position if it forms an independent constituent that is also licit in its base position. In other words, it is only licit if the missing parts of the partial verb phrase can be dropped independently in the base position. As shown in (274), the verb and its direct object form such a constituent with the indirect object being dropped (274-a), whereas this is not true for the verb and the indirect object (274-b). Hence, the contrast in (273) derives from a factor independent of scrambling.

(274) a. Marek chciał [dać   kwiaty] wczoraj.
          Marek wanted give.INF flowers yesterday
          'Marek wanted to give flowers yesterday.'
      b. *Marek chciał [dać   jej] wczoraj.
          Marek wanted give.INF her yesterday
          'Marek wanted to give her yesterday.'   (Bondaruk 2009: 73)

A further problem posed by ditransitive verb fronting as in (253), repeated in (275), is that it requires scrambling of both objects which is known to be marginal in Polish (276). We would expect the marginality to persevere into the verb fronting which it does not.

(275) **Dać**   (to) **dał**   jej kwiaty, ale prezentu nie kupił.
      give.INF TO   he.gave her flowers but present not bought
      'As for giving, he gave her flowers, but he didn't buy a present.'
                                                    (Bondaruk 2009: 73)

(276) ?Ania Tomkowi lody   kupiła.
       Ania Tomek   ice.cream bought
       'Ania bought Tomek ice cream.'
                              (Bondaruk 2009: 73, citing Tajsner 1998: 150)

As it stands, there is no plausible explanation for the lack of degradation in (275).

Summary

Polish shows both verb and verb phrase topic fronting with a copy of the verb appearing clause-internally. The fronted verb has to be infinitive and bear the same aspect as its lower copy. Fronting in embedded clauses is possible as well as fronting out of subjunctive *żeby* and infinitive clauses. Islands and embedded finite clauses with the complementizer *że*, however, may analogous to wh-extraction not be left by verbal fronting. Material that may accompany the verb (phrase) in fronted position includes low adverbs and prepositional phrases but not negation and high sentential adverbs. There are arguments that the fronted verb is not a bare head but a remnant *v*P. Auxiliaries may not be fronted, partial verb phrase fronting is possible, independent *v*P evacuating scrambling movement is attested, and idiomatic verb-complement expressions retain their reading under verb fronting. Table 8.14 provides a condensed overview over the properties of

Polish verbal fronting. Verbal fronting in Polish shows the same repair, a copy of the fronted verb, in both verb and verb phrase fronting. It therefore displays pattern I of Generalization I.

Tab. 8.14: Properties of verbal fronting in Polish

	Copy	Dummy	Unbound	Islands	GS	TAM	L-Adv	H-Adv	NEG	L/R	Top/Foc
V	✓	–	✓[26]	✓	n.d.	✓[27]	✓	–	–	L	Top
VP	✓	–	✓	✓	n.d.	✓	✓	–	–	L	Top

8.2.11 Russian

Russian, a Slavic language of the Indo-European phylum, is spoken by about 260 million people in Russia and neighbouring countries. Its basic word order is SVO.

The language shows a verb (277-a) and a verb phrase fronting construction (277-b), in which a copy of the fronted verb appears inside the clause. According to Abels (2001), the constituent in sentence-initial position is interpreted as an S-topic in the sense of Büring (1995) and, roughly speaking, acts as a contrastive topic in providing one non-exhaustive answer to a set of alternative questions.

(277)   a.   **Čitat'** (-to) Ivan eë **čitaet**, no ničego ne
 read.INF TO Ivan it.FEM.ACC reads but nothing not
 ponimaet.
 understands
 'Ivan does read it, but he doesn't understand a thing.'

(Abels 2001: 1)

     b.   [**Napisat'**-[to] stat'ju[-to]] ja (stat'ju)
 write.INFL(-TO) article.ACC(-TO) I.NOM article.ACC
 napisala,...
 write.PST.FEM.S
 'As for writing the article, I did write it.'

(Aboh & Dyakonova 2009: 1040)

---

26 Verbal fronting behaves parallel to wh-extraction in being unbounded from subjunctive *żeby* and infinitive clauses but not from embedded finite clauses with the complementizer *że*. The same holds for verb phrase fronting.

27 The fronted infinitive may be marked for aspect but not for tense. The same holds for verb phrase fronting.

However, there seems to be considerable variation with regard to the conditions that hold on these fronting constructions. On the one hand, Abels (2001: 14) asserts, contrary to what we see in (277-b), that it is not possible to have verb phrase fronting with a direct object, be it a pronoun as in (278) or a full NP object (though he gives no example showing the latter). Only PPs (279-a) and CPs (279-b) are licit as complements of the fronted verb.

(278) *[**Čitat'** eë] (-to) Ivan (eë) **čitaet** (eë), no…
 read.INF it.FEM.ACC TO Ivan it.FEM.ACC reads it.FEM.ACC but…
 (Abels 2001: 14)

(279) a. [**Dumat'** o ženit'be] (-to) on **dumaet** – no nikogda on
 think.INF about marriage TO he think3SG but never he
 ne ženitsja.
 not marry.self
 'He does think about marriage, but he will never marry.'
 b. [**Dumat'** čto Xomskij genij] on **dumaet** no čitat' ego
 think.INF that Chomsky genius he thinks but read.INF his
 knigi ne čitaet / no znat' ne znaet.
 books not reads / but know.INF not knows
 'He does think that Chomsky is a genius, but he doesn'T read his books / but he doesn't know for sure.' (Abels 2001: 4)

On the other hand, there are examples like (277-b) and (280), which clearly exhibit the direct object inside the fronted verb phrase.

(280) [**Kupit'** pomidory] ona **kupila**, no salat ne sdelala.
 buy.INF tomatoes.ACC she bought but salad not make.PERF
 'She bought the tomatoes but she hasn't made a salad.'
 (Verbuk 2006: 397)

Similar variation is found in verb fronting. While example (277-a) allows stranding of the direct object, the ungrammatical example (282) indicates that it is illicit.

(281) ***Napisat'**(-to) ja **napisala** stat'ju.
 write.INF(-TO) I.NOM write.PST.FEM.S article.ACC
 'As for writing the article, I did write it.'
 (Aboh & Dyakonova 2009: 1040)

This variation might of course be due to dialectal or even idiolectal variation. Nonetheless, if one disregards Abels' (2001) assertion that full NP objects cannot be fronted together with the verb and relies solely on the data provided above, the following generalization emerges: Verb fronting is only licit as long as the stranded object is not a full NP (282) whereas verb phrase fronting is allowed only in case the object is a full NP (283). This is again presented abstractly in (284).

(282) *Verb fronting*
    a. **Čitat'** (-to) Ivan *eë* **čitaet**, no ničego ne
        read.INF TO Ivan it.FEM.ACC reads but nothing not
        ponimaet.
        understands
        'Ivan does read it, but he doesn't understand a thing.'
        (Abels 2001: 1)
    b. *****Napisat'**(-to) ja **napisala** *stat'ju*
        write.INF(-TO) I.NOM write.PST.FEM.S article.ACC
        'As for writing the article, I did write it.'
        (Aboh & Dyakonova 2009: 1040)

(283) *Verb phrase fronting*
    a. *****[Čitat'** *eë*] (-to) Ivan (eë) **čitaet** (eë),
        read.INF it.FEM.ACC TO Ivan it.FEM.ACC reads it.FEM.ACC
        no...
        but... (Abels 2001: 14)
    b. [**Napisat'**-[to] *stat'ju[-to]*] ja (stat'ju)
        write.INFL(-TO) article.ACC(-TO) I.NOM article.ACC
        napisala,...
        write.PST.FEM.S
        'As for writing the article, I did write it.'
        (Aboh & Dyakonova 2009: 1040)

(284) *Interaction of verbal fronting and type of object in Russian*

	V fronting	VP fronting
full NP object	✗	✓
pronominal object	✓	✗

This pattern easily falls out if Russian disposes of an object movement akin to Object Shift in the Scandinavian languages. While full NPs (and other phrasal material like PPs or CPs) obligatorily stay inside the verb phrase, pronominal elements have to undergo object shift out of that verb phrase. Now, if in Russian, only verb phrases, not bare verbal heads, may be fronted, then the obligatory shift of pronominal elements accounts for the fact that they never appear with a fronted verb. Full NPs, on the other hand, cannot leave the verb phrase before it gets fronted and hence always accompany the verb into the left periphery. Whether this approach is correct or not, however, is not the point of this section. In any case, Russian shows verb and verb phrase fronting even if the former is only possible with pronominal objects while the latter is licit only when the object is not pronominal.

Turning to some other properties of the construction, we find that verb doubling is precluded when verbal fronting strands an auxiliary (285).

(285) a. On budet čitat'.
           he will read.INF
       b. ***Čitat'** (-to) on budet **čitat'**.
           read.INF TO he will read.INF
       c. Čitat' (-to) on budet.
           read.INF TO he will
           'He will read.' (Abels 2001: 4f.)

This also holds in cases where the verb appears in its participial form (286).

(286) a. Dom byl postroen.
           house was build.PTCP.PST.PASS
       b. ***Postroen** (-to) dom byl **postroen**.
           build.PTCP.PST.PASS TO house was build.PTCP.PST.PASS
       c. Postroen dom byl.
           build.PTCP.PST.PASS house was
           'The house was built.' (Abels 2001: 5)

Furthermore, like in Polish (see section 8.2.10), the verb in sentence-initial position and its copy inside the clause may not bear different aspects (287)

(287) a. ***Čitat'** (-to) on eë **pročitaet**…
           read.INF TO he it.FEM.ACC reads.PFV
       b. ***Pročitat'** (-to) on eë **čitaet**…
           read.PFV.INF TO he it.FEM.ACC reads (Abels 2001: 13)

Fronting is not limited to specific verb classes. We have already seen that it is possible with the transitive verb *čitat'* 'read'. Other frontable verbs are unergatives (288-a), unaccusatives (288-b), ditransitives (288-c), PP-embedding verbs (288-d), and CP-embedding verbs (288-e).

(288) a. Čto èto on? **Streljat'** ne **streljaet**, a ružë deržit?!
           what that he shoot.INF not shoots, but rifle hold.3SG
           'What's wrong with him? Holds a rifle but doesn't fire?!'
       b. **Rasti** -to Marina **rastët**, no často boleet.
           grow.INF TO Marina grow.3SG but often be.ill.3SG
           'Marina does grow, but she is ill a lot.'

c. **Dat'** (-to) ja eë emu **dal,** no...
   give.INF TO I her him gave, but...
   'I did give it to him, but...'
d. **Dumat'** o ženit'be (-to) on **dumaet** – no nikogda on ne
   think.INF about marriage TO he think3SG but never he not
   ženitsja.
   marry.self
   'He does think about marriage, but he will never marry.'
e. **Dumat'** čto Xomskij genij on **dumaet** no **čitat'** ego
   think.INF that Chomsky genius he thinks but read.INF his
   knigi ne **čitaet** / no **znat'** ne **znaet.**
   books not reads / but know.INF not knows
   'He does think that Chomsky is a genius, but he doesn't read his books
   / but he doesn't know for sure.' (Abels 2001: 3f.)

As far as $\bar{\text{A}}$-movement diagnostics are concerned, verbal fronting behaves like wh-movement in that it is not possible from embedded clauses with the complementizer *čto* (289).

(289) ***Kupit'** (-to) ty skazal [čto ja èto **kupil**...]
      buy.INF TO you said that I that bought (Abels 2001: 10)

And just like wh-movement is licit from embedded infinitives and subjunctives, verbal fronting is sometimes allowed to take place from infinitivals, too (asserted without examples in Abels 2001: 10). We can therefore safely accept that verbal fronting in Russian involves $\bar{\text{A}}$-movement.

With regard to the size of the initial constituent in verb fronting, it was already suggested that it might be a remnant verb phrase because verb fronting is only allowed when the object is a pronominal element that by assumption has to shift out of the verb phrase. Further evidence for the object shift (and remnant verb phrase) approach comes from verb phrases that contain a PP. According to our assumptions about object shift, PPs have to stay inside the verb phrase. Therefore, if verb fronting is actually remnant verb phrase movement rather than bare head movement, the verb should not be able to move to the left periphery on its own whilst stranding the PP. This is indeed what we find (290-b). The PP has to be fronted with the verb (290-a). However, as is well known from English Heavy-NP Shift, object shift is often influenced by the heaviness of the object, where heavier objects tend to shift easier than light ones. A similar situation is found in Russian. In (290-c), the object is quite heavy as it embeds a full relative clause. We thus expect it to exceptionally be able to shift out of the verb phrase creating a remnant verb phrase that might be fronted and result in the verb being located in clause-initial position with the PP being stranded. The example is therefore accepted although with a slight degradation.

(290) a. [**Dumat'** *o* *ženit'be* (-to)] on **dumaet** – no nikogda on
 think.INF about marriage TO he thinks but never he
 ne ženitsja.
 not marry.self
 b. ***Dumat'** (-to) on **dumaet** *o* *ženit'be* – no ...
 think.INF TO he thinks about marriage but ...
 'He does think about marriage, but he will never marry.'
 c. ?**Dumat'** (-to) on **dumaet** *o* *pesni, kotoruju pel Ivan*...
 think.INF TO he thinks about song which sang Ivan...
 'He does think about the song that Ivan sang, but...'

(Abels 2001: 7, 15)

These data thus receive a straightforward explanation under an approach involving object shift and remnant verb phrase fronting. Whether the fronted phrase is *v*P or VP, however, is not evident from the available data. The only thing we can state is that it is not larger than *v*P because while low VP-adjoined adverbs like *bystro* 'fast' are allowed with a fronted verb (291-a), high *v*P-adjoined adverbs like *čera* 'yesterday' are not (291-b).

(291) a. Bystro pečatat' (-to) on pečataet, no delaet mnogo ošibok.
 fast type.INF TO he types but makes many errors
 'He types fast, but he makes a lot of mistakes.'
 b. *Včera pečatat' (-to) on pečatal, no sdelal mnogo ošibok.
 yesterday type.INF TO he typed but made many errors
 'He did type yesterday, but he made a lot of mistakes.'

(Abels 2001: 7f.)

Summary

In conclusion, Russian shows both verb and verb phrase fronting with a copy of the displaced verb appearing in the base position. Both tokens of the verb may not mismatch in their aspectual values. No verb copy is found when an auxiliary is present inside the clause. The fronting exhibits a neat complementary pattern: In case the object is a pronominal element, only verb fronting, not verb phrase fronting is licit, whereas with non-pronominal object, the reverse is true. This pattern receives a simple explanation if Russian only allows verb phrases, not bare verbal heads, in clause-initial position and the relevant remnant creating movement is obligatory for pronominal elements but only exceptionally applicable to non-pronominal elements. As verbal fronting behaves similar to wh-movement in being precluded from finite clauses with the complementizer *čto* but allowed from embedded infinitives we are safe to assume that it involves $\bar{\text{A}}$-movement. The size of the moved verbal phrase is not exactly determined. It might be a VP or a *v*P but in any case cannot be larger than *v*P. The relevant results are summarized in table 8.15. Russian verbal fronting, thus, fits pattern I of Generalization I perfectly. It shows the same repair of verb doubling in both verb and verb phrase fronting.

Tab. 8.15: Properties of verbal fronting in Russian

	Copy	Dummy	Unbound	Islands	GS	TAM	L-Adv	H-Adv	NEG	L/R	Top/Foc
V	✓	–	–	n.d.	n.d.	–	✓	–[28]	n.d.	L	Top
VP	✓	–	–	n.d.	n.d.	–	✓	–	n.d.	L	Top

8.2.12 Spanish

Spanish, a Romance language of the Indo-European phylum, is one of the most widely spoken languages of the world. Its number of speakers lies at around half a billion worldwide. Due to its wide distribution there exist a number of dialects and varieties. As the discussion in this section is based on data from Vicente (2007, 2009) I have to remain agnostic as to whether the observations hold beyond Iberian peninsular Spanish.

The language shows both verb (292-a) and verb phrase fronting (292-b) with a copy of the displaced verb occupying he clause-internal verb position. The fronted constituent is interpreted as a topic while the whole construction receives a verum focus reading (Vicente 2009: 166).

(292)   a.   **Leer,**   Juan ha **leído** un libro.
               read.INF Juan has read   a   book
               'As for reading, Juan has read a book.'
       b.   [**Leer**   el libro], Juan lo ha **leído**.
               read.INF the book   Juan CL has read
               'As for reading the book, Juan has indeed read it.'
       c.   ?[**Leer** el libro], Juan ha **leído** el libro.   (Vicente 2009: 159, 167)

---

[28] The fronted copy may, as all infinitives in Russian, be marked for aspect. This also holds for verb phrase fronting.

Note that as in (292-c) it is marginally possible to double the object of a fronted verb phrase, although this option is dispreferred in comparison with (292-b). The presence of a left dislocated clitic *lo* in (292-b) is unsurprising when one considers that it also appears whenever a DP complement of the verb is topicalized on its own. In contrast, topicalization of a PP complement does not trigger the presence of a left dislocated clitic and, consequently, such a clitic is absent when the fronted verb phrase contains a PP complement (293).

(293)   [**Salir**   con Clara], Juan ha **salido**.
         go.out.INF with Clara   Juan has gone.out
         'As for going out with Clara, Juan has gone out (with her).'
                                                                            (Vicente 2009: 167)

It is not possible to omit the left-dislocated clitic in verb phrase fronting containing a DP object (294-a). However, there is the option of having an object clitic inside the fronted constituent, too (294-b). Doubling a fronted object clitic with a full DP clause-internally is ungrammatical (294-c).

(294)   a.   ?*[**Leer**   un libro], Juan ha **leído**.
                read.INF a   book   Juan has read
                'As for reading a book, Juan has read (it).'
       b.   **Leer**=lo,   Juan lo ha   **leído**.
                read.INF=CL Juan CL has read
                'As for reading it, Juan has read it.'
       c.   *****Leer**=lo,   Juan ha   **leído** un libro.
                read.INF=CL Juan has read   a   book
                'As for reading it, Juan has read a book.'   (Vicente 2007: 63)

In any case, the verb in the fronted portion must be infinitive. It can neither appear in a finite form (295-a) nor can it be a participle (295-b).

(295)   a.   *****Leyó**,   Juan **leyó**   el   libro.
                read.PST.3SG Juan read.PST.3SG the book
                'As for reading, Juan read the book.'
       b.   *****Leído**,   Juan ha   **leído** el   libro.
                read.PERF.PART Juan has read   the book
                'As for reading, Juan has read the book.'   (Vicente 2009: 165)

Dummy verb insertion is not possible in the abovementioned verbal fronting examples. Although Spanish does comprise of the construction in (296-a) where a fronted verb phrase is referred back to by a form of *hacer* 'do' and a pronoun *eso* 'that' (similar to the *fazer isso* periphrase in Brazilian Portuguese, see section 8.2.1)

Lipták & Vicente (2009) show that this is a different construction. First, it only allows verb phrase fronting, not verb fronting (296-b). Second, the *eso*-construction requires the fronted verb phrase to be embedded under a higher verb (like *suele* in (296)) whereas this is not necessary in the verb doubling construction. Third, this higher verb must independently be able to select for a nominal complement which is not the case with verb doubling. Finally, the two constructions differ semantically: While the verb-doubling verbal fronting construction receives a verum focus interpretation, the *eso*-construction simply expresses a (contrastive) topicalization.

(296)   a.   Regalarle libros a María, Juan suele hacer eso.
                 give.CL   books to María Juan HAB do.INF that
                 'To give books to María, Juan usually does that.'
         b.   *Regalarle, Juan suele hacer(le) eso libros a María.
                 give.CL   Juan HAB do.ING.CL that books to María
                                                                    (Lipták & Vicente 2009: 667)

Generally, all types of verbs can undergo fronting with verb doubling as long as their semantics are compatible with a topic interpretation. This includes among others raising and control verbs. However, the auxiliaries *haber* 'to have' and *ser* 'to be' are precluded from the sentence-initial topic position (297).

(297)   a.   **Haber,** Juan ha leído un libro.
                 have.INF Juan has read a book
                 'As for something being done, Juan has read a book.'
         b.   **Ser,** la puerta **fue** reparada.
                 be.INF the door was fixed
                 'As for being (done something), the door was fixed.'
                                                                        (Vicente 2009: 166)

Let us now turn to the arguments for the $\bar{\text{A}}$-nature of the dependency between the fronted constituent and the verb copy inside the clause. Unfortunately, Vicente (2007, 2009) provides the respective examples for verb fronting only. Since he does not mention anywhere that verb phrase fronting diverges from the pattern of verb fronting I will assume here that the relevant judgements for verb fronting also hold for the corresponding verb phrase fronting sentences. First, verbal fronting can take place across finite clause boundaries (298), a hallmark property of $\bar{\text{A}}$-movement.

(298)   a.   **Leer,** Juan ha dicho [que María ha **leído** un libro].
                 read.INF Juan has said   that María has read a book
                 'As for reading, Juan has said that María has read a book.'

b. **Venir,** me parece [que ya no **vienes**].
   come.INF me.DAT seems that already not come.2SG
   'As for coming, it seems to me that you aren't coming in the end.'
   (Vicente 2009: 168)

Second, the dependency is sensitive to islands. Thus, it is not possible to extract a verbal constituent across an island boundary like the Complex NP Island (299), the Adjunct Island (300), the Subject Island (301), the Relative Clause Island (302), or from one conjunct of a coordinated structure (303).

(299) *Complex NP Island*
   ***Comprar,** he oído [el rumor de que Juan ha **comprado** un libro].
   buy.INF have heard the rumour of that Juan has bought a book
   'As for buying, I've heard the rumour that Juan has bought a book.'
   (Vicente 2009: 168)

(300) *Adjunct Island*
   ***Comprar,** he ido al cine [después de **comprar** un libro].
   buy.INF have gone to cinema after of buy.INF a book
   'As for buying, I've gone to the movies after buying a book.'
   (Vicente 2009: 169)

(301) *Subject Island*
   *?**Ganar,** [que el Athletic **ganara** la Copa] sorprendería a mucha gente.
   win.INF that the Athletic wins the Cup surprise to many people
   'As for winning, that Athletic should win the Cup would surprise many people.'
   (Vicente 2009: 169)

(302) *Relative Clause Island*
   ***Comprar,** he visto al hombre [que ha **comprado** un libro].
   buy.INF have seen the man that has bought a book
   'As for buying, I've seen the man that has bought a book.'
   (Vicente 2009: 168)

(303) *Coordinate Structure Constraint*
   ***Leer,** Juan ha [visto una película y **leído** un libro].
   read.INF Juan has watched a film and read a book
   'As for reading, Juan has watched a film and read a book.'
   (Vicente 2009: 169)

The Wh-Island is not of any diagnostic use here because it can often be violated in Spanish without any deterioration of grammaticality. Vicente (2009) provides the following examples (304) taken from Lasnik & Uriagereka (2005) as evidence for the violability of a Wh-Island by wh-movement.

(304) [A quién]₁ no sabes [cuánto aprecia Pedro ___₁].
 to who not know.2SG how.much likes Pedro
 'Who do you wonder how much Pedro likes?'
 (Lasnik & Uriagereka 2005: 84)

A last indication that verbal fronting in Spanish involves (Ā-)movement rather than base generation is the absence of any genus-species effects.

(305) a. *[**Leer** *un tebeo japonés*], Juan ha **leído** *Akira*.
 read.INF a comic-book Japanese, Juan has read Akira
 'As for reading a Japanese comic book, Juan has read Akira.'
 b. ***Viajar**, Juan ha **volado** a Amsterdam.
 travel.INF Juan has flown to Amsterdam
 'As for travelling, Juan has flown to Amsterdam.'
 (Vicente 2009: 170)

Various elements besides the internal argument(s) (306-a, b) may be fronted together with the verb including secondary predicates (306-c, d), complement clauses (306-e, f), and locative complements (306-g, h).

(306) a. **Mandarle,** Juan le ha **mandado** *una carta a María*.
 send.INF.CL.DAT Juan CL.DAT has sent a letter to María
 'As for sending, Juan has sent María a letter.'
 b. [**Mandarle** *una carta a María*], Juan se la ha **mandado**.
 send.INF.CL.DAT a letter to María Juan CL CL.DAT has sent
 'As for sending a letter to María, Juan has sent it to her.'
 c. **Ver,** Juan ha **visto** a María *desnuda*.
 see.INF Juan has seen to María naked.FEM
 'As for seeing, Juan has seen María naked.'
 d. [**Ver** a María *desnuda*], Juan la ha **visto**.
 see.INF to María naked Juan CL has seen
 'As for seeing María naked, Juan has seen (her naked)'
 e. **Pensar,** Juan **piensa** *que mañana va a llover*.
 think.INF Juan thinks that tomorrow goes to rain
 'As for thinking, Juan thinks that it is going to rain tomorrow.'

f. [**Pensar** *que mañana va a llover*], Juan lo **piensa**.
   think.INF that tomorrow goes to rain   Juan CL thinks
   'As for thinking that it is going to rain tomorrow, Juan thinks (it).'
g. **Entrar,** Juan **entró** *en la casa*.
   enter.INF Juan entered in the house
   'As for going, Juan went into the house.'
h. [**Entrar** *en la casa*], Juan **entró**.
   enter.INF in the house Juan entered
   'As for going into the house, Juan did go.' (Vicente 2009: 167f.)

Unfortunately, Vicente (2007, 2009) does not provide examples of partial verb phrase fronting with ditransitive verbs. Hence, it is at this point not possible to investigate whether Spanish respects Landau's (2007) condition on fronted VP-portions.

Concerning the category of the fronted constituent, Vicente (2007, 2009) puts forward a number of arguments to the fact that what is fronted in verb phrase fronting must be a *v*P rather than a VP or TP. First, in contrast to Yiddish, Spanish does not allow a fronted verb to appear in a regularly derived infinitive form. That means, if a verb has an irregular infinitive form, this form occurs on a topicalized verb rather than some regularly constructed infinitive built from the stem of the finite verb plus a regular infinitive ending like *-ir, -ar,* or *-er*. Thus, the infinitive of the verb 'to go' is always *ir* (307-a–c) rather than *vir* (307-d) or *fu(i)r* (307-e).

(307) a. **Ir,** Juan **va**.
      go.INF Juan goes.PRS
      'As for going, Juan goes.'
   b. **Ir,** Juan **fue**.
      go.INF Juan went.PFV
      'As for going, Juan went.'
   c. **Ir,** Juan **iba**.
      go.INF Juan went.IPFV
      'As for going, Juan used to go.'
   d. *****Vir,** Juan va.
      go.INF Juan goes.PRS
      'As for going, Juan goes.'
   e. *****Fu(i)r,** Juan fue.
      go.INF Juan went.PFV
      'As for going, Juan went.' (Vicente 2007: 74)

As the stem allomorphs are conditioned by the presence of tense/aspect features usually hosted in a T/Asp head, the fronted verb not showing this kind of allomorphy cannot contain a T or Asp head. We can therefore conclude that the fronted constituent is smaller than AspP.

Second, low adverbs of manner like *rápido* 'quickly', which are usually assumed to adjoin below *v*P, may accompany the verb (phrase) in sentence-initial position (308-a). However, high adverbs of time like *ayer* 'yesterday' and sentential adverbs like *aparentemente* 'apparently', which are adjoined above *v*P, cannot be fronted with the verb (phrase) (308-b, c).

(308) a. [**Leer** el libro *rápido*], Juan lo **leyó**.
 read.INF the book quickly Juan CL read.PST.3SG
 'As for reading the book quickly, Juan read (it quickly).'
 b. ?*[**Leer** el libro *ayer*], Juan lo **leyó**.
 read.INF the book yesterday Juan CL read.PST.3SG
 'As for reading the book yesterday, Juan has read (it yesterday).'
 c. *[**Leer** el libro *aparentemente*], Juan lo **leyó**.
 read.INF the book apparently Juan CL read.PST.3SG
 'As for reading the book apparently, Juan has (apparently) read (it).'
 (Vicente 2007: 76f.)

Third, evidence that the fronted constituent cannot be smaller than *v*P comes from verbal topicalization in passive sentences. As shown in (309-a), when a verb is fronted in a passive clause, it cannot appear in the infinitive. Rather, it has to take the form of a passive participle. And just like any other passive participle it has to agree with the promoted internal argument in gender and number, hence, (309-b) is ungrammatical because the fronted participle is masculine while the promoted argument *puerta* 'door' is feminine.

(309) a. ***Reparar**, la puerta ha sido **reparada**.
 fix.INF the door has been fixed.FEM.SG
 'As for fixing, the door has been fixed.'
 b. ***Reparado**, la puerta ha sido **reparada**.
 fixed.MASC.SG the door.FEM has been fixed.FEM.SG
 'As for being fixed, the door has been fixed.'
 c. **Reparada**, la puerta ha sido **reparada**.
 fixed.FEM.SG the door.FEM has been fixed.FEM.SG
 'As for being fixed, the door has been fixed.' (Vicente 2009: 171)

Passive morphology is commonly assumed to reside in the *v* head (also sometimes called Voice, Kratzer 1996). As the fronted verb in a passive sentence exhibits regular passive morphology rather than being infinitive, the fronted constituent must contain the *v* head that encodes the passive information.

Addressing the question whether the verb in verb fronting is a bare head or a remnant verb phrase Vicente (2009) provides several arguments against a remnant movement analysis. Some of these have already been discussed in detail in section 4.1.1 (to which I refer the interested reader here to avoid unnecessary repetition). Here, we turn to three asymmetries in behaviour between verb and verb phrase fronting which indicate that at no point in the derivation of verb fronting the object has been part of the moved constituent. This precludes a remnant movement account as well as a selective deletion account as proposed for verb fronting in general by Fanselow & Ćavar (2002) and Nunes (2004). They suggest that it is always the whole vP that is fronted and only at PF is it determined which copy of the object (the one inside the fronted vP or the one in base position) is spelled out.

The first asymmetry concerns quantifier scope. Consider example (310-a) with two quantified NPs, the subject *dos chicas* 'two girls' and the object *todos los chicos* 'all the boys'. This sentence allows two readings, one where the numeral scopes over the universal quantifier and one where the scope is reversed. Now, verb and verb phrase fronting have different influences on the scoping options. While verb fronting does not affect the readings at all (310-b), verb phrase fronting makes unavailable the reading where the universal quantifier takes scope over the numeral (310-c).

(310) a. *Dos* chicas han salido con *todos* los chicos.
           two girls have gone.out with all the boys
           'Two girls have dated every boy.' $(2 > \forall, \forall > 2)$
       b. **Salir,** *dos* chicas han **salido** con *todos* los chicos.
           go.out.INF two girls have gone.out with all the boys
           'As for dating, two girls have dated every boy.' $(2 > \forall, \forall > 2)$
       c. [**Salir** con *todos* los chicos], *dos* chicas ha **salido**.
           go.out.INF with all the boys two girls have gone.out
           'As for dating all the boys, two girls have.' $(2 > \forall, {*}\forall > 2)$
                                                           (Vicente 2009: 181)

This is expected as phrasal movement is known to create scope islands (Sauerland 1998). However, it also means that verb fronting most likely does not involve phrasal movement at any point in the derivation of (310-b), as it does not exhibit the same scope island effect.

The second asymmetry manifests itself in the licensing of negative polarity items (NPIs). NPIs like *ningún* 'any' generally need to be licensed by a proper negative element like ngeation (311-a). While, given an NPI-licensing environment inside the clause, an NPI may appear in an object stranded by verb fronting (311-b), it may not appear inside a fronted verb phrase even if the clause from which it was fronted provides a licensing environment (311-c).

(311) a. Juan   no ha leído *ningún* libro.
           read.INF Juan not has read   any book
           'As for reading, Juan hasn't read any book.'
       b. **Leer,**   Juan no ha **leído** *ningún* libro.
           read.INF Juan not has read any   book
           'As for reading, Juan hasn't read any book.'
       c. *[**Leer**   *ningún* libro], Juan no lo ha **leído**.
           read.INF any   book Juan not CL has read
           'As for reading any book, Juan hasn't read it.' (Vicente 2009: 181)

Vicente (2009) suggests that this asymmetry is presumably due to a cross-linguistic restriction that precludes NPIs from occurring in a topicalized constituent. Though, again, we would expect this restriction to also hold in verb fronting if verb fronting actually involved the same phrasal movement as verb phrase fronting plus a different PF deletion since both structures should have the same logical form under this approach.

The last asymmetry seems to be quite a common one in languages that show both verb and verb phrase fronting. It concerns the availability of idiomatic readings of verb-complement combinations like *estirar la pata* 'to die'. While this idiomatic reading is accessible in verb phrase fronting (312-a), it is precluded in verb fronting, where the verb is separated from its complement (312-b).

(312) a. [**Estirar**   la pata], Juan la ha **estirado**.
           stretch.INF the leg   Juan CL has stretched
           Lit.: 'Juan has stretched his leg (as a warm-up exercise).'
           Id.: 'Juan has died.'
       b. **Estirar,** Juan ha **estirado** la pata.
           stretch.INF Juan has stretched the leg
           Lit.: 'Juan has stretched his leg.'
           Id.: *'Juan has died.'   (Vicente 2009: 182)

Again, this asymmetry is unexpected if verb fronting involved phrasal movement and PF deletion of the fronted copy of the object, because the logical form, and therefore the interpretation, of verb and verb phrase fronting should be the same. Thus, Vicente (2009) concludes that verb fronting is $\bar{\text{A}}$-head movement of the verbal head whereas verb phrase movement is standard phrasal movement.

Summary
Spanish shows verb and verb phrase fronting, both of which trigger the presence of a copy of the displaced verb in the base position. The fronted constituent is usually interpreted as a (contrastive) topic while the whole sentence receives a verum

focus reading. With verb phrase fronting, the object is doubled by a clitic inside the clause just in case it is also doubled by one when it undergoes topicalization on its own. The fronted verb has to be in the infinitive (or in a passive participle form in passive sentences). Generally, all types of verbs can be fronted with the exclusion of the auxiliaries *haber* 'to have' and *ser* 'to be'. Verbal fronting can span finite clause boundaries, is sensitive to islands, and does not allow genus-species effects. Hence, it plausibly involves proper $\bar{\text{A}}$-movement. Various elements can be part of the fronted constituent including indirect objects, secondary predicates, complement clauses and locative expressions. However, in contrast to low adverb, high adverbs are precluded from accompanying the topic, which indicates that the fronted constituent cannot be larger than *v*P. It can also not be smaller than *v*P because the *v* head encodes passive information which is needed to correctly derive the passive participle form of the fronted verb in passive sentences. Vicente (2009) argues at length that verb fronting cannot be regarded as remnant *v*P movement because there is no evidence of *v*P-evacuating object movement in the relevant verb fronting examples. Rather, due to certain asymmetries between verb and verb phrase fronting with regard to quantifier scope, NPI licensing, and idiomatic readings, he concludes that the former employs a different kind of $\bar{\text{A}}$-movement, namely $\bar{\text{A}}$-head movement, than the latter. The relevant properties of verbal fronting are summarized in table 8.16. In conclusion, Spanish verbal fronting behaves according to pattern I of Generalization I: Both types of fronting trigger the same repair, namely verb doubling.

Tab. 8.16: Properties of verbal fronting in Spanish

	Copy	Dummy	Unbound	Islands	GS	TAM	L-Adv	H-Adv	Neg	L/R	Top/Foc
V	✓	–	✓	✓[29]	–	–[30]	✓	–	n.d.	L	Top
VP	✓	–	✓	✓		–	✓	–	n.d.	L	Top

---

[29] Both verb and verb phrase fronting respect the Complex NP Island, the Subject Island, the Adjunct Island, the Relative Clause Island, and the Coordinate Structure Constraint. Wh-Islands have not been provided as they usually have no effect in Spanish. This also holds for verb phrase fronting.
[30] The fronted verb can be a passive/past participle only if it is fronted from a passive sentence.

8.2.13 Tiv

Tiv is a Southern Bantoid language of the Niger-Congo family and is spoken by over two and a half million speakers in Nigeria (Angitso 2015: 142, fn. 1). Its basic word order is SVO (313).

(313) M̀yọ́m yàm á-kóndó.
       Myom buy NCL-cloth
       'Myom bought clothes.'   (Táíwò & Angitso 2016: 98)

The language shows verb and verb phrase fronting (314-a, b). The focus marker *ká* precedes the fronted constituent while the emphatic marker *yé* appears clause finally. Instead of a gap we find a copy of the verb clause-internally in both cases.

(314) a. Ká [ù **náhá**-n] Sésùgh á   **náhá**   mátù yé.
          FOC to drive-IPFV Sesugh AGR.PRN.PST drive.IPFV car EMP
          'It is driving a car that Sesugh is doing.'
                                                      (Táíwò & Angitso 2016: 102)
       b. Ká [ù **yàm**-én kwàgh-yá-n] Sésùgh á   **yám**   yé.
          FOC to buy-IPFV thing-eat-IPFV Sesugh AGR.PRN buy.PST EMP
          'It is/was BUYING FOOD that Sesugh did.'   (Angitso 2015: 145)

The fronted constituent obligatorily occurs as a so-called infinitive nominal clause (Táíwò & Angitso 2016: 103) in which the verb has to be imperfective and is preceded by the infinitive particle *ù*. It is interpreted as either new information focus or contrastive/exhaustive focus (Táíwò & Angitso 2016: 102).

As mentioned above, focus is marked by the focus marker *ká* and the emphatic marker *yé*. If the latter is absent, the sentence is ungrammatical (315).[31]

(315) *Ká [ù **yàm**-én kwàgh-yá-n] Sésùgh á   **yám**.
        FOC to buy-IPFV thing-eat-IPFV Sesugh AGR.PRN buy.PST
        Intended: 'It is/was BUYING FOOD that Sesugh did.'   (Angitso 2015: 145)

Due to the scarcity of data on Tiv, however, nothing more can be said here.

Summary

Tiv disposes of a verb and verb phrase fronting construction where a copy of the fronted verb occurs in the canonical verb position. The fronted constituent, which is interpreted as a new information or contrastive/exhaustive focus, takes the shape

---

[31] The emphatic marker *yé* may only be absent in interrogative-focus questions or in truncated answers to focussed questions (Táíwò & Angitso 2016: 147f.).

of an infinitive nominal clause, that is, it is imperfective-marked and contains the infinitive particle *ù*. Table 8.17 shows the properties of the construction. From what we know at this point, Tiv instantiates pattern I of Generalization I.

Tab. 8.17: Properties of verbal fronting in Tiv

	Copy	Dummy	Unbound	Islands	GS	TAM	L-Adv	H-Adv	NEG	L/R	Top/Foc
V	✓	–	n.d.	n.d.	n.d.	✓[32]	n.d.	n.d.	n.d.	L	Foc
VP	✓	–	n.d.	n.d.	n.d.	✓	n.d.	n.d.	n.d.	L	Foc

8.2.14 Vietnamese

Vietnamese, a Viet-Muong language of the Austro-Asiatic family, is spoken by approximately 70 million speakers predominantly in Vietnam and neighbouring regions. Its neutral word order is SVO (Duffield 1999). The language disposes of a verb fronting (316-a) and a verb phrase fronting construction (316-b), in which a copy of the displaced verb appears clause-internally. The constructions trigger a contrastive topic interpretation, which is also indicated by the particle *thi* that usually acts as a contrastive topic marker in nominal fronting constructions (Tran 2011: 60ff.).[33]

(316) a. **Doc** thi toi co **doc** quyen sach nay, nhung khong hieu.
           read TOP I ASR read CL book this but not understand
           'As for reading this book, I read, but I don't understand.'

---

[32] The fronted verb is obligatorily marked with imperfective aspect as part of the overall morphology of an infinitive nominal clause. The presence of other TAM-markings can neither be confirmed nor excluded. This also holds for verb phrase fronting.

[33] Verb phrase topicalization is also possible clause-internally, where the topicalized constituent does not appear in the left periphery, but in a position below the subject's surface position. Nonetheless, there is a copy of the verb in an even lower position (i).

(i) Toi [**doc** quyen sach nay] thi co **doc**, nhung khong hieu.
     I read CL book this TOP ASR read but not understand
     'As for reading this book, I read, but I don't understand.' (Tran 2011: 60f.)

I will focus on the construction in (316) here, mainly because the data on (i) are not as rich in Tran (2011).

b. [**Doc** quyen sach nay] thi toi co **doc**, nhung khong
　　read CL　book this TOP I ASR read but　not
　　hieu.
　　understand
　　'As for reading this book, I read, but I don't understand.'

　　　　　　　　　　　　　　　　　　　　　　　(Tran 2011: 60f.)

While doubling of the verb is obligatory, repetition of the object in verb phrase fronting results in ungrammaticality (317).

(317)　*[**Doc** quyen sach nay] thi toi co **doc** *quyen sach nay*, ...
　　　　 read CL　book this TOP I ASR read CL　book this
　　　　　　　　　　　　　　　　　　　　　　　(Tran 2011: 63)

There are no restrictions on the type of verbs that may undergo fronting. Besides transitives (318-a) the fronted predicates can be unergatives (318-b), unaccusatives (318-c), ditransitives (318-d), statives (individual-level predicates) (318-e), and modals (318-f).

(318)　a.　[**Uong** ruou] thi toi co **uong**, nhung toi uong khong nhieu.
　　　　　 drink wine TOP I ASR drink but　I drink NEG　much
　　　　　 'As for drinking wine, I drink, but I can't drink much.'
　　　 b.　**Ngu** thi no co **ngu**, nhung khong say.
　　　　　 sleep TOP he ASR sleep but　not　sound
　　　　　 'As for sleeping, he slept, but he did not have a sound sleep.'
　　　 c.　**Lon** thi no co **lon**, nhung khong co khon.
　　　　　 grow TOP he ASR grow but　NEG　ASR wise
　　　　　 'As for growing, he grows, but growing with no wisdom.'
　　　 d.　[**Dua** tien　cho anh ay] thi toi co **dua**, nhung anh ay khong
　　　　　 give money for him　TOP I ASR give but　he　NEG
　　　　　 nhan.
　　　　　 take
　　　　　 'As for giving money to him, I gave, but he didn't take it.'
　　　 e.　**Yeu** thi co ay co **yeu**, nhung khong muon cuoi.
　　　　　 love TOP she ASR love but　NEG　want marry
　　　　　 'As for loving, she loves, but she doesn't want to marry.'
　　　 f.　**Dam** thi toi co **dam**, nhung toi khong thich.
　　　　　 dare TOP I ASR dar but　I NEG　like
　　　　　 'As for daring, I dare, but I don't like.'　　(Tran 2011: 67f.)

However, it is not possible to topicalize the copula (319).

(319) a. Co ay co phai la   giao vien khong.
         she ASR right COP teacher Q
         'Is she a teacher?'
     b. ??**La** thi co **la,** nhung khong di day nua.
         COP TOP ASR COP but   NEG go teach anymore
         'As for being a teacher, she is, but she does not teach anymore.'

(Tran 2011: 68)

In contrast to many other languages, but like in Hebrew (see section 8.2.4) when a lexical verb is fronted from under an auxiliary or a modal it is ungrammatical to omit its clause-internal copy (320). However, this does not hold for intransitive verbs, with which the copy is optional (321).

(320) **Doc** thi no nen   *(**doc**) sach.
      read TOP he should read   book
      'As for reading, he should read books.'   (Trinh 2009: 191)

(321) **Den** thi no se (**den**).
      come TOP he will (come)
      'As for coming, he will come.'   (Trinh 2009: 195, fn. 18)

A further difference compared to many other languages is the fact that the modal and the lexical can be topicalized as a unit (322-a) and even the modal alone may felicitously undergo fronting (322-b). In case modal and lexical verb are fronted together, either a copy of both appears inside the clause (322-a) or a copy of the modal alone (322-c). However, having only a copy of the lexical verb is not sufficient and results in ungrammaticality (322-d).

(322) a. [(Mon cay) **dam an**] thi toi co **dam an,** nhung khong thich
         dish spicy dare eat TOP I ASR dare eat but   NEG   like
         lam.
         very
         'As for daring eat spicy dishes, I dare eat, but I don't like very much.'
     b. [(Mon cay) **dam**] thi toi co **dam** an, nhung khong thich lam.
         dish spicy dare TOP I ASR dare eat but   NEG   like very
     c. [(Mon cay) **dam an**] thi toi co **dam,** nhung khong thich lam.
         dish spicy dare eat TOP I ASR dare but   NEG   like very
     d. *[(Mon cay) dam **an**] thi toi co **an,** nhung khong thich lam.
         dish spicy dare eat TOP I ASR eat but   NEG   like very

(Tran 2011: 69f.)

Turning to the diagnostics for $\bar{\text{A}}$-movement, we find that both verb and verb phrase fronting may cross finite clause boundaries (323).

(323) a. [**Doc** quyen sach nay] thi toi nghi [rang anh ay co **doc**], ...
read CL book this TOP I think that he ASR read
'As for reading this book, I think that he read.'
b. **Doc** thi toi nghi [rang anh ay co **doc** quyen sach nay], ...
read TOP I think that he ASR read book this
'As for reading, I think that he read this book.' (Tran 2011: 82)

In addition, fronting also occurs in embedded clauses (324).

(324) Nam nghi [rang **doc** thi toi co **doc** quyen sach nay], ...
Nam think that read TOP I ASR read CL book this
'Nam think that as for reading, I read this book, ...' (Tran 2011: 88)

Furthermore, verbal fronting from inside an island is ungrammatical, as shown for the Complex NP Island (325), the Subject Island (326), the Relative Clause Island (327), and the Adjunct Island (328).

(325) *Complex NP Island*
a. ***Doc** thi toi tin [chuyen anh ay co **doc** quyen sach nay].
read TOP I believe story he ASR read CL book this
'As for reading, I believe the story that he read this book.'
b. *[**Doc** quyen sach nay] thi toi tin [chuyen anh ay co **doc**],
read CL book this TOP I believe story he ASR read
...

'As for reading this book, I believe the story that he read.'
(Tran 2011: 83)

(326) *Subject Island*[34]
a. ***Doc** thi [chuyen anh ay co doc quyen sach nay] la tot, ...
read TOP story he ASR read CL book this COP good
'As for reading, that he read this book is good.'
b. *[**Doc** quyen sach nay] thi [chuyen anh ay co **doc**] la tot,
read CL book this TOP story he ASR read COP good
...

'As for reading this book, that he read is good.' (Tran 2011: 83)

---

[34] Tran (2011) presents this as a Subject Island although it looks suspiciously similar to the Complex NP Island example as it also contains the phrase *chuyen anh ay co doc* 'the story that he read'. It might thus be the case that the subject here is a complex NP and that the ungrammaticality of this example is not exclusively attributable to a violation of the Subject Island.

(327) *Relative Clause Island*
   a. *****Doc** thi toi quen [mot nguoi co **doc** quyen sach nay], ...
      read TOP I know a person ASR read CL book this
      'As for reading, I know a person who read this book.'
   b. *****[Doc** quyen sach nay] thi toi quen [mot nguoi co **doc**], ...
      read CL book this TOP I know a person ASR read
      'As for reading this book, I know a person who read.'

(Tran 2011: 83f.)

(328) *Adjunct Island*
   a. *****Doc** thi chung toi di an trua [sau khi co **doc** quyen sach nay].
      read TOP we go eat lunch after ASR read CL book this
      'As for reading, we went to lunch after reading this book.'
   b. *****[Doc** quyen sach nay] thi chung toi di an trua [sau khi co **doc**], ...
      read CL book this TOP we go eat lunch after ASR read
      'As for reading this book, we went to have lunch after reading.'

(Tran 2011: 84)

One additional indication that the construction involves movement comes from the fact that genus-species effects are absent (329).

(329) a. *****[Doc** quyen sach nay] thi toi co **xem**, nhung khong hieu.
         read CL book this TOP I ASR saw but NEG understand
         'As for reading this book, I saw, but I don't understand.'
   b. *****[Di My]** thi toi co **bay** den do, nhung khong di thuong xuyen.
         go America TOP I ASR fly there but NEG go frequently
         'As for going to America, I flew there, but I don't go frequently.'

(Tran 2011: 85)

Let us turn to the question of which additional material can appear with the fronted constituent. First, we observe that it is possible for both low adverbs like *cham* 'slowly' and prepositional phrases like *ve co ay* 'about her' to accompany the fronted verb. The difference between them is that while adverbs obligatorily leave a copy when they front with the verb (330-a) no such copy appears when the PP moves along (331-a). Of course, it is possible for both adverbs and PPs to stay with the lower copy of the verb (330-b) and (331-b).

(330) a. [**Viet** *cham*] thi anh ta co **viet** **(cham)*, nhung viet rat dep.
write slowly TOP he ASR write slowly but write very nicely
'As for writing slowly, he writes slowly, but writes very nicely.'
b. **Viet** thi anh ta co **viet** *cham*, nhung viet rat dep.
write TOP he ASR write slowly but write very nicely
'As for writing, he writes slowly, but writes very nicely.'

(Tran 2011: 63f.)

(331) a. [**Nghi** *ve co ay*] thi toi co **nghi**, nhung toi khong muon gap.
think about her TOP I ASR think but I not want see
'As for thinking about her, I think, but I don't want to see her.'
b. **Nghi** thi toi co **nghi** *ve co ay*, nhung…
think TOP I ASR think about her but
'As for thinking, I think about her, but…'

(Tran 2011: 64)

If the clause contains any overt tense or aspect particles, these are not allowed to be fronted with the verb phrase and must stay inside the clause (332).[35]

(332) a. **Doc** thi toi *da/dang/se* (co) **doc** quyen sach nay, nhung…
read TOP I PST/PRS/FUT ASR read CL book this, but
'As for reading this book, I read, but…'
b. *[*Da/Dang/Se* **doc** quyen sach nay] thi toi co **doc**, nhung…
PST/PRS/FUT read CL book this TOP I ASR read but

(Tran 2011: 64f.)

It is equally ungrammatical to modify the fronted constituent with negation (333-a) or a modal (333-b) unless a copy of that modal accompanies the copy of the lexical verb in base position (see example (322)).

---

35 Unfortunately, example (332) is not a true minimal pair. While (332-a) exhibits verb fronting, (332-b) is an example of verb phrase fronting. However, this should not impair the argumentation here.

(333) a. *[*Khong* **dep**] thi co ay *khong* (co) **dep**, nhung
 NEG beautiful TOP she NEG ASR beautiful but
 thong minh.
 intelligent
 b. *[*Dam* **an**] thi toi co **an**, nhung…
 dare eat TOP I ASR eat but (Tran 2011: 66)

The abovementioned examples do not shed light on the question whether the verb in verb fronting is a bare head or a remnant verb phrase. Although the presence of low adverbs and PPs with a fronted verb would favour a remnant verb phrase analysis the examples in (330) are inconclusive because they do not contain an overt direct object. Thus, they remain ambiguous between verb and verb phrase fronting with the presence of the adverb or the PP being expected in the latter case.

Nonetheless, there are arguments against a remnant movement account in the literature. Tran (2011: 103) straightforwardly asserts that scrambling, which is required to create a remnant verb phrase, does not exist in Vietnamese (334-b).

(334) a. Toi [$_{VP}$ doc quyen sach nay hom qua].
 I read CL book this yesterday
 'I read this book yesterday.'
 b. *Toi [quyen sach nay]$_1$ [$_{VP}$ doc ___$_1$ hom qua]
 I CL book this read yesterday (Tran 2011: 103f.)

Trinh (2009: 193), on the other hand, acknowledges that a scrambling operation distinct from topicalization is available (335).[36]

---

[36] The construction in (335) might be argued to be topicalization with a silent topic marker, which is possible in Vietnamese (i).

(i) Sach (thi) no nen doc.
 book TOP he should read
 'Books, he should read.' (Trinh 2009: 193, fn. 14)

Trinh (2009: 193, fn. 14), however, argues that this cannot be the case because although topicalization is not recursive (ii-a), topicalization of the subject in (335) does not result in ungrammaticality (ii-b).

(ii) a. *No thi sach thi nen doc.
 he TOP book TOP should read
 Intended: 'As for him, books he should read.'
 b. No thi quyen sach nay nen doc.
 he TOP CL book this should read
 'As for him, this book he should read.' (Trinh 2009: 193, fn. 14)

(335) [Quyen sach nay]₁ no nen [_VP_ doc ___₁].
      CL   book this he will   read
      'He should read this book.' (Trinh 2009: 193)

Two conditions hold on this scrambling: It must be to a position higher than SpecTP (i.e. above the modal but below the topic position) (336-a, b) and the object must be definite (336-c).

(336) a. *No nen   [quyen sach nay]₁ doc ___₁.
             he should CL   book this   read
             Intended: 'He should read this book.'
      b. No thi [quyen sach nay]₁ nen   doc ___₁.
             he TOP CL   book this should read
             'As for him, this book he should read.'
      c. *[Mot quyen sach]₁ no nen   doc ___₁.
             one CL   book he should read
             Intended: 'He should read a book.' (Trinh 2009: 193)

However, this scrambling cannot be responsible for the creation of the putative remnant VP in verb fronting since none of the two conditions hold for the stranded object. It must neither be definite nor does it have to appear in a position between the topic and the modal (337-a) but it can optionally undergo scrambling (337-b).

(337) a. **Doc** thi no nen   **doc** mot quyen sach.
             read TOP he should read one CL   book
             'As for reading, he should read a book.'
      b. **Doc** thi quyen sach nay no nen   **doc**.
             read TOP CL   book this he should read
             'As for him, this book he should read.' (Trinh 2009: 194)

Extraposition of the object is equally unsuitable to create a remnant verb phrase. Short bare nouns such as *sach* 'book' cannot extrapose in Vietnamese (338-a) but they can be stranded by verb fronting (338-b).

(338) a. *No doc ___₁ hom-qua sach₁.
             he read   yesterday book
      b. **Doc** thi no nen   **doc** *sach*.
             read TOP he should read book
             'As for reading, he should read book.' (Trinh 2009: 194,191)

Concerning the verb copy's status as a repair one might raise the objection that the topic structures in (339-a, b) might be derived from the low verb doubling construction in (339-c, d), respectively, by moving one of the verb copies into the left periphery of the clause.

(339) a. **Nhay** thi no co **nhay** mat,...
wink TOP he ASR wink eyes
'As for winking, he winked his eyes.'
b. **Gat** thi toi co **gat** dau,...
nod TOP I ASR nod head
'As for nodding, I nodded my head'
c. No **nhay nhay** mat.
he wink wink eyes
'He winked his eyes.'
d. Toi **gat gat** dau.
I nod nod head
'I nodded my head.' (Tran 2011: 89f.)

This cannot be the case, however, for this low doubling is for the most part restricted to verbs of bodily movement. If verbal topicalization were indeed derived from it, we would not expect the former to be applicable to such a wide range of different verbs. Additionally, verb phrase fronting would remain unexplained since low doubling is only available for heads, not phrases.

A more serious approach that might undermine the treatment of the lower verb copy as a repair is one that derives the verbal topicalization by movement of an independently available cognate object similar to what has been argued to happen in Edo (see section 7.1.3). Tran (2011: 91) states that cognate object constructions like (340) are prevalent in Vietnamese and do not seem to be restricted to a certain class of verbs.

(340) a. Toi **gap** cho no mot **gap** rau.
I pick for him a pick vegetable
'I picked for him a pick of vegetable.'
b. Anh ay **son** nha bang **son**.
he paint house by paint
'He painted the house with paint.' (Tran 2011: 91)

Nevertheless, Tran (2011) dismisses this construction as a possible base for topicalization.

We may therefore conclude that the appearance of the verb copy in verbal fronting is directly linked to the movement of the verb (phrase).

Summary

Vietnamese exhibits both verb and verb phrase fronting with a contrastive topic interpretation on the fronted constituent. In both constructions, a copy of the verb occupies the clause-internal verb position. Further, they both show evidence of $\bar{\text{A}}$-movement: They can cross finite clause boundaries and are sensitive to islands. Genus-species effects are unattested. The fronted constituent may not be accompanied by TAM-markers or negation. However, low adverbs and prepositional phrases may move along. Whether the latter only holds for verb phrase fronting or for verb fronting as well cannot be seen from the data available. The verb in verb fronting must be a bare head rather than a remnant verb phrase because the available remnant-creating operations underly restrictions that do not seem to be complied in verb fronting. The properties of both constructions are given in table 8.18. As it stands, Vietnamese verbal fronting falls under pattern I of Generalization I. Both verb and verb phrase fronting trigger verb doubling therefore behaving identically.

Tab. 8.18: Properties of verbal fronting in Vietnamese

	Copy	Dummy	Unbound	Islands	GS	TAM	L-Adv	H-Adv	Neg	L/R	Top/Foc
V	✓	–	✓	✓	–	–	✓	n.d.	–	L	Top
VP	✓	–	✓	✓	–	–	✓	n.d.	–	L	Top

8.2.15 Yiddish

Yiddish, a Germanic language of the Indo-European family, is spoken by approximately one and a half million people most of which live in America and Europe. Its basic word order is SVO.

The language famously disposes of both verb (341-a) and verb phrase fronting (341-b), in which a copy of the fronted verb appears in the canonical verb position. The fronted constituent is interpreted as a topic.

(341)   a.   **Essen est** Maks fish.
              eat.INF eats Max fish
              'As for eating, Max eats fish.'
       b.   [**Essen** fish] **est** Maks.
              eat.INF fish eats Max
              'As for eating fish, Max eats them.'   (Cable 2004: 2)

It is illicit to have a copy of the object besides the copy of the verb in base position in verb phrase fronting (342).

(342) *[**Essen** fish] **est** Maks fish.
eat.INF fish eats Max fish
'As for eating fish, Maks eats fish.'

While the verb in the sentence-initial constituent is usually an infinitive (342) and (343-a), it may also be a past participle in case the copy in the base position is a past participle too (see (343-b, c) vs. (343-d, e)).

(343) a. **Essen** hot Maks **gegessen** a fish.
eat.INF has Maks eaten a fish
'As for eating, Max has eaten a fish.'
b. **Gegessen** hot Maks **gegessen** fish.
eaten has Max eaten fish
'As for having eaten, Max has eaten fish.'
c. [**Gegessen** fish] hot Maks **gegessen**.
eaten fish has Max eaten
'As for having eaten fish, Max has eaten them.'
d. ***Gegessen est** Maks fish.
eaten eats Max fish
e. *[**Gegessen** fish] **est** Maks.
eaten fish eats Max (Cable 2004: 2)

Interestingly, the fronted infinitives are not regular infinitives. Rather, they are formed by suffixing -*n* to the stem of the verb copy inside the clause. Thus, in (344-a), where the verb *visn* 'to know' inside the clause is inflected and therefore ablauted, the fronted verb takes the form *veys+n* rather than the expected regular infinitive *visn*. A finite form in fronted position is ungrammatical. In example (344-b), this is not the case, because the clause-internal token of the verb is already in the regular infinitive form and hence the fronted verb also appears in that form.

(344) a. **Veysn**/*Visn/*Veyst veyst er gornit.
know.INF/know.INF/knows knows he nothing
'As for knowing, he knows nothing.'
b. **Visn**/*Veysn ken ikh nit **visn**.
know.INF/know.INF can I not know.INF
'Know I cannot.' (Davis & Prince 1986: 1f.)

Example (345) shows that this pattern of infinitive-forming holds for other verbs like *veln* 'to want' and *zayn* 'to be' as well. Other alternations include irregular *gibn* instead of regular *gebn* 'to give' and irregular *hobn* instead of regular *hubn, hobn* 'to have'. Due to the suppletive paradigm of *zayn* 'to be', this verb shows the most variation of irregular infinitives including *binen, bizn, izn, zenen*, and *zaynen* (Davis & Prince 1986: 5).

(345) a. **Viln vilst** du a sakh.
want.INF want.2SG you a lot
'As for wanting, you want a lot.'
b. **Izn** iz er yetst a kabtsn.
be.IRREG.INF is he now a pauper
'As for being, he's a pauper now.' (Källgren & Prince 1989: 53)

In sentences where a modal verb or an auxiliary embeds the main lexical verb/participle, it is possible to front that main verb without leaving an overt copy in the base position (346).

(346) a. **Getantst** *hob* ikh nekhtn (**getantst**).
danced have I yesterday danced
'Dance I did yesterday.'
b. **Tantsn** *vel* ikh morgn (**tantsn**).
dance will I tomorrow dance
'Dance I will tomorrow.'
c. **Visn** *ken* ikh nit (**visn**).
know can I not know
'Know I cannot.' (Davis & Prince 1986: 2)

Modal verbs themselves may also undergo topicalization and thereby leave a copy clause-internally (347).

(347) **Kenen ken** zi yo shvimen (nor **viln vil** zi nit).
can can she swim but want wants she not
'As for ability, she can swim, (but, as for wanting, she doesn't want to).'
(Davis & Prince 1986: 7)

In contrast, this option is not available for auxiliaries. The two temporal auxiliaries are *hobn* 'to have' and *zayn* 'to be'. As main verbs (348-a, b), these two may be topicalized without problems leaving a copy in their respective base position (348-c, d), whereas as auxiliaries (349-a, b), the same kind of fronting results in ungrammaticality (349-c, d).

(348) a. Ikh *hob* gelt.
I have money
b. Ikh *bin* in amerike.
I am in America

c. **Hobn hob** ikh gelt.
   have have I money
   'As for having, I have money.'

d. **Binen** bin ikh in amerike.
   be.IRREG.INF am I in America
   'As for being, I am in America.' (Davis & Prince 1986: 6)

(349) a. Ikh *hob* gekoyft a hunt.
          I have bought a dog
          'I (have) bought a dog.'

   b. Ikh *bin* ongekumen.
      I am arrived
      'I (have) arrived.'

   c. *****Hobn hob** ikh gekoyft a hunt.
      have have I bought a dog

   d. *****Binen** bin ikh ongekumen.
      be.IRREG.INF am I arrived (Davis & Prince 1986: 7)

In Yiddish there exist so-called compound verbs that consist of either *zayn* or *hobn* and a (in most cases Semitic) complement (350-a), (351-a). With these verbs, fronting exclusively affects the complement (350-c), (351-c), not the verb even though it is syntactically a main verb (350-b), (351-b). When fronted, the complement, like other non-verbal constituents, leaves a gap rather than a copy.

(350) a. Ikh *bin* dir *moykhl*.
          I am you forgive
          'I forgive you.'

   b. *****Binen** bin ikh dir moykhl.
      be.IRREG.INF am I you forgive

   c. *Moykhl* bin ikh dir,...
      forgive am I you...
      'As for forgiving, I forgive you,...' (Davis & Prince 1986: 7)

(351) a. Ikh *hob* dikh *lib*.
          I have you love
          'I love you.'

   b. *****Hobn hob** ikh dikh lib.
      have have I you love

   c. ...nor *lib* hob ikh dikh nit.
      ...but love have I you not
      '...but, as for loving, I don't love you.' (Davis & Prince 1986: 7f.)

Unlike in Fongbe (see section 7.1.5) and Haitian Creole (see section 7.1.7) there are no restrictions on the semantic or syntactic class of verbs that can undergo topicalization. As we have seen above both stage-level predicates like *essen* 'to eat' and individual-level predicates like *visn* 'to know' may appear in topic position. Similarly, intransitives like *tantsn* 'to dance' as well as transitives like *essen* 'to eat' can be fronted. The same is true for ditransitives like *gebn* 'to give' (352-a). They can undergo both verb (352-b) and verb phrase fronting (352-c, d). However, it is not possible to front a partial verb phrase, that is a verb and just one of its two internal arguments while stranding the other (352-e–g).

(352)   a.   Ikh gib *(di kinder) *(tsukerkes).
              I   give   the children   candies
              'I give the children candies.'
       b.   **Gibn gib** ikh di kinder tsukerkes.
       c.   [**Gibn** di kinder tsukerkes] **gib** ikh.
       d.   [**Gegebn** di kinder tsukerkes] hob ikh **gegebn**.
       e.   *[**Gibn** di kinder] **gib** ikh tsukerkes.
       f.   *[**Gibn** tsukerkes] **gib** ikh di kinder.
       g.   *[**Gegebn** di kinder] hob ikh tsukerkes **gegebn**.   (Cable 2004: 7)

This restriction of the fronting possibilities of ditransitive verb phrases has been observed in Hebrew (see section 8.2.4) and to some extent in Polish (see section 8.2.10). Landau (2007) formulates the underlying generalization as in (353).

(353)   *Condition on fronted VP-portions* (Landau 2007: 134)
        [[V Arg$_1$]…Subject…Arg$_2$] is grammatical iff [Subject…[$_{VP}$ V Arg$_1$]…] is grammatical (i.e., if Arg$_2$ may be dropped independently).

Apparently, this condition holds for Yiddish as well. As is evident from (352-a), it is not possible to independently drop one of the two internal arguments of the ditransitive verb *gebn* 'to give'. The impossibility of partial verb phrase fronting indicates that a single verb in clause-initial position cannot be a remnant verb phrase. In order for such a remnant phrase to be created the internal arguments would both have to be able to leave the verb phrase. In turn, this would lead us to expect that a verb phrase should be frontable after one of the two arguments has evacuated it giving rise to partial verb phrase fronting. As this is not grammatical in Yiddish, the remnant-creating movement must be unavailable (at least in the relevant fronting constructions). Therefore, the fronted verb cannot be a remnant verb phrase but must rather be a bare head.

This condition, however, only holds for verb phrase fronting in which a copy of the verb appears in the base position. Fronting of a partial verb phrase is perfectly fine in case the displaced material just leaves a gap (354).

(354) a. [Gegebn tsukerkes] hot er gor di kinder.
 given candies has he of.all.things the children
 'Of all things, he has given candy to the children.'
 b. [Gegebn di kinder] hot er gor tsukerkes (Cable 2004: 8)

The fact that both kinds of verbal fronting (the one with a copy and the one without) show distinct behaviour with regard to partial verb phrases suggests that their underlying structure or derivation is in fact distinct.

Verbal fronting behaves like other extractions such as nominal topicalization or verb preposing without leaving a copy: It may cross finite clause boundaries (355-a) and is sensitive to islands like the Wh-Island (356) and the Relative Clause Island (357). Unfortunately, I only found examples with verb fronting. As verb phrase fronting has not been explicitly mentioned to behave differently, I will assume that the diagnostics established for the former also hold for the latter.

(355) a. **Veysn** hos du mir gezogt [az er **veyst** a sakh].
 know.INF have you me told that he knows a lot
 'As for knowing, you told me that he knows a lot.'
 b. [Ot dem hunt]$_1$ host du mir gezogt [az er hot gekoyft ___$_1$].
 PRT the dog have you told me that he has bought
 'That dog you told me that he bought.'
 c. Koyfn$_1$ host du mir gezogt [az er vet ___$_1$ ot dem hunt].
 buy have you told me that he will PRT the dog
 'As for buying, you told me that he will buy that dog.'
 (Davis & Prince 1986: 4)

(356) *Wh-Island*
 a. ***Veysn** host du mir gezogt [ver es **veyst** a sakh].
 know have you me said who ES knows a lot
 'As for knowing, you told me who knows a lot.'
 b. *[Ot dem hunt]$_1$ host du mir gezogt [ver es hot gekoyft ___$_1$].
 PRT the dog have you me said who ES has bought
 'That dog you told me who bought.'
 c. *Koyfn$_1$ host du mir gezogt [ver es vet ___$_1$ ot dem hunt].
 buy have you me said who ES will PRT the dog
 'As for buying, you told me who will buy that dog.'
 (Davis & Prince 1986: 4)

(357) *Relative Clause Island*
    a. ***Veysn** hob ikh gezen dem yidn [vos **veyst** a sakh].
        know have I seen the man that knows a lot
        'As for knowing, I saw the man that knows a lot.'
    b. *[Ot dem hunt]$_1$ kenst du dem yidn [vos hot gekoyft ___$_1$].
        PRT the dog know you the man that has bought
        'That dog you know the man who bought.'
    c. *Koyfn$_1$ kenst du dem yidn [vos vet ___$_1$ ot dem hunt].
        buy know you the man that will PRT the dog
        'As for buying, you know th man who will buy that dog.'
                              (Davis & Prince 1986: 4)

Further, verbal fronting behaves like nominal topicalization (358-b) in being possible in embedded clauses (358-c)

(358) a. Ikh veys [az er iz a kabtsn].
        I know that he is a pauper
        'I know that he's pauper.'
    b. Ikh veys [az *a kabtsn* iz er].
        I know that a pauper is he
        'I know that a pauper, he is.'
    c. Ikh veys [az **izn** iz er a kabtsn].
        I know that be.IRREG.INF is he a pauper
        'I know that, as for being, he is a pauper.'
                              (Källgren & Prince 1989: 56)

However, an argument against movement of the fronted constituent is the (marginal) acceptability of genus-species examples. In (359), the lexical material in the fronted position is different from that in the base position. The denotation of the former, however, is a superset of the denotation of the latter. Hence, the topic is further specified by the corresponding elements in the comment.

(359) a. ?[Essen **fish**] est Maks **hekht**.
        eat.INF eats Max pike
        'As for eating fish, Max eats pike.'
    b. ?[**Forn keyn amerike**] bin ikh **gefloygn** keyn amerike.
        travel.INF to America am I flown to America
        'As for travelling to America, I have flown to America.'
    c. ?[**Forn keyn amerike**] bin ikh **gefloygn keyn nyu-york**.
        travel.INF to America am I flown to New York
        'As for travelling to America, I have flown to New York.'
                                    (Cable 2004: 9)

Under a movement approach to verbal fronting, this genus-species effect remains unexplained according to Cable (2004).

It is not possible to have the lexical material differ in such a way that the subset-superset relation holds in the opposite direction (360).

(360) *[Essen **hekht**] hob ikh gegessen **fish**.
eat.INF pike have I eaten fish
'As for eating pike, I have eaten fish.' (Cable 2004: 10)

Cable (2004) argues based on the existence of these genus-species effects that verbal fronting in Yiddish does not involve ($\bar{\text{A}}$-)movement of the verb (phrase) into sentence-initial position. Rather, he suggests that the fronted constituent is base-generated there. The movement-indicating island diagnostics above do not preclude such an approach as they all involve two CPs. The fronted verbal constituent might thus have been base-generated in the left periphery of the embedded clause from where it has subsequently undergone $\bar{\text{A}}$-movement to the left periphery of the matrix clause. Movement-diagnostics within a single CP, like the licensing of parasitic gaps, seem to support this view. Consider example (361), where verb phrase fronting of *leyenen dos bukh* 'to read the book' does not license a parasitic gap of *dos bukh* 'the book' in the adjunct.

(361) *[**Leyenen** dos bukh] **leyent** Bill eyder Maks leyent $pg_{\text{dos bukh}}$.
read.INF the book reads Bill before Max reads
'As for reading the book, Bill reads it before Max reads it.'
(Cable 2004: 14)

In effect, this analysis renders verbal fronting similar to left dislocation, where an element in the left periphery is linked to a lexically distinct element in the clause (362). This structure is usually assumed to be base-generated.

(362) Maks$_i$ – im$_i$ hob ikh gezen.
Max him have I seen
'Max$_i$, I've seen him$_i$.' (Cable 2004: 3)

Crucially, though, verbal fronting does not seem to pattern with left dislocation structures but rather with nominal topicalization which clearly involves $\bar{\text{A}}$-movement. In a Yiddish V2 sentence, only one constituent may precede the finite verb (363).

(363) a. [Er] leyent dos bukh.
he reads the book
'He is reading the book.'

b. [Efsher] leyent er dos bukh.
   maybe reads he the book
   'Maybe he is reading the book.'
c. *[Efsher] [er] leyent dos bukh.
   maybe he reads the book   (Davis & Prince 1986: 2f.)

Now, while a topicalized nominal may occupy this single preverbal position (364-a) and no other consituent may occur with it (364-b), the situation is the reverse with a left dislocated element. This may not be the single constituent before the verb (364-c), but actually requires there to be another constituent occupying the preverbal position (364-d).

(364) a. [Dos bukh] leyent er.
         the book reads he
         'The book he is reading.'
      b. *[Dos bukh] [er] leyent.
         the book he reads
      c. *[Dos bukh] leyent er dos.
         the book reads he this
      d. [Dos bukh] [dos] leyent er.
         the book this reads he
         'The book, he is reading it.'   (Davis & Prince 1986: 3)

This indicates that left dislocated elements occupy a structurally distinct position from that into which topicalized constituents move. If verbal fronting, as in Cable's proposal, is the result of a base-generation process akin to the one that produces left dislocation, we would expect it to pattern with the latter rather than with topicalization. However, this is not what we find. In contrast, a fronted verb that does not occur immediately left-adjacent to the finite verb in a V2 sentence leads to ungrammaticality (365-a). Like a topicalized nominal, the fronted verb has to appear in the preverbal position (365-b).

(365) a. *[**Leyenen**] [er] **leyent** dos bukh.
         read   he reads   the book
      b. [**Leyenen**] **leyent** er dos bukh.
         read   reads   he the book
         'As for reading, he is reading the book.'   (Davis & Prince 1986: 3)

These word order facts seem to favour a movement approach to verbal fronting over a base-generation account. Cable (2004), however, argues that this is not the case because despite their superficial similarity, nominal left dislocated elements and fronted verb (phrases) are base-generated in different positions. This is supposed to parallel the distinction between Clitic Left Dislocation (CLD) and left dislocation as found in English. The relevant diagnostics (Cinque 1977, 1990) show that Yiddish left dislocation is of the English type: There is a marked intonational break between the dislocated nominal and the following clause (366), there is no case matching between the dislocated nominal and the corresponding clause-internal element (367), only DPs can undergo left dislocation (368), and finally, dislocation is not possible in embedded clauses (369).

(366) a. Maks – im hob ikh gezen.
Max him have I seen
'Max – I've seen him.'
b. *Maks im hob ikh gezen (Cable 2004: 15)

(367) *Maksn – im hob ikh gezen. (Cable 2004: 15, without gloss)

(368) a. *In hoyzn – ikh bin gegangen ahin.
in house I am gone there
'To the house, I went there.'
b. *In hoyzn – ahin bin ikh gegangen. (Cable 2004: 15)

(369) *Maria meynt [az Maks – im lib ikh].
Mary thinks that Max him like I
'Mary thinks that May, I like him.' (Cable 2004: 15)

As verbal fronting is clearly distinct from this kind of left dislocation, it can, following Cable (2004), be regarded as the Yiddish incarnation of CLD targeting a position that is distinct from the English-type left dislocation of nominal elements in Yiddish. The fact that left dislocation and verbal fronting do not pattern together with regard to V2 sentences is therefore no longer an argument against the base-generation approach.

However, as verbal fronting differs from left dislocation with regard to the abovementioned diagnostics this makes it seem even more similar to non-verbal topicalization. In addition to the V2 word order facts, where both topicalized non-verbal constituents and fronted verbal constituents have to immediately precede the finite verb, verbal fronting and non-verbal topicalization behave alike in the sense that they do not exhibit a marked pause between the fronted constituent and the rest of the clause, that non-DP elements may be fronted, and that they may occur in embedded clauses. In my view, this makes it even more plausible to treat verbal fronting as an instance of $\bar{\text{A}}$-movement akin to non-verbal topicalization. Nonetheless, the genus-species effects remain problematic for such an approach, if they turn out to be robust. However, I would like to point out that it is not impossible to think of a movement analysis giving rise to these effects. First, under the copy theory of movement there is, usually implicitly assumed, an operation that creates a copy of the moving item. This copy operation, if properly defined, could be able to alter the featural constitution of the copy such that it only copies a subset of the semantic features of the original element. Assuming that the copy stays behind while the attracted original moves this could give rise to the observed genus-species effect. Alternatively, under a Late Insertion approach to morphological realization, post-syntactic operations like Impoverishment might change the features of a terminal such that only a more general Vocabulary Item can be inserted. These are just two rough suggestions meant to highlight the fact that genus-species effects do not immediately preclude a movement-based analysis.

Eventually, the issue of genus-species effects will have to await further elicitation with more than a handful of speakers and possibly even experimental evidence. For now, I will focus on the question marks of these examples and regard them as more ungrammatical than grammatical. In particular against the background that, even if they turn out to be robust, they do not immediately preclude a movement-based analysis of verbal fronting.

Summary
Yiddish exhibits both verb and verb phrase fronting, where the fronted constituent receives a topic interpretation and a copy of the verb appears in the base position. A copy of the object leads to ungrammaticality. The fronted verb usually appears as an infinitival form, although that form is not necessarily the same as the regular infinitive. It may also take the form of a past participle if the copy inside the clause is a past participle too, i.e. if the verb is embedded under an auxiliary. A copy becomes optional when the verb is fronted from below an auxiliary or a modal. Auxiliaries themselves cannot appear in sentence-initial position, but modals may. While there are not restrictions on the semantic class of verbs that may undergo fronting, topicalization of ditransitive verb phrases leaving a copy obeys a constraint against partial verb phrase fronting. Only complete (ditransitive) verb phrases may be displaced when a copy of the verb appears in the base position. Verbal fronting shows typical $\bar{A}$-properties: It takes place across finite clause boundaries but respects island conditions. However, the existence of genus-species effects is reported, though with decreased grammaticality. In the absence of clearly grammatical genus-species examples it is thus plausible to conclude that verbal fronting is an instance of $\bar{A}$-movement. Concerning the size of the fronted constituent, I was unable to find any examples testifying to the (un)availability of adverbs or negation within the sentence-initial verbal element. The reported properties are summarized in table 8.19. In conclusion, Yiddish verbal fronting, provided that it indeed involves $\bar{A}$-movement, instantiates pattern I of Generalization I. Both verb and verb phrase fronting trigger verb doubling.

Tab. 8.19: Properties of verbal fronting in Yiddish

	Copy	Dummy	Unbound	Islands	GS	TAM	L-Adv	H-Adv	Neg	L/R	Top/Foc
V	✓	–	✓	✓	✓	–[37]	n.d.	n.d.	n.d.	L	Top
VP	✓	–	✓	✓	✓	–	n.d.	n.d.	n.d.	L	Top

8.2.16 Yoruba

Yoruba, a Yoruboid language of the Niger-Congo family, is spoken by about 19 million speakers in Nigeria (Kobele 2006: 214). Its basic word order is SVO (370).

(370)   Ajé ra ìwé.
       Aje buy paper
       'Aje {is buying/bought} {a book/books}.'   (Manfredi 1993: 19)

The language shows both verb (371-a) and verb phrase fronting (371-b), where a copy of the displaced verb occupies the canonical verb position inside the clause. The fronted constituent is usually interpreted as a (contrastive) focus.

(371)   a.   Rí-**rà**   ni Ajé **ra** ìwé.
                NMLZ-buy FOC Aje buy paper
                'It is a buying that Aje {is doing/did} to {a book/books}.' [i.e. he didn't steal it/them]
       b.   Rí-[**rà**   ìwé] ni Ajé **ra** ìwé.
                NMLZ-buy paper FOC Aje buy paper
                'It is book-buying that Aje {is doing/did}.' [i.e. he didn't go yam-selling]
                                              (Manfredi 1993: 20)

Note that in contrast to many other languages in verb phrase fronting there is a doublet of the object present in addition to the copy of the verb.

The fronted constituent is nominalized by the reduplicative gerundive prefix that consists of the copied onset consonant of the first syllable of its host followed by the vowel *i*. This kind of nominalization is not restricted to fronting constructions. It is also found in certain echoic constructions of intransitive verbs (372).

---

[37] The fronted constituent does not exhibit finite morphology. However, the verb may appear in a past participle form if embedded under an auxiliary. This also holds for verb phrase fronting.

(372) Ajé lọ í-lọ ì-yà kò lọ **lí-lọ̀** kan.
Aje go going turning NEG go going one
'Aje went on a side trip, he didn't go [just] one going.'
(Manfredi 1993: 20)

Unfortunately, I was unable to find any examples testifying to the behaviour of verbal fronting with regard to (un)boundedness, islands, or other Ā-diagnostics. However, example (373) at least shows that it is allowed to front a verb that is embedded under a control predicate *fe* 'want'.

(373) Ri-**ra** ni Ayo o fe **ra** bata.
NMLZ-buy FOC Ayo AGR want buy shoes
'Ayo wants to BUY the shoes.' (Cho & Nishiyama 2000: 41)

Aspectual auxiliaries/particles may accompany the fronted verb (374-b). Whether they can also undergo fronting on their own remains unclear.

(374) a. Ajé {máa/n} ra ìwé.
Aje PROG buy paper
'Aje is buying {a book/books}.' (unambiguously non-past)
b. Mí-[**máa-ra** ìwé] ni Ajé **máa ra** ìwé.
NMLZ-PROG-buy paper FOC Aje PROG buy paper
'It is continuous book-buying that Aje does/did.' [i.e. not just occasionally] (Manfredi 1993: 20)

With serial verb constructions like (375), all verbs may be fronted together stranding their arguments (376-a).

(375) Ajé bá won dé Èjìgbò.
Aje accompany 3PL arrive Ejigbo
'Aje accompanied them to Ejigbo.' (Manfredi 1993: 20)

It is also allowed to front each verb together with its object separately (376-b, c). However, only the first verb may be fronted without its direct object (376-d) while this results in ungrammaticality when attempted for one of the other verbs (376-e).

(376) a. Bí-**bá-dé** (Èjìgbò) ni Ajé **bá** won **dé**
NMLZ-accompany-arrive Ejigbo FOC Aje accompany 3PL arrive
Èjìgbò.
Ejigbo
(without translation in source)

b. Bí-[**bá**   wọn] ni Ajé **bá**   wọn dé   Èjìgbò.
   NMLZ-accompany 3PL FOC Aje accompany 3PL arrive Ejigbo
   (without translation in source)

c. Dí-[**dé**   Èjìgbò] ni Aje   bá wọn **dé**   Èjìgbò.
   NMLZ-arrive Ejigbo FOC accompany 3PL arrive Ejigbo
   (without translation in source)

d. Bí-**bá**   ni Ajé **bá**   wọn dé   Èjìgbò.
   NMLZ-accompany FOC Aje accompany 3PL arrive Ejigbo
   (without translation in source)

e. *Dí-**dé**   ni Aje   bá wọn **dé**   Èjìgbò.
   NMLZ-arrive FOC accompany 3PL arrive Ejigbo

(Manfredi 1993: 20f.)

In contrast, the verb *fún* 'give' is not extractable independently of whether its direct object moves along (377-b, c) whereas with instrumental serial verb constructions, fronting is generally possible for all verbs with and without their direct object (378-b, c).

(377) a. Ajé mú   àpótí fún mi.
         Aje take.hold.of boy give 1SG
         'Aje gave a/the boy to me.'

   b. *Fí-**fún**   ni Ajé mí   àpótí **fún** mi.
       NMLZ-give FOC Aje take.hold.of box give 1SG

   c. *Fí-[**fún**   mi] ni Ajé mí   àpótí **fún** mi.
       NMLZ-give 1SG FOC Aje take.hold.of box give 1SG

(Manfredi 1993: 22)

(378) a. Ajé fi   òbe gé isu.
         Aje use knife cut yam
         'Aje used a/the knife to cut a/the yam.'

   b. Gí-**gé**   ni Ajé fi   ọ̀bẹ **gé** iṣu.
      NMLZ-cut FOC Aje use knife cut yam
      (without translation in source)

   c. Gí-[**gé**   iṣu] ni Ajé fi   ọ̀bẹ **gé** iṣu.
      NMLZ-cut yam FOC Aje use knife cut yam
      (without translation in source)   (Manfredi 1993: 22)

At this point, we cannot say more about verbal fronting in Yoruba as published data on that matter is scarce.

Summary

Yoruba comprises of both verb and verb phrase fronting where a copy of the fronted verb appears in the base position. Interestingly, there is also a copy of the object in verb phrase fronting. The fronted constituent receives a (contrastive) focus interpretation and is nominalized by a reduplicative prefix which also occurs outside of verbal fronting constructions. Aspectual auxiliaries/particles may be fronted together with the verb, in which case they also leave a copy in their original position. Due to the unavailability of any data on the matter, nothing can be said about whether verbal fronting is $\bar{\text{A}}$-movement or not. Some relevant properties are shown in table 8.20. Even though there is hardly any relevant data from the language, Yoruba verbal fronting seems to instantiate pattern I of Generalization I, namely symmetric verb doubling.

Tab. 8.20: Properties of verbal fronting in Yoruba

	Copy	Dummy	Unbound	Islands	GS	TAM	L-Adv	H-Adv	Neg	L/R	Top/Foc
V	✓	–	n.d.	n.d.	n.d.	✓	n.d.	n.d.	n.d.	L	Foc
VP	✓	–	n.d.	n.d.	n.d.	✓	n.d.	n.d.	n.d.	L	Foc

Bibliography

Abels, Klaus. 2001. The predicate cleft construction in Russian. In S. Frank, T. Holloway King & M. Yadroff (eds.), *Annual Workshop on Formal Approaches to Slavic Linguistics: The Bloomington Meeting*, 1–18. Michigan: Michigan Slavic Publications.

Aboh, Enoch Oladé. 1998. Focus constructions and the focus criterion in Gungbe. *Linguistique Africaine* 20. 5–50.

Aboh, Enoch Oladé. 2006. When verbal predicates go fronting. In I. Fiedler & A. Schwarz (eds.), *Papers on information structure in African languages* ZAS Papers in Linguistics 46, 21–48. Berlin: ZAS.

Aboh, Enoch Oladé. 2009. Delete: A phase-level property. *Theoretical Linguistics* 35. 229–238.

Aboh, Enoch Oladé & Marina Dyakonova. 2009. Predicate doubling and parallel chains. *Lingua* 119. 1035–1065.

Abraham, Werner & Annette Fischer. 1998. Das grammatische Optimalisierungsszenario von *tun* als Hilfsverb. In Karin Donhauser & Ludwig M. Eichinger (eds.), *Deutsche Grammatik – Thema in Variationen. Festschrift für Hans-Werner Eroms zum 60. Geburtstag*, 35–47. Heidelberg: Winter.

Ackerman, Farrell & Gregory Stump. 2004. Paradigms and periphrastic expressions: A study in realization-based lexicalism. In Andrew Spencer & Louisa Sadler (eds.), *Projecting morphology*, 111–158. Stanford, CA: CSLI Publications.

Aelbrecht, Lobke. 2012. What ellipsis can do for phases and what it can't, but not how. Talk given at: 'Ellipsis conference', Vigo University.

Ameka, Felix. 1992. Focus Constructions in Ewe and Akan. In C. Collins & V. Manfredi (eds.), *Proceedings of the Kwa Comparative Syntax Workshop*, vol. 17 MIT Working Papers in Linguistics, 1–25. Cambridge, MA: MIT Press.

Ameka, Felix K. 1991. *Ewe: Its grammatical constructions and illocutionary devices*. Canberra: Australian National University dissertation.

Ameka, Felix K. 2010. *Information packaging constructions in Kwa: Micro-variation and typology* chap. 7, 141–176. Dordrecht: Springer.

Anderson, Stephen R. 1981. Topicalization in Breton. In Danny K. Alford, Karen Ann Hunold, Monica A. Macaulay, Jenny Walter, Claudia Brugman, Paula Chertok, Inese Čivkulis & Marta Tobey (eds.), *Proceedings of the seventh annual meeting of the Berkeley Linguistics Society*, 27–39. Berkeley, CA: Berkeley Linguistics Society.

Anderssen, Merete & Kristine Bentzen. 2012. Norwegian object shift as IP-internal topicalization. *Nordlyd* 39(1). 1–23.

Angitso, Michael Terhemen. 2015. The limits of the DP/CP parallelism: Evidence from Tiv. *Semantics-Syntax Interface* 2(2). 141–156.

Ansah, Mercy Akrofi. 2009. *Aspects of Leteh (Larteh) grammar*. Manchester, UK: University of Manchester dissertation.

Ansah, Mercy Akrofi. 2010. Focus constituent interrogatives in Lɛtɛ (Larteh). *Nordic Journal of African Studies* 19(2). 98–107.

Ansah, Mercy Akrofi. 2014. Information packaging – focus marking and focus constructions in Leteh (Larteh). *Nordic Journal of African Studies* 23(3). 162–179.

Aoyagi, Hiroshi. 2006. On the predicate focus construction in Korean and Japanese. In Susumu Kuno, Ik-Hwan Lee, John Whitman, Joan Maling, Young-Se Kang, Peter Sells & Hyang-Sook Sohn (eds.), *Harvard studies in Korean linguistics XI*, 359–373. Seoul: Hanshin Publishing.

Arad, Maya. 1999. On 'little v'. In Karlos Arregi, Benjamin Bruening, C. Krause & V. Lin (eds.), *Papers in morphology and syntax: Cycle one; MITWPL 33*, 1–26. Cambridge, MA: MITWPL.

Arregi, Karlos & Andrew Nevins. 2012. *Morphotactics: Basque Auxiliaries and the Structure of Spellout*. Dordrecht: Springer.

Arregi, Karlos & Asia Pietraszko. 2020. Unifying long head movement with phrasal movement: A new argument from spellout. Talk given at WCCFL 38, UBC Vancouver, 7th of March.

Artiagoitia, Xabier. 1995. *Verb projections in Basque and minimal structure*. Donostia: Supplements of Anuario del Seminario de Filología Vasca "Julio de Urquijo" XXXVI, Gipuzkaoko Foru Aldundia.

Assmann, Anke, Doreen Georgi, Fabian Heck, Gereon Müller & Philipp Weisser. 2015. Ergatives Move Too Early: An Instance of Opacity in Syntax. *Syntax* 18(4). 343–387.

Badan, Linda. 2007. *High and low periphery: A comparison of Italian and Chinese*. Padua: Università degli Studi di Padova dissertation.

Baier, Nico. 2014. Spell-out, chains, and long-distance *Wh*-movement in seereer. Ms., University of California Berkeley.

Baker, Mark. 1988. *Incorporation. A theory of grammatical function changing*. Chicago/London: University of Chicago Press.

Baker, Mark C. 2009. Is head movement still needed for noun incorporation? *Lingua* 119. 148–165.

Baker, Mark C. 2014. Pseudo noun incorporation as covert noun incorporation. *Language and Linguistics* 15. 5–46.

Baltin, Mark. 2002. Movement to the higher V is remnant movement. *Linguistic Inquiry* 32. 653–659.

Bamgbose, Ayo. 1972. *The Yoruba verb phrase*. Ibadan: Ibadan University Press.

Barbiers, Sjef, Olaf Koeneman & Marika Lekakou. 2009. Syntactic doubling and the structure of wh-chains. *Journal of Linguistics* 45. 1–46.

Barnickel, Katja. 2017. *Deriving asymmetric coordination in German: A non-monotonic approach*. Leipzig: Universität Leipzig dissertation.

Bassong, Paul Roger. 2014. *Information structure and the Basa'a left peripheral syntax*. Yaoundé, Cameroon: University of Yaoundé I dissertation.

Bastos-Gee, Ana Claudia. 2009. Topicalization of verbal projections in Brazilian Portuguese. In Jairo Nunes (ed.), *Minimalist Essays on Brazilian Portuguese Syntax*, 132–155. Amsterdam: John Benjamins.

Bayer, Josef. 1996. *Directionality and logical form: On the scope of focusing particles and wh-in-situ*. Amsterdam: Kluwer.

Bayer, Josef. 2008. What is verb second? Ms., Universität Konstanz.

Bayer, Josef & Constantin Freitag. to appear. How much verb moves to second position? In Horst Lohnstein & Antonios Tsiknakis (eds.), *Verb second: Grammar internal and grammar external interfaces*, Berlin: De Gruyter.

Becker, Laura, Imke Driemel & Jude Nformi. 2019. Focus in Limbum. In Samson Lotven, Silvina Bongiovanni, Phillip Weirich, Robert Botne & Samuel Gyasi Obeng (eds.), *African linguistics across the disciplines: Selected papers from the 48th Annual Conference on African Linguistics*, vol. 5 Contemporary African Lingusitics, 219–237. Berlin: Language Science Press.

Becker, Laura & Jude Nformi. 2016. Focus and verb doubling in Limbum. In Katja Barnickel, Matías Guzmán Naranjo, Johannes Hein, Sampson Korsah, Andrew Murphy, Ludger

Paschen, Zorica Puškar & Joanna Zaleska (eds.), *Replicative Processes in Grammar*, vol. 93 Linguistische Arbeits Berichte (LAB), 57–84. Leipzig: Universiät Leipzig.
Bentzen, Kristine, Jason Merchant & Peter Svenonius. 2013. Deep properties of surface pronouns: Pronominal predicate anaphors in Norwegian and German. *Journal of Comparative Germanic Linguistics* 16. 97–125.
Berman, Ruth A. 1980. The case of an (S)VO language: Subject constructions in Modern Hebrew. *Language* 56(4). 759–776.
Bernabé, Jean. 1983. *Fondal-natal, Grammaire Basilectale Approchée des Créoles Guadeloupéen et Martiniquais*. Paris: L'Harmattan.
den Besten, Hans. 1983. On the interaction of root transformations and lexical deletive rules. In Werner Abraham (ed.), *On the formal syntax of Westgermania*, 47–131. Amsterdam: John Benjamins.
den Besten, Hans & Gert Webelhuth. 1990. Stranding. In G. Grewendorf & W. Sternefeld (eds.), *Scrambling and Barriers*, 77–92. Amsterdam: John Benjamins.
Biberauer, Theresa. 2009. Predicate-doubling in Afrikaans: Facts and comparison. Ms., University of Cambridge/Stellenbosch University.
Biberauer, Theresa, Anders Holmberg & Ian Roberts. 2007. Disharmonic word-order systems and the Final-over-Final-Constraint (FOFC). In A. Bisetto & F Barbieri (eds.), *Proceedings of XXXIII Incontro di Grammatica Generativa*, 86–105.
Biberauer, Theresa, Anders Holmberg & Ian Roberts. 2008. Structure and linearization in disharmonic word orders. In C. B. Chang & H. J. Haynie (eds.), *Proceedings of the 26th West Coast Conference on Formal Linguistics*, 96–104. Somerville, MA: Cascadilla Proceedings Project.
Biberauer, Theresa, Anders Holmberg & Ian Roberts. 2014. A syntactic universal and its consequences. *Linguistic Inquiry* 45(2). 169–225.
Bildhauer, Felix & Philippa Cook. 2010. German multiple fronting and expected topic-hood. In Stefan Müller (ed.), *Proceedings of the 17th international conference on Head-Driven Phrase Structure Grammar, Université Paris Diderot*, 68–79. Standford, CA: CSLI Publications.
Biloa, Edmond. 2013. *The Syntax of Tuki: A cartographic apporach*, vol. 203 Linguistik Aktuell/Linguistics Today. Amsterdam/Philadelphia: John Benjamins.
Boadi, Lawrence. 1976. A note on the historical antecedents of the obligatory pronoun-3-deletion rule in the Akan dialects. *Acta Linguistica Hafniensia* 16(1). 1–10.
Boadi, Lawrence. 2008. Tense, Aspect and Mood in Akan. In F. K. Ameka & M. E. Kropp Dakubu (eds.), *Aspect and Modality in Kwa Languages*, 9–68. Philadelphia: John Benjamins.
Bobaljik, Jonathan. 1993. On ergativity and ergative unergatives. In Colin Phillips (ed.), *Papers on case and agreement II, mitwpl 19*, 45–88. Cambridge, MA: MITWPL.
Bobaljik, Jonathan. 1995. *Morphosyntax: The syntax of verbal inflection*. Cambridge, MA: MIT dissertation.
Bobaljik, Jonathan. 2002. A-chains at the PF-interface: Copies and covert movement. *Natural Language and Linguistic Theory* 20. 197–267.
Boeckx, Cedric. 2001. Scope reconstruction and a-movement. *Natural Language and Linguistic Theory* 19. 503–548.
Boeckx, Cedric. 2008. *Understanding Minimalist Syntax: Lessons from locality in long-distance dependencies*. Oxford: Blackwell.
Boeckx, Cedric & Sandra Stjepanović. 2001. Head-ing toward PF. *Linguistic Inquiry* 32(2). 345–355.

Bondaruk, Anna. 2009. Constraints on predicate clefting in Polish. In G. Zybatow, U. Junghanns, D. Lenertová & P. Biskup (eds.), *Studies in Formal Slavic Phonology, Morphology, Syntax, Semantics, and Information Structure* Proceedings of FDSL 7, Leipzig 2007, 65–79. Frankfurt am Main: Peter Lang.

Bondaruk, Anna. 2012. Copy deletion in Polish predicate clefting. In E. Cyran, H. Kardela & B. Szymanek (eds.), *Sound, structure and sence. Studies in memory of Edmund Gussmann*, 55–70. Lublin: Katolicki Uniwersytet Lubelski.

Bonet, Eulalia. 1991. *Morphology after syntax: Pronominal clitics in Romance*. Cambridge, MA: MIT dissertation.

Borer, Hagit. 1984. Restrictive relatives in Modern Hebrew. *Natural Language and Linguistic Theory* 2. 219–260.

Börjars, Kersti, Nigel Vincent & Carol Chapman. 1997. Paradigms, periphrases and pronominal inflection: A feature-based account. In *Yearbook of Morphology 1996*, 155–180. Dordrecht: Kluwer.

Borsley, Robert D. & Andreas Kathol. 2000. Breton as a V2 language. *Linguistics* 38. 665–710.

Borsley, Robert D. & Jaklin Kornfilt. 2000. Mixed extended projections. In Robert D: Borsley (ed.), *The nature and function of syntactic categories*, vol. 32 Syntax and Semantics, 101–132. San Diego, CA: Academic Press.

Borsley, Robert D., Maria-Luisa Rivero & Janig Stevens. 1996. Long head movement in Breton. In Robert D. Borsley & Ian Roberts (eds.), *The syntax of Celtic languages: A comparative perspective*, 53–74. Cambridge: Cambridge University Press.

Borsley, Robert D., Maggie Tallerman & David Willis. 2007. *The syntax of Welsh*. Cambridge: Cambridge University Press.

Bošković, Željko. 1997. *The syntax of nonfinite complementation*. Cambridge, MA: MIT Press.

Bošković, Željko. 2004. Left branch extraction, structure of NP, and scrambling. In Joachim Sabel & Mamoru Saito (eds.), *The free word order phenomenon: Its syntactic sources and diversity*, 13–73. Berlin/New York: Mouton de Gruyter.

Bošković, Željko & Jairo Nunes. 2007. The copy theory of movement: A view from PF. In Norbert Corver & Jairo Nunes (eds.), *The Copy Theory of Movement*, 13–74. Amsterdam: John Benjamins.

Brody, Michael. 1995. *Lexico-Logical Form: A radically minimalist theory*. Cambridge, MA: MIT Press.

Brody, Michael. 2000. Mirror theory: Syntactic representation in perfect syntax. *Linguistic Inquiry* 31. 29–56.

Brody, Michael. 2003. *Towards an elegant syntax*. London: Routledge.

Broekhuis, Hans & Norbert Corver. 2015. *Syntax of Dutch: Verbs and verb phrases (volume 2)*. Amsterdam: Amsterdam University Press.

Brousseau, Anne-Marie, Sandra Filipovich & Claire Lefebvre. 1989. Morphological processes in Haitian Creole: The question of substratum and simplification. *Journal of Pidgin and Creole Languages* 4(1). 1–36.

Buell, Leston Chandler. 2012. Ewe VP fronting and derivation by phase. Ms., University of Amsterdam; LingBuzz/001486.

Büring, Daniel. 1995. *The 59th street bridge accent – on the meaning of topic and focus*. Tübingen: Universität Tübingen dissertation.

Büring, Daniel. 1997. *The meaning of topic and focus: The 59th street bridge accent*. London: Routledge.

Byrne, Francis. 1987. *Grammatical relations in a radical creole*. Amsterdam/Philadelphia: John Benjamins.
Cable, Seth. 2004. Predicate clefts and base-generation: Evidence from Yiddish and Brazilian Portuguese. Ms., MIT.
Cable, Seth. 2010. *The grammar of Q. Q-Particles, wh-movement, and pied-piping*. Oxford: Oxford University Press.
Carlson, Gregory N. 1977. A unified analysis of the English bare plural. *Linguistics and Philosophy* 1. 413–457.
Carnie, Andrew. 1996. *Non-verbal predication and head movement*. Cambridge, MA: MIT dissertation.
Carnie, Andrew. 2000. On the definition of X^0 and XP. *Syntax* 3. 59–106.
Cheng, Lisa Lai-Shen. 2008. Deconstructing the *shi…de* construction. *The Linguistic Review* 25. 235–266.
Cheng, Lisa Lai-Shen & Luis Vicente. 2013. Verb doubling in Mandarin Chinese. *Journal of East Asian Linguistics* 22. 1–37.
Childs, George Tucker. 1995. *A grammar of kisi*. Berlin: Mouton de Gruyter.
Childs, George Tucker. 2011. *A Grammar of Mani*, vol. 54 Mouton Grammar Library. Berlin/Boston: De Gruyter Mouton.
Childs, Tucker. 1997. Predicate clefting in kisi. *Proceedings of the Twenty-Third Annual Meeting of the Berkeley Linguistics Society* 23(2). 47–58.
Cho, Eun. 1997. VP (and TP) movement and verbal morphology. In Matthew L. Juge & Jeri L. Moxley (eds.), *Proceedings of the twenty-third annual meeting of the Berkeley Linguistics Society*, 38–49. Berkeley, CA: Berkeley Linguistics Society.
Cho, Eun & Kunio Nishiyama. 2000. Yoruba predicate clefts from a comparative perspective. In Vicki Carstens & Frederick Parkinson (eds.), *Advances in african linguistics* (Trends in African Linguistics 4), 37–49. Trenton, NJ: Africa World Press.
Cho, Sae-Youn & Jong-Bok Kim. 2002. Echoed verb constructions in Korean: A construction-based HPSG analysis. *Korean Journal of Linguistics* 27(4). 661–681.
Choi, Kiyong. 2000. Korean VP-focus constructions: Another case of base adjunction of X^0 to Y^0. *Studies in Generative Grammar* 10(2). 329–356.
Choi, Kiyong. 2003. The echoed verb construction in Korean: Evidence for V-raising. In Patricia M. Clancy (ed.), *Japanese/Korean linguistics 11*, 457–470. Stanford, CA: CSLI.
Chomsky, Noam. 1957. *Syntactic structures*. The Hague: Mouton.
Chomsky, Noam. 1965. *Aspects of the theory of syntax*. Cambridge, MA: MIT Press.
Chomsky, Noam. 1973. Conditions on transformations. In Stephen Anderson & Paul Kiparsky (eds.), *A Festschrift for Morris Halle*, 232–286. New York: Holt, Reinhart and Winston.
Chomsky, Noam. 1977. On wh-movement. In Peter W. Culicover, Thomas Wasow & Adrian Akmajian (eds.), *Formal syntax*, 71–132. New York: Academic Press.
Chomsky, Noam. 1980. On binding. *Linguistic Inquiry* 11(1). 1–46.
Chomsky, Noam. 1986. *Barriers*. Cambridge, MA: MIT Press.
Chomsky, Noam. 1991. Some notes on economy of derivation and representation. In Robert Freidin (ed.), *Principles and parameters in comparative grammar*, 417–454. Cambridge, MA: MIT Press.
Chomsky, Noam. 1993. A Minimalist Program for Linguistic Theory. In K. Hale & S. J. Keyser (eds.), *The View from Building 20: Essays in Linguistics in Honour of Sylvain Bromberger*, 1–52. Cambridge, MA: MIT Press.

Chomsky, Noam. 1995a. Bare phrase structure. In Gert Webelhuth (ed.), *Government and Binding Theory and the Minimalist Program*, 383–440. Oxford: Blackwell.
Chomsky, Noam. 1995b. *The Minimalist Program*. Cambridge, MA: MIT Press.
Chomsky, Noam. 2000. Minimalist inquiries: The framework. In R. Martin, D. Michaels & J. Uriagereka (eds.), *Step by step*, 89–155. Cambridge, MA: MIT Press.
Chomsky, Noam. 2001. Derivation by Phase. In M. Kenstowicz (ed.), *Ken Hale. A life in Language*, 1–52. Cambridge, MA: MIT Press.
Chomsky, Noam. 2004. Beyond explanatory adequacy. In Adriana Belletti (ed.), *Structures and Beyond. The cartography of syntactic structures, volume 3*, 104–131. Oxford: Oxford University Press.
Chomsky, Noam. 2008. On phases. In R. Freidin, C. P. Otero & M. L. Zubizarreta (eds.), *Foundational Issues in Linguistic Theory. Essays in Honor of Jean-Roger Vergnaud*, 291–321. Cambridge, MA: MIT.
Chomsky, Noam & Morris Halle. 1968. *The sound pattern of English*. Cambridge, MA: MIT Press.
Chumakina, Marina. 2013. Introduction. In Marina Chumakina & Greville G. Corbett (eds.), *Periphrasis: The role of syntax and morphology in paradigms*, 1–23. Oxford: Oxford University Press.
Chung, Sandra & William A. Ladusaw. 2004. *Restriction and saturation*, vol. 42 Linguistic Inquiry Monographs. Cambridge, MA: MIT Press.
Chung, Sandra, William A. Ladusaw & James McCloskey. 1995. Sluicing and logical form. *Natural Language Semantics* 3. 239–282.
Cichocki, Wladislaw. 1983. Multiple wh-questions in Polish: A two-COMP analysis. *Toronto Working Papers in Lingusitics* 4. 53–71.
Cinque, Guglielmo. 1977. The movement nature of left dislocation. *Linguistic Inquiry* 8. 397–411.
Cinque, Guglielmo. 1990. *Types of A-Bar Dependencies*. Cambridge, MA: MIT Press.
Cinque, Guglielmo. 1999. *Adverbs and functional heads: A crosslinguistic perspective*. Oxford: Oxford University Press.
Collins, Chris. 1993. *Topics in Ewe syntax*. Cambridge, MA: MIT dissertation.
Collins, Chris. 1994. The factive construction in Kwa. In Claire Lefebvre (ed.), *Travaux de recherche sur le creole haitien*, 31–65. Montréal: Departement de Linguistique Université du Québec à Montréal.
Cowper, Elizabeth. 2010. Where auxiliary verbs come from. In Melinda Heijl (ed.), *Proceedings of the 2010 Annual Conference of the Canadian Linguistic Association*, http://homes.chass.utoronto.ca/~cla-acl/actes2010/CLA2010_Cowper.pdf.
Cyrino, Sonia & Gabriela Matos. 2002. VP-ellipsis in European and Brazilian Portuguese: A comparative analysis. *Journal of Portuguese Linguistics* 1(2). 177–195. https://doi.org/10.5334/jpl.41.
Davis, Lori J. & Ellen F. Prince. 1986. Yiddish verb-topicalization and the notion of 'lexical integrity'. In Anna M. Farley, Peter T. Farley & Karl-Eric McCullough (eds.), *Proceedings of the 22nd annual meeting of the chicago linguistics society*, 90–97. Chicago, IL: University of Chicago, Chicago Linguistic Society.
Dayal, Veneeta. 2011. Hindi pseudo-incorporation. *Natural Language and Linguistic Theory* 29. 123–167.
Dekydspotter, Laurent. 1992. The syntax of predicate clefts. In Kimberly Broderick (ed.), *Proceedings of NELS 22*, 119–133. Amherst, MA: GLSA.
Diedrichsen, Elke. 2008. Where is the precore slot? mapping the layered structure of the clause and German sentence topology. In Robert D. Van Valin, Jr. (ed.), *Investigations of the*

Syntax-Semantics-Pragmatics Interface, vol. 105 Studies in Language Companion Series, Amsterdam/Philadelphia: John Benjamins.

Diesing, Molly. 1990. Verb movement and the subject position in Yiddish. *Natural Language and Linguistic Theory* 8(1). 41–79.

Diesing, Molly. 1992. *Indefinites*. Cambridge, MA: MIT Press.

den Dikken, Marcel. 2006. *Relators and linkers: The syntax of predication, predicate inversion and copulas*. Cambridge, MA: MIT Press.

Dobler, Eva. 2008. Creating as causing something to exist somewhere. Talk given at GLOW 31, Newcastle.

Donohue, Mark. 2004. A grammar of the Skou language of New Guinea. Ms., University of Sydney, (retrieved: April 27, 2016). http://pubman.mpdl.mpg.de/pubman/item/escidoc: 402710:4/component/escidoc:402709/skou_donohue2004_s.pdf.

Doron, Edit. 1999. V-movement and VP-ellipsis. In Shalom Lappin & Elabbas Benmamoun (eds.), *Fragments: Studies in ellipsis and gapping*, 124–140. New York: Oxford University Press.

Doron, Edit. 2003. Agency and voice: The semantics of the Semitic templates. *Natural Language Semantics* 11. 1–67.

Driemel, Imke. 2020. *Pseudo-noun incorporation across languages*. Leipzig: Universität Leipzig dissertation.

Duffield, Nigel. 1999. Final modals, adverbs and asymmetry in Vietnamese. *Revue québécoise de linguistique* 27(2). 91–129.

Dunigan, Melynda. 1994. *On the clausal structure of Wolof*. Chapel Hill, NC: University of North Carolina at Chapel Hill dissertation.

Einarsson, Stéfan. 1945. *Icelandic: Grammar, texts, glossary*. Baltimore: Johns Hopkins.

Elordieta, Arantzazu & Bill Haddican. 2016. Strategies of verb and verb phrase focus across Basque dialects. In Beatriz fernandes & Jon Ortiz de Urbina (eds.), *Microparameters in the Grammar of Basque*, 221–241. Amsterdam: John Benjamins.

Embick, David. 1997. *Voice and the interfaces of syntax*. Philadelphia, PA: University of Pennsylvania dissertation.

Embick, David. 2015. *The morpheme: A theoretical introduction*. Boston/Berlin: De Gruyter Mouton.

Embick, David & Rolf Noyer. 2001. Movement Operations after Syntax. *Linguistic Inquiry* 32(4). 555–595.

Embick, David & Rolf Noyer. 2007. Distributed morphology and the syntax-morphology interface. In G. Ramchand & C. Reis (eds.), *The oxford handbook of linguistic interfaces*, 289–324. Oxford: Oxford University Press.

Emonds, Joseph. 1970. *Root and structure preserving transformations*. Cambridge, MA: MIT dissertation.

Emonds, Joseph. 1976. *A transformational approach to English syntax*. New York, NY: Academic Press.

Emonds, Joseph. 1994. Two principles of economy. In Guglielmo Cinque, Jan Koster, Jean-Yves Pollock, Luigi Rizzi & Raffaella Zanuttini (eds.), *Paths toward Universal Grammar: Studies in honor of RIchard S. Kayne*, 155–172. Washington, DC: Georgetown University Press.

Etxepare, Ricardo. 2003. Valency and argument structure in the Basque verb. In Jose Ignacio Hualde & Jon Ortiz de Urbina (eds.), *A grammar of Basque*, 363–425. Berlin: Mouton de Gruyter.

Etxepare, Ricardo & Jon Ortiz de Urbina. 2003. Focalization. In Jose Ignacio Hualde & Jon Ortiz de Urbina (eds.), *A grammar of Basque*, 460–516. Berlin: Mouton de Gruyter.

Fanselow, Gisbert. 1987. *Konfigurationalität: Untersuchungen zur Universalgrammatik am Beispiel des Deutschen*. Tübingen: Narr Verlag.
Fanselow, Gisbert. 1991. Minimale syntax. Habilitationsschrift, Universität Passau.
Fanselow, Gisbert. 1993. Die Rückkehr der Basisgeneriere. *Groninger Arbeiten zur Germanistischen Linguistik* 36. 1–74.
Fanselow, Gisbert. 2002. Against remnant VP-movement. In A. Alexiadou, E. Anagnostopoulou, S. Barbiers & H.-M. Gärtner (eds.), *Dimensions of movement: From features to remnants*, 91–125. Amsterdam: John Benjamins.
Fanselow, Gisbert & Damir Ćavar. 2001. Remarks on the Economy of Pronunciation. In Gereon Müller & Wolfgang Sternefeld (eds.), *Competition in Syntax*, 107–150. Berlin: de Gruyter.
Fanselow, Gisbert & Damir Ćavar. 2002. Distributed deletion. In Artemis Alexiadou (ed.), *Theoretical approaches to universals*, 65–107. Amsterdam: John Benjamins.
Fanselow, Gisbert & Anoop Mahajan. 2000. Towards a Minimalist theory of wh-expletives, wh-copying and successive cyclicity. In Uli Lutz, Gereon Müller & Arnim von Stechow (eds.), *Wh-scope marking*, 195–230. Amsterdam: John Benjamins.
Felser, Claudia. 2004. Wh-copying, phases, and successive cyclicity. *Lingua* 114. 543–574.
Ferguson, K. Scott. 1993. Notes on the Shortest Move Metric and Object Checking. *Harvard Working Papers in Linguistics* 3. 65–80.
Fife, James & Gareth King. 1991. Focus and the Welsh 'abnormal sentence': A cross-linguistic perspective. In James Fife & Erich Poppe (eds.), *Studies in Brythonic word order*, vol. 83 Current Issues in Linguistic Theory, 81–154. Amsterdam: John Benjamins.
Filipovich, Sandra. 1987. *La morphologie de l'Haïtien*. Montréal Université du Québec à Montréal MA thesis.
Fleischer, Jürg. 2008. Zur topikalisierenden Infinitivverdoppelung in deutschen Dialekten: Trinken trinkt er nich, aber rauchen raucht er (mit einem Exkurs zum Jiddischen). In Peter Ernst & Franz Patocka (eds.), *Dialektgeographie der Zukunft: Akten des 2. Kongresses der Internationalen Gesellschaft für Dialektologie des Deutschen (IGDD) am Institut für Germanistik der Universität Wien, 20. bis 23. September 2006* Zeitschrift für Dialektologie und Linguistik Beihefte 135, 243–268. Stuttgart: Steiner.
Fowlie, Meaghan. 2010. More multiple multiple spell-out. In *Proceedings of GLOW 31: Principles of linearisation workshop*, Berlin: Mouton de Gruyter.
Fox, Danny. 2000. *Economy and semantic interpretation*. Cambridge, MA: MIT Press.
Fox, Danny & David Pesetsky. 2003. Cyclic linearisation and the typology of movement. Ms., MIT.
Fox, Danny & David Pesetsky. 2005. Cyclic linearisation of syntactic structure. *Theoretical Linguistics* 31. 1–45.
Fransen, Margo Astrid Eleonora. 1995. *A grammar of Limbum: A grassfields bantu language*. Amsterdam, The Netherlands: Vrije Universitet Amsterdam dissertation.
Freitag, Constantin. 2019. *Verb-second in grammar, processing, and acquisition: What you see is not what you get*. Konstanz: Universität Konstanz dissertation.
Gao, Qian. 1994. Focus criterion: Evidence from Chinese. In Jose Camacho & Lina Choueiri (eds.), *Proceedings of the 6th North American Conference on Chinese Linguistics (NACCL-6)*, 51–71. Los Angeles, CA: GSIL, University of Southern California.
Georgi, Doreen. 2014. *Opaque Interaction of Merge and Agree: On the Nature and Order of Elementary Operations*: Universität Leipzig dissertation.
Georgi, Doreen & Gereon Müller. 2010. Noun-Phrase Structure by Reprojection. *Syntax* 13(1). 1–36.
Gléau, René Le. 1973. *Syntaxe du breton moderne: 1710–1972*. La Baule: Editions La Baule.

Göksel, Aslı & Celia Kerslake. 2005. *Turkish: A comprehensive grammar*. London/New York: Routledge.
Goldberg, Lotus M. 2005. *Verb-stranding VP ellipsis: A cross-linguistic study*. Montreal: McGill University dissertation.
Grewendorf, Günther & Joachim Sabel. 1994. Long scrambling and incorporation. *Linguistic Inquiry* 25. 263–308.
Gribanova, Vera. 2013. Verb-stranding verb phrase ellipsis and the structure of the Russian verbal complex. *Natural Language and Linguistic Theory* 31(1). 91–136.
Gribanova, Vera. 2017. Head movement and ellipsis in the expression of Russian polarity focus. *Natural Language and Linguistic Theory* 35. 1079–1121.
Grimshaw, Jane. 1991. Extended projection. Ms., Brandeis University, Boston, MA.
Groat, Erich & John O'Neill. 1996. Spell-Out at the interface: Achieving a unified syntactic computational system in the minimalist framework. In W. Abraham, S. D. Epstein, H. Thráinsson & J.-W. Zwart (eds.), *Minimal ideas: Syntactic studies in the minimalist framework*, 113–139. Amsterdam: John Benjamins.
Haddican, Bill. 2005. *Aspects of language variation and change in contemporary Basque*. New York, NY: New York University dissertation.
Haddican, Bill. 2007. Do-support and VP focus in central and western Basque. *Natural Language and Linguistic Theory* 25(4). 735–764.
Hagstrom, Paul. 1995. Negation, focus and *do*-support in Korean. Ms., MIT.
Haider, Hubert. 1986. V-second in German. In Hubert Haider & Martin Prinzhorn (eds.), *Verb second phenomena in Germanic languages*, 49–76. Dordrecht: Foris.
Haider, Hubert. 2010. *The Syntax of German*. Cambridge: Cambridge University Press.
Hale, Ken & Samuel Keyser. 2002. *Prolegomenon to a Theory of Argument Structure*. Cambridge, MA: MIT Press.
Hale, Ken & Samuel J. Keyser. 1993. *On argument structure and lexical expression of syntactic relations*. Cambridge, MA: MIT Press.
Halle, Morris. 1962. Phonology in generative grammar. *Word* 18. 54–72.
Halle, Morris. 1992. Latvian declension. In G. Booij & J. van der Marle (eds.), *Morphology Yearbook 1991*, 33–47. Dordrecht: Kluwer.
Halle, Morris. 1997. Distributed morphology: Impoverishment and fission. In Benjamin Bruening, Yoonjung Kang & Martha McGinnis (eds.), *Papers at the Interface*, vol. 30 MIT Working Papers in Linguistics, 425–449. Cambridge, MA: MITWPL.
Halle, Morris & Alec Marantz. 1993. Distributed Morphology and the Pieces of Inflection. In Kenneth Hale & S. Jay Keyser (eds.), *The View from Building 20*, 111–176. Cambridge, MA: MIT Press.
Halle, Morris & Alec Marantz. 1994. Some key features of distributed morphology. In A. Carnie, H. Harley & T. Bures (eds.), *Papers on phonology and morphology*, vol. 21 MIT Working Papers in Linguistics, 275–288. Cambridge, MA: MITWPL.
Hankamer, Jorge & Line Mikkelsen. 2002. A morphological analysis of definite nouns in Danish. *Journal of Comparative Germanic Linguistics* 14(2). 137–175.
Hankamer, Jorge & Ivan Sag. 1976. Deep and surface anaphora. *Linguistic Inquiry* 9. 66–74.
Harbour, Daniel. 2008. Klivaj predika, or predicate clefts in Haitian. *Lingua* 118. 853–871.
Harizanov, Boris. 2019. Head movement to specifier positions. *Glossa* 4(1). 140.1–36.
Harizanov, Boris & Vera Gribanova. 2019. Whither head movement? *Natural Language and Linguistic Theory* 37(2). 461–522.

Harley, Heidi. 1994. Hug a tree: Deriving the morphosyntactic feature hierarchy. In Andrew Carnie & Heidi Harley (eds.), *Papers on phonology and morphology, mitwpl 21*, 275–288. Cambridge, MA: MITWPL.
Harley, Heidi. 2004. Merge, conflation, and head movement. The First Sister Principle revisited. In K. Moulton & M. Wolf (eds.), *NELS 34*, 239–254. Amherst: University of Massachusetts, GLSA.
Harley, Heidi. 2013. Getting morphemes in order: Merger, affixation, and head-movement. In Lisa Lai-Shen Cheng & Norbert Corver (eds.), *Diagnosing syntax*, 44–74. Oxford: Oxford University Press.
Harley, Heidi. 2014. On the identity of roots. *Theoretical Linguistics* 40. 225–276.
Harley, Heidi & Rolf Noyer. 1998. Licensing in the non-lexicalist lexicon: nominalinominal, Vocabulary Items and the Encyclopedia. In H. Harley (ed.), *Papers form the UPenn/MIT Roundtable on Argument Structure and Aspect*, vol. 32 MIT Working Papers in Linguistics, 119–137. Cambridge, MA: MIT Press.
Harley, Heidi & Rolf Noyer. 1999. Distributed Morphology. *GLOT International* 4(4). 3–7.
Harley, Heidi & Rolf Noyer. 2003. Distributed morphology. In Lisa Lai-Shen Cheng & Rint Sybesma (eds.), *The second GLOT International State-of-the-Article book*, 463–496. Berlin: Mouton de Gruyter.
Harris, James. 1997. Why *n'ho* is pronounced [li] in Barceloni Catalan. In Benjamin Bruening, Yoonjung Kang & Martha McGinnis (eds.), *Papers at the interface, mitwpl 30*, 451–479. Cambridge, MA: MITWPL.
Hartmann, Katharina. 2006. Focus constructions in Hausa. In Valéria Molnár & Susanne Winkler (eds.), *The architecture of focus*, 579–607. Berlin: Mouton de Gruyter.
Haugen, Jason D. & Daniel Siddiqi. 2013. Roots and the derivation. *Linguistic Inquiry* 44(3). 493–517.
Heck, Fabian. 2008. *On pied-piping: Wh-movement and beyond*. Berlin: de Gruyter.
Heck, Fabian. 2016. *Non-monotonic derivations*. Leipzig: Universität Leipzig dissertation.
Heck, Fabian & Gereon Müller. 2007. Extremely local optimization. In E. Brainbridge & B. Agbayani (eds.), *Proceedings of the 26th WECOL*, 170–183. Fresno, CA.
Hein, Johannes. to appear. Verb movement and the lack of verb doubling VP-topicalization in Germanic. *Journal of Comparative Germanic Linguistics* .
Hein, Johannes & Andrew Murphy. to appear. VP nominalization and the Final-over-Final-Condition. *Linguistic Inquiry* .
Heycock, Caroline. 1994. The internal structure of small clauses. In Jill Beckman (ed.), *Proceedings of NELS 25*, 223–238. Amherst, MA: GLSA, University of Massachusetts.
Hinterhölzl, Roland. 2002. Remnant movement and partial deletion. In A. Alexiadou, E. Anagnostopoulou, S. Barbiers & H.-M. Gärtner (eds.), *Dimensions of movement: From features to remnants*, 127–149. Amsterdam: John Benjamins.
Hiraiwa, Ken. 2003. Relativization in Buli. *Working Papers on ENdangered and Less Familiar Languages* 4. 45–84.
Hiraiwa, Ken. 2005a. *Dimensions of symmetry in syntax: Agreement and clausal architecture*. Cambridge, MA: MIT dissertation.
Hiraiwa, Ken. 2005b. Predicate cleft in Bùlì: The CP/DP symmetry. *Linguistic Analysis* 32. 544–583.
Hiraiwa, Ken & Adams Bodomo. 2008. Object-sharing as Symmetric Sharing: predicate clefting and serial verbs in Dàgáárè. *Natural Language and Linguistic Theory* 26. 795–832.

Hoge, Kerstin. 1998. The Yiddish double verb construction. In David Willis (ed.), *Oxford University Working Papers in Linguistics, Philology and Phonetics*, vol. 2, 85–97. Oxford: University of Oxford.
Höhle, Tilman. 1983. Subjektlücken in Koordinationen. Ms., Universität Köln.
Höhle, Tilman. 1990. Assumptions about asymmetric coordination. In Juan Mascaro & Marina Nespor (eds.), *Grammar in progress. glow essays for Henk van Riemsdijk*, 221–235. Dordrecht: Foris.
Höhle, Tilman. 1991. On reconstruction and coordination. In Hubert Haider & Klaus Netter (eds.), *Representation and derivation in the theory of grammar*, 139–197. Dordrecht: Kluwer.
Höhle, Tilman. 1992. Über Verum-Fokus im Deutschen. In Joachim Jacobs (ed.), *Informationsstruktur und Grammatik*, 112–141. Opladen: Westdeutscher Verlag.
Höhle, Tilman. 2000. The W-...W-construction: Appositive or scope indicating? In Uli Lutz, Gereon Müller & Arnim von Stechow (eds.), *Wh-scope marking*, 249–270. Amsterdam: John Benjamins.
Hoji, Hajime, Shigeru Miyagawa & Hiroaki Tada. 1989. NP-movement in Japanese. Ms., USC, OSU, and MIT.
Holmberg, Anders. 1986. *Word order and syntactic features in the Scandinavian languages and English*. Stockholm: University of Stockholm dissertation.
Holmberg, Anders. 1999. Remarks on Holmberg's Generalization. *Studia Linguistica* 53. 1–39.
Holmberg, Anders & Christer Platzack. 1991. On the role of inflection in Scandinavian syntax. In Werner Abraham, Wim Kosmeijer & Eric Reuland (eds.), *Issues in Germanic Syntax*, 93–118. Berlin: Mouton de Gruyter.
Holmberg, Anders & Christer Platzack. 1995. *The role of inflection in Scandinavian syntax*. Oxford: Oxford University Press.
Houser, Michael J., Line Mikkelsen, Ange Strom-Weber & Maziar Toosarvandani. 2006. Gøresupport in Danish. Ms., UC Berkeley.
Houser, Michael J., Line Mikkelsen & Maziar Toosarvandani. 2011. A defective auxiliary in Danish. *Journal of Comparative Germanic Linguistics* 23(3). 245–298.
Hsieh, I-Ta Chris. 2009. Even-focus and VP-fronting in Mandarin Chinese. In Yun Xiao (ed.), *Proceedings of the 21st North American Conference on Chinese Linguistics (NACCL-21)*, vol. 2, 494–507. Smithfield, RI: Bryant University.
Hualde, Jose Ignacio. 2003. Introduction. In Jose Ignacio Hualde & Jon Ortiz de Urbina (eds.), *A grammar of Basque*, 1–14. Berlin: Mouton de Gruyter.
Hutchinson, John. 2000. Predicate focusing constrcutions in African and Diaspora languages. In H. Ekkehard Wolf & Orin D. Gensler (eds.), *Proceedings of the Second World Congress of African Linguistics, Leipzig 1997*, 577–591. Köln: Rüdiger Köppe Verlag.
Iatridou, Sabine & Hedde Zeijlstra. 2010. On the scopal interaction of negation and deontic modals. In Maria Aloni, Harald Bastiaanse, Tikitu de Jager & Katrin Schulz (eds.), *Logic, language and meaning: 17th Amsterdam Colloquium, Amsterdam, The Netherlands, December 16–18, 2009, Revised Selected Papers*, 315–324. Berlin/Heidelberg: Springer.
Ishihara, Yuki. 2010. Non-identical verb forms in the Japanese predicate doubling construction. *Linguistic Research* 26. 39–65.
Jaggar, Philip J. 2001. *Hausa*. Amsterdam/Philadelphia: John Benjamins.
Jayaseelan, K. A. 1990. Incomplete VP deletion and gapping. *Linguistic Analysis* 20. 64–81.
Jo, Jung-Min. 2000. Morphosyntax of a dummy verb 'ha-' in Korean. *Studies in the Linguistic Sciences* 30(2). 77–100.

Jo, Jung-Min. 2013. Hpredicate contrastive topic constructions: Implications for morpho-syntax in Korean and copy theory of movement. *Lingua* 131. 80–111.

Johnson, Kyle. 2001. What VP-ellipsis can do, and what it can't, but not why. In Mark Baltin & Chris Collins (eds.), *The Handbook of Contemporary Syntactic Theory*, 439–479. London: Blackwell.

Jouitteau, Mélanie. 2005. *La syntaxe comparée du Breton*. Nantes: Université de Nantes dissertation.

Jouitteau, Mélanie. 2008. The Brythonic reconciliation. In Jeroen van Craenenbroek & Johan Rooryck (eds.), *Linguistic variation yearbook 2007*, 163–200. Amsterdam/Phildelphia: John Benjamins.

Jouitteau, Mélanie. 2011. Post-syntactic excorporation in realizational morphology, evidence from Breton. In Andrew Carnie (ed.), *Formal approaches to Celtic linguistics*, 115–142. Newcastle upon Tyne: Cambridge Scholars Publishing.

Julien, Marit. 2005. *Nominal phrases from a Scandinavian perspective*. Amsterdam: John Benjamins.

Kalin, Laura. 2014. *Aspect and argument licensing in Neo-Aramaic*. Los Angeles: University of California dissertation.

Kalin, Laura. 2018. Licensing and differential object marking: The view form Neo-Aramaic. *Syntax* 21. 112–159.

Källgren, Gunnel & Ellen F. Prince. 1989. Swedish VP-topicalization and Yiddish verb-topicalization. *Nordic Journal of Linguistics* 12. 47–58.

Kandybowicz, Jason. 2004. Predicate clefts, derivations, and Universal Grammar. In Akin Akinlabi & Oluseye Adesola (eds.), *Proceedings of the fourth world congress on african linguistics, New Brunswick 2003*, 211–223. Köln: Rüdiger Köppe Verlag.

Kandybowicz, Jason. 2008. *The Grammar of Repetition. Nupe grammar at the syntax-phonology interface*, vol. 136 Linguistik Aktuell/Linguistics Today. Amsterdam/Philadelphia: John Benjamins.

Kandybowicz, Jason. 2015. On prosodic vacuity and verbal resumption in Asante Twi. *Linguistic Inquiry* 46(2). 243–272.

Kandybowicz, Jason & Harold Torrence. 2016. Predicate focus in Krachi: 2 probes, 1 goal, 3 PFs. In K. Kim, P. Umbal, T. Block, Q. Chan, T. Cheng, K. Finney, M. Katz, S. Nickel-Thompson & L. Shorten (eds.), *Proceedings of the 33rd West Coast Conference on Formal Linguistics*, 227–236. Somerville, MA: Cascadilla Proceedings Project.

Karimi, Simin. 2005. *A Minimalist Approach to Scrambling: Evidence from Persian*, vol. 76 Studies in Generative Grammar. Berlin: Mouton de Gruyter.

Kayne, Richard. 1994. *The antisymmetry of syntax*. Cambridge, MA: MIT Press.

Keine, Stefan & Rajesh Bhatt. 2016. Interpreting verb clusters. *Natural Language and Linguistic Theory* 34(4). 1445–1492.

Kersten, Bart. 2015. *Does doen matter? An exploration of periphrastic doen in Dutch*. Nijmegen: Radboud University MA thesis.

Klecha, Peter & Martina Martinović. 2015. Exhaustivity, predication and the semantics of movement. In Anna E. Jurgensen, Hannah Sande, Spencer Lamoureux, Kenny Baclawski & Alison Zerbe (eds.), *Proceedings of the 41st Annual Meeting of the Berkeley Linguistics Society*, 267–286. Berkeley, CA: Berkeley Linguistics Society.

Kobele, Greg. 2006. *Generating copies*. Los Angeles: UCLA dissertation.

Kobele, Gregory M. 2005. Features moving madly: A formal perspective on feature percolation in the Minimalist Program. *Research in Language and Computation* 3(4). 361–410.

Kobele, Gregory M. & Harold Torrence. 2004. The syntax of complement clauses in Asante Twi. Paper presented at the 35th Annual Conference on African Linguistics.
Kobele, Gregory M. & Harold Torrence. 2006. Intervention and focus in Asante Twi. In Ines Fiedler & Anne Schwarz (eds.), *Papers on information structure in African languages*, vol. 46 ZAS Papers in Linguistics, 161–184. Berlin: ZAS.
Koopman, Hilda. 1984. *The syntax of verbs: From verb movement rules in the Kru languages to Universal Grammar*. Dordrecht: Foris.
Koopman, Hilda. 1997. Unifying predicate cleft constructions. *Proceedings of the Twenty-Third Annual Meeting of the Berkeley Linguistics Society* 23(2). 71–85.
Korsah, Sampson. 2017. *Issues in Kwa syntax: Pronouns and clausal determiners*. Leipzig: Universität Leipzig dissertation.
Korsah, Sampson & Andrew Murphy. 2019. Tonal reflexes of movement in Asante Twi. *Natural Language and Linguistic Theory* https://doi.org/10.1007/s11049-019-09456-9.
Koster, Jan. 1975. Dutch as an SOV language. *Linguistic Analysis* 1(2). 111–136.
Koster, Jan. 1987. *Domains and dynasties*. Foris: Dordrecht.
Kouwenberg, Silvia. 1994. *A grammar of Berbice Dutch Creole*. Berlin: Mouton de Gruyter.
Kouwenberg, Silvia & Eric Murray. 1994. *Papiamentu*, vol. 83 Languages of the World/Materials. München/Newcastle: Lincom Europa.
Kratzer, Angelika. 1995. Individual-level and stage-level predicates. In Gregory N. Carlson & Francis Jeffrey Pelletier (eds.), *The generic book*, 125–175. Chicago: Chicago University Press.
Kratzer, Angelika. 1996. Severing the external argument from its verb. In J. Rooryck & L. Zaring (eds.), *Phrase structure and the lexicon*, 109–138. Dordrecht: Kluwer.
Krifka, Manfred. 2007. Basic notions of information structure. In Caroline Féry, Gisbert Fanselow & Manfred Krifka (eds.), *The notions of information structure*, 13–55. Potsdam: Universitätsverlag Potsdam.
Kush, Dave & Terje Lohndal. 2017. Variable island sensitivity in Norwegian: Wh-extraction and topicalization. Talk given at the 32nd Comparative Germanic Syntax Workshop, Trondheim, 13–15 September.
Kush, Dave, Terje Lohndal & Jon Sprouse. 2018. Investigating variation in island effects: A case study of Norwegian wh-extraction. *Natural Language and Linguistic Theory* 36. 743–779.
Kuthy, Kordula De & Walt Detmar Meurers. 2001. On partial constituent fronting in German. *Journal of Comparative Germanic Linguistics* 3(3). 143–205.
LaCara, Nicholas. 2016a. Verb phrase movement as a window into head movement. *Proceedings of the Linguistics Society of America* 1(17). 1–14.
LaCara, Nicholas. 2016b. VP movement and verb doubling. Ms., University of Massachusetts Amherst.
Lahne, Antje. 2008a. Excluding SVO in ergative languages: A new view on Mahajan's Generalisation. In Fabian Heck, Gereon Müller & Jochen Trommer (eds.), *Varieties of Competition*, vol. 87 Linguistische Arbeits Berichte (LAB), 65–80. Leipzig: Universität Leipzig.
Lahne, Antje. 2008b. *Where There is Fire There is Smoke. Local Modelling of Successive-Cyclic Movement*. Leipzig: Universität Leipzig dissertation.
Laka, Itziar. 1990. *Negation in syntax. on the nature of functional categories and projections*. Cambridge, MA: MIT dissertation.
Landau, Idan. 2006. Chain Resolution in Hebrew V(P)-fronting. *Syntax* 9(1). 32–66.
Landau, Idan. 2007. Constraints on partial VP-fronting in Hebrew. *Syntax* 10. 127–164.

Landau, Idan. 2018. Missing objects in Hebrew: Argument ellipsis, not VP ellipsis. *Glossa* 3(1). 76–137.
Landau, Idan. 2020. On the non-existence of verb-stranding VP-ellipsis. *Linguistic Inquiry* https://doi.org/10.1162/ling_a_00346.
Larson, Richard & Claire Lefebvre. 1991. Predicate cleft in Haitian Creole. In *NELS*, vol. 21, 53–61. Amherst, MA: GLSA Publications.
Lasnik, Howard. 1981. Restricting the Theory of Transformations. In N. Hornstein & D. Lightfoot (eds.), *Explanation in Linguistics*, 152–173. London: Longman.
Lasnik, Howard. 1995. Verbal morphology: Syntactic structures meet the Minimalist Program. In Héctor Campos & Paula Kempchinsky (eds.), *Evolution and revolution in linguistic theory: Essays in honor of Carlos Otero*, 251–275. Georgetown, DC: Georgetown University Press.
Lasnik, Howard. 1999. Pseudogapping puzzles. In Shalom Lappin & Elabbas Benmamoun (eds.), *Fragments: Studies in ellipsis and gapping*, 141–174. Oxford: Oxford University Press.
Lasnik, Howard & Juan Uriagereka. 2005. *A course in minimalist syntax*. Oxford: Blackwell.
Law, Paul & Claire Lefebvre. 1995. On the relationship between event determiners and predicate cleft in Kwa languages: The case of Fongbe. *Linguistique Africaine* 14. 7–45.
Lechner, Winfried. 2001. Reduced and phrasal comparatives. *Natural Language and Linguistic Theory* 19(4). 683–735.
Lechner, Winfried. 2004. *Ellipsis in comparatives*. Berlin/New York: Mouton de Gruyter.
Lechner, Winfried. 2007. Interpretive effects of head movement. Ms., University of Cyprus/Stuttgart.
Lee, Chungmin. 2002. Contrastive topic and proposition structure. In Anna Maria di Sciullo (ed.), *Asymmetry in grammar. volume 1: Syntax and semantics*, vol. 57 Linguistik Aktuell/Linguistics Today, 345–371. Amsterdam: John Benjamins.
Lefebvre, Claire. 1987. On the interpretation of predicate cleft. *The Linguistic Review* 6. 169–194.
Lefebvre, Claire. 1992. Towards a typology of predicate cleft languages. *Journal of West African Languages* 22(1). 53–61.
Lefebvre, Claire. 1994. On spelling out e. In *Travaux de recherche sur le Créole Haitien*, 1–33. Montreal: Département de Linguistique, Université de Montréal.
Lefebvre, Claire & Anne-Marie Brousseau. 2002. *A grammar of Fongbe*. Berlin: Mouton de Gruyter.
Lefebvre, Claire & Elizabeth Ritter. 1993. Two types of predicate doubling adverbs in Haitian Creole. In F. Byrne & D. Winford (eds.), *Focus and grammatical relations in creole languages*, 65–94. Amsterdam: John Benjamins.
Legate, Julie Anne. 2003. Some interface properties of the phase. *Linguistic Inquiry* 34. 506–516.
Lema, José & Maria Luisa Rivero. 1990. Long head movement: ECP vs. HMC. In Juli Carter, Rose-Marie Déchaine, Bill Philip & Tim Sherer (eds.), *Proceedings of the 20th meeting of the North East Linguistic Society (NELS 20)*, vol. 2, 333–347. Amherst, MA: GLSA.
Lema, José & María-Luisa Rivero. 1991. Types of verbal movement in Old Spanish. *Probus* 3. 237–278.
Levin, Theodore. 2019. On the nature of differential object marking: Insights from Palauan. *Natural Language and Linguistic Theory* 37. 167–213.
Lipták, Anikó & Luis Vicente. 2009. Pronominal doubling under predicate topicalization. *Lingua* 119. 650–686.
Lobeck, Anne. 1995. *Ellipsis: Functional heads, licensing, and identification*. Oxford: Oxford University Press.

Lødrup, Helge. 1990. VP-topicalization and the verb *gjøre* in Norwegian. *Working Papers in Scandinavian Syntax* 45. 3–12.
Lötscher, Andreas. 1985. Syntaktische Bedingungen der Topikalisierung. *Deutsche Sprache* 13. 207–229.
Lumsden, John S. 1990. The biclausal structure of Haitian clefts. *Linguistics* 28. 741–759.
Lumsden, John S. & Claire Lefebvre. 1990. Predicate-cleft constructions and why they aren't what you might think. *Linguistics* 28. 761–782.
Mahajan, Anoop. 2003. Word order and (remnant) VP movement. In S. Karimi (ed.), *Word order and scrambling*, 217–237. Oxford: Blackwell.
Maling, Joan & Annie Zaenen. 1982. A phrase structure account of Scandinavian extraction phenomena. In Pauline Jacobson & Geoffrey K. Pullum (eds.), *The nature of syntactic representation*, 229–282. Dordrecht/London: D. Reidel Publishing.
Manfredi, Victor. 1993. Verb focus in the typology of Kwa/Kru and Haitian. In F. Byrne & D. Winford (eds.), *Focus and grammatical relations in Creole languages*, 3–51. Amsterdam: John Benjamins.
Marantz, Alec. 1997. No escape from syntax: Don't try morphological analysis in the privacy of your own lexicon. In A. Dimitriadis (ed.), *UPenn Working Papers in Linguistics*, vol. 4, 201–225. Philadelphia: University of Pennsylvania.
Marfo, Charles. 2005. *Aspects of Akan Grammar and the Phonology-Syntax Interface*. Hong Kong: University of Hong Kong dissertation.
Marfo, Charles & Adams Bodomo. 2005. Information structuring in Akan question-word fronting and focus constructions. *Studies in African Linguistics* 32(4). 179–208.
Martinović, Martina. 2015. *Feature geometry and head-splitting: Evidence from the morphosyntax of the Wolof clausal periphery*. Chicago, IL: University of Chicago dissertation.
Martinović, Martina. 2017. Wolof wh-movement at the syntax-morphology interface. *Natural Language and Linguistic Theory* 35. 205–256.
Massam, Diane. 1990. Cognate objects as thematic objects. *Canadian Journal of Linguistics* 35(2). 161–190.
Massam, Diane. 2001. Pseudo noun incorporation. *Natural Language and Linguistic Theory* 19(1). 153–197.
Matushansky, Ora. 2006. Head movement in linguistic theory. *Linguistic Inquiry* 37(1). 69–109.
McCloskey, James. 1991. Clause structure, ellipsis and proper government in Irish. *Lingua* 85. 259–302.
McCloskey, James. 2007. A language at the edge: Irish and the theory of grammar. Ms. for a talk at the University of North Carolina Linguistics Colloquium, March 24th 2007, available at http://ohlone.ucsc.edu/ jim/PDF/unc.pdf.
McCloskey, James. 2011. The shape of Irish clauses. In Andrew Carnie (ed.), *Formal approaches to Celtic linguistics*, 143–178. Newcastle upon Tyne: Cambridge Scholars.
Merchant, Jason. 2001. *The syntax of silence: Sluicing, islands, and the theory of ellipsis*. Oxford: Oxford University Press.
Merchant, Jason. 2002a. PF output constraints and elliptical repair in SAI comparatives. In Line Mikkelsen & Christopher Potts (eds.), *Proceedings of WCCFL 21*, 292–305. Somerville, MA: Cascadilla Press.
Merchant, Jason. 2002b. Swiping in Germanic. In Jan-Wouter Zwart & Werner Abraham (eds.), *Studies in comparative Germanic syntax. proceedings from the 15th Workshop on Comparative Germanic Syntax*, 289–316. Amsterdam/Philadelphia: John Benjamins.

Merchant, Jason. 2003. Subject-auxiliary inversion in comparatives and PF output constraints. In Kerstin Schwabe & Susanne Winkler (eds.), *The interfaces: Deriving and interpreting omitted structures*, vol. 61 Linguistik Aktuell/Linguistics Today, 55–77. Amsterdam: John Benjamins.
Merchant, Jason. 2008. Variable island repair under ellipsis. In Kyle Johnson (ed.), *Topics in ellipsis*, 132–153. Cambridge: Cambridge University Press.
Mikkelsen, Line. 2010. On what comes first in a verb-second language. Ms., UC Berkeley.
Moro, Andrea. 1997. *The raising of predicates: Predicate noun phrases and the theory of clause structure*. Cambridge: Cambridge University Press.
Müller, Gereon. 1998. *Incomplete category fronting: A derivational approach to remnant movement in German*. Dordrecht: Kluwer.
Müller, Gereon. 2002. Two types of remnant movement. In A. Alexiadou, E. Anagnostopoulou, S. Barbiers & H.-M. Gärtner (eds.), *Dimensions of movement: From features to remnants*, 209–241. Amsterdam: John Benjamins.
Müller, Gereon. 2004. Syncretism and iconicity in Icelandic noun declension: A distributed morphology approach. In Geert Booij & Jaap van Marle (eds.), *Yearbook of Morphology 2004*, 229–271. Dordrecht: Springer.
Müller, Gereon. 2007. Extended exponence by enrichment: Argument encoding in German, Archi, and Timucua. *UPenn Working Papers in Linguistics* 13(1). 253–266.
Müller, Gereon. 2009a. Ergativity, Accusativity, and the Order of Merge and Agree. In Kleanthes K. Grohmann (ed.), *Explorations of Phase Theory. Features and Arguments*, 269–308. Berlin: Mouton de Gruyter.
Müller, Gereon. 2009b. Notes on partial fronting and copy spell-out. *Theoretical Linguistics* 35. 289–306.
Müller, Gereon. 2014. *Syntactic Buffers*, vol. 91 Linguistische Arbeits Berichte. Leipzig: Institut für Linguistik, Universität Leipzig.
Müller, Gereon. 2016. Predicate doubling by phonological copying. In K. Barnickel, M. Guzmán Naranjo, J. Hein, S. Korsah, A. Murphy, L. Paschen, Z. Puškar & J. Zaleska (eds.), *Replicative processes in grammar*, vol. 93 Linguistische Arbeits Berichte, Universität Leipzig: Institut für Linguistik.
Müller, Stefan. 2005. Zur Analyse der scheinbar mehrfachen Vorfeldbesetzung. *Linguistische Berichte* 203. 297–330.
Müller, Stefan. 2015. *German Clause Structure: An Analysis with Special Consideration of So-Called Multiple Frontings*, vol. 2 Empirically Oriented Morphology and Syntax. Berlin: Language Science Press. With contributions by Felix Bildhauer and Philippa Cook.
Murasugi, Kumiko. 1992. *Crossing and nested paths*. Cambridge, MA: MIT dissertation.
Murphy, Andrew. 2016. What copying (doesn't) tell us about movement: Remarks on the derivation of wh-copying in German. In Katja Barnickel, Matías Guzm#'an Naranjo, Johannes Hein, Sampson Korsah, Andrew Murphy, Ludger Paschen, Zorica Puškar & Joanna Zaleska (eds.), *Replicative Processes in Grammar*, vol. 93 Linguistische Arbeits Berichte (LAB), 149–188. Leipzig: Universität Leipzig.
Murphy, Andrew & Zorica Puškar. 2018. Closest Conjunct Agreement is an Illusion. *Natural Language and Linguistic Theory* 36(4). 1207–1261.
Muysken, Pieter. 1977. Movement rules in Papiamentu. In Pieter Muysken (ed.), *Amsterdam creole studies*, vol. 1, 80–102. Amsterdam: Instituut vor Algemene Taalwetenschap.
Muysken, Pieter. 1978. Three types of fronting constructions in Papiamentu. In Frank Jansen (ed.), *Studies on fronting*, 65–79. Lisse: Peter de Ridder.

Ndayiragije, Juvénal. 1992. Structure syntaxique des clivées en Fòn. *Journal of West African Languages* 22(1). 63–95.
Ndayiragije, Juvénal. 1993. *Syntaxe et sémantique du clivage du prédicat en Fòngbè*. Montreal: Université du Québec à Montréal dissertation.
Newman, Paul. 2000. *The Hausa language: An encyclopedic reference grammar*. New Haven/London: Yale University Press.
Nformi, Jude. 2018. Complementizer agreement and intervention effects. Ms., Universität Leipzig.
Nishiyama, Kunio & Eun Cho. 1998. Predicate cleft constructions in Japanese and Korean: The role of dummy verbs in TP/VP preposing. *Japanese/Korean Linguistics* 7. 463–479.
Nkemnji, Michael Akamin. 1995. *Heavy pied-piping in Nweh*. Los Angeles, CA: University of California Los Angeles dissertation.
Norris, R. L. 2003. Embedded clauses in Bùlì. In G. Akanlig-Pare & Michael Kenstowicz (eds.), *Studies in Bùlì grammar*, vol. 4 MIT Working Papers on Endangered and Less Familiar Languages, 131–146. Cambridge, MA: MITWPL.
Nunes, Jairo. 1995. *The copy theory of movement and linearization of chains in the Minimalist Program*. College Park, MD: University of Maryland dissertation.
Nunes, Jairo. 2004. *Linearization of chains and sideward movement*, vol. 43 LI Monographs. Cambridge, MA: MIT Press.
Nylander, Dudley K. 1985. A new analysis of the krio cleft predicate. *Studies in African Linguistics*. Supplement 9.
Ordóñez, Francisco. 1997. *Word order and clause structure in Spanish and other Romance languages*. New York, NY: CUNY Graduate Center dissertation.
Ordóñez, Francisco. 1998. Postverbal asymmetries in Spanish. *Natural Language and Linguistic Theory* 16. 313–346.
Ørsnes, Bjarne. 2011. Non-finite *do*-support in Danish. In Olivier Bonami & Patricia Cabredo Hofherr (eds.), *Empirical issues in syntax and semantics 8: Papers from cssp 2009*, 409–434. Paris: CNRS. http://www.cssp.cnrs.fr/eiss8.
Ortiz de Urbina, Jon. 1989. *Parameters in the grammar of Basque*. Dordrecht: Foris.
Osam, Emmanuel Kweku. 1996. Animacy distinctions in Akan grammar. *Studies in the Linguistic Sciences* 23(2). 153–164.
Otani, Kazuyo & John Whitman. 1991. V-raising and VP-ellipsis. *Linguistic Inquiry* 22(2). 345–258.
Ott, Dennis. 2014. An ellipsis approach to contrastive left-dislocation. *Linguistic Inquiry* 45(2). 269–303.
Ott, Dennis & Mark de Vries. 2016. Right dislocation as deletion. *Natural Language and Linguistic Theory* 34(2). 641–690.
Pankau, Andreas. 2009. Eliminating delete: Copies at the interfaces. In A. Karasimos, C. Vlachos, E. Dimela, M. Giakoumelou, M. Pavlakou, N. Koutsoukos & D. Bougonikolou (eds.), *Proceedings of the Patras International Conference of Graduate Students in Linguistics 1*, 197–209. Patras: University of Patras.
Pankau, Andreas. 2013. *Replacing copies: The syntax of wh-copying in German*. Utrecht: University of Utrecht dissertation.
Paster, Mary. 2010. The verbal morphology and phonology of Asante Twi. *Studies in African Linguistics* 39(1). 77–120.
Pesetsky, David. 1997. Optimality Theory and syntax: Movement and pronunciation. In D. Archangeli & D. Terrence Langendoen (eds.), *Optimality Theory: An overview*, 134–170. Malden, MA: Blackwell.

Pesetsky, David. 1998. Some optimality principles of sentence pronunciation. In P. Barbosa, D. Fox, P. Hagstrom, M. McGinnis & D. Pesetsky (eds.), *Is the best good enough?*, 337–383. Cambridge, MA: MIT Press.
Phillips, Collin. 2003. Linear order and constituency. *Linguistic Inquiry* 34. 37–90.
Piou, Nanie. 1982. Le clivage du prédicat. In Claire Lefebvre, Hélène Magloire-Holly & Nanie Piou (eds.), *Syntaxe de l'Haïtien*, 122–152. Ann Arbor, MI: Karoma Publishers.
Platzack, Christer. 1986. COMP, INFL, and Germanic word order. In L. Hellan & K. Christensen (eds.), *Topics in Scandinavian syntax*, 185–234. Dordrecht: Reidel.
Platzack, Christer. 2008. Cross linguistic variation in the realm of support verbs. Ms., Lund University. LingBuzz/000766.
Platzack, Christer. 2012. Cross Germanic variation in the realm of support verbs. In Peter Ackema, Rhona Alcorn, Caroline Heycock, Dany Jaspers, Jeroen van Craenenbroek & Guido Vanden Wyngaerd (eds.), *Comparative Germanic Syntax: The state of the art*, vol. 191 Linguistik Aktuell/Linguistics Today, 279–310. Amsterdam/Philadelphia: John Benjamins.
Platzack, Christer. 2013. Head movement as a phonological operation. In Lisa Lai-Shen Cheng & Norbert Corver (eds.), *Diagnosing Syntax*, vol. 46 Oxford Studies in Theoretical Linguistics, 21–43. Oxford: Oxford University Press.
Pollock, Jean-Yves. 1989. Verb movement, universal grammar and the structure of IP. *Linguistic Inquiry* 20(3). 365–424.
Preminger, Omer. 2019. What the PCC tells us about "abstract" agreement, head movement, and locality. *Glossa* 4(1). 13.1–42. https://doi.org/10.5334/gjgl.315.
Press, Ian. 1986. *A grammar of modern Breton*. Berlin/New York: Mouton de Gruyter.
Puškar, Zorica. 2018. Interactions of gender and number agreement: Evidence from Bosnian/Croatian/Serbian. *Syntax* 21(3). 275–318.
Pylkkänen, Liina. 2008. *Introducing arguments*, vol. 49 LI Monographs. Cambridge, MA: MIT Press.
Rapp, Irene & Arnim von Stechow. 1999. *Fast* "almost" and the visibility parameter for functional adverbs. *Journal of Semantics* 16. 149–204.
Rebuschi, Georges. 1983. A note on focalization in Basque. *Journal of Basque Studies* 4(2). 29–42.
Reis, Marga. 1996. Extraction from verb-second clauses in German. In Uli Lutz & Jürgen Pafel (eds.), *On extraction and extraposition in German*, 45–88. Amsterdam: John Benjamins.
Reis, Marga & Inger Rosengren. 1992. What do *wh*-imperatives tell us about *wh*-movement? *Natural Language and Linguistic Theory* 10. 79–118.
Rett, Jessica. 2006. Pronominal vs. determiner *wh*-words: Evidence from the copy construction. In Olivier Bonami & Patricia Cabredo Hofherr (eds.), *Empirical issues in syntax and semantics 6*, 355–374. Paris: CNRS.
Richards, Marc. 2011. Deriving the edge: What's in a phase. *Syntax* 14(1). 74–95.
Richards, Norvin. 2001. *Movement in language: Interactions and architecture*. Oxford: Oxford University Press.
van Riemsdijk, Henk. 1978. *A case study in syntactic markedness: The binding nature of prepositional phrases*. Dordrecht: Foris.
van Riemsdijk, Henk. 1989. Movement and regeneration. In P. Benincá (ed.), *Dialectal variation and the theory of grammar*, 105–136. Dordrecht: Foris.
Ritter, Elizabeth. 1992. Cross-linguistic evidence for number phrase. *Canadian Journal of Linguistics* 37. 197–218.

Rivero, Maria Luisa. 1991. Long head movement and negation: Serbo-Croatian vs. Slovak and Czech. *The Linguistic Review* 8(2-4). 319–351.

Rivero, María-Luisa. 1993. Long head movement vs. V2 and null subjects in Old Romance. *Lingua* 89. 217–245.

Rizzi, Luigi. 1997. The fine-structure of the left periphery. In Liliane Haegeman (ed.), *Elements of grammar*, 281–337. Dordrecht: Kluwer.

Roberts, Ian. 1994. Two types of head-movement in Romance. In Norbert Hornstein & David Lightfoot (eds.), *Verb movement*, 207–242. Cambridge: Cambridge University Press.

Roberts, Ian. 2010. *Agreement and head movement: Clitics, incorporation, and defective goals*, vol. 59 LI Monographs. Cambridge, MA: MIT Press.

Römer, Raúl. 1977. Polarization phenomena in Papiamentu. *Amsterdam Creole Studies* 17. 69–79.

Rosen, Carol. 1976. Guess what about? In A. Ford, J. Reighard & R. Singh (eds.), *Proceedings of the 6th Annual Meeting of the North East Linguistic Society (NELS 6*, 205–211. Amherst, MA: GLSA.

Ross, John R. 1969. Guess who? In R. Binnick, A. Davidson, G. Green & J. Morgan (eds.), *Papers from the 5th Regional Meeting of the Chicago Linguistic Society*, 252–286. Chicago: Chicago Linguistic Society.

Rouveret, Alain. 2012. VP ellipsis, phases and the syntax of morphology. *Natural Language and Linguistic Theory* 30. 897–963.

Rudin, Catherine. 1988. On multiple questions and multiple wh-fronting. *Natural Language and Linguistic Theory* 6. 445–501.

Saah, Kofi. 1992. Null object constructions in Akan. In Chris Collins & Victor Manfredi (eds.), *Proceedings of the Kwa Comparative Syntax Workshop, MITWPL 17*, 219–244. Cambridge, MA: MITWPL.

Saah, Kofi. 2010. Relative clauses in Akan. In Enoch O. Aboh & James Essegbey (eds.), *Topics in Kwa Syntax* Studies in Natural Language and Linguistic Theory, 91–109. Dordrecht: Springer.

Saah, Kofi & Helen Goodluck. 1995. Island effects in parsing and grammar: Evidence from Akan. *The Linguistic Review* 12. 381–409.

Saah, Kofi K. 1994. *Studies in Akan syntax, acquistion and sentence processing*. Ottawa: University of Ottawa dissertation.

Sailor, Craig. 2014. VP ellipsis in tag questions: A typological approach. In *Proceedings of the 46th Annual Meeting of the Chicago Linguistic Society (CLS 46)*, 372–386. Chicago: The University of Chicago.

Sailor, Craig. 2018. The typology of head movement and ellipsis: A reply to Lipták & Saab. *Natural Language and Linguistic Theory* 36. 851–875.

Sauerland, Uli. 1998. Scope freezing. In P. Tamanji & K. Kusumoto (eds.), *Proceedings of NELS 28*, 169–182. Amherst, MA: GLSA Publications.

Sauerland, Uli. 2003. Intermediate adjunction with a-movement. *Linguistic Inquiry* 34. 308–314.

Sauerland, Uli & Paul Elbourne. 2002. Total reconstruction, PF movement, and derivational order. *Linguistic Inquiry* 33(2). 283–319.

Schafer, Robin. 1995. Negation and verb second in Breton. *Natural Language and Linguistic Theory* 13. 135–172.

Schippers, Ankelien. 2012. Some people are repeaters: Medial copy spell-out in long-distance wh-dependencies. In Camelia Constantinescu, Bert Le Bruyn & Kathrin Linke (eds.), *Proceedings of ConSOLE XVII*, 269–288. Leiden: Leiden University Centre for Linguistics.

Schoorlemmer, Erik. 2012. Definiteness marking in German morphological variations on the same syntactic theme. *Journal of Comparative Germanic Linguistics* 15. 107–156.

Schoorlemmer, Erik & Tanja Temmerman. 2012. Head Movement as a PF-Phenomenon: Evidence from Identity under Ellipsis. In J. Choi, E. A. Hogue, J. Punske, D. Tat, J. Schertz & A. Trueman (eds.), *Proceedings of the 29th West Coast Conference on Formal Linguistics*, 232–240. Somerville, MA: Cascadilla Proceedings Project.

Schuyler, Tamara. 2001. *Wh-movement out of the site of VP-ellipsis*. San Diego, CA: University of California San Diego MA thesis.

Schwarz, Christian. 2009. *Die tun-Periphrase im Deutschen. Gebrauch und Funktion*. Saarbrücken: VDM.

Selkirk, Elizabeth. 2011. The Syntax-Phonology interface. In J. Goldsmith, J. Riggle & A. Yu (eds.), *The Handbook of Phonological Theory*, 435–484. Oxford: Blackwell 2nd edn.

Sells, Peter. 2001. *Structure, alignment, and optimality in Swedish*. Stanford, CA: CSLI.

Shyu, Shu-Ing. 1995. *The syntax of focus and topic in Mandarin Chinese*. Los Angeles, CA: University of Southern California dissertation.

Shyu, Shu-Ing. 2004. (A)symmetries between Mandarin Chinese *lian-dou* and *shenzhi*. *Journal of Chinese Linguistics* 32(1). 71–128.

Soh, Hooi-Ling. 1998. *Object scrambling in Chinese*. Cambridge, MA: MIT dissertation.

Spencer, Andrew & Gergana Popova. 2015. Periphrasis and inflection. In Matthew Baerman (ed.), *The Oxford Handbook of Inflection*, 197–232. Oxford: Oxford University Press.

Speyer, Augustin. 2008. Doppelte Vorfeldbesetzung im heutigen Deutsch und im Frühneuhochdeutschen. *Linguistische Berichte* 216. 455–485.

Sproat, Richard. 1985. Welsh syntax and VSO structure. *Natural Language and Linguistic Theory* 3. 173–216.

von Stechow, Arnim. 1996. The different readings of *wieder* "again": A structural account. *Journal of Semantics* 13. 87–138.

Stewart, John. 1963. Some restrictions on objects in Twi. *Journal of African Languages* 2. 145–149.

Stewart, Osamuyimen Thompson. 2001. *The serial verb construction parameter*. New York: Garland.

Stewart, Osamyimen Thompson. 1998. *The serial verb construction parameter*. Montreal: McGill University dissertation.

Stump, Gregory. 2001. *Inflectional morphology*. Cambridge: Cambridge University Press.

Surányi, Balász. 2005. Head movement and reprojection. In *Annales Universitatis Scientiarum Budapestinensis de Rolando Eötvös Nominatae. Sectio Linguistica. Tomus XXVI*, 313–342. Budapest: ELTE.

Svenonius, Peter. 2004. On the edge. In David Adger, Cécile de Cat & George Tsoulas (eds.), *Syntactic Edges and their effects*, 261–287. Dordrecht: Kluwer.

Svenonius, Peter. 2005. Extending the extension condition to discontinuous idioms. *Linguistic Variation Yearbook* 5. 227–263.

Svenonius, Peter. 2008. The position of adjectives and other phrasal modifiers in the decomposition of DP. In Louise McNally & Christopher Kennedy (eds.), *Adjectives and adverbs: Syntax, semantics, and discourse*, 16–42. Oxford: Oxford University Press.

Táíwò, Oyè & Michael Terhemen Angitso. 2016. In-situ and ex-situ focusing in Tiv. *Journal of West African Languages* 43(1). 93–116.

Tajsner, Przemysław. 1998. *Minimalism and functional thematization. A cross-linguistic study*. Poznań: Motivex.

Takano, Yuji. 2000. Illicit remnant movement: An argument for feature-driven movement. *Linguistic Inquiry* 31. 141–156.
Tallerman, Maggie. 1996. Fronting constructions in Welsh. In Robert D. Borsley & Ian Roberts (eds.), *The syntax of the Celtic languages: A comparative perspective*, 97–124. Cambridge: Cambridge University Press.
Tateishi, Koichi. 1991. *The syntax of "subjects"*. Amherst, MA: University of Massachusetts Amherst dissertation.
Teleman, Ulf, Staffan Hellberg & Erik Andersson. 1999. *Svenska Akademiens grammatik*. Stockholm: Norstedts Ordbok.
Tenny, Carol. 1987. *Grammaticalizing aspect and affectedness*. Cambridge, MA: MIT dissertation.
Thiersch, Craig. 1978. *Topics in German syntax*. Cambridge, MA: MIT dissertation.
Thoms, Gary. 2012. Ellipsis licensing and verb movement in Scandinavian. Ms., University of Glasgow.
Thornton, Rosalind & Stephen Crain. 1994. Successive-cyclic movement. In Teun Hoekstra & Bonnie D. Schwartz (eds.), *Language acquisition studies in generative grammar*, 215–252. Amsterdam: John Benjamins.
Torrego, Esther. 1998. *The dependencies of objects*. Cambridge, MA: MIT dissertation.
Torrence, Harold. 2005. *On the distribution of complementizers in Wolof*. Los Angeles, CA: University of California Los Angeles dissertation.
Torrence, Harold. 2013a. *The clause structure of Wolof: Insights into the left periphery*, vol. 198 Linguistik Aktuell/Linguistics Today. Amsterdam/Philadelphia: John Benjamins.
Torrence, Harold. 2013b. A promotion analysis of Wolof clefts. *Syntax* 16(2). 176–215.
Tran, Thi Giang. 2011. *The contrastive predicate construction in Vietnamese*. Guangdong, China: National Sun Yat-Sen University MA thesis.
Travis, Lisa. 1984. *Parameters and effects of word order variation*. Cambridge, MA: MIT dissertation.
Travis, Lisa. 1991. Parameters of phrase structure and verb second phenomena. In Robert Freidin (ed.), *Principles and parameters in comparative grammar*, 339–364. Cambridge, MA: MIT Press.
Travis, Lisa. 2003. Reduplication feeding syntactic movement. In Sophie Burelle & Stanca Somesfalean (eds.), *Proceedings of the 2003 annual conference of the canadian linguistic association*, 236–247. Université du Québec à Montréal.
Trinh, Tue. 2009. A constraint on copy deletion. *Theoretical Linguistics* 35. 183–227.
Trinh, Tue. 2011. *Edges and Linearization*. Cambridge, MA: MIT dissertation.
Tucker, Matthew. 2011. Verb-stranding verb-phrase ellipsis in EgyptianArabic. Paper presented at the 25th Arabic Linguistics Symposium/UCSC Structure of Arabic, Tucson, Santa Cruz.
Tuller, Laurice Anne. 1982. Null subject and objects. *Journal of Linguistic Research* 2(2). 77–99.
Tuller, Laurice Anne. 1986. *Bijective relations in Universal Grammar and the syntax of Hausa*. Los Angeles, CA: University of California Los Angeles dissertation.
Tyler, Matthew. 2018. Differential object marking by a'-status. NELS 49 Poster.
Ürögdi, Barbara. 2006. Predicate fronting and dative case in Hungarian. *Acta Linguistica Hungaria* 53(3). 291–332.
Verbuk, Anna. 2006. Russian predicate clefts as S-topic constructions. In J. Lavine, S. Franks, M. Tasseva-Kurktchieva & H. Filip (eds.), *Annual Workshop on Formal Approaches to Slavic Linguistics: The Princeton Meeting 2005*, 394–408. Ann Arbor, MI: Michigan Slavic Publications.

Vicente, Luis. 2007. *The syntax of heads and phrases: A study of verb (phrase) fronting*. Leiden: Leiden University dissertation.
Vicente, Luis. 2009. An alternative to remnant movement for partial predicate fronting. *Syntax* 12(2). 158–191.
Vikner, Sten. 1995. *Verb movement and expletive subjects in the Germanic languages*. Oxford: Oxford University Press.
Weber, Thilo. 2017. *Die tun-Periphrase im Niederdeutschen: Funktionale und formale Aspekte*. Tübingen: Stauffenberg Verlag.
Weisser, Philipp. 2015. *Derived coordination: A minimalistic perspective on clause chains, converbs and asymmetric coordination*, vol. 561 Linguistische Arbeiten. Berlin: de Gruyter.
Weisser, Philipp. 2019. Telling allomorphy from agreement. *Glossa* 4(1). 86. http://doi.org/10.5334/gjgl.803.
Whitman, John. 1987. Configurationality parameters. In T. Imai & M. Saito (eds.), *Issues in Japanese linguistics*, 351–374. Dordrecht: Foris.
Whitney, William Dwight. 1889. *Sanskrit grammar, including both the classical language and the older dialects of Deda and Brahmana*. Cambridge, MA: Reprinted 1975 by Harvard University Press.
Wiltschko, Martina. 2014. *The universal structure of categories: Towards a formal typology*. Cambridge: Cambridge University Press.
Witkoś, Jacek. 1998. *The syntax of clitics. steps towards a minimalist account*. Poznań: Motivex.
Yakpo, Kofi. 2009. *A grammar of Pichi*. Berlin/Accra: Isimu Media.
Zabala, Igone & Juan Carlos Odriozola. 1996. On the relation between DP and TP: The structure of Basque infinitivals. *Catalan Working Papers in Linguistics* 5. 231–281.
Zaenen, Annie. 1997. Contrastive dislocation in Dutch and Icelandic. In Elena Anagnostopoulou, Henk van Riemsdijk & Frans Zwarts (eds.), *Materials on left dislocation*, 119–148. Amsterdam: John Benjamins.
Ziv, Yael. 1997. Infinitive initially: Theme/topic/focus. In J. H. Connolly, R. M. Vismans, C. S. Butler & R. A. Gatward (eds.), *Discourse and pragmatics in functional grammar*, 163–175. Berlin: Mouton de Gruyter.
Zubizaretta, Maria Luisa. 1998. *Focus, prosody, and word order*. Cambridge, MA: MIT Press.
Zwart, Jan-Wouter. 1991. Clitics in Dutch: Evidence for the position of INFL. *Groninger Arbeiten zur Germanistischen Linguistik* 33. 71–92.
Zwart, Jan-Wouter. 1997. *Morphosyntax of verb movement. a minimalist approach to the syntax of Dutch*. Dordrecht: Kluwer.
Zwart, Jan-Wouter. 2005. Verb-second as a function of Merge. In Marcel den Dikken & Christina M. TOrtora (eds.), *The function of function words and functional categories*, 11–40. Amsterdam: John Benjamins.
Zwart, Jan-Wouter. 2017. An argument against the syntactic nature of verb movement. In Laura Bailey & Michelle Sheehan (eds.), *Order and structure in syntax 1: Word order and syntactic structure*, vol. 1 Open Generative Syntax, 29–47. Berlin: Language Science Press.

Index

Ā-head movement, 4, 7, 105, 110, 119, 121, 126, 129, 131, 148, 174, 182, 185, 191, 205
– in Asante Twi, 51, 159
– in Limbum, 63
Ā-movement, 22, 44–49, 58–62, 78, 231–233, 247, 258, 259, 268, 269, 275, 276, 280, 283, 289–291, 295, 296, 299, 300, 308, 311–313, 321, 331, 333, 340, 346, 347, 354–356, 364–369, 375–379, 385, 386, 394, 398–400, 404, 405, 408, 417, 422–424, 426, 427, 435–437, 448, 452, 454, 463, 465, 475–478
Agree, 19, 130, 150, 151
amalgamation, 120
argument encoding, 149

Bare Phrase Structure, 127
base generation, 21, 23, 83, 84, 379
bleeding, 116, 117, 137, 157, 158, 169, 170, 173, 174, 180, 185, 206, 225

Chain Reduction, 85, 86
Chain Uniformity Condition, 119, 121, 127, 128
clitic doubling, 124, 125, 451
cognate objects, 24, 25, 54, 66, 83, 208, 209, 241–243, 250, 389–391, 413, 414, 469
Conflation, 111, 113, 115
copy deletion, 116, 117, 146, 148
Copy Theory of Movement, 5, 85, 91, 104, 130, 145
copying, 23, 130, 146, 147, 156, 159, 161
counter-bleeding, 117, 161, 164, 166, 177, 180, 185
cross-linguistic variation, 105, 107, 117, 149, 151, 153, 185, 186, 188, 189, 205, 212–215

do-periphrase, 24, 26–28, 54, 66, 70, 319, 328, 350, 356, 371–373, 410–413

do-support, 83, 101, 116
double definiteness marking, 151–153
dummy verb insertion, 409
– in Asante Twi, 38, 39, 157, 158
– in German, 16, 167, 169, 173
– in Limbum, 38, 55

Economy of Pronunciation, 91, 105
ellipsis, 137, 139
– verb-stranding VP-, 139, 140, 224, 226
– VP-, 224
Extension Condition, 128, 134

feature saturation, 128, 130, 131, 147, 157, 204
Final-over-Final Condition, 51, 212, 214
Freezing, 124, 441

Generalization I, 4, 71, 79, 154
Generalization II, 77, 79, 155, 181
genus-species effects, 23, 24, 47, 233, 276, 381, 400, 405, 422, 427, 454, 465, 476

haplology, 215–217
head, 127, 146, 148, 160, 165, 180, 182, 191, 205
head movement, 83, 116, 117
– blocking by auxiliaries/modals, 87, 95, 145, 192, 195, 199
– long, 100, 121
– post-syntactic, 108, 116, 117, 135, 137, 139, 142, 145
– syntactic, 117, 134, 145, 225
– V-to-Asp, 41, 99, 102, 157, 176, 179
– V-to-C, 114, 115, 136, 168
– V-to-T, 6, 41, 43, 90, 92, 102, 111, 113, 140, 145, 157, 162, 188, 192, 199, 224
Holmberg's Generalization, 21, 183

incorporation, 30, 43, 105, 139, 393

Index

individual-level predicates, 27, 51, 52, 64, 250, 259, 260, 270, 285, 329, 359, 372, 394, 438, 474
infinitive, 17, 193, 230, 282, 285, 294, 297, 320, 337, 338, 359, 395, 432, 451, 455, 460, 471
information structural features, 130, 204–206
information structure, 31
inherent complement verbs, 234, 251, 254

late insertion, 24, 42, 211
left dislocation, 300, 301, 315, 324, 326, 373, 477–479
Linear Correspondence Axiom, 85, 86
linearization, 85, 86
Local Dislocation, 151, 152

Merge, 127, 130, 149, 151
Merge-over-Move, 149
Minimal Link Condition, 132, 204
modifiers
– adverbial, 30, 31, 52, 53, 65, 236, 249, 261, 270, 278, 284, 292, 300, 313, 321, 322, 348, 356, 370, 381, 386, 401, 404, 418, 439, 449, 456, 465
– nominal, 29, 30, 238, 249, 270, 285, 341, 393, 417
morphological fusion, 86–91
movement-induced index, 146, 147, 156, 162, 171

nominalization, 17, 51, 56, 69, 206–208, 210, 211, 229, 230, 240, 242, 244, 248, 264, 267, 268, 292, 297, 383, 387, 388, 407, 417, 430, 481

Object Shift, 21, 183, 446
order of application, 117, 118, 137, 148–153, 173–175, 180, 185, 186, 189, 214–217, 226
– in Asante Twi, 157, 159
– in German, 167, 168, 171, 173
– in Hebrew, 162, 164, 166
– in Polish, 176, 179

P-recoverability, 92, 93
parallel chains, 98, 103, 108
participle, 20, 21, 193, 194, 324, 434
percolation, 130
Potential Complete VP Constraint, 126
predicate cleft, 83, 84, 246
projection, 130, 131, 164, 204, 205
prosodic vacuity, 41, 42
pseudogapping, 135

reconstruction, 49, 62, 78, 122, 145, 312, 369, 386, 436
remnant movement, 5, 105, 117, 119, 121–124, 170, 171, 174, 177, 185, 187, 190, 427–429, 440–442, 448, 467, 468, 474
resumption, 299, 380, 385

scrambling, 170, 187, 190, 427–429, 440, 441, 467, 468
serial verb construction, 237–239, 271, 278, 482, 483
sluicing, 136, 138
stage-level predicates, 250, 259, 260, 270, 285, 329, 394, 438, 474
Strict Cycle Condition, 103, 130
Structure Preservation Principle, 126
structure-building features, 130, 146, 156
swiping, 137–139

tense/aspect marking, 19, 29, 49, 62, 233, 236, 249, 254, 260, 261, 270, 278, 284, 292, 294, 300, 314, 320, 338, 359, 369, 414, 415, 418, 433, 447, 466
tonal reflex of movement, 46, 47

verb doubling
– in Asante Twi, 38, 159, 160
– in Hebrew, 164, 165
– in Limbum, 38, 55
– in Polish, 16, 177, 180
– optional, 63, 187, 195–197, 199–201, 203, 396
– under auxiliaries/modals, 16, 187, 192–196, 202, 396, 434, 463

verb second, 19, 114, 136, 167, 168, 214, 216, 294, 364, 365, 477
verbal identity requirement, 140

word order, 107, 110, 207, 212–216, 252, 387, 393

Language Index

Afrikaans, 69, 70
Asante Twi, 3, 38–55, 88, 96, 103,
    155–160, 207, 210–212, 219

Basaa, 74, 229–235
Basque, 191, 197–199, 337–345
Berbice Dutch Creole, 235–240
Bosnian/Serbian/Croatian, 2
Brazilian Portuguese, 35, 48, 374–383
Breton, 37, 191, 200, 201, 345–353
Buli, 18, 25, 35, 95, 206–210, 213,
    383–391

Dagaare, 29, 88, 89, 94, 113, 213,
    392–395
Danish, 19, 28, 114, 151, 225, 293–296
Dutch, 2, 17, 114, 141, 190, 217, 218,
    354–357

Edo, 26, 240–243
English, 101, 103, 135, 137–139, 224
Ewe, 244, 245

Faroese, 151
Fongbe, 22, 23, 30, 88, 246–251

Gã, 142–144
German, 14, 16, 17, 26–28, 37, 114, 138,
    167–170, 172, 190, 214, 217,
    357–374
Gungbe, 100, 102, 252, 254, 255

Haitian Creole, 67–69, 74, 256–264
Hausa, 18, 30, 297–305
Hebrew, 2, 14, 17, 93, 106, 108, 125, 126,
    161–164, 166, 196, 202, 218, 224,
    395–403
Hungarian, 403–406

Irish, 139–141

Japanese, 18, 305–309

Kisi, 18, 196, 264, 265
Korean, 35, 36, 109, 213, 406–416
Krachi, 29, 30, 214, 416–420

Leteh, 16, 266
Limbum, 3, 38, 55–66, 94, 103, 219

Mandarin Chinese, 420–430
Mani, 89, 113, 213, 430–432

Norwegian, 15, 19, 20, 28, 76, 115, 138,
    151, 183, 219, 225, 310–316
Nupe, 15, 24, 25, 94, 181, 206–208, 210,
    211, 218, 267–273
Nweh, 94, 273–275

Papiamentu, 29, 94, 276, 277
Pichi, 94, 278, 279
Polish, 16, 17, 109, 175–179, 192, 193,
    432–444

Russian, 101, 192, 444–449

Saramaccan, 18, 74, 280, 281
Skou, 76, 316–320
Spanish, 122–125, 127, 193, 450–459
Swedish, 19, 20, 28, 29, 114, 151, 225,
    320–325

Tiv, 460
Tuki, 18, 75, 89, 282–285
Turkish, 287

Vata, 86, 95, 287–293
Vietnamese, 89, 95, 106, 113, 195, 202,
    461–469

Welsh, 26, 27, 76, 327–330
Wolof, 18, 76, 331–336

Yiddish, 23, 48, 138, 214, 217, 470–480
Yoruba, 29, 214, 481–483

www.ingramcontent.com/pod-product-compliance
Lightning Source LLC
Chambersburg PA
CBHW022102290426
44112CB00008B/517